Evans and Smith:
The Law of
Landlord and Tenant

Third Edition

P F Smith BCL, MA
Lecturer in Law
University of Reading

Butterworths
London
1989

United Kingdom	Butterworth & Co (Publishers) Ltd, 88 Kingsway, LONDON WC2B 6AB and 4 Hill Street, EDINBURGH EH2 3JZ
Australia	Butterworths Pty Ltd, SYDNEY, MELBOURNE, BRISBANE, ADELAIDE, PERTH, CANBERRA and HOBART
Canada	Butterworths Canada Ltd, TORONTO and VANCOUVER
Ireland	Butterworth (Ireland) Ltd, DUBLIN
Malaysia	Malayan Law Journal Sdn Bhd, KUALA LUMPUR
New Zealand	Butterworths of New Zealand Ltd, WELLINGTON and AUCKLAND
Singapore	Butterworth & Co (Asia) Pte Ltd, SINGAPORE
USA	Butterworths Legal Publishers, ST PAUL, Minnesota, SEATTLE, Washington, BOSTON, Massachusetts, AUSTIN, Texas and D & S Publishers, CLEARWATER, Florida

A CIP Catalogue record for this book is available from the British Library

ISBN 0 406 57812 5

Typeset by Cotswold Typesetting Ltd, Gloucester
Printed and bound by Mackays of Chatham Ltd

Preface

The third edition of this book appears after a four-year period of great change in the law of landlord and tenant, and this of itself would have necessitated many alterations to the text. As well as undertaking the re-writing involved as a result of these changes, I have re-structured the common law sections of the book so as to devote as much space as possible to important topics such as licences, enforcement of covenants, assignments, rent and rent review, repairing obligations and forfeiture. As a result, there has been some re-arrangement of the chapters in Parts A and B of the book, and licences, rent and rent review and repairing obligations now have self-contained chapters. It has, in the process, been possible to expand the treatment of these subjects somewhat, a course of action necessitated in no small part by the sheer number of important recent cases in each of these areas. In addition, I have re-written the text of other Chapters in Parts A to C wherever necessitated by new case law, legislation, or in the interest of what I hope will be greater clarity of exposition. It has also been possible to include some reference in the text, wherever appropriate, to Law Commission reports and working papers on, for example, disposition covenants and forfeiture, both published in 1985.

Part D of the book, which deals with the statutory codes in relation to residential tenancies, has been largely re-written. Residential tenancies have been profoundly affected by the enactment of the Housing Act 1988. As from 15 January 1989 no new tenancies protected by the Rent Act 1977 may be created. The sole lettings in the private residential sector as from then are assured or assured shorthold tenancies. The broad result of having two systems, given that the Rent Act 1977 will or may still apply to residential tenancies granted before 15 January 1989, is that material (in Chapters 16 to 18) dealing with both systems has been inserted or retained, as the case may be. It so happens that, as regards scope of the legislation, main exemptions and some aspects of re-possession, the 1977 and 1988 Act codes have some similarities: where this is so, there are suitable cross-references between the Chapters concerned. Owing to major amendments to anti-harassment and eviction legislation by the Housing Act 1988 and the enactment of the Landlord and Tenant Act 1987, Chapter 19 was re-written almost completely. The Chapter on secure tenancies was re-written completely, to deal with some interesting recent cases, and to incorporate the relevant provisions of the Housing Acts 1985 and 1988.

The legislative framework for business tenancies, Part II of the Landlord and Tenant Act 1954, remains intact since the last edition of this book: but the publication, late in 1988, of the Law Commission Working Paper No 111 is a sign that reform proposals are on the way. In any event, major cases concerned, in particular, with the scope of protection, basic security and grounds of opposition have been digested in the appropriate places of Part E, whose first and last chapters also required amendment because of reform proposals. As for agricultural tenancies, dealt with in Part F, there has been consolidating legislation in the shape of the Agricultural Holdings Act 1986, which is reflected in the text, and, apart from general updating of the text, the opportunity has been taken to re-write most of the material dealing with security of tenure and succession.

Inevitably, it has been necessary to reduce the scope of some Chapters, so as to avoid unnecessary increases in the length of the work. The separate Chapters in the last edition dealing with housing association tenancies, retricted contracts and old-style assured tenancies have been removed, and any relevant material in them transferred elsewhere. This was because of the enactment of the Housing Act 1988. For the same reason, the treatment of rent regulation in Chapter 17 has been curtailed, as has that of premiums and some aspects of statutory tenancies.

I am grateful to the editorial staff at Butterworths for all their kind consideration during the progress of the present work, and also to Mr Ian Sainsbury and the other staff in the Law Library, University of Reading, for their unfailing help and patience with a seemingly endless series of queries and requests.

The text of the book endeavours to state the law as it stood on 1 January 1989, but it has been possible to incorporate some subsequent developments at proof stage.

P F Smith
Reading
March 1989

Contents

Table of statutes

References in this Table to *Statutes* are to Halsbury's Statutes of England (Fourth Edition) showing the volume and page at which the annotated text of an Act may be found.

List of cases

PART A
CREATION OF TENANCIES

Chapter 1

Introduction

I GENERAL

The law of landlord and tenant deals with those rules of law which
govern the relations between the parties to a lease. There are various
different ways in which this relationship may arise and these are
discussed later in this Chapter. The basis of the law of landlord and
tenant rests firmly in the common law; but as things stand today, there
are special statutory codes governing many aspects of the relationship
between landlord and tenant of certain types of land, notably, the Rent
Act 1977, the Housing Act 1985, the Housing Act 1988 in relation to
private-sector residential premises, the Landlord and Tenant Act 1954
Part II in relation to business premises and the Agricultural Holdings
Act 1986 governing agricultural holdings.

In this book, therefore, the first three Parts deal with the general
common law rules applicable to leases generally. The remaining four
Parts are concerned with the various statutory codes which apply to
particular classes of tenancy.

A short summary of the historical position is now given.[1] There
follows an outline of the effects of the property legislation and a short
terminological discussion.

Brief historical perspective

Strictly speaking, the law governing leaseholds was never part of the law
of real property. Logically, therefore, it is unnecessary in relation to
landlord and tenant to outline the feudal system of land tenure, because
it did not recognise leaseholds as real property, as they were classified as
personal property along with chattels and labelled 'chattels real'. In
consequence, leaseholds were purely contractual relationships, so that
the landlord merely hired his land to the tenant for a limited period, in

---

1 For a detailed discussion see Cheshire & Burn *Modern Law of Real Property* (14th
edn) chs 2 and 3.

return for the payment by the tenant of rent. The remedies of a freeholder who was wrongfully dispossessed from land were real or in rem; in contrast, a tenant in occupation was denied any real remedies for the recovery of the land following wrongful eviction by the landlord. The tenant did not have *seisin* (possession) so he was left to the contractual remedy of damages against the landlord for breach of contract. Later, the position of tenants was improved. In 1235, as a result of the introduction of an action in trespass, the tenant was enabled to recover his land specifically, if wrongfully ejected therefrom.[2] Owing to improvements to this particular form of action, it could be said that the action of ejectment in substance gave the tenant a real remedy. With a fully-fledged real remedy, the tenant could be said to have a real interest in land, as his right to possession was protected. As to the reasons why leaseholds were treated as chattels real, one may have been economic pressure, and in any case a leasehold was regarded as a valuable investment. It provided a means of evasion of the usury laws so that a debtor would lease land to his creditor at a nominal rent, and the creditor would draw the rents and profits from the land.

Certain further advantages were apparent from the classification of leaseholds as personal property: first, that leaseholders were exempted from the burdensome system of feudal incidents. Secondly, leaseholds, unlike real property, could be freely disposed of by will. Thirdly, the action for ejectment was originally limited to actions by the tenant against the landlord and his successors in title, but was later expanded to allow actions against any wrongful dispossessor of the tenant, and was so efficacious that freeholders in due course elected for it because of the more cumbersome and formalised (real) actions available to them: they did this by pleading (until 1852) the fiction that they held a leasehold.[3]

Nonetheless, in theory, possession remained with the landlord not the tenant. As time progressed, tenants came to acquire the status of (in substance) real property estate owners. While after the reforming legislation contained in the 1925 property statutes, all forms of tenure were abolished except one (socage tenure, the standard freehold tenure), in landlord and tenant, tenure has been stated in *Milmo v Carreras*[4] to be fundamental to the relationship of the parties to a lease. Lord Greene MR there said, of a tenant who purported to grant a sub-lease for a longer period than the length of his own lease,[5] that: '. . . from that moment he [the tenant] is a stranger to the land, in the sense that the

---

2 The action was called *quaere ejecit infra terminum*.
3 The enactment of the Common Law Procedure Act 1852 rendered pleading of this fiction unnecessary.
4 [1946] KB 306, [1946] 1 All ER 288, CA.
5 With the result that he was deemed to have assigned the whole residue of his leasehold interest to the so-called 'sub-tenant'.

relationship of landlord and tenant, in respect of tenure, cannot any longer exist between him and the so-called sub-lessee ... I find it impossible to conceive of a relationship of landlord and tenant which has not got that essential element of tenure in it,'[6]

Although, therefore, leaseholds were historically classified as chattels real, and thus as a hybrid between real property and chattels, they have steadily been assimilated into real property, and this process has been virtually completed by the 1925 property legislation, whose effects on leaseholds are next outlined.[7]

Effects of the 1925 property legislation

The 1925 legislation is a convenient label for a whole series of reforming and consolidating statutes passed in 1925, which resulted in the enactment, in particular, of the Law of Property Act 1925, the Land Registration Act 1925,[8] and the Land Charges Act 1925 (now the Land Charges Act 1972).[9]

A number of important reforms, partly with the overall aim of simplifying conveyancing, were incorporated into Part I of the Law of Property Act 1925 and these are discussed in the appropriate parts of the text of this book. One general reform was that the number of legal estates in land was reduced to two by s 1(1) of the 1925 Act: the fee simple absolute in possession and the term of years absolute. This second expression is statutory shorthand for all types of lease or tenancy with a few exceptions. 'Term of years absolute' is widely defined by s 205(1)(xxvii) as meaning: 'a term of years (taking effect either in possession or in reversion whether or not subject to a rent) . . . subject or not to another legal estate[10] and either certain or liable to determination by notice, re-entry, operation of law . . . or in any other event'.

This definition is, therefore, sufficient to include fixed-term leases; and the statutory definition proceeds, deliberately, to include legal short-term periodic tenancies by the concluding words: '. . . "term of years" includes a term for less than a year, or for a year or years and a fraction of a year or from year to year'. Excluded from legal terms of years within s 1(1) are terms determinable with life or lives and terms which infringe s 149(3) of the 1925 Act. The exclusion of terms determinable with life is deliberate as the policy of the 1925 legislation is to exclude any interest which subsists behind a trust from legal estates.

---

6 Ibid at 290–291.
7 For a more detailed appraisal, see *Wolstenholme and Cherry's Conveyancing Statutes* (13th edn) (Farrand) Vol. 1, p 32 ff.
8 Since amended, and the collective citation is the Land Registration Acts 1925 to 1986.
9 Also enacted were the Trustee Act 1925, the Settled Land Act 1925 and the Administration of Estates Act 1925.
10 This is to preserve concurrent legal terms, of which there may be any number.

The Law of Property Act 1925, having reduced the maximum number of legal estates to two, then provides in s 1(3) that: 'all other estates, interests and charges in or over land take effect as equitable interests'. Generally, the status of a lease (whether legal or equitable) makes no difference to the substantive rights of the parties thereunder.[11] As will be seen, however, the formalities of creation of legal and equitable leases differ and equitable leases require protection against third parties by registration.

Equitable substantive rules applicable to legal and equitable leases developed alongside relevant legal rules; equitable remedies, such as an injunction or specific performance are available to enable a landlord or tenant of a legal or equitable lease to enforce their respective rights, for example, under covenants restrictive of the user of the demised premises, which are often preferable to the standard common-law remedy of damages. Some rights in leaseholds are only recognised by equity, such as those of a tenant holding under a void legal lease or certain rights arising out of equitable estoppel.

There is a view, according to which equity and law have become fused since the passage of legislation now consolidated into the Supreme Court Act 1981 (especially s 49 and Sch 1).[12] This view overlooks the self-evident fact that there are differences in classification in property law as between legal and equitable estates and interests; there are important consequences from this for registration. Some of the substantive law, moreover, for example, that governing the enforcement of covenants, may be different for legal and equitable leases. There are clear differences between legal and equitable remedies. The 'fusion' theory does some violence to property law and is rather suspect.[13]

Main terminology

Those new to landlord and tenant find themselves confronted with a series of technical terms, some of which are interchangeable. These terms are used throughout this book and are outlined in what follows.

1   *Lease or demise*   Generally 'lease' is a noun to describe a formal document under which land or premises is 'demised' or 'leased' to a tenant. In the case of informal leases, such as weekly or monthly

---

11   *Walsh v Lonsdale* (1882) 21 Ch D 9, CA.
12   See dicta of Lord Diplock in *United Scientific Holdings Ltd v Burnley Borough Council* [1978] AC 904 at 925, [1977] 2 All ER 62 at 68, HL; and for a still more extreme version, dicta of Lord Denning MR in *Federal Commerce and Navigation Co Ltd v Molena Alpha Inc, The Nanfri* [1978] QB 927 at 975, [1978] 3 All ER 1066 at 1078, CA.
13   See PV Baker (1977) 93 LQR 529 for a detailed critique; also passim, J E Martin (ed) *Hanbury and Maudsley, Modern, Equity* (12 edn), pp 22–26.

tenancies, this process is sometimes spoken of as 'letting'. 'Demised premises' is a label for the land with a building or buildings, or land consisting of a building or part of a building or land with a defined boundary,[14] demised by the habendum of a lease.

2 *Landlord or lessor* These alternative terms describe the estate owner who grants the lease in question. 'Landlord' is a slightly flexible term, as it describes not only a head landlord, but also a mesne landlord where appropriate, as the following diagram shows:

A_____99_____B_____21_____C

A lets land to B for 99 years and B, the mesne landlord, who is also A's tenant, later sub-lets the land to C for 21 years.

3 *Tenant or lessee* Obviously these interchangeable words describe the person who accepts a lease. In the diagram above, both B and C are lessees, or, as the case may be, sub-lessees. B's lease may contain a covenant obliging him to notify A of any sub-leases granted by B.

4 *Assignor and assignee* Subject to any expressly imposed restrictions or limitations on the transfer of leases, leases are freely assignable. Likewise the freeholder's interest, his reversion expectant on the lease, is freely assignable. By assignment is meant the outright transfer (by deed) of the leasehold interest, or freehold reversion, as the case may be. The assignor is the person making the assignment and the assignee the person accepting it.

5 *Sub-demises or sub-leases* A sub-lease takes place where a mesne landlord (such as B in the above diagram) lets the demised premises or part to a tenant, who, vis-à-vis the head landlord (A) is a sub-tenant. The sub-tenant's interest depends on the continued existence of the head lease supporting it for its survival: in principle, the destruction of the head lease by forfeiture annihilates any sub-leases derived out of it.[15]

Many leasehold estates

Complex chains of assignments and sub-demises may readily build up where the head lease has been granted for a substantial term of years. Several leasehold estates in the same land may therefore exist. The position may be illustrated by the following diagram.

---

14 See eg *Whitley v Stumbles* [1930] AC 544, HL.
15 See *Moore Properties (Ilford) Ltd v McKeon* [1977] 1 All ER 262, [1976] 1 WLR 1278 (unlawful tub-tenancy granted to X held not binding on superior landlord).

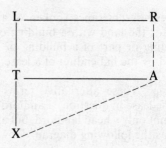

L was head landlord of T, but having assigned his freehold reversion to R, and T having assigned the residue of his lease to A, R occupies L's position as against A. Tenure exists between R and A. T has no tenure with R. X now holds as sub-lessee of A, with tenure between them. R is X's head landlord.

II   SCOPE OF THIS SUBJECT

Main methods of creation of leases

Leases and tenancies arise in a number of different ways which are fully explored in Chapter 2. For present purposes, they may arise in the following two ways, at common law:

1   By express agreement, as where L demises land to T1 for a 21-year fixed term.
2   By implied agreement, as where T2 enters L's land with L's consent, has exclusive possession and pays a weekly rent. T2 is weekly periodic tenant of L even though there may be only an oral agreement between the parties.

In the case of periodic tenants, T2 in the above example has a legal estate in land, derived from his exclusive possession and the payment and acceptance of rent for a periodic term.[16] This is as much a legal estate as that demised to a tenant holding under a 999-year fixed-term lease. The fact that the maximum duration of a periodic tenancy, which ends only following notice to quit from one party or the other, is inherently uncertain at the outset, is of no significance to this question.

---

16   A proposition emphatically restated by Lord Templeman in *Street v Mountford* [1985] AC 809 at 826, [1985] 2 All ER 289 at 299–300, HL.

Outline of effect of statutory rules

In the private sector of landlord and tenant law there are a number of statutory rules which are grafted onto the common law principles.

Residential tenancies are significantly affected by the Rent Act 1977, and Part I of the Housing Act 1988, which are discussed in Part D. The Rent Act 1977, which is relevant to all residential tenancies granted before the commencement of the Housing Act 1988, is enacted almost as if the common law rules governing termination of tenancies did not exist. Part I of the Housing Act 1988 is a specific code sui juris: parts of it seem to have been borrowed from legislation applicable to council tenancies, parts from the Rent Act 1977 and parts even from long residential tenancies legislation. It must be said that the proliferation of statutory rules and of different categories of letting within them does not make for simplicity. One additional matter of difficulty is the extent to which the parties may contract out of either of these two sets of provisions. Council tenancies are governed by a third code, Part IV of the Housing Act 1985, discussed in Part G of this book. Common to all these is security of tenure for the tenant, to a greater or lesser extent, but while the Rent Act 1977 controls the rent payable, the Housing Act 1988 does away with most rent controls.

The principal code affecting business tenants is Part II of the Landlord and Tenant Act 1954. The Act is generally thought to be satisfactory, though, as will appear from Part E, there are some defects in it. As with residential tenancies, attempts have been made to contract out of the provisions of Part II: some are frustrated by the 1954 Act Part II; some are allowed; some are dealt with by common law rules dealing with contractual licences designed to avoid Part II of the Act of 1954.

A third main set of statutory rules, which deals with the landlord and tenant of an agricultural holding, is the Agricultural Holdings Act 1986. This specialised branch of the law is dealt with in Part F of this book. Notably, the 1986 Act has express provisions dealing with avoidance of the 1986 Act by licences and other arrangements. These provisions are absent both from the Rent Act 1977, the Housing Act 1988 and from Part II of the 1954 Act, though not from Part IV of the Housing Act 1985. A further feature of the 1986 Act is the significant role allotted to arbitrations with regard especially to rents and dilapidations disputes. The 1986 Act security of tenure and succession provisions are, however, of considerable complexity.

Chapter 2

Relationship of landlord and tenant

I NATURE OF THE RELATIONSHIP

The relationship of landlord and tenant arises where one person, who possesses either a freehold or leasehold property interest expressly or impliedly grants to another, an estate in that property which is less than the freehold interest or for a shorter duration than the leasehold interest of the grantor, as the case may be.

Tenure

The granting of a lease creates tenure between the parties and the results of this are as follows.

1   The respective assignees of each party to the lease will be bound by its terms (under 'privity of estate') if, but only if, the covenant runs with the land.
2   Rent is an incident of tenure and so it issues out of the land, not simply out of any buildings on the land: this means that the landlord is entitled to distrain for unpaid rent over the land as a whole.
3   The landlord and tenant are mutually estopped from denying each other's title.

Grant of lease creates estate in tenant

Any express grant of a lease which follows the correct formalities (if any) required for the purpose, passes a legal or at least an equitable estate or interest to the tenant. Moreover, it follows from this that:

1   Throughout the tenant's estate, there must be two concurrent estates in the land, the lease and the landlord's reversion, which may itself be either freehold or leasehold.
2   The duration of the lease must be certain. it must either be a fixed-term lease (sometimes called a 'term certain') of a duration both as regards commencement and termination, which is certain. Or it must be a periodic tenancy, whose maximum duration is not fixed at the

commencement of the lease, but which is capable of being rendered certain by notice to quit from either party.

3 The tenant has the right, in principle, to assign or mortgage his lease, and to create sub-leases out of it, but no tenant may validly sub-let for a longer period of years than he is entitled to under his own lease at the date of the sub-lease. Moreover, leases commonly restrict and sometimes completely remove the ability of the tenant to dispose of his interest.[1]

4 On the termination of a fixed-term lease or periodic tenancy at common law (by effluxion of time or following a notice to quit as the case may be) the tenant's estate in the land ends. Statutory rules applicable to residential, business and agricultural tenancies severely restrict or modify this rule, as will become apparent from subsequent chapters. There is a dispute whether the interest of a tenant holding under the protection of the Rent Acts or as a secure tenant under the Housing Act 1985 Part IV is in any sense proprietary.[2]

Manner relationship arises

The relationship of landlord and tenant may arise in various different ways between the original parties. One has been mentioned: express or implied agreement. A tenancy may arise by estoppel, as will be mentioned later in this Chapter.

Another way in which the relationship of landlord and tenant may arise is by attornment. Attornment is a useful device for ensuring that tying covenants run with the land in question – as with a mortgage where the borrower attorns himself tenant of the mortgagee.[3] Under s 151 of the Law of Property Act 1925, attornments by existing tenants are generally not required.

The relationship of landlord and tenant may continue despite the wish of one of the parties to terminate it. For example, on expiry of a fixed-term or periodic tenancy of a dwelling house protected by the Rent Act 1977, a statutory tenancy automatically arises. The landlord has no choice but to accept this state of affairs.[4]

Finally, on the occasion of any assignment of a lease the relationship of landlord and tenant arises under 'privity of estate' between persons who by definition were not the original parties and in 'privity of contract'.

---

1 See ch 7.
2 See Hand [1980] Conv 351; but cf *Jessamine Investment Co v Schwartz* [1978] QB 264 at 270, [1976] 3 All ER 521 at 526, CA.
3 The burden of restrictive covenants (and positive covenants) does not run at law with freehold land: *Austerberry v Oldham Corpn* (1885) 29 Ch D 750, CA.
4 Another example of this process is the continuation of business tenancies under Part II of the Landlord and Tenant Act 1954.

II   SUBJECT MATTER

All land and interests in land lie in grant[5] and so may be leased. 'Land' is defined by s 205(1)(ix) of the Law of Property Act 1925 as including:

> 'land of any tenure, and mines and minerals, whether or not held apart from the surface, buildings or parts of buildings (whether the division is horizontal, vertical or made in any other way) and other corporeal hereditaments; also a . . . rent and other incorporeal hereditaments, and an easement, right, privilege, or benefit in, over, or derived from land; but not an undivided share in land . . . .'

Corporeal hereditaments consist of the land itself (including mines and minerals) and permanent structures on the land, such as buildings parts of buildings and fixtures.

Incorporeal hereditaments are rights issuing out of land, and include rights of way, easements generally, sporting rights and other *profits à prendre*, tolls, commons and estovers and so on: all these may be leased but a deed is required to pass the legal estate.[6]

If a lease of a right of way over land adjoining the tenant's premises is expressly granted, the grantor is not obliged by Part II of the Landlord and Tenant Act 1954 to renew the lease on its expiry.[7] If the tenant entitled to the lease of a right of way also holds a lease of adjoining premises protected by Part II of the 1954 Act, then the relevant holding for statutory purposes includes the lease of the right of way.[8]

Goods and chattels cannot be let as such. Plant and machinery may be leased by a separate agreement to that leasing the land where they are situated. If chattels and land are let in the same agreement, as with furnished lettings, the rent issues out of the land as a whole and so the whole rent – including any part payable for the use of the furniture – is distrainable.

Easements in a lease

A tenant may obtain the benefit of easements in the lease, by express or implied grant, or express or implied reservation. For present purposes 'easement' means: 'a right attached to a particular piece of land which allows the owner of that land (the dominant owner) either to use the land of another person (the servient owner) . . . or to restrict its user by that other person to a particular extent . . . .'[9]

---

5   Law of Property Act 1925 s 51(1).
6   Law of Property Act 1925 s 52(1). An equitable lease of an incorporeal hereditament may be validly granted.
7   *Land Reclamation Co Ltd v Basildon District Council* [1979] 2 All ER 993, CA.
8   *Nevill Long & Co (Boards) Ltd v Firmenich & Co* (1984) 47 P & CR 59, CA.
9   Cheshire & Burn, *Modern Law of Real Property* (14th edn) p 490.

The extent of any particular grant or reservation of an easement in favour of a tenant is a matter of construction,[10] and the question of whether the rights so conferred have been interfered with is a question of fact. Where, for example, the landlords of a block of flats to lessees (A) expressly reserved A a right of vehicular access over a driveway, and then demised the driveway to another lessee (B), it was held that A was entitled to an injunction against B to restrain the building of a car wash, whose erection would substantially interfere with the rights of access, though not render them impossible.[11] In the case of the right to erect signboards, these are generally construed as capable of passing, if at all, as an easement[12] but the right to erect a signboard may be spelt out of a demise 'with appurtenances'.[13]

The tenant may in the absence of express grant or reservation obtain certain easements by implication under one of four headings.

1   *An easement of necessity*   This is limited in principle to a right of access over the landlord's retained land (if any) if at the time of the demise there was no other means of access to the demised premises, however inconvenient: an easement of neccessity is limited to the purposes of the lessee at the date of the demise.[14]

2   *Intended easements*   are readily implied into leases to enable the purposes of the tenant, if known to the landlord, to be effectually carried out, as where a tenant was held entitled to instal a ventilation system in the basement kitchen of a restaurant, let as such.[15]

3   *Continuous and apparent quasi-easements*   are implied under the rule in *Wheeldon v Burrows*[16] but they must be continuous and apparent; necessary for the reasonable enjoyment of the demised

---

10 In *Civil Service Musical Instrument Association v Whiteman* (1899) 68 LJ Ch 484, a lessee with a right of way over a passage to the demised shop who to the landlord's knowledge spent money on the passage was held not bound to restore the passage to its original condition nor to remove his signboard.

11 *Celsteel Ltd v Alton House Holdings Ltd* [1986] 1 All ER 608, [1986] 1 WLR 512, CA.

12 In *Francis v Hayward* (1882) 22 Ch D 177, CA, signboards were construed as part of the demised premises, but this was a very special case.

13 *William Hill (Southern) Ltd v Cabras Ltd* (1986) 54 P & CR 42, CA. Such right may not be construed out of a qualified prohibition against putting up signboards, ibid.

14 *Pinnington v Galland* (1853) 9 Exch 1; *Titchmarsh v Royston Water Co Ltd* (1899) 81 LT 673; *Nickerson v Barraclough* [1980] Ch 325, [1979] 3 All ER 312.

15 *Wong v Beaumont Property Trust Ltd* [1965] 1 QB 173, [1964] 2 All ER 119, CA. The ventilation system, which had to be built against the landlord's back wall, was essential if public health regulations were to be complied with and in this sense 'necessary'.

16 (1879) 12 Ch D 31, CA.

premises; and used by the landlord up to the date of the grant of the lease, for the benefit of the demised land or premises. It was, for example, held that this rule enabled the equitable lessee of a house to use an unmetalled way over the landlord's land as a means of access to and from the house.[17]

4   *Section 62(1)*   of the Law of Property Act 1925. Any lease by deed automatically passes to the tenant a long list of easements, rights and reputed rights, 'at the time of conveyance demised, occupied or enjoyed with, or reputed or known as part or parcel of or appurtenant to the land or any part thereof'. This is supposed to be merely a word-saving provision in relation to leases and other conveyances. In fact, where land is demised to a tenant and he under the lease enjoys a precarious right, such as to use a coal-shed on the landlord's land, and the lease is renewed, the right, unless expressly excluded on renewal,[18] is converted on renewal into a full easement.[19] A precarious easement not known to the law will not pass under s 62, such as a right to a supply of hot water and central heating.[20] Subject to that, any right de facto enjoyed with the demised premises at the date of renewal of the lease, such as a way, will pass automatically on renewal under s 62.[1]

III   THE PARTIES

General

Any person[2] not under a legal disability may take or grant a lease. For present purposes, 'disability' means a restriction imposed on a person's capacity to grant or accept a lease. All relevant restrictions are statute-imposed except that in the case of a corporation, its own constitutive

---

17   *Borman v Griffith* [1930] 1 Ch 493.
18   The grant of a lease 'with appurtenances' is insufficient to exclude s 62: *Hansford v Jago* [1921] 1 Ch 322.
19   *Wright v Macadam* [1949] 2 KB 744, [1949] 2 All ER 565, CA. This rule applies to a licence to use a right of way or other advantage granted to a tenant let into occupation prior to the granting of a lease: on grant, the right becomes a full easement unless s 62 is excluded: *Goldberg v Edwards* [1950] Ch 247, CA.
20   *Regis Property Co Ltd v Redman* [1956] 2 QB 612, [1956] 2 All ER 335, CA; nor a right to have one's flank outside wall proofed against the elements: *Phipps v Pears* [1965] 1 QB 76, [1964] 2 All ER 35, CA, nor a right to unlimited grazing: *Anderson v Bostock* [1976] Ch 312, [1976] 1 All ER 560.
 1   *International Tea Stores Co v Hobbs* [1903] 2 Ch 165.
 2   Common law disabilities on the power of a married woman to grant or accept leases were removed by s 1 of the Law Reform (Married Women and Tortfeasors) Act 1935. A contract to grant a lease to an enemy alien is void at common law (but in any case war regulations would strike down such contract).

instrument may contain further restrictions on the ability to grant or accept leases. In general, therefore, a lease may be granted by any person with capacity to do so on any terms and conditions thought fit; but statute expressly prohibits any discrimination against potential lessees on the grounds of race and sex.[3]

A lease may be void or voidable for other reasons apart from disabilities. In particular, general contractual rules rendering any contract void or voidable apply as much to contracts for a lease as to any contract. Accordingly, a lease made under duress or undue influence is voidable by the other party. So too is a lease procured by fraud or innocent misrepresentation – in this latter case it makes no difference that the lease may have been executed.[4] A lease entered into when one of the parties was in such a state of intoxication as not to know what he was doing, is voidable, provided the other party knew of the fact.[5] A lease made under a genuine mistake of fact as to the identity of the parties or the property is void.[6]

If the grantor purports to grant a lease or sub-lease for a longer term than he himself is entitled to, the 'lease' operates as an out-and-out assignment of the residue of his term.[7] Moreover no person may validly grant a lease of any length to himself.[8] Such a transaction would be totally absurd: for example the notion of a person enforcing covenants in the lease against himself will not bear serious consideration.[9] By reason of s 72(3) of the Law of Property Act 1925, tenants in common of land are enabled validly to lease land, by deed, to themselves in another capacity.

Infants

At common law, leases made by infants were voidable, but by s 1(6) of the Law of Property Act 1925, no infant is capable of holding a legal estate in land. If an infant becomes entitled to any land whether in fee simple or a term of years, it is treated as settled land under the Settled Land Act 1925, and the legal estate will remain vested in the trustees of the settlement, or in the personal representatives (if the land was left to him by will) until or unless they are required by trustees to vest it in them. Trustees acting for infants have the statutory powers of a tenant for life

---

3 Race Relations Act 1976 s 21(1); Sex Discrimination Act 1975 s 30(1).
4 Misrepresentation Act 1967 s 1. See further ch 4.
5 *Gore v Gibson* (1845) 13 M & W 623.
6 The remedy is rectification once the lease has been executed and parol evidence of mutual mistake is admissible even though the lease appears complete in itself: *Craddock Bros v Hunt* [1923] 2 Ch 136, CA. See also ch 4.
7 *Milmo v Carreras* [1946] KB 306, [1946] 1 All ER 288, CA.
8 *Rye v Rye* [1962] AC 496, [1962] 1 All ER 146, HL.
9 See ibid at 506 (Viscount Simonds).

and also special powers of management under s 102 of the Settled Land Act, including the power to determine tenancies and accept the surrender of leases. A conveyance of a legal estate to an infant now operates only as an agreement for valuable consideration to execute a settlement in his favour (s 27(1)). A conveyance jointly to an infant and one or more other persons of full age vests the legal estate in the other persons as joint tenants under a trust for sale, on the statutory trusts (LPA 1925 s 19(2)). An infant is nevertheless free to grant an equitable lease of his beneficial interest but this would be voidable by him within a reasonable time of attaining his majority, in accordance with the ordinary law of contract. The age of majority was reduced to 18, by the Family Law Reform Act 1969, with effect from January 1970.

Patients

Where a legal estate in land is vested in a patient (i e by s 1 of the Mental Health Act 1983, a person suffering or appearing to suffer from a mental disorder), either solely or jointly with any other person, s 22 of the Law of Property Act 1925 provides that his receiver (or if none), any person authorised in that behalf, must, by order of the judge with jurisdiction under Part VII of the 1983 Act, make or concur in making all dispositions required to convey or create a legal estate in his name and on his behalf. By s 93 of the 1983 Act the judge[10] has all powers to do anything necessary or expedient in relation to the property which the patient would have had, and may in particular, under s 96, make orders or directions for the sale, charging, etc, of any of the patient's property; hence he may grant leases of such property.

Bankrupts

On bankruptcy, the bankrupt's estate, including all freehold and leasehold property[11] vests in a trustee in bankruptcy as soon as the latter's appointment takes effect.[12] When a person is adjudged bankrupt, he loses his power to grant leases: any lease (as a 'disposition') is void except to the extent that it is made with the consent of the court or was subsequently ratified by the court.[13] The statutory prohibition applies from the day of presentation of a petition for a bankruptcy order,

---

10   I e the Lord Chancellor, a judge of the Supreme Court appointed by him, the Master of the Court of Protection or any official thereof nominated by the Lord Chancellor (ss 93, 94).
11   Insolvency Act 1986 s 283 as amended by Housing Act 1988 s 117 so as to exclude from the bankrupt's estate most assured, protected and secure tenancies in particular from the bankrupt's estate.
12   Insolvency Act 1986 s 306.
13   Insolvency Act 1986 s 284(1).

and it ends with the vesting of the bankrupt's estate in the trustee in bankruptcy.[14] This is of little solace to the bankrupt since the trustee is invested by statute with the bankrupt's former power to grant leases.[15]

Executors and administrators

On a person's death, all his property, real and personal, vests in the executors of his will immediately on his death, or if none is appointed, or he dies intestate, upon his administrators when they are granted letters of administration (Administration of Estates Act 1925 s 1); until the distribution of the assets, they have all the powers of trustees for sale and tenant for life.[16] They have powers to grant leases, therefore, though they would not normally do so, except where the property vested in them, for example, during a minority. The concurrence of all personal representatives, if there are two or more, is required on the grant of a lease.[17]

Tenants for life

A tenant for life in whom the legal estate in settled land has been vested by deed will, if there are no express wider settlement powers conferred, have a statutory power of leasing under the Settled Land Act 1925. The following rules apply:

1 Save as mentioned in 5 below, notice of any intention to grant a lease must be given by the tenant for life to the settlement trustees before the granting of the lease (s 101 of the Settled Land Act 1925).[18]
2 The lease must comply with s 41 of the 1925 Act and, in particular, the length of the term must not exceed:
    (i) in the case of a building lease, 999 years;
    (ii) in the case of a mining lease, 100 years;
    (iii) in the case of a forestry lease, 999 years; and
    (iv) in any other case, 50 years.
3 The lease must comply with further formalities (s 42(1)):
    (i) it must be by deed, taking effect in possession not later than 12 months after its date;
    (ii) it must reserve the best rent that can reasonably be obtained.[19]

---

14 Insolvency Act 1986 s 284(3).
15 Insolvency Act 1986 s 314 and Sch 5 Part II para 12.
16 Administration of Estates Act 1925 s 39; Law of Property Act 1925 s 33.
17 Administration of Estates Act 1925 s 2(2).
18 The fact that no notice is given is of no concern to a lessee dealing in good faith with the tenant for life: Settled Land Act 1925 s 101(5).
19 See *Dowager Duchess of Sutherland v Duke of Sutherland* [1893] 3 Ch 169 at 195 and *Re Aldam's Settled Estate* [1902] 2 Ch 46 at 59, CA.

       though regard is had to any premium taken, to capital improvements and other circumstances;

    (iii) it must contain a covenant by the lessee for the payment of rent and a condition of re-entry on rent not being paid for a specified time of not over 30 days.[20]

4   If a premium is taken, it must be paid (s 42(4)) not to the tenant for life, but to the settlement trustees.

5   Notice to the trustees is not required where (s 42(5)) a lease is granted at the best rent which can reasonably be obtained without taking a premium for not over 21 years.

6   If a lease is not over three years in duration, s 42(5) provides that no deed is necessary, but writing and an agreement for payment of rent are essential.

7   A tenant dealing in good faith with a tenant for life[1] should be able generally to rely on s 110(1) of the Settled Land Act 1925 to protect his title as against aggrieved settlement beneficiaries even if the lease fails to comply with the above requirements.

8   If for some reason, s 110(1) is non-applicable, then the lease, if it fails on the face of it, to comply with the above rules, is liable to be set aside at the instance of the aggrieved settlement beneficiaries.[2] Yet even an invalid lease may take effect as a contract for a lease on the same terms, as varied where necessary to comply with the Act, under s 152 of the Law of Property Act 1925. This latter is only available if the tenant shows that he acted in good faith, and this is impossible if the best rent was not obtained.[3]

Trustees for sale

Where land is conveyed to two or more persons jointly, a trust for sale arises; the legal estate is vested in them (and in the first four named, if there are more than four) as joint tenants, on the statutory trusts, by s 34(2) of the Law of Property Act 1925. Section 28 confers on them the leasing powers of the tenant for life (see above).

Mortgagors and mortgagees

The mortgagor of land, at common law, has only a limited power of leasing once the land is mortgaged, since, to bind the mortgagee, any lease granted by the mortgagor will need the mortgagee's consent;

---

20 A counterpart of the lease must be executed by the lessee and delivered to the tenant for life: Settled Land Act 1925 s 42(2).

1 See *Re Morgan's Lease, Jones v Norsesowicz* [1972] Ch 1, [1971] 2 All ER 235.

2 *Kisch v Hawes Bros Ltd* [1935] Ch 102.

3 *Davies v Hall* [1954] 2 All ER 330, [1954] 1 WLR 855, CA.

though a lease granted prior to the mortgage will bind the mortgagee.[4] At common law, a lease made by the mortgagor after the mortgage was created will bind the mortgagor-landlord and the tenant though the mortgagee's paramount title, as explained, is unaffected.[5]

The mortgage deed almost certainly will exclude the following statutory power of leasing[6] and will require that any leases have the consent of the mortgagee; but some deeds may not do so and then the statutory power, in s 99 of the Law of Property Act 1925, is relevant.

Application of power   The statutory power enables a mortgagor in possession (s 99(1)) to grant leases or agreements for a lease, which will bind the mortgagor and mortgagee, of the whole or any part of the land in question.

Relevant leases   By s 99(3), after 1925 only two kinds of lease are allowed:

(a)   agricultural or occupation leases for up to 50 years; and
(b)   building leases for up to 999 years.

Formalities   Leases under the statutory power must comply with four formalities:

(a)   The lease must take effect in possession not later than 12 months after its start date (s 99(5)).
(b)   It must reserve the best rent reasonably obtainable in all the circumstances and no premium is allowed (s 99(6)).
(c)   The lease must contain a covenant by the lessee for payment of rent (s 99(7)).[7]
(d)   A counterpart of the lease must be executed by the lessee and delivered to the lessor (s 99(8)) and also, any counterpart of a lease granted by the mortgagor must, within one month of its making, be delivered to the mortgagee or first mortgagee (s 99(11)).[8]

None of these formalities applies to either oral leases or agreements for a lease. As with leases by a tenant for life under a settlement which are not formally valid, if the lack of formality is the sole reason for the

---

4   *Grace Rymer Investments Ltd v Waite* [1958] Ch 831, [1958] 2 All ER 777, CA; *Rhodes v Dalby* [1971] 2 All ER 1144, [1971] 1 WLR 1325.
5   *Dudley and District Benefit Building Society v Emerson* [1949] Ch 707, [1949] 2 All ER 252, CA.
6   Allowed by Law of Property Act 1925 s 99(13). The statutory power may also be extended: s 99(14).
7   And the lease must contain a condition for re-entry for non-payment of rent within a time of up to 30 days: Law of Property Act 1925 s 99(7).
8   The lessee is not concerned to see that this is complied with: Law of Property Act 1925 s 99(11).

invalidity, then the lease may be saved and take effect in equity under s 152(1) of the Law of Property Act 1925.[9]

Receivers

Receivers appointed by the High Court[10] have no powers of leasing, without the authority of the court. It is not usual for the court to insert, in the order appointing a receiver, a general authority to grant leases: as a rule each individual proposal for a lease must be considered by the court on its merits.[11] If a receiver is appointed by a mortgagee under s 101 of the Law of Property Act 1925, the leasing powers of the mortgagor (i e under the mortgage and under s 99) are thereby vested in the mortgagee (s 99(19)), and are only exercisable by the receiver with his written authority; and the lessee will not obtain a legal estate unless the legal owner is a party to the lease.

The Crown

By virtue of s 1 of the Crown Estate Act 1961, the Crown Estate Commissioners may lease any part of the Crown Estate at the best rent obtainable, for any term not exceeding 100 years. A lease must take effect in possession not later than 12 months after its date, or in reversion after a lease having at that date not more than 21 years to run; and no option or contract may be made for a lease to commence more than 10 years from the date of contract, unless the rent under such lease is left to be fixed as at the commencement of the term in such a manner as in their opinion is calculated to ensure the best consideration reasonably obtainable at that date. They may, with the royal assent, under the Sign Manual grant leases, either gratuitously or at such rent as they think fit, of land for development, improvement or general benefit of the Crown, if it is to be used for any of the purposes specified in s 5, or for any public or charitable purposes connected with Crown Estate Land, or tending to the welfare of persons residing or employed on it (s 5). Section 5 of that Act makes special provisions for maintaining the present character of the Windsor Estate. Other Acts affecting leases of Crown Land are the Crown Lands Acts 1808 and 1821, the Duchy of Cornwall Management Acts 1863 and 1893, the Dean Forest (Mines) Act 1838.

Government departments authorised to acquire land from time to time for public purposes are generally given power to lease any part of it

---

9   The onus is then on the lessee to show that, apart from non-compliance with the statutory power, the lease is otherwise valid: *Davies v Hall* [1954] 2 All ER 330, [1954] 1 WLR 855, CA.

10 See Supreme Court Act 1981 s 37.

11 *Kerr on Receivers* (15th edn) p 185. Leases will be granted in the name of the estate owner and the best terms must be obtained: *Wynne v Lord Newborough* (1790) 1 Ves 164.

that is not required for that purpose immediately. Their powers of leasing in such cases are limited strictly to the terms of the enabling Act.[12] Whether they can claim Crown privilege or not, e g whether such a lease is subject to the Rent Act, depends upon whether they can be regarded as acting as agents of the Crown, or merely servants of the Crown;[13] in the latter case they do not enjoy Crown privilege.

Corporations

A corporation is an artificial legal 'person' representing either the holder of an office (i e a corporation *sole*, e g a bishop and his successors) or a body of persons (i e a corporation *aggregate*, e g a mayor and corporation). The legal personality of a corporation is unchanging despite changes in the individuals who are its members. Corporations are either ecclesiastical or lay, and lay corporations are either eleemosynary or civil, and their leasing powers are governed by statute or by their constitutive instrument (e g charter, memorandum of association, etc.). A lease granted by a corporation must be by deed sealed with the corporate seal; but a tenant who goes into possession under an unsealed lease may become a tenant from year to year at law.[14]

The University and College Estates Act 1925 s 6, which applies to the Universities of Oxford, Cambridge and Durham and their colleges, and the colleges of Winchester and Eton, permits leases of any land for any term not exceeding 99 years in the case of building leases, 60 years in the case of mining leases and 21 years in the case of any other kind of lease.

Local authorities' powers of leasing

Section 123 of the Local Government Act 1972 governs the leasing powers of local authorities.[15] County councils, district councils and the councils of a London borough have power to grant leases of any length.[16] The consent of the Secretary of State for the Environment is required for the granting of a lease for a term not exceeding seven years, where, in particular, the consideration is less than the best rent reasonably obtainable. His consent is not required, however, in the case of the grant of a secure tenancy.[17] Certain other restrictions and

---

12 As in Civil Aviation Act 1982 s 41.
13 *Tamlin v Hannaford* [1950] 1 KB 18 at 22, CA, per Denning LJ.
14 *Ecclesiastical Comrs v Merral* (1869) LR 4 Exch 162.
15 By the Local Government Act 1985 s 57(7) and Sch 13 para 7, these powers are also conferred on residuary bodies, i e the London Residuary Body and the residuary bodies for the metropolitan counties.
16 For special leasing powers in relation to houses in National Parks etc see Housing Act 1985 ss 32 and 37.
17 Housing Act 1985 s 32. Provisions relating to leases granted under the right to buy fall outside the scope of this book. See passim Hughes *Public Sector Housing Law* (2nd edn) ch 2.

limitations are imposed on the powers of local authorities to lease land.[18]

Statutory corporations' leasing powers are governed by the statutes that created them. Thus, by s 14(1) of the Transport Act 1962, the British Railways Board, the London Transport Board, the British Transport Docks Board and the British Waterways Board may lease any property which in their opinion is not required by them for the purposes of their undertaking.[19] Non-statutory corporations have full leasing powers, subject only to any restrictions imposed by their charters or constitutions or by statute.

Companies registered under the Companies Act 1985, have full leasing powers except in so far as some restriction is imposed by virtue of the memorandum of association, which sets out the objects for which it was incorporated.

AGENTS

Prospective parties to a lease may authorise an agent to act on their behalf, with regard to negotiating its terms, and also to the granting and accepting of a lease, if they so desire. Authority to negotiate, to sign a binding contract, and even to enter into a lease that does not have to be by deed, requires no formality; but authority to execute a formal lease by deed must itself be given by deed, i e by a power of attorney. An agent should execute a lease in the name of his principal.[20]

An estate agent who is instructed to find a tenant, has no implied authority thereby to sign a contract for a lease, nor let prospective tenants into possession. A bailiff, on the other hand, may have a limited authority to grant leases, e g tenancies from year to year, by virtue of his contract of employment. An agent who exceeds his authority cannot bind his principal, though, of course, his unauthorised acts may be ratified, and such ratification will date back to them. A principal's knowledge will not be imputed to an agent, so that if an agent makes an innocent misrepresentation, an action will not lie against him in consequence, nor against the principal, unless the principal had

---

18 As, for example, land acquired under National Parks and Access to the Countryside Act 1949, or land acquired for planning purposes within Town and Country Planning Act 1971 s 290.

19 Similar leasing powers are given to the British Steel Corporation by the Iron and Steel Act 1982 s 14(1); also New Towns Act 1981 ss 17, 37 and 64 (leases for up to 99 years may be granted by New Towns and development corporations without ministerial consent).

20 See Powers of Attorney Act 1971 s 7.

deliberately kept his agent in ignorance (e g of a serious defect) in order to mislead the purchaser, i e fraudulently.[1] On the other hand, fraudulent mis-statements of an agent will be imputed to the principal. Similarly, where the agent, without the landlord's knowledge or authority, received an illegal premium from a tenant, the landlord was held liable, for the act was within the apparent authority of the agent.[2]

An agent employed to let property is under a duty:[3]

1 to make reasonable enquiries as to the solvency of a prospective tenant if, as a matter of construction, such a duty falls within the scope of his employment;[4]
2 to obtain the best price reasonably obtainable[5] (though in the case of a regulated tenancy, the rent registered under Part IV of the Rent Act 1977, is the maximum rent lawfully recoverable); and
3 until his principal accepts an offer, to disclose to him any other offers made to him.[5]

Agents normally charge the scale fees fixed by their professional bodies, but an agent's right to payment will depend upon any express terms of the agreement between himself and his principal. The contract may stipulate that he will be entitled to his fee on the introduction of a willing 'purchaser', for example, or only if a lease is granted. In such a case it is possible that a term will be implied that the principal will not dispose of the property himself or through other means, preventing the agent from receiving any commission.[6] A stipulation for sole letting rights will affect the position between the parties. Any deposit taken by the agent is held by him as agent for the landlord, and therefore, if the agent absconds with the money, the loss falls upon the landlord.[7]

It is unlawful for an agent to require or receive payment from prospective tenants of residential accommodation in certain circumstances: the Accommodation Agencies Act 1953.[8] See further Chapter 19.

---

1 *Armstrong v Strain* [1951] 1 TLR 856; affd [1952] 1 KB 232, [1952] 1 All ER 139, CA.
2 *Navarro v Moregrand Ltd* [1951] WN 335, CA; also *Saleh v Robinson* [1988] 2 EGLR 126, CA.
3 For statutory duties see Estate Agents Act 1979.
4 *Heys v Tindall* (1861) 1 B & S 296; *Bradshaw v Press* (1983) 268 Estates Gazette 565, CA (on facts estate agent not in breach of duty as nothing in (bogus) reference put him as reasonable agent on further inquiry).
5 *Keppel v Wheeler* [1927] 1 KB 577, CA.
6 *Luxor (Eastbourne) Ltd v Cooper* [1941] AC 108, [1941] 1 All ER 33, HL.
7 *Goding v Frazer* [1966] 3 All ER 234, [1967] 1 WLR 286.
8 *McInnes v Clarke* [1955] 1 All ER 346, [1955] 1 WLR 102; *Crouch and Lees v Haridas* [1972] 1 QB 158, [1971] 3 All ER 172, CA.

IV   TYPES OF LEASES AND TENANCIES

Since 1925, a term of years absolute is the only leasehold interest which is capable of existing as a legal estate (Law of Property Act 1925 s 1(1)). 'Term of years absolute' is defined by s 205(1)(xxvii) as meaning:

> 'a term of years (taking effect either in possession or in reversion whether or not at a rent) with or without impeachment for waste, subject or not to another legal estate, and either certain or liable to determination by notice, re-entry, operation of law, or by a provision for cesser on redemption, or in any other event (other than the dropping of a life, or the determination of a determinable life interest); but does not include any term of years determinable with life or lives or with the cesser of a determinable life interest, nor, if created after the commencement of this Act, a term of years which is not expressed to take effect in possession within twenty-one years after the creation thereof where required by this Act to take effect within that period; and in this definition the expression "term of years" includes a term for less than a year, or for a year or years and a fraction of a year or from year to year'.

Section 1(3) expressly provides that all other estates take effect as equitable interests. Since a lease for life or lives is expressly excluded from the statutory definition of 'term of years absolute' it must necessarily take effect in equity behind a trust, unless it is converted by s 149(6) of the 1925 Act (see below).

In any event, if the requisite formalities for passing the legal estate on the granting of a 'term of years absolute' are not followed[9] the tenant's interest takes effect if at all, in equity, with the result that if title to the land is unregistered, it must be protected by registration as a land charge.[10]

The statutory definition of a 'term of years absolute' is deliberately wide. It includes leases for a fixed number of years, for any length of time, long or short, provided the time span is less than perpetuity.[11] The fact that a 'term of years absolute' is or may be liable to determination by re-entry or forfeiture is, in this, of no significance. The statutory definition embraces all types of periodic tenancies, such as weekly, monthly, quarterly and yearly tenancies. Under the Rent Act 1977, a term of years is sometimes deliberately described so as to connote a 'term of years

---

9   Law of Property Act 1925 ss 52 and 54: see ch 4.
10   Ch 4.
11   See *Siew Soon Wah v Yong Tong Hong* [1973] AC 836, PC (tenancy described as 'permanent' held grant for longest period landlord had power to demise).

absolute'.[12] Similar results have been arrived at in relation to business tenancies in the context of court-approved tenancies outside statutory protection.[13]

Concurrent leases

A concurrent lease is a term limited to commence before the expiry of an existing lease of the same premises. It operates as an assignment of part of the head landlord's reversion. The concurrent lessee becomes entitled to the rent payable and to enforce the tenant's covenants under the earlier lease.[14] For example, where X held a concurrent lease on a flat occupied by T, it was held that X was 'lessor' for the purpose of recovery from T of a proportion of a service charge.[15] There is no limit on the number of concurrent legal leases which may be granted. Each subsequent term operates as a reversion expectant on the term next preceding it. The subsequent term may be longer than the term next above it or it may be shorter, in which case the legal reversion lasts until expiry of the shorter term. All concurrent leases must be by deed to pass a legal estate.[16]

Reversionary leases

By the Law of Property Act 1925 s 205(1)(xxvii) 'term of years absolute' includes a term taking effect in reversion, in other words at a future date. There is no requirement that a lease must take effect immediately. Though reversionary or future leases are therefore permitted, statute imposes some limits. By s 149(3) of the 1925 Act:

> 'A term, at a rent or granted in consideration of a fine, limited ... to take effect more than twenty-one years from the date of the instrument purporting to create it, shall be void, and any contract ... to create such a term shall likewise be void.'

This provision does not affect leases taking effect under a settlement. It was new in 1925.[17]

A contract to create a lease which, when granted, will not infringe s 149(3) is not invalidated by that provision, which only strikes down

---

12 Rent Act 1977 Sched 15 Part II Case 13 ('term certain not exceeding eight months'); Case 14 ('not exceeding 12 months').
13 *Re Land and Premises at Liss, Hants* [1971] Ch 986, [1971] 3 All ER 380 (six-month term certain within Landlord and Tenant Act 1954 s 38(4)).
14 *Re Moore and Hulm's Contract* [1912] 2 Ch 105.
15 *Adelphi (Estates) Ltd v Christie* (1983) 47 P & CR 650, CA
16 LPA 1925 s 52.
17 The rule against perpetuities does not preclude the granting of a lease to take effect at a remote future date.

contracts to create leases which will infringe it when granted.[18] Otherwise a renewal option in any lease for over 21 years in duration would be invalidated by s 149(3).[19] However, any contract made after 1925 to renew a lease for over 60 years after the termination of the current lease is void.[20]

The creation of reversionary leases taking effect as estates from the date of grant under s 149(3) would have been in direct conflict with the rule at common law that a tenant acquired no estate in the land until he had taken possession under the lease. Accordingly, s 149(2) abolished it, by providing that leases are capable of taking effect from the date fixed for commencement, without actual entry, and s 149(1) abolished the doctrine of *interesse termini*, which was the tenant's interest pending entry.

LEASES FOR A FIXED TERM

The simplest form of a term of years is a lease for a fixed term of a defined length, such as for six months, a year or 999 years. The term granted must be expressed either with certainty in the habendum of the lease or it must be capable of being rendered certain at the commencement date of the lease: if not the lease is void.[1] Therefore a lease for the duration of World War Two was held void.[2] Where, on the other hand, the tenant occupied rent-free, but subject to an undertaking to give up possession on three months' notice from the landlords certifying that they were ready to proceed with redevelopment, it was held that the term was certain and continued until determined by the landlords on a three-month notice, and the fact that the redevelopment might never occur was held not to affect this construction.[3]

In principle, a term certain commences only from execution of the lease, and liability under covenants in the lease runs from that date onwards, but the parties may expressly vary this general rule and define the commencement of the term or its expiration by reference to a date prior to the execution of the lease.[4]

---

18 *Re Strand and Savoy Properties Ltd, DP Development Co Ltd v Cumbrae Properties Ltd* [1960] Ch 582, [1960] 2 All ER 327, (1960) 76 LQR 352; *Weg Motors Ltd v Hales* [1962] Ch 49, [1961] 3 All ER 181, CA.

19 The renewal option in *Re Strand and Savoy Properties Ltd* supra was for one renewal of a 35-year term.

20 LPA 1922 Sch 15 para 7.

 1 *Lace v Chantler* [1944] KB 368, CA.

 2 *Lace v Chantler*, supra; reversed on facts by Validation of War Time Leases Act 1944, now itself repealed.

 3 *Ashburn Anstalt v Arnold* [1988] 2 All ER 147, CA. The court did not decide whether the tenants had a quarterly periodic tenancy or not.

 4 *Bradshaw v Pawley* [1979] 3 All ER 273 at 277–278.

The period of letting need not be continuous.[5] A lease may validly prohibit personal occupation by the tenant at specified periods such as weekends. Time share lettings are in principle valid: a person may be granted exclusive possession for one specified week in a specified number of years.[6]

The strict rule of certainty does not apply to periodic tenancies since their maximum life is inherently uncertain at their commencement: their duration depends on the time elapsing between commencement and service of a notice to quit by either side.[7]

A lease for a fixed term comes to an end automatically (i e without notice) when the term expires, i e by effluxion of time. In addition, such tenancies may be made terminable *before* the expiration of the term on notice given by one party or the other to terminate the tenancy at given intervals during its currency (i e an option to terminate, or 'break-clause' as it is often called, expressed to be exercisable, for example, at the end of the seventh and the fourteenth years of a 21-year lease). Fixed term leases may be also determinable on a condition (see ch 13). Leases for lives or until marriage raise special considerations.

Leases for life or lives or until marriage

Leases for life or lives or until marriage were in effect abolished by s 149(6) of the Law of Property Act 1925. Under s 149(6), a lease at a rent or in consideration of a fine 'for life or lives or for any term of years terminable with life or lives or on the marriage of the lessee' is automatically converted into a term of 90 years.[8] Such 90-year terms are determinable, by s 149(6), on either side, 'on the death or marriage (as the case may be) of the original lessee,' by at least one month's notice in writing given to determine the tenancy on one of the quarter days applicable to it – or if none, then on one of the usual quarter days. They are legal estates by statutory conversion.

Section 149(6) does not apply to any term taking effect in equity under a settlement or created out of an equitable interest under a settlement for mortgage, indemnity, or other like purposes, even if a rent is reserved. These terms take effect in equity behind a trust under s 1(3) of the 1925 Act.[9]

---

5 *Smallwood v Sheppards* [1895] 2 QB 627 (occupation for three successive Bank Holidays held agreement for single letting).
6 *Cottage Holiday Associates Ltd v Customs and Excise Comrs* [1983] QB 735. Query, whether a time-share period exceeding 21 years would infringe LPA s 149(3).
7 *Re Midland Rly Co's Agreement, Charles Clay & Sons Ltd v British Railways Board* [1971] Ch 725, [1971] 1 All ER 1007, CA.
8 A contract for a lease within s 149(6) is deemed to be a contract for the grant of a 90-year term terminable by notice.
9 See eg *Binions v Evans* [1972] Ch 359, [1972] 2 All ER 70, CA.

Section 149(6) applies to any term expressed to be determinable with any life or lives or on the marriage of the lessee,[10] whether the life is that of the landlord, the tenant, or the survivor of the tenant and some other person, no matter how short the term may be. Moreover, s 149(6) applies to any term of years determinable with life, as with a term granted by L to T for 21 years if he (T) so long lives. This will be automatically converted into a 90-year lease determinable at the earliest within one month of T's death.[11] The actual intentions of the parties therefore may count for little.

However, s 149(6) does not apply to a lease or tenancy determinable by notice after the dropping of a life or lives, such as a letting to T for three years with power in the landlord to terminate the tenancy by notice in the event of the death of the tenant during the currency of the term.[12]

Leases with a covenant or option for perpetual renewal

The lease may contain a covenant or option for renewal by the tenant. If the covenant or option are such that the right to renew must be reproduced perpetually in all further leases granted, perpetual renewal is created, with the following consequences.

The grant of a term, sub-term or other leasehold interest which is perpetually renewable takes effect as a term of 2,000 years from the commencement date of the term, or a sub-term of 2,000 years less one-day, calculated from the date of commencement of the head term out of which it was derived.[13]

Perpetually renewable leases or sub-leases take effect in substitution for the term originally granted. The rent, covenants and conditions of the substituted term are payable or enforceable during its 2,000-year span.[14] Special provisions apply of which the following[15] may be mentioned:

1   The lessee or under-lessee may on giving written notice to the landlord at least ten days before the date on which the lease would, but for its conversion, have expired, determine the lease on such expiry date (and on any subsequent dates provided in the original term for regular renewals).

---

10   Ie automatically on death (or marriage): *Bass Holdings Ltd v Lewis* [1986] 2 EGLR 40, CA.
11   The position if L at the date of the grant holds a leasehold reversion of (say) only 22 years is not solved by s 149(6).
12   *Bass Holdings Ltd v Lewis* [1986] 2 EGLR 40, CA.
13   LPA 1922 s 145 and Sch 15 paras 1 and 2. Identical provision is made for contracts for perpetual renewal: LPA 1922 Sch 15 para 7(1).
14   LPA 1922 Sch 15 paras 1 and 2.
15   Ibid paras 10(1),(2) and 11.

2 The lessee or underlessee must register all assignments of the converted term with the lessor, his agent or solicitor within six months of the assignment.
3 Each lessee or underlessee, whether the original party or not, is only liable for rent accruing and breaches of covenant taking place while the lease or sub-lease is vested in him.

Since the consequences of perpetual renewal are draconian – for example the rent originally fixed remains for the whole 2,000-year span of the converted term – the courts are reluctant to hold that perpetual renewal is intended except in the face of unambiguous language. Hence, a covenant to renew at the 'like' rent and all covenants in the lease, did not create perpetual renewal.[16] The question whether a particular form of words confers a right to perpetual renewal is one of construction and unambiguous language indicating an intention to include the entitlement to renewal in the terms of the renewed lease will be given effect to and perpetual renewal will be created: as with for example, a covenant to renew 'on identical terms' as the present lease;[17] or to renew at the same rent and with the like covenants 'including the present covenant for renewal'.[18] The same result followed where the relevant words clearly indicated that the covenant to renew must be included in the terms of any renewed lease on every renewal – the result being the conversion of a five-year term into a 2,000-year term at the same rent as that originally reserved.[19] A formula for renewal of a 21-year lease as often as every 11 years of the term expired was also held to create perpetual renewal.[20] The court may be able to decide what the parties' true intentions in the light of the surrounding circumstances were, and so it was held that words literally wide enough to confer perpetual renewal must be cut down to take these circumstances into account.[1]

Where a renewal covenant in a seven year lease provided that a renewed lease must contain a renewal covenant for a further seven year term on expiry of the renewed term, the tenant was held entitled merely to a double renewal – this on the basis that an obligation for perpetual renewal must be expressly spelt out of the lease.[2]

The safest course is to avoid any danger of perpetual renewal by

---

16 *Iggulden v May* (1804) 9 Ves 325.
17 *Northchurch Estates Ltd v Daniels* [1947] Ch 117, [1946] 2 All ER 524.
18 *Parkus v Greenwood* [1950] Ch 644, [1950] 1 All ER 436, CA.
19 *Re Hopkin's Lease, Caerphilly Concrete Products Ltd v Owen* [1972] 1 All ER 248, [1972] 1 WLR 372, CA.
20 *Wynn v Conway Corpn* [1914] 2 Ch 705, CA.
 1 *Plumrose Ltd v Real and Leasehold Estates Investment Society Ltd* [1969] 3 All ER 1441, [1970] 1 WLR 52 (the lease out of which the option derived was itself a once-only renewable lease).
 2 *Marjorie Burnett Ltd v Barclay* (1980) 125 Sol Jo 199.

providing expressly that renewal is to be on the same terms (for example) as the current lease excluding any further renewal covenant or option.[3]

PERIODIC TENANCIES

Periodic tenancies differ fundamentally from fixed-term tenancies. Instead of their total duration being fixed, right from the commencement of the tenancy, they continue automatically from period to period, until they are determined at the end of any period by a notice to quit given by one party to the other. Originally, they arose by implication, in the absence of any written agreement, and they still do; equally well, they may be created expressly. The periods most commonly found are weekly, monthly, quarterly and yearly tenancies, and whatever period is employed, that is bound to be the minimum duration of the tenancy, but until notice of termination is given, its total duration will not be certain. As the tenancy progresses through one period and another, the tenancy is regarded as one continuous tenancy, without break and without renewal; it is quite the converse of a renewable lease.

Any provision which is repugnant to the nature of a periodic tenancy will be void and unenforceable. In the main, these are likely to involve restrictions upon either party's rights to serve a notice to quit. Thus, a condition precluding the landlord from serving a notice to quit, as long as the tenant pays his rent and performs his covenants, could make it impossible for the landlord ever to serve notice, and is repugnant.[4] The same result follows if a tenancy provides for service of a notice to quit only by the tenant.[5] On the other hand, an agreement by the landlord not to serve notice to quit during the first three years of the tenancy unless he requires the premises for his own occupation, is not repugnant;[6] nor, it has been held, is an agreement precluding the landlord from terminating the tenancy at any time unless he requires it for the purposes of his own undertaking, even though, on the facts of the case, it would be unlikely that the landlord would ever wish to terminate for that reason.[7]

Yearly tenancies

Yearly tenancies (tenancies from year to year) may be created expressly

---

3 See 2 Forms and Precedents (4th edn) 340–341 Form 2.
4 *Doe d Warner v Browne* (1807) 8 East 165.
5 *Centaploy Ltd v Matlodge Ltd* [1974] Ch 1, [1973] 2 All ER 720.
6 *Breams Property Investment Co Ltd v Stroulger* [1948] 2 KB 1, [1948] 1 All ER 758, CA.
7 *Re Midland Rly Co's Agreement, Charles Clay & Sons Ltd v British Railways Board* [1971] Ch 725, [1971] 1 All ER 1007, CA.

or impliedly, and may be determined at the end of the first or any subsequent year by service of a valid notice to quit. In the absence of agreement to the contrary, six months' notice is required. Where rent is payable on the quarter days, and the tenant enters in the middle of a quarter, the courts will try to hold that the yearly tenancy commenced and is therefore terminable on a quarter day,[8] e g where on entry, the tenant pays a proportionate part of a quarter's rent, in respect of the period between the actual date of entry and the next quarter day.[9] A tenancy 'for one year, and so on from year to year' creates a fixed-term tenancy for one year, followed by a yearly tenancy; accordingly, it cannot be terminated before the end of the second year.[10]

A tenant holding over after the expiration of a fixed-term lease becomes a tenant at will or on sufferance. If he pays or expressly agrees to pay, a yearly rent, a tenancy from year to year may arise by implication of law, on terms not inconsistent with the previous lease.[11] The question of whether there is an intention impliedly to grant a yearly tenancy is one of evidence.[12] Solid evidence of intention on the landlord's part is required, and no implied grant will arise if the landlord had no choice, due to the Rent Act protecting the tenant, but to accept the rent,[13] or if he accepted the rent under a mistake.[14] No implied yearly tenancy arose where a landlord accepted two isolated payments of rent from an erstwhile service occupier (and licensee) with no real evidence of the intentions of the parties.[15] Where a tenant held over, at a rent, after expiry of a series of tenancies of business premises excluded from statutory security (under s 38(4) of the Landlord and Tenant Act 1954), he was a tenant at will only, despite the payment and acceptance of rent.[16]

In any case where statutory security of tenure for residential or business premises would apply to the tenant under a possible implied yearly tenancy, the common-law presumption of a yearly tenancy from payment and acceptance of rent is no longer the norm: further proof of an agreement for an implied yearly tenancy is required.[17]

A person who goes into possession under a void lease, or a mere

---

8   *Croft v William F Blay Ltd* [1919] 2 Ch 343 at 357, CA.
9   *Doe d Holcomb v Johnson* (1806) 6 Esp 10.
10 *Doe d Chadborn v Green* (1839) 9 Ad & El 658; *Addis v Burrows* [1948] 1 KB 444, [1948] 1 All ER 177, CA.
11 *Ladies' Hosiery and Underwear Ltd v Parker* [1930] 1 Ch 304, CA.
12 *Woodfall* 1–0632.
13 *Dealex Properties Ltd v Brooks* [1966] 1 QB 542, [1965] 1 All ER 1080, CA.
14 *Maconochie Bros Ltd v Brand* [1946] 2 All ER 778; *Sector Properties v Meah* (1973) 229 Estates Gazette 1097, CA.
15 *Thompsons (Funeral Furnishers) Ltd v Phillips* [1945] 2 All ER 49, CA.
16 *Cardiothoracic Institute v Shrewdcrest Ltd* [1986] 3 All ER 633, [1986] 1 WLR 368.
17 *Longrigg, Burrough and Trounson v Smith* (1979) 251 Estates Gazette 847 at 849, CA.

agreement for a lease, is a tenant at will, but when he pays, or agrees to pay, rent in accordance with the intended lease, he becomes a tenant from year to year at law upon the terms of the intended lease in so far as they are not inconsistent with a yearly tenancy. He may have other rights in equity, however, for if he has a specifically enforceable agreement, he is treated as holding from the date of entry on the terms of the lease intended by the parties, as if it had been granted, under the doctrine in *Walsh v Lonsdale*.[18] However, the common law presumption of a new yearly tenancy is relevant where for some reason the remedy of specific performance is unavailable, such as failure by either party to perform a condition precedent.[19]

There must be clear evidence of an agreement for a tenancy (or a new tenancy, as the case may be), and payment of rent is not in itself decisive; nor is it even essential, if there is other evidence to support the implication. Conversely, the implication of a yearly tenancy may be rebutted by evidence to the contrary, e g by calculation[20] (though not necessarily payment) of the rent by reference to weekly sums.

Where a tenancy from year to year arises by implication, the tenant holds under such of the terms of the former (or as the case may be, intended) lease as are not inconsistent with those of a yearly tenancy, e g covenants to pay rent in advance,[1] to keep the premises in good tenantable repair,[2] provisos for re-entry by the landlord on non-payment of rent or on breach of other covenants,[3] etc., but no onerous covenants to do repairs that would not normally be done by yearly tenants,[4] to paint every three years,[5] an agreement for two years' notice to quit,[6] nor an option for renewal.[7] A notice to quit given to terminate a yearly tenancy must be expressed to expire at the end of any year of the tenancy. If it arose by reason of the tenant holding over, it is terminable on the anniversary of the termination, and not of the commencement of the original term,[8] unless a contrary intention can properly be inferred.

---

18   (1882) 21 Ch D 9.
19   *Coatsworth v Johnson* (1885) 55 LJQB 220, CA.
20   *Adler v Blackman* [1953] 1 QB 146, [1952] 2 All ER 945, CA.
 1   *Lee v Smith* (1854) 9 Exch 662.
 2   *Richardson v Gifford* (1834) 1 Ad & El 52.
 3   *Thomas v Packer* (1857) 1 H & N 669.
 4   *Bowes v Croll* (1856) 6 E & B 255.
 5   *Pinero v Judson* (1829) 6 Bing 206.
 6   *Tooker v Smith* (1857) 1 H & N 732.
 7   *Re Leeds and Batley Breweries and Bradbury's Lease, Bradbury v Grimble & Co* [1920] 2 Ch 548.
 8   *Croft v William F Blay Ltd* [1919] 2 Ch 343; *Addis v Burrows* [1948] 1 KB 444, [1948] 1 All ER 177, CA.

Periodic tenancies for less than a year

Periodic tenancies for less than a year may be created expressly, or may arise by implication, in the same way as tenancies from year to year. They include weekly, monthly, three-monthly, quarterly, six-monthly and half-yearly tenancies, and the only reason for treating them separately from yearly tenancies is that they are terminable on one full period's notice at common law, ie in the absence of any express agreement to the contrary, and therefore, unlike tenancies from year to year, they would not normally be terminable at the end of the first period. The following statutory provisions apply to periodic tenancies for less than a year:

1 *Protection from Eviction Act 1977, s 5(1):* no notice to quit any premises let as a dwelling is valid unless it is given not less than four weeks before the date on which it is to take effect (see further Chapter 19);

2 *Landlord and Tenant Act 1985, s 4:* the landlord of any dwelling in respect of which rent is payable weekly is required to provide the tenant with a rent book (Chapter 19);

3 *Agricultural Holdings Act 1986, s 2(1):* agreements for less than a year of agricultural holdings take effect as tenancies from year to year (Chapter 29); and

4 *Law of Property Act 1925, s 61(a):* in any agreement made or taking effect after 31 December 1925, 'month' means calendar month, unless the context requires otherwise.

The period upon which a tenancy is based may be ascertained mainly by reference to the way in which the rent is calculated; thus, where the rent reserved is so much per year, a yearly tenancy will be implied, even though the rent is payable monthly. There is a distinction between a monthly or quarterly rent and monthly or quarterly instalments of a yearly rent;[9] and accordingly, where a tenant for a fixed-term at a weekly rent holds over and continues to pay the same weekly rent, the proper inference is that a weekly tenancy was intended.[10]

The difference between three-monthly and quarterly tenancies and between six-monthly and half-yearly tenancies relates to the date of their commencement, and hence to the dates on which they are terminable and the length of notice required. A tenancy commencing on one of the usual quarter days will normally be construed as a quarterly (or half-yearly tenancy) terminable on one quarter's notice on any quarter day

---

9 *Ladies' Hosiery and Underwear Ltd v Parker* [1930] 1 Ch 304, CA.
10 *Adler v Blackman* [1953] 1 QB 146, [1952] 2 All ER 945, CA.

(or on two quarters' notice, as the case may be, on either of the usual half-year days). But where such a tenancy commences in the middle of a quarter, it may be construed as a three-monthly or six-monthly tenancy, terminable on so many calendar months' notice given to expire in the middle of a quarter or half-year, though this may be rebutted by payment of a proportionate part of a quarter's rent (i e from the date of entry to the next quarter day) with the result that the tenancy will be deemed to have commenced on the quarter day next after the tenant's entry.

TENANCIES AT WILL

A tenancy at will arises where a person occupies land or premises with the consent, i e 'at the will', of the owner, under a tenancy of uncertain duration; and because the tenant has no certain estate, a tenancy at will is not within the definition of a 'term years absolute' (LPA 1925 s 205(1)(xxvii)). For the same reason, such an interest is terminable at any time simply by a demand for possession, or by implication of law, i e by any act which is inconsistent with the landlord's continuing consent, such as the death of either party, alienation of the landlord's interest with notice to the tenant,[11] or waste committed by the tenant.[12] The tenancy can, in effect, be terminated forthwith, and the tenant must quit immediately; he may in such cases re-enter upon the land within a reasonable time thereafter, to remove his goods or crops. Section 5 of the Protection from Eviction Act 1977 is inapplicable to tenancies at will.[13] Though the tenant has no estate, the relationship is one of tenure between the parties, and therefore where a rent has been agreed it is distrainable;[14] otherwise, the landlord may bring an action for damages for use and occupation.

An implied tenancy at will arises if a tenant holds over rent-free at the end of his lease, with the implied consent of the landlord, or where a tenant under a lease void at law,[15] or under an agreement for a future lease, enters into possession, rent-free, or where a person is let by the vendor into possession without special stipulations, pending completion of a purchase.[16] There was held to be an implied tenancy at will where a person took possession during negotiations for a lease, though the

---

11   E g by mortgage, *Jarman v Hale* [1899] 1 QB 994.
12   Co Lit 57a; *Countess of Shrewsbury's Case* (1600) 5 Co Rep 13b.
13   *Crane v Morris* [1965] 3 All ER 77, [1965] 1 WLR 1104, CA.
14   *Anderson v Midland Rly Co* (1861) 3 E & E 614.
15   *Dossee v Doe d East India Co* (1859) 1 LT 345, PC; *Meye v Electric Transmission* [1942] Ch 290.
16   *Wheeler v Mercer* [1957] AC 416 at 425, HL. This is thought to be unaffected by the dictum of Lord Templeman in *Street v Mountford* [1985] AC 809 at 820, [1985] 2 All ER 289 at 295, that the vendor-purchaser relationship involved a licence.

occupier paid sums towards the rent, because the rent was not calculable by reference to a year – and no lease was ever entered into.[17] Where tenants held over on various extensions of the last of a series of short-term tenancies outside Part II of the Landlord and Tenant Act 1954, paying rent, pending negotiations (which were abortive) for a new lease, they were held to have done so as tenants at will only.[18]

In relation to impliedly created tenancies at will, once rent calculated by reference to a year is paid and accepted then a yearly tenancy is created in principle. In the case of expressly created tenancies at will rent may be payable under them and its payment and acceptance will not necessarily convert the tenancy at will into a yearly tenancy.[19] Whether it does do so may depend on whether the tenancy at will is genuine or not, given that expressly (and impliedly) created tenancies at will lie outside the protection of Part II of the Landlord and Tenant Act 1954.[20]

It may be different where there is a non-business arrangement, as where a married couple was informally invited to live in part of a house, for so long as they wished, with the hope that it would be for the rest of their lives, which was held to create a tenancy at will, which was converted into a yearly tenancy on payment of rent.[1] In another case by contrast the owner allowed a family informally into occupation of his house and frequently visited them there: it was held that the occupiers were licensees: this is explicable today solely on the basis that there was no intention to create legal relations.[2] Generally, at least in the context of residential premises, if there is exclusive occupation rent-free for an indefinite period, this appears to indicate an implied tenancy at will as opposed to a licence.[3]

The title of the landlord is extinguished as from the expiry of 12 years uninterrupted rent-free occupation by a tenant at will. The 12 years run from the time when the tenancy at will comes to an end.[4]

TENANCIES ON SUFFERANCE

A tenancy on sufferance is said to arise where a tenant wrongfully holds over on termination of a previous tenancy, e g on the expiry of a fixed-term tenancy, without the landlord's consent, after surrender or on the

---

17 *British Railways Board v Bodywright Ltd* (1971) 220 Estates Gazette 651.
18 *Cardiothoracic Institute v Shrewdcrest Ltd* [1986] 3 All ER 633, [1986] 1 WLR 368.
19 *Manfield & Sons Ltd v Botchin* [1970] 2 QB 612, [1970] 3 All ER 143.
20 See *Hagee (London) Ltd v Erikson and Larson* [1976] QB 209 at 216, [1975] 3 All ER 234 at 237, CA (Scarman LJ).
1 *Young v Hargreaves* (1963) 186 Estates Gazette 355, CA.
2 *Heslop v Burns* [1974] 3 All ER 406, [1974] 1 WLR 1241, CA, as explained in *Street v Mountford* [1985] AC 809 at 824, [1985] 2 All ER 289 at 298.
3 *Street v Mountford*, supra.
4 Limitation Act 1980 s 15(6) and Sch I para 5.

determination of a tenancy at will. It is not really a tenancy at all, and is distinguisable from a tenancy at will by the lack of consent, express or implied, on the part of the landlord. There can then be no payment of rent, under a tenancy on sufferance, but the landlord can sue to recover *mesne* profits. By acceptance of rent, however, or other acknowledgement the tenancy may be converted into a tenancy from year to year.

The landlord may sue the tenant for possession without demand, for though he entered lawfully, he becomes, in effect, a trespasser, by wrongfully holding over; and if his occupation continues uninterrupted for 12 years, he will acquire a good title as against his landlord, as a squatter. As against the Crown, however, no tenancy on sufferance can arise, for such a tenancy continues only by the *laches* of the landlord (i e his delay or negligence), and the Crown cannot be guilty of *laches*.

TENANCIES BY ESTOPPEL

Non-denial of landlord's title

The tenant cannot deny the title of his landlord to grant a lease and the landlord cannot deny the tenant's right to occupation under it.[5] This recognition of the binding force of tenancies between the parties and their assigns applies no matter what the form of the lease.[6] The rule lasts for the duration of the lease; even after it expires, the tenant cannot set up a want of title in his landlord as a defence to an action for damages for breach of covenant unless the claim is by a third party.[7] On the other hand, once the lease has determined, a lessee paying rent to an ex-lessor thereafter is only estopped from setting up the ex-lessor's want of title if the lessee knew, or had notice of, the true facts as to the lessor's title.[8]

Effect of tenancies by estoppel

If a person with no legal estate in land purports to grant a lease to a tenant, it is enforceable between the parties, therefore, and their assigns, but not against third parties. If the landlord, after granting a lease or tenancy (i e a tenancy by estoppel) subsequently acquires a legal estate, out of which a legal tenancy could have been granted, at once the lease or tenancy becomes a legal tenancy and the title of the tenant is perfected:

---

5   *Tadman v Henman* [1893] 2 QB 168; generally, J Martin [1978] Conv (NS) 137.
6   *E H Lewis & Son Ltd v Morelli* [1948] 2 All ER 1021, CA.
7   *Industrial Properties (Barton Hill) Ltd v Associated Electrical Industries Ltd* [1977] QB 580, [1977] 2 All ER 293, CA.
8   *National Westminster Bank Ltd v Hart* [1983] QB 773, [1983] 2 All ER 177, CA; *Serjeant v Nash, Field & Co* (1903) 2 KB 304 at 312, CA.

the estoppel is 'fed'.[9] An estoppel is only 'fed' if the landlord later acquires the legal estate in his personal, as opposed to his representative, capacity.[10] A serious consequence for any mortgagee of the legal estate is that, assuming that the mortgage or charge takes effect only upon the landlord-mortgagor's acquisition of the legal estate, the landlord having previously to this granted tenancies by estoppel at a time when only entitled to the land in equity, the legal mortgagee will be postponed to the tenants. The feeding of the estoppel notionally precedes in point of time, the execution of the legal mortgage or charge.[11]

However, tenancies by estoppel may also be created by a landlord who previously charged the land by legal mortgage or charge even where the landlord's statutory power of leasing (above) is excluded. These tenancies will be binding as between the landlord and tenant and their respective assigns; but they will not bind the mortgagee or chargee as necessarily, they took effect after the mortgage or charge.[12] If the security becomes enforceable, the mortgagee may for instance sell the land free of the interests of the tenants and they will not have Rent Act protection against the mortgagee even if they did have it against the landlord.[13]

Attornment

This is a species of estoppel. Attornment is acknowledgment of the landlord's title: once it was necessary as between a tenant and an assignee of the reversion.

It is not so now.[14] Only in mortgages are attornments of use, as a means of enforcing restrictive trading agreements for a longer period than the mortgage would otherwise, in the general law, permit.[15]

---

9   *Universal Permanent Building Society v Cooke* [1952] Ch 95, [1951] 2 All ER 893, CA.

10 *Harrison v Wing* [1988] 29 EG 101, CA.

11 *Church of England Building Society v Piskor* [1954] Ch 553, [1954] 2 All ER 85, CA.

12 *Dudley and District Benefit Building Society v Emerson* [1949] Ch 707, [1949] 2 All ER 252, CA.

13 Ibid.

14 After Law of Property Act 1925 s 151.

15 See e g *Regent Oil Co v JA Gregory (Hatch End) Ltd* [1966] Ch 402, [1965] 3 All ER 673; *Shell UK Ltd v Lostock Garage Ltd* [1977] 1 All ER 481, [1976] 1 WLR 1187, CA.

Chapter 3

Leases and licences

I GENERAL PRINCIPLES

Introduction

A lease, because it confers an estate in land, is much more than a mere personal or contractual agreement for the occupation of a freeholder's land by a tenant. A lease, whether fixed-term or periodic, confers a right in property, enabling the tenant to exclude all third parties including the landlord, from possession, for the duration of the lease, in return for which a rent or periodical payment is reserved out of the land.[1] A contractual licence confers no more than a permission on the occupier to do some act on the owner's land which would otherwise constitute a trespass.[2] If exclusive possession is not conferred by an agreement, it is a licence.

The following are clear examples of licences: an agreement for the hiring of a concert hall for several days,[3] the grant of permission to erect advertisement hoardings,[4] or to run boats on a canal,[5] and the grant of 'front of house rights' in a theatre.[6] In all these cases, the agreements did not confer exclusive possession on the occupier, at a rent for a term, and were therefore held to be licences. In all cases, moreover, the user of the land by the licensee was for strictly limited purposes. There was no question of attempting to use the licences as devices to avoid tenant statutory protection, and the genuineness of the licences was not called into question. Where this is so, very different considerations may arise, dealt with particularly in the last two sections of this Chapter.

---

1 *Street v Mountford* [1985] AC 809 at 825, [1985] 2 All ER 289 at 299, HL.
2 *Thomas v Sorrell* (1673) Vaugh 330 at 351, Ex Ch.
3 *Taylor v Caldwell* (1863) 3 B & S 826. Also *Verrall v Great Yarmouth Borough Council* [1981] QB 202, [1980] 1 All ER 839, CA (licence to occupy hall for two specified days held enforceable by specific performance).
4 *Wilson v Tavener* [1901] 1 Ch 578.
5 *Hill v Tupper* (1863) 2 H & C 121.
6 *Clore v Theatrical Properties Ltd* [1936] 3 All ER 483, CA.

Agreements which are not tenancies

As seen above, the fundamental difference between a tenant and a licensee is that a tenant, who has exclusive possession, has an estate in land, as opposed to a personal permission to occupy. If, however, the owner of land proves that he never intended to accept the occupier as tenant, then the fact that occupier pays regular sums for his occupation does not make the occupier a tenant.[7] There are various circumstances where the nature of the occupation may be inconsistent with a tenancy such as, for example, where the occupier is a lodger and the landlord provides services or attendance, such as providing daily meals or changing linen regularly.[8] It is the owner's genuine requirement of unrestricted regular access to the premises, with a view to providing services or attendance, which in substance deprives the occupier of exclusive possession and hence of the status of tenant. These and other matters are considered in what follows.

General rules of construction

If a written agreement for the occupation of any land or premises, whether residential, business or agricultural, contains three elements then it will be a lease or tenancy, notwithstanding its language. Those elements are: (1) the grant of exclusive possession (2) at a rent or for periodical payments[9] (3) for a fixed or periodic term.[10] The presence or absence of exclusive possession is the decisive factor in deciding whether an agreement is a licence or a lease. This principle has been held to apply where the agreement confers a right to occupy on more than one occupier, the question being whether, in substance and in fact, the occupiers have exclusive possession of the whole accommodation or not.[11]

Licences not prohibited by statute

There is no general statutory provision invalidating the use of contractual licences as a means of avoiding statutorily-conferred security of tenure.[12] However, there is a difference between genuine and

---

7   *Isaac v Hotel de Paris* [1960] 1 All ER 348, PC.
8   *Marchant v Charters* [1977] 3 All ER 918, [1977] 1 WLR 1181, CA.
9   Even if no rent is payable, there may be a tenancy: *Ashburn Anstalt v Arnold*, supra. In *AG Securities Ltd v Vaughan* [1988] 3 All ER 1058, [1988] 3 WLR 1205, HL, Lord Templeman substituted the words 'periodical payments' for 'rent'.
10 *Street v Mountford*, supra.
11 *AG Securities Ltd v Vaughan*, supra.
12 However, the Agricultural Holdings Act 1986 s 2(2) (agricultural holdings) and the Housing Act 1985 s 79(3) (secure tenancies) deem certain licences to be tenancies: see chs 29 and 37 respectively.

contrived licence agreements. This aspect is taken up in later parts of this chapter. Suffice it here to note that, if an agreement is held to be a tenancy, terms in it which are inconsistent with, say, the Rent Act 1977 will be disregarded.[13] An example of such a term is a right enabling the landlord to use a room at any time with the tenant or to permit other persons to use the room with the tenant. Given that there are express statutory exceptions to full statutory security of tenure in the case of residential, business and agricultural land or premises, the possibility has been canvassed of generally extending the benefit of tenant protection statutes to licensees.[14] Such a step would involve difficulty and it is arguable that, after recent developments, no legislation is required or useful at present.[15]

Statutory background

In residential, business and agricultural land there are separate statutory codes in the private sector. These do not, generally, apply to licences. For instance, genuine licences of residential accommodation lie outside the full protection of the Rent Act 1977.[16] Genuine licences are incapable of being assured tenancies under the Housing Act 1988, and genuine licences of business premises are outside the protection of Part II of the Landlord and Tenant Act 1954.[17] There is an incentive on any owner of residential or business premises to draft, and have signed by an occupier, a document which asserts in terms that it is a licence, and which uses licence terms throughout, and attempts to avoid conferring exclusive possession on the occupier, with the result that on expiry or termination of the agreement, the occupier will lack statutory security of tenure. The principles of construction which have evolved in fairly recent years have addressed the problems thrown up by these documents. These principles of construction do not, it is thought, directly bear on the legitimate and long-established use of contractual licences for genuine purposes, such as the use of licences granting front of house rights in a theatre,[18] or an agreement licensing the use of refreshment rooms in a theatre.[19] In the residential sector, as will be seen, genuine licences to occupy are

---

13   *AG Securities Ltd v Vaughan*, supra.
14   Law Com No 162 (1987) Cm 145, para 4.9.
15   When the Housing Act 1988 was at the Committee stage of the House of Lords, it was said by the government that, if need be, sham licences might have to be dealt with in a future Bill: HL Deb 25 July 1988, cols 133–134.
16   *Fordree v Barrell* [1931] 2 KB 257, CA.
17   *Shell-Mex and BP Ltd v Manchester Garages Ltd* [1971] 1 All ER 841, [1971] 1 WLR 612, CA.
18   *Clore v Theatrical Properties Ltd* [1936] 3 All ER 483, CA.
19   *Edwardes v Barrington* (1901) 85 LT 650, HL; also *Frank Warr & Co v LCC* [1904] 1 KB 713, CA.

accepted, without serious question (unless they are shams) where an occupation, though exclusive, is due to family or domestic considerations with no intention to create legal relations,[20] or where as the result of a genuine surrender agreement, the status of the occupier is altered from tenant to licensee in return for rent-free occupation.[1] Similarly, a person occupying a room in an hotel or lodging-house is normally regarded as a lodger and, therefore, as a licensee, not a tenant.[2] The principles now discussed govern 'licence' agreements under challenge from the occupier at a later stage, where the latter claims that he has the status in substance of tenant, whatever the agreement may state on paper.

II CONSTRUCTION OF 'LICENCE' AGREEMENTS

Introduction

Whenever an agreement labelled a licence is challenged, the very difficult question arises as to how such an agreement is to be construed. Some questions of policy are necessarily involved, in particular, the question of how far it is permissible for parties to contract out of statutory security by using a licence as a device. In a recent decision, the House of Lords made it clear that courts must enforce the Rent Act and should observe the principle that the parties to an agreement, bogus or genuine, cannot contract out of it, if the net result of the agreement is to create a tenancy and also held that terms in what is in substance found to be a tenancy, which are inconsistent with the Rent Act, will be unenforceable except as provided in the Act.[3]

The key case of *Street v Mountford*[4] is a leading authority on this question. The limits on this case are: first, it dealt with an agreement where exclusive possession was conceded to exist, for occupation by one person. It applies, nonetheless, where there is an agreement for joint occupation, as will appear.[5] Second, rent was, in substance, payable by the occupier. Rent-free occupation of land may indicate a licence or it may indicate a tenancy this is a question of intention and the

---

20 See eg *Cobb v Lane* [1952] 1 All ER 1199, CA and also cases discussed below.
1 *Foster v Robinson* [1951] 1 KB 149, [1950] 2 All 342, CA. If the surrender had not been genuine then the court would clearly have disregarded it.
2 *Appah v Parncliffe Investments Ltd* [1964] 1 All ER 838, [1964] 1 WLR 1064, CA; *Luganda v Service Hotels Ltd* [1969] 2 Ch 209, [1969] 2 All ER 692, CA.
3 *AG Securities Ltd v Vaughan* [1988] 3 All ER 1058, [1988] 3 WLR 1205, HL.
4 [1985] AC 809, [1985] 2 All ER 289, HL. See Anderson (1985) 48 MLR 712; Tromans (1985) CLJ 351; Street [1985] Conv 328; Bridge [1986] Conv 344; Clarke [1986] Conv 39.
5 *AG Securities Ltd v Vaughan*, supra.

surrounding circumstances, but, as was said earlier, the payment of rent
has been held not to be an essential pre-requisite of a tenancy, although
the payment of periodical payments is usually required, save in the case
of tenancies at will.

To return to *Street v Mountford*[6] the facts were that M agreed to
occupy a furnished room in S's house at a so-called "licence fee' of £37
per week. The agreement, described as a 'licence' was careful to avoid
any overt suggestion of a tenancy and it consisted of ten numbered
paragraphs. At the foot of the agreement there appeared a separate
statement signed only by M 'I understand and accept that a licence in the
above form does not and is not intended to give me a tenancy protected
under the Rent Acts'. The House of Lords ruled that this agreement in
substance constituted a tenancy. It was conceded that the agreement
conferred exclusive possession on the occupier. Since the agreement
conferred exclusive possession, at a rent for a (periodic) term, it had the
hallmarks of a tenancy. The owner provided neither attendance nor
services. The actual language in which the agreement was dressed up,
that of a licence, had no effect on the result in law of the agreement. Two
general points are apparent.

1   The House of Lords adopted an approach which did not construe the
    agreement merely in accordance with its formal language, but under
    which the effect in substance of the agreement had to be decided.
    Moreover, the approach adopted was, apparently, intended to apply
    to residential, commercial and agricultural land and premises alike.
    It has been expressly held to apply to agreements for the joint
    occupation of residential premises: agreements must be construed
    objectively in the light of their language, factual matrix and
    surrounding circumstances, and these must include any relationship
    between the prospective occupiers, the course of the negotiations, the
    nature and extent of the accommodation and the intended and actual
    mode of occupation.[7]

2   Lord Templeman in *Street v Mountford*[8] warned courts to be 'astute
    to detect and frustrate sham devices and artificial transactions whose
    only object is to disguise the grant of a tenancy and to evade the Rent
    Acts'. No doubt the intention behind this statement was severely to
    limit the use of 'non-exclusive' licences as a means of wholesale
    avoidance of tenant protection statutes. Similarly, after some
    difficulties caused by conflicting decisions in the Court of Appeal

---

6   [1985] AC 809, [1985] 2 All ER 289, HL.
7   *AG Securities Ltd v Vaughan* [1988] 3 All ER 1058, [1988] 3 WLR 1205, HL.
8   [1985] AC 809 at 825, [1985] 2 All ER 289 at 299. In *AG Securities Ltd v Vaughan*,
    supra, at 1067, Lord Templeman said he would now substitute 'pretence' for 'sham
    device'.

following *Street v Mountford*,[9] the House of Lords reaffirmed its previous approach and ruled, in relation to agreements for the occupation of residential premises by, in one case, two, and in another, four, persons, that if an agreement created in substance, a tenancy and exclusive possession, the agreement would be a tenancy and terms which would destroy it and deprive the tenants of exclusive possession would be struck down, such as an owner's paper right to co-occupy the flat concerned.[10]

Traditional distinction

The House of Lords in *Street v Mountford*[11] restored the traditional distinction between leases and contractual licences. Lord Templeman, in criticising the reasoning of the Court of Appeal below, said:[12]

'In addition to the hallmark of exclusive possession there were the hallmarks of weekly payments for a periodical term. Unless these three hallmarks are decisive, it really becomes impossible to distinguish a contractual tenancy from a contractual licence save by reference to the professed intention of the parties or by the judge awarding marks for drafting.'

In other words, the question of whether an agreement for the occupation of land, whether for single or joint occupation, is a tenancy or a licence, rests on whether in fact and in substance a given agreement confers exclusive possession for periodical payments, for a term, whatever the labels of the quality of occupation and payments may be and whether the grant of a term is express or implied.[13] This issue is determined as a question of law, depending on the true construction of the agreement, in any case where it is not clear whether exclusive possession, the factor of paramount importance, is or is not present, and whether it is conferred in relation to the whole premises or not. Paper denials of the existence of a tenancy or of exclusive possession count for little or nothing if in substance a tenancy is created.

This approach is illustrated by a number of cases. Where a residential occupier had exclusive possession, and paid weekly sums for his occupation, and was not a service occupier, he was held a tenant despite an express denial in his agreement that he had a tenancy.[14] Similarly, an

---

9 See especially *Antoniades v Villiers* [1988] 2 All ER 309, [1988] 3 WLR 139, CA, and *AG Securities Ltd v Vaughan* [1988] 2 All ER 173, [1988] 2 WLR 689, CA.
10 *AG Securities Ltd v Vaughan*, supra. The actual result in each appeal is discussed at the end of this chapter.
11 [1985] AC 809, [1985] 2 All ER 289, HL.
12 Ibid at 826 and 299–300. For the decision below see (1985) 49 P & CR 324.
13 See eg *Taylor v Caldwell* (1863) 3 B & S 826 at 832.
14 *Facchini v Bryson* [1952] 1 TLR 1386, CA.

agreement for two years certain, relating to tennis courts, placing the 'licensee' under substantial repairing obligations and conferring in substance exclusive possession on the grantee was held a tenancy in the face of its careful and deliberate use of 'licence' terminology throughout: the agreement, significantly, reserved the ower a right to enter and inspect the premises, which was unnecessary if exclusive posession had not been conferred in reality.[15] Of this case, it was said in *Street v Mountford*,[16] that it was not clear until the whole document was examined that exclusive possession was granted. If the effect in law of any occupation agreement is unclear, it may accordingly, be necessary to examine the whole of it to see if it contains the ingredients of a tenancy.[17] Hence, an occupation agreement relating to a garage where the owner expressly and genuinely retained the right to possession and control of the premises was held a licence only.[18]

Scope of rules

It has been assumed from the fact that cases both in the residential and business sectors were cited and analysed in *Street v Mountford* that the approach of that case to the construction of so-called licence agreements was intended to apply both to residential and business land or premises and, where relevant, to agricultural land.[19] Nevertheless, it has been said, obiter, that the passages in *Street v Mountford* dealing with tenants and lodgers do not apply to business premises, and that the indicia for and against a tenancy in residential cases may have less effect in some business cases.[20] This matter cannot be resolved as the authorities stand but in the business sector there may be more reluctance to assume that a licence is not genuine, but if it confers exclusive possession, it will generally be held to be a tenancy.[1] If an agreement for the occupation of business premises is oral, the effect of the agreement is a question of the correct inference to be drawn from the facts and circumstances.[2] However, it is possible to derive a written agreement from a series of informal documents, such as letters.

---

15 *Addiscombe Garden Estates Ltd v Crabbe* [1958] 1 QB 513, [1957] 3 All ER 563, CA.

16 [1985] AC 809 at 823, [1985] 2 All ER 289 at 297, HL.

17 *AG Securities Ltd v Vaughan*, HL, supra.

18 *Shell-Mex and BP Ltd v Manchester Garages Ltd* [1971] 1 All ER 841, [1971] 1 WLR 612, CA. Also *Bahamas International Trust Co v Threadgold* [1974] 3 All ER 881, [1974] 1 WLR 1514, HL.

19 *London and Associated Investment Trust plc v Calow* [1986] 2 EGLR 80; *University of Reading v Johnson-Houghton* [1985] 2 EGLR 113.

20 *Dresden Estates Ltd v Collinson* (1987) 55 P & CR 47, CA.

 1 *London and Associated Investment Trust plc v Calow* [1986] 2 EGLR 80; Bridge [1987] Conv 137. For a sham agreement see *Dellneed Ltd v Chin* (1986) 53 P & CR 172.

 2 *Smith v Northside Developments Ltd* [1987] 2 EGLR 151, CA.

In residential cases, the new approach was rigorously applied in relation to single occupation agreements, so that a houseparent who was accepted to have exclusive possession of a house owned by his employer, paying rent, under an informal agreement, was held a tenant.[3] Likewise a person taking possession of a house paying weekly sums, to put the house into good condition and then buy it from the owner, was held in substance to have exclusive possession and a (protected) tenancy, not a licence.[4] At the risk of repetition, after a period of judicial fluctuation, it was held that the *Street v Mountford* approach governs joint occupation agreements, as well as single occupation agreements, in the residential sector.[5]

Exclusive possession but no tenancy

There are some circumstances where, though a grantee of occupation rights over residential property has exclusive possession, there is no tenancy. These circumstances were listed, apparently comprehensively, in *Street v Mountford*. They are as follows.

(i) *No intention to create legal relations*

If the circumstances and the conduct of the parties show that the occupier is to be granted a personal privilege, with no interest in the land, then he will be a licensee – even if apparently in exclusive possession.[6] However, this category is limited to family arrangements, or acts of friendship or generosity.[7] On these principles, a licence was created where an owner allowed a couple rent-free occupation as an act of generosity,[8] and also where there was occupation under what was, in substance, despite its tenancy labelling, an informal family arrangement.[9] The exact ambit of the principle is uncertain, but there have been cases outside family and similar arrangements where licences have been held to exist simply because of the absence of intention, in substance, to enter into legal relations. On this basis the occupier, apparently exclusively, of a room in an old people's home was held a licensee,[10] as was a war-time evacuee living in a house under informal

---

3 *Royal Philanthropic Society v County* [1985] 2 EGLR 109, CA; PF Smith [1986] Conv 215; also *Postcastle Properties Ltd v Perridge* [1985] 2 EGLR 107, CA.
4 *Bretherton v Paton* [1986] 1 ELGR 172, CA.
5 *AG Securities Ltd v Vaughan*, HL, supra.
6 *Errington v Errington and Woods* [1952] 1 KB 290 at 297–298, [1952] 1 All ER 149 at 154–155, CA.
7 *Facchini v Bryson* [1952] 1 TLR 1386 at 1389, CA.
8 *Heslop v Burns* [1974] 3 All ER 406, [1974] 1 WLR 1241, CA.
9 *Barnes v Barratt* [1970] 2 QB 657, [1970] 2 All ER 483, CA.
10 *Abbeyfield (Harpenden) Society v Woods* [1968] 1 All ER 352n, [1968] 1 WLR 374, CA.

arrangements with the owner.[11] Where parties negotiated for the grant of a lease 'subject to contract' but the negotiations broke down, it was held that the individual concerned was only a licensee as it was the mutual intention of the parties to enter into legal relations only if a lease was completed.[12] Where the tenant died, leaving a daughter in residence, and the landlords only accepted rent from her for a short time while considering their position, it was held, on the very special facts, arising under residential succession provisions, that the landlords had not intended to contract with the daughter at all, and she was held a licensee.[13]

(ii) *Exclusive possession exists but is referable to legal relations other than a tenancy*

Exclusive possession is not decisive in all cases, it was held in *Street v Mountford*, because an occupier with exclusive possession is not necessarily a tenant. The occupier may be a lodger or a service occupier or there may be other special circumstances, as where the occupier is a fee simple owner, a trespasser, a mortgagee in possession, or the object of charity, or where the parties are vendor and purchaser,[14] or where the owner such as a requisitioning authority,[15] has no power to grant a tenancy.

Service occupation   A person is a service occupier where he is a servant in occupation of the house of his master in order to perform his services: the occupation must be strictly ancillary to the performance of the duties of the servant-occupier, and the servant's occupation in this case is deemed to be that of his master.[16] That being so, the possession is that of the master, the servant is a licensee, and no tenancy is created.[17] Examples of service occupation include: a surgeon whose post required residence within the hospital concerned,[18] a soldier required to occupy military quarters,[19] a chauffeur lodged in part of his master's premises.[20] However, the mere fact that the servant occupies the master's house rent-free as part of his remuneration will not of itself make him a service occupier.[1]

---

11   *Booker v Palmer* [1942] 2 All ER 674, CA; also *Davies v Brenner* [1986] CLY 163.
12   *Isaac v Hotel de Paris* [1960] 1 All ER 348, [1960] 1 WLR 239, PC.
13   *Marcroft Wagons Ltd v Smith* [1951] 2 KB 496, [1951] 2 All ER 271, CA.
14   See *Essex Plan Ltd v Broadminster Ltd* [1988] 43 EG 84.
15   *Finbow v Air Ministry* [1963] 2 All ER 647, [1963] 1 WLR 697.
16   *Smith v Seghill Overseers* (1875) LR 10 QB 422.
17   *Mayhew v Suttle* (1854) 4 E & B 347, Ex Ch.
18   *Dobson v Jones* (1844) 5 Man & G 112.
19   *Fox v Dalby* (1874) LR 10 CP 285.
20   *Thompsons (Funeral Furnishers) Ltd v Phillips* [1945] 2 All ER 49, CA.
1   *Hughes v Chatham Overseers* (1843) 5 Man & G 54; *R v Spurrell* (1865) LR 1 QB 72.

Determining whether exclusive possession exists

It was conceded in *Street v Mountford*[2] that exclusive possession was conferred by the agreement in that case. There was no need for the court to embark on a detailed examination of the whole agreement, once it could spell out of it the three hallmarks of exclusive possession at a rent for a term. The court, if there is doubt as to whether exclusive possession is conferred, will, as noted, have to scrutinise the whole agreement to see whether exclusive possession is conferred by it, in fact and in substance, bearing in mind the requirement of the House of Lords in *Street v Mountford* to detect and frustrate shams or pretences.[3] This process had been applied, as noted above, to agreements to occupy business premises, for some time.[4] Further, and difficult, questions of construction arise where there is an agreement for the joint occupation of residential premises, for example, where there are separate agreements for the occupation of one or more rooms. In such cases, the court must examine the agreement in the light of the surrounding circumstances listed earlier and must conclude whether, in substance, there is joint exclusive possession of the whole premises on the occupiers' part. Important factors will be (1) whether the occupiers are related or cohabiting, or independent persons; (2) whether the owner genuinely intends to deprive them of exclusive possession by means of a common law power to do so; (3) the course of the negotiations.[5]

Occupation as lodger

In residential premises, a person's occupation may be as a lodger and for that reason, independently of the above, a licensee. It was held in *Street v Mountford*[6] that an occupier of residential accommodation is a lodger if the landlord provides attendance or services which require the landlord or his servants to exercise unrestricted access to and use of the premises. A plain example occurred where the landlord of a bed-sitting room provided daily cleaning of the room (and other rooms in the premises) and clean linen each week.[7] A lodger has exclusive use of his rooms; but he has no exclusive occupation, the occupation being retained by the landlord, except that exclusive enjoyment of the occupation is given to

---

2 [1985] AC 809, [1985] 2 All ER 289, HL.
3 Eg in *AG Securities Ltd v Vaughan* [1988] 3 All ER 1058, [1988] 3 WLR 1205, Lord Templeman treated a term, in *Hadjiloucas v Crean* [1987] 3 All ER 1008, [1988] 1 WLR 1006, CA, reserving an owner the right to require one of two co-occupiers to share the flat concerned with a stranger as a pretence.
4 See *Addiscombe Garden Estates Ltd v Crabbe* [1958] 1 QB 513, [1957] 3 All ER 563, CA and other cases discussed earlier.
5 *AG Securities Ltd v Vaughan*, HL, supra. See further section III of this chapter.
6 [1985] AC 809, [1985] 2 All ER 289 at 817–818 and 293, HL.
7 *Marchant v Charters* [1977] 3 All ER 918, [1977] 1 WLR 1181, CA.

the lodger for the time being.[8] In other words, the occupation of the landlord is paramount in this case, that of the lodger subordinate and the occupation rights of the landlord are (at least) co-extensive with those of the lodger.[9] However, it is not easy to frame an exhaustive definition of a lodger. For example, the fact that the landlord lives in part of the same premises will not automatically render the occupiers of other parts lodgers – especially if the landlord retains no control over the parts he does not occupy.[10] Where no attendance or services are provided, a person will be a lodger only if the landlord retains sufficient control over the occupier's part of the premises: how much control is retained is a question of fact.[11] Where an agreement in terms denied the 'licensees' the right to use their rooms at certain defined times of day, and gave the owner the right to remove or to substitute any furniture in any flat in the premises as he saw fit, it was held that these terms could be regarded as shams, rendering the whole agreement suspect.[12]

Reservation of rights

1   In relation to agricultural land, an occupier of gallops and land under a series of 'licences' was held to have exclusive possession and a tenancy: one factor was that he was obliged to take the land (which he did not really require) in return for the gallops.[13]

2   A reservation by an owner of co-extensive or exclusive control and possession of premises, which is genuine and really intended to be or in fact exercised, points to a licence, at least in the case of business premises, as where the owner reserved the right, without first determining the agreement, to transfer the occupier to other parts of the premises.[14] Similarly, a genuine reservation of co-extensive rights to the owner of occupation and control of agricultural land deprives the occupier of exclusive possession, and the occupation will then be under licence.[15]

---

8   *Allan v Liverpool Overseers* (1874) LR 9 QB 180 at 191–192 (Blackburn J). See also *Bradley v Baylis* (1881) 8 QBD 195, CA (landlord's retaining duplicate key equated with retention of control).

9   *Holywell Union v Halkyn District Mines Drainage Co* [1895] AC 117.

10   *Kent v Fittall* [1906] 1 KB 60, CA.

11   *Helman v Horsham and Worthing Assessment Committee* [1949] 2 KB 335, [1949] 1 All ER 776, CA.

12   *Crancour v Da Silvaesa* [1986] 1 EGLR 80, CA. In *AG Securities Ltd v Vaughan*, supra, Lord Templeman approved the analysis of Ralph Gibson LJ of shams in this case.

13   *University of Reading v Johnson-Houghton* [1985] 2 EGLR 113; Rodgers [1986] Conv 275.

14   *Dresden Estates Ltd v Collinson* (1987) 55 P & CR 47, CA; PF Smith [1987] Conv 220.

15   *Lampard v Barker* (1984) 272 Estates Gazette 783, CA.

3 In the case of residential premises, reservations entitling an owner to co-occupation of the premises, especially if there simply for the purpose of avoiding statutory protection, will be treated with considerable suspicion, and if not genuinely intended to be exercised, will be unenforceable under the Rent Act 1977 or the Housing Act 1988.[16]

III PRINCIPLES WHERE AN AGREEMENT IS SUSPECT – FURTHER ASPECTS

In *Street v Mountford*[17] the House of Lords disapproved of three decisions which had held that a residential occupier or occupiers had licence agreements.[18] Lord Templeman said that the courts should be astute to detect and frustrate sham devices and artificial transactions whose only object is to disguise the grant of a tenancy and to evade the Rent Acts. On this basis, the so-called licence in one case specially subjected to criticism was treated as creating a joint tenancy – in terms there were two separate 'licence' agreements, one each granted to an unmarried couple. In short, the House of Lords in *Street v Mountford* regarded this particular agreement as a sham, as creating a joint tenancy and as granting exclusive possession.

Some difficulty, since *Street v Mountford*, arose in determining the exact limits of the new approach. Prior to this case, the courts, at least in the residential sector, placed emphasis on the stated intentions of the parties, particularly in relation to agreements envisaging occupation by more than one person, and adopted a narrow test of what were to be sham agreements (and tenancies in disguise). This test, derived from a different context, required that the occupier prove that the parties said one thing in their agreement while really intending another, or to give the appearance of creating legal rights different from those actually created.[19] After *Street v Mountford* matters were not, at first, resolved, and there were conflicting decisions. It was held, for example, that *Street v Mountford* created no presumption of a joint tenancy.[20] As will be seen, this view is no longer sustainable. It has also been held that *Street v Mountford* may not necessarily apply with equal force to agreements for

---

16 *AG Securities Ltd v Vaughan*, HL, supra.
17 [1985] AC 809, [1985] 2 All ER 289 at 825–826 and 299–300.
18 Ie *Somma v Hazlehurst* [1978] 2 All ER 1011, [1978] 1 WLR 1014, CA; *Aldrington Garages Ltd v Fielder* (1978) 37 P & CR 461, CA and *Sturolson & Co v Weniz* (1984) 272 Estates Gazette 326, CA.
19 *Snook v London and West Riding Investments Ltd* [1967] 2 QB 786 at 802, [1967] 1 All ER 518 at 528, CA.
20 *Hadjiloucas v Crean* [1987] 3 All ER 1008, [1988] 1 WLR 1006, CA; also *Brooker Settled Estates Ltd v Ayers* [1987] 1 EGLR 50, CA.

the occupation of business premises,[1] although the mere fact that a business occupier shares a reception area with others will not of itself prevent him from having exclusive possession over the whole area granted to him.[2] It was also held that a business occupation agreement with, in reality, the hallmarks of exclusive possession at a rent for a term, constituted a tenancy irrespective of the parties' professed intentions.[3] In the latter case, a submission based on the sanctioning by the Court of Appeal[4] of the primacy of the parties' intentions was rejected as being inconsistent with *Street v Mountford*. However, the agreement in this particular case was an obvious sham.

In relation to joint occupation agreements of residential premises, judicial doubt was expressed that certain authorities had in fact been overruled by the House of Lords, enabling the Court of Appeal to re-emphasise the importance of the stated intentions of the parties, and to re-apply the narrow test mentioned earlier for holding an agreement which did not on its face confer exclusive possession to be a sham.[5] On this basis, separate flat-sharing agreements granted to an unmarried couple were held to be genuine non-exclusive licences: it was said that there was no reason why these agreements should not be made, and so, it seems, that the intention of the parties as stated in the documents was still a very important factor.[6] The result and reasoning in this case was overruled on appeal by the House of Lords, and the couple held to be joint tenants, for reasons explained above; in a related appeal, agreements for the occupation by four persons, none of them related, each paying a different rent, and none of them entitled, in fact, to exclusive possession of the whole premises, were held genuine licences because they did not confer exclusive possession.[7] The owner in the case of the unmarried couple had a power to require one of the two to share with him as a stranger: this was treated as a pretence and unenforceable except under s 98 of the Rent Act 1977. The fact that there were two agreements was dismissed – the two were treated as one. In contrast, in the case of the four occupiers, each agreement was taken separately and none was entitled to joint exclusive possession of the whole. The avoidance or evasion of statutory protection in the residential sector has been rendered more difficult, but not impossible, by these developments.

---

1   *Dresden Estates Ltd v Collinson* (1987) 55 P & CR 47, CA. This was a case where in reality there could be no exclusive possession.
2   *London and Associated Investment Trust plc v Calow* [1986] 2 EGLR 80.
3   *Dellneed Ltd v Chin* (1986) 53 P & CR 172; Bridge [1987] Conv 298.
4   *Matchams Park (Holdings) Ltd v Dommett* (1984) 272 Estates Gazette 549, CA.
5   *Hadjiloucas v Crean*, supra, CA.
6   *Antoniades v Villiers* [1988] 2 All ER 309, [1988] 3 WLR 139, CA; PF Smith [1988] Conv 305.
7   *AG Securities v Vaughan*; *Antoniades v Villiers* [1988] 3 All ER 1058, [1988] 3 WLR 1205, HL.

Chapter 4

Creation and form of leases

I LEASES AND AGREEMENTS FOR LEASES

A lease is a 'conveyance'[1] of an estate in land, and the same formalities are required by law as for a conveyance of the fee simple. It is, in effect, a sale of land, and by its very nature, differs from the sale of a chattel in this respect, that the legal title cannot (except in the case of certain short leases) pass to the purchaser by word of mouth, but must be effected by deed, i e an instrument under seal, which is duly executed. Thus, whereas under an ordinary contract for sale, title to a chattel passes on conclusion of the contract, title under a lease has to be passed formally, in performance of a prior contract. There are three distinct stages in the transaction:

1 preliminary negotiations;
2 a contract or agreement for a lease; and
3 the lease itself.

First, there are preliminary negotiations, when the bargaining goes on, the property is inspected, the rent and other terms discussed, references given on the part of the tenant, etc. At this stage, there is as yet no agreement cognisable in law, and the parties remain free to withdraw, with impunity. A contract is concluded when the prospective parties reach agreement on the granting of a lease. An enforceable contract for a lease which stipulates that a formal lease will be granted will be construed as a lease if its essential terms are fixed and if possession is to be taken under it: the covenants will then be binding at once.[2] If an existing term is to be repudiated and replaced with a new term, the conduct of the party in default must lead the other reasonably to conclude that he no longer intends to be bound by the agreement.[3]

A contract for the sale or other disposition of land is unenforceable

---

1 LPA 1925 s 205(1)(ii).
2 *Halsbury's Laws of England* (4th edn) Vol 27 para 51.
3 *Bush Transport Ltd v Nelson* [1987] 1 EGLR 71, CA.

unless it is in writing, or evidenced in writing (LPA 1925 s 40). Only then, is the second stage of the transaction complete, in the sense that there is an enforceable contract for a lease, which consists of mutual promises. The prospective landlord promises that he will grant the lease and the prospective tenant promises that he will take the lease upon the terms agreed. Finally, the lease is granted in performance of that prior contract.

The law recognises the disparity that exists between different kinds of leases by allowing certain legal leases not exceeding three years to be created informally, i e orally or simply in writing (LPA 1925 s 54(2)). This is the case, for example, where a weekly tenancy is granted orally, to commence immediately. A legal lease is thereby created without, apparently, going through the second stage above. A verbal promise of a weekly tenancy to commence next Saturday is quite another thing, however, for that is no more than an agreement for a future lease, which to be enforceable, must be in writing, or evidenced in writing, in accordance with s 40.

The expressions 'contract for a lease' and 'agreement for a lease' are in fact synonymous, though 'contract' perhaps more aptly describes an agreement which is enforceable in law because it satisfies s 40, if only because it is more likely to suggest a greater degree of formality than does the word 'agreement'. However, evidence in writing is the essential requirement of s 40, and a signed note containing the barest terms of the intended lease will suffice. The more valuable the interest to be created, of course, the more likely are the parties to have formal contracts drawn up for them, which will invariably contain express terms on a whole range of matters which would not be found in a mere note. Nevertheless, in the absence of express terms, the law will imply terms necessary to make the contract effective, and the mere note is enforceable just as well as a formal contract.

An enforceable contract for a lease also creates valuable equitable rights in the land for the benefit of the tenant. These have already been mentioned *à propos* the creation of legal tenancies from year to year by implication, by entry and by payment of rent by the tenant under a void lease, for example. The distinction between legal leases and equitable leases, however, will be postponed until the formalities for the creation of a lease and enforceable contract for a lease have been explained.

II   CREATION OF LEGAL LEASES UNDER LPA 1925 ss 52 AND 54

Section 52(1) of the Law of Property Act 1925, provides that:

'All conveyances of land or of any interest therein are void for the purpose of conveying or creating a legal estate unless made by deed'.

but s 52(2)(d) exempts from these formal requirements:

'leases or tenancies or other assurances not required by law to be made in writing'.

Further, s 54 provides that:

'(1) All interests in land created by parol and not put in writing and signed by the persons so creating the same, or by their agents thereunto lawfully authorised in writing, have, notwithstanding any consideration having been given for the same, the force and effect of interests at will only.

(2) Nothing in the foregoing provisions of this Part of this Act shall affect the creation by parol of leases taking effect in possession for a term not exceeding three years (whether or not the lessee is given power to extend the term) at the best rent which can be reasonably obtained without taking a fine.'

The combined effect of these provisions is four-fold:

1   The general rule is that for a lease capable of existing as a legal estate to be created, as such, it must be made by deed, unless it is a lease which falls within the exception under s 54(2).
2   A lease created orally, which by s 52(1) is required to be by deed, will take effect as a tenancy at will only, unless and until it is converted into a tenancy from year to year by implication of law. A lease which is void at law is enforceable between the parties in equity as an agreement for a lease, so as to effectuate the parties' intentions.[4] If the tenant takes possession and pays rent, the parties are in the same position as if a valid lease had been granted.[5]
3   No formality is required for a lease which:
      (i) takes effect in possession,
      (ii) for a term not exceeding three years,[6] whether or not the tenant is given power to extend the term,
      (iii) is at the best rent reasonably obtainable without taking a fine.[7]
4   A lease of incorporeal rights must generally be by deed.

In other words, an informal lease (ie whether created orally or in writing) will take effect as a legal lease if the three conditions are satisfied. 'Taking effect in possession' is to be contrasted with a reversionary lease;

---

4   *Parker v Taswell* (1858) 2 De G & J 559.
5   *Walsh v Lonsdale* (1882) 21 Ch D 9, CA.
6   Computed from the day the lease is made: *Foster v Reeves* [1892] 2 QB 255, CA.
7   See *Bush Transport Ltd v Nelson* [1987] 1 EGLR 71, CA (oral executory contract).

i e the lease must commence immediately, and not at some later date. 'Possession' does not require physical possession, but includes receipt of rents and profits, or the right to receive them,[8] e g from sub-tenants. A 'term not exceeding three years' includes weekly, monthly, yearly and other periodic tenancies, as well as tenancies for terms not exceeding three years, whether or not the latter contains an option for renewal beyond three years. It does not include a lease for a term exceeding three years, even though it contains an option to determine within the first three years.[9] The third condition is that the rent should be equivalent to the full value of the premises, whether payable as a rack rent or at a premium and a reduced rent.

Whilst an oral lease may create a legal estate by virtue of s 54(2), it is not a 'conveyance' within the definition of s 205(1)(ii) of the Act, and will therefore not operate to convey easements and other rights implied under s 62 on a conveyance.

Two important limitations to the operation of s 54(2) must not be overlooked: the sub-section does not apply to a contract for a lease or a contract of assignment, which must be in writing (s 40), nor does it apply to an assignment of a lease, however short, which must be by deed (s 52).

III   CONTRACTS ENFORCEABLE UNDER LPA 1925 s 40

Section 40 of the Law of Property Act 1925, provides:

'(1) No action may be brought upon any contract for the sale or other disposition of land or any interest in land, unless the agreement upon which such action is brought, or some memorandum or note thereof, is in writing, and signed by the party to be charged or by some other person thereunto by him lawfully authorised.

(2) This section applies to contracts whether made before or after the commencement of this Act and does not affect the law relating to part performance, or sales by the court.'

Section 40 applies to all terms which are part of the agreement for a lease; but rescission of the contract may validly be achieved orally. The provision renders contracts for a lease unenforceable unless evidenced either in writing or by a sufficient memorandum in writing, or where there is proof of a sufficient act of part performance. Even an oral contract may be admitted by the defendant, in which case it will be enforceable.

---

8   LPA 1925 s 205(1)(xix).
9   *Kushner v Law Society* [1952] 1 KB 264, [1952] 1 All ER 404.

It is established,[10] moreover, that unless the absence of writing is specially pleaded by the defendant, he is not entitled to rely on it, and the contract will then become enforceable against him. Further, it should be noted that s 40 does not apply to sales by order of the court, nor may it be relied on if the lack of writing is attributable to the fraud of the defendant.[11] If it is raised in defence, the effect is to render the entire contract unenforceable. 'Unenforceable' means unenforceable by action on the contract (e g for damages); nevertheless the plaintiff may be able to take advantage of the contract in some other way. If, for example, a deposit has been paid by the prospective tenant under an oral contract, and he afterwards refuses to proceed, the landlord is entitled to retain the deposit,[12] even though he would not have been entitled to damages for breach of contract;[13] moreover, the tenant would be entitled to recover it, if it were the landlord who refused to proceed.[14]

A contract that is sufficiently evidenced either in writing or by part performance may be enforceable at the discretion of the court in equity by specific performance, but only a contract evidenced in writing is enforceable at law by an action for damages. Apart from the question of the remedies available, enforceability of a contract under s 40 is dependent upon firm evidence or proof of an agreement between the parties to which the court can give effect. Section 40 does not render unenforceable collateral agreements to the contract for a lease.[15] Both limbs of s 40 will now be explained.

AGREEMENT OR MEMORANDUM IN WRITING

Section 40(1) requires, as a condition precedent to the enforceability of a contract for a lease, that either the agreement itself, or some memorandum or note of it, be in writing.

In the case of an agreement, the relevant document for s 40(1) purposes is the contract finally agreed between the parties. Normally, two copies are made of the contract: each party signs his counterpart and these are then simultaneously exchanged.[16] A formal contract is

---

10 See RSC Ord 18 r 8/21.
11 *Viscountess Montacute v Maxwell* (1720) 1 P Wms 616 at 620.
12 Under LPA 1925 s 49(2).
13 *Smith v Butler* [1900] 1 QB 694, CA.
14 *Pulbrook v Lawes* (1876) 1 QBD 284.
15 *City and Westminster Properties (1934) Ltd v Mudd* [1959] Ch 129, [1958] 2 All ER 733.
16 By post or other suitable method e g even by telephone if a mutually agreed means of exchange: *Domb v Isoz* [1980] Ch 548, [1980] 1 All ER 942.

complete in itself: as a rule oral evidence is inadmissible to admit other terms.[17]

Where a memorandum is relied on for s 40(1) purposes, it does not constitute the whole contract and either party may adduce oral evidence to show other terms of the oral contract not reproduced in the memorandum,[18] except that such terms cannot be essential terms: if they are, then the memorandum is insufficient and cannot be relied on.

Complete and binding contract

Even a series of complete terms reduced to writing cannot amount to a 'contract' within s 40(1) if the parties do not at a given stage intend a binding contract. So an oral contract reduced to writing but expressly stating that it is 'subject to contract' will not satisfy the statute, since it denies recognition of any contract.[19] If, further, the parties negotiate on the basis of all dealings and documents being 'subject to contract' then, no matter how far things have gone, either party may withdraw right up to the moment, if any, of exchange of contracts.[20] Moreover, once a 'subject to contract' qualification is introduced into negotiations, it ceases apparently to apply only if and when both parties expressly or impliedly agree to remove it, as might happen with the complete ending of one set of negotiations 'subject to contract' and the starting of a fresh set not expressly or impliedly so subject.[1]

Memorandum or note

Section 40(1) allows the enforcement of a contract not completely reduced to writing, provided there is a sufficient memorandum or note of the essential terms of the contract. The memorandum or note need not necessarily be contemporaneous with the contract but it must exist prior to the action on which it is based.[2] A pre-contract memorandum is acceptable in principle but if it formed the offer it must be shown to have been orally accepted.[3] A memorandum need not necessarily be a single document and may, if the documents refer to each other or are otherwise connected, be made up of several documents.[4]

---

17 *Henderson v Arthur* [1907] 1 KB 10, CA.
18 *Beckett v Nurse* [1948] 1 KB 535, [1948] 1 All ER 81, CA.
19 *Tiverton Estates Ltd v Wearwell Ltd* [1975] Ch 146, [1974] 1 All ER 209, CA.
20 *D'Silva v Lister House Development Co Ltd* [1971] Ch 17, [1970] 1 All ER 858; *Derby & Co Ltd v ITC Pension Trust Ltd* [1977] 2 All ER 890.
1 *Cohen v Nessdale Ltd* [1982] 2 All ER 97, CA.
2 *Barkworth v Young* (1856) 4 Drew 1.
3 *Watson v Davies* [1931] 1 Ch 455 at 468; *Parker v Clark* [1960] 1 All ER 93, [1960] 1 WLR 286.
4 *Chaproniere v Lambert* [1917] 2 Ch 356, CA; *Pearce v Gardner* [1897] 1 QB 688, CA.

No special form of memorandum is necessary since it does not have to be shown that, when drawn up, it was intended to satisfy s 40(1).[5] Thus, a letter to a third party,[6] an entry in a company minute-book,[7] and a note in a rent book[8] have all been held sufficient memoranda.

A causal link must be established between the various elements in question, if it is sought to rely on a composite memorandum rather than a single document. It is possible to take a single document signed by the defendant and to link it, by oral evidence, to a further written but unsigned document in existence at the time of the cross-reference, as with a cheque drawn by the defendant and a receipt, provided that there is reference in the cheque to the receipt.[9]

Subject to the points above as to composite memoranda, a memorandum is sufficient for s 40(1) only if it states all the material terms of the contract and shows that the parties agreed to these terms. If this is not so, then the defendant may bring oral evidence to show that the memorandum is incomplete.[10] But if a term is omitted from a memorandum which is for the benefit exclusively of one party, that party may sue on the contract provided he waives the term.[11] So may the other party, if he agrees to perform the term.[12]

The terms which a sufficient memorandum or note must include are, for the present purposes, as follows:

1 The names of the parties, or their agents, or other sufficient description which will identify them. A general description will not suffice unless it enables the particular party to be identified in the circumstances.[13]

2 The address of the property or a description sufficient to identify it, such as Mr O's house[14] or mentioning a given property in a given street.[15] A physical description suffices without it being necessary to describe the estate or interest.[16]

---

5 *Re Hoyle, Hoyle v Hoyle* [1893] 1 Ch 84 at 99, CA; *Hill v Hill* [1947] Ch 231, [1947] 1 All ER 54, CA.
6 *Moore v Hart* (1683) 1 Vern 110 at 201.
7 *Jones v Victoria Graving Dock Co* (1877) 2 QBD 314, CA.
8 *Hill v Hill,* supra.
9 *Timmins v Moreland Street Property Co Ltd* [1958] Ch 110, [1957] 3 All ER 265, CA.
10 *Beckett v Nurse* [1948] 1 KB 535, [1948] 1 All ER 81, CA; *Tweddell v Henderson* [1975] 2 All ER 1096, [1975] 1 WLR 1496.
11 *Hawkins v Price* [1947] Ch 645, [1947] 1 All ER 689; *Heron Garage Properties Ltd v Moss* [1974] 1 All ER 421, [1974] 1 WLR 148.
12 *Scott v Bradley* [1971] Ch 850, [1971] 1 All ER 583.
13 *Coombs v Wilkes* [1891] 3 Ch 77; *Lovesy v Palmer* [1916] 2 Ch 233.
14 *Ogilvie v Foljambe* (1817) 3 Mer 53.
15 *Bleakley v Smith* (1840) 11 Sim 150.
16 *Timmins v Moreland Street Property Co Ltd,* supra.

3   The term and its commencement date: the court will not assume that the term is to commence from the date of the agreement[17] nor within a reasonable time.[18]

4   The rent and any premium or fine. It is sufficient if the mode of calculation is specified[19] but it is not necessary to specify the time of payment.

5   Since only the usual covenants will be implied, any special covenants must be stated, if agreed on. Sufficient precision in specification is required.[20] What is sufficient is a question of fact and degree and an agreement for an option to take a lease was held enforceable where the method of calculating the rent and certain covenants remained to be agreed.[1]

Signed by the party to be charged

Section 40(1) requires the agreement or memorandum or note to be signed by the party to be charged, or by some other person thereunto lawfully authorised. Both parties need not necessarily sign. But if only one party has signed a memorandum, then, as he is the 'party to be charged', the contract is only enforceable against him and he cannot enforce it against the other party, who may repudiate it with total impunity.[2] 'Signed' has a wide connotation and includes not just a signature, but the defendant's initials[3] and names printed on the heading of notepaper (as opposed to at the foot of the document).[4] It also includes a recital by the defendant in the third person including a reference to his own name.[5] All that is required, therefore, is an acknowledgment by the defendant of the contract.

Registration of contracts

A contract for a lease is a contract to convey or create a legal estate, and in the case of unregistered land, is therefore registrable as an estate contract (as a Class C(iv) charge) under s 2(4) of the Land Charges Act 1972. As a registrable interest, it will be void against a purchaser for

---

17   *Fitzmaurice v Bayley* (1860) 9 HL Cas 78.
18   *Harvey v Pratt* [1965] 2 All ER 786, [1965] 1 WLR 1025, CA.
19   *Gregory v Mighell* (1811) 18 Ves 328.
20   *Baumann v James* (1868) 3 Ch App 508, CA (agreement to do repairs costing 'from about £150 to £200', sufficient).
1   *Trustees of National Deposit Friendly Society v Beatties of London Ltd* (1985) 275 Estates Gazette 54.
2   *Child v Comber* (1723) 3 Swan 423n.
3   *Hill v Hill* [1947] Ch 231, [1947] 1 All ER 54, CA.
4   *Selby v Selby* (1817) 3 Mer 2.
5   *Ogilvie v Foljambe, supra.*

money or money's worth of a legal estate in the land affected, unless it is registered before completion of that purchase.[6] In the case of registered land, the agreement may be capable of protection under s 48 of the Land Registration Act 1925, by entry of a notice, or a caution. If the tenant goes into occupation, however, under his contract for a lease, he will have an overriding interest under s 70(1)(g) of the Act, which will bind the registered proprietor and person claiming under him unless on enquiry from the tenant, his rights are not disclosed.

Stamp duties on contracts

Agreements (and also memoranda thereof) for leases must be stamped as leases. If the lease is made in conformity with a contract duly stamped, the duty on it is reduced by the amount of duty paid.[7]

Damages for breach of contract

The two remedies available for breach of contract, i e an action to compel specific performance of the contract and, where the contract is evidenced in writing, an action for damages are, generally speaking, alternative remedies, for specific performance is only granted where damages would not give an adequate remedy to the plaintiff. Nevertheless, damages may be awarded on a decree of specific performance, in respect of loss caused by the delay in performance of the contract.[8]

The measure of damages for breach of contract arising from a defect in the landlord's title, is generally limited to the losses actually incurred by the tenant,[9] but includes also damages for loss of bargain if the landlord is blameworthy, e g if he fails to take the necessary steps to secure possession,[10] or pay off a mortgage.[11] Damages are recoverable where the defendant failed to remove a blot on the title.[12] No damages are generally recoverable for mere delays in completion.[13] Expenses occasioned by such delays are recoverable generally, but not if solely due to conveyancing difficulties.[14] In addition, the tenant may sue for the recovery of any deposit or premium paid.

An action for damages may be brought either in the High Court or, if

---

6   LCA 1972 s 4(6).
7   Stamp Act 1891, s 75, as amended.
8   *Jacques v Miller* (1877) 6 Ch D 153.
9   *Keen v Mear* [1920] 2 Ch 574.
10   *Engell v Fitch* (1868) LR 3 QB 314.
11   *Re Daniel* [1917] 2 Ch 405.
12   *Malhotra v Chaudhury* [1980] Ch 52, [1979] 1 All ER 186.
13   Law of Property Act 1925 s 41; *Stickney v Keeble* [1915] AC 386.
14   *Rainieri v Miles* [1981] AC 1050, [1980] 2 All ER 145, HL.

the amount claimed does not exceed the county court limit, in the county court.[15] A High Court claim for under that limit may be transferred to the county court. At any stage in a county court action the court may, in certain circumstances, transfer the action to the High Court, irrespective of the amount claimed.[16]

DOCTRINE OF PART PERFORMANCE

Section 40(2) provides that s 40(1) does not affect the law relating to part performance, so that the equitable doctrine of part performance is statutorily recognised. Part performance enables a contract for a lease to be enforced in equity by a decree of specific performance, even though it is oral.

To establish acts amounting to part performance, it is necessary for a plaintiff to show that he acted to his detriment; that the defendant knew of the acts in question; and that the acts are such that on a balance of probabilities they have been performed in reliance on some contract with the defendant which was consistent with the contract alleged.[17] Proof of a sufficient act of part performance raises an equity in the plaintiff's favour and enables him to prove by oral evidence all the exact contractual terms,[18] including terms unconnected with the act of part performance, such as the existence of an option to purchase.[19]

For an action for specific performance based on part performance and consequent proof of contract to succeed and result in an enforceable contract for a lease, certain further conditions apply:

1   The oral contract alleged must be complete and binding and such that, if in writing, it would have been specifically enforceable.[20] Specific performance is discretionary and so if a discretionary bar to relief, such as fraud, misrepresentation, hardship or delay, applies, then part performance cannot be invoked by the plaintiff.
2   The acts of the plaintiff, as was seen, must refer to some contract for a lease; only certain acts count as sufficient. The payment of a ground rent in advance, when paid as a separate sum unrelated to normal rental payments, was recently held sufficient to amount to part

---

15   This is currently £5,000: SI 1981/1123.
16   County Courts Act 1984 s 42. One important ground is that some important question of law or fact is likely to arise.
17   *Steadman v Steadman* [1976] AC 536, [1974] 2 All ER 977.
18   *Kingswood Estate Co Ltd v Anderson* [1963] 2 QB 169, [1962] 3 All ER 593, CA.
19   *Brough v Nettleton* [1921] 2 Ch 25.
20   *Maddison v Alderson* (1883) 8 App Cas 467, HL. So, a contract void for uncertainty cannot be enforced: *Waring & Gillow Ltd v Thompson* (1912) 29 TLR 154, CA.

performance.[1] Likewise sufficient acts include: the taking of possession of the landlord's land with his consent;[2] the spending of substantial sums of money on property by the tenant, or sub-tenant;[3] the execution by the landlord of structural alterations on the faith of an oral agreement for a lease under the supervision and on the request of the defendant.[4]

Certain alleged acts of part performance have been held insufficient to raise an equity in the plaintiff's favour: for instance, the payment of a sum of general rental as an isolated act;[5] also the mere continuance by the tenant in occupation;[6] unless possibly, if this were at an increased rent.[7]

IV THE ACTION FOR SPECIFIC PERFORMANCE

The equitable remedy of specific performance is an order of the court compelling the defendant to perform his obligations under a contract, the effect of which, in relation to a contract for a lease, is the execution of a legal lease in proper form according to the contract. The remedy is available at the court's discretion for breach of a contract where there is:

1 a contract, or a memorandum or note thereof, in writing and signed by the defendant in the action, sufficient to satisfy s 40(1), LPA 1925, or
2 a sufficient act of part performance by the plaintiff in the action or at his request, to support the alleged contract.

The court exercises its discretion in accordance with established equitable principles, which find expression in the maxims of equity, e g 'he who seeks equity, must do equity', 'equity does nothing in vain', etc. Examples of the kind of considerations that the court will take into account in deciding whether to exercise its discretion in favour of the plaintiff may conveniently be classified under the following heads.

1 *Nature of the contract* There must be a complete and binding contract entered into by the parties, to which full effect could be given

---

1 *Cohen v Nessdale Ltd* [1981] 3 All ER 118. However, the tenant was refused specific performance on other grounds and on appeal this particular point was not considered (see [1982] 2 All ER 97, CA).
2 *Brough v Nettleton*, supra.
3 *Williams v Evans* (1875) LR 19 Eq 547.
4 *Rawlinson v Ames* [1925] Ch 96.
5 *Chaproniere v Lambert* [1917] 2 Ch 356, CA.
6 *Re National Savings Bank Association, Hebb's Case* (1867) 15 WR 754.
7 *Miller & Aldworth Ltd v Sharp* [1899] 1 Ch 622.

by an order of specific performance, and which is unobjectionable in other respects. The court will not enforce contracts which might result in further litigation, e g for sub-leases which are in breach of covenant,[8] or which contain stipulations unenforceable by the court, e g contracts for personal services,[9] or which are illegal, or would render the parties liable to criminal proceedings;[10] or which still leave something to be done by a third party, over whom the court has no control, e g fix rent,[11] give consent;[12] or which the plaintiff seeks to be performed in part, unless that part is separable from the rest, e g where successive building leases are to be granted to a builder as work proceeds.[13] In the case of a fully qualified covenant against assignments, specific performance of a contract to assign a term will not be granted if a head landlord's consent is refused where the tenant is able to show that he used his best endeavours to obtain consent.[14] The remedy is available, at discretion, even where only one side is able to obtain specific performance.[15]

2 *Title* A bad title will not be forced upon the defendant, and if the landlord has no title at the time of the action, specific performance will not be ordered against him,[16] but it is immaterial that he had no title at the time of the contract, if in the meantime he has acquired one, or can compel someone to make title.[17] The tenant is precluded from calling for proof of his landlord's title by s 44(2) of the Law of Property Act 1925, but if he can show by other means that it is bad, this is a good defence in an action by the landlord.[18] Where the landlord's title would determine before the expiration of the purported lease, specific performance has been ordered on the contract for a term that he had title to grant, and damages awarded

8   Or possibly in breach of covenant in the head lease, *Reeves v Greenwich Tanning Co Ltd* (1864) 2 Hem & M 54.
9   *Ogden v Fossick* (1862) 4 De G F & J 426.
10 *Hope v Walter* [1900] 1 Ch 257; but *quaere*, a covenant for rent in excess of the rent lawfully recoverable under the Rent Acts, *Brilliant v Michaels* [1945] 1 All ER 121.
11 *Milnes v Gery* (1807) 14 Ves 400.
12 *Forrer v Nash* (1865) 35 Beav 167.
13 *Wilkinson v Clements* (1872) 8 Ch App 96.
14 See Condition 11(5), National Conditions of Sale; *29 Equities v Bank Leumi (UK) Ltd* [1987] 1 All ER 108, (1987) 54 Pd CR 114, CA. Where the tenancy contains a requirement that any assignments by a sub-tenant require the consent of the mesne landlord and the approval of the head landlord, the latter is under a statutory duty to give approval, unless it is reasonable to withhold it, and to serve written notice of his decision on the parties: Landlord and Tenant Act 1988 s 3.
15 *Price v Strange* [1978] Ch 337, [1977] 3 All ER 371, CA.
16 *Baskcomb v Phillips* (1859) 29 LJ Ch 380; *Becker v Partridge* [1966] 2 QB 155, [1966] 2 All ER 266, CA.
17 *Elliott & H Elliott (Builders) Ltd v Pierson* [1948] Ch 452, [1948] 1 All ER 939.
18 *Jones v Watts* (1890) 43 Ch D 574, CA.

to the tenant in respect of that part of the term contracted for, that he had lost,[19] and similarly, where the landlord contracted to let an entire property, but had title only in respect of part, specific performance has been ordered in respect of that part only, with a proportionate abatement of rent.[20]

3   *Conduct of the plaintiff*   Specific performance will not be ordered where it would be inequitable to do so having regard to the conduct of the plaintiff. Misrepresentation, deceit, or concealment of material facts by the plaintiff will afford a good defence, as will unnecessary delay on his part in seeking to enforce the contract, especially if the circumstances and the defendant's position have changed in the meantime;[1] but, delay will be no bar to the landlord, if the tenant has been in possession for many years, paying rent.[2] Where time has been made of the essence of the contract by notice, the plaintiff is not entitled to specific performance if he was not ready at the time specified.[3] A landlord cannot enforce a contract if he has not completed works that he undertook to do before the lease commenced, e g to complete a new house;[4] nor can a tenant who, having gone into possession, has committed waste, or has failed to comply with what would have been covenants in the lease, thereby entitling the landlord to re-enter.[5] The court has power to settle any disputes arising from the allegation of breaches, in order to establish whether the landlord has a good defence to the action brought by the tenant.[6]

4   *Hardship to the defendant*   Specific performance will not be ordered against the defendant if it would cause him unreasonable and intolerable hardship. Considerations which arise after the contract was made are generally irrelevant, e g accidental damage or destruction to the property by fire,[7] as are mistakes of fact[8] or law, but material or substantial misdescription[9] will be defence to an action for specific performance.

5   *Absolute prohibition on assignments*   Where the tenant/assignor is under an absolute prohibition against assignments or sub-lettings, a

19   *Leslie v Crommelin* (1867) IR 2 Eq 134.
20   *Burrow v Scammell* (1881) 19 Ch D 175.
 1   *Hayes v Caryll* (1702) 1 Bro Parl Cas 126, HL; *Laurence v Lexcourt Holdings Ltd* [1978] 2 All ER 810, [1978] 1 WLR 1128.
 2   *Sharp v Milligan* (1856) 22 Beav 606.
 3   *Finkielkraut v Monohan* [1949] 2 All ER 234.
 4   *Tildesley v Clarkson* (1862) 30 Beav 419.
 5   *Gregory v Wilson* (1852) 9 Hare 683.
 6   Supreme Court Act 1981 s 49(2).
 7   *Paine v Meller* (1801) 6 Ves 349.
 8   *Jefferys v Fairs* (1876) 4 Ch D 448.
 9   *Dimmock v Hallett* (1866) 2 Ch App 21.

contract for a sub-lease cannot be specifically enforced.[10] If the tenant/assignee reasonably fears a forfeiture as the result of the proposed disposition specific performance will not lie to force his hand – but forfeiture must be a realistic possibility.[11]

An action for specific performance may be brought as soon as the date for completion has passed,[12] and before that date, if the defendant repudiates the contract (i e anticipatory breach).[13] No action for specific performance may be brought if the plaintiff elects to sue for damages; if he elects for specific performance, but it is not carried out, he may ask for dissolution of the order and for damages in lieu.[14] The High Court has power under s 50 of the Supreme Court Act 1981, to award damages either in addition to, or instead of, specific performance, in any action in which it is claimed. By para 1 of Sched 1 of that Act, jurisdiction is assigned to the Chancery Division of the High Court, and if the action arises by way of counter-claim in an action in the Queen's Bench Division, it may be transferred, if the terms of the lease are required to be settled by the court. If the value of the property does not exceed £30,000, the action may be brought in the county court.[15]

V   EQUITABLE LEASES

An order for specific performance of a contract for a lease will be complied with by the execution of a legal lease (if, of course, it is a lease capable of existing as a legal estate). Irrespective of any rights the intending tenant might have acquired at law (i e a tenancy from year to year, by going into possession under the contract) the courts of equity were prepared to enforce the terms of the intended lease between the parties, if the contract was specifically enforceable, for 'equity looks on that as done which ought to be done'. Hence the expression, 'equitable lease'.

So far, we have considered only contracts for leases specifically enforceable by virtue of a contract or memorandum sufficient to satisfy s 40(1) of the Law of Property Act 1925, or an act of part performance sufficient to take the contract outside s 40(1). In addition, both law and equity came to the aid of the parties to an imperfect lease. Leases that were required to be by deed were void at law under the Real Property Act

---

10   *Warmington v Miller* [1973] QB 877, [1973] 2 All ER 372, CA.
11   *Helling v Lumley* (1858) 3 De G & J 493.
12   *Marks v Lilley* [1959] 2 All ER 647, [1959] 1 WLR 749.
13   *Hasham v Zenab* [1960] AC 316, PC.
14   *Johnson v Agnew* [1980] AC 367, [1979] 1 All ER 883, HL.
15   County Courts Act 1984 s 23.

1845, if they were made in any other way. However, these could be treated in law and equity as if they were contracts for leases only, which would then be enforceable just as if they were contracts.[16] Thus, under the doctrine of *Parker v Taswell*,[17] a court of equity could treat an imperfect lease as a contract for a lease, and then order specific performance of that contract. In the case of a lease by deed, which for some defect could not take effect as such, a court of law could have awarded only damages before the Judicature Acts 1873–1875.

As long as law and equity were administered separately by different courts, a tenant in occupation under a contract for a lease could have conflicting rights in law and equity. Even if in law he was regarded as having a tenancy from year to year, he was in equity regarded as holding under the intended lease as if it had been properly granted, and thereby had an equitable lease. Since 1875, when the two systems were brought together in a single court, it was held, in the case of *Walsh v Lonsdale*,[18] that the conflict had been resolved by the Judicature Acts 1873–1875, since both parties could enforce their equitable rights against each other and that their equitable rights prevailed over their legal rights.

In *Walsh v Lonsdale*, the parties had agreed in writing to the grant of a lease for seven years of a mill, at a rent variable with the number of looms. The contract provided that one year's rent should be payable in advance, on demand. The tenant went into possession without the lease being executed, and, having paid rent quarterly in arrears for a year and a half, became a tenant from year to year by implication of law. The landlord subsequently distrained for a year's rent in advance, which the tenant had refused to pay when demanded of him. The tenant claimed damages for wrongful distress, for specific performance and for an injunction. The court held that the equitable rules prevailed over legal rules in all courts, with the result that the tenant's equitable lease prevailed over any yearly tenancy at law, and its terms were binding upon the parties as if it had been a lease properly executed. The doctrine was extended to enforce repairing covenants in an equitable lease from landlord to tenant (where the landlord was not entitled to but could call at any time for, the legal estate).[19]

The effect of the decision in *Walsh v Lonsdale* was to blur the distinction between equitable leases of this nature and legal leases. Indeed, it is often said that 'a contract for a lease is as good as a lease',[20]

---

16 *Bond v Rosling* (1861) 1 B & S 371; *Tidey v Mollett* (1864) 16 CBNS 298.
17 (1858) 2 De G & J 559.
18 (1882) 21 Ch D 9.
19 *Industrial Properties (Barton Hill) Ltd v Associated Electrical Industries Ltd* [1977] QB 580, [1977] 2 All ER 293, CA.
20 See *Re Maughan, ex p Monkhouse* (1885) 14 QBD 956 at 958.

but there remain a number of important differences, especially in relation to third parties, which are these.

1   *Specific performance*   There can be an equitable lease on the terms of a contract for a lease only if the contract is one which would be specifically enforceable by the court. Thus, the terms of a contract which would not be enforced for any of the reasons discussed above, could not be enforced under *Walsh v Lonsdale*, though the tenant might become a yearly tenant at law. Moreover, the court may not have jurisdiction to order specific performance in a particular case.[1] In the county court, a plaintiff's[2] (but not a defendant's)[3] rights to specific performance are limited.

2   *Third parties*   An equitable lease is binding and enforceable between the parties, but as against third parties it suffers the weakness of all equitable rights: they are good against all persons except a *bona fide* purchaser of a legal estate for value without notice. A contract for a lease is registrable as an estate contract (a Class C(iv) land charge) under s 2(4) of the Land Charges Act 1972. If the land is unregistered, therefore, a tenant under an equitable lease has no protection against an assignee of the landlord's reversion, for example, unless the estate contract had been registered, whether or not the assignee knew of the tenant's interest. In the case of registered land, the tenant can protect his interest by entering a notice on the register under s 48 of the Land Registration Act 1925. If he moves into possession, however, he will be protected against third parties by his occupation, for he will thereby have an 'overriding interest' under s 70(1)(g), LRA, which will bind them unless he does not disclose his rights to them if they enquire. In this context 'into possession' means that the tenant is physically present on the land, and occupation or possession, existing as a fact, may protect the tenant's rights, if he has any.[4]

Conversely, because his tenancy is only equitable, the tenant cannot plead that he is himself a *bona fide* purchaser of a legal estate for value without notice. Thus, he might, for example, be bound by pre-1926 restrictive covenants (which are unregistrable), or some other unregistrable interest.

3   *LPA 1925, s 62*   A contract for a lease is not a 'conveyance' within s 205(1)(ii) of the Law of Property Act 1925, and a tenant will not have the benefit of any of the easements, rights, etc, which would be

---

1   See *Cornish v Brook Green Laundry* [1959] 1 QB 394, [1959] 1 All ER 373, CA (unwaived condition precedent not complied with).
2   *Foster v Reeves* [1892] 2 QB 255, CA.
3   *Kingswood Estate Co Ltd v Anderson* [1963] 2 QB 169, [1962] 3 All ER 593, CA.
4   *Williams and Glyn's Bank Ltd v Boland* [1980] 2 All ER 408 at 413, HL.

deemed to be included on a conveyance by s 62 of the Act, though he may acquire easements under the rule in *Wheeldon v Burrows*.[5]

4 *Assignments* The benefits of covenants and rights in an equitable lease which run with the land are assignable, including the right to specific performance.[6] The burdens would appear, though this view is not uncontroverted,[7] to bind an assignee,[8] if capable of running with the land.

5 '*Usual covenants*' Only in a contract for a lease will the law imply 'usual covenants' (Chapter 6), and not in a lease.

VI FORMALITIES

We have already considered the kinds of tenancies which may take effect as legal estates, even though they are created informally (i e orally or in writing), under s 54(2) of the Law of Property Act 1925, by way of exception to the general rule contained in s 52(1), that 'all conveyances of . . . land are void for the purpose of conveying or creating a legal estate unless made by deed'. In other words, all leases, other than those within s 54(2), must be by deed.

In what follows 'lease' means a deed, i e an instrument which creates a term of years absolute. Leases are made in two parts: the lease, which is executed by the landlord and delivered to the tenant, and the counterpart, which is executed by the tenant. The counterpart may be sued on by the landlord, and it may be used as evidence to correct a clerical error in the lease itself.[9]

A deed must necessarily be written or printed; it may be in any character or language, but it must be on parchment or paper which are materials least susceptible of alteration. If several separate leaves are required, they must be bound together and paginated consecutively. It is common to draw up schedules or inventories of the contents or the state of the premises (the tenant covenanting to give them up in the same state at the end of the term) – these schedules should be attached physically to the lease, and *connected* to the lease by express terms in the lease. If this is not done, the courts will ignore the contents of the schedules in so far as they can, without making nonsense of the lease.

To take effect, a lease must be *executed*, i e signed, sealed and delivered. Section 73(1) of the Law of Property Act 1925, requires that a person executing a deed after 1925, 'shall either sign or place his mark

5 (1879) 12 Ch D 31, CA.
6 *Manchester Brewery Co v Coombs* [1901] 2 Ch 608.
7 See *Purchase v Lichfield Brewery Co* [1915] 1 KB 184.
8 *Boyer v Warbey* [1953] 1 QB 234, [1952] 2 All ER 976, CA.
9 *Matthews v Smallwood* [1910] 1 Ch 777.

upon the same and sealing alone shall not be deemed sufficient'. It should be signed at the bottom, and anything below that signature will be valid only if it is signed separately. Attestation of the execution of the lease in the presence of witnesses is not essential, unless the lease is made under a power of attorney.[10] The lease must also be *delivered* to take effect, either by the landlord personally, or, as is more usual, by his solicitor. Actual delivery is not necessary, for the requirement may be satisfied by any act which shows that intention. A deed is taken, in the absence of contrary proof, to be delivered on the day it bears as date.[11] A wafer or wax seal may be used for sealing a deed: it has been judicially noted that in practice today sealing is by a printed circle which the landlord signs across.[12] A lease may be delivered as an *escrow*, ie expressed to take effect, not upon delivery, but upon the happening of some event, or the performance of some condition. Where execution precedes the date of the deed, the condition may simply be the completion of the contract, by exchange of lease and counterpart, which must be done in a reasonable time.[13] When the conditions of an escrow are satisfied, rent is payable from the date of conditional delivery.[14] It is a question of fact and of the intention of the landlord whether a lease is intended to operate as an escrow.[15] Only when the condition or conditions of an escrow are performed will a lease delivered as an escrow vest the estate granted.[16] But a deed delivered in escrow is not recallable: it becomes binding once the condition is performed.[17] Even in the case of an unexecuted lease, which is enforceable in equity, covenants therein will bind the tenant immediately after the date the agreement is made.[18]

VII FORM OF A LEASE

No precise form is required by law for a lease, but a fairly standard layout tends to prevail. Precedents are widely used and standard forms

---

10 Cf LPA 1925 s 159.
11 *Woodfall* 1–0565. An undated but signed and sealed lease or underlease will bind both parties if it is proved that it was intended to be binding on delivery: see *Bentray Investments Ltd v Venner Time Switches Ltd* [1985] 1 EGLR 39.
12 *First National Securities Ltd v Jones* [1978] Ch 109, [1978] 2 All ER 221, CA.
13 *Kingston v Ambrian Investment Co Ltd* [1975] 1 All ER 120, [1975] 1 WLR 161, CA; *Glessing v Green* [1975] 2 All ER 696, [1975] 1 WLR 863, CA.
14 *Alan Estates v W G Stores Ltd* [1982] Ch 511, [1981] 3 All ER 481, CA.
15 *D'Silva v Lister House Development Ltd* [1971] Ch 17, [1970] 1 All ER 858.
16 *Beesly v Hallwood Estates Ltd* [1961] Ch 105, [1961] 1 All ER 90, CA; *Alan Estates Ltd v WG Stores*, supra.
17 *Beesly v Hallwood Estates Ltd, supra.* The landlords there could not recall the deed just because they thereafter discovered that the option to renew, the basis of the contract, was void for non-registration, the tenant having complied with the condition.
18 *Carrington Manufacturing Co v Saldin* (1925) 133 LT 432.

adopted by landlords letting many similar properties. An attempt was made by Parliament to standardise leases, and produced a standard form of lease in the Leases Act 1845.

The Law Commission[19] noted that the 1845 Act provided a series of key words for use in leases.[20] The 1845 Act, they admitted, has been largely neglected.

Standard clauses

There is no standard form of leases as such but obviously books of precedents contain precedents of leases for almost every conceivable purpose.[1] Whether standardisation of the various types of clauses used in residential, commercial and other leases is desirable is a difficult issue. The Royal Commission on Legal Services supported standardisation especially with regard to residential property.[2] A problem with standardisation is this: there are too many diverse problems to be capable of being solved by standard forms, which, in any case, will date rapidly.

Standard rent review clauses have in fact been produced by the Law Society.[3] Whether these clauses will be sufficient to stem the flood of litigation in rent review, is open to question. It is also questionable whether standardisation in other areas, such as repairing covenants, would really help, but the Law Commission felt able to recommend further study of the issue generally.[4]

Requirements of a valid lease

For there to be a valid lease, there must be a landlord, who has capacity to make the lease; and there must be a tenant with capacity to accept it. The lease must be of land (or premises), where necessary by deed. It must describe the landlord, the tenant, the land or premises demised, the term granted, the rent and all the covenants. The landlord must express an intention to demise, and the tenant, an intention to accept the land and the estate.

Parts of a lease

A lease by deed usually consists of five parts:

---

19 Landlord and Tenant: Reform of the Law, Law Com No 162 (1987) para 3.8–3.10.
20 They cite the example of a covenant to 'repair' by the tenant which would be taken as a covenant 81 words in length.
1   See especially *Encyclopaedia of Forms and Precedents* (Butterworths); *Precedents for the Conveyancer* (Sweet and Maxwell).
2   [1979] Cmnd 7648 Annex 21.1 para 13.
3   See e g (1979) 76 LS Gaz 564; revised (1980) 77 LS Gaz 82; revised (1985) 82 LS Gaz 3664.
4   Law Com No 162 para 3.18.

1   *The Premises* (i e that part of a lease which precedes the Habendum)
comprises the commencement, the date of the lease, the names and
description of the parties, the recitals (if any), the premium or fine (if
any), the operative words (i e the words of demise), the description of
the parcels demised and the appurtenances, and any exceptions or
reservations. Any exceptions to the thing demised must be stated. A
lease of 'land', which includes premises, will normally also include
the outside of external walls. Where a long lease demised buildings
and premises, it was held that the roof passed with the demise.[5] The
question of the scope of any particular demise is one of fact.[6] In the
case of flats, the demise of a flat is presumed to include the external
walls enclosing it[7] but not the external walls of other flats in the same
building.[8] A demise may also include any void spaces between the
actual and 'false' ceilings of a sub-divided house.[9] It is presumed that
a demise will include everything below ground level in a vertical line,
such as a cellar, in the absence of specific words of exclusion.[10]

   In a lease 'with appurtenances', 'appurtenances' includes only such
things as outhouses, yards and gardens.[11] However, for the purposes
of s 2(3) of the Leasehold Reform Act 1967, 'appurtenances' includes
any land within the curtilage of the house concerned.[12] If an upper
floor of premises is demised separately from lower floors, the use of
staircases passes (in principle) as an appurtenance to the upper floor
tenant, on the basis of necessity if the staircase is the sole means of
access as at the date of the demise.[13] A right of way in favour of the
demised premises will pass as an 'appurtenance' if enjoyed at the date
of the lease.[14]

   Leases generally contain exceptions and reservations.

Exceptions   A lease of land prima facie includes everything above
and beneath the surface but the landlord may limit the physical
extent of his grant by expressly excluding from it some part of the
land such as a field, a building, or mines and minerals, or sporting
rights.[15]

---

5   *Straudley Investments Ltd v Barpress Ltd* [1987] 1 EGLR 69, CA. Cf *Cockburn v
    Smith* [1924] 2 KB 119, CA.
6   *Douglas-Scott v Scorgie* [1984] 1 All ER 1086, [1984] 1 WLR 716, CA.
7   *Sturge v Hackett* [1962] 3 All ER 166, [1962] 1 WLR 1257, CA.
8   *Campden Hill Towers v Gardner* [1977] QB 823, [1977] 1 All ER 739, CA.
9   *Graystone Property Investments Ltd v Margulies* (1983) 47 P & CR 472, CA; cf
    Hatfield v Moss [1988] 2 EGLR 58, CA; *Wilkinson* (1989) 139 NLJ 235.
10 *Grigsby v Melville* [1973] 3 All ER 455, [1974] 1 WLR 80, CA.
11 *Trim v Sturminster RDC* [1938] 2 KB 508, [1938] 2 All ER 168, CA.
12 *Methuen-Campbell v Walters* [1979] QB 525, [1979] 1 All ER 606, CA.
13 *Altmann v Boatman* (1963) 186 Estates Gazette 109, CA; cf *Chappell v Mason* (1894)
    10 TLR 404, CA.
14 *Hansford v Jago* [1921] 1 Ch 322.
15 See eg *Mason v Clarke* [1955] AC 778, [1955] 1 All ER 914, HL.

Reservations These are new rights created in the lease in favour of the landlord subject to which the tenant will take the property, as with the landlord reserving himself a right of way over the demised premises, or reserving a right to build to any height on adjoining land notwithstanding that the buildings may obstruct any light on the demised premises.[16] Any reservations must be expressly made in the lease[17] except in the case of a way of necessity.[18] Reservations are construed against the landlord.[19]

2 *The Habendum* specifies the quantity and quality of the estate signified by 'to hold' or 'to have and to hold'. The habendum indicates the commencement date of the lease, which may precede or follow that date.[20] If no date is fixed for the commencement of the lease, it commences at the date of the lease. A lease from a given date, say 25 March, normally commences at midnight on 25 to 26 March,[1] but whether 'from' is inclusive or exclusive of the date fixed depends ultimately on the context.[2]

3 *The reddendum* is the reservation of rent clause, and indicates with certainty that rent is payable, by words such as 'yielding and paying'. Rent may be reserved throughout the term or for a fixed period, followed by a reference to rent review provisions.

4 *The covenants* are the obligations of the parties, and express covenants will be set out after the reddendum. If there are no express covenants, some may be implied or statute-implied.

5 *Provisos and conditions* for re-entry for non-payment of rent or breaches of covenant are the means of providing the landlord with a contractual remedy against the tenant whereby he can, in the last resort, terminate the tenancy for breach of covenant (i e forfeiture) or of giving either party the option to determine the lease at certain specified intervals during the term (i e break clauses). Conditions may be precedent or subsequent. A landlord's covenant to renew may be conditional on performance, by the tenant, of his covenants as at the date of the renewal notice.

6 *Schedules* Leases may well contain schedules dealing with various matters, for example:

---

16 *Foster v Lyons* [1927] 1 Ch 219.
17 *Re Webb's Lease* [1951] Ch 808, [1951] 1 All ER 131, CA.
18 *Liddiard v Waldron* [1934] 1 KB 435, CA.
19 *St Edmundsbury and Ipswich Diocesan Board of Finance v Clark (No 2)* [1975] 1 All ER 772, [1975] 1 WLR 468, CA; as in *Trailfinders Ltd v Razuki* [1988] 30 EG 59.
20 Subject to Law of Property Act 1925 s 149(3) (ch 2).
1 *Sidebotham v Holland* [1895] 1 QB 378, CA; also *Eyre v Price* [1954] JPL 595.
2 *WH Brakspear & Sons Ltd v Barton* [1924] 2 KB 88; *Ladyman v Wirral Estates* [1968] 2 All ER 197.

   (a) *Schedule of fixtures* Where the demised premises are let together with fixtures or furniture then a schedule of these items is normal. In this way the landlord will have remedies if the tenant fails to deliver up the items at the end of the lease (which he would be expected expressly to covenant to do). The items must, however, be specified with absolute certainty.

   (b) *Schedule of condition* In connection with a tenant's covenant to repair which obliges him to keep the premises in repair to a defined standard, a schedule of condition is recommended: this should be drawn up at the commencement of the term and annexed to the lease, or put into a separate document.[3]

VIII COSTS OF LEASES

The lease and counterpart are usually prepared on behalf of both parties by the landlord's solicitor, who sends the draft lease to the tenant or his solicitor for approval. In the absence of express agreement to the contrary, the normal practice has been for the expense of the lease to be borne by the tenant, and that of the counterpart, by the landlord,[4] but often the tenant was obliged by covenant to pay for both parties' costs. Section 1 of the Costs of Leases Act 1958 provides that, unless it is otherwise agreed in writing, a party to a lease is not under any obligation to pay either the whole or any part of any other party's solicitor's costs of the lease. And by s 2 of that Act, 'costs' include fees,[5] charges, disbursements (including stamp duty), expenses and remuneration. The Solicitors' Remuneration Order 1972[6] permits solicitors to charge such fees as may be fair and reasonable in all the circumstances, having regard, e g to the time spent, the complexity, difficulty or novelty of the matter, etc.

IX STAMPING OF LEASES

The Stamp Act 1891 requires all leases and all agreements for a lease to be impressed with a stamp in accordance with the prescribed scale.[7]

---

3 *Woodfall* 1–0536. In agricultural holdings see Agricultural Holdings Act 1986 s 22 (record of condition of holding).
4 *Re Negus* [1895] 1 Ch 73.
5 See Solicitors Act 1957 s 20.
6 SI 1972/1139 (L 14).
7 See Stamp Act 1891 Sched 1; *Woodfall* para 1–2311.

X REGISTRATION OF LEASES

The position regarding registration of leasehold titles in areas of compulsory registration of title may be summarised as follows.

1 The title of a leaseholder must be registered under the Land Registration Act 1925 on the first grant of a lease where the title of the leaseholder is a legal estate, the term granted is for more than 21 years and where the title of the freeholder is in an area of compulsory registration of title. Registration of the title of a leaseholder is also required where there is an assignment on sale, or the grant of an under-lease out of, a registered lease with or for an unexpired term of more than 21 years in any area of compulsory registration of title.[8]

2 Unless registration of title is applied for within two months of the grant, assignment or under-lease in question, these become void for the purpose of passing the legal estate in the land.[9]

3 Where the term granted, or the unexpired residue of the term assigned or sub-let, is just over 21 years at the date of application for registration, applications may be made for registration within the two-month period allowed even though by the time the lease is registered it will have less than 21 years to run.[10]

4 The registration of any lease or underlease originally created for a term not exceeding 21 years is prohibited even if the freehold or head leasehold is situated in an area of compulsory registration of title.[11]

5 Leases for a term exceeding 21 years which contain an absolute prohibition on assignments inter vivos are registrable.[12]

6 Any lease originally granted for a term not exceeding 21 years is incapable of being registered and overrides the registered title.[13]

Leaseholders may be registered with one of four kinds of title:

(a) *Absolute title* (under s 9 of the 1925 Act) where both the title to the

---

8 Land Registration Act 1925 s 123(1), as amended by Land Registration Act 1986 s 2. The 1986 Act, passed to implement the recommendations of Law Com No 125, came into force on 1 January 1987: SI 1986/2117. References are to the 1925 Act as amended.

9 Land Registration Act 1925 s 123(1). The Chief Land Registrar has power of discretion to extend the two month period: ibid. Where title to a lease etc is not registered, see *British Maritime Trust v Upsons Ltd* [1931] WN 7.

10 Land Registration Act 1925 s 8(1A) – otherwise, because of the two-month period for applications, if the term fell to below 21 years by the time of registration, s 8 would, prior to being amended, have precluded registration.

11 Land Registration Act 1925 s 22(2).

12 Land Registration Act 1925 s 8(2).

13 Land Registration Act 1925 s 70(1)(k).

leasehold, the freehold and any intermediate leasehold titles must be approved by the Registrar.

(b) *Good leasehold title*   (under s 10) which requires approval only of the leasehold title, and therefore the Registrar cannot guarantee that the lease was validly granted.

(c) *Qualified title*   (under s 12) where the title is subject to a specified defect – otherwise the effect is the same as absolute or good leasehold titles.

(d) *Possessory title*   (under s 11) in which case no guarantee is given as to the title prior to first registration.

Upgrading of these titles is possible under s 77 of the 1925 Act. In the case of a good leasehold title the registrar must on application by the proprietor convert the title to an absolute title provided he is satisfied as to the title to the freehold and the title to any intermediate leasehold (s 77(1)). In the case of a possessory title the registrar must similarly convert the title to good leasehold if he is satisfied as to the title or if the land has been registered as good leasehold for at least twelve years and he is satisfied that the proprietor is in possession (s 77(2)). The registrar must likewise convert a qualified title to good leasehold if satisfied as to the title (s 77(3)). In all cases just mentioned the registrar may convert titles without any application for conversion having been made. Where an adverse claim is pending, no conversion is possible until the claim is disposed of (s 77(4)).

XI   RECTIFICATION AND RESCISSION

Rectification

The court may, on parol evidence of mutual mistake, order the rectification of an executed lease because it fails to carry out the intention of both parties.[14] An example of such rectification is correcting clerical mistakes or other obvious slips in the preparation of the lease.[15] Rectification may be ordered against an assignee with notice.[16] The court may, in its discretion, order rescission, as opposed to rectification, of a lease for mutual mistake, as where there is a misdescription in the

---

14   *Craddock Bros v Hunt* [1923] 2 Ch 136, CA; *Dormer v Sherman* (1966) 110 Sol Jo 171, CA.
15   *Boots the Chemist Ltd v Street* (1983) 268 Estates Gazette 817.
16   *Equity and Law Life Assurance Society Ltd v Coltness Group Ltd* (1983) 267 Estates Gazette 949.

lease. Therefore, where by mistake a first floor was included in a lease, rescission was ordered and the tenant given an option to take a new lease without that floor.[17]

If the plaintiff has simply made a bad bargain, forgetting a material matter in negotiations, rectification is out of the question.[18] Rectification is possible where only one party is mistaken, but the plaintiff must prove each of the following elements. (1) There was a mistake by the plaintiff in executing the deed, so that the deed does not translate that party's subjective intention at the time of the execution of the deed. (2) There is no mistake by the other party, who intends the result in fact achieved. (3) The other party must be both aware of the plaintiff's mistake, and also, in standing back, his conduct must be unconscionable.[19]

In unregistered land, an equity of rectification appears to be unenforceable against a purchaser for value without notice of it.[20] In the case of registered land, an equity of rectification held by a person in 'actual occupation' within s 70(1)(g) of the Land Registration Act 1925, binds third parties.[1]

Rescission

By s 1 of the Misrepresentation Act 1967, the fact that a contract has been performed is no longer a bar to a claim for rescission, but the court has a discretion to award damages *in lieu* of rescission, and this is without prejudice to any claim that the plaintiff might otherwise have for damages if the representation was negligently made. But for rescission to be granted, the court must be satisfied that the parties can be put back into substantially the same position as before.[2] Moreover, there must be evidence of conduct verging on fraud, and this applies where rescission is asked for on the grounds of unilateral mistake, e g where plaintiffs claimed rectification or rescission of a lease in which they had failed to insert a term to protect their own interest.[3]

A party entitled to rescind a lease or a contract to assign a lease has an election and may affirm the lease or contract. For this to apply, the party must have knowledge of his legal rights and of the relevant facts. The

---

17 *Paget v Marshall* (1884) 28 Ch D 255.
18 *Harlow Development Corpn v Kingsgate (Clothing Productions) Ltd* (1973) 226 Estates Gazette 1960.
19 *Thomas Bates & Son v Wyndham's (Lingerie) Ltd* [1981] 1 All ER 1077, [1981] 1 WLR 505, CA; *Kemp v Neptune Concrete Ltd* [1988] 2 EGLR 87, CA.
20 *Smith v Jones* [1954] 2 All ER 823, [1954] 1 WLR 1089.
 1 *Blacklocks v JB Developments (Godalming) Ltd* [1982] Ch 183, [1981] 3 All ER 392.
 2 *Curtin v Greater London Council* (1970) 114 Sol Jo 932, CA.
 3 *Truman Aviation Ltd v Bingham* [1970] EGD 296.

sooner he thereafter elects to rescind the better. If a period elapses between knowledge of the facts and of entitlement to rescind, there can be no effective election to affirm during this period.[4] Once any such period elapses, any right to rescind must be promptly exercised. The commencement of negotiations which are inconsistent with an earlier right to rescind will deprive the party concerned of that right.[5] If a person takes possession knowing that the consent of the landlord to an assignment of a lease to him has not been obtained, this is not waiver of any right to rescind the contract for a lease.[6]

---

4   *Peyman v. Lanjani* [1985] Ch 457, [1984] 3 All ER 703, CA.
5   *Aquis Estates Ltd v Minton* [1975] 3 All ER 1043, [1975] 1 WLR 1452, CA.
6   *Butler v Croft* (1973) 27 P & CR 1 (rescission refused at discretion due to conduct of plaintiff).

PART B
RIGHTS AND OBLIGATIONS
OF THE PARTIES

Chapter 5

Covenants generally

I INTRODUCTION

The rights and obligations of the parties are governed by the covenants in the lease. There are three basic types of covenant. First, express covenants, which regulate, often in minute detail, the exact nature and scope of each party's rights and obligations.[1] Any well-drawn lease, at least for a substantial term, will contain a full range of covenants. Secondly, implied covenants: these, discussed in Chapter 6, apply if and so far as the lease fails to make express provision for a matter, and are limited in scope. Thirdly, statutorily-implied covenants, which usually, where applicable, override the terms of the lease, and which relate chiefly to repairs (see Chapter 9).

Covenants and conditions distinguished

A covenant governs the rights and obligations of a party during the tenancy, whereas a condition is a qualification of the estate granted, whereby the tenancy is not created until any condition *precedent* has been satisfied or more commonly, whereby the tenancy is made terminable if any condition *subsequent* is broken. The distinction is important mainly with regard to the right of re-entry (Chapter 13), in that on breach of a condition the tenancy is automatically terminable, giving to the landlord the right to re-enter (i e whether he has expressly reserved the right or not); but on breach of a covenant, the tenancy is not terminable except under an express proviso for re-entry. In practical terms, however, a covenant (e g not to do something) coupled with an express right of re-entry has much the same effect as a condition; thus, the distinction is vital where there is a covenant without an express right of re-entry. It is not always easy to recognise whether a particular

---

1 On drafting of such covenants, see generally M J Ross *Drafting and Negotiating Commercial Leases* (3rd edn Butterworths); also S Tromans *Commercial Leases* (1987, Sweet and Maxwell).

obligation constitutes a covenant or condition, especially since the words used are not in themselves conclusive.

No special form of words such as 'covenant' or 'agree' is necessary to create a covenant; the intention of the parties is paramount, and therefore it is a question of construction in each case, having regard to the lease as a whole. Words such as 'provided always, and it is agreed', and 'it is hereby agreed' create a covenant; so, too, 'yielding and paying' and 'yielding' amount to covenants to pay rent; and even 'provided always and these presents are upon the express condition, that' has been held to create a covenant.[2] Moreover, a covenant may be implied from the rest of the lease, as where a covenant to build was implied in what was clearly intended to be a building lease having regard to the recitals (which have no contractual force) from an express covenant to maintain and leave in repair only.[3] An agreement is not easily construed as a condition, however.

Dependent and independent covenants

A difficult point of construction often arises under a covenant (especially one for repairs) which imposes an obligation on one party, the other party having first performed some other obligation. The important question to be decided is whether the two limbs of the covenant are *dependent* or *independent*, in other words, whether the second obligation can be enforced only when the first obligation has been performed, or whether the two obligations can be enforced independently of each other. A dependent covenant is in effect one made conditional upon the prior performance of another covenant by the other party. In *Westacott v Hahn*,[4] where the tenant covenanted that he would 'from time to time during the said lease at his own cost, being *allowed* all the necessary materials for this purpose, . . . well and substantially repair and maintain' the premises in repair, the Court of Appeal held that the tenant's obligation to repair was conditional upon the materials first being provided by the landlord, and so the tenant would be liable only for those repairs for which the landlord agreed to supply the necessary materials.

In other cases, however, as a matter of construction, the covenants may be construed as independent. A tenant under an obligation to keep buildings in repair was held liable on his covenant even though the landlord failed, in breach of covenant, to find the necessary materials.[5] An agricultural tenant remained liable for rent despite his landlord's

---

2   *Brookes v Drysdale* (1877) 3 CPD 52.
3   *Sampson v Easterby* (1829) 9 B & C 505.
4   [1918] 1 KB 495, CA. Cf *Cannock v Jones* (1849) 3 Exch 233.
5   *Tucker v Linger* (1882) 21 Ch D 18, CA.

failure to execute repairs.[6] Similarly, in the context of service charges, the payment on time of tenants' service charges was held not to be a condition precedent to a landlord's liability to provide services under the lease.[7] On the other hand, a condition requiring the approval of tenants for what were in fact major repairs, was held a condition precedent to liability to pay a share of the cost as a service charge contribution.[8]

Covenants and collateral contracts distinguished

Covenants must be distinguished from contracts collateral to and not included in the terms of the lease. Contractual stipulations in the lease itself are covenants, and therefore the problem of collateral contracts arises principally in relation to representations allegedly made before the granting of a tenancy, or to agreements made during the lease for additional rent to be paid.

The terms of a lease are taken to be a complete statement of the agreement between the parties. In some circumstances a collateral contract or warranty may be established, as where prior to the execution of the lease, the landlord makes a representation to the tenant as to the state of repair or fitness of the premises; or as where he undertakes, prior to such execution, to put down rabbits,[9] or that the drains of the house are in order,[10] or that there was (contrary to the fact) the benefit of planning permission for the whole building.[11]

A tenant seeking to establish a collateral contract must establish, first, that the statement preceded the grant of the lease; secondly, that he would have refused to complete unless the representation was true; thirdly, the representation must not contradict the terms of the lease itself.[12] If a covenant in the lease deals with the matter inconsistently with the alleged statement, the lease will prevail unless it is possible to show that the landlord has estopped himself from enforcing the covenant concerned. Accordingly, where a landlord induced most sitting flat tenants to take 99-year leases with full repairing covenants by promising the tenants to pay for initial roofing repairs, the landlord was held unable to recover the cost of these repairs from any of the tenants or their assigns as a result.[13]

6　*Burton v Timmis* [1987] 1 EGLR 1, CA.
7　*Yorkbrook Investments Ltd v Batten* [1985] 2 EGLR 100, CA.
8　*CIN Properties Ltd v Barclays Bank plc* [1986] 1 EGLR 59, CA.
9　*Morgan v Griffith* (1871) LR 6 Exch 70.
10　*De Lassalle v Guildford* [1901] 2 KB 215, CA.
11　*Laurence v Lexcourt Holdings Ltd* [1978] 2 All ER 810, [1988] 1 WLR 1128.
12　*De Lassalle v Guildford, supra* (lease silent about the drains); *Henderson v Arthur* [1907] 1 KB 10, CA.
13　*Brikom Investments Ltd v Carr* [1979] QB 467, [1979] 2 All ER 753, CA (the costs were recoverable under the strict terms of the lease). For a case where deceit was proved see *Gordon v Selico & Co* [1986] 1 EGLR 71, CA.

The remedies of a tenant for misrepresentation are rescission – even if the lease has been executed[14] – or damages.[15]

II   CONSTRUCTION OF COVENANTS

Covenants are, as we have seen, the terms which govern the rights and obligations of the parties throughout the tenancy, and if any doubts arise as to their precise meaning, these are resolved by reference to rules of construction which are part of the general law. The more important ones may be summarised as follows:

1   The general rule of construction is that all covenants are to be construed according to the intention of the parties *as expressed by their own words*. By 'intention' is meant not what it is thought the parties might have wished to effect, but the intention they actually express; their words must be viewed objectively, and adhered to as closely as possible, and given their normal meaning unless from the context it is abundantly clear that the parties intended them to have some special meaning. In construing a particular covenant, the whole lease may be taken into consideration, in order to establish its precise meaning in the context.

2   If the meaning of a covenant cannot be established from the lease itself, then and only then may regard be had to surrounding circumstances, such as the nature of the property, but not the conduct of the parties or what they said or wrote prior to the lease. The contract for that lease may be referred to, but not the draft contract nor the draft lease, since any changes from the draft must be taken to have been intentional.

3   Where words of *generality* follow words of *particularity*, the words of *generality* cannot extend the scope of the covenant beyond the class of the *particular* things mentioned earlier. This rule (i e the *ejusdem generis* rule) confines an 'omnibus' clause at least to the class of things mentioned specifically in preceding clauses; so that if the tenant covenants to deliver up in repair at the end of the tenancy, for example, the 'doors, locks, keys, wainscott, hearths, stoves and *all other erections, buildings, improvements, fixtures and things which are now on or which at any time shall be fixed, fastened or belong to*' the demised premises, any trade fixtures he annexed would fall outside the 'omnibus' clause italicised, since the items previously specified in it are all landlord's fixtures.

---

14   Misrepresentation Act 1967 s 1.
15   Misrepresentation Act 1967 s 2.

4   Doubts as to the extent of a grant are generally construed against the grantor; this applies to the extent of the estate or of the property or land comprised in the grant, for example, or of a reservation or exception, since it was in his power to reduce the estate or property, or enlarge the reservation had he been so minded.

III   ENFORCEABILITY OF COVENANTS

The question of who is entitled to enforce a covenant in a lease and against whom, is of vital significance. As between the original landlord and tenant, liability is based on privity of contract. Therefore, all covenants in the lease and all collateral contracts thereto are enforceable.

However, if the leasehold term or the freehold reversion are assigned, there is no longer any privity of contract between the parties. The only way in which covenants may be enforced between the new parties is if the covenants 'run with the land'. This means that the benefit and burden of the covenants, whether at law or in equity, pass to successors in title of the covenantor or covenantee.[16]

The basis on which covenants are enforced between assignees of the lease or of the reversion is that of privity of estate. For privity of estate to exist between particular parties, the test is whether the parties hold directly as landlord and tenant. There is both privity of contract and of estate between the original landlord and tenant. Once the original tenant assigns the term, there is no privity of estate between him and the landlord. Privity of estate will exist between the landlord and the assignee currently entitled to possession: if the assignee re-assigns, he loses privity of estate and the new assignee acquires it. With that, the assignee comes under the primary liability to observe and perform all real covenants in the lease. There is no privity of estate between a head landlord and any sub-lessee of the whole or any part of the land concerned, though privity of estate exists between the sub-lessee and his immediate landlord.

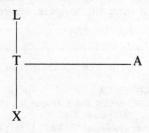

---

16   Law of Property Act 1925 s 80(4).

In the diagram, L and T are in privity of contract and estate (while T holds the lease). L and A, T's assignee, are now in privity of estate. X is in privity of contract with T and of estate with A, but not with L.

1   LIABILITY BETWEEN THE ORIGINAL PARTIES; PRIVITY OF CONTRACT; RIGHTS OF ORIGINAL TENANT AGAINST ASSIGNEES OF TERM

The original landlord and tenant are in privity of contract. If, however, the original tenant assigns his lease, he remains liable to the landlord and his successors in title (unless he is released) for breaches of real covenants in the lease committed by the assignee currently in possession. Accordingly, a lessee was held liable for rent arrears to the landlord notwithstanding the assignment of his (informal) lease.[1] The same rule applies to the landlord: he is under a continuing liability, despite an assignment of the reversion, to the original tenant.[2] Moreover, it has been held that an assignee of the lease is entitled to recover damages from the current landlord for breaches of the latter's covenant to repair committed while he held the lease, notwithstanding re-assignment of the term.[3] It has been suggested that the original landlord may be liable, on a real covenant, direct to an assignee who became tenant after the assignment of the reversion.[4]

The primary liability is that of the assignee currently in possession. On re-assignment, the assignee's liability ends, but not that of the original tenant. Double compensation to the landlord is not possible.[5]

Extent of original tenant's liability

The original tenant's continuing liability for breaches of real covenants is severe. If he is sued on the covenants as (in effect) a surety of the current assignee in breach, he has (in the absence of release) but three defences: (1) that the tenant has performed the covenants; (2) that the assignee has performed them; (3) that due to some operation on the land itself, such as surrender of the lease, all liability under the covenants is at an end.[6]

The original tenant's continuing liability is unaffected by the fact that the lessor has accepted from the assignee a surrender of part of the

---

1   *Betts & Sons Ltd v Price* (1924) 40 TLR 589. The fact that the lease was not under seal made no difference.
2   *Stuart v Joy* [1904] 1 KB 362, CA.
3   *City and Metropolitan Properties Ltd v Greycroft* [1987] 3 All ER 839, [1987] 1 WLR 1085; P F Smith [1987] Conv 374.
4   *Celsteel Ltd v Alton House Holdings Ltd (No 2)* [1987] 2 All ER 240 at 244, CA.
5   *House Property and Investment Co v Bernardout* [1948] 1 KB 314.
6   *Selous Street Properties v Oronel Fabrics Ltd* (1984) 270 Estates Gazette 643, 743.

demised premises,[7] or that the lessor and assignee agreed on a higher rent than the original rent reserved on a rent review – to which the original tenant by definition was not a party.[8] The original tenant's liability is irrespective of his ability, or rather lack of it, to enforce covenants, such as that to repair, by the assignee.[9] Obviously what applies to the original tenant applies to his guarantors – all the more so since the benefit of a covenant of guarantee passes automatically on any assignment by deed of the reversion.[10] Moreover, if a guarantor is released, this has no effect on the primary liability of the original tenant.[11] If the lease is assigned and the reversion is also assigned, the original tenant is liable to the assignee of the reversion for rent arrears due from the assignee of the lease.[12]

Indemnity covenants by assignees

The tenant, on assigning the term, may take an express indemnity covenant from the assignee. Clear words are required to achieve this, such as 'to pay the future rent and observe the covenants on the part of the lessee contained in the . . . lease'.[13]

Indemnity covenants on the part of the assignee are implied into any assignment for valuable consideration[14] by statute.[15] In the case of continuing breaches, such as of the covenant to repair, the statute-implied indemnity covenants relate to pre- and post-assignment breaches unless the bargain between the parties provides otherwise.[16] In the case of once-and-for-all breaches, the date of the assignment is the watershed for liability.

---

7 *Baynton v Morgan* (1888) 22 QBD 74, CA.
8 *Centrovincial Estates plc v Bulk Storage Ltd* (1983) 46 P & CR 393. This applies even though the value of the demised premises was increased by an improvement carried out by the assignee without the original tenant's knowledge: *Selous Street Properties v Oronel Fabrics Ltd, supra.*
9 *Thames Manufacturing Co Ltd v Perrotts (Nichol & Peyton) Ltd* (1984) 50 P & CR 1.
10 *Kumar v Dunning* [1987] 2 All ER 801, [1987] 3 WLR 1167, CA, approved in *P & A Swift Investments v Combined English Stores Group plc* [1988] 2 All ER 885, [1988] 3 WLR 313, HL.
11 *Allied London Investments v Hambro Life Assurance* (1985) 50 P & CR 207, CA.
12 *Arlesford Trading Co Ltd v Servansingh* [1971] 3 All ER 113, [1971] 1 WLR 1080, CA.
13 Formula of *Woodfall* 1–1746; see *Butler Estates Co v Bean* [1942] 1 KB 1, [1941] 2 All ER 793, CA.
14 I e an assignment attaching responsibility or liability to the assignee: *Johnsey Estates Ltd v Lewis & Manley (Engineering) Ltd* [1987] 2 EGLR 69, CA. A consideration of £1 for the assignment was accepted not to amount to 'valuable consideration' by itself: ibid.
15 Law of Property Act 1925 s 77 and Sched II Parts IX and X (unregistered land); Land Registration Act 1925 s 24 (registered land).
16 *Middlegate Properties Ltd v Bilbao* (1972) 24 P & CR 329.

If the lease is re-assigned by the assignee, the new assignee is primarily liable. The former assignee loses privity of estate and with it, in principle, all liability for post-assignment breaches. The original tenant, if liable to the landlord, retains his right of indemnity against all successive assignees.[17] This chain of indemnity covenants, as it is known, is useless if the assignee in possession is bankrupt.[18]

Covenants of indemnity provide some financial security but they do not entitle the original tenant to remedies apart from indemnity, such as an injunction to restrain alterations which might constitute a breach of covenant.[19]

2 BY OR AGAINST ASSIGNEES

The principles on which an assignee may be liable to indemnify the original tenant for breaches of covenant after the lease has been assigned have been considered above.

In what follows there are discussed the principles on which landlords' and tenants' covenants are enforceable by and against assignees of the reversion and of the lease.

Two general conditions must be satisfied. (1) There must be privity of estate between the parties. (2) The covenant must be a real covenant, or it must touch and concern the land. If this is not so, the covenant is a personal covenant and cannot be enforced by or against assignees, though it is enforceable between the original parties. The meaning of privity of estate and privity of contract have already been discussed.

Covenants touching and concerning land

Unless a covenant in a lease touches and concerns[20] the land (or in the case of the reversion, has reference to the subject-matter of the lease[1]) it cannot run with the land in the sense explained above. If a covenant does not run with the land then the mere existence of privity of estate between the parties makes no difference.

A covenant will not touch and concern the land in question if it is purely personal to the parties. In general, a covenant will run with the land if: (1) it is beneficial to the owner of the land for the time being; (2) it

---

17 *Moule v Garrett* (1872) LR 7 Exch 101; also *Becton Dickinson UK Ltd v Zwebner* [1988] 3 WLR 1376.

18 *Hardy v Fothergill* (1888) 13 App Cas 351.

19 *Harris v Boots Cash Chemists (Southern) Ltd* [1904] 2 Ch 376. If a sub-lessor is under covenant to his lessee to observe covenants in the head lease, this principle has no application: *Ayling v White* [1961] 2 QB 228, [1961] 2 All ER 399, CA; *Yorkbrook Investments Ltd v Batten* [1985] 2 EGLR 100, CA.

20 See *Spencer's Case* (1583) 5 Co Rep 16a.

1 Law of Property Act 1925 ss 141 and 142.

affects the nature, quality, user or value of the landlord's land; (3) it is not in terms personal; and (4) the fact that a covenant is to pay a sum of money does not prevent it touching and concerning the land if (1) to (3) apply and the covenant is concerned with something to be done on, or in relation to the land.[2]

All implied covenants touch and concern land.[3] Conditions for re-entry for breaches of covenant which themselves touch and concern the land also do so.[4]

Landlords' covenants which touch and concern land

The following are examples of landlords' covenants which touch and concern the land: for quiet enjoyment,[5] for title,[6] for renewal of the lease,[7] to supply a housekeeper to clean flats,[8] not to allow building on adjacent land in front of the building line,[9] and not to determine a quarterly tenancy during its first three years.[10]

Landlords' covenants not touching and concerning land

The following are examples of personal covenants by the landlord which do not run with the land: a tenant's right of pre-emption on adjoining land,[11] a tenant's option to purchase,[12] to buy chattels (as opposed to fixtures) at the end of the lease,[13] to pay the tenant £500 unless the lease is renewed,[14] allowing the tenant to display advertising signs on other premises,[15] not to open another public house within half a mile,[16] to keep in repair other houses in the district,[17] and a covenant to return a

---

2 *P & A Swift Investments v Combined English Stores Group plc* [1988] 2 All ER 885, [1988] 3 WLR 313, HL.
3 *Wedd v Porter* [1916] 2 KB 91, CA.
4 See *Horsey Estate Ltd v Steiger* [1899] 2 QB 79, CA.
5 *Campbell v Lewis* (1820) 3 B & Ald 392.
6 *Williams v Burrell* (1845) 1 CB 402.
7 *Weg Motors Ltd v Hales* [1962] Ch 49, [1961] 3 All ER 181, CA.
8 *Barnes v City of London Real Property Co* [1918] 2 Ch 18.
9 *Ricketts v Enfield (Churchwardens)* [1909] 1 Ch 544.
10 *Breams Property Investment Co Ltd v Stroulger* [1948] 2 KB 1, [1948] 1 All ER 758, CA.
11 *Collison v Lettisom* (1815) 6 Taunt 224; *Charles Frodsham & Co Ltd v Morris* (1972) 229 Estates Gazette 961.
12 *Woodall v Clifton* [1905] 2 Ch 257.
13 *Gorton v Gregory* (1862) 3 B & S 90.
14 *Re Hunter's Lease, Giles v Hutchings* [1942] Ch 124, [1942] 1 All ER 27.
15 *Re No 1 Albemarle Street W1* [1959] Ch 531, [1959] 1 All ER 250.
16 *Thomas v Hayward* (1869) LR 4 Exch 311.
17 *Dewar v Goodman* [1909] AC 72, HL.

deposit at the expiry of the lease, provided the tenant observed the covenants in the lease.[18]

Tenants' covenants touching and concerning land

The following are examples of tenants' covenants which run with the land: to pay rent, rates, taxes and other charges,[19] to repair or to leave in repair,[20] to repair tenants' fixtures,[1] to pay £40 towards redecoration on quitting,[2] to reside on the premises,[3] to use as a private dwelling-house only,[4] not to assign without consent,[5] not to carry on a particular trade,[6] to insure against fire,[7] not to sell beer or petrol on the premises, other than that supplied by the landlord,[8] and a covenant by a third party to guarantee the tenant's performance of his obligations.[9]

Tenants' covenants not touching and concerning land

The following are examples of tenants' covenants which do not run with the land: to pay rates in respect of other land,[10] to repair and renew chattels (not fixtures),[11] and to exclude a third party from the business on the premises.[12]

Reform

A Law Commission Report[13] takes the clear view that the privity of contract rule, under which the original tenant is liable throughout the rest of the term for breaches of covenant committed by his successors,

---

18   *Hua Chiao Commercial Bank v Chiaphua Industries Ltd* [1987] AC 99, [1987] 1 All ER 1110, PC. Cf *Moss Empires Ltd v Olympia (Liverpool) Ltd* [1939] AC 544, [1939] 3 All ER 460, HL (covenant to spend a stipulated sum on repairs ran with land).
19   *Parker v Webb* (1693) 3 Salk 5 (rent); *Wix v Rutson* [1899] 1 QB 474 (rates etc).
20   *Windsor (Dean and Chapter) v Hyde* (1601) 5 Co Rep 24a; *Anon* (1533) Bro NC 18.
 1   *Williams v Earle* (1868) LR 3 QB 739.
 2   *Boyer v Warbey* [1953] 1 QB 234, [1953] 1 All ER 269, CA.
 3   *Lloyds Bank v Jones* [1955] 2 QB 298, [1955] 2 All ER 409, CA.
 4   *Wilkinson v Rogers* (1864) 2 De GJ & SM 62.
 5   *Goldstein v Sanders* [1915] 1 Ch 549.
 6   *Mayor of Congleton v Pattison* (1808) 10 East 130 at 138.
 7   *Vernon v Smith* (1821) 5 B & Ald 1.
 8   *Manchester Brewery Co v Coombs* [1901] 2 Ch 608 (beer); *Cleveland Petroleum Co Ltd v Dartstone Ltd* [1969] 1 All ER 201, [1969] 1 WLR 116, CA (petrol).
 9   *Kumar v Dunning* [1987] 2 All ER 801, [1987] 3 WLR 1167, CA, approved *P & A Swift Investments v Combined English Stores Group plc* [1988] 2 All ER 885, [1988] 3 WLR 313, HL.
10   *Gower v Postmaster General* (1887) 57 LT 527.
11   *Williams v Earle* (1868) LR 3 QB 739.
12   *Lewin v American and Colonial Distributors Ltd* [1945] Ch 225, [1945] 1 All ER 592.
13   Law Com No 174; see generally [1987] Conv 103 (D Gordon).

should be abrogated, and the tenant's liability would apply to the period he was a lessee. A term in a lease which (if such a reform were enacted) purported to impose a continuing liability on the original tenant would not, in principle, be enforceable.

Assignment of the lease

An assignee of the lease may sue (take the benefit) or be sued (be subject to the burden) of real covenants in the lease, but there are three limitations to the operation of the rule.

(i) Only covenants in a lease by deed were formerly held to run under this rule;[14] where an assignee of an informal lease entered and paid rent, a new agreement was readily inferred on the same terms, so that the covenant was binding in contract,[15] and in equity the benefit (but not the burdens) could pass on the assignment of an equitable lease. In *Boyer v Warbey*,[16] the Court of Appeal held that the burden of a covenant passed on assignment of a legal but informal lease (i e for three years in writing).

(ii) For privity of estate to be created, there must be a legal assignment of the whole term.[17] An equitable assignee (i e under a contract to assign) takes the benefits only (though presumably he would have to accept the burden also if he should seek specific performance). If there is an assignment of part of the land under the tenancy, real covenants will bind his part in so far as they relate to his part. He will be liable only for an apportioned part of the rent, even though the landlord can *distrain* on his part for the whole rent.

(iii) An assignee is liable only for breaches of covenant committed whilst there is privity of estate between himself and the landlord. He is not liable for breaches committed before the assignment, unless they are continuing breaches,[18] nor for breaches committed after a further assignment of the lease by him. Unlike the original tenant, therefore, an assignee of the lease can divest himself of liability to the landlord for future breaches by assigning the lease.

The assignee of a lease is as a result under less onerous potential liabilities than the original tenant; but this may be varied by express

---

14 *Elliott v Johnson* (1866) LR 2 QB 120 at 127.

15 *Buckworth v Simpson* (1835) 1 Cr M & R 834.

16 [1953] 1 QB 234, [1953] 1 All ER 269, *quaere* the position of an assignee of a legal tenancy granted orally.

17 'Assignment' includes an assignment in breach of a covenant not to assign without consent: *Old Grovebury Manor Farm v W Seymour Plant Sales and Hire Ltd (No 2)* [1979] 3 All ER 504, [1979] 1 WLR 1397, CA.

18 *Granada Theatres Ltd v Freehold Investments (Leytonstone) Ltd* [1959] Ch 592, [1959] 2 All ER 176.

agreement, as where on taking an assignment the assignee covenants direct with the landlord to observe all the covenants in the lease and to pay the rent: in this case the assignee's liability for breaches of covenant commences with the date of the assignment and continues from then until the expiry of the term, co-extensively with the liability of the original tenant.[19] This process of direct covenanting with the landlord (say as a condition of the assignments) may take place each time the lease is re-assigned. If a breach of a continuing nature (say of the tenant's covenant to repair) starts prior to a first assignee's assignment and continues after he re-assigns to a second assignee, the second assignee will be solely liable in the absence of contrary stipulations.[20]

Assignment of the reversion

An assignee of the reversion may sue or be sued on any covenants in the lease which run with the land under ss 141 and 142 of the Law of Property Act 1925.

Section 141(1) of the 1925 Act (passing the benefit of real covenants) provides that rent reserved by a lease, and the benefit of every covenant therein, having reference to the subject matter thereof, 'shall be annexed and incident to and shall go with the reversionary estate in the land, immediately expectant on the term granted by the lease, notwithstanding severance of that reversionary estate . . .'

This provision accordingly enables an assignee by deed of the reversion immediately expectant on a lease to enforce lessees' real covenants such as to pay rent, to keep in repair and against assignments.

Section 142(1) of the 1925 Act (transmitting the burden of real covenants) is, in its first part, cast in similar language to section 141(1), but it further provides that the lessor's obligations 'may be taken advantage of and enforced by the person in whom the term is from time to time vested . . . .'

Again, only the burden of landlords' real covenants will automatically pass on an assignment by deed of the reversion expectant on the term in question.

Both provisions apply, it is thought, to enable the benefit and burden of real covenants in a written agreement for a lease[1] and oral tenancies[2] to pass automatically.

The effect of s 141(1) of the 1925 Act is to pass the full benefit of all the lessee's real covenants to an assignee of the reversion by deed. After the

---

19   *Lyons & Co v Knowles* [1943] 1 KB 366, [1943] 1 All ER 477, CA.
20   *Middlegate Properties Ltd v Bilbao* (1972) 24 P & CR 329.
 1   *Cole v Kelly* [1920] 2 KB 106, CA.
 2   Law of Property Act 1925 s 154 extends ss 141 and 142 ibid to 'an underlease or other tenancy'.

date of the assignment, the assignor loses all further right to enforce the covenants in the lease. In the case of breaches of a continuing nature, such as of a tenant's repairing covenant, which have not been enforced prior to the assignment date, the assignee of the reversion is statutorily entitled to enforce the covenant and to recover damages from the tenant; the damages will be for the whole period of the breach, both before and after the assignment date.[3] 'You cannot give any sensible meaning to the words of [s 141(1)] unless the entire benefit of a repairing covenant has passed, leaving the assignor without remedy against the lessee.'[4] This principle enables an assignee of the reversion to sue and re-enter for rent arrears when the right of re-entry arose prior to the assignment date.[5] Moreover, an assignee of the reversion is entitled to recover rent arrears, due prior to the date of the assignment, from an original tenant, though, given that the tenant had assigned his lease before the assignment of the reversion, there was neither privity of contract nor of estate between the parties. However, the original tenant's liability remained throughout the term and the right to enforce this passed automatically on assignment by deed of the reversion.[6]

Under s 142(1) of the 1925 Act, cited above, it would seem that a landlord who has assigned his reversion remains liable on express real covenants which run with the reversion.[7] If the tenant assigns the residue of the term and prior to and at the date of the assignment, the landlord is in breach of a continuing covenant, such as to repair, the tenant/assignor will be able to sue the landlord and recover damages for breach of the covenant to repair up to the date of the assignment. This is because s 142(1) does not in terms annex to the term the right to take advantage of landlords' breaches of real covenant which took place while the assignor was tenant, and so a landlord's liability to a tenant survives the assignment of the lease.[8] But an assignee of the reversion is not liable for his predecessor's breaches of covenant.[9] The original landlord may, it has been suggested, be liable on a real covenant, direct to an assignee, who became tenant after the assignment of the reversion.[10]

---

3 *Re King* [1963] Ch 459, [1963] 1 All ER 781, CA.
4 Ibid at 489 (Upjohn LJ).
5 *A and D London and County Ltd v Wilfred Sportsman Ltd* [1971] Ch 764, [1970] 2 All ER 600, CA.
6 *Arlesford Trading Co Ltd v Servansingh* [1971] 3 All ER 113, [1971] 1 WLR 1080, CA.
7 *Stuart v Joy* [1904] 1 KB 362, CA.
8 *City and Metropolitan Properties Ltd v Greycroft* [1987] 3 All ER 839, [1987] 1 WLR 1085.
9 *Pettiward Estates v Shephard* [1986] CLY 1861 (Cty Ct) s 142(1) was treated as not alike s 141(1).
10 *Celsteel Ltd v Alton House Holdings Ltd (No 2)* [1987] 2 All ER 240 at 244, CA.

Sections 141 and 142 apply 'notwithstanding severance of that reversionary estate' (i e where a part or parts of the reversion fall into separate hands), and apportionment of the benefits and burdens is provided by s 140. A tenant who is served with a notice to quit in relation to a part of his land (after the reversion of that part has been severed) is given the option under s 140(2) to quit the whole of the land if he so wishes, by serving a counter-notice within one month upon the reversioner in relation to the rest of the land.

Where a tenant surrenders his lease, leaving a sub-tenancy unexpired, s 139 of the Law of Property Act 1925, deems the superior landlord to be the reversioner vis-à-vis the sub-tenant, for the purpose of enforcing the covenants in the lease; the reversion is similarly 'kept alive' in the event of merger of the tenancy with some other interest.

Duty to notify tenants of dwellings of assignments

By s 3(1) of the Landlord and Tenant Act 1985, if the interest of the landlord of a tenancy[11] of premises consisting of or including a dwelling is assigned, the new landlord must give written notice of the assignment and of his name and address to the tenant not later than the next day on which rent is payable under the tenancy, unless that date is within two months of the assignment. In that case the period is the end of the period of two months. Failure without reasonable excuse to comply with this requirement is a criminal offence (s 3(3)).

If the above duty is broken, the old landlord remains liable, jointly and severally with the new landlord, to the tenant for any breaches of covenant until written notification is given to the tenant by the new landlord of the assignment and of the new landlord's name and address.[12]

3   BY OR AGAINST STRANGERS TO THE LEASE

We have considered above the rules for the enforcement of covenants in a lease as between the original parties and their respective assignees; and, as a general rule, they are the only persons who can sue or be sued in respect of them. There are, however, a number of limited exceptions whereby strangers, or persons who are apparently strangers, to the lease may enforce its terms.

---

11   By s 3(4), 'tenancy' includes a statutory tenancy. However, the duty to notify does not apply to tenancies to which Part II of the Landlord and Tenant Act applies (s 32(1)).

12   Landlord and Tenant Act 1985 s 3(3A) and (3B), added by Landlord and Tenant Act 1987 s 50 from 1 February 1988: SI 1987/2177.

(a) Under *s 56 of the Law of Property Act 1925*, 'a person may take an immediate or other interest in land or other property, or the benefit of any condition, right of entry, covenant or agreement over or respecting land or other property, although he may not be named as a party to the conveyance or other instrument'. Until recently, it could safely be said that s 56 entitled only those third parties with whom a covenant was expressed or intended to have been made, to sue upon it (even though they were not parties to the instrument creating it), and not merely parties for whose benefit the covenant was made.[13] So, for example, if a tenant covenanted with the landlord and 'also with the owners for the time being' of adjacent business premises specified, that he would not carry on a particular trade, they might sue him on the covenant. In *Beswick v Beswick*,[14] however, mere benefit was held enough to justify the claim of a third party, thus casting doubts upon a limited interpretation of the section; but it can still be said that such a claimant must be in existence and identifiable at the time when the covenant is made, and it would seem that it matters not that the covenant is not one that will run with the land.[15]

(b) Under *s 78(1) of the Law of Property Act 1925*, 'a covenant relating to any land of the covenantee shall be deemed to be made with the covenantee and his successors in title and the persons deriving title under him or them', and has effect as if such successors and other persons were expressed.[16] So, in respect of the benefit of a covenant (whether positive or negative) in the head lease, which runs with the land, the covenant may be sued upon by a sub-tenant, for example, even though he is a third party to that lease, because such a covenant is treated as if it had been made with him; but not so, in respect of the burden of a covenant under s 79[17] which has been taken to give an indemnity to the covenantee for acts of the covenantor's successors and those claiming under him (e g the sub-tenant in the above example).

(c) *Restrictive covenants* in a lease may be enforceable against persons who are not parties to it, as, for example, where there is a covenant in the head lease against a particular trade, and the sub-tenant in

---

13 *Re Foster, Hudson v Foster* [1938] 3 All ER 357 at 365.
14 [1968] AC 58, [1967] 2 All ER 1197.
15 *Re Ecclesiastical Comrs for England's Conveyance* [1936] Ch 430 at 438; also *Pinemain Ltd v Welbeck International Ltd* (1984) 272 Estates Gazette 1166.
16 If, as a matter of construction, the covenant is annexed to the land, it will run with it: *Federated Homes Ltd v Mill Lodge Properties Ltd* [1980] 1 All ER 371, [1980] 1 WLR 504; *Roake v Chadha* [1983] 3 All ER 503, [1984] 1 WLR 40.
17 It is assumed that s 79 is a mere 'word-saver': *Tophams Ltd v Earl of Sefton* [1967] 1 AC 50, [1966] 1 All ER 1039, HL.

occupation is carrying on that trade, his own sub-lease containing no such restriction. There being no privity of estate between the parties, the landlord can restrain the breach against the sub-tenant only if the covenant would be enforceable under the general law, i e under the rule in *Tulk v Moxhay*.[18] The covenant must therefore be negative in substance; it must have been intended to run with the land demised (but in covenants made since 1925, this will be presumed, by virtue of s 78 of the Law of Property Act 1925, unless a contrary intention appears);[19] and the sub-tenant must have had 'notice' of it, i e it will not bind a bona fide purchaser of a legal estate for value without notice. It would thus be enforceable against a squatter, but not against a sub-tenant without notice. Restrictive covenants in lease are not registrable.[20] Furthermore, under s 44 of the Law of Property Act 1925, a sub-tenant may be precluded from inspecting the lease imposing the covenant, even though he had covenanted to observe all the covenants in that lease. Where, however, a restrictive covenant in a superior lease is enforceable against a sub-tenant, under these rules, only equitable remedies are available. Where it is not enforceable directly, it may nevertheless be enforced indirectly, i e by threatening or bringing forfeiture proceedings against the tenant under the relevant lease, who in turn might be able to restrain the sub-tenant in breach.

(d)   *Adjacent tenants* under a letting scheme[1] are entitled to enforce inter se restrictive covenants imposed on them in their leases under the scheme, even though they are strangers, under rules laid down in *Elliston v Reacher*,[2] in connection with a 'building scheme', and applied to a block of flats:

(i)   the plaintiff and the defendant must derive their titles from the same landlord;

(ii)   the restrictive covenants must apply to all the tenants within the scheme;

(iii)   the restrictive covenants must be for the benefit of the tenants generally (and not merely to protect the landlord in relation to covenants in the head lease),[3] and,

(iv)   the restrictive covenants must have been intended to be enforceable by the tenants inter se.

Under these rules a tenant may thus have the terms of his own lease

---

18   (1848) 2 Ph 774.

19   *Re Royal Victoria Pavilion, Ramsgate* [1961] Ch 581, [1961] 3 All ER 83.

20   Land Charges Act 1972 s 2(4).

1   Cf *Newman v Real Estate Debenture Corpn Ltd* [1940] 1 All ER 131; *Kelly v Battershell* [1949] 2 All ER 830.

2   [1908] 2 Ch 374, in relation to 'building schemes', or 'schemes of development' as they are now preferably called: *Brunner v Greenslade* [1971] Ch 993, [1970] 3 All ER 833.

3   *Browne v Flower* [1911] 1 Ch 219; also *Andrews v Sohal* [1989] EGCS 12.

enforced against him in equity (i e by injunction) by another tenant of the common landlord; and to that extent, it is an exception to the general rule above. Positive covenants are never enforceable,[4] unless through privity of contract or estate.

(e) *Arrears of rent* and damages for breach of other covenants are recoverable from a tenant after he has assigned by an assignee of the reversion, even though there has never been privity of contract or estate between them (see the *Arlesford* case above). The tenant, *ex hypothesi*, is not, however, a stranger to the lease; and the right to recover arrears of rent from him passed to the assignee of the reversion under s 141 of the Law of Property Act 1925.

(f) *An option to purchase* the freehold contained in a lease, in so far as it is an agreement collateral to the lease, cannot be enforced under the rules given above after an assignment. The benefit of a contract is assignable under the general law, however, and on an assignment of the lease, the benefit of the option will pass to the assignee if the assignment is considered to extend to the option. Moreover, an option is an interest in land, and as such is assignable separately from the lease,[5] unless expressed to be exercisable by the tenant alone; but, for the same reason, it must be protected by registration as an estate contract under the Land Charges Act 1972,[6] or by the entry of a notice in the charges register[7] under the Land Registration Act 1925 as the case may be.

Third parties have a number of other rights and obligations which they can enforce against, or which can be enforced against them by, a landlord or a tenant under the general law. These are not to be confused with the enforcement of the contractual or quasi-contractual rights considered in this section; they involve the enforcement of rights relating to land which are universally enjoyed under the law, such as valid restrictive covenants upon the freehold, and, in particular, the right to claim damages in tort against the landlord or tenant as owner or occupier of the land, as employer, as 'builder' of a dwelling, etc. (See Chapter 10.)

IV REMEDIES

The purpose of this section is to offer a general overview of the various remedies available to the landlord or tenant for breaches of covenants in the lease.

---

4 See the Report of Committee on Positive Covenants affecting Land, 1965 Cmnd 2719.
5 *Griffith v Pelton* [1958] Ch 205, [1957] 3 All ER 75.
6 S 2(4); *Pritchard v Briggs* [1980] Ch 338, [1980] 1 All ER 294.
7 Land Registration Rules 1925 r 7.

Breaches by the landlord or tenant of covenants, express, implied or statutory, in a lease are enforceable by means of the normal remedies available at law and in equity for breaches of contract – albeit that, as was noted, third party assignees of the lease and of the reversion are entitled to seek these remedies provided the covenant sought to be enforced runs with the lease or the reversion.

The common-law remedy for breach of covenant is *damages*. Any breach is actionable per se: obviously a mere technical or trifling breach is not worth suing for because it sounds in nominal damages only. Substantial awards of damages are particularly suitable where the losses of the landlord or tenant are quantifiable in money, and where an award of money would be sufficient compensation for the breach. For example, a breach by the landlord of his covenant to repair or for quiet enjoyment may well entitle the tenant to substantial damages.

If the court considers it appropriate, it may order *equitable relief*, in the form of an injunction (mandatory or negative) or specific performance, to enforce landlords' or tenants' covenants. For instance an injunction might well be awarded to compel a tenant or sub-tenant to comply with a restrictive covenant in the lease.[8] The court has power, for example where the landlord is seriously in default with his repairing covenants, to order the appointment of a receiver and manager of the premises in certain serious cases, particularly, under statute, with blocks of residential flats held on long leases.[9]

Injunctions are also appropriate to enforce landlords' covenants (express or implied) for quiet enjoyment and against derogation from grant; and to enforce tenants' user covenants and covenants against assignments and sub-lettings, though in all cases the remedy is not automatic and its availability in a particular case is at the discretion of the court.[10]

In the case of breaches by the tenant of his covenant to repair, the landlord's measure (or quantum) of damages is limited by statute to the amount of the diminution in the value of his reversion.[11] In other cases the measure of damages is the actual loss suffered by the landlord. Some tenants' breaches, for example, of a covenant against the making of internal alterations, may actually raise the value of the landlord's reversion. In that case, assuming no injunction directing re-instatement of the premises to their former state is considered appropriate, the landlord may be entitled to the cost of restoring the premises to their

---

8   See eg *Sutton Housing Trust v Lawrence* (1987) 55 P & CR 320, CA (fact that tenant might disobey injunction not a bar to relief).

9   See Landlord and Tenant Act 1987 Part II.

10   See e g *Kehoe v Marquess of Lansdowne* [1893] AC 451, HL; *Achilli v Tovell* [1927] 2 Ch 243; *Talbot v Ford* (1842) 13 Sim 173; *Murray v Dunn* [1907] AC 283, HL.

11   Landlord and Tenant Act 1927 s 18(1).

original state plus any loss of rent incurred while the necessary works are carried out.[12]

The statutory limit on the amount of damages recoverable by the landlord for tenants' breaches of covenant to repair has no application to tenants, and the measure of damages for landlords' breaches of covenant to repair awarded to tenants is, essentially, the amount of the loss caused to the tenant, because the object of the award is to put the tenant in the same position as if no breach had taken place.[13]

The landlord has two remedies to enforce tenants' covenants in the lease which are not available to tenants. One is the right, subject to strict conditions (dealt with in Chapter 13) to forfeit the lease, that is, to bring the term to a premature end for tenants' breaches of covenant. Since forfeiture is a drastic process, and its effect, if an order for possession is made, is to deprive the tenant of what may be a valuable investment,[14] this remedy is hedged about with very important restrictions and limitations, which are particularly severe in the case of alleged breaches of the tenant's covenant to repair. Moreover, forfeiture will, if granted, annihilate the lease concerned and with that, the security of any mortgagees of the tenant and the immediate reversion expectant on any sub-leases. So mortgagees and sub-lessees alike are given important rights to protect their interests, as will be apparent from Chapter 13.

The other remedy unique to landlords is to levy a distress on the premises against the tenant's goods, for unpaid rent. This is a self-help remedy, and its abolition has been recommended.[15]

However, not even the worst possible conduct by a landlord (e g unlawful eviction) gives the tenant the right to end the tenancy; indeed a tenant wishing to do so could be deterred by the financial losses so drastic a step would occasion.[16] The doctrine of contractual repudiation has no application to an executed lease, the stated reason being that a lease creates an interest in land and is not just an ordinary contract.[17] It is true that the tenant is able, in particular cases, such as breaches by the landlord of his covenant to repair, or for quiet enjoyment, to withhold

---

12 *Eyre v Rea* [1947] KB 567, [1947] 1 All ER 415, as explained in *Duke of Westminster v Swinton* [1948] 1 KB 524, [1948] 1 All ER 248.

13 *Calabar Properties Ltd v Stitcher* [1983] 3 All ER 759, [1984] 1 WLR 287, CA.

14 As in *Di Palma v Victoria Square Property Co Ltd* [1986] Ch 150, [1985] 2 All ER 676, CA, where a 99-year term valued at £30,000 by the lessee was forfeited because of non-payment of £299.36 service charges rent: however, the case wholly lacked merit.

15 Law Com WP No 9 (1986). See Hill-Smith [1983] Conv 444.

16 See Law Com No 142 Forfeiture of Tenancies (1985) HC 279 Part XVII paras 17.2 and 17.4.

17 *Total Oil Great Britain Ltd v Thompson Garages (Biggin Hill) Ltd* [1972] 1 QB 318, [1971] 3 All ER 1226, CA.

rent and/or to seek injunctions, specific performance, or the appointment of a receiver, as well as damages. The Law Commission
nonetheless considered the tenant to be disadvantaged and recommended a termination order scheme for tenants, to be of use particularly
where the landlord's breaches are frequent.[18]

The position of tenants of long leases of residential flats was improved
by the Landlord and Tenant Act 1987 (see Chapters 9 and 19) which not
only contains a code for the appointment by the county court of a
manager where the landlord is in serious breach of his repairing
covenants, but provides for tenants' buy-outs in such a case.

Generally a tenant (or landlord) who considers that the terms of his
lease do not adequately reflect the present circumstances of the lease, is
simply locked into them, unless the landlord is prepared to accept a
surrender of the term.[19] However, Part IV of the Landlord and Tenant
Act 1987 may be a vehicle for general future changes. This enables the
county court to vary the terms of long leases of flats where they fail for
example to make adequate provision for repairs and service charges.

---

18 Law Com No 142, supra, Part XVIII.
19 This result is re-inforced by the narrow interpretation of Landlord and Tenant Act
    1954 s 35 in *O'May v City of London Real Property Co Ltd* [1983] 2 AC 726, [1982]
    1 All ER 660, HL – effectively precluding non-consensual variations of the incidence
    of liability for and to pay for repairs and maintenance. See, however, Law Com
    No 162 (1987) 4.54–4.56.

Chapter 6

Implied covenants

I AMBIT OF IMPLIED COVENANTS

Implied covenants fall into two classes: those implied at common law, and those implied by statute.

(a) Covenants implied in law

Covenants are implied in law not for the sake of filling in obvious lacunae in the lease as drafted, nor indeed in the hope of divining what terms the parties might have included, had they given more thought to the matter, for this would amount to a re-drafting of the lease;[1] they are implied in order to give a tenant the full benefit of the estate which he has (i e a legal estate) and for the reasonable protection of the landlord's interest (i e the reversion). In other words, they are the elemental rights and obligations necessary to give effect to the intention of the parties implicit in the very grant of the tenancy, unless the parties agree otherwise, the intention being that on payment of the rent the tenant shall enjoy the land as he finds it for the period limited by the lease, and hand it back, intact, at the end of that period.

Such covenants arise automatically by virtue of the creation of the relationship of landlord and tenant, and then, only in the absence of any express agreement in the lease in relation to that matter.[2] An express covenant for quiet enjoyment, however limited in its scope, for example, will exclude the operation of the corresponding implied covenant completely. Unlike express covenants which by their contractual nature continue in force for the whole of the term granted, implied covenants, by their attachment to the estate, can last for only as long as the estate;[3] and by the same reasoning, they are all deemed to be 'covenants that touch and concern the land', and will therefore run with the land on assignment.

---

1 See *Smith v Harwich Corpn* (1857) 2 CBNS 651.
2 *Miller v Emcer Products Ltd* [1956] Ch 304, [1956] 1 All ER 237.
3 *Baynes & Co v Lloyd & Sons* [1895] 1 QB 820; affd [1895] 2 QB 610.

(b)   Covenants implied by statute

Certain covenants are implied as the result of statute. In particular, the landlord of a dwelling-house or flat let for a term of less than seven years is, by s 11 of the Landlord and Tenant Act 1985, under a statute-implied duty to keep in repair the structure and exterior of the dwelling-house or flat. This obligation cannot be contracted out of directly or indirectly: see generally Chapter 9. Statute-implied covenants or warranties relate chiefly to repairs.

A   IMPLIED COVENANTS BY THE LANDLORD

II   QUIET ENJOYMENT

The covenant by the landlord for quiet enjoyment will arise from the relationship of landlord and tenant, however created, whether by deed, in writing, or by parol.[4] The covenant in law continues only for as long as the landlord's estate, and is excluded by any express covenant for quiet enjoyment contained in the lease. Originally described as a covenant to secure title and possession, its scope has been considerably extended. It entitles the tenant to be put into possession,[5] but it cannot be regarded as a full covenant for title. At most, it is qualified, to the extent that the landlord covenants that he has title at the commencement of the tenancy. The covenant extends to unlawful acts of the landlord and to lawful acts of other persons claiming under the landlord by way of entry, eviction, or interruption of the tenant's peaceful enjoyment of the land. It protects the tenant from acts which cause *physical* interference, whether those acts are done on the premises or not and, from any conduct of the landlord or his agent interfering with the tenant's freedom of action in exercising his rights as tenant.[6] It affords him no remedy in respect of acoustic or visual interference, for which his proper remedy if any, would lie in tort.[7] So that noise from machinery in the same building as an hotel has been held not to be a breach of the covenant,[8] but where noise, dust and dirt from building operations on adjacent premises were so intolerable as to render the tenant's premises uninhabitable, it may be otherwise.[9]

---

4   *Kenny v Preen* [1963] 1 QB 499, [1962] 3 All ER 814, CA.
5   *Miller v Emcer Products Ltd* [1956] Ch 304, [1956] 1 All ER 237.
6   *McCall v Abelesz* [1976] 1 All ER 727 at 730–731, CA; *Kenny v Preen* [1962] 3 All ER 814 at 820, CA. See now Housing Act 1988 s 29.
7   See *Mafo v Adams* [1970] 1 QB 548 at 557, per Sachs LJ, where the plaintiff succeeded under the tort of deceit for loss of possession by a fraudulent trick, and not force.
8   *Kelly v Battershell* [1949] 2 All ER 830.
9   *Matania v National Provincial Bank Ltd* [1936] 2 All ER 633.

The covenant protects ordinary reasonable use of the premises by the tenant, and not the latter's privacy or amenities. Where the landlord erected an external staircase which passed the tenant's bedroom window, destroying her privacy, she had no claim under the covenant,[10] nor could a tenant claim under the covenant where the landlord retained a cellar under the demised premises, let as a paper warehouse, and used it for the purposes of his own trade, even though the tenant's goods, special, not ordinary, paper were damaged as a result.[11] On the other hand where the entrance to the tenant's shop was barred by scaffolding erected by the landlord, damages were recovered for loss of custom.[12] If the landlord sends the tenant threatening letters and bangs on the door and shouts at the tenant,[13] or cuts off gas and electricity supplies,[14] or enters the premises and removes the doors and windows,[15] he will be in breach of the implied covenant for quiet enjoyment: it is not necessary to show actual physical irruption into the premises.

The implied covenant for quiet enjoyment is narrow in scope.

1 It is a qualified covenant and extends only to the acts of the landlord and those claiming under him. It does not extend to disturbance by title paramount, as where a sub-tenant finds that he is subject to a restrictive covenant in the head lease.[16] Therefore where an injunction was granted to flat tenants, to restrain another tenant, under a later lease, from building a carwash which would contravene a right of way granted by the present freeholder's predecessor in title to the flat tenants, it was held that the covenant for quiet enjoyment did not cover rights or interests granted by a predecessor in title of the current landlord.[17]

2 The implied covenant terminates with the landlord's interest, so that where a tenant with eight and a half years to run under his own lease, mistakenly granted a sub-lease for ten and a half years, the sub-tenant had no remedy when evicted by the superior landlord at the end of the eight and a half years.[18] On the other hand, the covenant includes an obligation to put the tenant into possession so that if the previous tenant wrongfully holds over, the new tenant may sue the landlord.[19]

---

10 *Browne v Flower* [1911] 1 Ch 219.
11 *Robinson v Kilvert* (1889) 41 Ch D 88, CA.
12 *Owen v Gadd* [1956] 2 QB 99, [1956] 2 All ER 28, CA.
13 *Kenny v Preen* [1963] 1 QB 499, [1962] 3 All ER 814, CA.
14 *Perera v Vandiyar* [1953] 1 All ER 1109, [1953] 1 WLR 672, CA.
15 *Lavender v Betts* [1942] 2 All ER 72.
16 *Jones v Lavington* [1903] 1 KB 253, CA.
17 *Celsteel Ltd v Alton House Holdings Ltd (No 2)* [1987] 2 All ER 240, [1987] 1 WLR 291, CA (express covenant).
18 *Baynes & Co v Lloyd & Sons* [1895] 1 QB 820.
19 *Miller v Emcer Products Ltd* [1956] Ch 304, [1956] 1 All ER 237, CA.

3   The covenant covers all unlawful acts of the landlord on the premises. However, acts done pursuant to rights under the lease itself cannot by definition constitute a breach of covenant, such as re-entry for breach of covenant or condition or entry to inspect the condition of the premises under a right expressly or statutorily conferred. On the other hand if the landlord lets adjoining premises, such as a flat above, for a purpose, and it is in such a state that no matter how it is used, it will interfere with the reasonable enjoyment of the tenant's adjoining premises below the landlord or his assignee will be in breach of the covenant.[20]

4   The covenant extends to acts of the landlord (or a person claiming under him) on adjoining, or adjacent land or premises which cause some physical interference with the ordinary enjoyment of the tenant, unless some special purpose of the tenant, which is interfered with, is known to the landlord: if at the date of the demise it is, he will also be liable.[1] Hence, a landlord was liable for interference with the tenant's access to the demised premises.[2] On the other hand, there is no implied term in a tenancy agreement compelling landlords to enforce a tenant's agreement not to cause a nuisance to their neighbours (and fellow tenants).[3]

5   The covenant extends to the lawful acts of persons claiming under the landlord such as other tenants, as with mining operations by a tenant causing the land under another's house to subside.[4] The acts of these tenants must be 'lawful'. Where the defendants let farms to A, B and C, and A suffered damage from the flooding of drains on B and C's land, the landlords were held liable only for C's proper use of defective drains, but not for B's excessive ('unlawful') use of drains which were in good order.[5]

The measure of damages for breach is the loss to the tenant resulting from it.[6] This includes removal expenses, damages for inconvenience and shock where appropriate, and legal costs.[7] Unless trespass or nuisance is shown, no exemplary damages for breach of the covenant for quiet enjoyment may be awarded.[8]

---

20   *Sampson v Hodson-Pressinger* [1981] 3 All ER 710, CA.
 1   *Robinson v Kilvert* (1889) 41 Ch D 88, CA.
 2   *Hilton v James Smith & Sons (Norwood) Ltd* (1979) 251 Estates Gazette 1063, CA.
 3   *O'Leary v London Borough of Islington* (1983) 9 HLR 83.
 4   *Markham v Paget* [1908] 1 Ch 697.
 5   *Sanderson v Berwick-upon-Tweed Corpn* (1884) 13 QBD 547.
 6   *Sutton v Baillie* (1891) 65 LT 528.
 7   *Grosvenor Hotel Co v Hamilton* [1894] 2 QB 836, CA; *Giles v Adley* [1987] CLY 2121.
 8   *Kenny v Preen* [1963] 1 QB 499 at 513, CA.

If the landlord commits a tort, such as trespass or nuisance, then an additional separate claim may be framed by the tenant in tort.[9] If the court considers that the conduct of the landlord has been particularly outrageous exemplary damages may be awarded: these need bear no relation to the tenant's losses. An example is where the landlord deliberately ignores the tenant's legal rights as by illegally evicting him.[10] It is not necessary for the tenant to plead trespass in his statement of claim as a condition precedent to an award of exemplary damages.[11] Nor is it necessary to show that the landlord made a profit or aimed at one.[12]

III NON-DEROGATION FROM GRANT

The landlord is subject to an implied covenant not to derogate from his grant, or, to adapt words from a different context,[13] he cannot agree to grant (a lease) and at the same time deny to (the tenant) what is, at the time of the grant, necessary for his reasonable and ordinary enjoyment of the land.[14] The landlord is bound not to interfere with any easements which he has granted, such as a right to use the airspace of adjoining land of his for advertising purposes,[15] nor may he interfere with profits à prendre.[16] Non-derogation from grant applies, moreover, where the landlord retains adjacent land, and gives the tenant remedies in respect of activities on the part of the landlord or any persons claiming under him, which adversely affect the use of the land let. An implied covenant for non-derogation from grant is not excluded by an express covenant for quiet enjoyment,[17] even though the two covenants serve related objects. An express covenant to let for residential purposes only may

---

9   As in *Guppys (Bridport) Ltd v Brookling* (1983) 14 HLR 1, CA, where the landlords cut off all water supplies and sanitation as part of their redevelopment of premises.
10   *Drane v Evangelou* [1978] 2 All ER 437, [1978] 1 WLR 455, CA (£1,000 award upheld). Also, *McMillan v Singh* (1984) 17 HLR 120, CA (award of £250 upheld despite tenant being in arrear with rent).
11   *Drane v Evangelou, supra.* Also *Breeze v Elden & Hyde* [1987] CLY 2120 (Cty Ct).
12   *Amrani v Oniah* [1984] CLY 1974.
13   *Sovmots Investments Ltd v Secretary of State for the Environment* [1979] AC 144 at 168, [1977] 2 All ER 385 at 391, HL.
14   If the tenant intends to make use of the land for a special purpose, e g the manufacture of paper of special sensitivity, the landlord will only break the present covenant if he knows of this special user: *Robinson v Kilvert* (1889) 41 Ch D 88, CA.
15   *Johnston & Sons Ltd v Holland* [1988] 1 EGLR 264, CA.
16   *Peech v Best* [1931] 1 KB 1, CA.
17   *Grosvenor Hotel Co v Hamilton* [1894] 2 QB 836, CA.

carry the implication that any letting of part for business purposes is a derogation from grant.[18]

The covenant is broken only if the landlord, or a person claiming under him, such as a tenant or assignee of adjoining land, does something which renders the premises less or substantially less fit for the particular purpose or purposes for which they were known to be let. Therefore, the covenant was broken where an assignee of the landlord built on adjoining land in such a way as to obstruct the flow of air to the drying sheds in the tenant's timber yard, the premises having been let for that purpose.[19] Where the plaintiff held a lease of land expressly for the purpose of storing explosives, and the defendant held a lease of adjoining land from the same landlord, with a view to working minerals, and the defendant built too near the plaintiff's magazine, so jeopardising the latter's statutory licence, the plaintiff obtained an injunction to restrain the breach.[20] Other examples of breaches of the implied covenant not to derogate from grant include: the endangering of the stability of the tenant's adjoining premises by vibration from heavy machinery on the landlord's premises,[1] and where the landlord built against an external wall of the tenant's premises, thereby making use of it as a party wall and blocking off the tenant's right to light.[2]

No action may be brought unless the tenant proves that at the time of granting the lease the landlord knew the purpose for which the land was to be used, and also, where relevant, knew that any particular user was special or sensitive.[3] The test for determining the existence of a breach is whether the premises are rendered less fit or materially less fit for the particular purpose of the lease: therefore, if the only complaint is of interference with the tenant's privacy,[4] or that adjoining premises have been let for a competing trade,[5] or that the insurance risks, such as for fire, have been increased by a letting of adjacent premises,[6] there is no breach of the present covenant.

---

18   *Newman v Real Estate Debenture Corpn Ltd* [1940] 1 All ER 131.
19   *Aldin v Latimer Clark, Muirhead & Co* [1894] 2 Ch 437.
20   *Harmer v Jumbil (Nigeria) Tin Areas Ltd* [1921] 1 Ch 200, CA.
 1   *Grosvenor Hotel Co v Hamilton*, supra.
 2   *Betts Ltd v Pickford's Ltd* [1906] 2 Ch 87. The extent of a tenant's right to light in any case is a question of fact and degree: *Birmingham, Dudley and District Banking Co v Ross* (1888) 38 Ch D 295, CA.
 3   *Robinson v Kilvert*, supra.
 4   See *Browne v Flower* [1911] 1 Ch 219.
 5   *Port v Griffith* [1938] 1 All ER 295.
 6   *O'Cedar Ltd v Slough Trading Co Ltd* [1927] 2 KB 123. It would obviously have been different if the letting of the adjoining premises had rendered it impossible for the tenant to insure their own premises.

IV RATES

(a) General rate

Generally the occupier is liable for the general rate under s 116 of the General Rate Act 1967, but under s 58, the landlord as owner must pay, or allow the rate, by way of deduction from rent, in the case of tenancies for a term not exceeding three months. The general rate is payable also by the owner where:

(i) the rateable value of the premises does not exceed £200 and the owner has been so directed (s 55); or,

(ii) the landlord has agreed to pay or collect the rate in tenancies where the rent is payable more frequently than quarterly (s 56), and in these cases he is entitled to an allowance equal to such proportion of the amount payable as the rating authority may by resolution determine.[7]

(b) Water rate

The owner may be directed to pay the water rate, where he has been directed to pay the general rate under para (1) above.

(c) Drainage rate

An owner's or occupier's drainage rate (as defined in s 63 of the Land Drainage Act 1976) is assessed on the relevant occupier of the land; but an internal drainage board (the responsible body) may resolve that, in certain cases, e g that of dwelling-houses, the rate is to be levied on owners not occupiers (s 73). The owner once assessed has a right to recover from the occupier any amount paid by him which, as between himself and the occupier, the latter is liable to pay (s 73(3)). By s 72(5), the internal drainage board likewise has the right to recover drainage rate from an occupier, who in turn is given the right to deduct the amount paid, if falling on the owner, from any rent payable under a lease or tenancy (s 75(5)(d)).

B IMPLIED COVENANTS BY THE TENANT

V RENT

In the absence of any express covenant by the tenant to pay rent (more fully discussed in Chapter 8 below), a covenant to pay rent will be

---

7 General Rate Act 1967 s 55(2).

implied from a good reservation by deed such as the words 'yielding' and 'paying', and from any words in an agreement which show a clear intention that rent shall be paid, such as 'at and under the rent of £80'.[8]

Liability under an express covenant to pay rent arises without entry by the tenant on the premises; under an implied covenant, however, a tenant is liable neither before entry nor after assignment.[9] Further, under an express covenant, the tenant is obliged to seek out a landlord who is *intra quatuor maria* to pay him, unless a place of payment has been specified; under an implied covenant, the tenant must be prepared to pay the rent on the premises. The amount of rent agreed must be 'certain', otherwise it will not be rent properly so-called, in which case there will be an implied promise by the tenant to pay a reasonable sum to the landlord by way of compensation for use and occupation.

VI RATES AND OTHER CHARGES IN RESPECT OF THE PROPERTY

The tenant is under an implied obligation to pay all rates, taxes, charges, etc, for which the landlord is not liable.[10] The incidence of liability for charges levied on land on the owner or occupier by public authorities or utilities is determined by statute, and the most important of these falling upon the tenant as occupier, in the absence of express agreement to the contrary are:

(a) General rate

The general rate (i e excluding water and drainage rates) which is levied on the basis of the annual value of the property by local authorities is payable by the occupier under s 116 of the General Rate Act 1867, except in the case of:

(i) tenancies for a term not exceeding three months and weekly tenancies (s 58);

(ii) premises with a rateable value nor exceeding £200 where the owner has been so directed (s 55); and

(iii) tenancies under which rent is payable more frequently than quarterly, where the landlord agrees to pay or collect the rate (s 56). In these cases, the rate is payable by the owner.

---

8 *Doe d Rains v Kneller* (1829) 4 C & P 3.
9 See *Paradine v Jane* (1647) Aleyn 26.
10 As from 1 April 1990, by the Local Government Finance Act 1988, domestic rates are abolished and replaced by a community charge.

(b) Water rate

The water rate is payable by the occupier under s 38 of the Water Act 1945, except where the owner has been directed to pay the general rate under para (ii) above.

(c) Landlord's income tax

Where the landlord defaults in default of payment of income tax assessed under Schedule A and the tenant is obliged to pay it, he may recover it from the landlord by way of deduction from his rent: s 23(5) of the Income and Corporation Taxes Act 1988.

VII DISCLAIMER OF THE LANDLORD'S TITLE

There is said to be an implied condition of every tenancy that the tenant shall not impugn (deny) his landlord's title or prejudice that title by acts that are inconsistent with the existence of a tenancy, which if broken, will automatically give the landlord the right to re-enter and terminate the lease by forfeiture. Certainly, a tenant cannot acquire good title to the land as against his landlord during the continuance of the tenancy by non-payment of rent, any more than a landlord can deny his own title if sued upon the covenants of a lease he has granted; but adverse possession is on the contrary an admission of title which has been barred by lapse of time. The condition has been held to be broken:

(a) *By matter of record*, i e by a positive denial of the landlord's title in court proceedings, as by the tenant claiming, in answer to a claim for rent, that the title is in him, or in a third party. In *Warner v Sampson*[11] the Court of Appeal held that the tenant's general denial of allegations made in the landlord's claim for possession did not, on the facts, amount to a denial of title. Lord Denning, however, in that case, went on to say that disclaimer by matter of record died with the feudal system of tenure.

(b) *By act in pais*, i e by a denial of the landlord's title implied from the tenant's conduct, as where he wrongfully pays rent to a third party, or purports to alienate the land, as happened in the case of *Wisbech Parish Council v Lilley*.[12] However, for there to be a breach of the implied condition, there must be proved a clear intention on the part of the tenant to deny the title, which there was not in that case, the tenant apparently being unaware of the fact that he had had no more than a tenancy.

11　[1959] 1 QB 297, [1959] 1 All ER 120, CA.
12　[1956] 1 All ER 301, CA.

VIII   LANDLORD'S RIGHT TO ENTER

It should be emphasised that in the absence of an express right reserved under the lease, the law implies no right on the part of the landlord to enter the premises to view the state of the premises, or even to carry out repairs (except those expressly covenanted for[13]) or for any other purpose except to distrain for arrears of rent;[14] and that should the landlord enter without an express or implied right or without the tenant's consent, he would be liable as a trespasser.[15] The tenant cannot however expect to be awarded damages for non-repair if he refuses the landlord and his workmen admittance.[16] A right of entry to inspect the premises and also, after notice to the tenant, to execute any necessary repairs required to comply with the tenant's covenant to repair should ideally be inserted in (at all events) a commercial lease, with an express right of recovery of the landlord's costs and expenses. A right of entry is conferred by statute wherever a statute-implied obligation to repair is imposed on the landlord: see Chapter 9.[17]

Apart from statutory provisions discussed later, in the case of a weekly tenancy there is an implied right on the part of the landlord to enter to view the premises and do necessary repairs, in the absence of express agreement to that effect.[18]

IX   USUAL COVENANTS

What covenants are 'usual' is a question that arises in connection with a contract for a lease (or for an assignment of a lease), either where the contract specifies that the lease shall contain the 'usual covenants', or where the contract is silent as regards what covenants shall be contained in the lease when granted (i e an 'open contract'), for in the latter case, the law will imply into the contract a term that the lease shall contain the *'usual* covenants'.[19] And if the lease as drawn up does not contain them, it may be rectified so that it does; conversely any covenants which are not *usual* may be struck out.

---

13   *Saner v Bilton* (1878) 7 Ch D 815.
14   *Doe d Worcester Trustees v Rowlands* (1841) 9 C & P 734.
15   If necessary the wrongful entry will be restrained by injunction: *Stocker v Planet Building Society* (1879) 27 WR 877, CA; *Regional Properties Ltd v City of London Real Property Co Ltd* (1979) 257 Estates Gazette 64.
16   *Granada Theatres Ltd v Freehold Investment (Leytonstone) Ltd* [1959] Ch 592, [1959] 2 All ER 176.
17   There are also statute-implied rights of entry and repair in the case of protected and statutory tenancies (ch 17), assured tenancies (ch 18) and agricultural holdings (ch 29). For general reform see Law Com No 151 (1985).
18   *Mint v Good* [1951] 1 KB 517, CA.
19   *Propert v Parker* (1832) 3 My & K 280.

Usual covenants add little more to the lease than the covenants which would in any event be implied at common law if it did not contain them already. They must not be confused with the expression 'covenants commonly found in leases', which refers to the sort of express covenant that one would expect to find in a particular type of lease.

The main test governing the nature in general of 'usual' covenants is derived from *Chester v Buckingham Travel Ltd*.[20] It was there held that the question of what are 'usual' covenants is one of fact, to be determined by the court, by looking at the nature of the premises, their situation, the purpose for which they are being let, the length of the term, the evidence of conveyancers and the books of precedents. It further appears from this decision and others that 'usual' means no more than 'occurring in ordinary use': if it is found that in nine out of ten cases a covenant of a particular sort would be in a lease of premises of a given nature and in a given district, the covenant may be 'usual' for the particular premises in question, for that reason.[1] Lists of what are or have been held to be 'usual' covenants are to be found in books of precedents, one of which has been judicially approved,[2] but this list – which is the basis of the enumeration below of what are 'usual' covenants – must today be regarded as extended and perhaps capable of further extension, to covenants not formerly accepted as 'usual'.[3]

Where the contract stipulates that the lease will contain 'proper' covenants, regard may be had to local custom and particular circumstances, but only in order to give full effect to the contract.[4] Any dispute as to what are usual and proper covenants in any case can be determined on a summons under s 49 of the Law of Property Act 1925; but, in view of the doubts which exist, it is safer when entering into a contract, to assume that only those covenants are *usual* which have been held to be so (see below), and safer still, to ensure that all the covenants to be contained in the lease are specified in the contract.

'Usual covenants'

The following have been held to be *usual* covenants:

(i) a covenant by the landlord for quiet enjoyment in the usual qualified form;[5]

(ii) a covenant by the tenant to pay tenants' rates and taxes;

---

20 [1981] 1 All ER 386 esp at 390–391.
1 *Flexman v Corbett* [1930] 1 Ch 672 at 678–679.
2 Davidson's *Precedents in Conveyancing* (13th edn) Vol 5 pp 51–54, approved in *Hampshire v Wickens* (1878) 7 Ch D 555.
3 *Chester v Buckingham Travel Ltd*, supra.
4 *Jones v Jones* (1803) 12 Ves 186 at 189.
5 *Hampshire v Wickens*, supra.

(iii)   a covenant by the tenant to keep the premises in repair and deliver them up in repair at the end of the term;

(iv)   a covenant by the tenant to permit the landlord to enter and view the state of repair (where the landlord has covenanted to repair);

(v)   a condition of re-entry for non-payment of rent (but not for breach of any other covenant);[6]

(vi)   not to alter or add to the demised premises without the lessor's consent;

(vii)   not to stop up, darken or obstruct windows or light belonging to the demised premises;

(viii)   not to permit easements to be acquired against the demised premises;

(ix)   not to permit the demised premises to be used for specified purposes;

(x)   a proviso for re-entry for breach of covenants, other than to pay rent.[7]

Onerous covenants

Covenants are onerous to the tenant if they qualify the rights he would have, or impose obligations which he would not otherwise have, at common law by virtue of the tenancy. The following covenants have therefore been held not to be usual (i e *onerous*):

(i)   to insure;[8]

(ii)   to repair and rebuild;[9]

(iii)   to pay solicitors' and surveyors' costs;[10]

(iv)   not to assign or sub-let without consent;[11]

(v)   not to exercise a particular trade (except in the case of a public house);[12]

(vi)   a proviso for re-entry extending to the bankruptcy of the lessee.[13]

---

6   *Hodgkinson v Crowe* (1875) 10 Ch App 622.

7   Covenants '(vi) to (x) were accepted as 'usual' on the facts and circumstances in *Chester v Buckingham Travel Ltd* [1981] 1 All ER 386, [1981] 1 WLR 96; they might not necessarily be accepted as 'usual', individually or as a whole, in all cases and circumstances.

8   *Cosser v Collinge* (1832) 3 My & K 283.

9   *Doe d Dymoke v Withers* (1831) 2 B & Ad 896.

10   *Allen v Smith* [1924] 2 Ch 308; *Chester v Buckingham Travel*, supra.

11   *Church v Brown* (1808) 15 Ves 258; *Chester v Buckingham Travel*, supra.

12   *Propert v Parker*, supra.

13   *Chester v Buckingham Travel*, supra.

Chapter 7

Express covenants

I INTRODUCTION

It is clear from Chapter 6 that no tenancy lacks covenants, but it should be equally clear that the covenants implied by law are basically the minimum necessary to maintain the leasehold estate and to protect the reversion, and that if a landlord wants to cut down or qualify the interest he gives to the tenant, or exercise greater control over the property, then he must do so expressly in the lease. To what extent, or how he does so varies enormously; indeed, the limits on his doing so varies, too. For whilst 100 or even 60 years ago one could have said as a general rule that the parties to a lease were free to include in it whatever terms they wished, that is far from being the case today.

This chapter attempts to cover those covenants *commonly found in leases*, and their most common forms. It should be borne in mind throughout, however, not only that every covenant is construed objectively, and therefore will depend for its meaning in every case upon the precise form of words expressed, but also that not every covenant will be allowed to have its meaning as expressed, by virtue of its conflict with protective legislation applicable to particular classes of tenancy. Moreover, certain agreements would not only be void on that account, but would also constitute criminal offences.

II RATES, TAXES, ASSESSMENTS AND OUTGOINGS

The incidence of liability for rates and other charges levied in respect of the premises is determined in the first instance by the statute under which the charge is imposed. In other words, *vis-à-vis* the public authority or utility to whom payment is owed, the relevant statute imposes liability for payment upon either the landlord or the tenant, generally depending on whether the charge has been incurred for the landlord's benefit, as owner, or the tenant's benefit as occupier. But, as between landlord and tenant, the burden of the statutory liability may usually be shifted from one party to the other by express agreement. To do so, however, the covenant must be clear and unequivocal, with regard not only to any existing charge in particular, but also to any new kind of charge which is imposed for the first time after the commencement of the tenancy. This section covers particular words and phrases commonly employed to vary the statutory incidence of liability already set out in Chapter 6. The abolition of land tax and the incorporation of highway, lighting and other separate rates under a single general rate has much simplified the position; moreover, in so many cases, the express covenant merely reiterates the statutory position, but it is nevertheless important to note the meaning of particular words and phrases used, and the cases in which no variation is permissible or there is statutory provision for apportionment.

(a)   Generally

Covenants vary from the simplest form, e g 'rates and taxes', to the more sophisticated, e g 'pay, bear and discharge all rates, taxes, duties, assessments, charges, impositions and outgoings whatsoever of an annual nature whether parliamentary, or of any other description, which now are or during the term shall be imposed or charged on the premises or the owner or occupier in respect thereof'. A covenant by the tenant to pay 'rates and taxes' and assessments, however, is enough to make the tenant liable for rates and taxes imposed in the first instance by statute on the landlord, but it is limited to those of a recurring nature. A tenant's liability for new taxes or charges imposed after the lease is granted depends on whether the new charge can be brought within one of the classes for which he is already liable, and if it can, he will still be liable therefor even if the statute imposes it upon the landlord 'in the absence of express agreement to the contrary'. The scope of a particular form of covenant may be qualified by other covenants in the lease. So that, even though the tenant agrees to pay 'all outgoings', he will not be liable for the cost of repairing outside drains required by the local authority where the landlord is responsible for external repairs.[1] On the other hand, where a sub-tenant covenants to pay all rates, etc, he cannot avoid liability by pointing to a covenant by the tenant (i e his landlord) to pay them.[2] A covenant in a sub-lease to perform all covenants (except for rent and to insure) contained in the head lease, will render the sub-tenant liable for all charges for which thereunder the tenant (i e his landlord) would be liable. The meaning of particular words may be more narrowly construed in a covenant purporting to vary statutory liability so that whereas a covenant by the tenant to pay 'rates' will usually include the

---

1   *Howe v Botwood* [1913] 2 KB 387.
2   *W H Read & Co Ltd v Walter* (1931) 48 TLR 15.

water rate, the same covenant by the landlord may exclude it. A covenant to pay rent, 'net' or 'without reduction' means just that: the tenant is not permitted to deduct charges which are statutorily recovered from the tenant but made deductible. But when it is fixed as '£X yearly (including rates and taxes)' the tenant is entitled to deduct all such payments he has made. If the tenant is made liable for a charge by covenant, then he is liable for sums levied during the tenancy even though the benefits of the charge will not accrue until after his tenancy has terminated.[3] And if he agrees to pay all rates, etc, he must pay them in full even if liability increases on account of improvements or new buildings of which he will benefit.[4] But where liability is on the landlord in such a case, the tenant will be liable for any increase attributable to the increased value.[5] Normal periodic increases (e g on a general revaluation) however will follow the original liability, unless the covenant clearly shows otherwise.

(b) Apportionment

Where special work is required to be done to the premises by statute (e g under the Factories Act 1961, the Building Act 1984, the Public Health Act 1936, the Fire Precautions Act 1971, etc), special provision is often made under the statute for an application to the county court to apportion the costs of executing the necessary work between the owner and occupier. The court should consider the terms of the tenancy, but may make such order as appears just and equitable under all the circumstances of the case. So, the court may apportion between landlord and tenant a local authority's costs incurred in demolishing premises under s 277 of the Housing Act 1985.

(c) Particular words

'*Rates*' covers the general rate, but whether it includes a water rate will depend very much on the circumstances. If the covenant is the tenant's, it will generally include the water rate,[6] but if the landlord's, it is thought that the water rate will be included only in special circumstances, as under a lease of one floor of a building where the building is assessed as a whole.[7] Drainage rates are not within the meaning of 'rates' so as to dispel the incidence of liability under the Land Drainage Act 1976. If the landlord agrees to pay rates 'on the demised premises', he will not be liable for increased rates in respect of buildings subsequently erected.

---

3   *Eastwood v McNab* [1914] 2 KB 361.
4   *Hurst v Hurst* (1849) 4 Exch 571.
5   *Mansfield v Relf* [1908] 1 KB 71.
6   *King v Cave-Brown-Cave* [1960] 2 QB 222, [1960] 2 All ER 751.
7   *Bourne and Tant v Salmon and Gluckstein* [1907] 1 Ch 616.

'*Taxes*' when used in conjunction with 'rates' is generally taken to refer only to Parliamentary taxes, but when used alone may be allowed a wider meaning in the context to include other charges levied by local authorities under statutory powers. As to deductibility from rent of landlord's income tax recovered from the tenant, see Chapter 6.

'*Assessments*' when used in conjunction with 'rates and taxes' only has been held not to refer to a sum assessed in respect of work for the permanent benefit of the property, such as paving a street,[8] but its meaning may be widened by the addition of wider terms such as 'duties', 'burdens', 'impositions', or 'outgoings'. '*Duties*' has a much wider meaning than 'assessments', and has been held to include the cost of paving and drainage, and the cost of removing a public nuisance. '*Impositions*' includes the cost of paving and drainage, but not expenses resulting from breach of duty, and otherwise is not distinguishable from 'duty'; and '*burden*' and '*charge*' are synonymous with 'imposition'. Where impositions, etc, are 'charged upon the property', the tenant will be liable only for charges imposed on the property during the tenancy, but where they are 'charged upon the landlord or upon the tenant', the tenant will be liable for a charge made upon the property before the tenancy, in respect of which the apportionment is made during the tenancy.

(d) Remedies

A landlord's remedy is by exercise of a right of re-entry where one is reserved in the lease, or by action on the covenant, and he may sue in respect of sums which he has not yet paid, if the tenant's liability is expressed to be for sums charged on the landlord or due from him. If, on the other hand, the landlord is liable for any sums already recovered from the tenant, they are deductible by the tenant from the rent next due, unless the right to deduct is precluded by any agreement. If, nevertheless, he deducts the charges, he will, in any action by the landlord, be entitled to counterclaim them. Alternatively, he can pay the rent in full, and sue upon the covenant.

III   QUIET ENJOYMENT

An express covenant for quiet enjoyment or for title in any form will displace the implied covenant in qualified form. An express covenant is usually qualified, and will have the same effects as the implied covenant, but will endure throughout the term granted. As long as it is limited to

---

8   *Wilkinson v Collyer* (1884) 13 QBD 1.

protecting the tenant from lawful eviction or interruption by the landlord or anyone claiming 'by, from or under' him, it will be construed as qualified, and will not protect the tenant from eviction by title paramount, i e by any one with a title superior to that of the landlord. Nor will such a covenant protect the tenant against claims made under a leasehold title granted at an earlier date by predecessors in title to the landlord.[9] Even an unqualified covenant (e g 'by the landlord, or any person claiming under him, or any other person') will thus not protect the tenant against mere claimants of a superior title,[10] for acts of strangers will only be included if they are mentioned expressly, either by name, or as claimants to the landlord's or a superior title. A covenant against acts of a single identifiable person, such as a head lessor, covers lawful and, in contrast to the implied covenant, unlawful (i e unauthorised) acts by the head lessor; but if the head lessor assigns his superior interest, it is not clear whether the assignee is liable for unlawful acts.[11]

IV INSURANCE

In the absence of agreement to the contrary, neither the landlord nor the tenant was liable at common law to reinstate the premises in the event of damage caused accidentally or negligently by fire, and s 86 of the Fires Prevention (Metropolis) Act 1774, which applies throughout England re-states the rule in effect with regard to accidental fires. It has long been the practice, therefore, except in short leases, to provide expressly for insurance of the premises against fire and other damage.

(a) Covenants to insure

If the covenant is by the landlord, it is usually to the effect that the landlord shall take out the policy but that the tenant shall pay the premiums, to be recoverable by the landlord by way of additional rent. A covenant by the tenant may require him to insure for a fixed sum, or to the full value,[12] in his own or the landlord's name, or jointly; he can be required to insure against fire and other specified damage. If the tenant insures for his own name only, his interest in the policy moneys is good to the extent only of his interest.[13] Commonly, he is required to place the

---

9 *Celsteel Ltd v Alton Holdings Ltd (No 2)* [1987] 2 All ER 240, [1987] 1 WLR 291, CA.
10 *Young v Raincock* (1849) 7 CB 310.
11 *Queensway Marketing Ltd v Associated Restaurants Ltd* [1988] 32 EG 41, CA (mesne landlord liable to sub-under-lessee where head landlord interrrupted latter's business).
12 See *Leppard v Excess Insurance Co Ltd* [1979] 2 All ER 668, [1979] 1 WLR 512.
13 *Re King, Robinson v Gray* [1963] Ch 459, [1963] 1 All ER 781, CA.

insurance with a named insurance company, or a company to be approved by the landlord, and from time to time produce receipts to the landlord. This may result in the property being doubly insured, for where the tenant has mortgaged his interest, he may under his mortgage agreement be also liable *vis-à-vis* the mortgagee to insure it with a named insurance company. In such a case, the tenant has no option but to insure twice over, unless he can induce either the landlord or the mortgagee to accept the other's insurance. The covenant is broken if the property is uninsured at any time, whether or not there is any damage caused, and it is broken if it is not insured to the value specified or in the name of the parties specified.[14] It is not broken, however, if the tenant insures with a named company under one of their normal policies, and damage that is caused is excepted by the policy.[15] A covenant to insure is commonly coupled with a covenant to apply any insurance moneys received in reinstatement of the property.[16] But, where the insurance moneys are insufficient, the insurer, under the covenant, will be required to make up the difference. The measure of damages for breach of covenant will be the actual loss incurred; so that if the landlord has insured, the tenant having failed to do so, the landlord will be entitled to recover the premium paid, but if the property is damaged, then the tenant is liable for the full cost of reinstatement up to the sum that should have been insured. Where underinsured premises burnt down, the tenant then surrendering the lease, after releasing half the insurance moneys, the tenant was taken to have impliedly released any right to require reinstatement.[17] Where insurers paid the sum assured after a fire caused by the tenant's negligence, and the policy had no express clause protecting the tenant, the insurers failed to recover the sum assured from the tenant, in subrogation to the landlord, as the event was within the contemplation of the parties.[18]

(b)   Insurance moneys

Because there is no liability at common law, a landlord or tenant who insures voluntarily cannot be required to reinstate the property with the insurance moneys received; but, where there is a covenant to insure by

---

14   See also *Naumann v Ford* [1985] 2 EGLR 70 (agreement between tenant and insurers did not affect measure of damages for landlord's breach of covenant).

15   *Upjohn v Hitchens, Upjohn v Ford* [1918] 2 KB 48, CA.

16   I e an implied duty to lay out the money within a reasonable time: *Farimani v Gates* (1984) 271 Estates Gazette 887, CA.

17   *Beacon Carpets Ltd v Kirby* [1985] QB 755, [1984] 2 All ER 726, CA. The moneys stood in place of the building and belonged to the parties in shares proportionate to their interests, valued at the date of the fire.

18   *Mark Rowlands Ltd v Berni Inns Ltd* [1986] QB 211, [1985] 3 All ER 473, CA; PF Smith [1986] Conv 47.

the landlord or tenant, and the property is damaged by fire, the other party may, under s 83 of the Fires Prevention (Metropolis) Act 1774, require that the insurance money be spent on reinstatement. Where it is the tenant who has insured, the landlord must make the request to the insurance company, before the money is paid out. In neither case can the request extend to the reinstatement of tenant's fixtures.

V ASSIGNMENT, SUB-LETTING AND PARTING WITH POSSESSION

At common law a tenant has freedom to dispose of his leasehold interest, by assignment, sub-letting, mortgaging, or allowing any persons into exclusive (or non-exclusive) occupation. The landlord may seek to limit or restrict the tenant's powers but no covenants seeking to achieve that object will regarded as usual.

This means that any disposition covenants must be expressly imposed. There are three basic forms: an *absolute prohibition* against all forms of disposition (assignments, sub-lettings or parting with the possession of the premises), a *fully qualified prohibition* (such dispositions being only allowed with the landlord's consent but the landlord covenants not to withhold his consent unreasonably) and a *qualified prohibition* (dispositions are to be carried out only with the landlord's consent). In this last case, statute[19] fully qualifies most qualified covenants, so that the landlord is only able to withhold his consent to a disposition if it would be reasonable for him to do so.

The law has been considered by the Law Commission, whose main reform proposals are summarised below.[20]

(a) Absolute covenants

An absolute 'disposition' covenant precludes any assignments, sub-lettings and other dispositions by the tenant. The landlord may give the tenant a licence to carry out a particular transaction: if he does, he cannot later bring a forfeiture. Such a licence (unless otherwise expressed) operates to make lawful only the particular transaction for which it was specifically requested.[1] The Law Commission recommended that with certain exceptions (particularly relating to special classes of tenancy such as agricultural holdings or short residential

---

19 Landlord and Tenant Act 1927 s 19.
20 Law Com No 141 (1985) HC 278; Waite [1986] Conv 240; PF Smith (1985) 135 NLJ 991, 1015.
1 Law of Property Act 1925 s 143(1): it will not entitle the tenant to rely on it in respect of future breaches.

lettings), landlords should be unable to make absolute disposition covenants.[2]

(b) Transactions prohibited by the covenant

The scope of the covenant will depend on the transactions expressly prohibited, the commonest of which are:

Assignment   A covenant against assignment is broken if the tenant, without licence, 'conveys' to a third party the whole of his interest as such, or does so in effect by granting a sub-lease coextensive with, or longer than, his term. It is broken only by a legal assignment of the whole (or of a part, if the covenant is so expressed), and not for example by deposit of the lease as security, nor an equitable assignment (but see 'parting with possession').

The prohibition extends to express assignments only and not to assignments by operation of law, e g on death or bankruptcy, unless there is a condition for example or proviso for re-entry in the event of an act of bankruptcy by the tenant.

Sub-letting   A covenant against sub-letting is broken if the tenant creates a legal sub-tenancy in respect of the whole of the premises (or of part if the covenant is so expressed), and this will include a mortgage by sub-demise. He cannot in any event, without licence, sub-let a part of the premises, and then sub-let the rest.[3]

Parting with possession extends in scope both a covenant against assignment and a covenant against sub-letting. So parting with possession will include a contract for an assignment and a contract for a sub-lease, where the assignee or sub-tenant is thereby given possession. Occupation by licencees, or paying guests is no breach of covenant as long as the tenant retains exclusive possession.

Charging   A covenant merely prohibiting sub-leases precludes the tenant from creating a mortgage by sub-demise,[4] but not his right to create a mortgage by charge, unless it expressly extends to charging.[5]

The extent to which covenants against assignment, sub-letting or parting with possession should be regarded as mutually overlapping is not wholly clear; however, assignment necessarily involves a parting with possession; if then a covenant prohibits parting with possession but not assignments, nonetheless it is taken as impliedly prohibiting assignments.[6] A covenant prohibiting assignments of any part of the demised premises necessarily prohibits assignments of the whole.[7]

---

2   Law Com No 141, paras 4.17 and 7.7–7.24.
3   *Chatterton v Terrell* [1923] AC 578.
4   *Serjeant v Nash, Field & Co* [1903] 2 KB 304, CA.
5   *Grand Junction Co Ltd v Bates* [1954] 2 QB 160, [1954] 2 All ER 385.
6   *Marks v Warren* [1979] 1 All ER 29.
7   *Field v Barkworth* [1986] 1 All ER 362, [1986] 1 WLR 137.   .

(c) Qualified covenants

A covenant against assignment, etc, is commonly found in a *qualified* form (i e 'without the landlord's consent'). In such cases (other than leases of agricultural holdings) the express covenants are *further* qualified by statute as follows:

(i) Where a building lease for more than 40 years contains a condition or covenant that the tenant shall not assign, sub-let, charge or part with possession without the landlord's licence or consent, s 19(1)(b) of the Landlord and Tenant Act 1927, dispenses with the requirement as to the landlord's consent or licence in respect of such transactions, as long as the lease has more than seven years to run and on condition that notice in writing of the transaction is given to the landlord within six months thereof. This provision does not apply to mining leases, nor leases by the Crown, Government Departments, local or public authorities or public utilities. Within the prescribed limits, a tenant is free to assign, etc, without asking for consent in accordance with the express covenant in the lease.

(ii) In other cases, s 19(1)(a) of the Landlord and Tenant Act 1927, provides that notwithstanding any express provision to the contrary, such covenant, condition or agreement shall be deemed subject to a proviso that the landlord's licence or consent shall not be unreasonably withheld. Moreover, by s 144 of the Law of Property Act 1925, such condition or covenant is deemed to be subject to the further proviso that unless the lease contains an express provision to the contrary, no fine or sum of money in the nature of a fine shall be payable for or in respect of the granting of such a licence or consent; but the provision does not preclude the right of the landlord to require payment of any legal or other expenses incurred in connection with such licence or consent.

The Law Commission recommended that no fines should be payable by a tenant as a condition of consent.[8] The tests for deciding whether a landlord's refusal of consent is reasonable or not, in the context of fully qualified covenants, are shortly considered.[9]

(d) General

The landlord cannot make the test of reasonableness subjective: the interpretation of reasonableness is a question of law.[10] However, any

---

8 Law Com No 141, paras 8.22 et seq.
9 The Law Commission saw no desire to alter these rules generally, nor to impose statutory guidelines: ibid para 8.8.
10 *Creery v Summersell and Flowerdew & Co Ltd* [1959] Ch 751.

self-imposed limits on grounds for refusal will be upheld, and will limit the landlord, as with a term that consent will not be withheld in the case of a respectable and responsible person.[11] This means that, if the tenant proposes to assign or sub-let to such a person, the landlord cannot refuse consent. Where the Landlord and Tenant Act 1988 applies, the landlord will be under a liability for breach of statutory duty if he refuses his consent in circumstances outside the limits of a provision specifying the circumstances in which consent will be given or refused (s 1(5)).

The provisions of s 19(1)(a) of the 1927 Act are capable of being avoided, by a surrender-back clause, under which the fully qualified covenant only comes into effect if the landlord decides not to accept a surrender of the lease, which must be offered as a condition precedent to asking for consent.[12]

(e)   Statutory duties

The landlord of any tenant, except a secure tenant, is under new statutory duties in relation to applications for consent to an assignment, under-letting, charging or parting with possession, imposed by the Landlord and Tenant Act 1988. The Act implements proposals of the Law Commission,[13] and it aims to prevent landlords, including mesne and superior landlords, from unduly delaying in dealing with consent applications by tenants, especially where the landlord decides to refuse consent. If any of the duties of the 1988 Act are broken, the landlord comes under a liability for damages for breach of statutory duty (s 4).[14] The 1988 Act imposes the following duties.

1   Where the tenant serves[15] on the landlord or other person who may consent[16] a written application for consent, or licence (s 5(1)) the landlord, by s 1(3), owes the tenant a duty, within a reasonable time:
    (a)   to give consent, except where it is reasonable not to do so;
    (b)   to serve on the tenant written notice of his decision whether or not to give consent.

---

11   *Moat v Martin* [1950] 1 KB 175, [1949] 2 All ER 646, CA.
12   *Adler v Upper Grosvenor Street Investment Ltd* [1957] 1 All ER 229, [1957] 1 WLR 227; *Bocardo SA v S and M Hotels Ltd* [1979] 3 All ER 737, [1980] WLR 17, CA. See Adams (1979) 252 Estates Gazette 897. The Law Commission recommended the abolition of such clauses in most tenancies: Law Com No 141, para 7.63.
13   Law Com No 161, (1987) Leasehold Conveyancing, HC 360. The Act came into force on 29 September 1988 (s 7(2)). See Shaw (1988) 138 NLJ 918.
14   The Act does not impose a liability for breach of covenant, as to do so would have meant that the landlord would have been liable therefor even after assignment of the reversion, for the rest of the term, according to the Law Commission, supra.
15   Either by any manner prescribed in the lease or under Landlord and Tenant Act 1927 s 23 (s 5(2)).
16   Such as a mortgagee: see Law of Property Act 1925 s 89(1).

Where a notice is served, it must specify any conditions attached to consent, or the reasons for withholding it, as the case may be (s 1(3)). The 1988 Act cannot be evaded by imposing an unreasonable condition on a consent: the duty is treated as broken where this is so (s 1(4)). The Act does not provide what is to be a reasonable time. The Law Commission changed their minds about this point: in their 1985 Report, they had recommended a 28-day period.[17]

2 If a landlord receives a written consent application, where, in addition to his own consent, the consent of a superior landlord (or, say, mortgagee) is required as well, then the recipient is bound to take reasonable steps to secure the receipt, within a reasonable time, of a copy of the application by that person (s 2(1)).

3 The superior landlord then comes under a mirror duty to that of the mesne landlord under s 1, in relation to giving consent within a reasonable time, and so on (s 3).

4 A landlord or superior landlord who is under the above duties must show, if challenged by the tenant, that he gave a consent within a reasonable time. Likewise, the onus is on the landlord or superior landlord to show that any condition is reasonable, where the 1988 Act applies, and if consent is refused, the onus is on the landlord etc to show that the refusal was reasonable (s 1(6) and 3(5)).

(f) Reasonableness: general principles

The relevant date for determining the reasonableness or otherwise of a landlord's refusal of consent is the date of the disposition or refusal, not that of the hearing.[18] The court will not limit the landlord to any particular grounds.[19] The tenant is, however, bound to ask for consent even if it could not reasonably be refused because the landlord must be given a reasonable opportunity to consider the matter.[20] If the landlord is not asked for consent he may bring a forfeiture, unless he waives the breach,[1] and if he could reasonably have refused his consent, no relief will be granted to the tenant.

The following general principles govern the question of whether a refusal is reasonable or not, but each case is considered on its own facts and circumstances.[2]

---

17 Law Com No 141 (1985) para 8.125.
18 *Bromley Park Garden Estates Ltd v Moss* [1982] 2 All ER 890, [1982] 1 WLR 1019, CA; Wilkinson (1982) 132 NLJ 658.
19 *West Layton Ltd v Ford* [1979] 2 All ER 657 at 662, CA.
20 *Wilson v Fynn* [1948] 2 All ER 40. It is no excuse that the tenant forgot: *Barrow v Isaacs & Son* [1891] 1 QB 417, CA.
1 As in *Welch v Birrane* (1974) 29 P & CR 102 (refusal held reasonable).
2 *International Drilling Fluids Ltd v Louisville Investments (Uxbridge) Ltd* [1986] Ch 513, [1986] 1 All ER 321, CA; Crabbe [1986] Conv 287. Also *Bickel v Duke of Westminster* [1977] QB 517, [1976] 3 All ER 801, CA.

1   A landlord is not entitled to refuse his consent to an assignment on grounds which have nothing to do with the relationship of landlord and tenant in regard to the subject-matter of the particular demise of the premises such as an alleged difficulty in re-letting other premises.[3]

2   If, therefore, the landlord refuses his consent to a proposed assignment or sub-letting because of general reasons of good estate management relating to the whole building, not the particular part let to the tenant, his refusal will be unreasonable – as where the landlord had a general policy of refusing consents to assignments of residential tenancies: the refusal of consent to a flat tenant was held unreasonable.[4]

3   It is not necessary for the landlord to prove that the conclusions which led him to refuse consent were justified, if they were conclusions which a reasonable man might reach in the circumstances. For example, it was held reasonable for a landlord to refuse consent where he had grounds for believing that the proposed assignee might well use its position as leaseholder to gain a share in the landlord's redevelopment scheme.[5]

4   It may be reasonable for a landlord to refuse his consent to a proposed assignment on the ground of the purpose for which the assignee intends to use the premises, even though that purpose is not forbidden by the terms of the lease.[6]

5   On the question as to what extent it is permissible in deciding whether a refusal is reasonable, to take into account the consequences to the current tenant of a refusal of consent, there is a divergence of authority.[7] In general, the landlord is entitled to consider only his own interests. There may be some exceptional cases where there is such a disproportion between the benefit to the landlord and the detriment to the tenant that a refusal of consent is on that ground unreasonable, and where, therefore, the tenants proved that unless consent to an assignment to a company, which would licence out various parts of the premises for short-life office accommmodation, was given, they would be virtually locked into the

---

3   *Re Gibbs and Houlder Bros & Co Ltd's Lease, Houlder Bros & Co v Gibbs* [1925] Ch 575, CA.

4   *Bromley Park Garden Estates Ltd v Moss*, supra.

5   *Pimms v Tallow Chandlers in the City of London* [1964] 2 QB 547, [1964] 2 All ER 145, CA.

6   *Bates v Donaldson* [1896] 2 QB 241 at 244, CA; *Rossi v Hestdrive Ltd* [1985] 1 EGLR 50.

7   See in favour of doing so, *Leeward Securities Ltd v Lilyheath Properties Ltd*, infra; against: *Viscount Tredegar v Harwood* [1929] AC 72, HL.

lease, and where the damage to the landlords' reversion was minimal, it was held that the landlords had unreasonably withheld their consent.[8]

(g) Examples of reasonable withholding of consent

A landlord's refusal of consent has been held to be reasonable where the landlord believed (reasonably) that the proposed assignee or sub-tenant was objectionable for some personal or financial reason,[9] or that the future earnings or the financial viability of the property would be endangered,[10] and he may reasonably refuse consent if the effect of a disposition would be to confer on an assignee the right to enfranchise under statute.[11] Consent was reasonably withheld where a sub-letting would have conferred a statutorily protected sub-tenancy under the Rent Acts,[12] and where a sub-letting would have altered the nature of the tenancy from a business to a mixed-user tenancy.[13] If the landlord has reasonably-held suspicions as to the manner in which the assignee might conduct the business concerned, he may reasonably withhold consent,[14] as where he has serious doubts about the ability of the assignees to pay the rent or to comply with the full repairing obligations of the lease.[15]

A landlord supplied with insufficient information (e g in references or accounts) to enable him to decide is entitled to refuse consent.[16]

(h) Examples of unreasonable withholding of consent

A refusal of consent has been held unreasonable where the sole reason was to obtain possession,[17] or where the reason was otherwise not bona fide,[18] or where, although the tenant was in breach of his repairing covenants, the assignee intended to spend a considerable sum in

---

8 *International Drilling Fluids Ltd v Louisville Investments (Uxbridge) Ltd*, supra.
9 *Re Gibbs and Houlder Bros Co Ltd's Lease*, supra.
10 *Re Town Investments Ltd Underlease, McLaughlin v Town Investments Ltd* [1954] Ch 301, [1954] 1 All ER 585.
11 *Bickel v Duke of Westminster*, supra; *Norfolk Capital Group Ltd v Kitway Ltd* [1977] QB 506, [1976] 3 All ER 787, CA.
12 *Leeward Securities Ltd v Lilyheath Properties Ltd* (1984) 271 Estates Gazette 279, CA. It matters not that the refusal is based on supervening legislation not originally foreseen.
13 *West Layton Ltd v Ford*, supra.
14 *Rossi v Hestdrive Ltd*, supra.
15 *British Bakeries (Midlands) Ltd v Michael Testler & Co Ltd* [1986] 1 EGLR 64. Also *Ponderosa International Development Inc v Pengap Securities (Bristol) Ltd* [1986] 1 EGLR 66.
16 See *Fuller's Theatre and Vaudeville Co v Rofe* [1923] AC 435, PC.
17 *Bates v Donaldson*, supra.
18 *Lovelock v Margo* [1963] 2 QB 786, [1963] 2 All ER 13, CA.

executing repairs.[19] It was held unreasonable to refuse consent because the proposed assignee had diplomatic immunity,[20] and it is not possible under statute to refuse consent on the grounds of race or sex.[1] A landlord was held unreasonably to have withheld consent where the lease required multiple occupation and the sub-lettings were not Rent-Act protected.[2]

The landlord cannot reasonably withhold consent for reasons wholly extraneous to the particular lease under consideration (see above), nor is it possible for him in any conditions of consent, to impose additional burdens on the tenant or assignee.[3] The fact that a superior landlord might unreasonably withhold his consent is no ground in itself for the landlord to withhold his.[4] A landlord who refused consent to an assignment because of his fears about the nature of future under-lettings was held to have acted unreasonably – his fears could be considered when appropriate.[5]

(i) Breach of covenant against changes of user

It is reasonable for a landlord to withhold consent if he establishes that a breach of a user covenant in the lease is actually taking place or will be a necessary consequence of the disposition.[6] He may also reasonably object to any proposed user of the assignee, as where it would compete with other tenants' user of neighbouring premises.[7] If the landlord's ability to enforce a user covenant will not fatally be prejudiced by consenting to the disposition, (as it might be where the user covenant is positive not negative) he may be unable to refuse his consent merely because of his fear that the assignee or sub-tenant might break a negative user covenant, because he may enforce it, after the assignment, by means of a negative injunction.[8] In no case will the landlord be able to obtain from a user covenant a collateral advantage outside its contemplation

---

19 *Farr v Ginnings* (1928) 44 TLR 249; cf *Orlando Investments Ltd v Grosvenor Estate Belgravia* [1988] 49 EG 85 (assignee intended to ignore repairs scheme agreed with tenant: refusal upheld).
20 *Parker v Boggon* [1947] KB 346, [1947] 1 All ER 46.
 1 Race Relations Act 1976 s 24; Sex Discrimination Act 1975 s 31.
 2 *Deverall v Wyndham* [1989] 01 EG 70.
 3 *Evans v Levy* [1910] 1 Ch 452; *Mills v Cannon Brewery Co Ltd* [1920] 2 Ch 38.
 4 *Vienit Ltd v W Williams & Son* [1958] 3 All ER 621, [1958] 1 WLR 1267.
 5 *Rayburn v Wolf* (1985) 50 P & CR 463, CA.
 6 *F W Woolworth plc v Charlwood Alliance Properties Ltd* [1987] 1 EGLR 53; Crabbe [1987] Conv 381.
 7 *Packaging Centre v Poland Street Estate* (1961) 178 Estates Gazette 189, CA.
 8 *Killick v Second Covent Garden Property Co Ltd* [1973] 2 All ER 337, [1973] 1 WLR 658, CA. When consenting the landlord should expressly reserve his right to enforce the user covenant.

– such as to try to maximise rents of surrounding premises by forcing a change of user to retail purposes.[9]

(j) Remedies of tenant

If the tenant is advised that a refusal of consent is unreasonable (or that unreasonable conditions have been imposed on the giving of consent) he may carry out the transaction concerned, risking forfeiture. The tenant may, in the alternative, apply to the court (generally the county court) for a declaration that the refusal was unreasonable.[10] Where the Landlord and Tenant Act 1988 applies, and the landlord unreasonably refuses consent, or is deemed to have done so, the tenant may claim damages from him, and any superior landlord under the statutory duty, for breach of statutory duty (s 4).

(k) Remedies of landlord

The landlord may, if he could have reasonably withheld his consent, provided the lease entitles him to, bring an action to forfeit the lease;[11] he may bring an action for damages to his reversion and he may claim injunctive relief. If, in forfeiture proceedings, the court rules that the landlord could not reasonably have withheld his consent, it has a discretion to grant relief from forfeiture, as where no damage to the landlord's reversion occurred.[12]

VI ALTERATIONS AND IMPROVEMENTS

The landlord may be content to rely on the law of waste to protect his reversion against any damage caused by the tenant making alterations or improvements to the demised premises, but only if substantial damage is proved will he obtain any satisfaction; and he will obtain none if the value of the reversion is enhanced.

Accordingly, it is common to insert express covenants against the making of alterations in leases. The exact form is for the parties to negotiate. Express covenants against alterations may be in terms *absolute, qualified* or *fully qualified*, as to the nature of which see the discussion of disposition covenants above. The Law Commission recommended no general ban on absolute alteration covenants.[13] In

---

9   *Anglia Building Society v Sheffield City Council* (1983) 266 Estates Gazette 311, CA.
10   Landlord and Tenant Act 1954, s 53(1).
11   Unless estopped: see *Troop v Gibson* [1986] 1 EGLR 1, CA.
12   *Scala House and District Property Co Ltd v Forbes* [1974] QB 575, [1973] 3 All ER 308, CA.
13   Law Com No 141, para 4.64; this also recommended that the Law of Property Act 1925, s 84 be extended to absolute covenants against alterations (para 4.53).

relation to protected and statutory tenants, absolute alteration covenants have been banned.[14]

(a) 'Alterations'

An alteration is a change in the form and constitution of a building, such as the conversion of a bedroom into a bathroom, the sub-division of two rooms, the making of two rooms into one, or the insertion of windows into walls, but not just a change in the appearance of the building, unless the covenant expressly so provides. Conversion of a house into flats[15] is a breach of a covenant against alterations, but not the erection of an advertising sign on an external wall unless the covenant extends to appearance.[16] And even a covenant against alterations to the building or the architectural elevation is not broken by changes in appearance which do not affect the fabric.[17]

(b) 'Improvements'

Section 19(2) of the Landlord and Tenant Act 1927, considered below, applies to a qualified covenant against the making of improvements, and converts it into a fully qualified covenant.

Therefore s 19(2) applies to any alteration which constitutes an improvement.[18] As to whether an alteration amounts to an improvement, this is to be judged from the point of view of the tenant.[19] Any alteration which would render the tenant's occupation and enjoyment of the demised premises more convenient and comfortable to him appears to constitute an improvement.[20]

A tenant's proposal to open apertures in the party-wall between the demised premises and adjoining premises, in both of which the tenant traded, was held to constitute an improvement to which the landlord could not reasonably withhold his consent.[1] Likewise, a tenant's proposed alterations which involved enlarging the demised shop premises, by demolishing a wall at the back, so connecting the shop with adjoining land, and then building an enlarged shop over the combined premises, moving the main staircase and staff accommodation to the extended premises, were held to be improvements within s 19(2) of the 1927 Act.[2]

---

14   Housing Act 1980 ss 81–83.
15   *Duke of Westminster v Swinton* [1948] 1 KB 524, [1948] 1 All ER 248.
16   *Heard v Stuart* (1907) 24 TLR 104.
17   *Joseph v LCC* (1914) 111 LT 276.
18   *Balls Bros Ltd v Sinclair* [1931] 2 Ch 325.
19   *Lambert v F W Woolworth & Co (No 2)* [1938] Ch 883, [1938] 2 All ER 664, CA.
20   *Woolworth & Co Ltd v Lambert* [1937] Ch 37, [1936] 2 All ER 1523, CA.
 1   *Lilley and Skinner Ltd v Crump* (1929) 73 Sol Jo 366.
 2   *Woolworth & Co Ltd v Lambert*, supra.

(c) Qualified covenants against improvements

Where there is a condition or covenant against the making of improvements without licence or consent, s 19(2) of the Landlord and Tenant Act 1927 provides that notwithstanding any express provision to the contrary, such condition or covenant shall be deemed to be subject to a proviso that such licence or consent is not to be unreasonably withheld; in other words, a *qualified* covenant is made *fully* qualified. The sub-section goes on to provide that this does not preclude the landlord's right to require as a condition of such licence or consent:

(i) the payment of a reasonable sum in respect of any damage to or diminution in the value of the premises or any neighbouring premises belonging to the landlord, and

(ii) the payment of any legal or other expenses properly incurred in connection with such licence or consent, nor, in the case of an improvement which does not add to the letting value of the holding,

(iii) an undertaking on the part of the tenant to reinstate the premises in the condition in which they were before the improvement was executed, where such a requirement would be reasonable.

Section 19(2) of the 1927 Act applies only to alterations which constitute improvements, and not to absolute prohibitions against the making of alterations.

If the landlord withholds his consent, the tenant may, as with disposition covenants, apply to the court for a declaration that consent has been unreasonably withheld.[3] If the tenant is advised that consent has been unreasonably withheld, he may, alternatively, simply proceed with the proposed alteration.[4] If consent could reasonably have been withheld, the landlord may bring a forfeiture, subject to the court's discretion to grant relief, which, in the case of a deliberate breach, will be refused.[5]

(d) Unreasonable and reasonable refusals

The onus of proving that the landlord has unreasonably refused his consent is on the tenant: hence, where a landlord demanded the payment of £7,000 before he consented to structural alterations proposed by the tenant, it was held that the tenant failed, on the facts, to prove that consent was unreasonably withheld.[6] However, if the landlord gives no

---

3 See Landlord and Tenant Act 1954 s 53 (generally the county court).
4 *Railway Comr v Avrom Investments Pty Ltd* [1959] 2 All ER 63, [1959] 1 WLR 389, PC.
5 *Duke of Westminster v Swinton* [1948] 1 KB 524, [1948] 1 All ER 248.
6 *Woolworth & Co Ltd v Lambert*, supra.

reason and merely refuses consent, this puts the onus of justifying the refusal on the landlord.[7] If the landlord demands compensation to cover any damage he may suffer, which sum is later determined in proceedings not to be reasonable, and refuses his consent unless that sum is paid, then it seems that he will be unable to require any sum, even a reasonable amount, ex post facto. If the landlord refuses consent, and so puts it out of his power to require reinstatement as a condition of giving consent, where the value of the reversion is diminished, he cannot later, if his refusal is held unreasonable, require re-instatement. Where therefore a landlord, having originally demanded the payment of £7,000 as a condition of consenting to tenants' improvements, later refused his consent unconditionally, and his refusal was held to be unreasonable, it was held that he could not then claim any money payments or re-instatement.[8] In any event, it may be that a requirement to pay an unreasonable sum in compensation, or the imposition of an unreasonable re-instatement requirement, as a condition of consent in either case, would amount to unreasonable withholding of consent. As to the grounds on which consent may reasonably be refused, there is little authority. It has been said that many reasons, aesthetic, historic or even personal, may be sufficient grounds.[9]

(e)   Non-compliance with reasonable re-instatement condition

A tenant who, having given an undertaking to re-instate, fails to carry it out when the time comes, is liable in damages, the measure of which is the reduction in value of the landlord's reversion: if the landlord proves that he intends and is able to carry out the re-instatement himself, and it would be reasonable for him to do so, he may recover the full cost of re-instatement. But, if the landlord suffers no actual damage, he is entitled to nominal damages only.[10]

VII   USER

Subject to planning and other statutory restrictions, the tenant may, in the absence of any agreement to the contrary, use the premises for any lawful purpose. A change of user on the premises may, however, have an adverse effect upon the value of the premises themselves or neighbouring premises, or upon the landlord's trading or other interests. It is therefore

---

7   *Lambert v F W Woolworth & Co Ltd (No 2)* [1938] Ch 883 at 906, CA (Slesser LJ).
8   Ibid.
9   *Lambert v F W Woolworth & Co Ltd (No 2)* [1938] Ch 883 at 907, CA (Slesser LJ).
10   *James v Hutton and J Cook & Sons Ltd* [1950] 1 KB 9, [1949] 2 All ER 243, CA; *Duke of Westminster v Swinton* [1948] 1 KB 524, [1948] 1 All ER 248.

common to find, for example, in leases of residential property covenants against use of the premises for any business or trade and in leases of business premises covenants against use for particular trades; such restrictive covenants are not invariably *usual*, however, and they are not contrary to public policy as being in restraint of trade. Such covenants run with the land and therefore bind all assignees of the tenant, and in equity bind all successors of the tenant (whether assignees or not) who have actual or constructive notice of them. Covenants against changes of user may be absolute, qualified or fully qualified. Note that merely qualified user covenants are not made fully qualified by legislation (see below), and the landlord is entitled to refuse his consent unreasonably under a qualified covenant.

(a) Qualified covenants

In the case of conditions or agreements against alteration of the user of the premises without licence or consent, s 19(3) (in contrast with sub-ss (1) and (2)) does *not* make the covenant 'fully' qualified, and therefore only if the covenant expressly provides that such licence or consent shall not be unreasonably withheld, will that be the case.[11] Section 19(3) provides only that if the proposed change of user does not involve any structural alteration of the premises, the covenant shall be deemed, notwithstanding any express provision to the contrary, to be subject to a proviso that no fine or sum of money in the nature of a fine, whether by way of increase of rent or otherwise, shall be payable for such licence or consent. The landlord is not precluded, however, from requiring payment of a reasonable sum in respect of any damage or diminution in the value of the premises or any neighbouring premises belonging to him and of any legal or other expenses incurred in connection with such licence or consent; but where a sum has been declared reasonable by the court, the landlord is bound to grant his consent, on payment of that sum.

If a user covenant is qualified, as opposed to fully qualified, the landlord is entitled to refuse his consent to any change in user unreasonably. The tenant may have to accept a new lease allowing the changed user, on terms more advantageous to the landlord. If the landlord requires the payment of money as a condition of consent, and the sum is declared to be reasonable by the court, then the landlord will have to consent upon payment. Section 19(3) of the 1927 Act may be avoided by surrender-back clauses – as to which, see the discussion of s 19(1).

If a change of user involves an alteration to the premises, the landlord

---

11   See *Guardian Assurance Co Ltd v Gants Hill Holdings Ltd* (1983) 267 Estates Gazette 678.

may validly require the payment of a fine in respect of the change of user, even though s 19(2) might preclude him from doing so in respect of the alteration.

(b) Fully qualified covenant

Where the covenant expressly provides that consent is not to be unreasonably withheld, then if the landlord refuses consent to a proposed change of user without giving a reason, or in the tenant's opinion on unreasonable grounds, the tenant's remedy is to apply to the county court under s 53 of the Landlord and Tenant Act 1954, for a declaration that consent has been unreasonably withheld. The reasonableness of the refusal to give consent will be judged in much the same way as a refusal to give consent to a proposed assignment, etc, and so, if the refusal seeks to exploit the user covenant to obtain a collateral advantage not contemplated by the parties in the covenant, it will be unreasonable, as where the landlord sought to exploit the user covenant in a lease to attempt to maximise the rents of surrounding premises.[12] A requirement by the landlord of payment of a sum which is not compensation for the matters specifically claimable under s 19(3) will constitute unreasonable refusal. If the landlord's refusal is declared unreasonable, the tenant will thereupon be entitled to go ahead with the proposed change of user. If on the other hand the landlord makes an apparently excessive demand for compensation in respect of the matters for which he is entitled to claim under s 19(3), the unreasonableness of the amount demanded is not a matter for a declaration by the county court under s 53 of the 1954 Act, and therefore the tenant is not entitled to proceed without paying any compensation; in other words, he will be required to pay whatever sum is determined to be reasonable.

(c) Reform

The Law Commission[13] considered whether absolute user covenants should be made fully qualified and decided on balance not to recommend any change in the law. They thought that, first, to impose full qualification would create difficulties, where covenants were imposed for a purpose wider than that of protecting the landlord's reversion, and secondly, because of the danger that full qualification might raise rents. They did recommend extending section 84 of the Law

---

12 *Anglia Building Society v Sheffield City Council* (1982) 266 Estates Gazette 311, CA; also *Tollbench Ltd v Plymouth City Council* [1988] 1 EGLR 79, CA (holding also that the procedure used by the landlord for making a decision is not relevant to reasonableness).

13 Law Com 141, paras 4.32–4.53.

of Property Act 1925 to user covenants of all kinds, and the abolition of qualified (as opposed to fully qualified) user covenants.[14]

(d)   Modification and discharge of restrictive covenants

Two special provisions enable restrictive covenants in leases to be modified. Under s 610 of the Housing Act 1985, the county court may vary the terms of any covenant in the lease restrictive of user or prohibiting conversions or alterations, where it is in effect the case that such works would enable letting after conversion into two or more tenements where letting as a single tenement is difficult. The provision applies to a single house which the tenant wishes to convert by subdivision into two or more units.[15]

An obsolete restrictive covenant may be modified by the Lands Tribunal on application by a tenant under a long lease (of over 40 years initially with at least 25 having run) on various grounds, such as changes in the neighbourhood.[16]

(e)   Covenants for or against a particular user

In leases of residential property, tenants commonly covenant to use the premises as a private residence only, or not to use them for the purpose of any trade. Such a covenant would be broken by the erection of a studio and classroom for pupils,[17] the presence of a notice signifying that the premises included an office,[18] the letting of a wall for advertising,[19] the conversion of the house into flats,[20] the taking in of lodgers or paying guests,[1] or the garaging of a taxi which was used by the tenant in his business.[2] A covenant for private residence in the occupation of one household only, has been held not to be broken where one paying guest was taken in as a member of the family.[3] A similar covenant was broken where occupation licences were granted to members of the public by a lessee of four flats in a block of flats, though the lessee was not conducting a trade or business.[4]

---

14   *Report* para 6.16.
15   This does not apply to a scheme for division of adjoining terraced houses into flats, each of which would extend beyond the original houses: *Josephine Trust Ltd v Champagne* [1963] 2 QB 160, [1962] 3 All ER 136, CA.
16   Law of Property Act 1925 s 84.
17   *Patman v Harland* (1881) 17 Ch D 353.
18   *Wilkinson v Rogers* (1863) 3 New Rep 145.
19   *Tubbs v Esser* (1909) 26 TLR 145.
20   *Day v Waldron* (1919) 88 LJKB 937.
 1   *Thorn v Madden* [1925] Ch 847.
 2   *Jones v Christy* (1963) 107 Sol Jo 374.
 3   *Segal Securities Ltd v Thoseby* [1963] 1 QB 887, [1963] 1 All ER 500.
 4   *Falgor Commercial SA v Alsabahia Inc* (1985) 18 HLR 123, CA.

A covenant against causing a nuisance to the landlord, his tenants or to adjoining occupiers is broken by creating an actionable nuisance in the strict sense, but one against causing annoyance is much wider, and has been held to have been broken by the establishment of a hospital for out-patients.[5]

Where the tenant covenants not to permit or suffer a particular activity, he must neither authorise a breach, nor wilfully ignore the commital of a breach;[6] but a tenant who has no control in respect of the breach cannot be said to have permitted it.[7]

In business leases, covenants against particular trades or for no trade other than a particular trade are common, but the latter does not oblige the tenant to carry on that trade. The prohibited businesses or trades may be specific or the covenant may prohibit only noisy, offensive or dangerous trades, or it may disallow the sale of certain types of product, such as goods not usually sold in a food supermarket.[8] The onus of proving a breach will be on the landlord.

Where the covenant is for business purposes only or a particular business only, it is a matter of construction whether residence on the premises will be allowed, but the past history of the premises, prior to the execution of the lease, is irrelevant; the nature of the premises and their suitability for use as a dwelling are both relevant to the construction of the user covenant.[9]

(f) Covenants 'in restraint of trade'

Agreements which had they been made between vendor and purchaser of freehold land, or between mortgagor and mortgagee would be unenforceable in law as being in restraint of trade are not so treated if they are included in a lease. 'If one who seeks to take a lease of land knows that the only lease which is available to him is a lease with a restriction, then he must either take what is offered (on the appropriate financial terms) or he must seek a lease elsewhere. No feature of public policy requires that, if he freely contracted, he should be excused from honouring his contract'.[10] So in *Cleveland Petroleum Co Ltd v Dartstone Ltd*[11] a covenant by the sub-tenant not to sell or distribute motor fuels

---

5　*Tod-Heatly v Benham* (1888) 40 Ch D 80, CA.

6　*Borthwick-Norton v Romney Warwick Estates Ltd* [1950] 1 All ER 798, CA.

7　*Tophams v Earl of Sefton* [1967] 1 AC 50, [1966] 1 All ER 1039, HL.

8　*Basildon Development Corpn v Mactro Ltd* [1986] 1 EGLR 137, CA.

9　*City and Westminster Properties (1934) Ltd v Mudd* [1959] Ch 129, [1958] 2 All ER 733.

10　*Esso Petroleum Co Ltd v Harper's Garage (Stourport) Ltd* [1967] 1 All ER 699 at 714, per LORD MORRIS OF BORTH-Y-GEST.

11　[1969] 1 All ER 201; see also *Total Oil Great Britain v Thompson Garages (Biggin Hill)* [1972] 1 QB 318, [1971] 3 All ER 1226.

other than those supplied by the plaintiff (the tenant) was held to be enforceable as against an assignee of the sub-tenancy. Only if the landlord cannot satisfy supply requirements is the tie unenforceable and the tenant entitled to seek his supplies elsewhere. It would appear to be difficult to obtain an injunction if the tie, though broken, operates unfairly and unreasonably, but it cannot be reduced to a dead letter.[12] However, if in reality, an agreement is a loan finance transaction by means of demise and sub-demise, rather than by mortgage, the doctrine of restraint of trade will apply to the agreement, as it would to any mortgage.[13]

VIII OPTIONS IN THE LEASE

1 OPTIONS FOR RENEWAL

(a) Construction

Quite apart from any statutory rights for continuation of the tenancy or to a new lease on the termination of the current tenancy, the lease itself not uncommonly provides expressly for renewal at the end of the term by way either of a covenant by the landlord to renew, or of an option on the part of the tenant for renewal. The difference may be one of form only, but it may be one of intention also, inasmuch as an option may be construed as personal, as for example where a tenant covenants to renew a sub-lease if he himself gets an extension of his own term.[14] Unlike options to purchase, options for renewal (but not an option for payment of a sum of money in *lieu* of renewal)[15] run with the land and with the reversion, and cannot be revoked as long as the option is exercisable under estoppel or otherwise; in unregistered land they are registrable as Class C(iv) land charges.[16] If, however, an option would otherwise be void for want of registration, it may still be enforceable if the landlord is estopped from asserting its invalidity.[17] In the case of registered land, an option to renew must generally be protected by means of a notice or caution, and, this should be done even if the grantee is in actual occupation of the land (in which case the option will also override by

---

12 *Shell UK Ltd v Lostock Garage Ltd* [1977] 1 All ER 481, [1976] 1 WLR 1187, CA.
13 *Alec Lobb (Garages) Ltd v Total Oil GB Ltd* [1985] 1 All ER 303, [1985] 1 WLR 173, CA.
14 *Muller v Trafford* [1901] 1 Ch 54.
15 *Re Hunters Lease, Giles v Hutchings* [1942] Ch 124, [1942] 1 All ER 27.
16 *Beesly v Hallwood Estates* [1960] 2 All ER 314, [1960] 1 WLR 549.
17 *Taylors Fashions v Liverpool Victoria Trustees* [1982] QB 133n, [1981] 1 All ER 897. The tenant must prove that the landlord has acted unconscionably: *Phillips v Mobil Oil Ltd* [1988] EGCS 105.

virtue of s 70(1)(g) of the Land Registration Act 1925).[18] Options are not subject to the rule against perpetuities,[19] as long as they form part of the lease or are part of the same transaction,[20] but options to renew granted after 1 January 1926 for a term exceeding 60 years from the expiry of the current lease are void.[1]

An option to renew 'for seven or fourteen years' will be construed as an option to renew for 14 years subject to an option to terminate at the end of the seventh year;[2] but generally an option will be construed strictly. On options for perpetual renewal see Chapter 2. Where the court orders specific performance on an option simply for 'renewal', it will not order another option to be included in the new lease.

(b) Exercise of option

The exercise of the option is generally conditional on the observance of the covenants in the lease, and as a rule, a trivial breach debars the tenant from exercising the option.[3] By 'breach' is meant a breach which is subsisting, at or by the date when the option is exercisable by the tenant. If, at either date, the breach is spent (i e it lies at some time in the past history of the lease), the tenant will still be entitled to exercise his option, whether to renew, purchase or determine. Moreover, this rule applies to all breaches of covenant, be they positive or negative.[4] So, if at some time in the past, the landlord tried to forfeit the lease and failed, the tenant having obtained relief, and at the date of exercise of the option the tenant is not in breach of covenant, the tenant will not be disentitled from exercising his rights, at least not where the terms of the option require that the tenant, at the date for its exercise, has paid the rent and observed the covenants. On the other hand, if the tenant is guilty, at that date, of even a trifling breach of covenant, which is easily remediable, this, as noted, will disentitle him to exercise his right to renew. Such was the position in two cases where at the relevant date there were subsisting but trivial breaches of the tenant's covenant to repair.[5] However, where a tenant had twice withheld rent to pressure his landlord into carrying out repairs, but owed no rent by the end of the term and was not otherwise in breach of covenants, the right to renewal at the expiry of the term was

---

18   See *Webb v Pollmount Ltd* [1966] Ch 584, [1966] 1 All ER 481.
19   *Re Strand and Savoy Properties* [1960] Ch 582, [1960] 2 All ER 327.
20   *Weg Motors Ltd v Hales* [1962] Ch 49, [1961] 3 All ER 181, CA.
 1   LPA 1922 Sch 15 para 7(2).
 2   *Gardner v Blaxill* [1960] 2 All ER 457, [1960] 1 WLR 752.
 3   *West Country Cleaners (Falmouth) Ltd v Saly* [1966] 3 All ER 210, [1966] 1 WLR 1485, CA.
 4   *Bass Holdings Ltd v Morton Music Ltd* [1987] 2 All ER 1001, CA.
 5   *Finch v Underwood* (1876) 2 Ch D 310, CA; *Kitney v Greater London Properties Ltd* (1984) 272 Estates Gazette 786.

held unaffected.[6] If the option specifies a rent under the new lease, a notice purporting to exercise the option is bad if it states a lower rent.[7] Normally, the option will be expressed to be exercisable upon notice, which must be complied with, but otherwise it will be exercisable throughout the tenancy, and even after the expiry of the tenancy if the tenant remains in occupation.[8]

In the absence of express terms of renewal, the new lease will generally be for the same period and upon the same terms as the current tenancy. The parties may agree on the rent payable under the new lease. If they do not, the rent will likely be the same as the old rent. The parties may simply agree that the new rent is such as to be agreed by some means or other, say by two valuers, one appointed by each party. If one party tries to frustrate the machinery agreed, then the court will determine what is a fair and reasonable rent.[9] Whether the parties' formula enables an arbitrator to include rent reviews in the new term is entirely a matter of construction.[10]

2 OPTIONS TO DETERMINE LEASE

(a) Construction

It is often provided in a lease for a fixed term that the tenant (most commonly) or the landlord or both shall have the right to determine the lease at a time (or times) specified before the expiration of the term or on the happening of a specified event. A lease for 21 years, for example, might contain a *break-clause*, as it is called, exercisable by the tenant at the end of the seventh and the fourteenth years of the lease; or such an option might be exercisable by the tenant in the event of the premises becoming unfit for habitation, or the proposed user becoming unlawful, or by the landlord in the event of planning permission being granted for development or re-development (resumption for building purposes). If the lease is silent as to the person by whom the option is exercisable, it is exercisable by the tenant alone.[11]

(b) Exercise of option

Since the exercise of an option to determine the lease will in effect deprive the landlord of rent for the rest of the term, or, as the case may be, the

---

6   *Bassett v Whiteley* (1983) 45 P & CR 87, CA.
7   *Murray v Durley Chine (Investments) Ltd* [1953] 2 QB 433, [1953] 2 All ER 458.
8   *Moss v Barton* (1866) LR 1 Eq 474.
9   *Sudbrook Trading Estate Ltd v Eggleton* [1983] 1 AC 444, [1982] 3 All ER 1, HL.
10 *National Westminster Bank v BSC Footwear* (1980) 42 P & CR 90, CA.
11 *Wingfield v Clapton Construction Co* (1967) 201 Estates Gazette 769.

tenant from the rest of his term, it is construed strictly. An option is exercisable only by the person in whom the term is legally vested, and only in strict accordance with the terms of the option. A landlord's notice requiring the tenant to quit 'within' three months of the date of service of the notice was construed as meaning the full three-month period, where the option to determine was exercisable on three months' notice at any time during the lease.[12]

(c) Notices to exercise option to determine

An option to determine is generally exercisable, as was seen, by a notice served a given period in advance of a date specified in the lease, for example by notice served prior to the six months before the break-clause date.

The courts generally refuse to correct errors in such notices, since they are not consensual documents: hence, a notice to determine served by a landlord which gave an incorrect date of termination was not upheld and was ineffective.[13] The results of serving an ineffective notice may be disastrous, however: if it can be shown that the mistake would have been obvious to a reasonable landlord or tenant as the case may be, then there is a jurisdiction to uphold the notice; it will be effective and the mistake is simply ignored.[14]

3   OPTIONS TO PURCHASE

(a) Construction

Unlike an option to renew, an option to purchase the reversion is treated not as part of the lease, but as a separate agreement between the parties collateral to the lease. It cannot as such run with the land, and will not bind an assignee of the reversion unless it is protected by registration as an estate contract under s 2(4) of the Land Charges Act 1972,[15] or, as the case may be, by entry of a notice under the Land Registration Act 1925. If the land is registered, however, an option exercisable by a tenant in occupation constitutes an overriding interest within s 70(1)(g) of the Land Registration Act 1925, which is consequently binding upon an assignee of the reversion without registration.[16] As an interest in land, the rights under an option are freely assignable,[17] unless they are limited

---

12   *Manorlike Ltd v Le Vitas Travel Agency and Consultancy Services Ltd* [1986] 1 All ER 573, CA.

13   *Hankey v Clavering* [1942] 2 KB 326, [1942] 2 All ER 311, CA.

14   *Carradine Properties Ltd v Aslam* [1976] 1 All ER 573, [1976] 1 WLR 442; *Germax Securities Ltd v Spiegal* (1978) 37 P & CR 204, CA.

15   See *Pritchard v Briggs* [1980] Ch 338, [1980] 1 All ER 294, CA.

16   *Webb v Pollmount Ltd* [1966] Ch 584, [1966] 1 All ER 481.

17   *Re Button's Lease* [1964] Ch 263, [1963] 3 All ER 708.

by the terms of the option; but to be exercisable by a third party they must be assigned expressly to him, unless he falls within the class of persons to whom the option was originally granted (e g the tenant, 'his executors, administrators and assigns').[18] Provided it is exercisable only between the parties and successors in title and before the expiry of one year after the end of the lease,[19] it cannot be void for perpetuity; but where the option is expressed to be assignable separately from the lease, or exercisable outside that period, enforceability is subject to the perpetuity period of 21 years, i e it will be exercisable for a maximum of 21 years, even as between the original parties.

(b) Exercise of option

An option is not generally exercisable after the expiration of the term, as for example where the tenant has become a statutory tenant under the Rent Acts,[20] but since the option may be independent of the lease, forfeiture of the lease will not necessarily destroy the option.[1] Nor will a breach of covenant necessarily debar the tenant from exercising an option unless performance of that covenant is under the terms of the option, a condition precedent to its exercise; indeed, all conditions precedent must be strictly observed, unless waived by the landlord. It is usually provided that the option shall be exercisable in writing, and if not, it is implied, for the exercise of an option to purchase the reversion constitutes a contract for its sale. The terms of the option therefore will usually stipulate the price, but if not, it will be the open market value of the reversion subject to the existing lease.[2] The parties may even provide that the price is to be a fair and reasonable one, to be subsequently agreed or determined by arbitration; should the machinery provided by the parties to settle the price break down, it appears that the court may itself substitute its own machinery objectively to ascertain what is a fair and reasonable price, and then on this basis decree specific performance of the option.[3] Whether the terms of the lease will be enforceable after the exercise of the option will depend upon the terms of the option; the lease itself will not be terminated thereby, but in equity its terms will be unenforceable once the relationship of vendor and purchaser has been created, which may be implied, for example, from an agreement for the payment of interest on the purchase money.[4]

---

18 *Griffith v Pelton* [1958] Ch 205, [1957] 3 All ER 75.
19 Perpetuities and Accumulations Act 1964 s 9.
20 *Longmuir v Kew* [1960] 3 All ER 26, [1960] 1 WLR 862.
 1 *Rafferty v Scholfield* [1897] 1 Ch 937.
 2 *Grimes v Grayshott Motor Co* (1967) 201 Estates Gazette 586.
 3 *Sudbrook Trading Estate Ltd v Eggleton* [1983] 1 AC 444, [1982] 3 All ER 1, HL; cf *Taylor Barnard Ltd v Tozer* (1983) 269 Estates Gazette 225.
 4 *Nightingale v Courtney* [1954] 1 QB 399, [1954] 1 All ER 362, CA.

Chapter 8

Rent and rent review

I DEFINITION OF RENT

Rent is a certain profit issuing out of land and tenements corporeal. First, it issues from and is reserved out of land, as a compensation for possession during the term by the tenant.[1] Secondly, it is an acknowledgement by the tenant of his landlord's title, based on tenure. Rent has been defined, accordingly, as a contractual sum which the landlord is entitled to receive from the tenant in return for the latter's use and occupation of his land.[2]

Because of this second rule, rent is due (unless some express exception appears in the lease) even if buildings on the land are destroyed or requisitioned during the term.[3] If the lease is frustrated, all liability to pay rent, after the frustrating event, ceases, but a frustrating event must be so grave that no substantial use is possible for the purposes permitted or contemplated by the parties, for the residue of the term, and frustration will seldom apply to relieve the tenant from his obligation to pay rent, even if his enjoyment of the demised land is severely dislocated.[4]

Rent issues out of the whole or any part of the demised land so that the rent due under a head lease of the whole land let to several sub-tenants may be distrained for on the land of any one of them. In the absence of clear express contrary provision, it is payable in arrear.[5] Moreover, the dates on which rent is due must be clearly expressed – see further below. As a rule, rent is payable in money.[6]

---

1 It is only against land that distress may be levied.
2 *C H Bailey Ltd v Memorial Enterprises Ltd* [1974] 1 All ER 1003, [1974] 1 WLR 728, CA.
3 *Paradine v Jane* (1647) Aleyn 26; *Redmond v Dainton* [1920] 2 KB 256.
4 *National Carriers Ltd v Panalpina (Northern) Ltd* [1981] AC 675, [1981] 1 All ER 161, HL.
5 *Coomber v Howard* (1845) 1 CB 440.
6 A rent may validly be payable as either goods or services: Co Lit 142 a; *Montague v Browning* [1954] 2 All ER 601, [1954] 1 WLR 1039, CA.

The old rule, which still applies for the purposes of distress, is that a rent must be certain to be recoverable: only a certain sum is capable of being distrained for.[7] Other than for the purposes of distress, if a rent is certain or capable of being rendered certain at the time it is due, it is recoverable. Insufficiently certain was a, rent based on as many hours' services as the landlord required from time to time,[8] but a rent calculated by reference to the index of retail prices was regarded as sufficiently certain,[9] as was a sum representing ten per cent of the turnover of a business.[10] In connection with rent review clauses, the position is this. The rent does not necessarily have to certain when it falls due, provided that it is ascertained in due course under a rent review procedure. The new rent is thereafter substituted for the old rent.[11]

Sums may be rent even though there is no power of distress in the lease, provided they are for use and occupation.[12] Equally, service charges (see further Chapter 19) – under which the landlord of a multi-occupied office building or block of flats may have the right to charge the tenants for repairs, maintenance and insurance, for example – may be expressly recoverable as rent, so that they may, in default, be distrained for.

II OTHER PERIODICAL PAYMENTS DISTINGUISHED

Certain money payments cannot be regarded as rent, but in modern leases, this may be overcome by reserving the sum concerned as rent – as indeed with service charges, which, as noted, may be reserved as rent.

1 *Rentcharges and rent seck* A rent charge is charged on land in perpetuity or for a term, with an express power of distress, but the owner of the rentcharge has no reversion on the land charged.[13] A rent seck is similar to a rent charge but there is no power of distress.[14]

---

7 *Walsh v Lonsdale* (1882) 21 Ch D 9, CA. There were two rents in this case, one fixed and one fluctuating, but when the latter amount became certain, no doubt it could have been distrained for.
8 *Barnes v Barratt* [1970] 2 QB 657, [1970] 2 All ER 483, CA.
9 *Blumenthal v Gallery Five Ltd* (1971) 220 Estates Gazette 483, CA.
10 *Smith v Cardiff Corpn (No 2)* [1955] Ch 159, [1955] 1 All ER 113.
11 *C H Bailey Ltd v Memorial Enterprises Ltd*, supra, approved in *United Scientific Holdings Ltd v Burnley Borough Council* [1978] AC 904, [1977] 2 All ER 62, HL.
12 *T & E Homes Ltd v Robinson* [1979] 2 All ER 522, [1979] 1 WLR 452, CA.
13 By Rentcharges Act 1977 s 2, rentcharges cannot be created after 22 August 1977.
14 Such power is conferred on chargees by Law of Property Act 1925 s 121.

2   *Premiums* Even if payable in instalments, a premium[15] is not rent,[16] though it is likely to represent the capitalised value of the land.[17]

3   *Payments for insurance* Although, at common law these are not rent, this may be overcome by the landlord expressly reserving them as part of the rent – so as to enable a distress to be levied for unpaid premiums.

III   CONSTRUCTION OF A RESERVATION

1   *Reddendum* It is usual, though not essential, for a lease to contain a formal *reddendum* using such words as 'yielding up and paying' or 'rendering' (i e the reservation) followed by an express covenant to pay the rent reserved. If there is a good reservation, then a covenant to pay the rent reserved will be implied on execution by the tenant of the counterpart, but being an implied covenant, no libility can arise under it before he goes into possession or after he has assigned. Any form of words, such as an express covenant or a proviso, that shows an intention to create an agreement to pay rent will be considered a good reservation.

2   *Kinds of rent* A *best rent* is the highest rent that can reasonably be obtained for the duration of the lease.

A *rack-rent* is a rent of the full annual value of the property, or within a reasonable margin of it, at the commencement of the lease. If the maximum rent lawfully recoverable is less than the market rent then the rack-rent is that lawfully recoverable.[18]

A *ground rent* is less than a rack-rent, the difference having been 'capitalised' in the form of a premium taken by the landlord on the granting of the lease. It is more usual to find this method of payment under long leases, and it is commonly used in building leases.

A *peppercorn rent* is, in effect, a nominal ground rent, in fact so nominal that it is scarcely ever collected.

A *corn rent* is simply rent paid in kind. Corn rents, where they still exist, are liable to redemption under s 30(1) of the Tithe Act 1936.[19]

A *dead rent* is the part of the rent reserved on the lease of a mine or other wasting asset which is payable throughout the term, whether or not the mine or whatever is worked. It is boosted by *royalties* which are

---

15   As distinct from a premium rent, i e an inflated rent paid by the tenant where there is no rent review in the lease.

16   *Regor Estates Ltd v Wright* [1951] 1 KB 689, [1951] 1 All ER 219, CA.

17   For statutory controls see Rent Act 1977 Part IX.

18   *Newman v Dorrington Developments Ltd* [1975] 3 All ER 928, [1975] 1 WLR 1642.

19   See also Corn Rents Act 1963.

payable over and above that, in relation to the amount of coal, etc, extracted or sold. A royalty is a true rent if properly reserved.

A *variable* or *sliding scale rent* is one fixed by reference to the cost or value of some commodity which is itself variable on a recognised scale, such as the value of gold in sterling,[20] or the cost-of-living index.[1] Such modes of fixing rent are very rare compared with rent review clauses which have fundamentally similar objects; they are an attempt to ensure that the rent reserved keeps pace with the value of currency other than sterling, the cost of living or the market value of property throughout the term.

Rents are also termed 'variable' where the *quantum* reserved is fixed by reference to a factor (usually in relation to the tenant's trade, such as his turnover, his net profits, his gross profits, etc), which itself is likely to vary from one rental period to another. Generally speaking, such a rent may nevertheless be 'certain', provided that when the rent for each period falls due, the amount is 'ascertainable', i e calculable by reference to the profits, etc already accrued. Thus, where rent is payable in arrears, the reservation will be good, even if the factor is the turnover during that period; but where the rent is payable in advance, the factor must necessarily be the turnover, etc, during the previous period. By their nature, variable rents in this sense are most likely to be reserved in mining leases and business tenancies; they are found too in family arrangements, or in relationships where there is an element of patronage, e g where the tenant could not afford to pay a full market rent, at least at the commencement of the tenancy.

A *penal rent* may, in effect, be either a pre-agreed assessment of damages payable in the event of a breach of a particular covenant (i e *liquidated damages*), or a *penalty*, which is also specified to be payable in the event of breaches of possibly several covenants, but which in amount is apparently arbitrary, bearing no relation to the damages likely to be suffered by the landlord in the event of a breach. The distinction is important, and the terminology used in the lease is by no means conclusive. A penalty is unenforceable as it stands, in so far as, though judgment will be given, execution cannot be levied in respect of it, and the landlord will be limited to the damage he actually suffered by the default.

A penal rent by way of liquidated damages or 'additional rent', on the other hand, is recoverable as rent,[2] and is incident to the reversion. In case of a specified breach, the landlord can sue either for the penal rent

---

20 *Treseder-Griffin v Co-operative Insurance Society* [1956] 2 QB 127, [1956] 2 All ER 33, CA.

 1 *Blumenthal v Gallery Five Ltd* (1971) 220 Estates Gazette 31.

 2 Penal rent clauses are ineffective in the case of agricultural holdings: Agricultural Holdings Act 1986 s 24.

on the grounds that it is due and has not been paid, or he can sue for damages for the breach, but not both. Liquidated damages are to be found most commonly in connection with restrictive user covenants, the tenant agreeing to pay additional rent, for example, if he uses the premises for purposes other than those specified. Provision for payment of additional rent does not necessarily entitle the tenant to break the covenant on payment; an injunction would therefore be granted to restrain a breach in respect of which a single sum is payable, but if additional rent is payable for the rest of the term, it suggests that the tenant is thereby given the option to break the covenant and pay the increased rent.

3　*Cesser of rent clauses*　Provision is often made in the lease for the suspension or extinction of liability for rent in certain events, and is especially common in relation to damage to the premises by fire. The precise effect of such a proviso depends upon the wording of the particular clauses. The words 'damage by fire excepted', for example, have been held to entitle the tenant to an abatement in proportion to the damage caused,[3] and the word 'suspended' only, to mean postponement of liability. If it is intended that the liability should be extinguished during any period, then such words as 'cease' or 'abate' should be used, and only if the lease expressly so provides will the tenant be entitled to elect to bring the tenancy to an end, in case of total destruction, for example, since the contractual doctrine of frustration seldom applies to leases.

IV　RENT REVIEW CLAUSES[4]

Introduction

The aim of rent review clauses is to provide machinery to determine progressive rents – to enable the initial rent, which may or may not be reserved throughout the whole term granted, to be reviewed, and usually increased, on one or more fixed occasions during the lease. Most rent reviews are to the open market rent. Rent reviews are generally upwards only, to the higher of the current rent or the open market rent at the date of review.[5] The object of rent review clauses is, no doubt, to shield the landlord from inflation, because, as time passes, a fixed rent will erode in

---

3　*Bennett v Ireland* (1858) EB & E 326.
4　See Bernstein and Reynolds *Handbook of Rent Review* (1981); Clark and Adams *Rent Reviews and Variable Rents* (2nd edn, 1987), and the journal *Rent Review and Lease Renewal*.
5　This has been criticised: Law Com No 162 (1987) para 4.62.

real value. Rent review gives the landlord an opportunity to charge an open market rent from time to time. If validly arrived at or determined, a new rent determined on review will take effect in place of the old rent. Most rent review clauses provide for a range of possibilities to be considered as part of the review procedure. Two preliminary matters deserve mention before analysing the main aspects of rent review clauses.

1 The interpretation of words in one rent review clause is not necessarily definitive guidance on the interpretation of similar words in a differently worded clause.[6] Rent review clauses have not yet attained the status of standard contract terms, though some standard forms of rent review clauses have been produced.[7]

2 There are many forms of rent review clauses. Some of the assumptions required to be made in evaluating the rent payable for the period after the date of review may be artificial, such as a term requiring it to be assumed, contrary to the fact, that the tenant is free to use the premises for any purpose he likes. The court will enforce terms clearly requiring a rent over the market level to be determined.[8] The presumption is, however, that the landlord is not intended to get any extra benefit from an artificial assumption which does not expressly have to be made.[9]

(a) Main elements of clause

The following elements have commonly appeared in rent review clauses.

(i) The *periods* of rent review, as identified by reference to definite intervals, by defining the review date or dates and the review periods.

(ii) There may well be a *formula* by which the new rent is to be measured, which may first provide that the new rent is to be finally agreed between the parties.[10] If no agreement is possible, it may be stated that the premises are to be assumed to be let on the open market with vacant possession by a willing landlord to a willing

---

6 *Equity and Law Life Assurance Society plc v Bodfield Ltd* (1987) 54 P & CR 290, CA; Pryor (1985) 273 Estates Gazette 953.

7 See e g Law Society/RICS Model Forms of Rent Review Clause in *Precedents for the Conveyancer* 5–61.

8 *General Accident Fire and Life Assurance plc v Electronic Data Processing Co plc* (1986) 53 P & CR 189.

9 *British Gas Corpn v Universities Superannuation Scheme Ltd* [1986] 1 All ER 978, [1986] 1 WLR 398 (lease assumed to have future rent reviews); *Basingstoke and Deane Borough Council v Host Group Ltd* [1988] 1 All ER 824, [1988] 1 WLR 348, CA (letting to be on same terms after review as before).

10 As against an agreement 'subject to contract'; *Henderson Group plc v Superabbey Ltd* [1988] 2 EGLR 155.

tenant for a given term.[11] If this figure is higher than the current level of rent, then the new figure becomes the reviewed rent: if not the old rent usually continues to be payable.[12] It is presumed, where an open market rent formula is used, that the rent is to be fixed as at the date of the arbitrator's decision, as against that fixed for review, if earlier.[13]

(iii)   Any *assumptions* to be made about the premises and the terms and conditions of the lease as at the review date ought to be clearly stated.[14] Some examples of assumptions, which will be enforced if clear and workable, are: that the premises are let subject to the same terms as the lease; that the tenant is free to make any user he likes of the demised premises (even if this is contrary to the fact); that the effect on rental value of any improvements made by the tenant or his predecessors in title in the tenancy must be disregarded; that the effect of the occupation of the tenant or any sub-tenant must be disregarded; and that the effect of any work diminishing the value of the demised premises must be ignored.

(iv)   There is likely to be *machinery* for ascertaining the new rent, for example, to provide that if no agreement is reached between the parties as to the new rent, within stated time-limits, then there is to be arbitration in default, by an arbitrator or independent valuer agreed by the parties or, failing that, nominated by, say, the President of the RICS. The arbitration procedure itself may have to be started off by a landlord's notice: if so there may be specific provisions as to whether time is of the essence or not.

(v)   The clause may contain procedures for the initiation of rent review by *landlords' trigger notices* – i e notices, sometimes in the form of letters, served on the tenant, before the first or any subsequent review period. There will sometimes be a timetable under which a trigger notice must be served a given number of months before the review period starts: if so, the clause may state whether or not late service is allowed, i e whether time is of the essence in relation to trigger notices.

(b)   Whether time is of the essence

The question of whether time is of the essence in relation to landlords' trigger or arbitration notices is one of construction of the rent review

---

11   The length of the term to be assumed should be stated: see *Pugh v Smiths Industries Ltd* (1982) 264 Estates Gazette 823.

12   The court may supply its own machinery: *R & A Millett (Shops) Ltd v Leon Allen International Fashions Ltd* [1988] 1 EGLR 45.

13   *Webber v Halifax Building Society* [1985] 1 EGLR 58; *Glofield Properties Ltd v Morley (No 2)* [1988] 2 EGLR 149.

14   *Guys 'n' Dolls Ltd v Sade Bros Catering Ltd* (1983) 269 Estates Gazette 129, CA.

clause. The presumption, in the absence of express counter-indications in the clause itself, or in the surrounding circumstances, is that time is not of the essence either in relation to trigger or arbitration notices.[15] Where, therefore, the landlords served a trigger notice two months after the last date for service under the rent review timetable had expired, it was held that they could still rely on the notice to initiate a rent review.[16] This presumption applies whether the clause gives a timetable for rent review procedures or merely requires the ascertainment of the rent by a certain date. There are no fixed guidelines for deciding whether, having regard to the presumption, time is or is not of the essence, but a provision that failure to serve a notice on time renders it void indicates that time is of the essence.[17] Where certain steps, such as the conclusion of an arbitration, are out of the control of the parties then it will be difficult to argue that even apparently mandatory language such as 'as soon as practicable' or 'not later than' in relation to an arbitration notice renders time of the essence.[18] The courts will enforce very clear indications that time is to be of the essence, examples being where the landlord was able to serve an arbitration notice within a given time 'but not otherwise',[19] or where, if no application for an arbitrator was made within a 15-month time-limit, the old rent must continue.[20]

(i) Time will generally be deemed to be of the essence where the rent review trigger procedures are clearly linked up to, or are expressly subject to, the exercise by the tenant of an option to determine the lease.[1] A simple correlation between a rent review clause and a tenant's option to determine is not of itself sufficient to render time of the essence, at least in relation to an arbitration notice where the event relied on to make time of the essence is the decision of the arbitrator.[2]

(ii) If time is not of the essence then the tenant may make it so by

---

15 *United Scientific Holdings Ltd v Burnley Borough Council* [1978] AC 904, [1977] 2 All ER 62, HL; *Amherst v James Walker (Goldsmith and Silversmith) Ltd* [1983] Ch 305, [1983] 2 All ER 1067, CA; *Panavia Air Cargo Ltd v Southend-on-Sea Borough Council* [1988] 1 EGLR 124, CA (statement that time not of essence in part of clause governed whole process).

16 *United Scientific Holdings Ltd v Burnley Borough Council*, supra; *Dean and Chapter of Chichester Cathedral v Lennards Ltd* (1977) 35 P & CR 309, CA.

17 *Power Securities (Manchester) Ltd v Prudential Assurance Ltd* [1987] 1 EGLR 121.

18 *Touche Ross & Co v Secretary of State for the Environment* (1982) 46 P & CR 187, CA; *Thorn EMI Pension Trust Ltd v Quinton Hazell plc* (1983) 269 Estates Gazette 414.

19 *Drebbond Ltd v Horsham District Council* (1978) 37 P & CR 237. Also *Norwich Union Life Insurance Society v Sketchley plc* [1986] 2 EGLR 126.

20 *Greenhaven Securities Ltd v Compton* [1985] 2 EGLR 117.

 1 *United Scientific Holdings Ltd v Burnley Borough Council*, supra; *Coventry City Council v J Hepworth & Son* (1982) 46 P & CR 170, CA.

 2 *Metrolands Investments Ltd v J H Dewhurst Ltd* [1986] 3 All ER 659, CA.

serving a counter-notice, say a clearly-worded letter, on the landlord giving him a reasonable time, say one month, in which to trigger the review or require arbitration.[3] The right to serve such a notice may well be contained in the rent review clause itself.

(iii)   Some rent review clauses have provided that the landlord's trigger notice may state the new rent and that, if the tenant fails within stated time-limits to challenge the landlord's figure, it will be deemed to be the new rent; and that if the tenant by counter-notice states a new rent and the landlord fails within stated time limits to apply for arbitration, the latter figure takes effect. The question of whether time is of the essence in these cases is one of construction, but only if finality is clearly intended, will time be held to be of the essence in relation to the notice procedures.[4] Possibly if the landlord (or tenant) alone is able to serve a deeming notice, time will not be of the essence for the reply.[5]

(iv)   Where time is of the essence, failure to serve a requisite notice or counter-notice within the stated time-limit will be fatal – and a late notice will be of no effect. The review procedure may in consequence collapse.[6] Accordingly, where a surveyor was appointed out of time, his award was of no effect and the old rent continued to be payable.[7]

(v)   Mere delay in the service of rent review notices, where time is not of the essence, will not preclude review, even if coupled with hardship to the tenant. Accordingly, review was allowed 18 months and even 23 months out of time.[8] Where the tenant is able to show mutual abandonment of review, repudiation by the landlord, or conduct by him amounting to estoppel, a review out of time, even where time is not of the essence, will be impossible.[9]

(c)   Implied terms and rectification

Where a rent review clause failed to provide a suitable formula for the ascertainment of the new rent, a term was implied that, failing

---

3   *British Rail Pension Trustee Co Ltd v Cardshops Ltd* [1987] 1 EGLR 127; *Glofield Properties Ltd v Morley* [1988] 1 EGLR 113.
4   *Henry Smith's Charity Trustees v AWADA Trading and Promotion Services Ltd* (1984) 47 P & CR 607, CA; *Mecca Leisure Ltd v Renown Investments (Holdings) Ltd* (1984) 49 P & CR 12, CA.
5   *Taylor Woodrow Property Co Ltd v Lonrho Textiles Ltd* [1985] 2 EGLR 120.
6   *Beer v Bowden* [1981] 1 All ER 1070, [1981] 1 WLR 522n, CA. If the landlord misses the review date in these circumstances, the old rent will continue to be payable: *Weller v Akehurst* [1981] 3 All ER 411.
7   *Darlington Borough Council v Waring & Gillow (Holdings) Ltd* [1988] 2 EGLR 159.
8   *Accuba v Allied Shoe Repairs* [1975] 3 All ER 782, [1975] 1 WLR 1559; *Printing House Properties Ltd v J Winston & Co Ltd* (1982) 263 Estates Gazette 725.
9   *Amherst v James Walker (Goldsmith and Silversmith) Ltd*, supra; *Esso Petroleum Co Ltd v Anthony Gibbs Financial Services Ltd* (1983) 267 Estates Gazette 351, CA.

agreement, the reviewed rent was to be a fair market rent for the premises at the review date.[10] If it is clearly shown that due to mutual mistake, a rent review clause is defective, then the court may rectify the lease, to give effect to the common intention of the parties, and insert the words omitted.[11] Even a complete rent review clause has been inserted on this basis.[12] This jurisdiction is even exercisable against an assignee, unless he can show that he is a purchaser for value, without notice of the right to rectify.[13] The general rules governing rectification apply to rent review clauses, as to which see the discussion in Chapter 4.

(d) Assumptions in rent review clauses

Many rent review clauses require assumptions to be made in a review, about the premises and other terms of the lease after the review. But except and in so far as a particular clause requires specific assumptions to be made on a rent review, a valuer must base his valuation on the assumption that the hypothetical lease, after review, will be on the same terms, other than as to amount of rent, as those in the existing lease.[14]

(i) *Improvements* The question of whether tenants' improvements prior to review should be taken into account is one of construction of the clause in question. It may provide that the effect of tenants' improvements carried out with the landlord's consent during the term should be disregarded.[15] There may be uncertainty about which persons count as 'tenant' (for example, is only the current tenant included, or are future tenants) and if so, the question is one of construction of the disregard clause.[16] The disregard clause may incorporate s 34 of the Landlord and Tenant Act 1954, and should make it clear whether this is the originally enacted or amended provision because if this is not done the question is one of construction.[17] Any uncertainties as to what is to be understood by the 'demised premises' in this connection are again questions of construction: structures put up during the term have been held to fall

---

10 *Beer v Bowden* [1981] 1 All ER 1070, [1981] 1 WLR 522n, CA.

11 *Thomas Bates & Son Ltd v Wyndham's (Lingerie) Ltd* [1981] 1 All ER 1077, [1981] 1 WLR 505, CA; also *Kemp v Neptune Properties Ltd* [1988] 2 EGLR 87, CA.

12 *Central and Metropolitan Estates Ltd v Compusave* (1983) 266 Estates Gazette 900.

13 *Equity and Law Life Assurance Society Ltd v Coltness Group Ltd* (1983) 267 Estates Gazette 949.

14 *Basingstoke and Deane Borough Council v Host Group Ltd* [1988] 1 All ER 824, [1988] 1 WLR 348, CA; *Trusthouse Forte Albany Hotels Ltd v Daejan Investments Ltd (No 2)* [1989] 03 EG 78.

15 If so, and the landlord unreasonably withholds consent, the disregard clause will cover the work concerned: see *Hamish Cathie Travel England Ltd v Insight International Tours Ltd* [1986] 1 EGLR 244.

16 *Hambros Bank Executor and Trustee Co Ltd v Superdrug Stores Ltd* [1985] 1 EGLR 99.

17 *Brett v Brett Essex Golf Club Ltd* (1986) 52 P & CR 330, CA.

outside a disregard clause.[18] If the disregard clause refers to the current term and the improvements are carried out under a licence granted prior to the grant of the term, it will not apply to the improvements.[19]

Where there is no disregard clause, the question of taking tenants' improvements into account in the rental value depends on the formula which describes the rent. If it is a rent payable for the demised premises, without any qualification, tenants' improvements prior to review become part of the demised premises and are to be taken into account.[20] If the clause requires the rent to be agreed between the parties, then a subjective assessment of a fair rent is required, and the question of disregarding tenants' improvements prior to review depends on all the circumstances: in particular, whether the tenant or assignee proves that he paid for their cost.[1]

(ii)   *User restrictions*   The question of whether it is to be assumed in assessing the reviewed rent that existing user restrictions, if any, in the lease, will continue, is one of construction but if an open market rent simpliciter is to be determined, then it is to be assumed that existing user restrictions will not be unilaterally waived or relaxed and that they will continue into the period after the review date.[2] This is merely a rule of construction: a narrow user clause will not be assumed to be carried into the review period in the face of clear language indicating that an open market rental free of existing user restrictions is intended.[3] If a clause requires absurd assumptions then it will be construed to produce a sensible result, having regard to the user the tenant is entitled to make of the demised premises.[4]

(iii)   *Future rent reviews*   The question of whether future rent reviews are to be taken into account (if no express provision exists) is one of construction of each rent review clause, so that, in one line of cases, provisions to the effect that the current terms must be assumed to continue 'other than as to rent' were held to mean that the existence of

---

18   *Panther Shop Investments Ltd v Keith Pople Ltd* [1987] 1 EGLR 131.
19   *Euston Centre Properties Ltd v H and J Wilson Ltd* (1981) 262 Estates Gazette 1079.
20   *Ponsford v HMS Aerosols Ltd* [1979] AC 63, [1978] 2 All ER 837, HL; also *Goh Eng Wah v Yap Phooi Yin* [1988] 32 EG 55, PC. Cf *Ipswich Town Football Club v Ipswich Borough Council* [1988] 2 EGLR 146 ('land' assumed free of buildings put up during term). Also *Ravenseft Properties Ltd v Park* [1988] 2 EGLR 164.
1   *Lear v Blizzard* [1983] 3 All ER 662.
2   *Plinth Property Investments Ltd v Mott, Hay and Anderson* (1978) 38 P & CR 361, CA; *James v British Crafts Centre* [1987] 1 EGLR 139, CA; *SI Pension Trustees Ltd v Ministerio de la Marina de la Republica Peruana* [1988] 1 EGLR 119, CA (user clause in lease prevailed over wider licence to assign).
3   *Law Land Co Ltd v Consumers' Association Ltd* (1980) 255 Estates Gazette 617, CA.
4   *Pearl Assurance plc v Shaw* (1984) 274 Estates Gazette 490.

future rent reviews must be ignored.[5] This approach has not been consistently applied.[6] and it has been held more recently, and, with respect, more realistically, that a literal construction should be avoided so that, if possible, the realistic assumption will be made that there are to be future rent reviews – though this result will be displaced by clear contrary language.[7]

(iv) *Miscellaneous points*

1   In some cases, a review formula will state that the effect of the tenant's occupation is to be disregarded: if so, it is to be assumed that the premises are let to a willing lessee by a willing lessor with vacant possession.[8] This is to be assumed even in the face of the facts, unless the clause clearly requires a contrary result.[9] The length of the term to be assumed in deciding on the new rent is presumed to be the whole length of the term originally granted, as opposed to the unexpired term at the review date.[10]

2   The court has no jurisdiction to determine a reviewed rent varying, from time to time, with the state of repair of the demised premises,[11] and any diminishing effect on an open market rent of a tenant's breaches of his repairing covenant must be disregarded.[12] However, a 27.5% downward adjustment on review due to an onerous repairing and rebuilding covenant was upheld.[13] Where a rent review clause required the comparison of the rights and obligations of the demised premises and of equivalent freehold land, it was held

---

5   *Equity and Law Life Assurance Society plc v Bodfield Ltd* (1987) 54 P & CR 290, CA. Also *National Westminster Bank plc v Arthur Young McClelland Moores & Co* [1985] 1 EGLR 61.

6   See *Arnold v National Westminster Bank plc* [1988] 3 All ER 977, where it was held that the *Arthur Young* decision, supra, did not preclude re-litigation of the same question, in view of later cases.

7   See e g *British Gas Corpn v Universities Superannuation Scheme Ltd* [1986] 1 All ER 978, [1986] 1 WLR 398 following earlier first-instance cases, approved *Basingstoke and Deane Borough Council v Host Group Ltd*, CA, supra and followed in *British Home Stores plc v Ranbrook Properties Ltd* [1988] 1 EGLR 121.

8   *F R Evans (Leeds) Ltd v English Electric Co Ltd* (1977) 36 P & CR 185; also *Royal Exchange Assurance v Bryant Samuel Properties (Coventry) Ltd* [1985] 1 EGLR 84 (valuation regardless of any sub-lettings); *Cornwall Coast Country Club v Cardgrange Ltd* [1987] 1 EGLR 146.

9   *Dennis & Robinson v Kiossos Establishment* (1987) 54 P & CR 282, CA.

10   *Norwich Union Life Insurance Society v Trustee Savings Bank Central Board* [1986] 1 EGLR 136.

11   *Clarke v Findon Developments Ltd* (1983) 270 Estates Gazette 426.

12   *Harmsworth Pension Funds Trustees Ltd v Charringtons Industrial Holdings Ltd* [1985] 1 EGLR 97.

13   *Norwich Union Life Insurance Society v British Railways Board* [1987] 2 EGLR 137.

that only rights attached to the freehold had to be compared.[14] If a rent review clause does not in terms deal with tenants' fixtures, these must be left out of account in fixing an open market rent.[15]

3   Whether a rent determined or agreed after a rent review is to be backdated to the date of review, given that some delays will be almost inevitable, is a question of construction.[16] The clause may make express provisions for backdating (ie making up the difference between the old rent and the reviewed rent once determined) and for the payment of interest on back-dated reviewed rent arrears.[17] If, after the review date, the lease is surrendered, the lessee remains liable to pay the reviewed rent from the review date up to the date of surrender.[18]

(v)   *Arbitrations*   If the valuer or surveyor acts as an arbitrator, an appeal may be mounted against his decisions. There is statutory power to extend the time-limits in a rent review clause for commencing arbitration proceedings if undue hardship is proved to exist.[19] An arbitrator acts in a quasi-judicial capacity with immunity from actions in negligence; if an arbitrator acts as an expert (whether he does is a matter of construction) then he is amenable to such actions.[20] On applications for leave to appeal, leave will be given only if the court is satisfied that there is real doubt the arbitrator is right in law.[1] If the arbitrator acts as an expert then only if there is a discernable error of law will the court interfere.[2]

---

14   *Wallace v McMullen & Sons Ltd* [1988] 2 EGLR 143; also *Leigh v Certibilt Investments Ltd* [1988] 1 EGLR 116.

15   *Young v Dalgety plc* (1986) 130 Sol Jo 985, CA. Also *Jefferies v O'Neill* (1983) 46 P & CR 376.

16   *South Tottenham Land Securities Ltd v R & A Millett (Shops) Ltd* [1984] 1 All ER 614, [1984] 1 WLR 710, CA; also *Parry v Robinson-Wyllie Ltd* [1987] 2 EGLR 133; *Parkside Knightsbridge Ltd v German Food Centre Ltd* [1988] 8/2 RRLR 131 (new rent payable from last date landlord's trigger notice could be given).

17   Interest is not presumed to be payable: *Trust House Forte Albany Hotels Ltd v Daejan Investments Ltd* (1980) 256 Estates Gazette 915.

18   *Torminster Properties Ltd v Green* [1983] 2 All ER 457, [1983] 1 WLR 676, CA.

19   Arbitration Act 1950 s 27. The provision does not apply unless there are bilateral rights of reference: *Tote Bookmakers Ltd v Development and Property Holding Co Ltd* [1985] Ch 261, [1985] 2 All ER 555.

20   *Palacath v Flanagan* [1985] 2 All ER 161; *North Eastern Co-operative Society Ltd v Newcastle upon Tyne City Council* [1987] 1 EGLR 142.

1   *Lucas Industries plc v Welsh Development Agency* [1986] Ch 500, [1986] 2 All ER 858. On procedure, see *Control Securities plc v Spencer* [1989] 07 EG 82.

2   *Hudson Pty Ltd v Legal and General Life of Australia Ltd* [1986] 2 EGLR 130, PC.

V PAYMENT OF RENT

(a) Time of payment

Rent is payable in arrear unless there is a clear express contrary provision in the lease.[3] Moreover, it is presumed, again subject to the terms of the lease, that a yearly rent is payable.[4] In the case of a periodic weekly or monthly tenancy, the assumption is that the rent is payable for the same periods as those of the tenancy. Where a rent is expressly payable quarterly, the quarters are calculated from the date of the lease,[5] and to get round this the lease may specify the usual quarter days. These are: 25 March (Lady Day); 24 June (Midsummer); 29 September (Michaelmas) and 25 December (Christmas). Rent is due on the morning of the day specified for payment, but it is not in arrear until midnight.[6] Rent due on a bank holiday is only due on the following day.[7]

Rent paid before the appointed day is not strictly satisfaction of the obligation, though it will be a good defence to an action by the landlord or his personal representatives on the covenant. However, it will not discharge the tenant's obligation against anyone who in the meantime acquires the landlord's reversion, unless the tenant has had no notice of the assignment before the day appointed for payment.[8]

(b) Manner of payment

Payment must be made by the tenant to the landlord, or their duly authorised agents respectively; and payment by a stranger does not acquit the tenant of his obligation unless the payment is so authorised by him or subsequently ratified. By Landlord and Tenant Act 1985 s 3, where the landlord of premises consisting of or including a dwelling-house assigns his interest, the new landlord must give written notice of his name and address to the tenant, not later than the next day on which rent is payable, or if that is within two months of the assignment, the end of two months. Failure to comply with this duty is an offence and the old landlord remains under a continuing liability for breaches of covenant from the assignment date until due notification. Tender by a lawful assignee is good,[9] and the landlord is bound to accept it. The proper

---

3 *Coomber v Howard* (1845) 1 CB 440.
4 *Turner v Allday* (1836) Tyr & GR 819. This rule was not altered by an oral agreement to pay the rent quarterly.
5 2 Roll 450.
6 *Re Aspinall, Aspinall v Aspinall* [1961] Ch 526, [1961] 2 All ER 751.
7 Banking and Financial Dealings Act 1971 s 1.
8 *De Nicholls v Saunders* (1870) LR 5 CP 589.
9 *Re House Property and Investment Co Ltd* [1954] Ch 576 at 586.

place at common law for payment is the land itself, since the rent issues from it, but the contractual aspect of a covenant for rent requires the tenant to pay at any place appointed, or otherwise to seek out the landlord. Payment by post, therefore, is not strictly proper, and unless the tenant is instructed to send the rent by post,[10] any loss is the tenant's. The rent must be paid in lawful currency, and a reservation such as 'yielding and paying' implies payment in cash. A landlord therefore can refuse to accept payment by cheque unless by prior agreement, but if it is accepted, payment is conditional upon it being honoured.[11]

(c) Deductions

A landlord is entitled to his rent in full, minus any deductions specifically authorised by the lease or by statute as are allowed by their nature. Commonly, however, the reservation tends the other way, and reserves the rent free of certain or even all deductions (i e a 'net rent'), which precludes the tenant from deducting sums he would otherwise have been entitled to in the absence of any agreement.[12] In the absence of any agreement to the contrary, or with such an agreement but by way of set-off or counterclaim to an action by the landlord for the full rent, certain sums are allowable against the rent owed by the tenant. They include payments for which the landlord, and not the tenant, is liable, but which are recoverable on the land, such as rent-charges, and the owner's drainage rate, and payments made by the tenant to avoid ouster from the land or distress[13] for the landlord's rent, and payments for repairs.[14] The difference between a right of deduction and a right of set-off is this: the amount of a lawful deduction is *pro tanto* satisfaction of the rent due, and therefore cannot be distrained for; but where payment by a tenant gives a right of set-off, distress can be brought for the full rent, even though if sued for the full rent, the tenant could set off those payments. A strange anomaly, however, arises from the fact that where a deduction is allowed, it is to be treated *pro tanto* as payment of rent: where the tenant by mistake deducts a payment for which under the lease the landlord is not liable, and the landlord gives a receipt showing the deduction, he cannot afterwards recover the difference.[15]

---

10 *Warwicke v Noakes* (1791) Peake 98.
11 *Beevers v Mason* (1978) 37 P & CR 452, CA; and cashed: *Official Solicitor v Thomas* [1986] 2 EGLR 1, CA.
12 *Bradbury v Wright* (1781) 2 Doug KB 624.
13 See Law of Distress Amendment Act 1908 s 3.
14 See *Waters v Weigall* (1795) 6 Term Rep 488.
15 *Waller v Andrews* (1838) 3 M & W 312; *Bramston v Robins* (1826) 4 Bing 11.

(d)   Agreements for reduction of rent

If the landlord promises to accept, for a limited period (or for the residue of the term), without consideration, a reduction or abatement in the rent, equitable promissory estoppel will preclude him from resiling from his promise. Accordingly, where the tenant of premises held under a long lease was unable, owing to war-time conditions, to let profitably, the landlord accepted an annual reduction in rent of £250 from 1941 to 1945. Later, his trustee in bankruptcy claimed the difference between the rent paid during these years and the full rent and failed. However, once the special circumstances of the War had ended, it was held that the original promise was revocable by notice, i e service of the writ.[16] Likewise a defence to an action for rent arrears succeeded to the extent of 12 months' arrears where the tenant held a memorandum signed by the landlord reducing the rent.[17]

The tenant may only invoke equitable promissory estoppel (which overcomes the difficulty that there is no deed)[18] as a defence, based on an express or implied promise of the landlord, intended to be binding, to accept a reduced rent. The tenant must prove that he acted in reliance on the promise – as by not assigning or surrendering the lease.

(e)   Receipt of rent

Clearly, it is advisable to require a receipt for payments in cash, and where payments are frequent, entries in a rent book are in certain respects to be preferred to individual receipts, since they form a proper and complete record of payments under the lease, period by period. The provision of rent books is compulsory, however, only where the rent is paid weekly (Chapter 19).

VI   APPORTIONMENT OF RENT

Apportionment of rent is the proportional division of liability for rent under a lease, as where the landlord's reversion of the land under the lease is split up between several people, e g by assignment of part. Accordingly, the rent is apportioned in respect either of estate, or of time.

---

16   *Central London Property Trust Ltd v High Trees House Ltd* [1947] KB 130, [1946] 1 All ER 256.
17   *Dorkins v Wright* [1983] CLY 1364. After the 12 months expired, the full rent became due and payable.
18   If the agreement for reduction in rent is by deed, then there will be consideration and it will be enforceable at law.

(a)   Apportionment in respect of estate

 (i)   *Severance of the reversion*   Where part of the landlord's reversion is assigned, or his estate is divided between several people, the rent is apportioned between them, but the apportionment is binding on the tenant only with his consent or by order of court.

 (ii)   *Severance of the term*   Where the tenant gives up to the landlord or loses part of his land (e g by surrender, eviction by title paramount, by invasion of the sea[19]) the tenant has a right to a reduction of rent in proportion, not to the amount, but to the value of the land lost. In addition, there are a number of statutory apportionments in the event of compulsory purchase.[20]

 On the other hand, where the tenant has assigned part of his interest at an apportioned rent, he remains liable on covenant for rent in respect of the whole, but may seek contribution (see LPA 1925 s 190(3), (4)).

(b)   Apportionment in respect of time

The position is governed by the Apportionment Act 1870, unless the lease expressly excludes the right of apportionment. The Act does not apply, however, where the rent is expressed to be payable in advance, since the right to receive the whole of it has already accrued.

 (i)   *Section 2* provides that rent and other periodical payments shall 'be considered as accruing from day to day', so that if the tenancy is forfeited, assigned, or otherwise terminated, in the middle of a period, only a proportionate part of the rent for that period will be due.[1]

 (ii)   *Section 3* provides that even though there is an apportionment of rent, liability for the portion payable shall not thereby arise any sooner than it would otherwise have done.

VII   EFFECT OF NON-PAYMENT OF RENT

It may be thought that since payment is an acknowledgement by the tenant of his tenure, the effect of non-payment of rent would be to set up in him a good title to the land by limitation against the landlord. This is not so. On the contrary, the general rule is that during the currency of a lease the tenant cannot acquire title against the landlord; but this will not

---

19   1 Roll Abs 236 (C) 1, 2.
20   E g under the Lands Clauses Consolidation Act 1845; Small Holdings and Allotments Act 1908; Agriculture Act 1947; Leasehold Reform Act 1967.
 1   See *Parry v Robinson-Wyllie Ltd* [1987] 2 EGLR 133 (assignee liable for rent, accordingly, only in post-assignment period).

prevent third parties from doing so. The land must be in the adverse possession of some person in whose favour time may run; in this context it means wrongful receipt of rent by a person wrongfully claiming the reversion.[2]

(a) *Lease in writing* Where the lease is in writing,[3] the tenant himself cannot begin to acquire a good title against his landlord as long as the lease continues; but when it expires, he can. The only effect of non-payment of rent is to bar recovery of each instalment of rent after six years.[4] However, where the rent is £10 p a or more, payment of rent to a third person for 12 years[5] will bar the landlord's title to the reversion against that third person.

(b) *Lease not in writing* Non-payment of rent by a yearly or periodic tenant without a lease in writing, however, for 12 years,[6] will debar his landlord from recovering possession from him. Time begins to run from the end of the first year or other period of the tenancy, and will start to run again after any payment of rent or written acknowledgement.

(c) *Tenancies at will on sufferance* Tenants at will are in a similar position to a yearly tenant without a lease, time beginning to run after the date of determination of the tenancy. In favour of a tenant on sufferance, time begins to run from the commencement of the tenancy.

VIII REMEDIES FOR NON-PAYMENT OF RENT

The landlord has three remedies against the tenant for non-payment of rent. The first is distress on the tenant's goods, followed, ultimately by sale, to pay off any unpaid rent arrears. The second is to sue the tenant on his personal covenant to pay rent. Thirdly, the landlord may try to forfeit the lease for non-payment of rent. In relation to any period after the expiry of the lease, the landlord is entitled to, but must claim separately, compensation for use and occupation, or mesne profits.

1 DISTRESS

Distress is an ancient remedy which is hedged about with a large number of restrictions, both at common law and under statute. Its abolition was

---

2 Limitation Act 1980 s 15(6) and Sch I para 8(3).
3 A rent-book is not a 'lease' in writing; *Moses v Lovegrove* [1952] 2 QB 533, [1952] 1 All ER 1279.
4 Limitation Act 1980 s 19.
5 Ibid, s 15(6) and Sch I para 6.
6 Ibid, s 15(6) and Sch I para 5.

recommended by the Law Commission.[7] Distress may nonetheless have some advantages over other methods of recovery of rent arrears.[8]

Distress entitles the landlord to enter the premises as soon as rent is in arrear and then to take possession of the tenant's goods without legal process, to satisfy the amount of the rent due. If, within five days of the seizure of the goods, the rent remains unpaid, the goods may be sold. Should the landlord himself not act as distrainor, he must employ a certificated bailiff.[9]

The landlord or bailiff may impound the goods, either on the premises or in another place; should the tenant then interfere with the goods he is guilty of pound-breach. The remedy of the landlord is then recapture and a civil action for treble damages.[10] The tenant, however, at the time of distress, must be given a notice of distress by the distrainor;[11] and the distrained goods may thereafter, as was seen, be sold (in the event of continued non-payment of rent) not less than five days after service of a notice of distress.[12]

If a distress is illegal, the tenant may act in one of two ways. First, he may recapture the goods, a process called rescue, but this must be done before they are impounded. Or he may bring a county court action, at any time before sale, in replevin (for return of the goods on his giving security for costs and rent arrears). Neither of these remedies is however available for an irregular or excessive distress (an irregular distress would for instance involve a sale of goods in less than five days; an excessive distress involves taking more goods than are necessary to satisfy the rent arrears). In such cases the landlord is liable for wrongful interference with goods.[13]

Distress is hedged about in other ways. In particular, many goods of the tenant are privileged against distress, i e they cannot be seized at all (absolute privilege) or only if no other goods are available (conditional privilege). For example, at common law, any tenants' fixtures, wild animals, loose money, milk, fruit and things in actual use at the time of the distress, cannot be distrained against at all. Tools and implements of the tenant's trade or profession may not be distrained, nor may certain farm animals (such as sheep or stock which the tenant is fairly paid to feed and pasture) unless there are not other sufficient goods on the premises to satisfy the distress.

---

7   Law Com WP No 9 (1986). In *Abingdon RDC v O'Gorman* [1968] 3 All ER 79 at 82, CA, Lord Denning MR described distress as 'an archaic remedy'.
8   See passim Hill-Smith [1983] Conv 444.
9   See Law of Distress Amendment Act 1888 ss 7 & 8; Distress for Rent Rules 1988, SI 1988/2050.
10   Distress for Rent Act 1689, s 3.
11   Distress for Rent Act 1689. Distress for Rent Rules, supra.
12   Distress for Rent Act 1689 s 1, extended to 15 days by Law of Distress Amendment Act 1888 s 6, following tenant's written request for security and costs.
13   Torts (Interference with Goods) Act 1977 s 1.

Further important restrictions on distress are imposed by statute. In the case of agricultural holdings, for instance, distress must be made within one year of the default.[14] In the case of a dwelling-house which is let on a protected or subject to a statutory tenancy, s 147 of the Rent Act 1977 provides that the leave of the county court is required before any distress may be levied; and even if leave is given, the wide powers of adjournment, staying, suspension or postponement, which govern possession actions against protected or statutory tenants, apply to distress.[15]

Third parties have some protection from distress under the Law of Distress Amendment Act 1908. This relates to the goods of a third party (anyone other than the tenant, such as his spouse or lodger) which are on the premises. The person in question makes a written declaration in the prescribed form[16] on the distraining landlord or bailiff once distress is threatened, to the effect that the tenant has no beneficial interest in the goods and that they are not goods excluded from the act by s 4. An inventory of the goods is required. Service of this declaration renders illegal any future proceedings in distress against the relevant goods, and the third party will have an action for damages against the bailiff, if any, as well as the landlord.[17] The protection of the 1908 Act is not total as there are specific exclusions from it.[18]

Other specific statutory provisions protect against distress particular kinds of goods, for instance, to take just two examples, the stock and machinery of third parties on agricultural holdings[19] and railway rolling stock.[20]

2 ACTIONS FOR RENT AND COMPENSATION

(a) Action for rent

Rent is a debt, and as such is recoverable by an action in contract. The action is based on:

(i) an express covenant in a lease by deed;

---

14 Agricultural Holdings Act 1986, s 16.
15 Rent Act 1977 s 100. Also Housing Act 1988 s 19 (assured tenancies).
16 See also *Lawrence Chemical Co Ltd v Rubenstein* [1982] 1 All ER 653, [1982] 1 WLR 284, CA; also footnote 9, supra.
17 *Lowe v Dorling & Son* [1906] 2 KB 772, CA.
18 Law of Distress Amendment Act 1908 s 4 (e g goods of the tenant's spouse; also goods in reputed ownership of the tenant with the consent of the true owner). See *Perdana Properties Bhd v United Orient Leasing Co Sdn Bhd* [1982] 1 All ER 193, [1981] 1 WLR 1496, PC; if the true owner withdraws consent, e g by withdrawing the tenant's continued right to possession, s 4 will not apply and the goods will thereafter be privileged against distress.
19 Agricultural Holdings Act 1986 s 18.
20 Railway Rolling Stock Protection Act 1872.

(ii) an express agreement in a simple contract (in writing or by parol); or,

(iii) an agreement implied by law from the conduct of the parties, as for example, where the words 'yielding up and paying' are relied upon in the *habendum*, in the absence of a *reddendum*.

1   *The action*   The action is for a debt, and therefore the plaintiff is suing for the specific sum agreed to be paid.

2   *The parties*   The action is basically an action in contract; but by virtue of privity of estate, assignees of the reversion and of the lease can sue and be sued respectively upon the covenant; as may a surety of the tenant by the original landlord.[1]

3   *Jurisdiction*   The appropriate court will be the county court if the claim does not exceed £5,000,[2] otherwise, the High Court. At any stage in proceedings, the county court may itself, or on the application of either party, transfer the whole or part of proceedings to the High Court if, inter alia, the court considers that some important question of law or fact is likely to arise.[3]

4   *The claim*   The action is commenced by writ on originating summons in the High Court and by summons in the county court. The statement of claim must set out the facts that will give the plaintiff a right of action. It need not show title, since the tenant cannot deny it, but it must allege the existence of the letting, the standing of the defendant (e g whether he is the tenant, or assignee), the substance of the obligation, the sum claimed, and the performance of a condition precedent, if any. Under RSC Ord 14 a summary procedure is available against the tenant and the landlord may include as part of his claim thereunder a claim for interim payments of rent under Ord 29 (r 10). Leave to defend, conditional or unconditional, may be given and if so, the procedure is as for an ordinary action.[4]

5   *Defences*   In answer to a claim for rent, the tenant may allege that:

(a) the landlord's title has ceased since the demise (e g by his assignment of the reversion expressly or by operation of law);

(b) he has been evicted by the landlord or by title paramount;

(c) the letting was known to be for illegal or immoral purposes, and is therefore void;

---

1   *Associated Dairies Ltd v Pierce* (1982) 265 Estates Gazette 127, CA (mesne profits).

2   And even if it does, where the tenancy is a statutory tenancy under the Rent Act 1977; *Woolfe v Clarkson* [1950] 2 All ER 529.

3   County Courts Act 1984 s 42.

4   If there is an arguable case for relief to be tried, leave will be granted: *Central Street Properties Ltd v Mansbrook Rudd & Co Ltd* [1986] 2 EGLR 33.

(d) the deed itself is void, together with any covenants contained in it;

(e) the rent due has been paid or tendered;[5]

(f) goods taken in distress have been sold in satisfaction of the arrears or remain impounded;

(g) the landlord is estopped from claiming the contractual rent;

(h) the claim is barred by s 19 of the Limitation Act 1980 (i e on the expiration of six years after the rent became due, or after any acknowledgment in writing,[6] whichever is the later);

(i) a frustrating event which is so serious that it destroys the term and the foundation of the claim for rent.[7]

He may on the other hand admit the claim, and plead a counterclaim or set-off.

6 *Interest* In the absence of an express agreement to pay interest on rent overdue, the court may, if it thinks fit, award interest on the arrears from the day the rent fell due to the date of judgment.[8] Interest is calculated from the date when each payment of rent fell due – and may be recovered from the original lessees despite a subsequent assignment of the term.[9]

(b) Action for compensation for use and occupation

At common law, a landlord was entitled to recover damages from a tenant who occupied premises in circumstances which would preclude an action for rent (i e in the absence of a covenant or any express agreement to pay rent; with his permission or on sufferance) based on an implied promise by the tenant to pay reasonable compensation for the landlord's loss of use of the premises by reason of his occupation. S 14 of the Distress for Rent Act 1737, provides that the action will still lie notwithstanding that a demise in writing or by parol (but not by deed) is proved, and that any express agreement as to rent is to be taken as evidence of the *quantum* of damages awarded.

1 *The action* The action can be used as an alternative to an action for rent, but this is unnecessary. In practice, its use is confined to cases where an action for rent would not be maintainable, as where the

---

5 *Morris Gore v Westbourne Hill Properties Ltd* (1982) 262 Estates Gazette 768, CA.

6 Payment of part of the rent does not extend the period for claiming the remainder then due: Limitation Act 190 s 29(6).

7 *National Carriers Ltd v Panalpina (Northern) Ltd* [1981] AC 675, [1981] 1 All ER 161, HL.

8 Law Reform (Miscellaneous Provisions) Act 1934 s 3.

9 *Allied London Investments Ltd v Hambro Life Assurance Ltd* (1984) 270 Estates Gazette 948.

tenant has gone into occupation without an express agreement as to rent, or holds over after the expiry of his tenancy in circumstances which do not give rise to a tenancy from year to year. It is maintainable against a tenant who goes into occupation under an unexecuted lease or a lease delivered as an escrow but before it can take effect,[10] and against a purchaser who goes into possession pending completion.[11] It cannot be maintained (unlike an action for rent) against a tenant who has never entered,[12] nor against a tenant after eviction or the commencement of proceedings for the recovery of possession[13] (e g on the expiry of the lease, for forfeiture, etc). The action for damages for occupation after an action for possession has been commenced is an action for mesne profits.

2 *Measure of damages*   By the very nature of the action the landlord's claim is for an unliquidated sum to be fixed by the court having regard to the letting value it puts upon the premises.[14] By s 14 of the Distress for Rent Act 1737, any express agreement as to rent may be used in evidence of the question of damages. Where the claim is based on holding over, the rent under the previous tenancy is evidence of its rental value, but is not conclusive, since it is open to the landlord to show a change of circumstances tending to increase the rental value.[15]

3 *Defences*   It is a good defence to an action for use and occupation for the tenant to show that:

(a) the plaintiff's title ceased after the tenant went into occupation;

(b) the claim has been satisfied or is statute-barred;

(c) his occupation was adverse to the plaintiff.

(c) Action for mesne profits

As has been stated above, a landlord cannot sue for damages for use and occupation once he has commenced proceedings in ejectment, since he is considered as having thereby elected to treat the tenant as a trespasser. Instead, his remedy is an action for mesne profits, from that date on which he commenced proceedings (i e the date on which he served the writ),[16] or for double value under the Landlord and Tenant Act 1730. In either case, he may sue for any rent owed in respect of any period before service of the writ.

---

10 *Gudgen v Besset* (1856) 6 E & B 986.
11 *Howard v Shaw* (1841) 8 M & W 118.
12 *Lowe v Ross* (1850) 5 Exch 553.
13 *Birch v Wright* (1786) 1 Term Rep 378.
14 *Tomlinson v Day* (1821) 2 Brod & Bing 680.
15 *Alford v Vickery* (1842) Car & M 280.
16 *Elliott v Boynton* [1924] 1 Ch 236; *Associated Deliveries Ltd v Harrison* (1984) 50 P & CR 91, CA.

In an action for mesne profits, damages may be claimed up to the date of judgment and also up to the date of the order for possession. The measure of damages is usually the market value of the premises, and the rent under the determined tenancy will be taken as evidence of market value, if no actual loss is shown.[17]

(d) Statutory duty of landlords to notify tenants

Under Part VI of the Landlord and Tenant Act 1987,[18] a landlord of premises consisting of or including a dwelling[19] must comply with ss 47 and 48 of the 1987 Act.

Section 47(1) requires that any demand for rent or other sums payable to the landlord under the tenancy, such as service charges, must contain the landlord's name and address, and, if this is not in England and Wales, an address in England and Wales at which notices (including those in proceedings) may be served on the landlord.

If this is not done, or any notice does not contain the relevant information, any part of the amount demanded which consists of a service charge is to be treated for all purposes as not being due from the tenant to the landlord, until compliance (s 47(2)). The only exception to this is where there is a receiver or manager currently appointed, whose functions include receipt of service charges (s 47(3)).

Section 48(1) requires a landlord who lets any dwelling to furnish the tenant with an address in England and Wales at which notices (including notices in proceedings) may be served on him by the tenant. If this is not complied with, any rent or service charge otherwise due from the tenant to the landlord is treated for all purposes as not being due from the tenant to the landlord (s 48(2)). This does not apply where there is an appointment of a receiver or manager whose functions include receipt of rent or service charges (s 48(3)).

There is no prescribed form for a s 48 notice and any relevant landlord is obliged to serve one on the tenant before he can enforce recovery of rent or service charge arrears. It makes no difference that the tenancy does not provide expressly for any written demand.

As regards service by a tenant to whom ss 47 and 48 apply of a notice on the landlord, s 196 of the Law of Property Act 1925 is amended, so as to include an address furnished by the landlord under s 48 or that last furnished under s 47 (s 49).

---

17 Cf *Swordheath Properties Ltd v Tabet* [1979] 1 All ER 240, [1979] 1 WLR 285, CA.
18 In force on 1 February 1988: Landlord and Tenant Act 1987 (Commencement No 1) Order 1987 SI 1987/2177.
19 Lettings to which Part II of the Landlord and Tenant Act 1954 applies are excluded (s 46(1)).

3 FORFEITURE

As we have seen above, a landlord cannot distrain *and* exercise a right of re-entry for forfeiture for non-payment of rent, but he may, and usually does, join an action for arrears in an action for forfeiture. Unlike the right of distress and the right of action on the covenant to pay rent, which arise automatically whenever rent falls into arrear, a right of re-entry for forfeiture, arises *only* where such a right is expressly reserved in the lease, with one exception,[20] or where payment of rent is made a condition. This section deals with those aspects of re-entry and forfeiture which are peculiar to their exercise for non-payment of rent.

1 *Formal demand for rent*   It is important to note at the outset that s 146(1) of the Law of Property Act 1925, does not apply to the exercise of a right of re-entry for non-payment of rent. However, even though payment of rent is expressed as a condition, the right of re-entry does not arise at common law unless a formal demand for the rent has properly been made, unless this requirement has been dispensed with[1] (see below). The rules for a formal demand are exacting. The demand must be made:

(a) by the landlord or his duly authorised agent;
(b) at the place specified in the lease for payment, or otherwise on the land (i e at the front door of a dwelling-house);
(c) before and until sunset;
(d) on the last day for payment; and,
(e) *only* for the sum due in respect of the last period.

2 *Formal demand dispensed with*   A formal demand required by the common law is dispensed with by s 210 of the Common Law Procedure Act 1852, or, as is invariably the case, by express agreement in the lease.

(a) *Section 210 of the Common Law Procedure Act 1852*, renders unnecessary a formal demand for rent prior to the exercise of a right of re-entry
  (i)   between landlord and tenant;
  (ii) when one half-year's rent is in arrear;
  (iii) where no sufficient distress is to be found on the premises to pay off all the arrears due; and,
  (iv) where the landlord has reserved the right to re-enter and determine the lease for non-payment of rent.

Section 210 does not require an actual distress, but it would seem

---

20 Under Distress for Rent Act 1737 s 16.
1   *Doe d Harris v Masters* (1824) 2 B & C 490; cf *Treseder-Griffin v Co-operative Insurance Society Ltd* [1956] 2 QB 127 at 143, CA.

that a landlord will not waive his right to re-enter under the Act by levying distress.[2]

(b) In view of the strict requirements as to a formal demand at Common Law, leases should, and invariably do, expressly dispense with the need for it. Express dispensation is effective simply by words such as "without demand".

4 RELIEF AGAINST FORFEITURE[3]

Relief against forfeiture in equity has long been granted to tenants in actions for rent arrears or non-payment of rent, the basis of relief being that the landlord's right of re-entry is merely security for the observance by the tenant of his covenant to pay rent.

There are two sets of rules governing relief. One set applies to High Court actions, and is based on the old equitable jurisdiction of the Court of Chancery to grant relief. The continuing existence of these rules is confirmed by s 38 of the Supreme Court Act 1981. The grounds of relief are based on the former practice of the old Court of Chancery and this fundamentally differentiates relief against forfeiture in the High Court from all other forms of relief.[4] Applications by the tenant to the High Court for relief must by statute be made within six months of the landlord's actual entry under a court order.[5] Another set of rules applies to county court actions, these applying where the rateable value of the premises does not exceed £1,000.[6] They are totally different from the High Court rules because their basis is suspended orders for possession, as will appear.

Relief in the High Court

1 *Automatic stay* If the tenant pays into court or to the landlord at any time, before judgment is given,[7] all the rent arrears and costs, he obtains an automatic stay on all proceedings.[8] This applies only if at

---

2 *Brewar d Lord Onslow v Eaton* (1783) 3 Doug KB 230.
3 For a critique of the present rules see Law Com No 142 especially paras 3.11–3.13. The reform proposals would abolish the separate rules relating to rent.
4 *Belgravia Insurance Co v Meah* [1964] 1 QB 436, [1963] 3 All ER 828, CA.
5 Common Law Procedure Act 1852, s 210.
6 In the case of High Court *and* county court actions, note that forfeiture at common law will not necessarily destroy the tenant's right to remain in occupation and that further procedures, under Rent Act 1977 s 98 and Sch 15 or Housing Act 1988 Part I and Sch 2 will be required to achieve that result. The two claims should be heard by the same court: *Peachey Property Corpn v Robinson* [1967] 2 QB 543, [1966] 2 All ER 981, CA.
7 See *Gill v Lewis* [1956] 2 QB 1, [1956] 1 All ER 844, CA.
8 Common Law Procedure Act 1852 s 212.

least half a year's rent is in arrear.[9] Where this is not so, then relief is based on the equity jurisdiction, as it is where there is peaceable re-entry and hence no proceedings by writ.[10]

2   *Applications for relief*   The court's power to grant or refuse relief is discretionary but only exceptionally[11] will relief be refused (assuming the application is within the six-month time-limit) where all the rent and costs have been paid before judgment or if the tenant or other applicant for relief (such as an underlessee or mortgagee[12]) pays off the rent arrears, costs and undertakes, where relevant, to perform the covenants in the lease.[13] The arrears, and costs must be paid within a time-limit set by the court (which no doubt in suitable cases may be extended after application).[14] On the other hand, where it is inequitable to grant relief, then it will be refused, as where the landlord, after judgment for possession, had reasonably re-let the premises to a third party.[15] The effect of relief, if given, is that no forfeiture is deemed to have taken place.[16] The power to grant relief cannot be excluded by a term in the lease which operates as a disguised forfeiture clause.[17]

3   *Interim payments*   When a landlord issues a writ claiming forfeiture for non-payment of rent and the tenant remains in occupation, the High Court and county court have power to award interim payments under RSC Ord 29 r 10.

Relief in the county court

The county court's jurisdiction to grant relief is under s 138 of the County Courts Act 1984 as amended. If the tenant pays rent arrears into court not less than five days before the return day, s 138(2) entitles him to automatic relief.[18] If this is not done, then the jurisdiction of the

---

9   *Standard Pattern Co Ltd v Ivey* [1962] Ch 432, [1962] 1 All ER 452.

10   *Thatcher v C H Pearce & Sons (Contractors) Ltd* [1968] 1 WLR 748 (no time limit applies in this case but a rough limit of six months applies under *laches*).

11   *Public Trustee v Westbrook* [1965] 3 All ER 398, [1965] 1 WLR 1160, CA.

12   Who apply under Law of Property Act 1925 s 146(4), and who are entitled to notification of forfeiture proceedings by the landlord under RSC Ord 6 r 2 as amended. In *Ladup Ltd v Williams & Glyns' Bank plc* [1985] 2 All ER 577, [1985] 1 WLR 851, it was held that mortgagees etc could apply outside the statute in certain cases – say deliberate non-notification by the landlord.

13   *Belgravia Insurance Co v Meah*, supra; *Re Brompton Securities Ltd (No 2)* [1988] 3 All ER 677.

14   *Barton, Thompson & Co v Stapling Machines Co* [1966] Ch 499, [1966] 2 All ER 222.

15   *Silverman v AFCO (UK) Ltd* [1988] 1 EGLR 51, CA, applying *Stanhope v Hawarth* (1886) 3 TLR 34, CA.

16   Supreme Court Act 1981 s 38(2); *Dendy v Evans* [1910] 1 KB 263, CA.

17   *Richard Clarke & Co Ltd v Widnall* [1976] 3 All ER 301, [1976] 1 WLR 845, CA.

18   There is no minimum six-month limit on automatic relief as in the High Court.

county court is based on suspended possession orders. By s 138(3), if the court is satisfied that the landlord is entitled to forfeit, it must order possession to be given not less than four weeks from the date of the order, the length of the suspension being at the court's discretion. If during the suspension period the tenant pays into court all the arrears and costs then the order does not take effect and then he gets automatic relief. The court has a discretion to extend the suspension period – at any time before (but not after) possession is recovered by the landlord (s 138(4)). If within this extended period the tenant pays off the rent arrears and costs then, again, he gets automatic relief (s 138(5)).

If the tenant fails during the original and any extended period of suspension to pay off all the rent arrears and costs, then by s 138(7) the order will be enforced and so long as it is unreversed the tenant will be barred from all relief. This means just that: where a tenant's lease was forfeited for service charges rent arrears of £299, and the order was enforced, it was held that she could not, in view of the plain language of s 138(7), obtain any relief either in the county court, where the order was made, or in the High Court.[19]

Underlessees and mortgagees may apply in the county court for relief against forfeiture of a lease under s 146(4) of the Law of Property Act 1925.[20]

---

19 *Di Palma v Victoria Square Property Ltd* [1986] Ch 150, [1985] 2 All ER 676, CA.
20 They are entitled to notification of the proceedings by the landlord under CCR Ord 6 r 3 as amended.

Chapter 9

Repairing obligations[1]

In this Chapter, the repairing obligations of both landlord and tenant are considered, and the remedies available to each party to enforce the other's repairing obligations are also dealt with. The Chapter concludes with an account of the procedures available to a local authority to compel repairs to unfit houses and to deal with nuisances arising from disrepair.

1   LANDLORD'S IMPLIED WARRANTIES AS TO FITNESS AND SUITABILITY AND IMPLIED REPAIRING OBLIGATIONS

General principles

There was, at one time, a rule of law that there could be no implied covenant by a landlord of any premises or land, that he would do any repairs, and also that the landlord did not impliedly warrant that the premises or land were fit for human habitation, occupation or cultivation, or for any other purpose.[2] The landlord was, therefore, held to be under no implied obligation to put premises into repair at the commencement of a tenancy, nor under any implied obligation to keep them in repair during the term.[3]

Recently, on special facts, it has been held that there is no rule of law to the effect that the landlord cannot be under any implied repairing obligations, and that, if business efficacy required it, the court would imply repairing obligations on ordinary principles; accordingly, the

---

1   See passim *West's Law of Dilapidations* (9th edn 1988) P F Smith, Estates Gazette Ltd.

2   *Woodfall* 1–1465; *Hart v Windsor* (1844) 12 M & W 68; *Sutton v Temple* (1843) 12 M & W 52; *Duke of Westminster v Guild* [1985] QB 688, [1984] 3 All ER 144, CA; *Tennant Radiant Heat Ltd v Warrington Corpn* [1988] 1 EGLR 41 at 43, CA.

3   See *Gott v Gandy* (1853) 2 E & B 845; *Sleafer v Lambeth Borough Council* [1960] 1 QB 43, [1959] 3 All ER 378, CA, and cases cited above.

landlord of a statutory periodic tenant was held to be impliedly liable to carry out structural and exterior repairs to an old house in very poor condition.[4] Despite this, it is thought that if a lease makes apparently comprehensive provision about repairs and dilapidations, there will be no room for any implied repairing obligations.[5]

There are, however, a number of instances, which cannot be regarded as closed, where a repairing obligation or an obligation as to fitness or suitability is either implied against a landlord or imposed by statute or tort on him, and these are as follows.[6]

Implied obligations of landlord

1 *Houses in the course of erection* In a lease of a dwelling-house which is still in the course of erection at the date of the lease, there is an implied warranty that it will be built with proper materials in a workmanlike manner, and that when it is completed, it will be fit for human habitation.[7]

2 *Landlord builder* If the landlord builds an unfurnished dwelling-house or flat to his own design and specification (where he is a local authority for instance), he will be liable in negligence for dangerous defects causing personal injury to occupiers – as where a tenant was injured by a defective glass panel. The scope of the duty is to see that the occupiers, such as the tenant and his family, are reasonably safe from personal injury due to dangerous defects; and the duty is not avoided by the mere fact that the person to whom it is owed knows of the danger unless it would be reasonable to expect him to remove or avoid it.[8] If the landlord is not the builder then there remains no liability at common law for dangerous defects.[9] In such cases, recourse must be had (if any) to the Dangerous Premises Act 1972, discussed in Chapter 10.[10]

---

4   *Barrett v Lounova (1982) Ltd* [1989] 1 All ER 351, CA. The tenancy was first granted in 1941. In such a case, if a similar tenancy is granted on or after 24 October 1961, Landlord and Tenant Act 1985, s 11 would apply on the facts – see section III of this Chapter; P F Smith [1988] Conv 448.

5   *Duke of Westminster v Guild,* supra; also *Gordon and Teixeira v Selico Co Ltd* [1986] 1 EGLR 71 at 76, CA.

6   For Landlord and Tenant Act 1985 s 11, see section III of this Chapter.

7   *Perry v Sharon Development Co Ltd* [1937] 4 All ER 390, CA.

8   *Rimmer v Liverpool City Council* [1985] QB 1, [1984] 1 All ER 930, CA. The defective glass panel was standard-design and built-in: so the tenant could not remove or avoid it.

9   *Cavalier v Pope* [1906] AC 428, HL; *McNerny v Lambeth London Borough Council* [1988] EGCS 169, CA.

10 The Defective Premises Act came into force on 1 January 1974.

3   *Furnished houses*   There is an implied condition in a tenancy of a furnished house or flat that the premises shall be fit for habitation at the commencement of the tenancy.[11] If on the day the tenancy commences, the premises are not fit for human habitation, the tenant may repudiate the lease – or he may elect to keep the lease and sue for damages.[12] The implied condition is very limited. It does not oblige the landlord to keep the premises fit for human habitation during the tenancy.[13] Infestation with bugs,[14] and defective drainage,[15] are examples of breaches of this implied condition.

4   *Statute*   In the case of any letting of a house[16] on or after 6 July 1957[17] at a rent[18] not exceeding £80 p a in London and £52 p a elsewhere, statute implies conditions and undertakings by the landlord.[19] Section 8(2) of the Landlord and Tenant Act 1985 implies a condition that the house is at the commencement of the tenancy, and an undertaking that the house will be kept by the landlord during the tenancy, fit for human habitation. This applies notwithstanding any stipulation to the contrary (s 8(1)). However, in the case of a lease for three years or more, which is not determinable at the option of either party before the expiration of three years, and upon terms that the premises be put by the tenant into a condition reasonably fit for human habitation, section 8 does not apply (s 8(5)). The landlord, or a person authorised by him in writing, has a right on giving 24 hours' written notice to the tenant or occupier, to enter the premises at reasonable times of the day to view their state and condition (s 8(2)).

In determining for the purposes of s 8 whether a house is unfit for human habitation, s 10 directs that regard is to be had to its condition in respect of the following matters: repair, stability, freedom from damp, internal arrangement, natural lighting, ventilation, water supply, drainage and sanitary conveniences and facilities for preparation and cooking of food and for the disposal of waste water. The house is to be regarded as unfit for human habitation if, and only if, it is so far defective

---

11   *Smith v Marrable* (1843) 11 M & W 5; *Collins v Hopkins* [1923] 2 KB 617.
12   *Wilson v Finch Hatton* (1877) 2 Ex D 336.
13   *Sarson v Roberts* [1895] 2 QB 395, CA.
14   *Smith v Marrable*, supra.
15   *Wilson v Finch Hatton*, supra; also *Collins v Hopkins* [1923] 2 KB 617 (previous occupant infected with TB).
16   Includes a part of a house and any yard, garden and appurtenances belonging to the house or usually enjoyed with it (s 8(6)).
17   For pre-6 July 1957 rent figures see s 8(4).
18   I e the contractual rent whether or not inclusive of rates.
19   By s 9, contracts of employment of agricultural employees are made subject to the same conditions and undertaking in relation to their houses, if provided as part of their remuneration.

in one or more of those matters that it is not reasonably suitable for occupation in that condition.

The standard imposed by these provisions is low and their scope is narrow. In any case it has been judicially noted that the provisions, by reason of the effect of inflation on the low rental limits, must nowadays have remarkably little application.[20] The landlord's duty is less than an obligation to keep in good tenantable repair and was described as requiring that the house be decently fit for human beings to live in.[1] Repairs over and above that obligation may validly be cast on the tenant. The obligations imposed by s 8 do not apply to any common user parts of the premises. The landlord is not in breach of his obligations unless and until he has notice of the disrepair from the tenant or a third party such as his rent collector or employee and he fails within a reasonable time thereafter to remedy the condition in question.[2] The landlord is not liable if he proves that the house is incapable of being rendered fit for human habitation at reasonable expense.[3]

5 *Common parts* In the case of lettings of blocks of residential flats, where the landlord retains possession and control of the common parts, such as rubbish chutes, common stairways and the like, there is implied against the landlord (in the absence of express provision in the lease) an obligation to keep the common parts in repair. The obligation is limited to taking reasonable care in all the circumstances to repair and maintain the common parts and is not absolute: where therefore the lifts failed and rubbish chutes became blocked due partly to vandalism, the landlords were held not to have broken their implied covenant.[4] It has been stated, obiter, that this exception is limited to high-rise blocks of residential flats and comparable special cases.[5]

6 *Correlative obligations* Where the tenant of an old house let on a periodic tenancy was under an express obligation to keep the inside in good repair, it was held that, to make it possible for him to perform that obligation, the landlord was under an implied obligation to keep the structure and exterior in repair.[6]

---

20 *Quick v Taff-Ely Borough Council* [1986] QB 809 at 817, [1985] 3 All ER 321 at 324, CA.
1 *Jones v Geen* [1925] 1 KB 659. Also *Summers v Salford Corpn* [1943] AC 283, [1943] 1 All ER 68, HL.
2 *Morgan v Liverpool Corpn* [1927] 2 KB 131, CA; *O'Brien v Robinson* [1973] AC 912, [1973] 1 All ER 583, HL; *McGreal v Wake* (1984) 128 Sol Jo 116, CA; *Dinefwr Borough Council v Jones* [1987] 2 EGLR 58, CA.
3 *Buswell v Goodwin* [1971] 1 All ER 418, [1971] 1 WLR 92, CA.
4 *Liverpool City Council v Irwin* [1977] AC 239, [1976] 2 All ER 39, HL.
5 *Duke of Westminster v Guild* [1985] QB 688, [1984] 3 All ER 144, CA.
6 *Barrett v Lounova (1982) Ltd*, supra.

7 *Landlord retains adjoining premises*   If the landlord retains part of premises, and lets part to the tenant, he may be liable to the latter in tort if a disrepair on the landlord's part of the premises causes damage to the tenant's part.[7]

8 *Licensor and licensee*   For the sake of completeness, note that as between licensor and licensee, it was held that the licensor of a new industrial unit gave an implied warranty of suitability and of soundness of construction to the licensee, for breach of which he was liable in damages.[8] If business efficacy does not warrant an implied term as to fitness, as where the premises were a 100-year-old oven, no term will be implied.[9]

II   TENANT'S IMPLIED OBLIGATIONS TO REPAIR

1   WASTE

Meaning of waste

The obligations of a tenant, where the lease or tenancy contains no express obligations with regard to repair or maintenance of the demised premises, are based on the tenant's implied obligation to use the premises in a tenant-like manner (discussed below) and upon his implied duty not to commit waste.

A tenant commits waste if he causes, by act or omission, any lasting alteration to the land or premises to the prejudice of the reversioner, by way of damage, destruction, addition, improvement or neglect. The obligation not to commit waste is founded in tort; it is independent of any contract express or implied. Liability for waste, despite what was said above, is therefore unaffected by express covenants to repair, to re-instate, or against structural alterations in the lease. Accordingly, if the landlord has an express covenant which applies to the damage, he may elect whether to sue in contract on the covenant, or in waste (an action in tort).[10]

Nonetheless, where there is an express covenant for alterations (for instance) the landlord cannot give a licence to break the covenant and then sue for damages for waste. On the other hand an injunction will be

---

7   *Tennant Radiant Heat Ltd v Warrington Development Corporation*, supra; also *Gordon v Selico Co Ltd*, supra.
8   *Wettern Electric Ltd v Welsh Development Agency* [1983] QB 796, [1983] 2 All ER 629; J Martin [1983] Conv 319.
9   *Morris-Thomas v Petticoat Lane Rentals Ltd* (1986) 53 P & CR 238, CA.
10 *Mancetter Developments Ltd v Garmanson Ltd* [1986] QB 1212, [1986] 1 All ER 449, CA.

granted to restrain acts of ameliorating waste, which would amount to a breach of express covenant or to restrain substantial alterations in the character of the property[11] or the conversion of a house into a shop,[12] and an injunction may be granted to restrain further acts of waste, coupled with an award of damages to compensate the reversioner for past acts of waste.[13] No injunction will be granted if the acts of waste are too trivial to warrant the remedy.[14] The tenant is entitled to remove tenants' trade fixtures after the termination of his lease and before quitting; but it is part and parcel of his right to do so that, if the building is left exposed to the weather, because the removal of the fixtures leaves holes in the building, the tenant is bound to make good the damage to the fabric of the building by in-filling the holes: if he fails to do this, he will be liable in voluntary waste, as will any occupier of the premises who buys the fixtures from the tenant.[15] However, the user of a building, apparently reasonably and properly, for the purpose it was intended to be let, is not waste.[16]

There are various types of waste. *Voluntary waste* is committed by any act causing damage, such as ploughing up pasture, felling or maiming trees or shrubs, negligently or wilfully damaging or destroying buildings,[17] removing tenants' trade fixtures and leaving the building concerned exposed to the weather,[18] or altering or converting premises.

Ameliorating or meliorating waste is a form of voluntary waste which improves the value of the land, buildings or premises, such as by building on land or extending an existing building. Only if substantial damage is proved will an injunction be awarded in such a case.[19]

Permissive waste is based on negligence and omission, such as by allowing a building to fall down for want of necessary repairs, but if a house is in ruins at the start of a lease, e g it has no roof, it is not permissive waste to let it fall down, but it would be different if the tenant pulled down the house.[20] To leave land uncultivated is not waste at common law.[1]

---

11 *Countess of Shrewsbury's Case* (1600) 5 Co Rep 13b.
12 *Marsden v Edward Heyes Ltd* [1927] 2 KB 1, CA.
13 *West Ham Central Charity Board v East London Waterworks Co* [1900] 1 Ch 624.
14 *Grand Canal Co v M'Namee* (1891) 29 LR IR 131 (IRCA).
15 *Mancetter Developments Ltd v Garmanson Ltd*, supra. A director of the occupier , a company, was held personally liable in waste for having procured the removal of the fixtures by the occupier, which was in liquidation.
16 *Manchester Bonded Warehouse Co v Carr* (1880) 5 CPD 507.
17 *Cole v Green* (1672) 1 Lev 309. Also overloading the floor of premises: see *Manchester Bonded Warehouse Co v Carr*, supra.
18 *Mancetter Developments Ltd v Garmanson Ltd*, supra.
19 *Doherty v Allman* (1878) 3 App Cas 709 at 722, HL; *Meux v Cobley* [1892] 2 Ch 253.
20 Co Litt 53a.
 1 *Hutton v Warren* (1836) 1 M & W 466. It may be bad husbandry.

Liability of various types of tenant for waste

Tenants for a term certain are liable both for voluntary and for permissive waste.[2] Such tenants must, even in the absence of express covenant, carry out such repairs as will keep the premises in as good a state of repair as at the outset of the tenancy, subject to allowances for changes due to ageing and reasonable user.

A periodic tenant is liable for voluntary but not for permissive waste.[3] The extent of the liability of a periodic tenant depends on the nature of his tenancy and he is not liable for mere wear and tear of the premises.[4] A weekly tenant is only liable to use the premises in a tenant-like manner.[5]

A tenant at will is not directly liable for voluntary waste but if committed, voluntary waste terminates the tenancy and renders him liable for trespass.[6] A tenant at will is not liable for permissive waste.[7] A tenant on sufferance is liable for voluntary waste,[8] but clearly not for permissive waste.

Defences to an action for waste

It is a good defence to an action for waste to show:

1   The damage resulted from the ordinary reasonable and proper use of the premises.[9]
2   The damage was caused by an Act of God, such as floods or lightning, or fire.[10]
3   Where the claim is that wood and timber have been cut, the tenant was entitled to do so by reason of his common-law right to estovers.[11]

Remedies for waste

Reference should be made to the earlier discussion. Two further additional points must be made.

---

2   2 Co Inst 145 – Coke's interpretation of the Statute of Marlborough 1267, accepted in *Yellowly v Gower* (1855) 11 Exch 274.
3   *Torriano v Young* (1833) 6 C & P 8.
4   Ibid.
5   *Warren v Keen* [1954] 1 QB 15, [1953] 2 All ER 1118, CA.
6   *Countess of Shrewsbury's Case* (1600) 5 Co Rep 13b.
7   *Harnett v Maitland* (1847) 16 M & W 257.
8   *Burchell v Hornsby* (1808) 1 Camp 360.
9   *Manchester Bonded Warehouse Co v Carr*, supra.
10   *Woodfall* 1–1516.
11   I e the right to take reasonable quantities of wood and timber for (a) repairing the house or burning in it (house-bote); (b) making and repairing agricultural implements (plough-bote); or repairing fences (hay-bote).

1   *Damages*   The measure of damages is the loss of value to the reversion.[12] This may be the depreciation in the selling value of the reversioner's interest. It may be the cost of making good the injury or damage to the building or premises or land.[13] If damages are nominal then judgment will, it seems, be given for the defendant.[14] The fact that the lease has expired is no defence,[15] and if the tenant holds over the landlord may still sue for waste.[16]

2   *An injunction*   will be granted to restrain the tenant from acts likely to cause substantial damage, and may be granted, in addition to damages, to restrain the tenant from further acts of waste, but it is not available to restrain permissive waste. See further the previous discussion.

2   TENANT-LIKE USER

Apart from any tortious liability for permissive waste, there is a contractual duty on a periodic tenant, in the absence of any express agreement to the contrary, to use the premises in a tenant-like manner, and to deliver up possession to the landlord at the termination of the tenancy in the same condition as when the tenant took them, fair wear and tear excepted.[17] An express agreement merely to *leave* the premises in repair, however, will not affect the first limb of the implied covenant.[18]

The liability of a weekly tenant was considered in *Warren v Keen*[19] and it appears from this case that a periodic tenant for less than from year to year is not liable for permissive waste, nor to keep the premises wind and watertight, nor for fair wear and tear. It was held that a weekly tenant is bound only to use the premises in a tenant-like manner. For example, if he goes away in winter, he may, if this is reasonable, have to turn off the water and empty the boiler and do minor repairs. The tenant must not wilfully or negligently damage the house – nor must his family or guests, and he must replace any breakages. He is not bound to execute

---

12   *Whitham v Kershaw* (1886) 16 QBD 613, CA.
13   *Mancetter Developments Ltd v Garmanson Ltd*, supra, where the damages award was based on the cost of making good the damage caused to the building by the careless removal of the tenants' fixtures.
14   *Governors of Harrow School v Alderton* (1800) 2 Bos & P 86.
15   *Kinlyside v Thornton* (1776) 2 Wm Bl 1111.
16   *Burchall v Hornsby* (1808) 1 Camp 360.
17   *Marsden v Edward Heyes Ltd* [1927] 2 KB 1, CA.
18   *White v Nicholson* (1842) 4 Man & G 95.
19   [1954] 1 QB 15, [1953] 2 All ER 1118, CA.

any repairs caused by items, such as windows, wearing out or decaying due to old age.

This standard does not compel the tenant to lag internal water-pipes as a precaution against freezing in winter, nor to turn off the stop-cock or drain the water system, unless in the circumstances, such as the severity of the cold, the conditions in the premises and the length of the tenant's absence, it would be reasonable to expect this.[20]

III LANDLORD'S STATUTE-IMPLIED OBLIGATION TO REPAIR DWELLING-HOUSES AND FLATS

Application of 1985 Act

Section 11 of the Landlord and Tenant Act 1985 imposes repairing obligations on landlords of dwelling-houses[1] or flats, where the lease is for a term of less than seven years.[2] Excluded from the 1985 Act are any leases granted on or after 3 October 1980 to a local authority and certain other public sector bodies (s 14(4)).[3] Tenancies to which Part II of the Landlord and Tenant Act 1954 applies are also excluded from the 1985 Act (s 32(2)), as are leases granted to the Crown (s 14(5)).[4]

A lease is caught by the Act where it is determinable at the landlord's option before seven years from the commencement of the term (s 13(2)(b)).[5] If the lease contains a tenant's option to renew which, if exercised, would prolong the lease over seven years, the Act does not apply (s 13(2)(c)). Any part of the term falling before the date of the grant of the lease is ignored in computing the statutory period which starts from the date of the grant or agreement for a lease (s 13(2)(a)).[6] This is to counter artificial backdating of leases with a view to extending the term beyond seven years. If the landlord obtains and accepts a registered rent on the basis that he is responsible for structural repairs under the 1985 Act, when in fact he is not, because the lease is for a term over seven

---

20   *Wycombe Health Authority v Barnett* (1982) 47 P & CR 394, CA (short absence, tenant not liable when pipe burst); cf *Mickel v M'Coard* 1913 SC 896 (long absence in mid-winter, tenant liable).

1   Defined Landlord and Tenant Act 1985 s 16(b).

2   Landlord and Tenant Act 1985 s 13(1). The date of grant must be on or after 24 October 1961.

3   As amended by Housing Act 1988 s 116(3) to exclude housing action trusts.

4   Nor is the Crown bound by the 1985 Act where it is landlord: *Department of Transport v Egoroff* [1986] 1 EGLR 89, CA. This result was criticised by the Law Commission, Law Com No 162 paras 4.28 ff.

5   See *Parker v O'Connor* [1974] 3 All ER 257, [1974] 1 WLR 1160, CA (lease for over seven years with right to determine lease on death of landlord outside this provision as right to determine not unfettered).

6   *Brikom Investments Ltd v Seaford* [1981] 2 All ER 783, [1981] 1 WLR 863, CA.

years, as long as he demands the full rent, or rent arrears, he will be estopped from denying liability under the 1985 Act.[7]

Scope of landlord's duty

Section 11(1) implies a covenant by the landlord:

(a) to keep in repair the structure and exterior of the dwelling-house (including drains, gutters and external pipes) (s 11(1)(a)); and

(b) to keep in repair and proper working order the installations in the dwelling-house for the supply of water, gas and electricity, and for sanitation (including basins, sinks, baths and sanitary conveniences but not, except as aforesaid, fixtures, fittings and appliances for making use of water, gas or electricity) (s 11(1)(b)) and installations for space heating or heating water (s 11(1)(c)).

If the lease is of a flat – or any other 'dwelling-house' forming part only of a building – the duty in s 11(1)(a) extends to any part of the structure or exterior of the building in which the landlord has an estate or interest (s 11(1A)(a)).[8] An example would be the common parts or the roof, if these are not demised to the individual lessees.

In the case of installations, where the landlord lets only part of the building (again for example, where flats are let and the landlord retains the common parts and/or the roof), the landlord must keep in repair and proper working order an installation which directly or indirectly serves the flat, provided that the installation is in part of a building in which the landlord has an estate or interest or which is owned or controlled by him (s 11(1A)(b)).

The extended obligations only apply if the disrepair or failure to maintain affect the tenant's enjoyment of the flat or common parts (s 11(1B)).[9] The landlord has a statutory defence in proceedings if he is able to show that he has no sufficient right to enable him to execute the repairs and he has unsuccessfully used all reasonable endeavours to obtain necessary rights (s 11(3A)).

Any covenant by the tenant for the repair of the premises (including any covenant to put in repair or deliver up in repair, to paint, point or render or to pay money in lieu of repairs by the tenant or on account of repairs by the landlord) is nullified (s 11(4)), in so far as it relates to matters covered by s 11(1).

---

7 *Brikom Investments Ltd v Seaford*, supra, CA.
8 This and also ss 11(1A)(b) and 11(3A), below, were added by Housing Act 1988 s 116(1). These amendments do not apply to leases entered into before 15 January 1989 nor to leases entered into under pre-1988 Act contracts: s 116(4).
9 The definition of 'common parts' in the Landlord and Tenant Act 1987 s 60(1) is expressly applied.

Exceptions

Section 11(2) expressly absolves the landlord from liability:

(a) for repairs attributable to the tenant's failure to use the premises in a tenant-like manner;
(b) to rebuild, or reinstate the premises as a result of damage by fire, tempest, flood or other inevitable accident; or
(c) to repair or maintain any tenants' fixtures.

Section 11(3) provides that in determining the standard of repair required to satisfy the obligations, regard is to be had to the age, character and prospective life of the house and the locality in which it is situated.[10]

The landlord's obligation is coupled with a right of entry, conferred on the landlord or a person authorised by him in writing, to view the state of repair of the premises, exercisable at reasonable times of the day and on giving 24 hours' written notice (s 11(6)).

No contracting out

Covenants by the tenant which purport to apply to the tenant the landlord's statute-implied duties are of no effect (s 11(4)). Accordingly, a covenant by the tenant to pay service charges or money in lieu of repairs is nullified in so far as it relates to landlords' statutory obligations (s 11(5)).[11] Express contracting out of the landlord's statute-implied duties is forbidden by s 12(1), except under the procedure laid down in s 12(2) by way of a joint application to the county court, prior to the granting of the lease. The court may authorise the inclusion in the proposed lease or in an agreement collateral thereto, of agreements excluding or modifying these statutory obligations, if, having regard to the other terms of the lease (such as an adjustment in rent) and in all the circumstances of the case, it is reasonable to do so.

Meaning of structure, exterior and installations

Structure and exterior Steps and a path giving access to the dwelling-house concerned were held to be part of the exterior,[12] but not a path at

---

10 This adopts the standard of repairs in *Proudfoot v Hart* (1890) 25 QBD 42, CA; *Jacquin v Holland* [1960] 1 All ER 402, [1960] 1 WLR 258, CA; also *McClean v Liverpool City Council* [1987] 2 EGLR 56, CA.
11 Or a tenants' covenant to spend a stated sum annually on repairs and decorations, in so far as caught by s 11(1) of the 1985 Act: see *Moss' Empires Ltd v Olympia (Liverpool) Ltd* [1939] AC 544, [1939] 3 All ER 460, HL.
12 *Brown v Liverpool Corpn* [1969] 3 All ER 1345, CA.

the back not giving access.[13] Any part of the structure and exterior of a house which does not form part of the demise to the tenant, such as drains or gutters on adjacent land, lies outside the statute-implied obligations of the landlord and any obligations on him in relation to those parts must be expressly imposed if at all.[14] Unopenable plate-glass windows which are structural fall within s 11,[15] as will any external-facing window which is out of repair.[16]

Installations Sanitary conveniences are 'installations' within s 11(1).[17] Otherwise the term includes such things as pipes, radiators, boilers, or even refrigeration equipment. The landlord is bound to keep installa-tions of the prescribed type in repair 'and proper working order' so that while he is not thereby obliged to lag water-pipes,[18] the landlord must see to it that the installation is in such a condition that it works properly as an installation.[19]

Limits on landlord's duty

1   In the case of lettings of flats, the landlord's obligation was judicially limited. 'Exterior' referred to the exterior of the particular flat and not the exterior of the whole building. The same limit applied to 'structure'.[20] This has been reversed by statute (s 11(1A)). Whether the roof of a top-floor flat falls within the landlord's obligation under s 11(1) is a question of fact: if the ceiling and roof are an inseparable unit then they may well both be within s 11(1).[1] If not, then s 11(1A) of the 1985 Act would require the landlord to keep the roof of a building containing flats, where this was retained by the landlord, in repair in any case.

2   The landlord is not bound to undertake to insert any new thing, by way of an improvement, which was not there before, so that he is not liable under s 11(1) to instal a new damp-proof course where the 'dwelling-house' never had one.[2] Nor is he bound to improve the

---

13   *Hopwood v Cannock Chase District Council* [1975] 1 All ER 796, [1975] 1 WLR 373, CA.

14   *Peters v Prince of Wales Theatre (Birmingham) Ltd* [1943] KB 73, [1942] 2 All ER 533, CA. In the case of leases of *flats*, s 11(1A), above, would appear to reverse this result, in relation to parts of the demised premises retained by the landlord in the same building, though not, presumably, in relation to adjoining land of his.

15   See *Boswell v Crucible Steel Co* [1925] 1 KB 119, CA.

16   See *Quick v Taff-Ely Borough Council* [1986] QB 809, [1985] 3 All ER 321, CA.

17   *Sheldon v West Bromwich Corpn* (1973) 25 P & CR 360, CA.

18   *Wycombe Health Authority v Barnett* (1982) 47 P & CR 394, CA.

19   *Liverpool City Council v Irwin* [1977] AC 239, [1976] 2 All ER 39, HL.

20   *Campden Hill Towers Ltd v Gardner* [1977] QB 823, [1977] 1 All ER 739, CA.

1   *Douglas-Scott v Scorgie* [1984] 1 All ER 1086, [1984] 1 WLR 716, CA.

2   *Wainwright v Leeds City Council* (1984) 82 LGR 657, CA.

design of the house, or to cure inherent defects, provided that the actual items which the tenant is trying to force the landlord to replace are themselves in repair: hence a local authority landlord was held not bound to replace metal windows nor to insulate lintels so as to cure severe condensation in a house where neither item was out of repair.[3]

3   The landlord is not liable under s 11 unless and until he has actual notice – i e notification by letter, or report – of the want of repair, no matter whether the defect is patent or latent, from the tenant personally, or some third party such as a landlord's rent-collector (or agent) or officer or employee.[4] Notice is required even in relation to defects in existence prior to the commencement of the term.[5] If notice is not given then the tenant has no right to damages for any injuries suffered, and moreover, the landlord is only in breach of covenant if, after a reasonable time from his being given notice, he fails to remedy the defect.[6] What is a reasonable time is a question of fact and it will be short in the case of urgently required repairs.[7] A notice which may be a letter or report,[8] need not give details, but it must state in general terms, what is required of the landlord.[9]

On the general meaning and scope of repair, see the next following section of this chapter, which applies to s 11.

IV   CONSTRUCTION OF EXPRESS COVENANT TO REPAIR

(a)   Scope of express covenants

Subject to the effect of statute, as to which see above, the parties are free to negotiate any repairing covenants they please. If none is inserted in the lease, then the question of liability for repairs is regulated either by

---

3   *Quick v Taff-Ely Borough Council*, supra, CA. If, as part of a repair to a damaged item, an inherent design fault is cured, the landlord cannot escape liability for the work, but in this case it was conceded that the house was built according to the requirements of current regulations at the time.

4   *O'Brien v Robinson* [1973] AC 912, [1973] 1 All ER 583, HL; *McGreal v Wake* (1984) 128 Sol Jo 116, CA; *Dinefwr Borough Council v Jones* [1987] 2 EGLR 58, CA.

5   *Uniproducts (Manchester) Ltd v Rose Furnishers Ltd* [1956] 1 All ER 146, [1956] 1 WLR 45.

6   *Porter v Jones* [1942] 2 All ER 570, CA (landlord who failed for eight months from notice to remedy disrepair held liable in damages); also *Morris v Liverpool City Council* [1988] 1 EGLR 47, CA (a few days' wait for emergency repairs not on facts unreasonable).

7   *McGreal v Wake*, supra (eight weeks from repair notice held a reasonable time on facts).

8   E g a valuation report sent to the landlord: *Hall v Howard* [1988] 2 EGLR 75, CA.

9   *Al Hassani v Merrigan* (1987) 20 HLR 238, CA.

the common law (in which case it will be minimal or non-existent), or by statute, or by the law of waste.

It would be usual to expect the tenant to undertake full repairing obligations on a long lease, except in the case of multi-occupied flats and office-blocks, where the scheme may be for the landlord to undertake structural and exterior repairs in return for service charges contributions from individual tenants. In the case of a short residential tenancy the provisions of s 11 of the Landlord and Tenant Act 1985 (above) will very likely apply to the landlord, leaving interior repairs and decorations alone as the liability of the tenant.[10]

Similar general principles apply to the interpretation of landlord's and tenant's express covenants to repair.[11] The court looks at the particular building, at its state at the date of the lease, the terms of the repairing covenant as a whole and then comes to a conclusion as to whether the requisite work is repair.[12] Moreover, as will be seen, no covenant to repair any item operates unless that item is in a condition of disrepair, so that inherent faults in a building cannot be required to be cured by asking a party to replace an item, itself in repair, with another item which will, indirectly, cure the inherent defect.[13] Accordingly, the tenants of an office building who were under a general covenant to repair, were held not liable to waterproof the basement, to protect it from its propensity, caused by an inherent design fault, to allow water penetration, where at the date of the hearing the basement was dry and apparently undamaged by an earlier entry of water: the fact that the basement suffered from an inherent design fault made no difference.[14]

The landlord is not liable under an express covenant to repair unless he has notice of the want of repair and he then fails within a reasonable time thereafter to execute the necessary repairs – see section III of this Chapter, which applies here.

'Repair' connotes, essentially, the renewal of subordinate and damaged parts of the building or premises concerned, so as to leave them, as far as possible, as though not damaged; but in the absence of clear language, an obligation to repair does not include an obligation to

---

10 It may be that, where the landlord is liable, expressly or impliedly, for outside repairs, and the tenant for interior repairs, the latter's obligation only arises if and so far as the landlord complies with his own obligation: see *Barrett v Lounova (1982) Ltd* [1989] 1 All ER 351, CA.

11 *Torrens v Walker* [1906] 2 Ch 166.

12 *Brew Bros v Snax (Ross) Ltd* (1970) 1 QB 612 at 640, [1970] 1 All ER 587 at 602, CA; *McDougall v Easington District Council* (1989) Times, 2 February, CA.

13 *Quick v Taff-Ely Borough Council* [1986] QB 809, [1985] 3 All ER 321, CA.

14 *Post Office v Aquarius Properties Ltd* [1987] 1 All ER 1055, CA, P F Smith [1987] Conv 224. As a result, no-one was liable at that stage to cure the defect.

rebuild the premises as a whole.[15] This matter will be returned to later in this part of this Chapter.

(b) Meaning of particular covenants

To put in repair

A covenant[16] by the tenant to put the demised premises into repair, at the commencement of the lease[17] or within a reasonable time thereafter, which is appropriate where the premises are dilapidated at the date of the demise, may specify a particular standard of repairs. If not, the standard is that required to render the premises fit for the particular purpose for which they are let, and no more.[18] If the premises are dilapidated at the date of the demise, a covenant to keep them in repair impliedly involves a covenant first to put them into repair in any event.[19] In relation both to a covenant to put and to keep in repair, however, if the landlord cannot prove a condition of disrepair, i e deterioration from a former better condition, this particular rule has no application.[20]

To keep in repair

A covenant by the tenant to keep premises in repair presupposes that the premises have first been put by him, where they are dilapidated at the commencement of the term, into repair, and thereafter the tenant must keep them in repair throughout the term.[1] A covenant to keep in repair also necessarily requires the tenant to deliver up the premises in repair at the end of the lease. The standard of repairs is either that laid down in the lease, or that under the general law (below), and if a schedule of condition of the premises at the date of the demise is drawn up, it may be a guide to the required standard.[2] On the interpretation of a covenant to keep in repair, see below.

To leave in repair

A separate obligation may be imposed on the tenant to leave the premises in repair, whether or not an obligation to keep in repair has

---

15 *Post Office v Aquarius Properties Ltd*, supra; *Plough Investments Ltd v Eclipse Radio and TV Services Ltd* [1989] EGCS 1.

16 Such a covenant is imposed on the landlord by Landlord and Tenant Act 1985 s 8, above, in the form of a condition. In this case, exceptionally, the tenant is entitled to repudiate the lease if the condition is not complied with.

17 I e within a reasonable time: *Doe d Pittman v Sutton* (1841) 9 C & P 706.

18 *Belcher v M'Intosh* (1839) 2 Mood & R 186.

19 *Proudfoot v Hart* (1890) 25 QBD 42, CA.

20 *Post Office v Aquarius Properties Ltd* [1987] 1 All ER 1055, CA.

1 *Proudfoot v Hart*, supra; also *Luxmore v Robson* (1818) 1 B & Ald 584.

2 In the case of agricultural holdings, either party may require a record of the condition of the holding to be made at any time: Agricultural Holdings Act 1986 s 22.

been imposed. If only an obligation to leave in repair is imposed, then until the lease ends, the landlord cannot make any claim against the tenant for dilapidations.[3]

Fair wear and tear excepted

An exception for fair wear and tear is sometimes found, particularly in short leases. The basic effect of this exception is to relieve the tenant from liability for disrepair arising both from the normal action of time and the elements, and from the normal and reasonable use of the premises by the tenant for the purpose for which they were let.[4] If the wind and weather have a greater effect on the premises, than if they were sound, the tenant is not liable to repair so as to cure the extra dilapidations so caused.[5] Therefore, an exception for fair wear and tear will excuse the tenant from liability for any repairs required solely due to the passage of time, but not from liability for repairs necessitated as the result of abnormal or extraordinary phenomena such as lightning, storm, flood, earthquake, fire or accident. Nor does this exception excuse the tenant if the damage is caused by his actively injuring the premises by non-normal user, as by overloading a warehouse floor, so that it fell in.[6]

A severe limit has been placed on the scope of a fair wear and tear exception, because otherwise a tenant could claim that it excused him from virtually all liability, where damage originally due to ageing or weathering, led to further, indirect damage to the demised premises. Therefore, an exception for fair wear and tear applies, if at all, only to direct damage which the tenant proves is the result of the reasonable use of the premises and the ordinary operation of natural forces, and the tenant must see to it that the premises do not suffer more than the operation of time and nature would produce.[7] If further, and in that sense indirect, dilapidations result from a cause which may ultimately be traceable back to fair wear and tear, the tenant is not excused by a fair wear and tear exception from doing repairs necessary to cure the indirect damage. If this means that the best or only way to cure the damage permanently is to replace the item which has worn out, then the tenant is bound to replace it as part of his duty to cure indirect damage.[8]

---

3 A breach of a covenant to leave in repair gives a separate cause of action to the landlord, even if the tenant covenanted to keep in repair: *Ebbetts v Conquest* (1900) 16 TLR 320.
4 *Terrell v Murray* (1901) 17 TLR 570; *Gutteridge v Munyard* (1834) 1 Mood & R 334.
5 *Miller v Burt* (1918) 63 Sol Jo 117.
6 *Manchester Bonded Warehouse Co v Carr* (1880) 5 CPD 507.
7 *Gutteridge v Munyard*, supra.
8 *Haskell v Marlow* [1928] 2 KB 45, approved in *Regis Property Co v Dudley* [1959] AC 370, [1958] 3 All ER 491, HL.

Structural repairs

Either party may undertake responsibility for structural repairs. The lease itself may well define the meaning of 'structural', and where s 11 of the Landlord and Tenant Act 1985 applies to the landlord, some authority has built up around the term.[9] It is thought that structural repairs mean any repairs to the essential structure or fabric of the premises, as opposed to the mere provision of equipment.[10] So, repairs to the roof, the main outside walls and load-bearing internal walls would be structural repairs. Other than that, no general definition has really been attempted, except that in one case structural repairs were described as repairs of or to a structure.[11] Some examples on either side may be taken. Large unopenable plate-glass windows fixed into a building were held to be structural within an exception from a tenant's liability to repair,[12] and a dividing wall between premises was held to be structural,[13] as has defective outside plumbing.[14] On the other hand, ordinary wooden frame windows were held not to be part of the main walls.[15]

Any repairs to fittings within the demised premises, and decorative repairs, cannot be structural, though where a central heating system was installed, and connected to the fabric of the house, this was held a structural alteration.[16]

(c)   Standard of repair

The standard of repair required of a landlord or tenant may well be laid down in terms in the covenant to repair. The first point is that it is an obligation to repair, however worded, which the court is looking for.[17] Secondly, the length of the term is a relevant factor, and a lower standard of repairs may be expected, depending on the circumstances, under a short lease as opposed to a long lease. In one case, this went to the extent of holding that a tenant's obligation to keep the interior of a flat held on a three-month protected tenancy obliged the tenant only to use the premises in a tenant-like manner.[18] Thirdly, the principles to be

---

9   See section III of this Chapter, which applies here.
10   See West's *Law of Dilapidations* (9th edn) pp 52–53.
11   *Granada Theatres Ltd v Freehold Investment (Leytonstone) Ltd* [1959] Ch 592, [1959] 2 All ER 176, CA (held that the replacement of a large number of slates was structural since the framework of the premises was interfered with).
12   *Boswell v Crucible Steel Co* [1925] 1 KB 119, CA.
13   *Green v Eales* (1841) 2 QB 225.
14   *Samuels v Abbints Invesments* (1963) 188 Estates Gazette 689; also outside drains; *Howe v Botwood* [1913] 2 KB 387.
15   *Holiday Fellowship v Hereford* [1959] 1 All ER 433, [1959] 1 WLR 211, CA.
16   *Pearlman v Harrow School Governors* [1979] QB 56, [1979] 1 All ER 365, CA.
17   *Anstruther-Gough-Calthorpe v McOscar* [1924] 1 KB 716, CA.
18   *Firstcross Ltd v Teasdale* (1982) 47 P & CR 228.

discussed presuppose that the premises have been proved to be in a state of disrepair, i e to have deteriorated from a former condition of good repair, and the onus of proving any disrepair falls on the party alleging it.[19] Fourthly, the date from which a covenant to repair takes effect is the relevant date for judging the condition of the premises, i e the date of the demise or sub-demise, with the result that a head and sub-lease with apparently identical repairing covenants may not necessarily impose identical standards of repair.[20]

In the case of a short lease, the tenant may be under an obligation to keep the demised premises in 'good tenantable repair', or a similar obligation. General guidance was given as to the meaning of this term in *Proudfoot v Hart*,[1] shortly to be discussed, but, as indicated earlier, the intentions of the parties and the context of the lease prevail where necessary,[2] and it should also be stressed that, in the case of any lease, particularly a long lease, the fact that there may have been a deterioration in the general standards or nature of the neighbourhood surrounding the demised premises affords of itself no defence to an action for breach of covenant to repair.[3] In the case of a long lease, the proper standard, if none is laid down in the lease, is that arrived at by assuming that the tenant has kept the premises in the same condition as a reasonably-minded owner would have kept them in, with full regard to the age of the building, its locality, the class of occupying tenant, and the maintenance of the property in such a way that an average amount of annual repair only was necessary.[4]

In the case of a short lease, the basic rule, as given by *Proudfoot v Hart*[5] is this, given in the context of a letting for three years of a house. 'Good tenantable repair' is such repair as, having regard to the age, character and locality of the house, would make it reasonably fit for the occupation of a reasonably minded tenant of the class who would be likely to take it. It was said that the age of the house must be taken into account because a 200-year-old house would not be expected to be in the same condition as a new house. Its locality was relevant because houses in Grosvenor Square required a wholly different standard of repair to those in Spitalfields. The character of the house was relevant, because repairs appropriate for a palace would not be so for a cottage. If a reasonably-minded incoming tenant would not require redecorations

---

19 *Post Office v Aquarius Properties Ltd* [1987] 1 All ER 1055, CA; also *Plough Investments Ltd v Eclipse Radio and TV Services Ltd* [1989] EGCS 1.

20 See *Ebbetts v Conquest* [1895] 2 Ch 377, CA.

1   (1890) 25 QBD 42, CA.

2   The standard in *Proudfoot v Hart*, supra, applies where the landlord is subject to s 11 of the Landlord and Tenant Act 1985 (s 11(3)).

3   *Anstruther-Gough-Calthorpe v McOscar*, supra.

4   *Anstruther-Gough-Calthorpe v McOscar*, supra.

5   Supra at 52–55.

then these need not be done; however, if damp had caused the paper to peel off the walls, it would have to be replaced. The quality of decorations need not be better than the original quality, it was held. The standard of repair imposed by this case is a subjective one, in the sense that it may be that, during the life of the lease, the requirements of incoming tenants will be greater or lower than those prevailing at the start of the lease. That is partly why it has no direct application to long leases.

(d)   Repair involving renewal[6]

Any covenant to repair will involve subordinate renewal; and the question to ask in deciding the extent of such covenant is whether the work is, as a matter of fact and degree, properly described as repair or whether it involves substantially renewing the whole, or almost the whole, of the demised premises.[7] The answer essentially depends on interpreting the intentions of the parties as expressed in the repairing covenant.[8] It was noted above that no liability to execute any remedial work can possibly arise unless there is proved to be a condition of disrepair in the premises in relation to the item or items concerned. A further preliminary matter is that the parties may well agree to exclude or limit any liability they might otherwise be under to cure inherent design faults in the structure of the premises, where newly-built: express words are required to achieve this.[9] Otherwise, liability to cure design faults is a question of interpretation of the particular covenant to repair. If a design fault produces a condition of disrepair, and the only sensible way of executing the work is, in the process, to cure the design fault, then a repairing covenant will require the party subject to it to pay for all the remedial work, though to some minor extent he is improving the design of the premises, without wholly renewing them.[10] Accordingly, a landlord was held liable to replace a worn out (and originally defectively-designed) front door with a new one of a different design as the only sensible way of complying with his repairing covenant,[11] but not liable to replace metal-frame windows or to insulate lintels, neither of which items were out of repair, in order to cure a design fault in a council house, which produced severe condensation.[12] The extent of

---

6   See P F Smith [1979] Conv 429.
7   *Ravenseft Properties Ltd v Davstone (Holdings) Ltd* [1980] QB 12, [1979] 1 All ER 929; approved in *Quick v Taff-Ely Borough Council* [1986] QB 809, [1985] 3 All ER 321, CA; also *McDougall v Easington District Council* (1989) Times, 2 February, CA.
8   *Lurcott v Wakely and Wheeler* [1911] 1 KB 905, CA.
9   See e g *Precedents for the Conveyancer* (Sweet & Maxwell) Vol 1, 5–66.
10   *Quick v Taff-Ely Borough Council* [1986] QB 809, [1985] 3 All ER 321, CA.
11   *Stent v Monmouth District Council* [1987] 1 EGLR 59, CA.
12   *Quick v Taff-Ely Borough Council*, supra.

repairs, if required, will be a question of fact: sometimes a repair will involve replacing the whole of the damaged article, say the whole roof,[13] but sometimes mere patching-up of an admittedly old roof or other item will suffice.[14]

Repair involves renewal of subordinate parts of the premises so as to leave the damaged article so far as possible as though not damaged.[15] Repair therefore may involve replacing a worn-out or damaged article with one which is brand new, corresponding as closely as possible to the original. In no case is a tenant under a covenant to repair required to give back at the end of the lease premises different in kind from the original subject matter of the demise, such as a house with properly-built foundations where it had poorly-built ones formerly; but equally, the mere fact that remedial work involves the replacement of a faultily-constructed *subordinate* part of the premises, is no defence to liability to pay for the full cost of the remedial work.[16]

In deciding on the scope of the covenant to repair in whatever precise form, it may be that the end result will differ where extensive work is required, as between old premises and newly-built ones.

In relation to older premises, it has been held that a covenant to repair does not bind a party to give back totally new premises, but only premises in proper repair, allowing for the effects of time.[17] The terms of the covenant and the age of the premises are relevant factors.[18] If therefore, the result of works of renovation would be to give the landlord premises totally different in kind from those let at the outset, such works lie outside the scope of repairs. This results from *Lister v Lane and Nesham*[19] where the tenants of a 100-year-old house on a seven-year lease covenanted that they 'when and where and as often as occasion shall require will sufficiently and substantially repair, uphold, sustain, maintain, amend and keep' the premises. The house was demolished at the end of the lease due to its dangerous condition. To have saved it would have required – in place of the old foundations which were a timber platform resting on muddy ground – underpinning of the house with new and proper foundations through 17 feet of mud to solid ground. The tenant was held not liable to pay for the costs of re-building the house; in no case, held the Court of Appeal, is a tenant bound under

---

13 As in *Elite Investments Ltd v T I Bainbridge Silencers Ltd* [1986] 2 EGLR 43.
14 *Murray v Birmingham City Council* [1987] 2 EGLR 53, CA.
15 *Anstruther-Gough-Calthorpe v McOscar* [1924] 1 KB 716, CA.
16 *Ravenseft Properties Ltd v Davstone (Holdings) Ltd*, supra.
17 *Lister v Lane and Nesham* [1893] 2 QB 212 at 216–217, CA.
18 *Gutteridge v Munyard* (1834) 1 Mood & R 334.
19 [1893] 2 QB 212; also *Sotheby v Grundy* [1947] 2 All ER 761 and *Halliard Property Co Ltd v Nicholas Clarke Investments Ltd* (1983) 269 Estates Gazette 1257.

repair, to pay for work which would give back to the landlord a new and different thing from the premises as let at the start of the tenancy.

Similarly, a landlord has been held not liable under repair, to rid an old house of damp, which was built without a damp course.[20] A tenant, likewise, was held sufficiently to have complied with a covenant to repair by replacing an elaborate but unsafe bay window with a new window, flush with the main walls: he was not obliged to provide new supports where the old were improperly built in the first place.[1] This is because neither the landlord nor the tenant is bound, under a covenant to repair to improve the design of the premises or items therein. Accordingly, a landlord who replaced wooden windows with double-glazed windows, where the old windows could at half the cost, have been repaired, failed to recover any part of the cost of the work from the tenant.[2] If a covenant enables work going beyond mere repairs to be carried out, the basic design of the premises or part may be improved.[3]

Equally, the mere fact that remedial work is shown to involve substantial but subordinate renewal, will not of itself take the matter out of the covenant to repair. Whether one is dealing with older or new premises, the matter is to be decided by looking at the particular building, its state at the time of the lease, the particular covenant and its precise interpretation, taking into account of the age of the building and comparing the cost or estimated cost of the work with the cost of rebuilding the premises as a whole. This is ultimately a matter of fact and degree,[4] but the view has been expressed that the cost of the work rather than the value of the building as repaired should be stressed if the two are seriously divergent.[5] Of necessity, repair involves subordinate renewal, and if at the completion of the work, what is done has left the premises substantially the same as when let, then the work normally falls on the repair side of the line. The main case is *Lurcott v Wakely and Wheeler*.[6] The front wall of a 200-year-old house had to be demolished following a dangerous structure notice, and it was re-built from ground level, in compliance with modern requirements, but it was a similar wall to that it replaced. The tenants had to pay for the cost: what was done being the renewal or replacement of a defective part. The covenant in that case was

---

20   *Pembery v Lamdin* [1940] 2 All ER 434, CA; also *Wainwright v Leeds City Council* (1984) 82 LGR 657, CA (council house); but cf *Elmcroft Developments Ltd v Tankersley-Sawyer* (1984) 270 Estates Gazette 140, CA (defective damp-course to be replaced with proper course at cost of landlord under general covenant).

1   *Wright v Lawson* (1903) 19 TLR 510, CA.

2   *Mullaney v Maybourne Grange (Croydon) Management Co Ltd* [1986] 1 EGLR 70.

3   *Sutton (Hastoe) Housing Association v Williams* [1988] 1 EGLR 56, CA (old windows could be replaced, accordingly, with windows of a better design).

4   *Brew Bros Ltd v Snax (Ross) Ltd* [1970] 1 QB 612, [1970] 1 All ER 587, CA; *Ravenseft Properties Ltd v Davstone (Holdings) Ltd*, supra.

5   *Elite Investments Ltd v T I Bainbridge Silencers Ltd* [1986] 2 EGLR 43.

6   [1911] 1 KB 905.

very strong, requiring the tenant to repair and keep in thorough repair and good condition: this meant that if need be, the tenant must replace part after part until the whole was, in due course, replaced.[7] Further, while the age and nature of a building may qualify the meaning of a covenant, of themselves they cannot relieve a tenant (or landlord) from his obligation. Hence, a tenant under a general covenant to repair was held liable to pay for the cost of replacing a defective outside stone cladding with new and properly constructed stone cladding, the cost of this being only a small fraction of the total replacement cost of the whole building.[8] Extensive and costly work may be required by a general covenant to repair, as where the roof of an old industrial unit had to be replaced (as the only way to repair it) at a cost of some £84,000, the value of the building with a new roof being about £140,000. After the work was done, the landlords would not get a different building, but the same building, with the roof in repair.[9]

These principles apply a fortiori to a new building, as where the landlord of a restaurant covenanted to keep the main walls and roof in good structural repair and condition throughout the lease and to make good all defects due to faulty materials or workmanship, but then the foundations being inadequate, extensive work of a supportive nature followed: rebuilding of the restaurant took place and the landlords were held liable in full. The obligation imposed was construed as being unqualified and the work done to comply with it was within the contemplation of the parties at the outset.[10]

(e) Repair involving painting

The tenant may expressly undertake a separate obligation to repaint the exterior and interior of the demised premises, at stated intervals, in the case of long leases, or at the end of the term, in the case of short leases.[11] An obligation to paint in a specific year operates as soon as that year commences.[12]

Even where the tenant is not under a specific obligation to paint, but only a general covenant to keep in good tenantable repair (or some similar obligation), he will be obliged to carry out whatever painting is necessary to preserve the woodwork and decorations from decay, to a

---

7   Ibid 915 (Fletcher Moulton LJ).
8   *Ravenseft Properties Ltd v Davstone (Holdings) Ltd* [1980] QB 12, [1979] 1 All ER 929.
9   *Elite Investments Ltd v T I Bainbridge Silencers Ltd* [1986] 2 EGLR 43; P F Smith [1987] Conv 140; cf *Plough Investments Ltd v Eclipse Radio and TV Services Ltd*, supra.
10 *Smedley v Chumley and Hawke Ltd* (1982) 44 P & CR 50, CA; cf *Halliard Property Co Ltd v Nicholas Clarke Investments Ltd* (1983) 269 Estates Gazette 1257 (no obligation on tenants to re-build to correct standards a 30-year-old 'jerry-built' utility room).
11 For precedents see e g *Precedents for the Conveyancer* Vol 1, 5-3, cll 4(6) and 4(7).
12 *Kirklinton v Wood* [1917] 1 KB 332.

standard sufficient for the requirements of reasonably-minded incoming tenants, bearing in mind the standard of the locality of the premises.[13]

V LANDLORD'S REMEDIES FOR BREACH OF TENANT'S COVENANT TO REPAIR

The landlord has various remedies to enforce the tenant's covenant to repair, namely, entering and executing the repairs, forfeiture, and claiming damages. Each of these remedies and their associated complications are considered in what follows.

(a) Right of entry to do repairs

Leases may entitle the landlord to enter and execute repairs and then to charge the tenant with their cost. In that case, the statutory restrictions on damages, discussed below, do not apply to the landlord. The sums spent will be recoverable as a contract debt.

Where statute imposes obligations to repair on the landlord, rights of entry, inspection and repair are conferred.[14] The landlord also has an implied licence, where he has no express right of entry and repair, to execute repairs for which he is liable.[15] This right is limited to what is strictly required to enable the work to be done, and no more. A right of entry to execute landlords' repairs is also implied in the case of weekly tenancies.[16] If there is no express, implied or statute-conferred right of entry to do repairs, the landlord has no implied right to enter and execute tenants' repairs which the tenant has failed to execute.[17]

(b) Leasehold Property (Repairs) Act 1938

The special rules imposed by the Leasehold Property (Repairs) Act 1938 apply both to forfeiture actions and to damages claims against the tenant for breach of covenant to repair.[18]

The original object of the 1938 Act was to prevent speculators buying up small property in an indifferent state of repair and serving schedules

---

13 *Proudfoot v Hart* (1890) 25 QBD 42, CA.

14 See Landlord and Tenant Act 1985 s 11(6), Rent Act 1977 ss 3(2) and 148, Housing Act 1988 s 15, Agricultural Holdings Act 1986 s 23.

15 *Granada Theatres Ltd v Freehold Investment (Leytonstone) Ltd* [1959] Ch 592, [1959] 2 All ER 176, CA; *McGreal v Wake* (1984) 128 Sol Jo 116, CA.

16 *Mint v Good* [1951] 1 KB 517, [1950] 2 All ER 1159, CA.

17 *Stocker v Planet Building Society* (1879) 27 WR 877, CA; *Regional Properties Ltd v City of London Real Property Co Ltd* (1979) 257 Estates Gazette 64.

18 See Blundell (1938/9) 3 Conv (NS) 10; P F Smith [1986] Conv 85. The Law Commission (Law Com No 142 (1985) paras 8.33 ff) recommended retaining an overhauled version of the 1938 Act for repairs, but the reversal of the rule, below, that no damages can be claimed where the landlord remedied the tenant's breach of covenant but cannot claim the cost under the lease.

of dilapidations on the tenants, with which the tenants could not comply.[19] Since the 1938 Act applies to most commercial and residential leases, the Act may have unfortunate consequences for perfectly innocent landlords, offering tenants who are in serious breach of covenant an opportunity for some tactical delays. The 1938 Act does not apply to a lease of an agricultural holding within the Agricultural Holdings Act 1986 (s 7(1)). It only applies to leases granted for a term of seven years or more (s 7(1)), of which at least three years are unexpired (s 1(1) and (2)). The 1938 Act does not apply where the breach of covenant is that of not putting the premises into repair at the beginning of the lease or within a reasonable time thereafter (s 3).[20] The Act applies to breaches of covenant to keep or put into repair, but not to breaches of tenants' covenants to carry out internal decorative repairs.[1]

By s 1(1), where the landlord serves an LPA 1925 s 146(1) notice on the tenant alleging breach of a covenant to keep or put into repair and at the date of the service of the notice three years or more of the term remain unexpired, the tenant may within 28 days from that date claim the benefit of the 1938 Act, by a counter-notice.

Similarly, by s 1(2), a right to claim damages for a breach of covenant to repair cannot be enforced by action commenced at any time when the lease has an unexpired residue of three years or more to run, unless the landlord serves on the tenant not less than one month before the commencement of the action a s 146(1) notice. Again, the tenant may then by a 28 day counter-notice claim the benefit of the 1938 Act.

By s 1(4) of the 1938 Act, in the case both of damages and forfeiture, the requisite s 146(1) notice must, on pain of invalidity, contain a statement, in characters not less conspicuous than those used in any other part of the notice[2] to the effect that the tenant is entitled to serve on the landlord within 28 days of service of the s 146(1) notice, a counter-notice claiming the benefit of the 1938 Act; and the s 146(1) notice must also state a name and address for service of the counter-notice on the landlord. (Section 196 of the Law of Property Act 1925 applies to the service of a counter-notice under the 1938 Act.) The effect of service within the 28-day period of a counter-notice by the tenant is that no proceedings by action or otherwise may be taken by the landlord for forfeiture or for damages without the leave of the court (s 1(3)).[3]

---

19 *National Real Estate and Finance Co Ltd v Hassan* [1939] 2 KB 61 at 78, CA.
20 This excludes an obligation to put into repair, premises which are dilapidated at the commencement of the lease.
1   The Law Commission recommended extending the 1938 Act procedure to these latter breaches: Report, supra, para 8.49.
2   I e equally readable or equally sufficient: *Middlegate Properties Ltd v Messimeris* [1973] 1 All ER 645, [1973] 1 WLR 168, CA.
3   A leave application is registrable under the Land Charges Act 1972 as a pending land action: *Selim Ltd v Bickenhall Engineering Ltd* [1981] 3 All ER 210, [1981] 1 WLR 1318.

By s 1(5), there are only five gateways under which leave may be given.

(a)   that the immediate remedying of the breach is requisite for preventing substantial diminution in the value of the reversion, or that the value thereof has been substantially diminished by the breach;[4]

(b)   that the immediate remedying of the breach is required for giving effect in relation to the premises to the purposes of any enactment, or of any by-law or other provision having effect under an enactment, or for giving effect to any order of a court or requirement of any authority under an enactment or any such by-law or provision as aforesaid;

(c)   where the tenant is not in occupation of the whole premises in respect of which the covenant or agreement is proposed to be enforced, that the immediate remedying of the breach is required in the interests of the occupier of those premises or of part thereof;

(d)   that the breach can be immediately remedied at an expense that is relatively small in comparison with the much greater expense that would probably be occasioned by postponement of the necessary work; or

(e)   special circumstances which in the opinion of the court render it just and equitable that leave should be given.

On an application for leave to proceed, the landlord is required to show only a prima facie case,[5] and in granting or refusing such leave, the court may impose such terms and conditions as it thinks fit. If relief is given, the effect is not usually to determine liability under the covenant for the rest of the lease, but to postpone the landlord's right to enforce it until such time as he should reasonably be allowed to enforce it, i e when he is likely to suffer actual damage thereby.

The terms of leave, if granted, are at the discretion of the court (s 1(6)). The court's discretion to grant leave is unfettered, and it has been said that is up to the landlord to persuade the court to grant leave, even if the landlord has made out a ground[6] under s 1(5).[7]

Various further aspects of the 1938 Act remain to be discussed.

---

4   See *Associated British Ports v C H Bailey plc* [1988] EGCS 134.
5   *Sidnell v Wilson* [1966] 2 QB 67, [1966] 1 All ER 68; this rule applies to all paragraphs of s 1(5): *Land Securities plc v Receiver for Metropolitan Police District* [1983] 2 All ER 254 at 258.
6   Proof of any one ground suffices for the purpose: *Phillips v Price* [1959] Ch 181, [1958] 3 All ER 386.
7   *Land Securities plc v Metropolitan Police District Receiver* [1983] 2 All ER 254, [1983] 1 WLR 439; contra, dicta in *Metropolitan Film Studios Ltd v Twickenham Film Studios Ltd* [1962] 3 All ER 508, [1962] 1 WLR 1315, that the discretion to refuse leave should be exercised only if the court was 'clearly convinced' that, despite compliance with s 1(5), leave should be refused; but see fn 4, supra.

1 Certain persons cannot claim the benefit of 1938 Act, notably, mortgagees or chargees of the lessee's interest in the premises.[8] However, an assignee in possession is entitled to claim the 1938 Act.[9]

2 A landlord's claim for costs and expenses in the preparation and service of a s 146 notice is a claim for a contract debt, where the tenant is under express covenant to pay these costs, and is outside the 1938 Act.[10]

3 If the landlord has the right to enter and execute repairs under the lease, but no express right to charge the tenant with their cost, no part of the cost will be recoverable unless, prior to acting, the landlord serves a s 146 notice on the tenant, which will allow him to claim the 1938 Act. This is because the landlord's claim is for damages.[11] This problem may be overcome, possibly, in a serious case, by the landlord obtaining a mandatory injunction against the tenant, requiring him to execute the works.[12]

4 If the lease enables the landlord, following a notice to repair to the tenant, to enter, execute the work and charge the tenant with the cost, the costs of the repairs may be treated as contract debt, and, in principles already discussed, the landlord has been held entitled, in three first instance decisions, to recover the costs without having to concern himself with the 1938 Act.[13] Although the numerical weight of authority favours this approach,[14] the opposite result has been reached in one earlier first instance decision, which held that the 1938 Act applied in the case of this type of clause, otherwise the tenant would lose the protection of the 1938 Act, and would lose the right himself to do the work.[15]

5 The 1938 Act applies only to repairing covenants, not, for example, to a covenant to cleanse,[16] nor to a covenant to lay out insurance moneys on the premises, if these are destroyed by fire.[17]

---

8 *Church Comrs for England v Ve-Ri-Best Manufacturing Co Ltd* [1957] 1 QB 238, [1956] 3 All ER 777.

9 *Kanda v Church Comrs for England* [1958] 1 QB 332, CA.

10 *Bader Properties Ltd v Linley Property Investments Ltd* (1967) 19 P & CR 620, approved in *Middlegate Properties v Gidlow-Jackson* (1977) 34 P & CR 4, CA.

11 *SEDAC Investments Ltd v Tanner* [1982] 3 All ER 646, [1982] 1 WLR 1342; P F Smith [1983] Conv 72. The repairs were urgent, and the conclusion was reached with 'surprise and regret'.

12 Suggestion of J Martin [1982] Conv 71.

13 *Hamilton v Martell Securities Ltd* [1984] Ch 266, [1984] 1 All ER 665, followed in *Colchester Estates (Cardiff) v Carlton Industries plc* [1986] Ch 80, [1984] 2 All ER 601, and *Elite Investments Ltd v T I Bainbridge Silencers Ltd* [1986] 2 EGLR 43. Work of renewal is outside a recovery of costs clause.

14 As do the Law Commission (Report, supra, para 8.66), who recommended its approval by legislation.

15 *Swallow Securities v Brand* (1983) 45 P & CR 328.

16 *Starrokate Ltd v Burry* (1982) 265 Estates Gazette 871, CA.

17 *Farimani v Gates* (1984) 128 Sol Jo 615, CA.

6   A s 146 notice which contains the statements required by s 1(4) of the 1938 Act will be valid even if it refers to alleged breaches of non-existent covenants.[18] If a s 146 notice is bad for want of compliance with the 1938 Act, but is good as respects other alleged breaches of covenant, it will be severed and valid as respects the latter breaches.[19]

(c)   Law of Property Act 1925 s 147

Where a s 146 notice served on a tenant relates to internal decorative repairs, the tenant may apply to the court for relief,[20] and if, having regard to all the circumstances, including in particular the length of the tenant's unexpired term, the court is satisfied that the notice is unreasonable, it may, by order, wholly or partially relieve the tenant from liability for these repairs.

If any of the four following exclusions apply, the relieving power of s 147(1) is excluded. These are, by s 147(2):

1   Where the liability arises under an express covenant or agreement to put the property into a decorative state of repair, which has not been performed.
2   Where any matter is necessary or proper for putting or keeping the property in a sanitary condition, or for the maintenance or preservation of the structure.
3   To any statutory liability to keep a house in all respects reasonably fit for human habitation.
4   To any covenant or stipulation to yield up the house or other building in a specified state of repair at the end of the term.

Where s 147 applies, the tenant[1] may apply to the court immediately he receives the notice concerned, and the court may, exceptionally, relieve him completely from liability for internal decorative repairs. Section 147 does not apply to a tenant's covenant to carry out regular exterior redecoration at stated intervals, because, no doubt, the execution of that work is essential to protect the exterior from weather attack.

(d)   Landlord and Tenant Act 1927 s 18

By s 18(1) of the Landlord and Tenant Act 1927, damages in an action by the landlord for breach of a covenant to put, keep or leave in repair are in

---

18   *Silvester v Ostrowska* [1959] 3 All ER 642, [1959] 1 WLR 1060.
19   *Starrokate v Burry*, supra.
20   I e the county court if the rateable value of the premises does not exceed the county court limit (s 147(5)).
 1   Or, where appropriate, any sub-tenant (s 147(3)).

no case to exceed the amount (if any) by which the value of the reversion (whether immediate or not) in the premises is diminished as a consequence of the breach of covenant. Where the action for damages is brought during the term, the measure of damages will consequently be less than if it had been brought at the end of the lease, and where the landlord has re-entered by forfeiture, it is the difference between the value of the property as he finds it and as it would have been had the repairs been done, no account being taken of any increase in value to the landlord by virtue of the fact that the tenancy is terminated prematurely; and the provision fixes a maximum limit on the amount of damages recoverable and does not alter their measure.[2] The assessment of damages is no easy matter, but if the landlord intends to carry out the repairs or has in fact done so, prima facie the estimated cost or cost of repairs is the proper measure of damages.[3] That an incoming tenant has undertaken to do repairs will not of itself, diminish the liability of an outgoing tenant.[4] A landlord selling at a good price for conversion into flats may be quite unable to prove damage.[5] If the premises are occupied by a business tenant entitled to statutory security of tenure, who will, on the grant of a new tenancy, have to pay an open market rent, which is fixed regardless of the state of repair of the premises, the landlord will be deemed to suffer no damage to his reversion, even though repairs are required to the premises, and recovery of damages will be barred by s 18(1).[6] It may for some reason be impossible to re-let the premises for the same purpose as under the former lease: for example, residential letting may be impossible. This may well reduce the damages otherwise recoverable by the landlord: the diminution in value to his reversion will not be the cost of repairs literally required to comply with the covenants in the old lease: the damages will have regard to the intended or possible future user of the premises, which may require a less onerous standard of repairs.[7] In addition, if the landlord re-lets to a tenant under a covenant to execute improvements, albeit that the initial rent is reduced due to the disrepair, it seems his damage is nil, if the improvements raise the value of the reversion.[8] Section 18(1) expressly provides that no damages shall be recovered for breach of any covenant to leave or put in repair at the end of the lease, if it can be shown that the premises have been or soon will be pulled down or such structural alterations made as to render

---

2 *Hanson v Newman* [1934] Ch 298, CA.
3 *Jones v Herxheimer* [1950] 2 KB 106, [1950] 1 All ER 323, CA; *Smiley v Townshend* [1950] 2 KB 311, [1950] 1 All ER 530, CA; *Drummond v S & U Stores Ltd* (1980) 258 Estates Gazette 1293.
4 *Haviland v Long* [1952] 2 KB 80, [1952] 1 All ER 463, CA.
5 *Landeau v Marchbank* [1949] 2 All ER 172.
6 *Family Management v Gray* (1979) 253 Estates Gazette 369, CA.
7 *Portman v Latta* (1942) 86 Sol Jo 119.
8 *Mather v Barclays Bank plc* [1987] 2 EGLR 254.

valueless the repairs in question. Where a local authority resolves before the end of the lease to acquire the premises compulsorily, the landlord cannot claim any diminution in value even though the compulsory purchase order is not made until afterwards.[9]

The date for determining the landlord's intention to demolish etc is the termination of the lease; and the intention must be definite and not conditional;[10] and if definite at the relevant time, it is irrelevant that the landlord's intention is later set at naught.[11] The second limb of s 18(1) contemplates a demolition rendering repairs nugatory, as opposed to acts by a tenant (and local authority) whose compulsory purchase of the premises could reward them for their breaches of covenant.[12]

Some concluding points may be made. First, the date down to which damages for breaches by the tenant of his covenant to repair is measured is, in the case of forfeiture, the date of service of the writ claiming forfeiture, which effects notional re-entry, as opposed to the date when the landlord eventually recovers possession of the premises.[13] Any claim for dilapidations during the post-writ period must be made in tort. Secondly, s 18(1) does not apply to a covenant by the tenant to spend a stated sum on repairs, nor to a covenant to pay the landlord the difference between the stated sum and any amount actually expended.[14] Thirdly, s 18(1) only limits landlords' damages claims in relation to the covenant to repair: it does not affect the measure of damages in other cases, such as covenants not to alter the internal planning of the premises,[15] or building leases.[16]

VI TENANT'S REMEDIES FOR BREACH OF LANDLORD'S COVENANT TO REPAIR

(a) Introduction

The landlord is not in breach of covenant to repair unless he has notice from the tenant (or a third party) of the want of repair (see above). The tenant remains liable to pay rent even if the landlord is in breach of his covenant.[17]

---

9 *London County Freehold and Leasehold Properties Ltd v Wallis-Whiddett* [1950] WN 180.

10 *Cunliffe v Goodman* [1950] 2 KB 237, [1950] 1 All ER 720, CA.

11 *Salisbury v Gilmore* [1942] 2 KB 38, [1942] 1 All ER 457, CA.

12 *Hibernian Property Co Ltd v Liverpool Corpn* [1973] 2 All ER 1117, [1973] 1 WLR 751.

13 *Associated Deliveries Ltd v Harrison* (1984) 50 P & CR 91, CA.

14 *Moss' Empires Ltd v Olympia (Liverpool) Ltd* [1939] AC 544, [1939] 3 All ER 460, HL.

15 *Eyre v Rea* [1947] KB 567, [1947] 1 All ER 415.

16 *Lansdowne Rodway Estates Ltd v Potown Ltd* (1983) 272 Estates Gazette 561.

17 *Surplice v Farnsworth* (1844) 13 LJCP 215.

(b) Damages

Section 18(1) of the Landlord and Tenant Act 1927 has no application to breaches by a landlord of the covenant to repair. The object of awarding damages to the tenant is to restore him to the position he would have been in had there been no breach by the landlord of his covenant to repair. This rule applies to landlords' express and statute-implied covenants alike. If the tenant has realised his lease by sale, the measure of damages is prima facie the amount of any loss in value of his interest due to the disrepair.[18] If the tenant remains in occupation, he may, for example, recover the cost of occupying alternative premises if the demised premises become uninhabitable, also for the personal inconvenience in living in premises out of repair, and for the cost of restoring decorations and of storing furniture pending repairs.[19] The landlord may be able, as a defence, to prove that the cause of damage is subsidence or some other cause which has nothing to do with a breach of his covenant; if this is so, he will not be liable for damages.[20] However, an award of damages will be disturbed only if erroneous in principle or so grossly excessive or insufficient as to demonstrate an error of law.[1]

Once the landlord has notice of a want of repair for which he is liable, he must remedy the breach within a reasonable time, failing which the tenant may claim damages or do the repairs himself and claim the cost from the landlord. Damages will be calculated on the basis of reasonably required repairs as opposed to extravagant repairs: extravagance means that nothing will apparently be recoverable. Prior to acting, the tenant must allow the landlord a reasonable opportunity to act himself and if he refuses access to the landlord, nothing is recoverable.[2]

(c) Deduction of cost of repairs from rent[3]

There are circumstances in which, where a landlord is in breach of covenant to repair and the tenant carries out the repairs, he may set off the cost of repairs against his future liability for rent. Where occupiers spent £630 on repairs for which the landlord was liable, it was held that they could recoup themselves out of future rents for the sum spent.[4] The sum must be certain for the right, which is at common law, to exist; and it must be unchallenged or unchallengeable, e g awarded in arbitration;

---

18   *Calabar Properties Ltd v Stitcher* [1983] 3 All ER 759, [1984] 1 WLR 287, CA.
19   *Calabar Properties Ltd v Stitcher*, supra; *McGreal v Wake* (1984) 128 Sol Jo 116, CA.
20   See *Minchburn Ltd v Peck* (1987) 20 HLR 392, CA.
  1   *Chiodi's Personal Representatives v De Marney* [1988] 41 EG 80, CA; *Davies v Peterson* [1989] 06 EG 130, CA.
  2   *Granada Theatres Ltd v Freehold Investment (Leytonstone) Ltd* [1959] Ch 592, [1959] 2 All ER 176, CA.
  3   See Waite [1981] Conv 199; also Rank (1976) 40 Conv (NS) 196.
  4   *Lee-Parker v Izzet* [1971] 3 All ER 1099, [1971] 1 WLR 1688.

and any excess over a proper amount will be disallowed; and the sum must be spent only on matters falling within the landlord's covenant to repair, where he has notice and is in breach.[5]

In equity, it is possible, provided a sufficiently close connection exists between the tenant's claim to set off and the landlord's claim for rent, for a tenant, in an action for rent arrears, to set off an estimated sum representing the cost of landlords' repairs, against the claim for rent arrears. The equity must go to the root of the claim for rent; it must not be covered by a common-law remedy; but the sum to be set off need not necessarily be certain, and the tenant need not necessarily have spent money on the repairs.[6]

(d) Specific performance

While the landlord cannot obtain an order for specific performance of the tenant's covenant to repair,[7] the remedy is available to force any landlord in breach of his covenant to repair, to execute the repairs specified in the order. The court has a general jurisdiction in equity and also a specific jurisdiction under statute which applies to dwellings.[8] An order is at the discretion of the court; it will be awarded with care and only in relation to definite and specific work. In a plain case of breach where there is no doubt what is to be done, an order will be made.[9] The mere fact that the landlord is insolvent is no bar of itself to relief.[10]

(e) Appointment of a receiver

General jurisdiction   Under s 37 of the Supreme Court Act 1981, the High Court has power to appoint a receiver in all cases where it appears just and convenient to do so. A receiver was accordingly appointed under this jurisdiction over residential blocks of flats, in one case, where the premises were seriously out of repair, due to the landlord's neglect to collect and apply to repairs service charges from the tenants, and in other cases, simply to support the covenant to repair, of which the landlord

---

5   *British Anzani (Felixstowe) Ltd v International Marine Management (UK) Ltd* [1980] QB 137, [1979] 2 All ER 1063; *Asco Developments v Gordon* (1978) 248 Estates Gazette 683.

6   *Melville v Grapelodge Developments Ltd* (1978) 39 P & CR 179 and cases cited in last note.

7   *Hill v Barclay* (1810) 16 Ves 402.

8   Landlord and Tenant Act 1985 s 17.

9   *Jeune v Queens Cross Properties Ltd* [1974] Ch 97, [1973] 3 All ER 97 (reinstatement of collapsed balcony); also *Gordon and Teixeira v Selico Co Ltd* [1986] 1 EGLR 71, CA (order to force landlords to perform covenant in relation to parts of block of flats).

10 *Francis v Cowlcliffe Ltd* (1976) 33 P & CR 368 (repairing lifts).

was in serious breach.[11] Such an order is capable of being protected by a caution against the landlord's title under s 54 of the Land Registration Act 1925 – a means, effectively, of blighting the landlord's ability to dispose of his interest in the premises while a receivership is in force.[12] If, however, the assets turn out to be insufficient to meet the receiver's expenses, he cannot recover these from the landlord.[13]

Statutory jurisdiction The county court (1987 Act s 52) is given the power, by Part II of the Landlord and Tenant Act 1987,[14] to appoint a manager over a building containing two or more residential flats (s 21). (It should be noted that the general jurisdiction is not in terms limited to residential flats.) The power arises on the application of one or more tenants. This jurisdiction is summarised in what follows. It does not apply to a tenant under a tenancy to which Part II of the Landlord and Tenant Act 1987 applies (s 21(7)).

A notice procedure must be gone through by the applicant tenant or tenants before an order may be applied for. This procedure, governed by s 22, is akin in many ways to the forfeiture notice procedure required of landlords by s 146(1) of the Law of Property Act 1925. The s 22 notice must be served on the immediate landlord (s 60).

(1) *Notice formalities* The preliminary notice must, in particular (s 22(2)):

(a) specify the grounds on which a management order is being requested and the matters relied on to establish it by the tenant;
(b) require the landlord to remedy the breach, within a specified reasonable period, by specified steps.[15]

The landlord must, as soon as reasonably practicable, after receipt of a s 22 notice, serve a copy on any mortgagee of his (s 22(4)).

However, the court has power to make a management order despite the fact that the tenant's notice is not served on the landlord because it was not reasonably practicable to do so (s 22(3)).

(2) *Reasonable time* After service of a notice, the tenant must

---

11 *Hart v Emelkirk Ltd* [1983] 3 All ER 15, [1983] 1 WLR 1289; *Daiches v Bluelake Investments Ltd* [1985] 2 EGLR 67; *Blawdziewicz v Diadon Establishment* [1988] 2 EGLR 52.
12 *Clayhope Properties Ltd v Evans* [1986] 2 All ER 795, [1986] 1 WLR 1223, CA.
13 *Evans v Clayhope Properties Ltd* [1988] 1 All ER 444, [1988] 1 WLR 358, CA. Under the statutory jurisdiction, this problem should not arise: Landlord and Tenant Act 1987 s 24(5)(c).
14 In force on 18 April 1988: Landlord and Tenant Act 1987 (Commencement No 2) Order 1988 SI 1988/480.
15 By s 22(2)(e), the tenant's notice must also contain prescribed information.

generally allow the reasonable time specified in the notice to expire, before making any application to the court (s 23(1)(a)). If the landlord, in this time, remedies the breaches, no application will be possible. If the breaches are incapable of remedy – as with breaches of covenant to insure – the tenant may apply without waiting.

(3) *Scope of power*   The court may make an interlocutory or final order, under s 24. The order may cover the whole premises or part only; and it may cover more extensive premises than those the subject-matter of the application (s 24(3)). An example might be where one or more individual flat tenants in a block apply for a management order and the court order is made applicable to the entire block.

(4) *Terms of order*   These are that a manager is appointed, to carry out management or receivership functions, or both (s 24(1)).[16] The terms of the order are generally at the discretion of the court: it may, for example, order that the manager's powers are to be exercised for a limited or for an unlimited period.

(5) *Grounds for making an order*   A management order is available on one of two grounds (s 24(2)).

(a) The court is satisfied that the landlord is in breach of a management obligation in the lease to the tenant, which breach is likely to continue. It must, in addition, be just and convenient to make the order.
(b) Other circumstances exist making it just and convenient to make the order.

A Part II order is registrable as a pending land action or as a caution, depending on whether the title to the freehold is unregistered or registered (s 24(8)).

(6) *Discharge*   Under s 24(9), the court may vary or discharge a management order on the application of any person interested, such as, no doubt, a new landlord or mortgagee. However, the fact that, after the making of an order, the premises cease to be covered by Part II of the 1987 Act, does not operate as an automatic discharge (s 24(10)).

If a management order is in force for three years, the tenants, subject to certain conditions, may apply to the court for the compulsory acquisition of the landlord's interest under Part III of the 1987 Act. They may also make such an application where it appears to the court that a management order would not be an adequate remedy. See further Chapter 19.

---

16 'Management' includes repair, maintenance or insurance of the premises (s 24(11)).

VII REPAIR NOTICES

Under Part VI of the Housing Act 1985 a local housing authority has power, by a repair notice under s 189, to compel repairs to houses, or parts of buildings where flats have been let, which are unfit or seriously dilapidated.[17] Repair notices may further be served to require a sub-standard but not unfit house to be brought up to standard (s 190(1)(a)) and to cure a condition in a house which materially interferes with the personal comfort of an occupying tenant (s 190(1)(b)). Repair notices may also be served under ss 189(1A) or 190(1A), as the case may be, where there are lettings of flats in a block, and the part of building containing the flats, but reserved from the demise, is unfit or seriously out of repair.[18] Where a local authority is satisfied that a house or part of a building is unfit, it is obliged to serve a repair notice.[19] In other cases, it has a discretion.

A repair notice must be served on the person having control of the house, defined by s 207 as, essentially, the person in receipt of the rack rent of the premises.[20] Where a large building was let to various long leaseholders, it was held that the freeholder was not the person having control of the house.[1] However, the leaseholder of a flat is the person having control of his part of the building for the purpose of disrepair within the individual flat and within s 207.[2] A repair notice may be served on the person retaining structural and common parts of the building, for example, from the demise of individual flats.

A repair notice must require the person concerned, within a specified reasonable time, to begin the works not earlier than seven days from the operative date of the notice (s 189(2)).[3] The notice must require the works to be completed by the person concerned within a specified reasonable time. A repair notice becomes operative when 21 days from the date of service expire (s 189(4)) unless it is appealed against. A copy of the notice must be served on other persons with an interest in the

---

17　The standard is laid down by Housing Act 1985 s 604, as extended to require regard to be had, in the case of flats, not just to the condition of the flat, but also to the condition of any other part of the building as it affects the flat. The flat may be deemed unfit if a part of the building not demised is unfit. For prescribed forms of notice see SI 1988/2189.

18　This is as a result of amendments in Housing Act 1988 Sch 15 paras 1 and 2.

19　*R v Kerrier District Council, ex p Guppy's* (1976) 32 P & CR 411, CA.

20　Where a block of flats is let, the person having control of parts of the building not let is, generally, the freeholder in respect of the part of the building retained, or a head lessee of the building – whichever the authority think appropriate.

1　*Pollway Nominees Ltd v Croydon London Borough Council* [1987] AC 79, [1986] 2 All ER 849, HL; also *White v Barnet London Borough Council* (1989) Times, 11 March, CA.

2　*R v Lambeth London Borough Council, ex p Clayhope Properties Ltd* [1988] QB 563, [1987] 3 All ER 545, CA.

3　The following rules apply also to notices served under s 190.

house, such as mortgagees and lessees (s 189(4)) and an operative notice is a local land charge (s 189(5)).

There is a statutory defence to a person aggrieved by a repair notice that the house is incapable of being rendered fit at reasonable expense (s 191). The general rule is to compare the open market value of the house if sold with vacant possession in repair, compared to its present value, but other factors may be taken into account, such as the means or financial position of the owner and the cost of the repairs as compared to the open market value.[4] However, a realistic approach to the value of the house as a saleable asset in the landlord's hands must be taken, so that if there are sitting tenants with Rent Act protected tenancies, the effect of their continuing rights of occupation should generally be taken into account in deciding on the value of the house as compared to the cost of the work of repair.[5] Where the cost of repairs compared to the value of the house meant that the work cost three times the value of the house, a repair notice was quashed.[6]

Where s 190 is concerned, it may be that slightly different considerations apply, as the whole object of s 190 is to prevent a house from sinking into so dilapidated a state that it cannot be repaired at reasonable expense. Therefore, a repair notice which required work to bring a house up to standard, where the cost of compliance was double the value of the house as repaired, was upheld.[7]

Once the period stated in the notice for the execution of repairs has passed, the authority have enforcement powers (s 193) which, broadly, entitle it to enter the premises, after a further notice, to execute the work and charge the person having control, and secondarily, any other person on whom the notice was served, with the cost. These powers also arise where the authority is satisfied that reasonable progress is not being made with the works. If unrecovered, the expenses are a charge on the house, enforceable by sale. Intentional failure to comply with a repair notice is a criminal offence (s 198A).

VIII   ABATEMENT NOTICES AND DANGEROUS BUILDINGS

Under s 93 of the Public Health Act 1936, a local authority is required to serve on the landlord of premises which are in such a state as to be prejudicial to health or a nuisance, an abatement notice requiring the

---

4   *Hillbank Properties Ltd v Hackney London Borough Council* [1978] QB 998, [1978] 3 All ER 343, CA.
5   *FFF Estates Ltd v Hackney London Borough Council* [1981] QB 503, [1981] 1 All ER 32, CA.
6   *Phillips v Newham London Borough Council* (1981) 43 P & CR 54, CA.
7   *Kenny v Kingston upon Thames Royal London Borough Council* [1985] 1 EGLR 26, CA.

landlord (as 'owner') to abate the nuisance. Blocked drains, leaking roofs and infestation are capable of being statutory nuisances, but not a mere want of decoration.[8] If the landlord fails to comply with the notice, a nuisance order may be granted by a magistrates' court on the local authority's application (s 94) and failure to comply therewith is a criminal offence (s 95). The authority have the power, in default of compliance, to abate the nuisance and recover the cost of so doing from the 'owner'. The discretion of the magistrates is wide, and an order requiring a landlord to effect improvements was upheld.[9] It is a not sufficient compliance with an order that the landlord obtained vacant possession of the building,[10] but if the damage is the fault of the tenant, no order can be made.[11] As with repair notices, where there is a block of flats, a nuisance order cannot be made against the landlord in relation to the entire block, unless the nuisance relates to every flat in the building.[12]

The 1936 Act procedure is not mandatory,[13] and there are limits on it. First, the question of its application must be considered in terms of fitness for human habitation, as opposed to human comfort,[14] which is why the repair notice procedure (above) needs to be invoked where interference with comfort is concerned. Secondly, the 1936 Act procedure applies only to nuisances which would be nuisances at common law, so that the defects in the premises must interfere for a substantial period with neighbouring premises, as well as the premises concerned; or that a class of the public are affected by the defects, not just the tenants.[15]

There is also a speedy procedure under s 76 of the Building Act 1984, under which a local authority may serve a so-called 'nine days' notice' on the landlord, if premises are in a defective state, specifying the repairs necessary. At the end of this time the authority is empowered to enter and execute the repairs and recover their cost from the landlord. If, within seven days of the service of the notice, he serves a counter-notice of his intention to do the repairs, he is entitled to a reasonable time to begin and to make reasonable progress.

If it appears to a local authority which is outside Inner London[16] that

8   *Springett v Harold* [1954] 1 All ER 568, [1954] 1 WLR 521.
9   *Birmingham District Council v Kelly* (1985) 17 HLR 572.
10 *Lambeth London Borough Council v Stubbs* (1980) 78 LGR 650, CA.
11 *Dover District Council v Farrar* (1982) 2 HLR 32.
12 *Birmingham District Council v McMahon* (1987) 151 JP 709; Hoath [1988] Conv 377.
13 *Nottingham Corpn v Newton* [1974] 2 All ER 760. It may be initiated by the tenant (s 92).
14 *Salford City Council v McNally* [1976] AC 379, [1975] 2 All ER 860, HL.
15 *National Coal Board v Neath Borough Council* [1976] 2 All ER 478.
16 In the case of Inner London special, but similar, rules apply: see London Building Acts (Amendment) Act 1939 Part VII.

202   *Repairing obligations*

a building or structure is in a dangerous condition, the authority may apply under s 77 of the Building Act 1984, to a magistrates' court. The court has power to order the landlord (as an owner) to do the necessary work to get rid of the danger or to demolish the building or structure. If an order is not complied with, the authority have default powers of entry and execution, and non-compliance is also an offence.[17] An order does not necessarily have to specify the works in detail.[18]

17   Where urgent action is required, s 78 of the 1984 Act confers emergency powers on the authority. Special rules apply to listed buildings.
18   *R v Bolton Recorder, ex p McVittie* [1940] 1 KB 290, [1939] 4 All ER 236, CA.

Chapter 10

Rights and liabilities as between landlord or tenant and third parties

I ON THE PART OF A LANDLORD

1 RIGHTS AGAINST THIRD PARTIES

On the granting of a term of years, the tenant acquires almost all of the *proprietary* rights in respect of the land from the landlord by subrogation, and he retains them until the lease expires and as long as he retains possession; and as the tenant has enjoyment of the land it is he who would normally have *personal* causes of action against a third party. With regard to both *real* and *personal* claims, however, the landlord may bring an action if his reversionary interest is injured or imperilled.

Adverse possession

A person who acquires a squatter's title under the Limitation Act 1980, by adverse dispossession of the tenant for 12 years, does not by this means acquire a title against the landlord. This is due to the fact that the landlord's right of action to recover the land is deemed to accrue only when his reversion falls into possession.[1] Therefore, time begins to run against the landlord from the termination of the lease, and the landlord's title is only barred after the expiry of 12 years from that date.[2] If the landlord begins proceedings for the recovery of possession of the land before the expiry of the 12-year limitation period, his right of action will be unaffected by any subsequent expiry of the 12-year period while the proceedings are pending: any judgment for possession given after the expiration of the 12-year period will be enforceable for a further 12 years from the date of the judgment before a title can be acquired by the tenant in adverse possession.[3]

---

1 Limitation Act 1980 s 15(6) and Sch 1 para 4.
2 Limitation Act 1980 s 15(1).
3 *BP Properties Ltd v Buckler* [1987] 2 EGLR 168, CA.

Title may be acquired against the landlord if adverse possession is taken by a third party of the rent due under a lease in writing with a rent of £10 per year or upwards: if the rent is paid to the third party for 12 years, the third party is able to bar the landlord's right to the reversion.[4] The receipt of rent by the third party is deemed to be adverse possession of the land.[5]

If a squatter acquires title against the whole, or part, of premises demised to a tenant, and title is unregistered, the estate of the tenant is not, as against his landlord, destroyed. Therefore, the tenant may validly surrender his lease to the landlord, and time will begin to run for limitation purposes, against the landlord, only as from the date the lease is determined by the surrender. Accordingly, the landlord is entitled to take possession proceedings against the squatter, provided he brings his action within the statutory period of 12 years from the date of the surrender.[6] The position with regard to registered land differs somewhat and is discussed elsewhere.[7]

Prescription

A third party cannot generally claim an easement or *profit-à-prendre* for a tenant has no power to grant easements,[8] since 'user' must be by or on behalf of a fee simple owner against a fee simple owner, except possibly under the doctrine of lost modern grant.[9] Where an easement is claimed by prescription over land held under a lease, the claim must fail, unless it can be shown that user as of right had been enjoyed against the landlord *before* he created the tenancy.[10] To this rule there is a statutory exception in the case of the acquisition of a right of light under the Prescription Act 1832, where such a right becomes indefeasible after 20 years. To bar the acquisition of a right of light, the landlord should register a notice under the Rights of Light Act 1959.

Trespass

For a landlord to be able to maintain an action for trespass, he would have to show injury to the reversionary interest, ie injury of such a permanent nature as to affect the value of his reversion adversely.[11]

---

4 Limitation Act 1980 s 15(6) and Sch 1 para 6.
5 Limitation Act 1980 s 15(6) and Sch 1 para 8(3).
6 *Fairweather v St Marylebone Property Co Ltd* [1963] AC 510, [1962] 2 All ER 288, HL.
7 See ch 4.
8 Except a tenant for life: Settled Land Act 1925 s 38(1).
9 See 74 LQR 82 (VTH Delany).
10 *Palk v Shinner* (1852) 18 QB 568; *Pugh v Savage* [1970] 2 QB 373, [1970] 2 All ER 353, CA.
11 See *Jones v Llanrwst UDC* [1911] 1 Ch 393.

Alternatively, he might be entitled to claim any loss from the tenant under a covenant, express or implied, for, redelivery, if the tenant cannot deliver up the land as it was at the commencement of the tenancy, even without there being any negligence on his part.[12]

Nuisance

The same principles apply in respect of nuisance, so that the cause of the nuisance will be actionable only by the tenant unless some permanent injury has been caused to the reversion. Smell and noise are not normally permanent, though a landlord has been granted an injunction against a third party against carrying on works which caused structural damage to the property let.[13] Although the claim is based on the damage to the reversion, the extent of that loss where the nuisance is continuing, is not the measure of damages, but as much as is necessary to ensure abatement of the nuisance.[14]

2   LIABILITY TO THIRD PARTIES

By the same token as above, any claims by third parties in respect of the land are maintainable against the tenant, and not against the landlord except where the landlord has himself caused the injury, and under certain statutory provisions.

Nuisance

Where the landlord lets property in a derelict or ruinous state, he will be liable to any third party injured as a result,[15] unless he had no reason to suspect that it was in fact dangerous;[16] so, too, if the lease expressly contemplates acts that will inevitably result in a nuisance.[17] He will be liable even if the nuisance was in fact created by a tenant under a previous tenancy and he re-lets, and even though he has no right to enter on the land to remove it.[18] If a latent defect in the premises manifests itself during the lease, the landlord will only be liable in nuisance in respect of it, if the third party proves that he was aware of the existence of the defect at the date of the lease.[19]

---

12   *Phillimore v Lane* (1925) 133 LT 268 (damage by burglars).
13   *Shelfer v City of London Electric Lighting Co* [1895] 1 Ch 287.
14   *Battishill v Reed* (1856) 18 CB 696.
15   *Sampson v Hodson-Pressinger* [1981] 3 All ER 710, CA; cf *Guppys (Bridport) Ltd v Brookling* (1983) 269 Estates Gazette 846, 942.
16   *St Anne's Well Brewery Co v Roberts* (1928) 140 LT 1.
17   *Harris v James* (1876) 45 LJQB 545.
18   *Thompson v Gibson* (1841) 7 M & W 456.
19   *Brew Bros v Snax (Ross) Ltd* [1970] 1 QB 612, [1970] 1 All ER 587, CA.

In the case of a public nuisance, where injury is caused on the highway as a result of his failure to repair, whether he has agreed to repair,[20] or merely reserved a right to enter and repair,[1] he will be liable. So onerous are his duties considered with regard to public nuisance, that in *Mint v Good*,[2] the court was prepared to imply an agreement to repair on his part in what was there a weekly tenancy. Denning LJ obiter, doubted even whether a landlord could escape liability today by taking a repairing covenant from the tenant.[3]

Damage by third parties – landlord's liability

If the tenant's premises are damaged due to the vandalisation of adjoining premises controlled by the landlord (as where these latter are vacant), a high degree of probability of injury as a result of the landlord's inaction must be shown, to render the landlord liable in negligence to the tenant for resulting losses. In one case, it was held that, where the landlords allowed a house next to the plaintiff tenant's to collapse, leading to serious damage by vandals to the plaintiff's house, the landlords were liable in damages – but negligence liability was admitted.[4] By contrast, where the action of vandals in a flat above the tenant's caused flooding in the tenant's flat, the landlords, who were held unable to take effective steps to defeat the vandals, were not liable in negligence to the tenant.[5]

Negligence

It is well settled that at common law, express contractual liability apart, a landlord is under no liability to his tenant in respect of the safety or condition of unfurnished premises at the commencement of the tenancy;[6] the doctrine of caveat emptor applies and the tenant cannot sue on any implied covenant for loss, nor in fact for any injury. A fortiori, a third party injured on the premises is at common law precluded from suing the landlord in negligence, so that the daughter of a tenant was unable to recover damages for injuries suffered as a result of the landlord's breach of his statutory obligations as to fitness for human habitation.[7] This harsh rule is modified in several respects by the Occupiers' Liability Act 1957, and the Defective Premises Act 1972.

---

20 *Wringe v Cohen* [1940] 1 KB 229, [1939] 4 All ER 241.
1 *Heap v Inde Coope and Allsop Ltd* [1940] 2 KB 476.
2 [1951] 1 KB 517, [1950] 2 All ER 1159.
3 Ibid at p 528; but cf *Pretty v Bickmore* (1873) LR 8 CP 401.
4 *Ward v Cannock Chase District Council* [1986] Ch 546, [1985] 3 All ER 537.
5 *King v Liverpool City Council* [1986] 3 All ER 544, [1986] 1 WLR 890, CA; see also *Smith v Littlewoods Organisation Ltd* [1987] 1 All ER 710, HL.
6 *Bottomley v Bannister* [1932] 1 KB 458.
7 *Ryall v Kidwell & Son* [1914] 3 KB 135.

(a) *Under s 2 of the Occupiers' Liability Act 1957* the occupier of premises owes to all his visitors the 'common duty of care', i e a duty to see that the visitor will be reasonably safe in using the premises for the purposes for which he is invited or permitted by the occupier to be there. Where the landlord lets off premises in their entirety, this duty will fall on the tenant as 'occupier' unless it is cast back upon the landlord by s 4 of the 1972 Act. However, if he retains control over any part of the premises, such as the entrance hall, staircase, lift, forecourt, lavatories or other common parts, he will be under that duty as occupier. If the occupier is bound under contract to allow strangers to the contract (see s 3(3)) to enter or use the premises, his duty to them as visitors cannot be restricted or excluded by the contract but includes the duty to perform his obligations under the contract whether undertaken for their protection or not (subject to any contractual provision to the contrary) in so far as those obligations go beyond obligations otherwise involved in that duty (s 3(1)). Generally, however, any exclusion of liability clause for visitors must by ss 1 and 2(1) of the Unfair Contract Terms Act 1977[8] be shown by the landlord etc to be reasonable and he cannot purport to exclude liability for death or personal injury. In relation to other loss or damage, the landlord may only restrict his negligence liability by notice if it satisfies a statutory requirement of reasonableness (s 2(2)) of the 1977 Act). The 1977 Act, however, applies to business liability only, and a purely domestic occupier is free to restrict, modify or exclude his liability for negligence.[9]

The degree of care required to satisfy the duty is relative to the particular visitor so that he must be prepared for children to be less careful than adults, for example, but he is entitled to expect that a person, in the exercise of his calling, will appreciate and guard against any special risks ordinarily incident to it (s 2(3)).

The duty is to take reasonable care to see that the visitor will be reasonably safe from injury, and his goods from damage. In the case of a known defect that is potentially dangerous, he can often discharge it by giving the visitor adequate warning, e g by means of prominent notices. Any warning, however, is not to be treated without more as absolving him from liability, unless in all the circumstances it was enough to enable the visitor to be reasonably safe (s 2(4)(a)). Moreover, he is regarded as having discharged the duty if the danger has been caused as a result of the faulty work of

---

8 As modified by Occupiers Liability Act 1984 s 2 to allow exclusion of liability for persons obtaining access for recreational or educational purposes unless these are within the business purposes of the occupier.
9 See Mesher [1979] Conv 58.

an independent contractor employed by him in carrying out any construction, maintenance or repairs, provided that he can show that he had taken such steps as could reasonably be expected of him in order to satisfy himself that the contractor was competent and that the work had been properly done (s 2(4)(b)). The Act mentions specifically only these two factors for consideration in determining whether he has discharged his duty; but regard must be had to 'all the circumstances'. Whether the landlord knew or ought to have known of the danger and how long it has existed, must both be relevant factors.

(b) *Under s 4 of the Defective Premises Act 1972*, which imposes a general duty on the landlord to all persons[10] who might reasonably be expected to be affected by defects in the state of the premises to ensure that the persons are reasonably safe from personal injury and damage to their property caused by a relevant defect (s 4(1)). The duty arises (s 4(3)) where the landlord is under a contractual or statutory obligation or duty to repair or maintain the premises; and also where the landlord has a right, express or implied, to enter the premises[11] to do repairs (s 4(4)). The duty applies to all types of tenancy (s 6(1)) and cannot be contracted out of (s 6(3)). The duty arises as soon as the landlord has notice from the tenant or otherwise or if he ought to have known of the defect (s 4(2)). Notice is deemed to arise where the landlord could have obtained it due to a right to enter and carry out repairs (s 4(4)).[12] The landlord is under no duty for defects arising from any failure by the tenant to carry out repairs under his obligations under the tenancy (s 4(4)). The duty imposed by s 4 is, in appropriate circumstances, enforceable by injunction.[13]

II ON THE PART OF A TENANT

1 RIGHTS AGAINST THIRD PARTIES

As stated above, it is generally the tenant who has any right of action against a third party for the infringement of rights in respect of the land,

---

10 Including a tenant: *Smith v Bradford Metropolitan Council* (1982) 44 P & CR 171, CA; *McDonagh v Kent Area Health Authority* (1984) 134 NLJ 567.

11 This is a wide term and includes a patio: *Smith v Bradford Metropolitan Council*, supra. Where there is no breach of a covenant to repair etc by a 'bare' landlord, he is under no general duty in tort to repair: *McNerny v Lambeth London Borough Council* [1988] EGCS 169, CA.

12 Whether express or under statute or by implication (e g in the case of weekly tenancies: *Mint v Good* [1951] 1 KB 517, [1950] 2 All ER 1159, CA).

13 *Barrett v Lounova (1982) Ltd* [1989] 1 All ER 351, CA.

by virtue of his possession, except as regards permanent damage to, or jeopardy of, the reversion. So, for example, if a trespasser cuts down trees, or damages landlords' fixtures and fittings, the tenant can sue in trespass, but he can recover only the loss of their amenity value to him; he cannot recover damages for their intrinsic value, for property in them is vested in the reversion. The same is true for actions in negligence, nuisance, breach of statutory duty and under the rule in *Rylands v Fletcher*. As regards squatters, there is only a tenant's title at risk if he is dispossessed, and it is for him to bring ejectment, in order to prevent anyone acquiring a good title to the leasehold interest by adverse possession.

Easements

Easements (except rights of light) and *profits-à-prendre* cannot be acquired over the land during a tenancy, and therefore the tenant would have an action in trespass against any person claiming such rights by prescription (where no such right was enjoyed before the tenancy was created); he may nevertheless be under an obligation, under the terms of the lease, to notify the landlord of, or to pass on to him, any claims adverse to the land comprised in the tenancy. To prevent the acquisition of an easement of light, he should register a notice under the Rights of Light Act 1959.

Conversely, a tenant can acquire easements and profits over other land in fee simple. He can do so for a term of years by express grant only from the owner of the *servient* land, or in fee simple by prescription; and in either case, such rights may give rise to an action against third parties. In claiming the right by prescription by virtue of his own user and enjoyment only, he is necessarily claiming it for the benefit of the owner in fee simple of the *dominant* land, i e the landlord.[14] A tenant cannot therefore acquire an easement over adjacent land owned by the landlord,[15] for the landlord cannot acquire rights against himself. By the same token, and for the reason given above, a tenant cannot prescribe against another tenant of his own landlord.[16]

If the lease grants the tenant an easement, for example, a right of way, over adjoining land demised by the same landlord to other tenants, an injunction against the landlord will not be an appropriate remedy to enforce the right of way because by demising the adjoining land, the landlord has put it out of his power to interfere with the tenant's easement. Naturally, an injunction against the adjoining tenants, if they interfere with the relevant easement, is entirely appropriate.[17]

---

14 He is not required to plead the landlord's title: Prescription Act 1832 s 5.
15 *Gayford v Moffat* (1868) 4 Ch App 133.
16 *Kilgour v Gaddes* [1904] 1 KB 457.
17 *Celsteel Ltd v Alton House Holdings Ltd* [1986] 1 All ER 608, [1986] 1 WLR 512, CA.

Benefit of covenants taken for the land

For a tenant to be able to enforce a covenant taken for the benefit of his land, against a third party, two conditions must be satisfied: not only must the third party be subject to the *burden* of the covenant; but the tenant must show that he is himself entitled to claim the benefit. Whether he is so entitled depends inter alia on whether the covenant is *positive* or *negative* (i e restrictive) in nature; and if he is, what remedies the tenant will have against a third party who is in breach of an enforceable covenant will depend on whether his rights are legal or equitable. The main rules in respect of the *burden* of covenants are set out below, in connection with a tenant's liabilities to third parties. Here we are concerned with the tenant's claim to the *benefit* of any covenants.

(a)   The tenant can claim the benefit of a covenant (whether positive or negative) under s 56 of the Law of Property Act 1925, on the grounds that the covenant was made *with* him, even though he was not a signatory to the deed creating the covenant, e g a freehold covenant taken by the landlord expressed to be for himself, 'his tenant' and their respective successors in title. He can claim under s 56 only if he was tenant when the covenant was created;[18] *his* successors must rely on (b) or (c) as assignees.

(b)   He can claim the benefit of any covenant *at law*, as tenant of a landlord who is, or is a successor in title of, the original covenantee if the covenant is one that touches and concerns the land and was created after 1925.[19]

(c)   He can claim as tenant[20] the benefit of a restrictive covenant *in equity* if he can show that it is one that touches and concerns his land and, if his landlord was not the original covenantee, that the benefit of the covenant has been passed to the landlord by express agreement or by *annexation* (express or implied) of the benefit of the covenant to the land.

(d)   *In equity* he can enforce a restrictive covenant in the lease of another tenant under a 'letting scheme', in the circumstances explained above (Chapter 5).

Where a covenant is enforceable at law, the tenant's remedy is an action for damages; in equity the only remedy is an injunction restraining the breach, which is necessarily discretionary.

---

18   Re *Foster, Hudson v Foster* [1938] 3 All ER 357.
19   By virtue of LPA 1925 s 78; *Smith and Snipes Hall Farm v River Douglas Catchment Board* [1949] 2 KB 500, [1949] 2 All ER 179; *Federated Homes Ltd v Mill Lodge Properties Ltd* [1980] 1 All ER 371, [1980] 1 WLR 594, CA. For the pre 1926 position see e g *J Sainsbury plc v Enfield London Borough Council* [1989] EGCS 4.
20   *Westhoughton UDC v Wigan Coal and Iron Co Ltd* [1919] 1 Ch 159.

Defective Premises Act 1972 s 1

By s 1 of the Defective Premises Act 1972, anyone who takes on work[1] for or in connection with the provision of a dwelling, is under a duty to see that the work taken on is done in a workmanlike or, as the case may be, a professional, manner, with proper materials, so that, as regards that work, the dwelling will be fit for habitation when completed. The duty is owed to any person to whose order the dwelling is provided and also to any person acquiring any interest, legal or equitable, in the dwelling. For the purposes of limitation of time, by s 1(5) of the 1972 Act, time begins to run from the completion of the dwelling; or, if the person who originally undertook work carries out further work of rectification, then time begins to run from the completion of that work. Section 6(3) prohibits any contracting out of any of the above duties.

The duty falls (s 1(4)) primarily on builders, developers, local authorities, architects, specialist contractors and those who manufacture equipment to order, but not suppliers or manufacturers of general building materials (s 1(3)). Nor does the duty apply where the builder is a registered member of the National House Builders' Registration Council and the work is 'guaranteed' by the Council on completion, i e under an approved scheme (s 2).

The 1972 Act came into force on 1 January 1974 and is not retrospective.

2 LIABILITIES OF TENANTS TO THIRD PARTIES

Except to the extent that the landlord may be liable, e g for breach of statutory duty in certain cases, it is generally the tenant, as occupier, upon whom is likely to fall any liability under the general law in respect of the land let.[2] So, if the tenant interferes with an easement of a third party over the land, or if he creates a nuisance, he can be restrained by injunction or sued for damages by the third party. Whether or not the tenant may have obligations to third parties under covenants entered into between the landlord and owners of other land (i e positive and restrictive covenants affecting the freehold) and covenants contained in any lease superior to his own, depends on a number of important distinctions which should be noted.

Liability to owners of other land

For a third party to be able to enforce a covenant taken for the benefit of his land, either by himself or by a predecessor in title, against a tenant,

1 *Alexander v Mercouris* [1979] 3 All ER 305, [1979] 1 WLR 1270, CA.
2 *Sampson v Hodson-Pressinger* [1981] 3 All ER 710, CA.

two conditions must be satisfied: the claimant must be entitled to the *benefit* of the covenant, and he must show that the tenant is subject to the *burden*. The position with regard to the *benefit* of covenants has already been covered (in the context of a tenant's rights to enforce covenants against third parties). The rules for the passing of the *burden* of covenants are markedly different, though here too, there is the primordial distinction to be made between positive covenants (i e which require some positive act) and restrictive covenants (i e which are negative by nature in that a certain activity is prohibited or restricted). Generally, the correct classification of a covenant will be apparent, but a covenant may be expressed positively, and yet be negative in substance, as in *Tulk v Moxhay*[3] where the covenant was one to maintain Leicester Square Garden 'in an open state, uncovered with any buildings'. In effect, this was no more than a covenant not to build thereon. A useful test is whether the covenant would oblige the covenantee to expend money in its performance; if it does, then the covenant is not negative in nature.[4] But the converse is not necessarily true, for not all positive acts involve expenditure.

(a) *Positive covenants*   The burden of a positive covenant has never been assignable by itself *at law*,[5] and therefore a tenant cannot be sued on such a covenant by a claimant trying to enforce it, unless he elects to take some reciprocal benefit, as in *Halsall v Brizell*[6] where it was held that an assignee of a building plot would have to pay his contribution towards the expenses of roads and sewers on an estate, if he wished to use them, the original purchasers having covenanted to do so. Otherwise, a positive covenant in favour of other land will be unenforceable against the tenant.

(b) *Restrictive covenants*   The burden of restrictive covenants cannot pass *at law*, but under the rule first formulated in *Tulk v Moxhay*[7] and later developed, it is allowed to pass *in equity*, provided that the four following conditions are satisfied:

    (i) The covenant must be negative in substance (see above), and where parts of the covenant are separable, this limb of the rule will be applied to the parts separately, with the result that the covenant as expressed may be enforceable in parts, as indeed was a part of the covenant in *Tulk v Moxhay* which provided for maintenance of the garden.

    (ii) The covenant must be made for the benefit and protection of

---

3   (1848) 2 Ph 774.
4   *Haywood v Brunswick Benefit Building Society* (1881) 8 QBD 403.
5   The position was not changed by LPA 1925 s 79.
6   [1957] Ch 169, [1957] 1 All ER 371.
7   (1848) 2 Ph 774.

adjacent land retained by the covenantee, as for example, by preserving its value. Apart from the original covenantee, therefore, successors in title to that land can enforce the restriction only as long as they retain the land for whose benefit the covenant was imposed. This limb is frequently invoked in justification of covenants taken by vendors of business premises purporting to restrict certain trades for the purpose of protecting local trading interests. Each case must be taken on its merits, having regard to the nature of the trade, the nature of the area and the proximity of the respective premises.

(iii) The burden of the covenant must have been *intended* to run with the land, so distinguishing it from a personal covenant. A covenant made expressly, or impliedly, as it is under s 79 of the Law of Property Act 1925, on behalf of himself his successors in title and persons deriving title under him or them, is prima facie evidence of such intention, for the covenantor thereby gives an indemnity against breaches committed when he no longer has possession.

(iv) A purchaser without notice is not bound by a restrictive covenant. Thus:

(a) Where the covenant was created before 1926, a bona fide purchaser of a legal estate for value without notice (actual, imputed or constructive) will not be bound;

(b) Where the covenant was created after 1925, it will be void against a subsequent purchaser of a legal estate for money or money's worth unless it is protected by registration under the Land Charges Act 1972,[8] or, if the land is registered, by entry of a notice under the Land Registration Act 1925.[9] Not only does registration of such covenants constitute 'actual' notice;[10] it constitutes the only form of notice, and if the covenant is not registered, he will take free of it, even though he knew of it *aliunde*.[11]

By way of exception to the rule in *Tulk v Moxhay* limb (ii) above is waived in relation to 'schemes of development' under the principles laid down in *Elliston v Reacher*[12] (see above); and no longer is the exception confined to covenants under a formal scheme as defined in that case, but

---

8 LCA 1972 ss 2(5), 4(6). See *Midland Bank Trust Co Ltd v Green* [1981] AC 513, [1981] 1 All ER 153, HL.

9 LRA 1925 s 50.

10 LPA 1925 s 198 (unregistered land); LRA 1925 s 50(6) (registered land).

11 LPA 1925 s 199(1)(i) (unregistered land); LRA 1925 s 59(6) (registered land).

12 [1908] 2 Ch 374.

will be allowed where common interests and intentions are expressed in the respective conveyances.

A restrictive covenant may be enforceable against a tenant, therefore, by injunction, within the rules of *Tulk v Moxhay* or *Elliston v Reacher*. This can, and often does, produce harsh results, partly in consequence of s 44[13] of the Law of Property Act 1925, which provides that in the absence of agreement to the contrary, he may call for any superior title other than the lease under which his immediate landlord holds. As he never has a right to inspect the freehold title, he may have no means of discovering the names of possible covenantees by which to search for covenants in the land charges register. He may therefore find, albeit too late if he has already taken the lease, that he is bound by a restrictive covenant of which he had no means of knowing. In respect of pre-1926 covenants only will he be 'immune' by virtue of his ignorance of them when he took the lease.[14] Clearly this can produce disastrous results with regard to user covenants.

Liability to superior landlord

Restrictive covenants in superior leases are binding on a sub-tenant under the rule in *Tulk v Moxhay* just as freehold covenants, but he does not run quite the same risks of being bound by such covenants without having had knowledge of them; indeed, his very ignorance may be his protection. Section 44 of the Law of Property Act 1925, precludes him from inspecting any title superior to that of his own landlord; furthermore, he is not affected by notice of any incumbrances that would have been revealed by any title so denied to him.[15] Therefore, since restrictive covenants in leases are not registrable, he cannot be bound by such a covenant unless he has actual, or constructive notice. However, he is not by s 44 precluded from calling for his immediate landlord's title, and under the rule in *Patman v Harland*[16] he will be deemed to have constructive notice of all matters that inspection of that title would have revealed. Thus it is a foolhardy thing to take a sub-lease without calling for title, and the courts will show little sympathy.[17]

---

13 Sub-ss (2)–(4).
14 *Shears v Wells* [1936] 1 All ER 832.
15 LPA 1925 s 44(5).
16 (1881) 17 Ch D 353.
17 For refusal of relief against forfeiture where a tenant accepted title without investigation, see *Imray v Oakshette* [1897] 2 QB 218, CA.

Chapter 11

Devolution of title

I BY ACT OF THE PARTIES

We have already considered the rights and liabilities of successors in title to the original parties to a lease, which depend for their enforceability upon privity of estate. In this chapter, it remains to summarise briefly the various ways in which title to the lease and to the reversion can devolve. Such devolution is by act of the parties[1] or by operation of law.

Assignment of the term

In the absence of an absolute covenant in his lease prohibiting assignment, any tenant (other than a tenant at will and a tenant on sufferance, who *ex hypothesi* have no terms) may assign the residue of his term, whenever and to whomsoever he pleases. We have seen, however, that the original tenant cannot (except in the case of a perpetually renewable lease), by virtue of an assignment, rid himself of his contractual liability under the terms of the tenancy *vis-à-vis* the landlord, and that his liability will continue – enforceable albeit in the last resort only (i e in default of satisfaction by the tenant for the time-being) – for the duration of the tenancy. In effect, this is a practical limitation upon his freedom to assign, for if he assigns to an irresponsible person, or towards the very end of the term, he does so at his own risk. On the other hand, he may be restricted in his powers of assignment by a 'qualified covenant' against assignment (i e that he may not assign except with the landlord's consent) the effect of which we have already considered. Lack of consent in such cases will not invalidate the assignment *per se*, but if the landlord has reserved the right to re-enter for forfeiture for breach of the covenant, the assignee risks forfeiture. For that reason, it is incumbent on the assignor to procure the necessary consent in the form required (e g in writing).

A tenancy is assigned in much the same way as a tenancy is created,

---

1 See LPA 1925 s 4(2).

and the formalities are the same. So, for a contract for an assignment to be enforceable between the parties, it must satisfy the requirements of s 40 of the Law of Property Act 1925, and for it to be binding on third parties, it must be registered as an estate contract under the Land Charges Act 1972 (Class C(iv)), or, in the case of registered land, be protected by notice under the Land Registration Act 1925. So, too, the assignment must be by deed in order to transfer a legal estate to the assignee, under s 52 of the Law of Property Act 1925, even if the tenancy is one which was not required by law to be by deed. By s 72(1) of the 1925 Act, a person may assign a lease to himself jointly with another person, and by s 72(4), two or more persons may assign a lease to one or some of themselves only. By s 72(3), a person holding a lease in one capacity may effectively assign it to himself to hold in another capacity, but a tenant cannot assign the lease to himself.[2]

An assignment of the term is an out-and-out transfer (whether intentionally or not) of all the rights that the tenant has under the lease. Thus, if a tenant purports to grant a sub-lease of a term which is equal to, or longer than, his own term, this operates as an assignment, and not as a sub-lease.[3] Where a periodic tenant grants a sub-tenancy for a fixed term, the transaction may create a sub-tenancy initially, but will operate as an assignment should his own tenancy be terminated by a notice to quit before the expiration of the sub-tenancy. (In the case of business tenancies to which Part II of the Landlord and Tenant Act 1954 applies, however, a continuing tenancy (under s 24) will apparently support an under-lease for a longer term than that of the original and continuing head lease.[4])

An assignment by deed is a conveyance, and therefore s 62 of the Law of Property Act 1925 will operate to transfer to the assignee the benefit of all rights, easements, etc, enjoyed with the land. Formerly, the deed set out the covenants entered into between the assignor and the assignee, but this is no longer necessary where the assignment is for consideration since by virtue of s 77 (and Schedule 2), if the assignor expressly conveys as 'beneficial owner', the assignor is deemed automatically to covenant with the assignee:

(a)   that the lease is in full force;
(b)   that all the rent, covenants and conditions have been paid, performed and observed up to the date of the assignment;
(c)   that he has power to assign;
(d)   that the assignee shall have quiet enjoyment for the rest of the term

---

2   See *Rye v Rye* [1962] AC 496, [1962] 1 All ER 146, (1962) 78 LQR 175, HL.
3   *Milmo v Carreras* [1946] KB 306, [1946] 1 All ER 28, CA.
4   *William Skelton & Son Ltd v Harrison & Pinder Ltd* [1975] QB 361, [1975] 1 All ER 182. In the case of periodic assured tenancies, cf Housing Act 1988 s 18(3).

(ie that he will not be dispossessed by the assignor or any person claiming under him);

(e)   that the property is free from incumbrances; and

(f)   that he will execute any further assurances necessary to vest the property in the assignee.

The assignee, for his part, is deemed to covenant with the assignor that he will pay the rent and perform the covenants in the lease and keep the assignor indemnified against non-payment of rent and breaches of covenant for the rest of the term.

At common law, there is no obligation on the parties to an assignment to give notice of the assignment to the landlord, but express covenants to that effect are commonly found.[5] Such a provision may even require that a copy of the assignment be given to the landlord, or that the assignment itself be prepared by the landlord's solicitor.

Severance of the term

Severance of the term occurs where part of the land under the tenancy is assigned to a third party, or where the whole of the land is assigned to several different people in parts. In that event, an assignee of part may be sued on a proportionate part of the rent due on the whole,[6] though he is liable to a distress for rent due on any part of the land. Consequently, if an assignee of part of the land suffers distress, or pays rent under threat of distress, in respect of arrears due on the whole of the land, he is entitled to recover a proportionate contribution from the tenants of the other parts.[7]

Mortgage of the term

By s 86(1) of the Law of Property Act 1925, all mortgages of leaseholds must be by sub-demise or charge by deed by way of legal mortgage; and any purported assignment of a term of years absolute by way of mortgage takes effect as a sub-lease for a term ten days less than the term purported to be assigned (s 86(2)). A mortgagee by sub-demise is not himself liable on the covenants in the lease, for there is no privity of estate between the mortgagee of the term and the landlord. The mortgagee's position is that of a sub-tenant; accordingly, he has the same rights to seek a vesting order under s 146(4) of the Law of Property Act 1925, in forfeiture proceedings (Chapter 13).

---

5   For such a requirement in the case of perpetually renewable leases, see LPA 1922 s 145 and Sch 15.

6   *Curtis v Spitty* (1835) 1 Bing NC 756.

7   See *Witham v Bullock* (1939) 55 TLR 617.

Section 101(1) of the 1925 Act confers upon a mortgagee by deed a power of sale, and in the event of its exercise, s 89(1) provides that the conveyance by him will operate to convey not just the term of the mortgage (i e the term of the sub-tenancy) but the full term of the tenancy (i e an enlarged interest) unless the conveyance expressly provides otherwise with leave of the court. This applies also to mortgagees with a legal charge.

An equitable mortgagee by deposit of the title deeds cannot come within the above provisions; nor has the landlord any remedies against him.

Assignment of the reversion

We are concerned with the assignment of the reversion only as regards the enforceability of the tenant's rights and obligations under the lease, and this has already been discussed (Chapter 5).

II BY OPERATION OF LAW

Bankruptcy of the landlord

Together with all the other property belonging to the landlord, a reversion upon a lease vests, by virtue of ss 283, 306 and 436 of the Insolvency Act 1986, in his trustee in bankruptcy. If the reversion is a liability, rather than an asset, the trustee may disclaim it under s 314 and Sch 5 as being land burdened with onerous covenants; and on such disclaimer the tenant would be entitled to have the reversion vested in him.

Bankruptcy of the tenant

It is common for the landlord to insert in the lease a proviso for re-entry or forfeiture in the event of the tenant becoming bankrupt and such a covenant is perfectly valid, but it is not a 'usual' covenant. The way in which the proviso is framed, however, is important, for as with all provisos for re-entry, it will be construed against the landlord. So where the proviso is reserved 'if the tenant or his assigns become bankrupt', there can be no forfeiture if the tenant becomes bankrupt after he has assigned the tenancy,[8] for it is assumed that it was intended to operate only on the bankruptcy of the tenant for the time being.

In the absence of a proviso for re-entry for forfeiture the lease will vest, under s 306, automatically in the official receiver on the tenant being

---

8 *Smith v Gronow* [1891] 2 QB 394.

adjudged bankrupt, and in the bankrupt's trustee from the time of his appointment.[9] The trustee then becomes liable on the covenants until he disposes of the lease.

One of the duties of a trustee in bankruptcy is to realise the assets of the bankrupt, by sale of his property. But this may raise a problem if the lease contains a covenant against assignment.

The trustee himself takes the lease by operation of law, which involves no breach of a covenant against assignment, but when he assigns it, the problem is to know whether such an assignment is a breach of the covenant. The law is not certain on this point. In some cases a trustee in bankruptcy has been held entitled to assign without the landlord's consent, even where it would otherwise be required.[10] But it would be dangerous to suppose that this can be stated as a general proposition of law, for such cases can usually be explained by reference to the precise wording of the covenants used. For example, a covenant expressed to bind the tenant and his assigns has been held to bind his trustee in bankruptcy.[11]

The landlord is apparently entitled, under s 345, to apply to the court for rescission of the lease, on such terms as to payment of damages for non-performance of covenants under the lease as may seem equitable.

If, on the other hand, the bankrupt tenant's lease is onerous, unprofitable, unsaleable, or not readily saleable, the trustee may disclaim it under s 315 of the 1986 Act and the Bankruptcy Rules 1986[12] within 12 months of his appointment as trustee.

The trustee may, on giving notice in the prescribed form, disclaim an onerous lease[13] or an unprofitable contract for a lease, without the leave of the court, notwithstanding that he has taken possession, endeavoured to sell the property or otherwise exercised rights of ownership over it (s 315(1)). A copy of the disclaimer must, in principle, be served on every person claiming under the bankrupt tenant as mortgagee or underlessee. If such a copy is not served, the disclaimer is ineffective. The mortgagee or underlessee may apply to the court for an order under s 320, with a view to having the lease vested in him. However, the court may nonetheless direct that the disclaimer is to take effect. In such a case, and also where an order under s 320 is made, the court may make any order it thinks fit with regard to fixtures, tenants' improvements and other

---

9 This automatic vesting applies to a protected tenancy under the Rent Act 1977: *Smalley v Quarrier* [1975] 2 All ER 688, [1975] 1 WLR 938, CA; but not, since it is purely a personal right of occupation, to a statutory tenancy thereunder: *Sutton v Dorf* [1932] 2 KB 304; also *Eyre v Hall* [1986] 2 EGLR 95, CA.

10 *Doe d Goodbehere v Bevan* (1815) 3 M & S 353.

11 *Re Wright, ex p Landau v The Trustee* [1949] Ch 729, [1949] 2 All ER 605.

12 SI 1986/1925.

13 I e a lease subject to onerous covenants by the tenant, such as to repair or restricting the user of the premises: see *Eyre v Hall*, supra.

matters (s 317(2)). Special rules apply to disclaimers of leases of dwelling-houses (s 318).

A liquidator winding up a company has a similar power of disclaimer under ss 178–182 of the 1986 Act, to that of a trustee in bankruptcy.

Disclaimer has the same effect as surrender, but is different in nature because the landlord's consent is not necessary. Its effect is to extinguish the right and liabilities between the landlord and the trustee.[14]

If the assignee is a company in liquidation or an individual bankrupt as the case may be, whose liquidator or trustee disclaims the lease, the term is not thereby destroyed; the original lessee remains liable for rent throughout the remainder thereof: he is not by the assignment of the term reduced merely to a surety for the discharge of the company's or individual's obligations.[15]

Where the trustee proposes to disclaim, any person interested (including the lessor himself, the mortgagee, and a sub-tenant) has a right to apply to the court to have the lease vested in him.

Under s 347 the landlord may distrain for up to six months' rent. If on sale of the tenant's goods seized, he realises *more* than the six months' due, he will have to hand over the surplus to the trustee in bankruptcy, even if the rent is more than six months in arrears. For the difference, he must prove in pari passu with the other creditors, and therefore gets no priority. Alternatively, he can forego his right to distrain altogether and bring an action for *all* arrears like all other creditors.[16]

Death of the landlord

On the death of the landlord, his reversion will vest, together with all his other property, in his personal representatives, under the Administration of Estates Act 1925, i e the executors of his will, if any, or otherwise, in the President of the Family Division of the High Court and then in his administrators, on the grant of letters of administration. Once a lease has vested in personal representatives, they are in the same position as was the deceased landlord, and may, for example, sue the tenant for breaches of covenant committed before the landlord's death. When they come to dispose of the reversion in accordance with the will or under the law of intestate succession, they do so by simple 'assent' in writing.

---

14 But the trustee remains liable for rent until notice of disclaimer is served on the landlord: *Re HH Realisations Ltd* (1975) 31 P & CR 249.

15 *Warnford Investments Ltd v Duckworth* [1979] Ch 127, [1978] 2 All ER 517.

16 If the landlord serves a notice on any underlessee to pay rent, by Law of Distress Amendment Act 1908 s 6, he gains priority over a mortgagee's receiver: *Rhodes v Allied Dunbar (Pension Services) Ltd* [1988] EGCS 152, CA.

Death of the tenant

A deceased tenant's lease similarly vests in his personal representatives under the Administration of Estates Act 1925. They are liable to the landlord in respect of any liabilities under the lease, but only to the extent of the value of any assets. The landlord has no priority over other creditors. When they have satisfied all the deceased tenant's debts and claims the personal representatives should vest the remainder of his property in the person beneficially entitled under his will or by virtue of his intestacy. Vesting of the lease is by simple 'assent' in writing. As in the case of bankruptcy, it is a matter of construction whether a covenant against assignment will bind the personal representatives.

III EXECUTION UPON LEASEHOLDS

Fieri facias

If the tenant fails to satisfy a judgment debt, the sheriff, under a writ of *fieri facias* may levy the debt on his land or goods, and so may seize his leasehold interest. The leasehold may be sold, whereupon title will be transferred from the tenant to the purchaser by an assignment executed by the sheriff.[17] If a purchaser cannot be found to take the fixtures with the leasehold, they must be sold separately.[18]

Execution under the writ of *fieri facias* results in an assignment by order of the court. The original tenant remains liable on all the covenants for the rest of the term as assignor, but by the same token, he is indemnified against future breaches by the assignee.

Charging order

The court has the power to impose a charging order, under the Charging Orders Act 1979, on any leasehold interest of the debtor, whether such interest is legal or equitable. The aim of the charge is to secure the payment of any moneys due or to become due under a judgment or order. The full details of the 1979 Act lie outside the scope of this book; but a charging order must be protected by registration. In the case of registered land, this is achieved by either a creditor's notice or a caution (s 59 of the Land Registration Act 1925). In the case of unregistered land, a charging order must be registered in the register of writs and orders affecting land (s 6 of the Land Charges Act 1972). In either case, failure to register renders the charging order in principle unenforceable against third parties.

---

17 *Playfair v Musgrove* (1845) 14 M & W 239.
18 *Barnard v Leigh* (1815) 1 Stark 43.

PART C
TERMINATION OF TENANCIES

Chapter 12

Introduction

I TERMINATION AT COMMON LAW

Part C of this book is concerned with an enumeration of the methods by which, at common law, a fixed-term lease or periodic tenancy may be terminated. It will be seen that an important method for determining a fixed-term lease before its expiry date is forfeiture, which, because of the potentially serious financial loss to the tenant it may entail, is hedged about with statutory and equitable restrictions.[1] Periodic tenancies are terminable, on the part of either side, by means of a notice to quit, which may, in the absence of contractual or statutory restrictions (see below) be served at any time.

For the sake of simplicity, the rules governing termination at common law are discussed separately from the rules laid down by statute, in the case of residential, business and agricultural tenancies, for the determination of tenancies within each code. Sometimes, as with business tenancies, common-law methods of determination are expressly preserved as fully efficacious: accordingly, tenants' notices to quit, surrender and forfeiture, are all preserved as effective means of determining a business tenancy to which Part II of the Landlord and Tenant Act 1954 applies, and thus of obtaining physical repossession of the premises (s 24(2)).[2] By contrast, in the private residential sector, generally, the landlord may obtain physical repossession of the demised premises only if he proves one or more statutory grounds for possession (see Chapters 17 and 18 and also Part G). In that sector, therefore, even if the common law lease or tenancy has ended by effluxion of time, the tenant is entitled to retain possession under one of three statutory codes.

In short, the common law methods of termination of leases and tenancies must be considered because, unless they are understood, it is not possible to deal with statutory security; but the various statutory codes conferring security of tenure on business, residential and agricultural tenants override, to a greater or lesser extent, the common

---

1 Forfeiture for non-payment of rent is considered in ch 8.
2 See further ch 24.

law methods to be discussed. Security of tenure despite the determination of the lease or tenancy at common law is a personal right of occupation given by Parliament. In the case of business tenancies, 'continuation' is a method of prolonging the occupation of the tenant pending the grant of a new tenancy or his removal from the premises. In the case of agricultural holdings, the tenant's tenancy is prolonged artificially. In the case of statutory tenancies under the Rent Act 1977, the rights of continuing occupation given to tenants are purely personal. As was put in one case, the Act prevented the landlord from evicting the tenant without a county court order, but was only a barrier in the landlord's right of action for possession.[3]

II FRUSTRATION

Frustration is one means by which it is possible, though not very likely, that an executed lease may be brought to an end, if a frustrating event takes place during the currency of the lease. In the present context, frustration is some event, such as the total destruction of the land itself, or the rendering of the land totally or substantially unusable for a mutually contemplated purpose throughout the lease, which destroys the whole basis of the contractual relationship of landlord and tenant.[4] Should frustration take place, the tenant is relieved thereafter from any liability to pay rent.

Since an executed lease creates an estate in land, the relevant event may only amount to frustration if it is very grave indeed. The following have been insufficiently so: destruction of buildings on the land; utter impossibility of building on the land due to wartime regulations;[5] the fact that some part of the land could not be used at all for quite a significant part of the lease, or that there will be severe disruption to the user of the demised premises for the purpose or purposes contemplated in the lease, for part of the term.[6] In none of these instances was the event regarded as serious enough to undermine the whole basis of the lease.

If an event is so serious that it goes to the whole foundation of the lease, such as those mentioned earlier, it may amount to frustration; and thus, even if the bare legal estate in the land granted by the lease continued, it would then be worthless and useless.[7]

---

3 *Moses v Lovegrove* [1952] 2 QB 533 at 544, [1952] 1 All ER 1279 at 1285, CA.
4 *National Carriers Ltd v Panalpina (Northern) Ltd* [1981] AC 675, [1981] 1 All ER 161, HL. Frustration may also apply to a contract for a lease: *Rom Securities Ltd v Rogers (Holdings) Ltd* (1967) 205 Estates Gazette 427.
5 *Cricklewood Property and Investment Trust Ltd v Leighton's Investment Trust Ltd* [1945] AC 221, [1945] 1 All ER 252, HL.
6 *National Carriers Ltd v Panalpina (Northern) Ltd*, supra.
7 See Lord Wilberforce in *National Carriers Ltd v Panalpina (Northern) Ltd* [1981] 1 All ER 161 at 171.

Chapter 13

Modes of termination

I EFFLUXION OF TIME

The estate in land granted by a fixed-term lease comes to an end automatically when the initial term agreed expires, and at common law, the tenant becomes a trespasser after such expiry. Should the former tenant hold over, the landlord may, for example, grant him a new tenancy for a term certain or there may be a tenancy at will; or, if the landlord accepts rent for a period, the former tenant is impliedly granted a periodic tenancy.[1]

As indicated later (Parts D–G), statute has profoundly affected the position in relation to business, residential and agricultural tenancies. In the case of business tenancies, for example, a fixed-term lease which has ended at common law, by effluxion of time, does not terminate but is continued by s 24(1) of the Landlord and Tenant Act 1954 on, in principle, the same terms as before. The continuing tenancy, a creature of statute, may only be determined in accordance with a specific notice procedure laid down by the 1954 Act Part II.

Residential tenants may well be fully protected by one of three separate statutory codes, two of which, the Rent Act 1977 and the Housing Act 1988 Part I, which are mutually exclusive, apply to private sector tenants[2] and one of which, the Housing Act 1985 Part IV, applies to public sector tenants. If there is any general notion behind the conferral of security by these codes, it is that, once the common law fixed-term lease[3] has determined, by effluxion of time (or by any other means such as forfeiture), the tenant has a *personal* right to remain in occupation of the residential premises concerned, thanks to the relevant statutory code. Accordingly, it was said that 'the statutory tenant [under the Rent Acts) has no estate as tenant, but a personal right to retain the

---

1 See further ch 2.
2 See Part D chs 16–18. The date of creation of the tenancy is crucial.
3 This point applies with equal force to periodic tenancies – the codes apply to these as much as to terms certain.

property'.[4] Strikingly, it was suggested that a statutory tenant 'is not a tenant at all; although he cannot be turned out of possession so long as he complies with the provisions of the statute, he has no estate or interest in the premises.'[5] The general security[6] given by all three codes is that, even if the landlord may be entitled to possession owing to the term certain having expired, he is only able to obtain physical repossession of the residential premises concerned if he is able to establish one of a number of statutory grounds, and, in some cases, only if he is able to satisfy the court that it is reasonable to order possession.

In other words, merely because a fixed-term lease has expired by effluxion of time, this does not *ipso facto* entitle the landlord to regain physical possession if the tenant refuses to quit voluntarily and the landlord is unwilling to grant a new tenancy. The result is, *and this applies to all common-law methods of termination*, that while, at common law, the lease may well have determined, owing to the effect of statute, the reverse applies,[7] and the tenant remains in occupation, provided he continues to comply with the requirements of the statutory code concerned, unless and until the landlord is able to evict him on statute-based grounds.

II EXERCISE OF AN EXPRESS POWER

Just as the parties to a lease may fix its duration, so too they may agree to confer on one or both parties an express power under the lease to determine it before it would otherwise expire. Such is the nature of an option to determine the lease or a proviso for resumption for building purposes, etc. A reservation of a right of re-entry for breach of a covenant in the lease is no less a reservation of such a power, but because the law of forfeiture is subject to special statutory provisions, it is considered below, under a separate head.

Tenants may be conferred, in the lease, an option to determine the lease early, on notice. See further Chapter 7. Likewise, the landlord may have an option to determine the lease, either at stated dates, or by so many months' advance notice given at any time during the lease.[8] The

---

4 *Jessamine Investment Co v Schwartz* [1978] QB 264 at 274, [1976] 3 All ER 521 at 527, CA.
5 *Keeves v Dean* [1924] 1 KB 685 at 694, CA.
6 For the exceptions to this principle, see chs 17 and 18.
7 For a case where this result was itself reversed because the parties validly agreed that a statutory protection was not applicable to the lease in question, see *Syed Hussain v Abdullah Sahib & Co* [1985] 1 WLR 1392, PC. Once the lease expired, the tenant became a trespasser.
8 See e g *Manorlike Ltd v Le Vitas Travel Agency and Consultancy Services Ltd* [1986] 1 All ER 573, CA.

landlord may reserve a right to resume possession, rather than granting himself an option to determine, as for example, where an agricultural tenancy reserves him the right to resume possession of the land if he requires it for building purposes. Such a right is normally exercisable on prior notice at any time during the lease, but it is construed strictly against the landlord and therefore if expressed to be for 'building, planting, accommodation or otherwise', it cannot be exercised for the purposes of sale.[9] The landlord must have a bona fide desire and intention to use the land for the specified purposes.[10]

III OPERATION OF A CONDITION

Leases may be limited conditionally, i e by condition subsequent. The commonest example arises where payment of rent or performance of some other obligation is made a condition of the continuation of the lease. In such cases the law implies a right of re-entry on the part of the landlord whereby he may forfeit the lease on breach of the condition. Other conditions commonly found are death, marriage, non-occupation or bankruptcy by the tenant, and termination of the tenant's contract of employment. A landlord may only resume possession for breach of a condition (e g in the event of the lessee's or his surety's bankruptcy) if first he serves a notice complying with s 146(1) of the LPA 1925 on the lessee.[11] In these cases, the tenancy is terminated on the happening of the event, and the landlord is entitled to resume possession.

A lease granted for a term, conditional on the tenant's continuing occupation of the premises, will terminate automatically if, for whatever reason, even bankruptcy, he parts with possession.[12] Service tenancies often make the continuation of the tenancy conditional on the continuation of the tenant's contract of employment. Again, therefore, cesser of the employment ipso facto, at common law, destroys the tenancy. If the tenant is protected under the Rent Act 1977, the Rent (Agriculture) Act 1976, or Part I of the Housing Act 1988, the landlord will only obtain an order for possession on grounds set out in these Acts: see Part D of this book.

---

9 *Johnson v Edgware etc Rly Co* (1866) 35 LJ Ch 322.
10 *Southend-on-Sea Estates Co Ltd v IRC* [1914] 1 KB 515, CA; affd *sub nom IRC v Southend-on-Sea Estates Co Ltd* [1915] AC 428, HL.
11 *Halliard Property Co Ltd v Jack Segal Ltd* [1978] 1 All ER 1219, [1978] 1 WLR 377.
12 *Doe d Lockwood v Clarke* (1807) 8 East 185.

IV　NOTICE TO QUIT

Common law general rules

A periodic tenancy is determinable, at common law, by a notice to quit of
the correct length, served by either the landlord or the tenant on the
other party. The length of a notice to quit is, if no express provision is
made in the tenancy, that which corresponds to the length of a period of
the tenancy. So, in the case of a weekly tenancy, the length of a notice is
one week, in the case of a monthly tenancy, one month, and in the case of
a quarterly tenancy, one quarter, these periods to run from the date of
entry.[13] In the case of a tenancy from year to year, and for a tenancy for a
greater period than that, however, the rule is that six months notice to
quit is required. 'Month' is to be taken as meaning a calendar month,
and where a notice of one month is required, therefore, it ends in the
corresponding date in the appropriate subsequent month, no matter
that some months are longer than others.[14]

A periodic tenancy is generally terminable only on one day in any
period, and an agreement to the contrary must be clear. It is therefore
possible to use express provisions as to termination to identify the length
of the relevant periods, as with a tenancy for an apparently indefinite
period, terminable at any time on one month's notice: this takes effect as
a monthly tenancy.[15]

Provisions purporting completely to preclude one party or the other
from serving a notice to quit are void, but provisions fettering but not
totally precluding a landlord's or tenant's power to serve a notice to quit
are upheld. See further Chapter 2. At the same time, the parties may
validly agree to a different period of notice than that prescribed by the
common law, subject to any statutory restrictions which apply in the
case of residential tenancies and agricultural holdings. So, a yearly
tenancy was validly made terminable on three months' notice, instead of
at the end of any year of the tenancy,[16] and it is possible, no doubt, to
make a monthly tenancy determinable at the will of the landlord, which
renders the tenancy a monthly tenancy determinable at any time, not a
tenancy at will.

Statutory restrictions

In the case of residential tenancies and agricultural holdings, special
rules as to the length of notice apply, considered elsewhere in this
book.[17] Notices to determine business tenancies are likewise governed

---

13　If a quarterly tenant enters during a quarter, his tenancy is terminable on the usual
　　quarter days, not on dates referable to the date of entry: *Croft v William F Blay Ltd*
　　[1919] 2 Ch 343, CA.
14　*Dodds v Walker* [1981] 2 All ER 609, HL.
15　*Doe d Lansdell v Gower* (1851) 17 QB 589.
16　*King v Eversfield* [1897] 2 QB 475, CA.
17　Chs 2, 19 and 31.

by specific rules.[18] These rules override the common law rules and also any inconsistent stipulations of the parties.

Expiry of a notice to quit

Even though a periodic tenancy strictly expires at midnight of the day before the anniversary, a notice will be valid if it is expressed to expire either on the anniversary of the commencement of the tenancy or on the previous day,[19] whether the tenancy is a yearly, monthly or weekly tenancy.[20] A notice to quit at noon, however, is bad at common law, by virtue of the strict rule as to expiry.[1]

The notice need not specify the date of expiry, provided that the date is clearly identifiable, as for example 'at the expiration of the present year's tenancy'.[2] Moreover, if the date of the commencement of the tenancy is uncertain, it may be advisable for the notice not only to specify what is thought to be the proper date of expiry, but also to provide further that if that is not the proper date, the notice will expire on the first date thereafter upon which the tenancy could lawfully be terminated.[3] Where the date of commencement of the tenancy is unknown or cannot be proved by the landlord, it would be dangerous for him to rely solely on a date specified in the notice, for such a notice is not even prima facie evidence that that is the proper date, and if the tenant can show that it is not, the notice will be bad. In such cases, it would be advisable to get the tenant to accept notice for a specified date or to state the date of the commencement of the tenancy, for presumably he would thereby be estopped from denying the validity of a notice given accordingly.

The length of the notice required need not be exclusive of the date that is given and the date of its expiry. Unless *clear notice* is stipulated in the lease, therefore, a weekly tenancy which commenced on a Saturday may be terminated on a Saturday by a notice given on the previous Saturday. So too, a notice given on Friday, 4 March, to expire on Friday, 1 April, has been held to satisfy the requirements of s 5 of the Protection from Eviction Act 1977.[4]

Form of notice

A parol notice is good at common law, though it is advisable that it

---

18 Ch 24.
19 *Sidebotham v Holland* [1895] 1 QB 378.
20 *Crate v Miller* [1947] KB 946, [1947] 2 All ER 45.
1   *Bathavon RDC v Carlile* [1958] 1 QB 461, [1958] 1 All ER 801.
2   *Doe d Gorst v Timothy* (1847) 2 Car & Kir 351.
3   *Addis v Burrows* [1948] 1 KB 444, [1948] 1 All ER 177 but see *P Phipps & Co (Northampton and Towcester Breweries) Ltd v Rogers* [1925] 1 KB 14.
4   *Schnabel v Allard* [1967] 1 QB 627, [1966] 3 All ER 816. In *Harler v Calder* (1989) Independent, 2 January, CA, held that a notice to quit in a monthly tenancy must take effect on a rent day.

should be in writing to avoid disputes that might otherwise arise; but, even then, it need not be signed or witnessed. In the case of a landlord's notice to quit a dwelling, the notice must contain prescribed information, for example, informing the tenant that if he does not quit, an order for possession from the court will be required to evict him.[5] The object and contents of a notice must be clear and unambiguous. It must show a clear intention to terminate the tenancy, and must not itself be made conditional. On the other hand, it may be accompanied by an offer of a new tenancy at higher rent.[6] A landlord's notice to quit 'on or before . . .' a specified date is valid and is construed as entitling the tenant to leave sooner, if he so desires.[7]

The notice must extend to the whole of the land comprised in the tenancy, except by express agreement, or by virtue of s 140 of the Law of Property Act 1925 (severance of the reversion) or in cases to which s 31 of the Agricultural Holdings Act 1986 applies.

Errors in notice to quit

A notice to quit which states the wrong date of expiry, without any further qualification, is bad.[8] An error in a notice to quit which is due to an obvious slip, such as a typing mistake, may be ignored and the court has the power to substitute the correct date provided that it would have been clear to a reasonable tenant from the terms of the lease, what the correct date should have been.[9] A notice to quit business premises which failed to mention part of the premises was, accordingly, held to apply to the whole.[10] The tenant must, however, be given sufficient information as to what he is required to quit, and a notice which failed to mention storage and other facilities to which the tenant was entitled under his lease was held bad.[11]

Service of notice

A notice to quit may be given either by the landlord or by the tenant, or by their authorised agents. A notice given by or to one joint tenant will bind them all.[12] If served personally, it need not be directed to the party

---

5   Notices to Quit (Prescribed Information) Regulations SI 1988/2201.
6   *Ahearn v Bellman* (1879) 4 Ex D 201.
7   *Dagger v Shepherd* [1946] KB 215, [1946] 1 All ER 133.
8   *Doe d Spicer v Lea* (1809) 11 East 312; cf *P Phipps & Co v Rogers*, supra.
9   *Carradine Properties Ltd v Aslam* [1976] 1 All ER 573, [1976] 1 WLR 442; *Germax Securities Ltd v Spiegal* (1978) 37 P & CR 204.
10 *Safeway Food Stores Ltd v Morris* (1980) 254 Estates Gazette 1091.
11 *Herongrove Ltd v Wates City of London Properties plc* [1988] 1 EGLR 82.
12 *Greenwich London Borough Council v McGrady* (1982) 81 LGR 288, CA; *Leek and Moorlands Building Society v Clark* [1952] 2 QB 788, [1952] 2 All ER 492, CA; *Parsons v Parsons* [1983] 1 WLR 1390; *Annen v Rattee* [1985] 1 EGLR 136, CA; F. Webb [1983] Conv 194. Thus, one joint tenant may effectually end an assured tenancy under the Housing Act 1988.

served, by name, and if sent to him, it may be addressed to him by description. It is sufficient to leave the notice with the addressee's wife or servant, provided that the recipient is made to understand that it should be delivered, whether or not it ever is.[13] A notice that is just left on the premises, e g under the door of the tenant's house, will be validly served if it can be shown that it came into his hands in time.[14]

A notice may be served on a company under the Companies Act 1985 by leaving it at or sending it by post to the registered office of the company.

Leases not infrequently incorporate the provisions of s 196 of the Law of Property Act 1925. This provision may usefully be made to apply to any notices required under the lease. It provides that a notice:

1 must be in writing;
2 is sufficient if addressed by designation and not by name;
3 is sufficiently served if it is left at the last-known place of abode or business in the United Kingdom of the addressee, or in the case of a notice served on the tenant, if it is affixed or left for him on the land or any house or building comprised in the lease;
4 is sufficiently served if sent by registered post or recorded delivery and not returned undelivered; and,
5 if so posted, is deemed to have been delivered at the time it would, in the ordinary course of post, be delivered.

Waiver of notice

Strictly speaking, a valid notice to quit cannot be waived,[15] but will terminate the current tenancy on its expiry, and therefore if the tenant stays on after that date with the landlord's consent, he does so under a new agreement. A new tenancy in such circumstances may be implied from any conduct of the parties that indicates that they recognise the creation of a new tenancy after the expiration of the old tenancy, as where the landlord accepts rent accruing after that date, distrains for arrears of rent, or serves a second notice to quit for a later date.[16] There must, however, have been an intention to create a new tenancy,[17] and where the occupier is claiming a statutory tenancy under the Rent Act 1977, the inference may be that the former landlord is simply considering his position, rather than intent on granting a new tenancy.[18] A second

---

13 *Tanham v Nicholson* (1872) LR 5 HL 561.
14 See also *Lord Newborough v Jones* [1975] Ch 90, [1974] 3 All ER 17, CA.
15 *Clarke v Grant* [1950] 1 KB 104, [1949] 1 All ER 768, CA.
16 *Lowenthal v Vanhoute* [1947] KB 342, [1947] 1 All ER 116.
17 See e g *Baron v Phillips* (1978) 38 P & CR 91.
18 *Marcroft Wagons Ltd v Smith* [1951] 2 KB 496, [1951] 2 All ER 271, CA, as explained in *Street v Mountford* [1985] AC 809, [1985] 2 All ER 289, HL.

notice to quit expressed to expire at an earlier date than the first, is valid, if served in time.[19]

V   SURRENDER

A surrender has been defined[20] as the 'yielding up of an estate for life or years to him that hath an immediate estate in reversion or remainder, wherein the estate for life or years may drown by mutual agreement between them'. Such surrender may be made expressly or may be brought about by operation of law.

Surrender by express terms

An express surrender of a term of more than three years must be by deed (s 52 of the Law of Property Act 1925); otherwise, the surrender must be in writing (s 53). No particular form of words is necessary,[1] but 'surrender and yield up', and 'assign and surrender' are appropriate. A surrender, however, must operate immediately, and cannot, it would seem, be expressed to operate in the future;[2] a purported future surrender may, however, be treated as an enforceable contract to surrender, which is valid.

A tenant's rights to surrender his contractual tenancy are not restricted by the Rent Act nor Part I of the Housing Act 1988; Part II of the 1954 Act, however, provides certain safeguards for the tenant.[3]

Surrender by operation of law

Section 52(2)(c) of the Law of Property Act 1925, excepts surrenders by operation of law from the requirement of a deed, and s 53(1)(a) excepts them from the requirement of writing. In the case of surrender by operation of law, surrender is implied from any unequivocal conduct of the parties, which is inconsistent with the continuance of the existing tenancy. It is not necessary for the tenant physically to quit the premises, at least not where the surrender takes the form of acceptance of a new lease of the same premises, to commence during the currency of the first lease.[4] There must, generally, be the giving up of the right to possession under the old lease, whether orally or in writing.[5]

---

19   *Thompson v McCullough* [1947] KB 447, [1947] 1 All ER 265.
20   Co Litt 337b.
1   *Weddall v Capes* (1836) 1 M & W 50.
2   *Doe d Murrell v Milward* (1838) 3 M & W 328.
3   Landlord and Tenant Act 1954 s 24(2), and s 38(4). See further, chap 23.
4   *Dibbs v Campbell* (1988) 20 HLR 374, CA; also below.
5   *Bush Transport Ltd v Nelson* [1987] 1 EGLR 71, CA.

A surrender of the current lease will not be implied where the tenant accepts from the landlord a new lease which is void or voidable;[6] indeed, surrender is subject to an implied condition that the new lease is valid, and that, if it is not, the current lease will remain in force.[7] Generally speaking, the purpose of the new lease will be to increase the tenant's terms, or vary the land comprised in the tenant's holding; surrender will not normally be implied, however, if the only variation effected is in relation to the rent payable[8] nor if the only variation is giving the tenant a new rent book with broadly similar terms therein but some slight variations.[9]

A mere temporary abandonment of possession by the tenant will not justify an inference of implied surrender; but a permanent abandonment of possession, say after an order for possession, where the landlord thereafter changes the locks and re-lets the premises, may well amount, depending on the facts, to an implied offer by the tenant and acceptance by the landlord of a surrender of the tenancy.[10] It may be otherwise where the tenant simply abandons possession but the landlord has not formally ended the tenancy nor re-let the premises.[11] The act relied upon, from which the landlord's consent to a surrender is to be inferred, must be incapable of any other construction. Thus, the landlord may have taken the keys merely to carry out repairs, and this cannot bring about a surrender by operation of law.[12] So too, in the case of a tenancy from year to year, it has been held that an oral licence from the landlord to the tenant to quit in the middle of a quarter, and the tenant's quitting, were not sufficient for a surrender to be implied.[13]

Operation of a surrender

The effect of a surrender is to transfer to the landlord the whole of the tenant's interest, but subject to any lesser interests which the tenant may have created, e g equitable charges.[14] He cannot prejudice the rights of any sub-tenants, for example, by surrender, any more than he could by an assignment of the lease, and in effect, by s 139 of the Law of Property Act 1925, the landlord is put in the position of an assignee of the lease, for

---

6   *Barclays Bank v Stasek* [1957] Ch 28, [1956] 3 All ER 439.
7   *Knight v Williams* [1901] 1 Ch 256.
8   *Jenkin R Lewis & Son Ltd v Kerman* [1971] Ch 477, [1970] 3 All ER 414.
9   *Smirk v Lyndale Developments Ltd* [1975] Ch 317, [1975] 1 All ER 690, CA. As a result the tenant was able, by squatting, to extend his tenancy to a strip of land not demised to him.
10 *R v London Borough of Croydon Council, ex p Toth* (1986) 18 HLR 493.
11 *Preston Borough Council v Fairclough* (1982) 8 HLR 70, CA.
12 *Boynton-Wood v Trueman* (1961) 177 Estates Gazette 191.
13 *Mollett v Brayne* (1809) 2 Camp 103.
14 *ES Schwab & Co Ltd v McCarthy* (1975) 31 P & CR 196, CA.

the purpose of preserving the rights and obligations under any sub-lease. On the other hand, where the lease is surrendered by operation of law in view of the acceptance of a new lease the respective positions of the landlord and any sub-tenant *vis-à-vis* the tenant are maintained by s 150, as if the original lease had continued.

The effect of surrender upon liabilities for breach of covenant before the surrender is not without doubt. It is generally taken as settled that the tenant will remain liable, for such breaches, even after surrender;[15] nevertheless, in the case of an express surrender, it would be advisable to put the matter beyond all doubt by express agreement in the instrument. This is particularly so where the landlord gives valuable consideration for the surrender, for one would expect the valuation of the leasehold interest to reflect, for example, the condition of the premises, and unless the tenant's liabilities for non-repair are waived, he might find himself bearing the consequential loss in the value of the property twice over.

As regards rent, the tenant is not entitled to recover any part of any rent paid in advance,[16] and before the Apportionment Act 1870, any rent accruing before the surrender, but not yet due, was lost to the landlord,[17] but s 3 may allow apportionment in such cases. The tenant remains liable for any arrears due before the surrender under any personal covenant, if any; if not, the landlord will be able to maintain an action for use and occupation.[18]

Where a new rent is determined followed a rent review, and the lease is surrendered after the review date, the lessee (or his sureties) may remain liable for the reviewed rent from the review date to that of the surrender, depending on the construction of the review clause.[19]

Prima facie, a surrender includes that of the right to remove tenants' fixtures in the absence of express contrary agreement; but where there is surrender by operation of law and the tenant remains in possession under a new lease, the right to remove such fixtures continues throughout the tenant's possession.[20]

VI   MERGER

Where a term of years and the reversion immediately expectant upon it become vested in the same person, the lesser estate is merged with the

---

15   *Richmond v Savill* [1926] 2 KB 530; but see F. E. Farrer, *Conveyancer*, vol xi, pp 73, 81.

16   *William Hill (Football) Ltd v Willen Key and Hardware Ltd* (1964) 108 Sol Jo 482.

17   *Grimman v Legge* (1828) 8 B & C 324.

18   *Shaw v Lomas* (1888) 59 LT 477.

19   *Torminster Properties Ltd v Green* [1983] 2 All ER 457, [1983] 1 WLR 676, CA.

20   *New Zealand Government Property Corpn v HM and S Ltd* [1982] 1 All ER 624, CA.

greater estate, and the term is extinguished. For the two estates to be merged, however, they must be both legal or both equitable. Moreover, by s 185 of the Law of Property Act 1925, there can be no merger where formerly there would have been no merger in equity. In equity the two separate estates were preserved if it was in the interest of the party concerned to keep them separate or if it was his duty to ensure that they should not be merged. Thus, there can be no merger where the two estates vest in one person in different rights, e g one beneficially and the other as tenant for life under a trust.

Where the term is extinguished by merger, all the covenants in the lease are also extinguished. So, where in a lease a landlord entered into a covenant restricting his rights to build on an adjacent plot, and the estates were subsequently merged, the covenant was extinguished, and held to be unenforceable against the purchaser of the plot, in due course.[1]

Surrender is just one example of merger, and the effects of the transaction *vis-à-vis* any sub-tenant, under s 139 of the Law of Property Act 1925, have already been explained. Merger also occurs by act of the parties to a lease where the tenant exercises an option to purchase the landlord's reversion, and by statute, where the tenant has the right to acquire the freehold by enlargement or by enfranchisement.

Enlargement

Enlargement – a forerunner of enfranchisement – was introduced in 1881 as a means of enlarging into freeholds certain long leases at peppercorn rents, or whose rents had not been collected for so long that the identity of the landlord was unknown. Most of the leases affected were granted in Elizabethan times.

The statutory provisions are in s 153 of the Law of Property Act 1925. If by s 153(1):

(a) the original term was for not less than 300 years; and
(b) not less than 200 years of the term are left to run; and
(c) either no rent is payable, or merely a peppercorn rent or other rent having no money value,

the lease can be enlarged into a freehold, whereupon the lease is extinguished. A rent of 'one silver penny if demanded', falls within the section[2] but not a rent of three shillings, for that has value. For the purposes of the section an annual rent not exceeding £1 which has not been paid for 20 years is deemed to be no longer payable (s 153(4)).

---

1 *Golden Lion Hotel (Hunstanton) v Carter* [1965] 3 All ER 506, [1965] 1 WLR 1189.
2 *Re Chapman and Hobbs* (1885) 29 Ch D 1007.

Enfranchisement

Enfranchisement is the term applied to the statutory right of a tenant to acquire the landlord's reversionary freehold interest in the land, on payment of compensation. The Leasehold Reform Act 1967 creates rights to enfranchise in favour of tenants of certain dwelling-houses granted on long leases at low rents. The provisions of the 1967 Act are explained in Part D below.[3]

VII RECOVERY OF DERELICT RENT

Where the tenant leaves, without terminating the tenancy, and cannot be traced, the landlord will presumably wish to terminate the tenancy to enable him to re-let the premises. He may be unable to serve a notice to quit, however, unless the terms of the tenancy provide expressly for the service of notices by leaving them on the premises, as for example, by the incorporation of s 196 of the Law of Property Act 1925, into the lease.

Under s 54 of the Landlord and Tenant Act 1954, the county court may, if it thinks fit, determine a tenancy if the landlord satisfies the court:

(a) that he has taken all reasonable steps to communicate with the person last known to be tenant, and has failed to do so;
(b) that for at least six months immediately prior to the application, no one has been in occupation of any part of the property; and
(c) that during the same period either no rent was payable, or the rent payable has not been paid.

An alternative, but seldom used, method of recovery is under s 16 of the Distress for Rent Act 1737.

VIII DISCLAIMER

Apart from disclaimer of an onerous lease by a trustee in bankruptcy, or by the liquidator of a limited company (see Chapter 11), the tenant of premises used by him for residential or business purposes, or both, which are requisitioned, would, if requisitioning powers are assumed, be entitled to disclaim his lease, provided that it has less than five years to run.[4]

---

3 There is also a right to buy in the public sector in favour of, for instance, local authority tenants. See generally, Hughes *Public Sector Housing Law* (2nd edn, 1987) Butterworths, ch 2.
4 Landlord and Tenant (Requisitioned Land) Act 1942 s 1.

In addition to these statutory rights to disclaim, on the part of the tenant, a lease may be forfeited by the tenant if he disclaims or denies the landlord's title, either by matter of record or by an act *in pais* (see further, Chapter 6).

IX FORFEITURE

1 RIGHT OF RE-ENTRY

A tenant may incur a forfeiture of his lease either by breach of a condition in the lease or by a breach of covenant in the lease. A condition may be express, i e where the lease is made conditional upon the performance of an obligation, or implied, e g disclaimer of the landlord's title. On breach of a condition by the tenant, the landlord's right of re-entry arises automatically, i e even though such a right is not reserved in the lease. A breach of covenant on the other hand, does not entitle him to re-enter, unless the right has been reserved to him in the lease; and in practice, a lease generally contains a proviso for re-entry for breach of any covenant by the tenant. When a right of re-entry accrues, by virtue of a breach, its effect is not to render the lease void, but voidable only, at the landlord's option; and therefore the tenant cannot himself bring the lease to an end, even though he is in breach of condition. Moreover, the right, whether express or implied is lost to the landlord after 12 years from the breach in respect of which it accrued (Limitation Act 1980 s 15(1)), or by *waiver*. The landlord may bring a forfeiture or exercise a right of re-entry as to part only of the demised premises; and relief may in any event be granted in respect of a physically separate part.[5]

Provisos for re-entry, though they may not be construed with the same strictness as conditions, are nevertheless construed against the landlord. Thus, a proviso expressed to take effect if the tenant 'shall do or cause to be done any act, matter or thing contrary to and in breach of any of the covenants' has been held not to apply to a breach of a covenant to repair, since failure to repair is itself an *omission* and not an *act* in breach of a covenant.[6] And a proviso in relation to covenants *thereinafter* contained in the lease has been rendered nugatory for the only covenants by the tenant were contained above.[7] 'Failure to perform', 'breach' and 'non-observance' are phrases commonly used and will apply to both positive and negative covenants, but care should be taken not to qualify an otherwise effective form of words so as to exclude

---

5 *GMS Syndicate Ltd v Gary Elliott Ltd* [1982] Ch 1, [1981] 1 All ER 619.
6 *Doe d Abdy v Stevens* (1832) 3 B & Ad 299.
7 *Doe d Spencer v Godwin* (1815) 4 M & S 265.

one or other kind. A proviso for re-entry has been held not to apply, for example, to a covenant against sub-letting, when expressed to arise 'if the tenant shall commit any breach of the covenants hereinbefore contained and on his part to be performed'.[8]

A proviso for re-entry for breach of any covenant other than a covenant to pay rent is not a *usual* covenant,[9] though in practice, as observed above, it is commonly extended to other covenants in the lease, and the right is commonly reserved in the event of the tenant's or his surety's bankruptcy.

By s 141 of the Law of Property Act 1925, the benefit of every condition of re-entry is annexed and incident to the reversion and passes to an assignee of the reversion. An assignee of the reversion is therefore entitled to re-enter for breaches committed before the assignment to him,[10] unless the breach has already been waived (s 141(3)).

Exercise of a right of re-entry

If a landlord wishes to forfeit the lease for breach of covenant or condition, he must in either case take positive steps to show unequivocally that he intends to terminate the lease, which is not void, but voidable. His right of re-entry is exercisable either by taking possession peaceably, or by bringing an action in ejectment. Therefore, unless the tenant is prepared to give up possession voluntarily,[11] which is rare, the landlord will be obliged to commence proceedings for forfeiture. It is unlawful to enforce a right of re-entry or forfeiture otherwise than by proceedings in court while any person is lawfully residing on the premises or any part of them (Protection from Eviction Act 1977 s 2).

The issue and service of the writ for possession is a conclusive indication that the landlord has irrevocably decided to treat the breach as giving rise to forfeiture.[12] The lease is notionally forfeited at the date the writ is served.[13] At this date, all the covenants in the lease cease to be enforceable by the landlord by injunction or otherwise.[14] The tenant continues to possess an as yet ill-defined interest in the premises pending

---

8 *Harman v Ainslie* [1904] 1 KB 698.
9 *Re Anderton and Milner's Contract* (1890) 45 Ch D 476.
10 *Re King, Robinson v Gray* [1963] Ch 459, [1963] 1 All ER 781; *London and County (A & D) Ltd v Wilfred Sportsman Ltd* [1971] Ch 764, [1970] 2 All ER 600, CA.
11 There is no forfeiture by peaceable re-entry of a head tenant's interest where the landlord does not challenge the continuation of any sub-lease: *Ashton v Sobelman* [1987] 1 All ER 755, [1987] 1 WLR 177.
12 *Serjeant v Nash, Field & Co* [1903] 2 KB 304.
13 *Canas Property Co Ltd v KL Television Services* [1970] 2 QB 433, [1970] 2 All ER 795, CA; *Associated Deliveries Ltd v Harrison* (1984) 50 P & CR 91, CA.
14 *Wheeler v Keeble (1914) Ltd* [1920] 1 Ch 57.

any order for possession.[15] This is sufficient to enable him to claim relief against forfeiture and also to enable a sub-lessee to enforce tenants' covenants.[16]

Waiver of forfeiture

The landlord will lose his right to forfeit a lease by express or implied waiver of the breach. As soon as he becomes aware, himself or by reason of knowledge imputed to him from his agent or servant,[17] of the basic facts which in law constitute a breach of covenant,[18] then the landlord is put on his election. Should he, or his agent then communicate to the tenant his fixed intention not to forfeit (express waiver), or should he or his agent do some unequivocal act which is consistent only with the continued existence of the lease (implied waiver), then the landlord is deemed to have waived the breach, which renders the lease voidable only rather than void *ab initio*. An absolute and unqualified demand for rent[18] or a similar acceptance of rent[19] where, in both cases, it is rent due in a period after the breach, is an automatic implied waiver despite the landlord's assertion, if any, that the demand or acceptance is without prejudice to any right of his to forfeit.[20] This is because implied waiver takes place if the landlord or his agent unequivocally affirms the lease despite the breach. Once the landlord has elected to forfeit, this is regarded as conclusive.[1] Because service of a notice under s 146(1) of the Law of Property Act 1925 is an essential preliminary to forfeiture, it cannot operate as waiver.[2] An offer to purchase the tenant's interest, if made with the requisite knowledge of the breach, may, however, amount to waiver.[3] A mere entry into negotiations cannot do so, however.[4]

Waiver is judged strictly objectively: it is the landlord's acts and not his words or intentions which count; and his agent's acts are imputed to him, as where rent was accepted, in error, by the landlord's agent's servant: waiver took place automatically as the rent was due for a period after the breach.[5] It may be that cases of acceptance of rent fall into a

---

15 *Liverpool Properties Ltd v Oldbridge Investments Ltd* [1985] 2 EGLR 111, CA. See also *Capital and City Holdings Ltd v Dean Warburg Ltd* [1988] EGCS 174, CA.
16 *Peninsular Maritime Ltd v Padseal Ltd* (1981) 259 Estates Gazette 860, CA.
17 *Metropolitan Properties Co Ltd v Cordery* (1979) 39 P & CR 10, CA.
18 *David Blackstone Ltd v Burnetts (West End) Ltd* [1973] 3 All ER 782, [1973] 1 WLR 1487.
19 *Central Estates (Belgravia) Ltd v Woolgar (No 2)* [1972] 3 All ER 610, [1972] 1 WLR 1048, CA; also *Welch v Birrane* (1974) 29 P & CR 102.
20 *Segal Securities Ltd v Thoseby* [1963] 1 QB 887, [1963] 1 All ER 500.
 1 *Expert Clothing Service and Sales Ltd v Hillgate House Ltd* [1986] Ch 340, [1985] 2 All ER 998, CA.
 2 *Church Comrs for England v Nodjoumi* (1985) 51 P & CR 155.
 3 *Bader Properties Ltd v Linley Property Investments Ltd* (1967) 19 P & CR 620 at 641.
 4 *Re National Jazz Centre Ltd* [1988] 2 EGLR 57.
 5 *Central Estates (Belgravia) Ltd v Woolgar (No 2)*, supra.

specific category: it has been held that, in other cases, the court is free to look objectively at all the circumstances of the case, in order to decide whether a landlord's act is so unequivocal as to amount to waiver.[6]

If, having become aware of circumstances which might entitle him to forfeit the lease, the landlord reasonably accepts an explanation from the tenant, his continued acceptance of rent thereafter will not disentitle him or his successor in title, from bringing a forfeiture based on the circumstances in question, if later it emerges that the tenant's explanation was false.[7]

The effect of waiver depends to a degree on the nature of the covenant broken. In the case of negative covenants, such as against assignments or under-lettings, a waiver of a given breach is final in relation thereto; but not in relation to any later breach, which gives rise to a separate cause of action.[8] Where there is a breach of a continuing covenant, such as to repair or as to user, a continuing breach after a waiver gives rise to a fresh cause of action.[9] The question as to at what, if any, point in time, a waiver comes to an end and a fresh cause of action arises, is one of fact.[10]

Generally, in no case will the silence of the landlord amount of itself to waiver.[11] An assignee of the reversion does not, by taking subject to the lease, waive any breaches of covenant.[12]

Where the tenant is a statutory tenant under the Rent Act 1977, the severe principles of implied waiver apply only in part to the landlord. A demand or acceptance of rent, with full knowledge of a breach, is not necessarily waiver, because a statutory tenant is entitled to retain possession unless and until his tenancy is determined by the court.[13] Whether a demand or acceptance of rent, in such cases, constitutes waiver is, accordingly, a question of fact for the county court judge. Hence, where a landlord who did not consent to a sub-letting of part of the premises, with full knowledge accepted two payments of rent from the head tenant, it was held that he had waived the breach and his action against the sub-tenant failed.[14]

Section 148 of the Law of Property Act 1925, limits 'any actual waiver

---

6 *Expert Clothing Service and Sales Ltd v Hillgate House Ltd*, CA, supra.
7 *Chrisdell Ltd v Johnson* [1987] 2 EGLR 123, CA.
8 Contra, *Chelsea Estates Ltd v Kadri* (1970) 214 Estates Gazette 1356 (special facts).
9 *Penton v Barnett* [1898] 1 QB 276, CA. No new statutory notice is required in such cases. See also *Farimani v Gates* (1984) 128 Sol Jo 615, CA.
10 See *Cooper v Henderson* (1982) 263 Estates Gazette 592, CA.
11 *West Country Cleaners (Falmouth) Ltd v Saly* [1966] 3 All ER 210, [1966] 1 WLR 1485, CA.
12 *London and County (A & D) Ltd v Wilfred Sportsman Ltd* [1971] Ch 764, [1970] 2 All ER 600, CA.
13 *Trustees of Henry Smith's Charity v Willson* [1983] QB 316, [1983] 1 All ER 73, CA (no evidence on facts that landlord's agent's rent demand reached tenant). The same rule might apply to assured tenancies under Part I of the Housing Act 1988.
14 *Oak Property Co Ltd v Chapman* [1947] KB 886, [1947] 2 All ER 1, CA.

by a lessor or the persons deriving title under him of the benefit of any covenant or condition in any lease . . . proved to have taken place in any particular instance' to any breach 'to which such waiver specially relates', and provides that such waiver shall not 'operate as a general waiver of the benefit of any such covenant or condition'.

Once the landlord has unequivocally exercised his right of re-entry, i e by serving a writ for possession, that operates as a final election to determine the lease, and acceptance of rent (or distress for rent) subsequently due, 'without prejudice to the proceedings in respect of the earlier arrears', will not amount to a waiver of the ejectment. So where a landlord brought ejection on 21 July, and subsequently distrained for rent due on 24 June, it was held that the landlord was entitled in the forfeiture proceedings to rely on non-payment of rent due before 24 June, and that the distress was no waiver, but a trespass.[15]

Forfeiture is hedged about with many statutory and other restrictions. The rules to be explained apply to all breaches of covenant except that to pay rent (these rules are discussed in Chapter 8).[16]

2   RESTRICTIONS ON AND RELIEF AGAINST FORFEITURE

While even prior to the Judicature Acts 1873 and 1875, equity was prepared to grant relief from forfeiture for non-payment of rent, only in very limited circumstances could the courts grant relief in other cases.[17] The present-day restrictions on forfeiture and also the general power to grant relief against forfeiture[18] are contained in s 146 of the Law of Property Act 1925, applying to all covenants other than that to pay rent.

The general policy of the main statutory restriction, s 146 of the 1925 Act, is as follows:

(a)   to give the tenant warning of a breach of covenant;
(b)   to enable the tenant to have a reasonable opportunity to remedy the breach, where remediable;
(c)   to enable the court, at its discretion, which is very wide, to relieve the tenant from forfeiture;
(d)   to give sub-leesees and mortgagees special protection against loss of their respective interests where the lease is forfeited.

---

15   *Grimwood v Moss* (1872) LR 7 CP 360.
16   Special notice and associated rules governing repairs are discussed in ch 9.
17   In application for relief, regard is still to be had to the practice of the court prior to 1873: *GMS Syndicate Ltd v Gary Elliott Ltd* [1981] 1 All ER 619 at 625.
18   Relief applications are part of the process of forfeiture: *Meadows v Clerical Medical and General Life Assurance Society* [1981] Ch 70, [1980] 1 All ER 454.

3   LAW OF PROPERTY ACT 1925 S 146

General

Section 146 of the 1925 Act, as noted above, restricts the landlord's right of re-entry or forfeiture in various ways, as discussed below. Generally, compliance with s 146(1) is an essential preliminary to forfeiture.

Section 146, in principle, applies to any lease which contains a right of re-entry or forfeiture under a proviso or stipulation for breach of any covenant or condition.[19] The right of re-entry or forfeiture is rendered unenforceable by action or otherwise unless and until the landlord serves a s 146(1) notice on the tenant.[20] The contents of this notice are discussed below. By s 146(12), any express stipulation to the contrary in the lease is overridden.[1]

Total exclusions of s 146

Section 146 does not apply to forfeiture for non-payment of rent (s 146(11)), though sub-lessees and mortgagees have the right to request a vesting order under s 146(4) where a lease is forfeited for non-payment of rent, as well as in the case of breaches of other covenants and conditions.

Section 146 does not apply, by s 146(9) to a condition for forfeiture on the bankruptcy of the lessee, nor on taking in execution of the lessee's interest if contained in a lease of:

(a)   agricultural or pastoral land;
(b)   mines or minerals;
(c)   a house used or intended to be used as a public-house or beershop;
(d)   a house let as a dwelling-house, with the use of any furniture, books, works of art, or other chattels not being in the nature of fixtures;
(e)   any property with respect to which the personal qualifications of the tenant are of importance for the preservation of the value or character of the property, or on the ground of the neighbourhood to the lessor, or to any person holding under him.[2]

---

19   This includes voluntary and involuntary acts by the lessee, and a lessee must be served with a s 146(1) notice if his surety is bankrupt: *Halliard Property Co Ltd v Jack Segal Ltd* [1978] 1 All ER 1219, [1978] 1 WLR 377.
20   For wide definitions of 'lease' and other terms see s 146(5).
1   By s 146(13), the county court has jurisdiction where the value of the premises falls within the county court limit.
2   Cf *Earl Bathurst v Fine* [1974] 2 All ER 1160, [1974] 1 WLR 905, CA where relief against forfeiture was refused because the tenant had shown himself to be personally unsuitable.

Section 146 is also excluded, by s 146(8), in two further specific cases:

(i) where there was a breach of a covenant against assignment, subletting or parting with possession of the demised premises before the commencement of the 1925 Act;

(ii) in the case of a mining lease, to a covenant or condition allowing the lessor to have access to or inspect books, accounts, records, weighing machines or other things, or to enter or inspect the mine or its workings.

The Law Commission[3] stated that the justification for the exception in s 146(8)(ii) may lie in the fact that the rent payable under a mining tenancy is usually dependent on the amount of minerals produced by a mine, and the covenant mentioned in s 146(8)(ii) is of particular importance.

Partial exception in other cases of bankruptcy

Section 146 is partially excluded, where s 146(9) does not apply, by s 146(10), whose net effect is this. Section 146 applies for one year from the date of the tenant's bankruptcy or the taking in execution of his lease. If the tenant's interest is sold during the year referred to, the protection of s 146 continues without time limit for the new tenant. If the tenant's interest is not sold within the year, the protection of s 146 ceases completely.[4]

We now deal with the notice requirements, relief against forfeiture, recovery of costs and vesting orders for sub-tenants and mortgagees. There are further special notice provisions in the case of repairs, as well as the general provisions, which apply to them: see as to the special rules, Chapter 9. The rules governing forfeiture for non-payment of rent, which are quite separate from the present rules, are dealt with in Chapter 8.

4 RESTRICTIONS ON ENFORCEMENT OF RIGHT OF RE-ENTRY: S 146(1)

No right of re-entry or forfeiture for breach of any covenant or condition in the lease is enforceable by action or otherwise unless and until the landlord has served on the tenant a notice complying with s 146(1) of the 1925 Act. Section 146(1) provides that the notice must:

(a) specify the particular breach complained of;

---

3 Law Com No 142 (1985), Forfeiture of Tenancies, para 2.51.
4 The time-limit is strictly enforced as far as the tenant's interest is concerned, but it has no effect on any right of a mortgagee to apply for a s 146(4) order outside the one-year period: *Official Custodian for Charities v Parway Estates Developments Ltd* [1985] Ch 151, [1984] 3 All ER 679, CA.

(b)   if the breach is capable of remedy, require the tenant to remedy the breach (a reasonable time must be allowed for a remedy); and

(c)   in any case, it must require the tenant to make compensation in money for the breach.

A letter containing the requisite points will suffice, but special requirements must be observed in the case of breaches of the covenant to repair (see Chapter 9).[5] Strictly speaking, a s 146(1) notice is required whether re-entry is by service of a writ or peaceable, due to the words 'or otherwise' in s 146(1).[6] The purpose of a s 146(1) notice is to operate as a necessary preliminary to actual forfeiture.[7]

Any attempt to avoid s 146(1) will be invalidated by the courts, who are astute to detect disguised forfeiture clauses. For example, a term in a lease that, in the event of failure to comply with a covenant in the lease, the landlord could fill in the date on an undated deed of surrender previously executed, did not avoid the need to serve a s 146 notice prior to forfeiture proceedings.[8] Similarly, a clause enabling the landlord to terminate the lease for breaches of covenant by a three months' notice served on the tenant did not preclude the court from exercising its jurisdiction to grant relief against forfeiture.[9] Not every term entitling the landlord to terminate a tenancy is a disguised forfeiture: for example a provision in a weekly tenancy agreement enabling either party to terminate it on four week's notice was not treated as a disguised forfeiture clause: however, the tenancy was a weekly tenancy terminable on a minimum four weeks' notice and no considerations of policy required the court to go behind the term.[10]

A s 146(1) notice must be served on the lessee in possession at the time of service;[11] this means (s 146(5)) an original or derivative under-lessee, where relevant; and all joint lessees, if any, must be served with a notice; as must any assignee, even where the assignment was in breach of covenant.[12]

When preparing a s 146(1) notice, the landlord has two predictions to make. If he gets either wrong, any proceedings based on his notice will fail. First, he must decide whether the breach in question (or, if there is more than one, then *each* breach in question) is capable of remedy. As a rule of thumb, positive covenants, such as to repair, are capable of

5   For forms see *Woodfall* 1–2604–2605.
6   *Re Riggs, ex p Lovell* [1901] 2 KB 16.
7   *Church Comrs for England v Nodjoumi* (1985) 51 P & CR 155.
8   *Plymouth Corpn v Harvey* [1971] 1 All ER 623, [1971] 1 WLR 549.
9   *Richmond Clarke & Co Ltd v Widnall* [1976] 3 All ER 301, [1976] 1 WLR 845, CA.
10 *Clays Lane Housing Co-operative Ltd v Patrick* (1984) 49 P & CR 72, CA.
11 *Kanda v Church Comrs for England* [1958] 1 QB 332, [1957] 2 All ER 815, CA.
12 *Old Grovebury Manor Farm Ltd v W Seymour Plant Sales and Hire Ltd (No 2)* [1979] 3 All ER 504, [1979] 1 WLR 1397, CA.

remedy and negative covenants are incapable of remedy. There is no absolute rule and in marginal cases difficult questions of construction arise, there being no guarantee that the landlord will be correct in law. Where a breach is capable of remedy and the landlord's notice fails to require one, it will be bad.[13] Secondly, a reasonable time must be allowed from service of the notice for all breaches to be remedied: if the landlord issues a writ too soon then proceedings will fail.[14] The time for remedy must be allowed, even if it is an empty formality, as where it is plain that the tenant has no intention of doing anything.

Particular breach

In relation to certain covenants (e g against sub-letting) it is necessary for the landlord to indicate no more than the particular covenant that has been broken. Breaches of other covenants, on the other hand, should be specified with greater particularity. In relation to breaches of repairing covenants especially is it necessary to identify the respects in which the covenant has been broken. In *Fox v Jolly*[15] it was held that a notice which mentioned repairs needed under various headings, such as 'roofs' was sufficiently informative in relation to a covenant to repair in a lease of a row of six houses, without indicating which house or houses were referred to. It is common practice for the landlord to have the property inspected by a surveyor for the purpose of drawing up a s 146 notice in relation to breaches of repairing covenants, in which case the notice itself will refer to a schedule of dilapidations compiled by the surveyor and appended to the notice. The schedule will comprise a detailed list of the repairs necessary and an itemised estimate of their cost.[16]

If the breach is capable of remedy

The general policy behind s 146 is to give time to the lessee to remedy the breach; but there are certain breaches which are incapable of remedy. In particular, breaches of a covenant against assignment or underletting are incapable of remedy[17] as are those of a covenant against illegal user of the premises.[18] A breach of a covenant not to cause or permit immoral user of the premises is incapable of remedy by mere cesser of the user, if

---

13 As in *Expert Clothing Service and Sales Ltd v Hillgate House Ltd* [1986] Ch 340, [1985] 2 All ER 998, CA (failure to reconstruct premises by certain date held capable of remedy and landlord's notice which failed to require remedy held bad).
14 As in *Horsey Estate Ltd v Steiger* [1899] 2 QB 79, CA (two days held insufficient).
15 [1916] 1 AC 1.
16 See generally Malcolm Hollis, *Surveying for Dilapidations* (1988) Estates Gazette, ch 6.
17 *Scala House and District Property Co Ltd v Forbes* [1974] QB 575, [1973] 3 All ER 308, CA.
18 *Hoffman v Fineburg* [1949] Ch 245, [1948] 1 All ER 592.

the breach has cast a stigma in the premises, which is only removable by the eviction of the offending tenant.[19]

Where a lessee was personally innocent, and, at the date of service of the s 146(1) notice, lacked any knowledge of the breach or breaches, and had not deliberately shut his eyes thereto, a prompt cesser of the breach, procured by his removal of offending sub-lessees, was held to amount to a remedy on the facts and a s 146(1) notice which failed to require a remedy was held bad.[20] Whenever a breach is incapable of remedy, a s 146(1) notice need not require one.[21]

Require the lessee to remedy the breach

As noted above, the question of whether a particular breach is capable of remedy is one of construction. Generally, a breach of a positive covenant is capable of remedy, but not of a negative covenant.[1] Moreover, if the landlord, after service of his s 146(1) notice, fails to allow the tenant a reasonable time to elapse in which to remedy the breach, any action based on his notice will fail. In the case of breaches of covenant which are incapable of remedy, no reasonable time at all need be allowed to elapse for any remedy and it was held in order for a writ to follow service of a s 146(1) notice in 14 days.[2]

There is no guidance on what exactly does amount to a reasonable time for the purpose of remediable breaches, but what is quite clear is that if there are a number of remediable breaches alleged in the notice, a reasonable time sufficient to enable each breach to be remedied must be allowed.[3]

Require the lessee to make compensation

This requirement is often regarded as superfluous, for in many cases no damages would be recoverable in respect of the breach for the reason that the landlord had thereby suffered no loss in the value of the reversion (e g by virtue of the Landlord and Tenant Act 1927 s 18); and in any event, a notice is not bad for not requiring compensation.[4]

---

19 *Governors of Rugby School v Tannahill* [1935] 1 KB 87, CA (user as a brothel); *Dunraven Securities Ltd v Holloway* (1982) 264 Estates Gazette 709, CA; *British Petroleum Pension Trust Ltd v Behrendt* [1985] 2 EGLR 97, CA.
20 *Glass v Kencakes Ltd* [1966] 1 QB 611, [1964] 3 All ER 807.
21 *Governors of Rugby School v Tannahill*, [1935] 1 KB 87, CA.
 1 *Expert Clothing Service and Sales Ltd v Hillgate House Ltd*, CA, supra.
 2 *Scala House and District Property Co Ltd v Forbes* [1974] QB 575, [1973] 3 All ER 308, CA (relief granted on facts).
 3 *Hopley v Tarvin Parish Council* (1910) 74 JP 209.
 4 *Governors of Rugby School v Tannahill*, supra.

Service of a notice

The service of a s 146 notice is governed by the provisions of s 196 of the Act (as to which, see above). In the case of repairs, by virtue of s 18(2) of the Landlord and Tenant Act 1927, however, delivery alone is not sufficient. In effect, that sub-section modifies s 146(1) to the extent that a right of re-entry is not enforceable unless the lessor proves that the fact that notice has been served on the tenant was known either to the tenant or certain other persons and that a reasonable time for executing the repairs has elapsed since the tenant (or other person) learned of the service of the notice. Further, if the notice is sent by registered post or recorded delivery to a person at his last known place of abode in the United Kingdom, he will be deemed to have had knowledge of the fact that the notice had been served as from the date on which the letter would have been delivered in the ordinary course of post, unless he shows proof to the contrary.

5 RELIEF AGAINST FORFEITURE: S 146(2)

By s 146(2), where, because the breach complained of is irremediable, or has been remedied by the tenant when the time allowed him has expired, the landlord is proceeding,[5] by action or otherwise (i e including by peaceable re-entry), to enforce a right of re-entry or forfeiture, the tenant may, by counterclaim in the lessor's action, if any, or in an action brought by himself, apply to the court for relief against forfeiture of the lease. There is no right of relief after judgment, which contrasts with the provisions for relief in the case of non-payment of rent.

The court may grant or refuse the relief applied for, as it thinks fit, having regard to the proceedings and conduct of the parties and to all other circumstances. If the court grants relief, then s 146(2) provides that it may do so on any terms as to damages, compensation or otherwise, as the court thinks fit. The remedies may include the granting of an injunction to restrain any like breach in the future. The critical point is the width of the court's discretion.

Relief is based on the notion that, if the tenant is able and willing to take effective steps within a time-limit specified in the court's order, to remedy the breach or breaches in question, forfeiture should not be ordered: a forfeiture clause is regarded as a security for the compliance by the tenant with his covenants.[6] In many cases, therefore, whether the

---

5 Once the landlord serves a s 146 notice, the court's power to grant relief under s 146(2) arises: *Pakwood Transport Ltd v 15 Beauchamp Place* (1978) 36 P & CR 112, CA.

6 *Hyman v Rose* [1912] AC 623, HL; *Shiloh Spinners Ltd v Harding* [1973] AC 691, [1973] 1 All ER 90, HL; *Re Brompton Securities Ltd (No 2)* [1988] 3 All ER 677 (past record of tenant, a bad payer of rent, irrelevant).

court will grant relief or not will depend on whether the tenant is prepared to accept or comply with the terms that the court imposes as a condition of the giving of relief: the court cannot force the tenant to accept relief on its terms.[7] Whether or not it grants relief to the tenant against forfeiture of his lease may also depend on the respective merits of the tenant and any sub-tenants involved in the proceedings.[8] The court has jurisdiction to grant relief in respect of part of the premises if physically separated from the remainder and a separately re-lettable unit.[9] If a covenant against immoral user is deliberately broken, generally, no relief will be granted, and this strict rule has not been relaxed.[10] Only in very limited and exceptional cases, such as, possibly, isolated breaches, is it ever considered appropriate to grant relief in this instance.[11] Indeed, a deliberate breach of any covenant, especially a negative covenant, will seriously prejudice the tenant's chances of relief.[12]

Two limits on applicants for relief are worthy of note. In the case of joint tenants, all must apply for relief: an application by one or more of a number of joint tenants cannot be entertained.[13] A person holding a possessory title to unregistered land cannot apply for relief.[14]

If relief is granted, the effect is as if there had never been a forfeiture of the lease, which will continue in force, so that any sub-tenant will be unaffected by the proceedings.[15] If possession is granted by the High Court, but the Court of Appeal reverses the forfeiture (say by ordering relief to be granted to the tenant), the clock is not totally put back because any acts of the landlord under the order for possession, until its reversal, are considered lawful.[16] If the court imposes time-limits, it has an inherent jurisdiction to extend them from time to time.[17] If relief is not granted, and an order for possession is made, the lease will be treated as having been forfeited with effect from the service of the writ.

Apparently, there is no inherent equitable jurisdiction in the High

---

7   *Talbot v Blindell* [1908] 2 KB 114.
8   *Duke of Westminster v Swinton* [1948] 1 KB 524, [1948] 1 All ER 248.
9   *GMS Syndicate Ltd v Gary Elliott Ltd* [1982] Ch 1, [1981] 1 All ER 619.
10 *Borthwick-Norton v Romney Warwick Estates Ltd* [1950] 1 All ER 798, CA; *British Petroleum Pension Trust Ltd v Behrendt* [1985] 2 EGLR 97, CA.
11 As in e g *Central Estates (Belgravia) Ltd v Woolgar (No 2)* [1972] 3 All ER 610, [1972] 1 WLR 1048, CA, but the breach was waived in any event.
12 *St Marylebone Property Co Ltd v Tesco Stores Ltd* [1988] 2 EGLR 40.
13 *T M Fairclough & Sons Ltd v Berliner* [1931] 1 Ch 60. The Law Commission Report on Forfeiture, infra, recommended abolishing this rule: para 3.63.
14 *Tickner v Buzzacott* [1965] Ch 426 [1965] 1 All ER 131. Query whether this applies to registered titles in view of Land Registration Act 1925 s 75(1).
15 *Dendy v Evans* [1910] 1 KB 263.
16 *Hillgate House Ltd v Expert Clothing Service and Sales Ltd* [1987] 1 EGLR 65.
17 *Chandless-Chandless v Nicholson* [1942] 2 KB 321, [1942] 2 All ER 315.

Court, independently of statute, to grant relief against forfeiture: at first instance it was held, in relation to a totally unmeritorious application, that any equitable jurisdiction had been swept aside by s 146(2).[18] The result in this case conflicts with two other first-instance decisions, one dealing with rent arrears,[19] the other with relief for mortgagees.[20] It is consistent with dicta in the Court of Appeal insisting that statute has, in this particular area, ruled out any inherent equitable jurisdiction,[1] but these dealt with s 146(9) and (10) of the 1925 Act, to which special considerations apply, and it is submitted that in cases such as of fraud, accident or surprise, there should in principle be a residual jurisdiction to allow applications outside the statute. It must be conceded that the prospects of the Court of Appeal ever acceding to such a jurisdiction are slender, to judge by their attitude in relation to county court forfeitures for non-payment of rent.[2]

Costs

Under s 146(3) a landlord is entitled to recover from the tenant all reasonable costs he has properly incurred 'in the employment of a solicitor and surveyor or valuer, or otherwise', if the tenant is given relief, or if the breach is waived at the request of the tenant. Consequently, if the tenant remedies the breach on notice and there are no court proceedings, the landlord is not entitled to any costs incurred, for example, in the preparation of his s 146 notice.[3] In the case of repairs, if the tenant claims the benefit of the Leasehold Property (Repairs) Act 1938 (see Chapter 9), the landlord may only recover costs under s 146(3) with the leave of the court (1938 Act s 2). An express covenant is commonly imposed upon the tenant to pay all costs and expenses in or in contemplation of any proceedings under ss 146 or 147 of the Law of Property Act 1925.[4]

---

18 *Smith v Metropolitan City Properties Ltd* [1986] 1 EGLR 52; P F Smith (1986) 136 NLJ 339.
19 *Ladup Ltd v Williams & Glyn's Bank plc* [1985] 2 All ER 577, [1985] 1 WLR 851. As to the county court position in relation to rent see ch 8.
20 *Abbey National Building Society v Maybeech Ltd* [1985] Ch 190, [1984] 3 All ER 262.
 1 *Official Custodian for Charities v Parway Estates Developments* [1985] Ch 151 at 155, CA.
 2 See *Di Palma v Victoria Square Property Ltd* [1986] Ch 150, [1985] 2 All ER 676, CA, the result of which led to amendments to County Courts Act 1984 s 138.
 3 See *Nind v Nineteenth Century Building Society* [1894] 2 QB 226.
 4 The costs will then be recoverable as a contract debt: see e g *Bader Properties Ltd v Linley Property Investments Ltd* (1967) 19 P & CR 620.

6 PROTECTION OF SUB-LESSEES AND MORTGAGEES; S 146(4)[5]

At common law, a sub-tenancy is destroyed automatically if the head tenancy is forfeited.[6] Section 146(4) of the 1925 Act enables any sub-lessee, and hence any legal mortgagee by demise or charge, of any part of the property to apply to the court for a vesting order, either in the forfeiture proceedings or a separate action. An order will, if granted, create a new tenancy and vest in the applicant the part of the property occupied by the sub-lessee for a term not exceeding the remaining term of the original sub-lease, the length of the term being, subject to that, at the court's discretion. The conditions for the grant of a vesting order are at the court's discretion. Section 146(4) refers to the position immediately before forfeiture: if then a sub-lessee occupies the whole or part of the premises for business purposes, he will be entitled, if appropriate, to a vesting order, not only in relation to the residue of his contractual term but also in respect of its continuation by Part II of the Landlord and Tenant Act 1954, after expiry of the sub-term at common law, of appropriate length.[7] The sub-section applies where the landlord *is proceeding* to enforce, by action or otherwise, a right of re-entry or forfeiture under *any* covenant, proviso, etc, in the lease, or *for non-payment of rent*. In other words, a sub-tenant may be entitled to an order under s 146(4) even though his own landlord (i e the tenant) is not, under s 146(2). A mortgagee by way of legal charge[8] is entitled to an order, as is a guarantor who has a right to call for a legal charge or mortgage.[9]

In granting an order, on the application of a sub-lessee or mortgagee, the court has a discretion as to the imposition of terms. As a general rule, relief will be granted provided the applicant pays off all rent arrears owing to date, undertakes to comply with the covenants in the head lease, pays off the landlord's costs, and remedies any outstanding breaches of covenant, in relation to the premises or part to which the application relates.[10] The idea is to put the landlord back into the same position as he was in before the forfeiture took place.[11] If the

5 See generally S Tromans [1986] Conv 187.
6 *Moore Properties (Ilford) Ltd v McKeon* [1977] 1 All ER 262, [1976] 1 WLR 1278.
7 *Cadogan v Dimovic* [1984] 2 All ER 168, [1984] 1 WLR 609, CA, where the contractual sub-term expired prior to the hearing but was extant immediately prior to forfeiture.
8 *Grand Junction Co Ltd v Bates* [1954] 2 QB 160, [1954] 2 All ER 385; *Purley Automobile Co Ltd v Aldon Motors Ltd* (1968) 112 Sol Jo 482, CA. Such an order will not *ipso facto* re-instate sub-lessees: *Hammersmith and Fulham London Borough v Top Shop Centres Ltd* (19 December 1988, unreported).
9 *Re Good's Lease, Good v Wood* [1954] 1 All ER 275, [1954] 1 WLR 309.
10 *Belgravia Insurance Co Ltd v Meah* [1964] 1 QB 436, [1963] 3 All ER 828, CA; *Official Custodian for Charities v Mackey (No 2)* [1985] 2 All ER 1016, [1985] 1 WLR 1308.
11 *Chatham Empire Theatre (1955) Ltd v Ultrans* [1961] 2 All ER 381, [1961] 1 WLR 817.

circumstances warrant it, relief will be refused at discretion. For example, relief was refused where rent had not been paid to the head landlord for 22 years and it had been assumed that the sub-leases had gone.[12] The same result followed where a sub-lessee held only a monthly tenancy of a basement, which was badly out of repair: he refused to undertake admittedly onerous repairing obligations in relation thereto, which the head lease had cast on the lessee: if relief had been granted in these circumstances, the landlords would have had less extensive rights regarding repairs than originally.[13]

If the court makes an order under s 146(4), its effect is not retroactive, as the forfeited interest is not revived, and any conditions attached to a vesting order are conditions precedent to actual vesting: hence, any rights accrued in the landlords prior to an order, such as to rent in the twilight period from service of the writ down to the date of a s 146(4) order, are unaffected by the order.[14] If a receiver was in possession of the tenant's interest, however, during the twilight period between notional and actual forfeiture, he is entitled to rents for that period to the exclusion of the landlord.[15]

Section 146(4) suffers from certain defects, for example:

(a) It does not enable the court, for reasons explained earlier, to preserve existing tenancies, nor indeed may the landlord elect to do so. The effect of relief under s 146(4) is to create a new tenancy – as is shown by the fact that if the successful applicant is a mortgagee, he holds a substituted security.[16]

(b) Subject to special considerations applicable to business tenancies, the court can never grant to the applicant a new tenancy for a longer term than he had originally under his old sub-lease.[17] As was seen, this may work harshly where the original sub-tenancy was merely periodic, or for a short fixed term.

(c) The sub-section contains no guidelines as to the rent payable under the new tenancy, but it has been held that the court has power to vary the rent.[18]

(d) After forfeiture has been ordered, no applications under s 146(4) may be entertained. A landlord is under a duty, both in High Court

---

12 *Public Trustee v Westbrook* [1965] 3 All ER 398, [1965] 1 WLR 1160, CA.

13 *Hill v Griffin* [1987] 1 EGLR 87, CA. The applicant was not prepared to undertake onerous liabilities for repairs on a periodic tenancy, which was all the court could grant him.

14 *Official Custodian for Charities v Mackey* [1985] Ch 168, [1984] 3 All ER 689.

15 *Official Custodian for Charities v Mackey (No 2)* [1985] 2 All ER 1016, [1985] 1 WLR 1308.

16 *Chelsea Estates Investment Trust Co Ltd v Marche* [1955] Ch 328 at 339.

17 *Factors (Sundries) Ltd v Miller* [1952] 2 All ER 630, CA; *Hill v Griffin*, supra.

18 *Ewart v Fryer* [1901] 1 Ch 499, CA (higher rent commanded due to fact that premises ceased, with forfeiture of head lease, to be a tied house).

and county court proceedings, to indorse his writ with a statement giving the name and address of any underlessee or mortgagee, known to him, and he must then send these persons a copy of the writ.[19] There may be sub-lessees and mortgagees unknown to the landlord – not a likely situation if the lease requires due notification of any sub-leases or mortgages to the landlord. These unknown persons, if such there be, may still not be notified of pending forfeiture proceedings, and the landlord is under no implied obligation to notify them.[20] In these exceptional circumstances it is likely that the court has an inherent jurisdiction in equity to accede to an application for relief even after it has ordered forfeiture.[1]

7   REFORM

A complete reform of the present system governing forfeiture for all breaches of covenant has been proposed by the Law Commission.[2] A brief digest of their recommendations is now given.[3]

(a) There should be brought into force, in place of the current systems, a new termination order scheme. It would apply to all breaches of tenants' covenant, whether non-payment of rent or all other breaches, and to insolvency events.

(b) Certain archaic doctrines, which operate either harshly or capriciously, would be abolished. These include the doctrine of re-entry and waiver. The latter doctrine would be replaced by a new rule that the landlord would lose his right to forfeit only if his conduct would lead a reasonable tenant (and the actual tenant) to believe that he would not seek a termination order. (It might be noted that the doctrine of waiver antedates the availability of statutory relief and is a less flexible instrument designed to attain that object.)

(c) Rent would be due down to the date the court terminated the

---

19 RSC Ord 6 and CCR Ord 6, as amended by SI 1986/1187 and SI 1986/1189, from 1 October 1986.

20 *Egerton v Jones* [1939] 2 KB 702, [1939] 3 All ER 889, CA.

1 *Abbey National Building Society v Maybech Ltd* [1985] Ch 190, [1984] 3 All ER 262, despite *Smith v Metropolitan City Properties Ltd* [1986] 1 EGLR 52, which dealt with s 146(2) of the 1925 Act. A sub-lessee may invoke equitable estoppel to save his interest: *Hammersmith and Fulham London Borough v Top Shop Centres Ltd*, supra.

2 Law Com No 142 (1985) Forfeiture of Tenancies. A special notice rule in cases involving repairs (ch 9) would, generally, be retained, though there would be modifications: paras 8.33 et seq.

3 See further P F Smith [1986] Conv 165.

lease – not, as at present, down to the date of notional re-entry and no further.

(d) The court would have power to grant either (i) an absolute termination order, reserved for very serious and irremediable cases, or (ii) a remedial termination order, which would operate to end the tenancy unless the tenant took specified remedial action.

(e) The power to save sub-leases and the interests of mortgagees would be retained and improved. For example, the landlord would be enabled to elect to retain some, or all, of any derivative interests in the premises.

The Law Commission's scheme also proposed granting tenants, for the first time, the right to terminate their tenancies on the ground of landlords' breaches of covenant. At present tenants cannot terminate their leases, even if the landlord is a serious and persistent defaulter, save by surrender, for example, which the landlord may not accept.

The enactment of this reform package might in some ways be advantageous. For example, the doctrine of re-entry causes uncertainty as to the position of the parties after service of a writ claiming forfeiture. Waiver is technical, and operates irrespective of the merits of the case.

The landlord would, if the scheme were adopted, be spared the necessity of guessing accurately whether a given breach was remediable and also how much time to allow the tenant to remedy the breach before serving a writ. Moreover, the separation between the rules governing rent and breaches of all other covenants, and the different schemes for relief, in the former case, between the High and county courts, seem difficult to justify.

Chapter 14

Landlord's rights on termination

I INTRODUCTION

On the termination of a lease or tenancy, the tenant must, at common law, deliver up to the landlord peaceably the possession of the whole of the demised premises, together with all erections, buildings, improvements and fixtures, save fixtures which he is entitled to remove, and all growing crops. The lease, or the custom of the country (see Chapter 29) may provide to the contrary in relation to all or any of these matters.[1]

Moreover, at common law, if the tenant fails to remove any sub-tenant before the termination of his tenancy, he is liable to the landlord for the costs incurred by the latter in recovering possession and for any damages he has to pay for breach of contract, if he agreed to re-let the premises to a third party. This is because possession means vacant possession.[2]

The common law rules are profoundly affected by statutory protection afforded to business, residential and agricultural tenants: see the first parts of Chapters 12 and 13 for some general guidance and Parts D to G of this book for further details. The effect of these codes is to put off the right of the landlord to possession until the time when the court orders possession, or the tenancy is otherwise validly determined, in accordance with the statutory code concerned.

If there is a lawful sub-tenant in occupation under the Rent Act 1977 (see Chapter 17), or a sub-tenant protected by Part II of the Landlord and Tenant Act 1954 (Chapter 22), the common law rule rendering the head tenant liable in damages to the landlord, where the sub-tenant remains in occupation, cannot apply. The head tenant is liable, however, if the landlord shows that the sub-tenancy was granted in breach of covenant: it is outside statutory protection, unless the landlord waived the breach.[3]

---

1 For tenants' rights to remove emblements, see ch 32.
2 See *Henderson v Van Cooten* (1922) 67 Sol Jo 228; *Bramley v Chesterton* (1857) 2 CBNS 592.
3 *Reynolds v Bannerman* [1922] 1 KB 719.

II REMEDIES ON TERMINATION

The landlord has remedies for the recovery of damages for breaches of covenant committed by the tenant, and for waste, which have been considered (Chapter 9) and for holding over – see below.

Remedies for breach of obligation

The landlord may bring an action for rent accruing before the termination of the tenancy. He may also bring an action for damages for waste, mesne profits, breach of covenant and for use and occupation, as appropriate. He may also distrain for arrears of rent due before the termination of the tenancy under ss 6 and 7 of the Landlord and Tenant Act 1709, within six calendar months after termination, provided the tenant is still in occupation.

Remedies for recovery of possession

1 The landlord may enforce his claim to possession by peaceable re-entry[4] but the effect of the Protection from Eviction Act 1977 should be noted (see Chapter 19).
2 The landlord may enforce his right to possession by an action for the recovery of land. He may, in a High Court action, issue a writ endorsed with a claim for possession. (See below for the summary procedure in the High and county courts.) The county court has jurisdiction if the net annual value of the premises at the time of commencement of proceedings does not exceed £1,000 (s 21 of the County Courts Act 1984), or where the parties agree, or by reason of s 141 of the Rent Act 1977, or s 40 of the Housing Act 1988.[5]

III REMEDIES FOR HOLDING OVER

It is a question of fact whether a tenant holding over after a fixed-term is to be taken to be holding as a tenant from year to year by implication of law. If so, he will hold on such of the terms of his former tenancy as are consistent with a yearly tenancy. In practice, however, statutory rights of tenants to continue in occupation will generally make it impossible to imply the creation of a new tenancy. Moreover, on the proper termination of any statutory rights it will rarely be possible to establish the mutual consent necessary for the creation of a new tenancy. Where

---

4 It is a criminal offence to use or threaten violence for the purpose of securing entry to premises: Criminal Law Act 1977 s 6.
5 For recovery of deserted premises, see ch 13; recovery of derelict land where the landlord is unable to serve a notice to quit, see ch 13.

no new tenancy is created, but the tenant stays in possession after the proper determination of his tenancy, he may do so as a tenant at will (i e with the landlord's consent), or on sufferance (i e wrongfully, without the landlord's consent), or the landlord may elect to treat him as a trespasser. In any event, the landlord has appropriate remedies if the tenant fails to give the landlord vacant possession.

(a)   Action for use and occupation

Where a tenant has been in occupation by permission or sufferance of the landlord, in the absence of an express lease or agreement for a lease at a fixed rent, the law will imply a promise by the tenant to pay a reasonable sum for use and occupation.[6]

(b)   Action for mesne profits

Whenever a landlord brings an action for possession he is entitled in the action to claim *mesne profits* which have or might have accrued from the date of the expiration or termination of the tenancy (e g re-entry) down to the time of judgment, and thereafter down to the day of delivery of possession, under s 214 of the Common Law Procedure Act 1852. The claim for *mesne profits* must be endorsed on the writ.[7] In proceedings for forfeiture, this is the appropriate action for the recovery of compensation from the date of re-entry, i e the date of the service of the writ.[8] The action is an action for damages, i e the fair value of the premises. The rent payable immediately prior to the termination of the tenancy may be evidence of the value of the premises, but if the fair value is higher, the rent must be ignored.[9] In the case of a regulated tenancy, the amount would not exceed the lawfully recoverable rent.[10]

The landlord may, alternatively, claim *mesne profits* in a subsequent action for trespass, or bring an action for double value or double rent.

(c)   Action for double value

Under s 1 of the Landlord and Tenant Act 1730, the landlord may bring an action for double the yearly value of the premises if a tenant holds over wilfully after the landlord has given notice under the Act before (or as soon as possible after) the expiry of the tenancy requiring the tenant to give up possession. The tenant must hold over wilfully and

---

6   See *Churchward and Blight v Ford* (1857) 2 H & N 446.
7   RSC Ord 6 r 2.
8   *Elliott v Boynton* [1924] 1 Ch 236; *Associated Deliveries Ltd v Harrison* (1984) 272 Estates Gazette 321, CA.
9   *Clifton Securities v Huntley* [1948] 2 All ER 283.
10 See *Rawlance v Croydon Corpn* [1952] 2 QB 803 at 813.

contumaciously,[11] and not by mistake or under a bona fide claim of right, such as statutory protection. The section applies to both tenancies for a fixed-term and to periodic tenancies of not less than year to year, and to tenancies for life or lives; it does not apply to weekly, monthly or quarterly tenancies. In the case of a yearly tenancy, a valid notice to quit in writing is sufficient for the requirements as to prior notice.

The action is for double *value*, and not for double rent. It is a penalty which cannot be distrained for, and in respect of which there can be no relief in equity. The amount payable is at the rate of double the yearly value of the premises from the date of termination or the date of the written notice, whichever is the later, for as long as the land is detained. No previous action for possession is necessary though the two actions may be joined.

(d) Action for double rent

The landlord may bring an action for double rent against a tenant who gives a valid notice to quit (whether or not in writing) and holds over, whether wilfully or not, after the notice has expired under s 18 of the Distress for Rent Act 1737. Double rent is recoverable notwithstanding that the tenancy is a protected tenancy.[12] It is recoverable in the same manner (i e by action or distress), and at the same time as rent would have been payable, up to the time that the tenant quits; but the right is lost by acceptance of single rent, even though a new tenancy cannot be implied.

(e) Ord 14 RSC procedure

A summary procedure is available against a tenant holding over, which also applies to a tenant liable to forfeiture for non-payment of rent. The defendant must have given notice of his intention to defend and a statement of claim must have been served on him. The application for judgment must be made by summons returnable not less than 10 clear days after service. Unless either the application is dismissed or the defendant satisfies the court that there is a triable issue or question, judgment may be given for the landlord. The defendant may be given leave to defend. The landlord's summons may include an application for interim rent under Ord 29 r 10, to cover this eventuality.

---

11 See *French v Elliott* [1960] 1 WLR 40 at 51.
12 *Flannagan v Shaw* [1920] 3 KB 96, CA.

Chapter 15

Tenant's rights to fixtures

I INTRODUCTION

The word 'fixtures' is applied to articles which would normally be classified as *personalty* under English law (e g furniture), as opposed to *realty* (i e land, together with the buildings on the land), but which by virtue of their annexation to the land are treated as part of the land and classified accordingly as *realty*. The law of fixtures is not confined to the law of landlord and tenant, but as between a landlord and a tenant its importance lies in the tenant's right to remove what in law has become a fixture, should he wish to do so either during or on the termination of his tenancy.

According to the rule of common law, *quicquid solo plantatur, solo cedit*, whatever is affixed to the land becomes part of the land, and becomes the property of the owner in fee simple of the land. Consequently, it cannot lawfully be detached and removed by any temporary owner or occupier of the land, even though it was he who put it there. Originally, a tenant was therefore obliged by this ancient rule of law to deliver fixtures up at the end of the tenancy together with the land of which they then formed part. In the course of time, the hardship of this inflexible rule became manifest, and the courts of law came to recognise the right of a tenant to detach and remove articles that he had affixed to the land for the purpose of trade or domestic convenience. In relation to trade and agricultural tenancies, local custom played a big part in the development of what is the modern law of fixtures.

In any dispute as to whether a tenant has the right to remove a thing that he has attached to the premises, it is first necessary to determine whether it has thereby become a fixture in law,[1] for though physical attachment will raise a presumption to that effect – and non-attachment will raise a presumption to the contrary – the question must be resolved by the test of *annexation*. If the thing has never been annexed, it is not in

---

1 *Reynolds v Ashby & Son* [1904] AC 466, HL.

law a fixture, and the tenant may at any time remove it, as he may any of his personal belongings such as clothes and furniture. If it has become a fixture, by annexation, it is then necessary to determine whether it is a fixture which, by way of exception to the basic rule, the tenant is entitled to remove. Three categories of fixture are removable at common law or by statute:

(a) domestic and ornamental fixtures,
(b) trade fixtures, and
(c) agricultural fixtures.

II NATURE OF A FIXTURE

'Land' is defined by s 205(1)(ix) of the Law of Property Act 1925, as including buildings and parts of buildings (whether the division is horizontal, vertical or made in any other way) and other corporeal hereditaments. Buildings of a permanent and substantial character, though erected by the tenant, cannot be fixtures, as such; nor is the word 'structure' properly applicable to anything which forms part of the structure of the building. It was said, in the case of *Boswell v Crucible Steel Co*[2] 'A fixture, as that term is used in connection with a house, means something which has been affixed to the freehold as an accessory to the house. It does not include things which were part of the house itself in the course of its construction'. In that case, some heavy plate-glass windows were held to be part of the structure and therefore not fixtures. Likewise, a greenhouse bolted to a concrete plinth which lay on the ground on its own weight was not a fixture.[3] In contrast, fluorescent light fittings in glass boxes fitted securely into ceiling plaster, and fitted carpets were fixtures, due to their permanent attachment to the premises.[4] Nor is the word 'fixture' applicable to tress, shrubs and things which grow on the land.

A fixture is a thing which is capable of having a separate identity as a chattel in its detached state, as opposed to a useless pile of constituent parts, which loses its separate identity as a chattel and assumes the character of realty as long as it remains fixed to the land or to a building on the land. It may be defined as a thing of chattel nature, which by virtue of its annexation to land, is regarded in law as being part of the land, notwithstanding that there may be a right, vested in some person

---

2 [1925] 1 KB 119; also *New Zealand Government Property Corpn v HM & S Ltd* [1982] 1 All ER 624 at 627.
3 *Dean v Andrews* (1986) 52 P & CR 17.
4 *Young v Dalgety plc* (1986) 130 Sol Jo 985, CA. See *passim* Adams (1986) 136 New Law J 652.

other than the landowner, to sever the article from the land and thereby restore its chattel nature.

III   ANNEXATION

Annexation is a legal concept which is not synonymous with physical attachment, for whilst most fixtures are physically attached either directly (i e to the land) or indirectly (i e to a building on the land), the law recognises certain things as so closely connected with the identity of the land itself that they are constructively annexed, such as keys, title deeds, grid covers, dry stone walls, and depending on the circumstances, garden seats and statues. Physical attachment, however, is not to be disregarded, for it raises a presumption of annexation; and conversely non-attachment raises a presumption to the contrary. Both may be rebutted by the party against whom they are raised, as follows.

Degree of annexation

Formerly, the degree of annexation was all-important; indeed, it was regarded as the only test, with the result that if the chattel was substantially attached to the land, it was legally annexed, but not if it merely rested on the land under its own weight. Accordingly, such things as fireplaces, chimney-pieces, panelling, and wainscoting have been held to have been annexed, so as to become fixtures,[5] but not a Dutch barn, the supports of which rested in sockets let into the ground.[6] In the more recent case of *Jordan v May*[7] the Court of Appeal, upholding the decision of the county court judge that a generator sunk into concrete was a fixture, but not the batteries attached to it by wires, approved a *dictum* of BLACKBURN J in *Holland v Hodgson:*[8] 'Articles not otherwise attached to land other than by their own weight are not to be considered as part of the land, unless the circumstances are such as to show that they were intended to be part of the land, the onus of showing that they were intended being on those who assert that they have ceased to be chattels; and that, on the contrary, an article which is affixed to the land even slightly is to be considered as part of the land, unless the circumstances are such as to show that it was intended all along to continue a chattel, the onus lying on those who contend that it is a chattel.'

---

5   *Buckland v Butterfield* (1820) 4 Moore CP 440.
6   *Culling v Tufnal* (1694) Bull NP 34.
7   [1947] KB 427, [1947] 1 All ER 231.
8   (1872) LR 7 CP 328 at 335.

In other words, the fact of attachment gives rise to a presumption that the thing is a fixture, and the more damage that will be caused by its removal, both to itself and to the premises, the stronger that presumption will be; and conversely, non-attachment gives rise to a presumption that the thing is a chattel. The test of annexation is therefore to a large extent a question of intention, which must in each case be gathered mainly from a consideration of the nature of the article and of the purpose for which it was attached to or placed upon the land.

Object and purpose

Intention is clearly of paramount importance for the purpose of rebutting the presumptions raised by attachment and non-attachment. In rebuttal or support of them, it may be necessary to consider whether the chattel was attached simply for the purpose of making use of it (e g where a machine is required to be bolted to the floor, to avoid vibration) or for the purpose of display (e g a large picture or tapestry), or whether it was attached with the object of making a permanent improvement to the premises (e g central heating). On the other hand, the presumption raised against annexation by non-attachment is much stronger; it may be rebutted if it can be shown that the chattels were intended to be part of a permanent improvement of the land, as where statues, stone vases and garden seats resting under their own weight upon the ground were essentially a part of an architectural scheme (*D'Eyncourt v Gregory*).[9]

Thus the following have been held to be chattels: a collection of stuffed birds in cages nailed to the walls (*Viscount Hill v Bullock*),[10] and an electric light bulb (*British Economic Lamp Co Ltd v Empire Mile End Ltd*)[11] and an army hut bolted to the ground (*Billing v Pill*)[12] and tapestries nailed to battens on the walls (*Leigh v Taylor*);[13] and the following have been held to be fixtures: a set of tapestries in a dining-room designed specially to accommodate them (*Norton v Dashwood*),[14] petrol pumps and tanks (*Smith v City Petroleum Co*)[15] and panelling (*Spyer v Phillipson*).[16]

It is not surprising that some things may in different circumstances be regarded as fixtures or chattels; but it should be observed that the main

---

9 (1866) LR 3 Eq 382.
10 [1897] 2 Ch 482.
11 (1913) 29 TLR 386.
12 [1954] 1 QB 70, [1953] 2 All ER 1061; but, cf *Webb v Frank Bevis Ltd* [1940] 1 All ER 247 where a similar hut was held to be a fixture.
13 [1902] AC 157; affg *sub nom Re De Falbe, Ward v Taylor* [1901] 1 Ch 523.
14 [1896] 2 Ch 497.
15 [1940] 1 All ER 260, though the pumps were held to be trade fixtures.
16 [1931] 2 Ch 183.

issue in cases concerning fixtures is the question of the tenant's right to remove them. And in practice, the courts often ignore the preliminary question of annexation, and taking that for granted, concentrating on the question of the right to remove and the question of damage likely to be caused by removal. Consequently, the rules for annexation tend to be somewhat blurred. Moreover, it is clear that as a general rule, the courts deal more favourably with a tenant (i e in disputes with the landlord) than with a tenant for life (i e in disputes with the remainderman), and therefore cases decided in favour of remaindermen are not necessarily good authority for disputes between landlord and tenant. The commercial aspect of the relationship of landlord and tenant makes it unlikely that a tenant would voluntarily and consciously benefit his landlord by installing valuable fixtures which he himself would not be able to enjoy for more than a few years, and the courts' approach is well illustrated by the leading case of *Spyer v Phillipson*.[17] Eleven years before the end of a 21-year lease of a house, the tenant in that case installed antique panelling, together with mantelpieces, ceilings, etc, worth £5,000, with the landlord's consent. They were held to be fixtures, for they were substantially attached, the existing furbishings having had to be removed and cornices and brickwork cut into, to accommodate them. Nevertheless, in view of their value in relation to the length of the lease, the tenant was held entitled to remove them, despite the considerable cost that would have to be incurred in reinstating the premises.

Consequences of annexation

Once it has been established that a chattel has become a fixture by annexation, it follows that:

1   ownership of the fixture will pass with the freehold on a conveyance, under s 62 of the Law of Property Act 1925;
2   it will be classified as realty until or unless it is detached and removed, and ownership will pass to the devisee of the land under the landlord's will, or to the remainderman on the death of the tenant for life (as opposed to the latter's executors);
3   it will be considered part of the land under a lease, and therefore will not be distrainable; and
4   the tenant will not be entitled to remove it, except by agreement with the landlord, or unless it is either a domestic, trade or agricultural fixture. Such fixtures as the tenant is entitled to remove are referred to as 'tenant's fixtures'; all other fixtures are 'landlord's fixtures'.

---

17   [1931] 2 Ch 183, CA; also *Berkley v Poulett* (1976) 241 Estates Gazette 911, CA.

IV TENANT'S RIGHTS TO REMOVE FIXTURES

Domestic and ornamental fixtures

It has long been the right of tenants to detach and remove articles which they have annexed to the premises for ornament or convenience. In relation to such fixtures, the original object and purpose of attaching the fixture is again relevant, in determining whether he is entitled to do so under this exception, as is the amount of damage that would be caused by its removal, both to the thing itself, and to the premises. These considerations are well illustrated by the case of *Spyer v Phillipson* discussed above.

Fixtures under this exception have been held to include tapestries and pier-glasses, chimney-pieces, panelling, wainscoting, grates, stoves, beds fastened to the wall or ceiling, cupboards and bookcases fixed with ties to the wall, central heating pipes in a greenhouse, but not the boiler built into the floor of the greenhouse to which the pipes were attached.

Whilst it is generally agreed that the courts tend to show great latitude in favour of a tenant's claim to remove a fixture, anything which can properly be regarded as a permanent improvement to the premises will for that reason be regarded as irremovable. Any improvement which causes the rateable value of the property to be increased would prima facie seem to be irremovable, such as a sun-lounge, bathroom, garage, verandah, conservatory or greenhouse, provided that there is a sufficient degree of attachment. In view of current trends in interior design towards built-in furniture, there is a surprising lack of authority with regard to some of the expensive fitments and appliances which make up the modern kitchen, for example.[18] A tenant's rights to remove them would in many cases be doubtful, though the problem is often avoided in practice the the tenant, by the substitution of less expensive units on quitting the premises, or replacement of the landlord's original fitments, if he has bothered to retain them.

Trade fixtures

Trade fixtures have been held to include engines and boilers, pipes and transmission gear, vats and coppers, fixed machinery, shop and office fittings, including partitions, light buildings, greenhouses erected by a market gardener and petrol pumps.

Less significance would appear to be attached to the amount of

---

18 See however in a commercial context *La Salle Recreations v Canadian Camdex Investments Ltd* (1969) 4 DLR (3d) 549 (fitted carpets held fixtures in view of intention to improve hotel as such); cf *Berkley v Poulett* (1976) 241 Estates Gazette 911, CA.

damage likely to be caused by the removal of trade fixtures than in the case of domestic fixtures; moreover, an intention to remove them at the end of the tenancy is more readily inferred in relation to their attachment thus negating any intention of permanent improvement. On the other hand, the fixture may constitute or form part of an improvement for which the tenant is entitled to compensation on quitting, under the Landlord and Tenant Act 1927 (see Chapter 28). That, together with a business tenant's rights to a new tenancy under Part II of the Landlord and Tenant Act 1954, which in due course might enable him to 'sell' his fixtures to an assignee of the lease, effectively reduce the number of instances where he might wish to remove fixtures.

In relation to structures erected by the tenant for the purposes of trade, the courts have gone some way towards resolving the problem, from the tenant's point of view, that buildings are not fixtures. No building of a substantial and permanent character that would be incapable of being removed without reducing it to its constituent parts is removable by the tenant.[19] On the other hand, a tenant has been held entitled to remove the superstructure of a shed that could readily be dismantled in sections and re-erected elsewhere, even though it was bolted to iron straps let into a concrete floor, on the grounds that the shed and the floor did not constitute a single unit.[20]

Agricultural fixtures

An agricultural tenant has special rights to remove fixtures under s 10 of the Agricultural Holdings Act 1986. Under this provision, two types of fixtures become the property of the tenant of an agricultural holding and are removable by him at any time during the tenancy or before the expiry of two months from its termination (s 10(1)):

(a)   any engine, machinery, fencing or other fixture (of whatever description) affixed, for the purposes of agriculture or not to the holding, by the tenant, and

(b)   any building erected by him on the holding.

If the tenant is in arrear with rent or is otherwise in breach of any obligations under the tenancy, his right of removal is not exercisable (s 10(3)(a)).

The tenant must, both before the exercise of the right to remove and the termination of the tenancy, give the landlord at least one month's notice of his intention to remove the fixture or building (s 10(3)(b)). If the landlord, before the expiry of the tenant's notice, elects by a written

---

19   *Pole-Carew v Western Counties General Manure Co* [1920] 2 Ch 97, following the distinction drawn in *Whitehead v Bennett* (1858) 27 LJ Ch 474.
20   *Webb v Frank Bevis Ltd* [1940] 1 All ER 247.

counter-notice to purchase a particular fixture or building, the tenant cannot remove it (s 10(4)). The landlord is then bound to pay the tenant the fair value of the fixture or building to an incoming tenant (s 10(5)). Any disputes as to the amount payable are to be settled by arbitration under the 1986 Act (s 10(6)).

If the fixture or building was erected in pursuance of an obligation to the landlord, it cannot be removed (s 10(2)(a)): this limit on the tenant's right of removal extends to certain other cases, notably where the fixture or building replaces a fixture or building of the landlord's (s 10(2)(b)) or where the tenant is entitled to compensation under the 1986 Act in respect of the item (s 10(2)(c)).

The tenant must not, in exercising his right of removal, do any unavoidable damage, and must make good any damage he does (s 10(5)).

Section 10 cannot be contracted out of.[1] An agricultural tenant has the same rights to remove trade fixtures as any other tenant.

V REMOVAL OF FIXTURES

Agricultural fixtures apart, the general rule is that the tenant may remove such fixtures as he is entitled to remove at any time during the lease and during such further period of possession by him as he holds the possession of premises under a right to consider himself a tenant. It seems certain that once the landlord resumes possession, the tenant's rights will be lost,[2] except where the term itself is an uncertain one (e g a tenancy, at will), in which case the tenant will have a reasonable time after its termination within which to remove them. Similarly, a stipulation in the lease that the tenant may remove fixtures 'at the end of the term', will be construed as extending the time for a reasonable period thereafter.[3]

Where an existing lease expires or is surrendered, expressly or impliedly, and is then followed immediately by another lease to the same tenant, who throughout remains in possession, the tenant will not lose his right to remove tenants' fixtures and will be entitled, at the end of the new tenancy, to remove them.[4] On the other hand, as was seen failure to remove tenants' fixtures in due time extinguishes the tenant's right of

---

1 *Premier Dairies Ltd v Garlick* [1920] 2 Ch 17.
2 *Penton v Robart* (1801) 2 East 88; *Weeton v Woodcock* (1840) 7 M & W 14; *New Zealand Government Property Corpn v HM & S Ltd* [1982] QB 1145, [1982] 1 All ER 624, CA. See Kodilinye [1987] Conv 253.
3 *Stansfield v Portsmouth Corpn* (1858) 4 CBNS 120.
4 *New Zealand Government Property Corpn v HM & S Ltd* [1982] QB 1145, [1982] 1 All ER 624, CA.

removal on expiry of the relevant lease unless the landlord consents to removal, and the fixtures then become part of the freehold. Then the tenant's sole remedy is damages.

In removing his fixtures, the tenant must ensure that as little damage as possible is done to the premises, and any damage that is done, he is liable to repair.[5]

VI REMEDIES IN RESPECT OF FIXTURES

The landlord has an action for damages for waste in respect of any fixtures wrongfully removed by the tenant, as where for example he removes trade fixtures, such as fans and pipes, from a building, without making good the consequential damage to the structure of the building.[6] The obligation to make good such damage is regarded as part and parcel of the tenant's right to remove fixtures. Only where damages would not be an adequate remedy will a mandatory injunction be granted to replace the fixture wrongfully removed, as, for example, where a tenant was ordered to put back an Adam door that he had removed, having substituted a new one in its place.[7]

Although a tenant has no right in law to remove any fixture whatsoever belonging to the landlord, it is generally recognised that a tenant may remove a landlord's fixture and substitute for it one of his own, and may subsequently remove his own fixture provided that he replaces the landlord's fixture, or one of at least equal value, and makes good any damage caused by the substitution. The landlord cannot reasonably complain of an act committed during the tenancy which, though technically an act of waste, has resulted in no loss or damage to his reversion.

---

5 See *Mancetter Developments Ltd v Garmanson Ltd*, CA infra.
6 *Mancetter Developments Ltd v Garmanson Ltd* [1986] QB 1212, [1986] 1 All ER 449, CA.
7 *Phillips v Lamdin* [1949] 2 KB 33, [1949] 1 All ER 770.

PART D
RESIDENTIAL TENANCIES

Chapter 16

Introduction to residential tenancies

I GENERAL

Residential tenancies have been subjected to statutory controls and regulations since 1915. The statutory rules which have been enacted ever since then, have resulted in a very complex mass of provisions. For this reason, some general introduction to the subject-matter seems appropriate. A detailed examination of the rules is contained in the three next following chapters.

It is possible to compile a list of all the various enactments passed since 1915 in this area.[1] Such a list serves little real purpose, other than to emphasise the chequered history of this sector in the last seventy years or so, and is accordingly not attempted here. It is, however, possible that some general trends may be found in the legislation, which today consists mainly of two sets of provisions, the Rent Act 1977 and the Housing Act 1988. At the very outset, it is worth pointing out that in many, though not all, respects the aims of the 1977 and 1988 Acts differ. This is evident from the fact that, for example: (1) rent control, a key feature of the 1977 Act, is more or less absent from the 1988 Act; (2) the 1988 Act has no controls on premiums, unlike the 1977 Act; (3) short-term lettings are encouraged by the 1988 Act; (4) re-possession is generally easier under the 1988 Act.

Mutually exclusive codes

The 1977 Act regime, governing protected tenancies, applies only to tenancies granted before 15 January 1989. Conversely, the 1988 Act regime, which creates new-style assured tenancies, applies only to tenancies granted on or after 15 January 1989.[2]

---

1 See *Woodfall* 3-0001 et seq.
2 Old-style assured tenancies, converted by the 1988 Act to new-style assured tenancies, were, until conversion, governed by Part II of the Landlord and Tenant Act 1954 as modified.

II CONSTRUCTION OF THE TWO CODES

The Rent Act 1977 is a consolidating statute and is to be interpreted without reference to legislative antecedents.[3] Consolidation has rendered drafting vices in the 1977 Act a permanent feature of the legislation. The original rent restriction legislation was passed as emergency legislation, and after World War One, it became permanent owing to the housing shortage which followed that war. The Housing Act 1988 was obviously not passed with easing a general housing shortage in mind: it had other objects, such as to revive the private rented sector, particularly by removing rent control and allowing the landlord to charge a market rent, which, during the contractual term, the tenant cannot challenge.[4]

Whether these considerations mean that language used in the 1988 Act, where similar to that in the Rent Act 1977, will be similarly construed, is a question to which no definite answer may be given in the absence of authority.[5] Presumably, the question depends on whether the provision or provisions under consideration are akin to those of the 1977 Act, as with exclusions from assured tenancy status, or whether they are quite new, as with provisions dealing with fixing of the terms of an assured tenancy.

III AIMS OF CODES

The present government has deregulated the rent payable by a private sector residential tenant. It is clear, however, that the 1988 Act regime which creates new-style assured tenancies has security of tenure provisions akin in general, though not in many details, to those of the Rent Act 1977. It is notable, to anticipate, that the landlord's position is significantly eased in relation to security of tenure and the terms on which a residential tenant will hold after expiry of his initial term. Residential tenants are offered, both by the 1977 and 1988 Acts, in very

---

3 *Farrell v Alexander* [1977] AC 59, [1976] 2 All ER 721, HL; for a case where the House of Lords went back to previous, repealed enactments, see *Maunsell v Olins* [1975] AC 373, [1975] 1 All ER 16, HL.
4 Income tax relief under the business expension scheme has been extended to unquoted companies specialising in letting residential property under assured tenancies under the 1988 Act: for details, see Finance Act 1988 s 50 and Sch 4, applying to shares issued after 29 July 1988 and before 1 January 1994. This scheme does not apply to assured shorthold tenancies. The market value of the letting at the date of issue of the shares must not exceed £125,000 in Greater London and £85,000 elsewhere.
5 The secure tenancies code has been held to be *sui generis*: *Hammersmith and Fulham London Borough v Harrison* [1981] 2 All ER 588, at 597, CA.

general terms, some factors which have remained a fairly constant feature of the private residential sector.

1 A wide-ranging catchment of residential tenancies, with a number of very significant exceptions. Residential sub-tenants are capable of being protected, but not business tenants or tenants of agricultural holdings.
2 Security of tenure and succession rights.
3 Provisions as to rent. In the case of the 1977 Act, the contractual rent could be challenged by the tenant as well as the rent payable once the original term is at an end; in the case of assured tenancies, the contractual rent cannot be so challenged, except in the case of assured shorthold tenancies, and the rent payable under a periodic tenancy is only referable following a notice of increase from the landlord.

There have, therefore, been modifications to every one of the above three matters ever since legislation protecting private residential tenants was first enacted. These reflect moves away from blanket, catch-all protection; also some wish to give the landlord a rent which is near the open market, or which, at least, is not fixed for all time at the outset of the tenancy; and a desire to encourage short-term lettings without the landlord having to worry about losing his right to regain possession of the dwelling concerned for a significantly longer period than the term of the original lease or tenancy.

IV ASSESSMENT AND COMPARISON OF SYSTEMS

General background

There is no real consensus as to whether private sector rents should be controlled or not. Not many major moves away from rent control have, in the past, survived for long, without being later reversed by a government of the opposite political persuasion. Whether the latest moves, in the Housing Act 1988, will prove an exception, is a matter of conjecture. On the other hand, the creation (especially since 1974) of new exclusions from full protection from the Rent Act 1977, which are incorporated with necessary modifications into the Housing Act 1988 for assured tenancies, has been a more successful and enduring process. With regard to rents, in 1957 the Conservative government passed the Rent Act 1957 which aimed at creeping de-control of rent. This process was abruptly halted by the Rent Act 1965, passed by a Labour government. Decontrol was not attempted by the Conservative government which was in power from 1970–1974. Until 1988, rent control was not further significantly amended. The Labour government's amendments to the Rent Acts so as to allow lettings by resident landlords and for holidays, in particular, to be outside full Rent Act protection have been adopted for assured tenancies in the Housing Act 1988. As was said earlier, amendments to basic security of tenure provisions have sometimes survived changes of government. However, changes enacted in the Housing Act 1988 go beyond the creation of new exemptions from protection and attack rent restriction or control itself.

Policy since 1979

The Conservative government, which has been in power since 1979 did not, until the Housing Act 1988, tackle rent de-control, for fear, perhaps, of the resulting controversies. Until 1988, it followed a policy of expanding rules allowing for lettings within the Rent Acts during their life but also allowing the landlord the right mandatorily to recover possession on the determination of the term, an example being old-style shorthold tenancies, and a further example being the amendments to the Rent Act 1977 owner-occupier provision.[6] After the return of a third successive Conservative government in 1987, more radical ideas seem to have taken hold and these resulted in the Housing Act 1988.

Market rents

By preventing the grant, after its commencement, of any new protected tenancies, the 1988 Act prospectively abolishes rent control under the Rent Act 1977 for residential tenancies granted on or after 15 January 1989 (with limited exceptions, see Chapters 17 and 18). Assured tenancies and assured shorthold tenancies, the sole means of letting within the private sector after the commencement of the 1988 Act, are not subject to old-style rent control or regulation. The assumption is that the tenant will have to pay the market rent – and if he cannot afford it, so be it. As noted, an assured tenant cannot challenge the rent payable during the assured contractual tenancy. The current government thinks that once it frees up the market in rents, more private sector landlords will let their empty houses. The belief will be tested by events. One further point. There are no provisions in the Housing Act 1988 disallowing or controlling the taking of premiums on the grant, renewal or assignment of assured or assured shorthold tenancies. This is deliberate. Therefore, the parties will be freely able to agree on the payment and receipt of premiums with no restrictions corresponding to those applicable to protected tenancies under the Rent Act 1977.

No blanket protection

Apart from rent de-control, the latest move away from blanket restriction of private residential tenancies manifested itself in cautious,

---

6   Rent (Amendment) Act 1985.

but quite significant forms, in those parts of the Housing Act 1988 Part I which deal with the scope of the assured tenancies scheme and security of tenure. As will be seen from Chapter 18, in many respects, the scope of the 1988 Act regime is very similar to the 1977 Act regime, but there are points of real difference. Some initial points deserve mention.

Overview of some further differences

1 As with the difference under the 1977 Act between protected tenancies and restricted contracts,[7] there is a difference between assured tenancies on the one hand, and tenancies which cannot be assured on the other. The latter are devoid of full 1988 Act protection – as were restricted contracts – but they are, however, divided into tenancies to which s 3 of the Protection from Eviction Act 1977 applies and those, neatly labelled 'excluded tenancies or licences', to which the protection of s 3 does not apply. The details of this matter follow in Chapter 19: it is significant that the underlying idea, in this respect, of the 1988 Act amendments to the Protection from Eviction Act 1977 appears to be that, if a landlord lets off rooms to someone and he or his relatives share living accommodation with the tenant (or licensee), then the landlord should be able to recover possession without court proceedings – though illegal methods of removing the tenant, such as force, remain subject to criminal and civil sanctions. At the same time, licences and tenancies alike, apart from these cases, require a court order to terminate them.

2 A further subtle shift in the 1988 Act, with regard to security of tenure, is as follows. An assured tenant is offered security from eviction (as with the Rent Act 1977). However, some of the grounds for possession which, under the 1977 Act, are discretionary, so that the court is not bound to order possession even if the ground is made out, are mandatory in the 1988 Act. This is so, for example, both with rent arrears and persistent delay in paying rent. In the case of a mandatory ground, the court cannot refuse possession once that ground is made out by the landlord. So it should be often easier for landlords to succeed in eviction assured tenants. If a landlord has redevelopment proposals, he will be able to rely on a new ground for possession which resembles that applicable to business tenants.[8]

3 A further difference between the 1977 and 1988 Act regimes is that the 1977 Act continues the terms of the original tenancy on an indefinite plane. The rent is 'regulated', and the contractual rent may be reduced by a rent officer if referred to him by the tenant. Under the 1988 Act there is no rent control of this kind, except that excessive

---

7 Which have been abolished from 15 January 1989.
8 Housing Act 1988 Sch 2, ground 6 (ch 18).

rents of shortholds in relation to the market may be referred, as may the rent under an assured periodic tenancy if the landlord serves a notice of increase on the tenant.

4   The 1988 Act system and the 1977 Act systems alike have succession provisions of some complexity. There is some apparent inconsistency in the matter: in the case of agricultural tenancies, successions have been abolished, but a single succession is allowed for in the case of secure tenancies.

Concluding remarks

The rules governing residential tenancies are most involved and this is likely to continue for a long time. Two sets of relevant provisions need to be discussed because the Rent Act 1977 system will continue to apply to any tenancy created before 15 January 1989, but after then the 1988 Act system begins, and the two systems are mutually exclusive. To prevent landlords from forcing existing tenants from the old into the new system, rules have been enacted to discourage unlawful eviction and harassment, discussed in Chapter 19. The Housing Act 1988 contains no provisions limiting or disallowing the use of licences as a means of avoiding the assured tenancy scheme. This omission is deliberate. The official view is that landlords will not need to use sham licences to get round statutory security because they will be able to use assured shorthold tenancies instead.[9] The principles on which the courts deal with licences as avoidance of security devices are, no doubt, applicable to assured tenancies and are discussed in Chapter 3 of this book. Nor are lettings to companies, which will avoid the 1988 Act, disallowed: on the contrary, a company cannot hold an assured tenancy. This may lead to avoidance of the 1988 Act, if landlords think it right to try to do so.

---

9   In the House of Lords Committee, the government spokesman, Earl of Caithness, stated that, if need be, sham licences might be dealt with in a future Landlord and Tenant Bill: HL debates 25 July 1988, cols 133–134.

Chapter 17

Rent Act protected tenancies[1]

A SCOPE OF RENT ACT PROTECTION

I INTRODUCTION

Tenancies to which the full protection of the Rent Act 1977 applies are known as protected tenancies. If a residential tenancy is granted on or after the commencement of Part I of the Housing Act 1988, it cannot, generally, be protected, and must either be assured or assured shorthold.[2] This means that protected tenancies may only exist in one of the following circumstances. If any of these apply, the tenancy must not, further, be excluded from protection under the terms of 1977 Act itself. If it is, it cannot be a protected tenancy in any event and may be a restricted contract – but then only if entered into before the commencement of the 1988 Act. After that date, generally, no new restricted contracts may be entered into.[3]

Where Rent Act protection may apply

1 The tenancy was granted to the original tenant *before* the commencement date of Part I of the Housing Act 1988 (15 January 1989), and it is not excluded by reason of the high rateable value of the dwelling-house concerned, nor by any of the excluded categories from 1977 Act protection, as listed below. In this case the tenancy will be a protected tenancy under the Rent Act 1977.
2 The tenancy was granted to a tenant of a dwelling-house before the commencement of the 1988 Act and he was a protected tenant, but he died, whether before or after such commencement, and has been succeeded by a person qualified to succeed as statutory tenant.

---

1 See further: Farrand and Arden *Rent Acts and Regulations* (2nd edn, 1981); Jill E Martin *Security of Tenure under the Rent Act* (1986); Megarry's *Rent Acts* (11th edn, 1988).
2 Housing Act 1988 s 34, the relevant date being 15 January 1989 (s 141(3)). For a special rule where the landlord is a new town corporation see s 38(4).
3 Housing Act 1988 s 36(1).

3   The tenancy is granted under a contract entered into before the commencement of the 1988 Act (1988 Act s 34(1)(a)).

4   The tenancy is granted to a person (alone or jointly with others) who, immediately before the grant, was the protected or statutory tenant (or one of them) by the landlord[4] under that tenancy (s 34(1)(b)). The aim of this is, evidently, to counteract any possibility that landlords of existing protected or statutory tenants would, but for the present rule, try to grant their sitting protected or statutory tenants new tenancies under the 1988 Act regime, which is more favourable to landlords than that of the 1977 Act.

5   Before the tenancy was granted, possession of the dwelling-house concerned was ordered by the court against the tenant on the ground that suitable alternative accommodation is available to the tenant[5] and the tenancy is of the suitable alternative accommodation and in the proceedings for possession the court directs that the tenancy is to be Rent Act protected because it considers that the grant of an assured tenancy would not afford the required security (s 34(1)(c)).

Position of shorthold tenants

It is possible, after the commencement of the 1988 Act, for a landlord with a protected shorthold tenant to grant the tenant an assured tenancy (or an assured shorthold tenancy) of the same premises as previously held under the shorthold tenancy.[6] After the commencement of the 1988 Act, protected shorthold tenancies cannot be created.[7]

Notes on restricted contracts

Two-tier protection

The Rent Act 1977, where it still applies, involves two-tier protection for residential tenants. One is full protection, which is discussed fully in this Chapter. The other tier is under a restricted contract. After the commencement of Part I of the 1988 Act, no new restricted contracts may, generally, be created, but their abolition is not retrospective, and

---

4   If there were joint landlords, then at least one (but not all) of them must have been the landlord under the previous tenancy.

5   Or under corresponding provisions for agricultural workers (Rent Act 1977 s 99 and Sch 16 Case 1).

6   Housing Act 1988 s 34(2). This extends to the case where the original shorthold term, which is a protected tenancy, has expired, and the shorthold tenant has held over without the grant of a new tenancy, or, if there is such a grant, to him or his successor. The landlord may by notice to the tenant indicate that the new tenancy is to be an assured tenancy (s 34(3)).

7   But they have been replaced by assured shorthold tenancies (ch 18).

some short further details are appropriate. A restricted contract arises where, in particular:

1 The resident landlord exception from full Rent Act protection applies under s 12 of the 1977 Act.
2 Where the rent includes payment for the use of furniture or services, provided in this latter case that the payments are for board or substantial attendance. A furnished tenancy granted prior to the coming into force of Part I of the 1988 Act may be fully protected.

Some further considerations

Tenancies which are held from a resident landlord (s 12) or where there are substantial payments for attendance as part of the rent (s 7) are restricted contracts; but not holiday lettings, for example. Another example of restricted contracts is where there is no tenancy but only a contractual occupation with furniture or services, an example being the exclusive occupation of an hotel room.[8] A further example still is where there is a residential licence, which cannot be a protected tenancy, under which furniture or services are provided.

Effect of Housing Act 1988

By s 36(1) of the Housing Act 1988, no tenancy or other contract entered into after the commencement of the 1988 Act can generally, except for transitional cases, be a restricted contract. Where a tenancy or contract is entered into after 15 January 1989, under a pre-commencement contract to do so, a restricted contract will be created.

If the rent under a pre-1988 Act restricted contract is varied, after 15 January 1989, a new contract comes into being at the time of the variation, and the contract ceases thereafter to be restricted (s 36(2) and (3)).[9] After that, any rent controls and security of tenure rules in the 1977 Act over the contract will cease to apply. To most intents and purposes, therefore, restricted contracts cannot be created, as from the commencement of the 1988 Act, and those existing at that date will probably quite rapidly come to an end.

Rent controls on restricted contracts created before Part I of the 1988 *Act came into force*

The rent controls under restricted contracts are very similar to those applicable to regulated tenancies and need not further be considered, save to note the following specific points.

---

8 *Luganda v Service Hotels Ltd* [1969] 2 Ch 209, [1969] 2 All ER 692, CA.
9 If the variation is by a rent tribunal or the parties, in the latter case in order to bring the rent the level of the registered rent, then a pre-1988 Act contract continues to be restricted.

1   Either party has the right to refer the rent to a Rent Tribunal (i e a Rent Assessment Committee) under s 77 of the 1977 Act.[10] In principle, the Tribunal must consider any reference which is not withdrawn before the Tribunal enters into a consideration of it is 78(1)).[11]

2   It is open to any party to challenge the jurisdiction of the Rent Tribunal – as where it is alleged either that a tenancy, for example, is protected, or that it is assured, or that the contract post-dates the commencement of the 1988 Act. The Tribunal must then give the party concerned a reasonable opportunity to raise the question before the county court under s 141 of the Rent Act 1977; but if this is not done, the Tribunal must itself decide the jurisdictional issue.

3   The Tribunal, if it decides that it has jurisdiction, has duties laid down by s 78(2), including making inquiries. It may then approve the rent, reduce or increase it, or dismiss the reference. The Tribunal must assess a reasonable rent (s 78(2)) but no statutory guidance beyond this is given, and it is thought that similar considerations will apply to reasonable rents as would apply to fair rents under regulated tenancies.

4   The procedure before the Tribunal is governed by statutory instrument.[12] A register of reasonable rents must be kept (s 79) in accordance with particulars supplied by Tribunals to the President of Rent Assessment Panels. There is a two-year bar on a further reference of a rent as from the date when the rent was last considered by the Tribunal (s 80(2)).[13] There are provisions precluding the recovery of any excess over the registered rent (s 81) with criminal penalties for non-compliance. There are controls over premiums where there is a registered rent, similar to those applicable to protected tenancies (s 122).

Security of Tenure

A tenant or licensee under restricted contract entered into before 15 January 1989, and which was created after 28 November 1980[14] has the following limited security of tenure.

---

10   But not, after the commencement of the 1988 Act, a local authority (Housing Act 1988 Sch 17 para 23).

11   I e as soon as the members start to read the relevant papers: *R v Tottenham District Rent Tribunal, ex p Fryer Bros (Properties) Ltd* [1971] 2 QB 681, [1971] 3 All ER 563, CA.

12   Rent Assessment Committees etc Regulations 1980 SI 1980/1700 (amended SI 1981/1483 and SI 1988/2200).

13   Changes in circumstances or in the condition of any furniture provided or in the terms of the contract are exceptions to this rule.

14   For restricted contracts entered into prior to this date, see Rent Act 1977 ss 103 and 104.

1   Four weeks' minimum notice to quit, under s 5 of the Protection from Eviction Act 1977, must be given by the landlord.

2   The county court has limited powers of postponement in proceedings for possession by the landlord under s 106A of the 1977 Act. The court has power to stay or suspend the execution of an order for possession for up to a total period of three months after making the order, either all at once, or up to that amount of time in a series of applications (s 106A(2) and (3)). The court has a discretion to impose any conditions (s 106A(4)). In the case of arrears of rent and rent and mesne profits, the court must impose conditions as to the repayment or payment, as the case may be, unless it considers that to do so would either impose exceptional hardship on the occupier or otherwise be unreasonable (s 106A(4)).

Housing association tenancies

Under Part VI of the Rent Act 1977, tenancies granted by housing associations, housing trusts and the Housing Corporation, though excluded from protection, were subject, while the landlord's interest was held by one of these groups of quasi public sector bodies, to rent regulation under Part IV of the 1977 Act. These tenancies were known as 'housing association tenancies'; and certain tenancies granted by co-operative housing associations were, and are, not subject to rent regulation.[15]

A tenancy granted by a 'housing association', in the above extended sense, on or after the commencement of Part I of the Housing Act 1988 cannot be a housing association tenancy, subject to the same exceptions, in principle, as exclude post-commencement private-sector residential tenancies from the Rent Act 1977.[16]

Any tenancy granted by a housing association, after the commencement of Part I of the 1988 Act, will be either assured, or assured shorthold, and the reader is referred to Chapter 18.

Relevant dates

To summarise, the relevant dates for the two statutory codes are:

Rent Act 1977:   this commenced on 29 August 1977, but it consolidated legislation which came into force on 8 December 1965.[17]
Housing Act 1988:   Part I of the 1988 Act, dealing with assured tenancies and related matters, came into force on 15 January 1989,

---

15   Rent Act 1977 ss 86 and 87.
16   Housing Act 1988 s 35.
17   The commencement date of the Rent Act 1965, consolidated by the Rent Act 1968, in turn replaced by the 1977 Act.

Royal Assent having been received on 15 November 1988. As from 15 January 1989, the only forms of new tenancy in the private residential sector are assured or assured shorthold tenancies.

II   BRIEF HISTORY AND POLICY OF THE RENT ACTS

Private sector residential tenants have had statutory controls since 1915. On occasions, the legislation has been codified: the first time was in the Rent and Mortgage Interest (Restrictions) Act 1920, eventually there were the Rent Acts 1968 and 1977.

The enactment of the Housing Act 1988 means that as from its commencement date, no Rent Act protected tenancies may (in general) be granted. There was therefore a complete break with the whole past series of Rent Acts. However, in relation to any pre-1988 private sector residential tenancy, the controls imposed by the Rent Acts are still relevant. Moreover, statutory controls of private residential tenants, whether under the pre- or post-1988 rules, will continue for the foreseeable future.

The policy of Parliament has, in general, been to confer controls of one sort or another on most private residential tenants, with only the most expensive properties escaping the net. However, in more recent years, even before the enactment of the 1988 Act, certain types of short-term tenancies and tenancies granted by certain types of landlord, have been either excluded from full protection[18] or, while there is full protection for the initial term, after this ends, possession is recoverable mandatorily, subject to compliance with formal notice conditions, in particular.[19] Full protection under the Rent Act 1977 may well, by 1988, have become an anachronism or the accidental result of a landlord not letting in one of a number of ways which would cause full protection not to apply to the tenancy, or where a so-called licence in fact creates a tenancy (see Chapter 3).

Whenever the full protection of the Rent Act 1977 applies to a tenancy, the tenant has a status of irremovability, as will be seen. Many of the provisions of the 1977 Act, which will continue to affect the residential sector for many years, for reasons explained earlier, are open to the criticism that there is 'inadequate definition, hidden meanings, missing principles, incautious superimposition, and plain mistakes.'[20] Sometimes the meaning of a given word can only be discovered by going back

---

18   As with resident landlord, or local authority tenancies – see below.
19   As with shorthold tenancies (in the pre-1988 form) or tenancies granted by an owner-occupier landlord – see below.
20   *Megarry's Rent Acts* (11th edn) p 15.

to earlier, now repealed legislation, even though the Rent Act 1977 was supposedly a consolidating measure.[1]

In the rest of this Chapter, reference is made to a large number of cases decided since 1915 – this is because wherever an identical or similar word is used in the 1977 Act to a previous Act, the word generally bears the same meaning as it did originally.[2]

Is there any general policy behind the Rent Act 1977? Perhaps with the enactment of the Housing Act 1988, with a rather different code, this question is otiose. Briefly, it seems that the aims of the old-style residential tenancies legislation, as one might now call the 1977 Act, are to protect a residential tenant from eviction, from extortion of premiums for the grant or renewal of his tenancy, and from the full effect of the market on his rent. The courts appear to regard many aspects of the 1977 Act regime (and its progenitors) as an interference with common-law rights. It has been held that any unavoidable interference necessarily resulting from the legislation must be to the smallest possible extent.[3]

B PROTECTED TENANCY DEFINED

I GENERAL PRINCIPLES

Tenancies to which the full protection of the Rent Act 1977 applies are protected tenancies (s 1). Subject to the narrow exceptions listed in section A above, after the commencement of the Housing Act 1988, viz, 15 January 1989 (s 141(3)) no residential tenancy granted on or after that date is capable of being protected by the 1977 Act (1988 Act, s 34).

Where the Rent Act 1977 applies to a tenancy, the following terminological points must be noted.

1 A tenancy is *protected* if it complies with three requirements laid down in s 1 of the Rent Act 1977 (i e there is a *dwelling-house let* as a *separate dwelling*).
2 If the *rateable value* of the dwelling-house concerned is too high then the tenancy will not qualify for protection.
3 If the tenancy is excluded by ss 5–16 from protection then it cannot

---

1 On general principles of construction, see *Farrell v Alexander* [1977] AC 59 at 73, [1976] 2 All ER 721 at 726, HL; for a reference to earlier legislation, see *Maunsell v Olins* [1975] AC 373, [1975] 1 All ER 16, HL.
2 *Smalley v Quarrier* [1975] 2 All ER 688, [1975] 1 WLR 938, CA.
3 See e g *Landau v Sloane* [1981] 1 All ER 705 at 707–708, HL. Similarly, statutory tenancies (qv) have been held to be purely personal rights: e g *Jessamine Investment Co v Schwartz* [1978] QB 264, [1976] 3 All ER 521, CA.

be protected.[4] An exclusion may relate to the nature of the landlord or because of the very nature of the tenancy.

4   Where a tenancy is protected, its protected status lasts only for the *contractual period of the tenancy* (i e the common-law term, whether fixed-term or periodic). Once the tenancy is terminated by forfeiture or notice to quit, as the case may be, it becomes a *statutory* tenancy.

5   *Statutory tenancies* (governed by ss 2 and 3) are the creature of the 1977 Act; they confer a *personal* right of occupation on the tenant.[5] They arise where a prior protected tenancy is determined or ends by effluxion of time (s 2(1)(a)).

6   Both protected and statutory tenants enjoy full Rent Act security of tenure and other protections, such as against the charging of premiums.[6]

7   Both protected and statutory tenancies are covered by rent control and are therefore referred to as *regulated* tenancies (s 18(1)).

II   THE QUALIFYING CONDITIONS

General

The following conditions must be satisfied for a tenancy of residential premises to be protected by the Rent Act 1977:

1   The tenancy, subject to the exceptions listed earlier in this chapter, must have been created before the commencement of Part I of the Housing Act 1988, i e 15 January 1989.

2   It must be a tenancy which complies with s 1 of the 1977 Act (below); and the rateable value of the dwelling-house must be within defined limits.

3   The tenancy must not be excluded from protection by ss 5–16.

Therefore, s 1 of the 1977 Act provides that: 'a tenancy under which a dwelling-house (which may be a house or a part of a house) is let as a separate dwelling is a protected tenancy for the purposes of this Act'. This provision may be sub-divided up into its principal component parts as follows.

Tenancy

There must be a contractual tenancy for there to be full protection, but 'tenancy' expressly includes sub-tenancy (s 152(1)). If assigned, a tenancy retains protected status. On the other hand, as noted above, if a tenancy is terminated by forfeiture or notice to quit as the case may be, it

---

4   It may be a restricted contract: see section A of this chapter for a brief account.

5   See *Jessamine Investment Co v Schwartz* [1978] QB 264, [1976] 3 All ER 521, CA.

6   The two types of tenancy are treated, where one follows the other, as a single continuing (regulated) tenancy by s 18(2) of the 1977 Act.

loses its protected status and becomes a statutory tenancy (s 2(1)(a)). Thereafter, the tenant's occupation rights depend on the 1977 Act.

Section 1 of the 1977 Act applies to any kind of common law tenancy: therefore, tenants at will paying rent[7] and even tenants on sufferance[8] are protected, as are tenants by estoppel – at least as against the landlord.[9] If a prior mortgage has been created by the landlord, the tenant, though protected as against the landlord, cannot claim protection as against the mortgagee.[10]

The Act deals with premises of which the person in possession is in a real sense tenant of a landlord and so, a purchaser going into possession pending completion and a vendor remaining in occupation pending completion cannot have protected status even if they pay sums for their use and occupation labelled as rent.[11] A mortgagor in possession who attorns tenant to the mortgagee is not within the scope of s 1 of the 1977 Act.[12]

The form of the tenancy is immaterial to whether protection is conferred by s 1: it may apply to periodic tenancies of any length, be they for one week, one month or yearly, and to fixed-term leases. Moreover, s 1 appears to apply to legal and equitable tenancies alike. The relationship of landlord and tenant must exist, and this matter is governed by the common law rules.

A genuine licence is outside the protection of s 1 of the 1977 Act: in particular, lodgers and service occupiers are not protected but a term in a tenancy which is inconsistent with the Rent Acts will be disregarded (see Chapter 3). If there is a genuine letting to a company, which has power to allow an individual to occupy, this is not a protected tenancy.[13]

Dwelling-house

'Dwelling-house' includes, obviously, both entire houses and self-contained flats; but it seems that almost any permanent buildings designed or adapted for living in are capable of being a dwelling-house.

---

7   *Chamberlain v Farr* [1942] 2 All ER 567, CA.
8   *Artizans, Labourers and General Dwellings Co v Whitaker* [1919] 2 KB 301.
9   *Mackley v Nutting* [1949] 2 KB 55, [1949] 1 All ER 413, CA.
10 *Dudley and District Benefit Buidling Society v Emerson* [1949] Ch 707, [1949] 2 All ER 252, CA. It is otherwise if the mortgagee's interest is created after the granting of the tenancy: *Church of England Building Society v Piskor* [1954] Ch 553, [1954] 2 All ER 85, CA.
11 *Hopwood v Hough* [1944] 11 LJCCR 80. Cf *Bretherton v Paton* [1986] 1 EGLR 172, CA.
12 *Portman Building Society v Young* [1951] 1 All ER 191, CA.
13 *Hilton v Plustitle* [1988] 3 All ER 1051, CA; *Estavest Investments Ltd v Commercial Express Travel* [1988] 49 EG 73, CA. These cases must be read subject to *A G Securities v Vaughan* [1988] 3 All ER 1058, [1988] 2 WLR 1205, HL, and in *Crampad International Marketing Co Ltd v Thomas* [1989] 11 LS Gaz 43, PC, a company let was held within the statutory protection.

A house cannot be let as a dwelling-house if it is constructed to consist of a number of units of habitation, all of which are to be sub-let.[14] Therefore, the question whether given premises are a 'dwelling-house' within s 1 is one of fact, and where premises had been converted from a warehouse into a garage with living rooms above, the living rooms fell within s1.[15] But a tenant under a letting of a barn, for example, is outside s 1.[16] Even one or two rooms in a house may, if self-contained, fall within s 1.[17] A caravan, house-boat or other mobile structure is capable of coming within s 1 but only if rendered completely immobile and, presumably, capable of being used by the tenant as his permanent home.[18]

Let as a separate dwelling

The premises let may comprise two or more physically separate units, let together in one lease to the tenant for use as his home, and the whole then constitutes a 'separate dwelling'.[19] Likewise, where a house, cottage and land attached thereto were let in one lease, the combined unit was a separate dwelling protected by s 1.[20]

A tenancy may be protected notwithstanding that: (1) the tenant never dwells in the house or any part of it; (2) the tenancy includes land or buildings not used as a dwelling, as well as the premises used as a dwelling[1] and (3) the premises are partly used for business purposes.[2] But a genuine letting to a company, which may have power to allow a person to occupy, is outside the protection of the Act.[3]

It is implicit in the statutory requirement of letting as a separate dwelling that the tenant is able to go, as of right, to all the rooms in the dwelling concerned.[4] Moreover, the accommodation let must be a separate unit in which it is possible for the tenant to carry on all the major activities of life, particularly sleeping, cooking and eating: if one or

---

14 *Horford Investments Ltd v Lambert* [1976] Ch 39, [1974] 1 All ER 131, CA.
15 *Gidden v Mills* [1925] 2 KB 713.
16 Example of Bankes LJ in *Epsom Grand Stand Association Ltd v Clarke* [1919] WN 170 at 171.
17 *Curl v Angelo* [1948] 2 All ER 189, CA.
18 *R v Rent Officer of Nottinghamshire Registration Area, ex p Allen* [1985] 2 EGLR 153.
19 *Langford Property Co Ltd v Goldrich* [1949] 1 KB 511, [1949] 1 All ER 402, CA (two separate flats let together); also *Grosvenor (Mayfair) Estates v Amberton* (1982) 265 Estates Gazette 693.
20 *Whitty v Scott-Russell* [1950] 2 KB 32, [1950] 1 All ER 884, CA.
1   This must be read subject to the statutory exclusions set out later in this chapter.
2   *Horford Investments Ltd v Lambert* [1976] Ch 39 at 51, [1974] 1 All ER 131 at 138, CA.
3   *Hilton v Plustitle Ltd* [1988] 3 All ER 1051, CA. A company cannot obtain a statutory tenancy on termination of the protected (contractual) tenancy: *Carter v SU Carburetter Co* [1942] 2 KB 288, [1942] 2 All ER 228, CA. But see n 13, supra.
4   *St Catherine's College v Dorling* [1979] 3 All ER 250, [1980] 1 WLR 66, CA.

more of these cannot be carried out, the tenancy is not protected.[5] 'Let as a separate dwelling' is confined to the singular, so that where all parts of a house, consisting of single rooms and a flat, were let off by the tenant to other persons, the tenant did not have a protected tenancy.[6] By contrast, where a tenant was let a penthouse and sub-let part, and remained in occupation of part, he was protected in respect of the whole at the relevant time since he was entitled to possession of the sub-let part.[7]

If part of a house is let, the part need not necessarily be self-contained for there to be a protected tenancy: but, in any event, the tenant must have the exclusive right to use essential living rooms, which include the kitchen, and sharing of other accommodation, in particular a bathroom and wc, does not deprive the tenant of protection.[8] But where the tenant had exclusive possession of two rooms only in a house and shared the kitchen and other accommodation with the landlord, he did not have a protected tenancy.[9] Special rules govern sharing (see below) and if the landlord is resident, s 12 excludes the tenancy from protection in any event.

If the tenant is tenant of different parts of the same house under different lettings from the same landlord, and carries on some of his living activities in one part of the house and the rest of them in the other part (as where he sleeps in one part and eats meals etc in the other part) neither tenancy will be protected. If there is a single composite letting of the two parts as a whole, the tenancies, as also noted above, may be protected.[10] The difference between these two results is one of fact and degree.

Which code?

If the tenant uses the premises partly for business and partly for residential purposes, questions arise as to which of the Rent Act 1977 or the Landlord and Tenant Act 1954 Part II apply.[11]

1   The chief consideration is to have regard to the terms of the lease. If they state the purpose of the letting, that is decisive.[12] Likewise, a

---

5   *Wright v Howell* (1947) 92 Sol Jo 26, CA.
6   *Horford Investments Ltd v Lambert*, supra.
7   *Regalian Securities Ltd v Ramsden* [1981] 2 All ER 65, [1981] 1 WLR 611, HL.
8   *Cole v Harris* [1945] KB 474, CA; also *Horford Investments Ltd v Lambert*, supra.
9   *Neale v Del Soto* [1945] KB 144, [1945] 1 All ER 191, CA.
10   *Hampstead Way Investments Ltd v Lewis-Weare* [1985] 1 All ER 564 at 568, HL; also *Kavanagh v Lyroudias* [1985] 1 All ER 560, CA.
11   See further ch 22. In *Henry Smith's Charity Trustees v Wagle* [1989] 11 EG 75 at 80, CA, Taylor LJ said that 'let as a separate dwelling' no longer included partial use for business purposes; but the context was total abandonment of business user by the lessee.
12   *Wolfe v Hogan* [1949] 2 KB 194, [1949] 1 All ER 570, CA.

description of the premises as being let for business purposes will exclude the Rent Acts.[13]

2   If 1 above does not apply, regard should be had to any user covenants in the lease, and a covenant to use the premises only as a residence excludes the business tenancies code,[14] just as, conversely, a covenant debarring residential user takes the tenancy out of the Rent Acts.[15]

3   If neither 1 nor 2 applies, the intention of the parties may be examined, and if this fails to produce any result, actual de facto user, at the time possession is sought by the landlord, becomes relevant.[16]

4   The lease may allow the user of the premises both for residential and business purposes. If so, the Rent Act cannot apply if business user is significant rather than purely incidental to residential user.[17] If the conclusion is that the tenancy is for business purposes, the mere continuation in residence by a tenant who has closed down the business will not attract the protection of the Rent Acts.[18] It is different if the alteration in de facto user from business to residential is with the landlord's knowledge and express or implied consent.[19]

Sharing of accommodation

Where the tenant shares accommodation with the landlord, if the tenancy was granted on or after 14 August 1974 it will be a restricted contract because the landlord will be a resident landlord.[20] However, as from the commencement of Part I of the Housing Act 1988, i e 15 January 1989, s 36 of that Act prevents any new restricted contracts from being created on or after that date, with limited exceptions.

Where the tenant shares accommodation with other tenants, s 22 applies. It confers protected tenancy status on the separate accommodation which the tenant holds exclusively, and also has the consequence that the tenant cannot be evicted from the shared accommodation by an order for possession unless the order also relates to the separate accommodation (s 22(5)). Moreover, the landlord cannot, by any term in the tenancy, terminate the right of the tenant to share, nor modify the terms of the tenancy with regard thereto (s 22(3)), except that, if the

---

13   *Ponder v Hillman* [1969] 3 All ER 694, [1969] 1 WLR 1261.
14   *Whitty v Scott-Russell* [1950] 2 KB 32, [1950] 1 All ER 884, CA.
15   *Levermore v Jobey* [1956] 2 All ER 362, [1956] 1 WLR 697, CA; *Cooper v Henderson* (1982) 263 Estates Gazette 592, CA.
16   *Wolfe v Hogan*, supra.
17   *Cheryl Investments Ltd v Saldanha* [1979] 1 All ER 5, [1978] 1 WLR 1329, CA.
18   *Pulleng v Curran* (1980) 44 P & CR 58, CA; applied *Henry Smith's Charity Trustees v Wagle* [1989] 11 EG 75, CA (the lease expressly required use for a business purpose).
19   *Russell v Booker* (1982) 263 Estates Gazette 513, CA.
20   Where the tenancy was granted before 14 August 1974, see Rent Act 1977 s 21, repealed by Housing Act 1988 Sch 18.

terms of the tenancy allow this, he may vary or increase the number of persons entitled to share (s 22(4)). The county court has power, on the landlord's application, to terminate the tenant's right to use the whole or any part of the shared accommodation other than living accommodation (s 22(8)), or modifying the tenant's right to use the shared accommodation, to the extent it thinks just (s 22(6)). No order may be made, however, which could not be effected by or under the terms of the tenancy (s 22(7)).[1]

III RATEABLE VALUE LIMITS

By s 4(1) of the 1977 Act, a tenancy is not protected if the dwelling-house has a rateable value which falls outside defined rateable value limits. 'Appropriate day' in these limits means, generally, 23 March 1965 (s 25(3)(a)). If the dwelling-house did not then appear on the valuation list (as where it was built after 23 March 1965), the 'appropriate day' means the first date when a rateable value is shown on the list (s 25(3)(b)).

Clearly, if a dwelling-house has very high rateable value, it would scarcely merit Rent Act protection; but there is a rebuttable presumption that a dwelling-house is caught by one or more of the various rateable value limits (s 4(3)), and only a small percentage of dwellings escape the net.

If a dwelling-house is part of a larger hereditament, the rateable value is apportioned; if it is more than one hereditament, there must be aggregation (s 25(1)(b)). Where the rateable value is altered after the appropriate day so as to take effect not later than the appropriate day, the altered value is taken, not the original value (s 25(4)).[2]

The following shows the relevant rateable values (s 4(2)) but to escape protection, the rateable values must be outside all those laid down, which depends on the appropriate day in question. If the dwelling-house is caught by one figure and is outside others, it is caught by the 1977 Act. The higher figure in each Class applies to dwelling-houses in Greater London and the lower one to those elsewhere.

Class A

The appropriate day falls or fell on or after 1 April 1973 and the dwelling-house on the appropriate day has or had a rateable value exceeding £1,500 or £750.

---

1 See *Lockwood v Lowe* [1954] 2 QB 267 at 270, CA – the aim of this rule is that, on a change of occupants, the hours during which the tenant can use the shared accommodation are not to be varied to his disadvantage.
2 See *Rodwell v Gwynne Trusts Ltd* [1970] 1 All ER 314, [1970] 1 WLR 327, HL.

Class B

The appropriate day fell on or after 22 March 1973 but before 1 April 1973 and the dwelling-house:

(a) on the appropriate day had a rateable value exceeding £600 or £300, and

(b) on 1 April 1973 had a rateable value exceeding £1,500 or £750.

Class C

The appropriate day fell before 22 March 1973 and the dwelling-house:

(a) on the appropriate day had a rateable value exceeding £400 or £200, and

(b) on 22 March 1973 had a rateable value exceeding £600 or £300, and

(c) on 1 April 1973 had a rateable value exceeding £1,500 or £750.[3]

IV TENANCIES EXCLUDED FROM PROTECTION

If a tenancy falls within any of the following specific statutory exclusions from protection, it is not a protected tenancy.

In the case of a tenancy with substantial rent attributable to attendance (s 7) and a tenancy granted by a resident landlord (s 12), these may be restricted contracts.

The following is a list of the principal tenancies which cannot be protected.[4]

PRINCIPAL EXCLUSIONS FROM PROTECTED TENANCY STATUS

1 Tenancies at a low rent (Rent Act 1977 s 5).
2 Dwelling-houses let with other land (ss 6 and 26).
3 Tenancies with payments for board and attendance (s 7).
4 Lettings to students (s 8).
5 Holiday lettings (s 9).
6 Tenancies of agricultural holdings (s 10).
7 Tenancies of licensed premises (s 11).
8 Tenancies granted by a resident landlord (s 12 and Sch 2).

---

3 Note that Local Government Finance Act 1988 s 119 confers on the Secretary of State a regulatory power to delete references in legislation to rateable value limits. This is owing to the introduction of the community charge.

4 Old-style assured tenancies still in being at the commencement of the Housing Act 1988 were converted into new-style assured tenancies by s 1(3) and (4) and no new old-style assured tenancies may thereafter be created: s 37(1).

9 Crown tenancies (s 13).
10 Local authority etc tenancies (s 14–16).
11 Business tenancies (s 24(3)).

Post 1988 Act tenancies

If the tenancy was granted on or after 15 January 1989, it cannot in any event be protected, unless, by s 34(1) of the 1988 Act, one of three very limited exceptions apply. These are:

(a) the tenancy is entered into in pursuance of a pre-commencement contract; or

(b) it is granted to a person who was the previous protected or statutory tenant of the same (or substantially the same) dwelling-house as that being let by the landlord (or one of them) under the previous tenancy; or

(c) it is granted to a person alone or jointly with others where, before the grant of the tenancy, the court ordered possession on the ground of suitable alternative accommodation being available. This only applies, however, if the court directs that the tenancy will be protected, because it considers that an assured tenancy would not afford the required security.

(a) Tenancies at a low rent

(i) *General rule* By s 5(1) of the 1977 Act, a tenancy is not a protected if under the tenancy either no rent is payable or the rent payable is less than two-thirds of the rateable value of the dwelling-house on the appropriate day. The clear object of s 5 is to exclude long tenancies at a low rent from the Rent Act 1977, but they are given some protection under Part I of the Landlord and Tenant Act 1954. The onus of proving, where relevant, that rent was in fact paid is on the tenant – there is no presumption that s 5 applies.[5] The relevant date for deciding whether s 5 applies is that of the hearing. If so, a progressive rent under a rent review could, in time, bring a tenancy originally at a low rent within the full protection of the 1977 Act.[6]

(ii) *Meaning of rent* There is no direct definition of 'rent' in the Rent Act 1977 for the purposes of s 5. The test appears to be that 'rent' within the 1977 Act refers to the total money payment payable by the tenant to the landlord.[7] If, rather than money payments, the tenant provides

5 *Bracey v Pales* [1927] 1 KB 818.
6 *Woozley v Woodall Smith* [1950] 1 KB 325, [1949] 2 All ER 1055, CA.
7 *Sidney Trading Co Ltd v Finsbury Borough Council* [1952] 1 All ER 460 at 461 (rates payable by tenant included); *Markworth v Hellard* [1921] 2 KB 755, CA.

services such as cooking and cleaning, then no rent is payable for the purposes of s 5.[8] Capital payments such as genuine premiums or fines do not count as 'rent' within s 5 unless the payments are rent in disguise.[9]

(iii) *Miscellaneous*   Service charges payable under long tenancies[10] do not count towards the two-thirds figure for rent if expressed to be payable as service charges (s 5(4)).[11] In the case of a variable rent, apparently the premises may enter and leave protection, dependent on the level of rent at any given time. If the rent of a protected tenancy is reduced below the two-thirds limit, s 5 may deprive the tenant of protection; but if the tenancy is statutory, this result is not possible.[12]

(b)   Dwelling-houses let with other land

(i) *General rule*   By s 6 of the Rent Act 1977, a tenancy is not a protected tenancy if the dwelling-house subject to the tenancy is let together with land other than the site of the dwelling-house. This is expressly subject to s 26: and s 26(1) provides that any land or premises let together with a dwelling-house shall, unless it consists of agricultural land exceeding two acres, be treated as part of the dwelling-house. The broad effect of s 26 is that, where it applies, the whole of the composite entity, dwelling-house plus land, is protected.[13]

(ii) *General test*   Sections 6 and 26 appear at first sight self-contradictory. Accordingly, a dominant purpose test applies: one asks whether the land is an adjunct to the dwelling-house or, on the other hand, whether the dwelling-house is an adjunct to the land.[14] Therefore, where a house occupied merely one-quarter of the land, the rest of which comprised buildings used for business purposes, there was no protected tenancy,[15] nor where there was a letting of a camping site which had a bungalow on it.[16]

---

8   *Barnes v Barratt* [1970] 2 QB 657, [1970] 2 All ER 483, CA (licence on facts).
9   *Samrose Properties Ltd v Gibbard* [1958] 1 All ER 502, [1958] 1 WLR 235, CA, where a 'premium' was added to a nominal rent and as a result took the total rent, including the premium, over the two-thirds mark.
10   Defined by s 5(5) as terms certain exceeding 21 years, other than those terminable by earlier landlords' notice.
11   See *Investment and Freehold English Estates Ltd v Casement* [1988] 1 EGLR 100, CA.
12   See *J & F Stone Lighting and Radio Ltd v Levitt* [1947] AC 209, [1946] 2 All ER 653, HL; *McGee v London Rent Assessment Panel Committee* (1969) 113 Sol Jo 384, for these assumptions.
13   *Langford Property Co Ltd v Batten* [1951] AC 223, [1950] 2 All ER 1079, HL.
14   *Pender v Reid* 1948 SC 381.
15   *Pender v Reid*, supra; *Cargill v Phillips* 1951 SC 67.
16   *Feyereisel v Turnidge* [1952] 2 QB 29, [1952] 1 All ER 728, CA.

(iii) *Agricultural land* It has been held that if at the date of the hearing or application the land is not used for agricultural purposes[17] but is used in conjunction with the user of the dwelling-house, then the tenancy of both house and land will be protected.[18] But if the land is let for use as agricultural land, mere unilateral abandonment of such user will not of itself attract the Rent Acts.[19]

(iv) *'Let together with'* This requires a reasonably close connection between the letting of the dwelling-house and the land[20] but the two do not have to be necessarily contemporaneously let in the same document,[1] and the landlord of one entity let need not necessarily be the same landlord as that of the other part so let.[2] The lettings should however presumably be to the same tenant.

(c) Tenancies with payments for board or attendance

By s 7(1) of the Rent Act 1977, a tenancy is not a protected tenancy if under it the dwelling-house is bona fide let at a rent which includes payments in respect of board or attendance. By s 7(2), a dwelling-house is not to be taken to be bona fide let at a rent which includes payments in respect of attendance unless the amount of rent fairly attributable to attendance, having regard to the value of attendance to the tenant, forms a substantial part of the whole rent. The reason for this latter requirement is that, but for it, a landlord could easily provide services which were more of a burden than a benefit to tenants, and be able to evade the Rent Act 1977.[3]

If board is provided within s 7(1), the tenancy is not protected nor, if substantial, is it a restricted contract. If attendance in the statutory sense is provided, there will be a restricted contract.[4]

(i) *General* The first point is that the term bona fide applies to the whole of s 7(1) so that the rent must genuinely include payments for board or attendance, and the provision of either of them must not just be

---

17 Defined by Rent Act 1977 s 26(2) by reference to the General Rate Act 1967 s 26(3)(c) as extended, i e any arable meadow or pasture ground.
18 *Bradshaw v Smith* (1980) 255 Estates Gazette 699, CA.
19 *Russell v Booker* (1982) 263 Estates Gazette 513, CA.
20 Farrand and Arden, loc cit, citing *Gaidowski v Gonville and Caius College, Cambridge* [1975] 2 All ER 952, [1975] 1 WLR 1066, CA.
1 *Mann v Merrill* [1945] 1 All ER 708, CA; *Wimbush v Cibulia* [1949] 2 KB 564, [1949] 2 All ER 432, CA.
2 *Jelley v Buckman* [1974] QB 488, [1973] 3 All ER 853, CA.
3 *Woodward v Docherty* [1974] 2 All ER 844 at 848, CA. No exclusion from assured tenancy status corresponding to s 7 exists in Housing Act 1988 Sch 1.
4 Note that as from the commencement of Part I of the Housing Act 1988, no new restricted contracts are possible – see section A of this Chapter.

a device or a matter of words.[5] Secondly, the relevant date for the conditions in s 7 to be complied with, i e at which the tenant is contractually entitled to board or attendance, is the date of commencement of the tenancy.[6] Thirdly, 'rent' refers to the total monetary payment made by the tenant.[7]

(ii)   *Meaning of board*   There is no definition of 'board' in s 7(1) but the term is not confined to full board, and the daily provision of continental breakfast (with no other meals) in a dining room in the same building as the tenant's room was held to be sufficient board.[8] The provision of one meal other than breakfast will suffice, but the de minimis principle applies, and insufficient is a morning cup of tea.[9] Nonetheless, provided there is a meal, it may be that board in the form of one sandwich suffices.[10]

(iii)   *Meaning of attendance*   This means a service personal to the tenant performed by the landlord under covenant for the benefit or convenience of the individual tenant in his use or enjoyment of the demised premises.[11] Examples include carrying coal,[12] delivery of letters,[13] and the provision of a resident housekeeper who cleaned the tenant's room daily, provided clean linen weekly and from whom food could be obtained on request and payment.[14] Services provided to all tenants in common do not qualify as attendance, as for instance, the provision of common central heating, hot water or general porterage.

As noted, the amount of rent fairly attributable to attendance must, having regard to the value of the attendance to the tenant, form a substantial part of the whole rent (s 7(2)). There is no statutory guidance as to what this rule means. The key notion is 'fairly' and a broad, commonsense approach is to be taken. Each step must be proved by the landlord, i e (1) that the rent includes payments in respect of attendance and (2) that the amount of rent fairly attributable to attendance is a substantial part of the whole rent and (3) regard must be had, in deciding on (2), to the use to the tenant of the attendance. What is fair and the

5   *Palser v Grinling* [1948] AC 291, [1948] 1 All ER 1, HL; *Otter v Norman* [1989] AC 129, [1988] 1 All ER 531, CA; affd [1989] AC 129, [1988] 2 All ER 897, HL.
6   *Woodward v Docherty* [1974] 2 All ER 844, [1974] 1 WLR 966, CA; also *Property Holding Co Ltd v Mischeff* [1946] KB 645, [1946] 2 All ER 294.
7   *Wilkes v Goodwin* [1923] 2 KB 86, CA.
8   *Otter v Norman*, supra.
9   *Wilkes v Goodwin*, supra.
10   According to dicta in *R v Battersea, Wandsworth, Mitcham and Wimbledon Rent Tribunal, ex p Parikh* [1957] 1 All ER 352 at 354.
11   *Palser v Grinling* [1948] AC 291, [1948] 1 All ER 1, HL.
12   *Nye v Davis* [1922] 2 KB 56.
13   *Wood v Carwardine* [1923] 2 KB 185.
14   *Marchant v Charters* [1977] 3 All ER 918, [1977] 1 WLR 1181, CA.

value to the tenant are not questions to be dealt with on a precise arithmetical basis.[15] Therefore, much is left to the discretion of the county court judge and only if there is an error of law in his decision would the Court of Appeal interfere. The critical matter is that it is the value to the tenant of the covenant to provide (personal) services that counts,[16] i e value to the tenant or original tenant at the date of the grant of the tenancy.[17]

The attendance must be substantial – i e considerable, solid or big, and more than just enough to escape the de minimis rule: whether attendance is substantial in a given case is a question of fact and degree.[18]

(d) Lettings to students

By s 8(1) of the Rent Act 1977, a tenancy is not a protected tenancy if it is granted to a person who is pursuing, or who intends to pursue, a course of study provided by a specified educational institution and the tenancy is granted either by that institution or by another specified institution or body of persons. Specified institutions[19] include universities, university colleges, polytechnics and certain higher education institutions. As will be seen, as well as pursuant to s 8, it is possible to let off student-let property in vacations, and then mandatorily to recover possession after expiry of the tenancy.[20] Private landlords cannot directly take advantage of s 8, but if they let to a specified educational institution and it sub-lets the whole premises, in parts, to different students, it may be that the head tenancy is not protected on general principles as there is no letting as a separate dwelling within s 1.[1] There is a similar exemption from assured tenancy status under the Housing Act 1988 (see Chapter 18).

(e) Holiday lettings

By s 9 of the 1977 Act, a tenancy is not a protected tenancy if the purpose of the tenancy is to confer on the tenant the right to occupy the dwelling-house for a holiday. A holiday letting is incapable of being a restricted

---

15 *Woodward v Docherty* [1974] 2 All ER 844, [1974] 1 WLR 966, CA.
16 *Palser v Grinling*, supra; *Woodward v Docherty*, supra. The two are not necessarily the same, but the cost to the landlord may be evidence of the value to the tenant – perhaps by comparing what the landlord is charging with what it might cost the tenant to obtain the service aliunde: *Eagle v Robinson* (8 April 1987, unreported), CA.
17 *Artillery Mansions Ltd v Macartney* [1949] 1 KB 164, [1948] 2 All ER 875, CA.
18 *Palser v Grinling*, supra; cf *Jozwiak v Hierowski* [1948] 2 All ER 9, CA (25 per cent accepted as substantial), *Woodward v Docherty* (14 per cent not substantial).
19 I e specified in regulations: Rent Act 1977 s 8(2). See SI 1988/2236.
20 Under Rent Act 1977 Sch 15 Part II Case 14.
 1 *St Catherine's College v Dorling* [1979] 3 All ER 250, [1980] 1 WLR 66, CA.

contract. Out of season lettings are protected, but possession may be recovered after termination of them under a mandatory ground.[2] There is a similar exclusion of holiday lettings from assured tenancies (see Chapter 18).[3]

(i) *General*   Clearly, the policy of s 9 is to deny Rent Act protection to holiday houses or flats; but even before the enactment of s 9, there were dicta that a tenant of a holiday home could not enjoy full protection, owing to non-compliance with the statutory residence requirement.[4]

There is no definition in s 9 of 'holiday' and two judicial definitions may be cited. In one case,[5] a dictionary definition was accepted – i e 'holiday' meant 'a period of cessation of work or period of recreation'. This, as has been forcefully pointed out,[6] omits to deal with working holidays or long holidays and further guidance has been given on the word 'holiday'. According to this, a holiday is a suspension of one's normal activities not necessarily implying a period of recreation.[7]

(ii) *Genuine or sham agreements*   The present exemption confers an incentive on landlords to avoid the protection of the 1977 Act.[8] The question is how the courts will deal with statements in tenancies such as: 'it is mutually agreed that the letting hereby made is solely for the purpose of the tenant's holiday in the London area'.[9] Apparently, while the labels of the parties are not conclusive, a statement of the purpose of the tenancy is evidence of the parties' purpose, and takes effect unless the tenant proves that the statement does not correspond with the true purpose. If a statement is proved to be a sham by the tenant, i e a term inserted by the landlord to avoid the 1977 Act by a misstatement of fact or intention, the tenancy will be outside s 9 and fully protected.[10] Accordingly, where a landlord was proved by the tenants to have known that, despite a statement in the agreement that it was (in effect) a holiday letting, the tenants intended to occupy the premises as students, i e for

---

2   Rent Act 1977 Sch 15 Part II Case 13.
3   In the absence of authority, it is conceived that the present discussion applies both to the Rent Act 1977 and the Housing Act 1988 regimes.
4   *Walker v Ogilvy* (1974) 28 P & CR 288 at 293, CA. This raises the question of the necessity of a specific exclusion of holiday lettings in the case of either regime: cf Farrand and Arden *Rent Acts and Regulations* notes to s 9.
5   *Buchmann v May* [1978] 2 All ER 993 at 995, CA.
6   Lyons [1984] Conv 286.
7   *Francke v Hakmi* [1984] CLY 1906 discussed in Lyons, loc cit.
8   Or that of the 1988 Act as the case may be.
9   The statement of purpose in *Buchmann v May*, supra.
10   *Buchmann v May*, supra.

work, the letting fell outside s 9.[11] By contrast, where a tenant held under a three-month tenancy which stated that it was for the purpose of the tenant's holiday in the London area, it was held that the tenancy fell within s 9; the statement was evidence of the purpose of the agreement, which could properly be described as a holiday letting; and the tenant, whose attention was not drawn to the statement, was held to have failed to discharge the onus of proving that the statement was untrue, did not represent the parties' common intention and was a sham.[12] However, it may be that if the tenant is a foreign visitor with little knowledge of English, the onus on him is less than that on a person fully conversant with English.[13] As noted earlier, a letting for a working holiday is capable of falling within s 9, as where a flat in Maida Vale was let on a 'holiday' letting to several foreign persons, who failed to prove that the statement of the purpose of the letting was a sham.[14]

(f) Agricultural holdings

Section 10 of the 1977 Act provides that a tenancy is not protected if the dwelling-house is comprised in an agricultural holding (as defined by Agricultural Holdings Act 1986 s 1)[15] This is because agricultural tenancies are protected by the 1986 Act. For s 10 to apply, the dwelling-house must be occupied by the person responsible for the control (whether as tenant or as a servant or agent of the tenant) of the farming of the holding.

Where a sub-tenancy of part of a house (itself excluded by s 10 from protection) is granted s 137(3) of the 1977 Act provides that the sub-tenancy is treated as protected, if it is of a separate dwelling, both as against the tenant and the head landlord.[16]

A problem arises where a tenancy is of an agricultural holding originally, but the user is mixed agricultural and residential, and later the protection of the 1977 Act is claimed owing to abandonment of

---

11 *R v Rent Officer for London Borough of Camden, ex p Plant* (1980) 257 Estates Gazette 713. The rent officer was later held to have jurisdiction to register a fair rent on the basis that the tenancy was protected: *R v Rent Officer for Camden, ex p Ebiri* [1981] 1 All ER 950.

12 *Buchmann v May*, supra.

13 This is based on dicta in *Francke v Hakmi*, supra, but there, the agreement contained self-contradictory provisions, so that it was doubtful whether the presumption about the 'holiday statement' actually applied: see Lyons [1984] Conv 286 at 294.

14 *McHale v Daneham* (1979) 249 Estates Gazette 969; also *Ryeville Properties v Saint-John* [1980] CLY 1598.

15 Similarly, agricultural tenancies cannot be assured (ch 18). The discussion of changes of user (below) appears to be relevant to assured tenancies.

16 This reverses, as regards the head landlord, *Maunsell v Olins* [1975] AC 373, [1975] 1 All ER 16, HL.

agricultural user. First, unilateral cesser of agricultural user and commencement of purely residential user will not bring the tenancy within the 1977 Act.[17] Secondly, if at the date of proceedings (which is the relevant date) a letting of an agricultural holding has been superseded by a new contract providing for different (i e solely residential) user, either expressly, or by implication, as where a change of user is known to and accepted by the landlord, the new contract will be Rent Act protected if a separate dwelling is let.[18]

(g) Licensed premises

By s 11 of the 1977 Act, a tenancy of a dwelling-house which consists of or comprises premises licensed for the sale of intoxicating liquors on the premises cannot be protected or statutory.[19] Off-licensed premises are excluded by s 24(3) from being business tenancies within Part II of the Landlord and Tenant Act 1954.

(h) Resident landlords

Tenancies granted by resident landlords, which fall within s 12 of the Rent Act 1977 are not protected tenancies. They are, however, restricted contracts (see section A of this Chapter).

Because of s 36(1) of the Housing Act 1988, no new restricted contracts may be entered into, with a few exceptions, after the commencement of Part I of the 1988 Act. Therefore, s 12 cannot be resorted to in relation to tenancies granted on or after 15 January 1989.

However, tenancies granted by resident landlords after the commencement of Part I of the 1988 Act are excluded from being assured tenancies.[20] The terms of this exclusion are identical in relevant respects to those of s 12, and it is thought that the discussion of s 12 of the 1977 Act is applicable also to the resident landlord exclusion from assured tenancies.[1]

The idea behind the resident landlord provisions is that an owner should be able to let off rooms in his house or flat without conferrring statutory protection on the tenant.[2] A company landlord, however, cannot very well reside personally on the premises, and so the exemption is confined to individual landlords. To retain exemption, the landlord or

---

17   It may well deprive the tenant of the protection of the 1986 Act: *Wetherall v Smith* [1980] 2 All ER 530, [1980] 1 WLR 1290, CA.

18   *Russell v Booker* (1982) 263 Estates Gazette 513, CA.

19   A similar exclusion exists from assured tenancies (ch 18).

20   Housing Act 1988 Sch 1 para 10. See further ch 18.

1   If a tenancy is granted by a resident landlord after the commencement of Part I of the 1988 Act, it may also be an excluded tenancy from s 3 of the Protection from Eviction Act 1977 (s 31 of the Housing Act 1988, inserting s 3A into the 1977 Act): see ch 18.

2   *Cooper v Tait* (1984) 48 P & CR 460, CA.

his successor must remain in residential occupation of other parts of the same premises, and, as will appear, there are complex provisions to facilitate the transfer of the reversion from one resident landlord to another, without loss of the exemption.

(i) *The rule* Section 12(1) of the Rent Act 1977 provides that, subject to s 12(2), a tenancy of a dwelling-house granted on or after 14 August 1974 shall not be a protected tenancy at any time if

1   the dwelling-house forms part only of a building and, except in a case where the dwelling-house also forms part of a flat, the building is not a purpose-built block of flats; and
2   the tenancy was granted by a person who, at the time when he granted it, occupied as his residence another dwelling-house:
    (a) where part of a flat is let, the part occupied by the landlord forms part of the same flat; or
    (b) in any other case, it also forms part of the same building; and
3   subject to para 1 of Sch 2 to the Act, at all times since the tenancy was granted the interest of the landlord under the tenancy has belonged to a person who, at the time he owned that interest, occupied as his residence another dwelling-house which:
    (a) is either part of the same flat in which the tenant resides; or
    (b) is part of the same building in which the tenant resides.

The exception may accordingly be taken advantage of only in relation to tenancies granted on or after 14 August 1974, and it does not apply, due to s 12(2), to renewed tenancies in the same building granted to any sitting, protected or statutory tenant. Each of the main points raised by these provisions is considered.

(ii) *Condition* (1) *'building'* There is no statutory definition of 'building' but the exception only applies if at the time of the grant and subsequently, the landlord is resident in another part of the same building. The question of what is a building is one of fact: if the landlord lives in an extension to a house where the tenants live, and the extension is separated from the house, has no internal communication with it and its own front entrance, then the landlord is not living in the same 'building'.[3] The mere fact that there is a continuous roof common to a number of separate units of dwelling does not automatically mean that all units together form one 'building';[4] but if the appearance of the property is that it is one large continuous building with various

---

3   *Bardrick v Haycock* (1976) 31 P & CR 420, CA.
4   Cf *Humphrey v Young* [1903] 1 KB 44.

extensions in which landlord and tenant reside, then there may be one single building.[5]

(iii) *Condition* (1)*'purpose-built blocks of flats'* By statutory definition (Sch 2 para 4) a building is a purpose-built block of flats if as constructed it contained and contains, two or more flats. 'Flat' means a dwelling-house which:

1 forms part only of a building; and
2 is separated horizontally from another dwelling-house which forms part of the same building.

Hence, a two-storey building with a shop on the ground-floor and a flat on the upper floor is not a 'purpose-built block of flats'. In any event the exception covers the case where part of a flat is let though it is in a purpose-built block of flats (s 12(1)(a)). It seems that the question whether there is a purpose-built block of flats is to be tested as at the date of the original design and construction of the building: if as originally designed and constructed, there was no purpose-built block of flats, later conversion into flats will not take a tenancy granted by a resident landlord in another part of the same building out of the exception.[6]

(iv) *Residence requirement* This is in s 12(1)(b) and (c) discussed above. The residential occupation by the landlord[7] must be (a) continuous at all times since the grant of the tenancy and (b) in another dwelling-house. It is provided (Sch 2 para 5) in the latter connection, that a person is treated as occupying a dwelling-house as his residence if he fulfils the same conditions as are required by s 2(3) for a statutory tenant. Moreover, to occupy 'another dwelling-house' the landlord must occupy different essential living accommodation from the tenant: if this is not so and he shares with the tenant, then the resident landlord exemption will not apply.[8]

The requirement of continuous occupation is relaxed so as to allow for periods of disregard, which enable transfer of the landlord's interest and also, following his death, to the same end. In all cases during a period of disregard the residence requirement is treated as satisfied.

---

5 *Griffiths v English* (1982) 261 Estates Gazette 257, CA; also *Guppy v O'Donnell* (1979) 129 NLJ 930.
6 *Barnes v Gorsuch* (1982) 43 P & CR 294, CA.
7 Residence by one of several joint landlords suffices for s 12(1): *Cooper v Tait* (1984) 48 P & CR 460, CA.
8 *Lyons v Caffery* (1982) 266 Estates Gazette 213.

(v) *Periods of disregard:*

(1) *Owner-occupier transfer*

(a) A period of up to 28 days is disregarded, from the date when the landlord's interest becomes vested in a non-resident person. The 28 days, in the case of sale, run from the completion of the contract.[9]

(b) Within the 28 day period, the disregard period may be extended for a maximum period of six months, following notice by the non-resident individual to the tenant of intention to occupy.[10]

(2) *Transfer to trustees as such* If the resident landlord's interest becomes vested in trustees as such and remains so vested, there is a two-year period of disregard.[11] During any period when the interest of the landlord is so vested and the landlord's interest or its proceeds of sale are held in trust for a resident beneficiary, the residence requirement is satisfied and no part of this period is disregarded.[12] Trustees as such' include bare trustees for the landlord, who may thus absent himself for up to two years and vest his interest in trustees for himself. In addition, the term includes cases where trustees hold under a trust for sale or settlement, and also trustees holding under a trust arising under a will or intestacy.[13]

The effect of the disregard periods in the last two cases is that no order for possession can be made against the tenant during a disregard period save on grounds applicable to a regulated tenancy.[14] However, it has been held that during a disregard period (or period of transition) the tenant is only a person holding over without any right to do so, while *temporarily* protected by the rule just mentioned from an order for possession; and that, when the transitional period of time ends, two things may happen. First, by then the tenancy may not have been determined by notice to quit (if periodical) or otherwise: if so the tenant becomes a protected tenant.[15] Second, however, the non-resident landlord-to-be or trustees may have validly determined the tenancy (e g if periodic, by notice to quit served on the tenant) during the period of disregard: if so, vacant possession may be obtained after the period of disregard.[15]

---

9 Rent Act 1977 Sch 2 para 1(a).
10 Ibid para 1(b).
11 Ibid para 1(c)(ii).
12 Rent Act 1977 Sch 2 para 2.
13 *Williams v Mate* (1982) 46 P & CR 43, CA.
14 Rent Act 1977 Sch 2, para 3.
15 *Landau v Sloane* [1982] AC 490, [1981] 1 All ER 705, HL; *Williams v Mate*, supra.

(3)   *Vesting in personal representatives*   Where a resident landlord's interest becomes vested in his personal representatives acting as such after his death, the residence requirement is deemed to be satisfied for two years from the vesting of the landlord's interest in his personal representatives.[16] This raises different considerations to the disregard period applicable to owner-occupiers and trustees.

If, *during the two-year extension period*, the tenancy expires (where it is fixed-term) or is determined by notice to quit (where it is periodic) served by the non-resident personal representatives, possession may be recovered from the tenant, without the need to prove any ground for possession,[17] not only after the end of the extension period, but actually while it is continuing.[18] There is no guidance as to this in the provisions themselves.

If a beneficiary, during the two-year extension period, moves into personal occupation (even without a formal assent) or if the landlord's interest is vested in such a beneficiary, the tenancy will be not protected so long as the new landlord satisfies the residence requirement.[19]

If the two-year extension period runs out and possession has not been recovered during or after it by the personal representatives (based on expiry of the tenancy or a notice to quit served during the extension period) and no beneficiary has moved into residential occupation, then the tenancy becomes protected or statutory as the case may be.[20]

(i)   Landlord's interest belonging to the Crown

Section 13(1) of the Rent Act 1977 provides that a tenancy is not protected at any time when the landlord's interest belongs to Her Majesty in right of the Crown or belongs to a government department or is held in trust for Her Majesty for the purposes of a government department. A person is not a statutory tenant if the interest of the immediate landlord is held by one of the above. However, by s 13(2), there may be a protected or statutory tenancy, if the interest of the Crown is managed by the Crown Estate Commissioners.[1] The operation of the 1977 Act between tenants and sub-tenants is unaffected by s 13 and sub-tenancies held indirectly from the Crown are also unaffected by

---

16   Rent Act 1977 Sch 2 para 2A (inserted by Housing Act 1980 s 65, the two-year period, but *not* the deeming of residence, being with retrospective effect: *Caldwell v McAteer* (1983) 269 Estates Gazette 1039, CA).

17   Under Rent Act 1977 Sch 15.

18   *Landau v Sloane*, supra; also Martin, *loc cit* p 40.

19   *Beebe v Mason* (1980) 254 Estates Gazette 987, CA.

20   *Landau v Sloane*, supra.

1   The text is of s 13 as substituted by Housing Act 1980 s 73, which is not retroactive: *Crown Estate Comrs v Wordsworth* (1982) 44 P & CR 302, CA.

its provisions.[2] Moreover, if the reversion becomes vested in any non-exempt landlord then there will be full protection for any existing tenancy.

(j) Miscellaneous

The following tenancies are not protected tenancies. They are excluded because, in the first two instances, they are public or quasi-public sector tenancies, and, in the third instance, by reason of another statute.[3]

1 *Shared ownership leases* A shared ownership lease granted under Part V of the Housing Act 1985 (under the 'right to buy') is not, by s 5A of the 1977 Act,[4] a protected tenancy.

2 *Exclusion of tenancies where landlord is a local authority etc* If the immediate landlord's interest is held by one of a number of bodies listed in ss 14–16 of the 1977 Act, the tenancy is not protected. If the landlord assigns his reversion to another landlord who is not within ss 14–16, exemption by reason of these provisions will be lost and the tenancy will become protected, unless for some other reason it is excluded from the 1977 Act.

The landlords listed include the following: local authorities generally,[5] the Commission for the New Towns, development corporations and the Development Board for Rural Wales and urban development corporations (all in s 14); also certain housing associations,[6] the Housing Corporation and charitable housing trusts (all listed in s 15); also housing co-operatives (s 16).[7]

3 *Tenancies of Parsonage Houses* Tenancies of these, in so far as they belong to the Church of England, are excluded from the 1977 Act by the overriding effect of the Pluralities Act 1838. Denominations other than the Church of England do not benefit from this exemption, but have a mandatory ground for possession.[8]

---

2 Rent Act 1977 s 154.
3 Old-style (i e pre-Housing Act 1988) assured tenancies were excluded from the Rent Act 1977 (s 16A) but from the commencement of Part I of the 1988 Act, old-style assured tenancies are converted to new-style assured tenancies (1988 Act s (3)).
4 Added by Housing and Planning Act 1986 s 18 and Sch 4 paras 1 and 11, in force on 11 December 1987: SI 1987/1939.
5 Tenancies granted by local authorities are generally secure tenancies, as to which see Part G of this book.
6 Tenancies granted by these bodies fell within the 'fair rent' system (Part VI of the 1977 Act) but, as from the commencement of Part I of the Housing Act 1988, this regime ceased to apply to new tenancies (1988 Act s 35).
7 Tenancies granted by these latter bodies may be secure: see Part G of this book.
8 Rent Act 1977 Sch 15 Part II Case 15, which applies to regulated tenancies.

(k)   Business tenancies

A tenancy is not regulated if it is one to which Part II of the Landlord and Tenant Act 1954 applies (s 24(3)). This provision expressly has no effect on the applicability of the Rent Act 1977 to a sub-letting of part of business premises. These sub-lettings must be considered separately. On the question of whether the 1977 or 1954 Act applies to mixed user tenancies of the whole premises, see above and also Chapter 22.

(l)   Tenancies of overcrowded dwellings

By s 101 of the 1977 Act, at any time when a dwelling-house is overcrowded within Part X of the Housing Act 1985 in such circumstances as to render the occupier guilty of a criminal offence, the occupier's immediate landlord is enabled to recover possession of the dwelling-house free from the restrictions of the 1977 Act. This lifting of re-possession restrictions is no longer limited to a dwelling-house used as a separate dwelling by members of the working class or a type suitable for such use.

(m)   Release from 1977 Act

The Secretary of State has the power under s 143(1), by regulations, to release all dwelling-houses in a particular area from being the subject of a regulated tenancy if satisfied that, in every part of the area, there is no scarcity. This power has not so far been exercised.

C   RENT REGULATION

I   RENT REGULATION UNDER THE RENT ACT 1977

1   OUTLINE OF SYSTEM

Rent regulation applies to protected and statutory tenancies under the Rent Act 1977, these being jointly referred to, for this purpose, as regulated tenancies. This form of rent control has no application to assured and assured shorthold tenancies under the Housing Act 1988. The 1977 Act system of rent control will slowly die out, in view of the fact that after the commencement of Part I of the 1988 Act, no new protected tenancies may, in principle, be created.

During a protected tenancy, if no rent is registered for the dwelling-house concerned, the parties may agree on any rent they wish. Either party alone, or the parties jointly, may apply for the registration of a fair rent to the Rent Officer of the appropriate local authority area. The Rent Officer has some limited statutory guidelines and a wide discretion in the matter. Notably, however, s 70(2) of the 1977 Act requires that he must ignore any scarcity element when assessing a fair rent. Once he has determined a fair rent, the Rent Officer must cause it to be registered – and the registered rent has a two-year life, running from the date of registration. There is a right of appeal to a Rent Assessment Committee, and further rights to require either a case stated to the High Court[9] or to apply for judicial review for error of law.

2 REMOVAL OF RENT CONTROL BY HOUSING ACT 1988

As from the commencement of the Housing Act 1988, rent control in the form outlined above and dealt with in the rest of this part of this Chapter has been abolished. Assured and assured shorthold tenants will have to pay market rents.[10] Rent control in the old form will, as noted above, continue to apply to any pre-1988 Act protected or statutory tenancies, and some discussion of it has been retained in the present book, though concentrating on the statutory and judicial guidelines as to the fixing of 'fair rents' rather than on procedural and related issues.

II RENT LIMIT DURING CONTRACTUAL PERIODS

Various matters arise concerning the maximum amount of rent lawfully recoverable from the tenant during a contractual period, i e while a tenancy is protected (s 61(1)). The position varies depending on whether there is a registered rent for the dwelling-house or not.

(a) *Previous uncancelled registered rent* By s 44(1) of the Rent Act 1977, where a rent for a dwelling-house is registered under Part IV of the 1977 Act, the rent recoverable for any contractual period of a regulated tenancy of the dwelling-house (i e while the tenancy is *protected* as opposed to *statutory*) is limited to the registered rent. If the amount of rent payable under the tenancy exceeds the registered rent limit then the excess is, by s 44(2), irrecoverable from the tenant. This is backed up s 57(1) which provides that a tenant who pays an excessive amount of rent is entitled to recover that amount from the landlord who received it or from his personal representatives.[11] There is a time-limit on this right of recovery to two years from the date of the payment (s 57(3)).

---

9 Tribunals and Inquiries Act 1971 s 13.
10 See ch 18.
11 Or the tenant may deduct the excess from any rent payable to the landlord: Rent Act 1977 s 57(2).

(b)   *Registered rent but 'dwelling-house' not the same*   The register must specify the dwelling-house for which the rent is registered (s 66(2)(b)). Therefore, if the premises let to the tenant are different, as where a tenant who is new is let additional rooms in a building with a rent registered only for the rooms previously let, or where a new tenant is let the whole of a dwelling-house where a rent is registered only for part of it, or for all parts separately but not the whole, then the previously registered rent, if any, will not apply to these new lettings.[12] Where, however, a landlord carried out substantial works of refurbishment and modernisation to a flat, a registered rent for a previous tenancy was held applicable to a new tenancy, because, it was held, the prescribed particulars on the register were the same as before.[13] Where a flat was first held under an unfurnished tenancy and then was let, after refurbishment, furnished, the previously registered rent for the unfurnished tenancy did not apply to the furnished tenancy.[14]

(c)   *Position if no registered rent*   There is no statutory rule governing the rent limit in such cases, and therefore the rent limit is the amount of rent agreed between landlord and tenant.

In two cases, a rent agreement is required to raise the rent, i e where a new regulated tenancy of the same dwelling-house is granted to an existing regulated tenant or to any successor of his, and where the rent of an existing protected tenancy is to be increased (s 51(1)). Failure to enter a rent agreement, where required, renders any excess over the previous rent limits irrecoverable from the tenant. Rent agreements must comply with formal requirements (s 51(4));[15] if not, the excess over the previous rent is irrecoverable.

III   RENT LIMIT DURING STATUTORY PERIODS

The position depends on whether there is a registered rent or not at the time of the statutory tenancy, i e where the protected (contractual) tenancy ends.

(a)   *No registered rent*   The rent limit here is the rent recoverable under the last contractual period of the regulated tenancy (s 45(1)) and any excess is irrecoverable from the tenant.

---

12   *Gluchowska v Tottenham Borough Council* [1954] 1 QB 438, [1954] 1 All ER 408.
13   *Waddock v Cheniston Investments Ltd* [1988] 2 EGLR 136, CA.
14   *Kent v Millmead Properties Ltd* (1982) 44 P & CR 353, CA.
15   The agreement must be written, with statements to the effect that the tenant's security and right to apply for a fair rent are unaffected.

(b) *Registered rent* If there is a registered rent for the last contractual period of the regulated tenancy then the rent limit for the statutory periods (i e under the statutory tenancy) is fixed at the rent registered for the last contractual period (s 45(1)) and the excess if any, over the registered rent is irrecoverable from the tenant (s 45(2)(a)). If the amount of registered rent under this rule exceeds the actual amount of rent payable for a statutory period, then s 45(2)(b) enables the rent to be brought up to the registered rent by means of a notice of increase in the prescribed form, served by the landlord on the tenant and specifying the date on which the increase is to take effect. This must be not earlier than the effective date of registration nor earlier than four weeks before service of the notice (s 45(3)). If a notice of increase is served while a periodical tenancy is contractual, it becomes thereafter a statutory tenancy (s 49(4)) from the date specified in the notice.[16]

(c) *Adjustments* Where no rent is registered and the rent is limited as a result to the rent payable in the last contractual period, adjustments may be made to the rent where:

1   the landlord pays rates and they rise, after suitable service of a notice of increase under s 49;[17]
2   the landlord's rates fall – this adjustment down is automatic however;[17]
3   where the quality or quantity of services or furniture provided have altered since the ending of the contractual tenancy (s 47).

IV APPLICATION FOR REGISTRATION OF RENTS

General

An application for the registration of a fair rent under Part IV of the Rent Act 1977 must be made to the Rent Officer in the prescribed form.[18] An application may be by the landlord or tenant alone or by the parties jointly (s 67(1) and (2)).[19]

A registered rent generally takes effect for two years from the date of registration (s 72(1)) but the landlord alone may apply, within the last

16   Phasing (up to the full amount of the registered rent) was abolished by Rent (Relief from Phasing) Order 1987 SI 1987/264, commencing 4 May 1987 and by Housing Act 1988 Sch 18, the phasing provisions remaining were repealed.
17   Rent Act 1977 s 46. See *Aristocrat Property Investments v Harounoff* (1982) 263 Estates Gazette 352 (notice of increase must always be in prescribed form).
18   Rent Act 1977 (Forms etc) Regulations 1980 SI 1980/1697 as amended, SI 1988/2195.
19   Provisions (ss 68, 69 and Sch 11 Part II and 12) enabling applications for registration by local authorities and persons intent on providing new dwellings for renting were repealed by Housing Act 1988 Sch 18.

three months of that period, for a different rent (s 67(4)). This will take effect as from the end of the two-year period. See further below.

An application may be made by a protected tenant who is not himself in occupation,[20] or in the name of a tenants' association.[1] Unless the application form is duly completed, the application will be a nullity, and the amount of rent proposed must be stated.[2] An application by one of a number of joint tenants is apparently not valid[3] unless one has authority to sign for the others.

Outline of duties of Rent Officer

The procedure for applications for registration of a fair rent is governed by Sch 11 Part I to the 1977 Act. In the case of a single application (i e by the landlord or tenant alone), the Rent Officer must offer the parties an opportunity for consultation; if this is not requested, he may either determine and register a fair rent or confirm the existing rent. If consultation is requested, it must take place and thereafter the duties of the Rent Officer are the same as where it does not take place. If the application is either joint or not objected to, the Rent Officer has power to register the rent stated in the application.

Rent Assessment Committees

Both parties may appeal to a Rent Assessment Committee from a Rent Officer's decision.[4] The appeal is in effect a re-hearing, and the Committee may either confirm the rent or itself determine a different rent.[5] The registration takes effect from the date of the Committee's decision (s 72(1)(b) and 72(2)(b)).

The High Court may be asked to review a decision of a Committee for error of law and will quash a decision whose reasons are unintelligible or insufficient.[6] Committees should state which of a given set of valuation methods they prefer, but they are entitled to rely on their own knowledge and experience and may proceed, if they think fit, on their own figures, as

---

20 *London Housing and Commercial Properties Ltd v Cowan* [1977] QB 148, [1976] 2 All ER 385.

1 *Feather Supplies Ltd v Ingham* [1971] 2 QB 348, [1971] 3 All ER 556, CA.

2 *Chapman v Earl* [1968] 2 All ER 1214, [1968] 1 WLR 1315; also *Druid Development Co (Bingley) Ltd v Kay* (1982) 44 P & CR 76, CA (prescribed particulars requirement as opposed to rent statement not mandatory).

3 *Turley v Panton* (1975) 29 P & CR 397; *R v Rent Officer for the London Borough of Camden, ex p Felix* (1988) 21 HLR 34.

4 The procedure is governed by Rent Assessment Committees etc Regulations 1971 SI 1971/1065 as amended.

5 Rent Act 1977 Sch 11, para 9.

6 See e g *Guppys Properties v Knott (No 3)* (1981) 258 Estates Gazette 1083.

opposed to those proffered by either party.[7] If it is shown that a rent has been determined on a fundamental misapprehension of the true state of affairs, as with the use of seriously faulty comparables, the court may interfere.[8] No Committee is bound to have regard to the cost of services; if it decides to, it is an error of law not to include some allowance for depreciation of the landlord's equipment and for profit.[9]

V DETERMINATION OF A FAIR RENT

Introduction

Section 70(1) of the 1977 Act provides that in determining a fair rent under a regulated tenancy, regard is to be had to all the circumstances, but not to personal circumstances. The circumstances include, in particular, the following, and they include only relevant circumstances. It has been said that what circumstances are relevant circumstances is a matter of valuation governed by the professional skill and experience of the valuer.[10]

1 The age, character, locality and state of repair of the dwelling-house (s 70(1)(a)).
2 The quantity, quality and condition of any furniture provided for use under the tenancy (s 70(1)(b));[11]
3 Any premium or sum in the nature of a premium, which has been or may be lawfully required or received on the grant, renewal, continuance or assignment of the tenancy (s 70(1)(c)).[12]

The effect of s 70(1)(c) is that any right of a tenant to charge a premium on assignment is a matter properly to be taken into account.[13]

Disregards

As well as personal circumstances, the following matters must be disregarded.

---

7 See e g *R v London Rent Assessment Panel, ex p Cliftvylle Properties Ltd* (1982) 266 Estates Gazette 44. They must not disregard totally the landlord's figures, however: *Daejan Properties Ltd v Chambers* [1986] 1 EGLR 167.
8 *London Rent Assessment Committee v St George's Court Ltd* (1984) 48 P & CR 230, CA.
9 *Perseus Property Co Ltd v Burberry* [1985] 1 EGLR 114.
10 *Mason v Skilling* [1974] 3 All ER 977 at 983, HL.
11 See *R v London Rent Assessment Panel, ex p Mota* (1987) 20 HLR 159: furniture 'provided' if available to the tenant, even if not used by him.
12 Added by Housing and Planning Act 1986 s 17, which also added s 70(4A), defining 'premium' and 'sum in the nature of a premium'.
13 It is statutory affirmation of *Crown Estate Comrs v Connor* [1986] 2 EGLR 97.

1   Any element of scarcity in the neighbourhood,[14] by assuming that there are substantially the same number of houses to let as there are prospective tenants (s 70(2)). This provision is dealt with later on; but it requires an artificial assumption of market equilibrium, and is a feature which is deliberately absent from the rent provisions relating to assured tenancies (Chapter 18). Scarcity is distinct as a concept from questions of specific amenities or inherent advantages in the particular dwelling-house, which latter is a factor which may properly be taken into account, in so far as it raises or lowers the rent.[15] Scarcity is therefore a concept requiring a survey of a wider area than the immediate confines of the dwelling-house.

2   Any disrepair or other defect attributable to a failure by the tenant or any predecessor in title of his to comply with the terms of the tenancy (s 70(3)(a)).[16]

3   Any improvement[17] carried out, otherwise than in pursuance of the terms of the tenancy, by the tenant under the tenancy or any predecessor in title of his (s 70(3)(b)).[18]

4   If furniture is provided under the tenancy, any improvement to it by the tenant or any predecessor in title of his; and any deterioration in the condition of the furniture due to any ill-treatment by the tenant, and person residing or lodging with him or any sub-tenant of his (s 70(3)(e)).

Some further aspects

(1)   *Repairs*   A landlord's failure to enforce a tenant's covenant to repair cannot be taken into account, and the premises must then be valued as they are at the date of the determination.[19] A low rent may be registered where the state of repair is not due to any fault of the tenant.[20] It is not obligatory for a nil rent to be registered merely because the house is subject to a closing order.[1] The statutory disregard of disrepair due to a tenant's fault does not extend to a tenant's failure to comply with some lesser obligation, such as an express duty to use furnished premises

---

14   See generally Watchman [1985] Conv 199.
15   *Metropolitan Property Holdings Ltd v Finegold* [1975] 1 All ER 389, [1975] 1 WLR 349.
16   See *Sturolson & Co v Mauroux* (1988) 20 HLR 332, CA.
17   This includes the replacement of any fixture or fitting (s 70(4)).
18   'Predecessor in title' in these rules means the predecessor in title to the tenant in the premises, as against a person who improves and then obtains a lease: *Trustees of Henry Smith's Charity v Hemmings* (1982) 45 P & CR 377.
19   *Metropolitan Properties Co Ltd v Wooldridge* (1969) 20 P & CR 64.
20   *McGee v London Rent Assessment Panel Committee* (1969) 113 Sol Jo 384 (unexplained fire).
1   *Williams v Khan* (1980) 43 P & CR 1, CA.

in a tenant-like manner, and failure in that regard was held to be a proper matter for a Rent Officer to take into account.[2]

(2) *Services* Any services provided by the landlord, certainly those under contract, should presumably be taken into account.[3] If a service is inefficiently provided by the landlord, any allowance made for it will be reduced (the basis of valuation being the value of the service to the tenant).[4] The landlord is in principle able to claim some allowance for depreciation of his equipment which provides services and for profit,[5] and also in respect of the cost of replacement, based on its original cost.[6] The landlord's figures may, after due consideration, be disregarded by the Rent Officer or Rent Assessment Committee in favour of some other set of figures.[7]

(3) *Personal circumstances* As noted above, these must be left out of account. The expression is inherently uncertain, but has been held to include the tenant's right to remain in possession.[8] It may also refer to the length of the tenancy.

(4) *Inflation* There has been some difficulty in deciding whether inflation should, in principle, be taken into account, and as to whether a price index should then be used as, after all, valuation is involved and this is a matter for the Rent Officer or Rent Assessment Committee.[9] It is generally regarded as permissible for inflation to be taken into account in such manner as an Officer or Committee deem reasonable, provided cogent reasons are given.[10]

Determination of fair rents – basic rules

Subject to what has already been mentioned, the principles applicable may be summarised as follows.

1   The best evidence of a fair rent is for an Officer or Committee to have regard to registered comparable fair rents for the relevant locality

---

2   *Firstcross Ltd v Teasdale* (1982) 47 P & CR 228.
3   *R v Paddington North and St Marylebone Rent Tribunal, ex p Perry* [1956] 1 QB 229, [1955] 3 All ER 391.
4   *Metropolitan Properties Co v Noble* [1968] 2 All ER 313, [1968] 1 WLR 838.
5   *Perseus Property Co Ltd v Burberry* [1985] 1 EGLR 114.
6   *Regis Property Co v Dudley* [1958] 1 QB 346, [1958] 1 All ER 510, CA.
7   *R v London Rent Assessment Panel, ex p Cliftvylle Properties Ltd* (1982) 266 Estates Gazette 44.
8   *Mason v Skilling* [1974] 3 All ER 977, [1974] 1 WLR 1437, HL.
9   See *Metropolitan Property Holdings Ltd v Laufer* (1974) 29 P & CR 172.
10 *Wareing v White* [1985] 1 EGLR 125, CA; also *R v London Rent Assessment Panel, ex p Chelmsford Building Co Ltd* [1986] 1 EGLR 175.

– as against unregistered rents, which will not have a built-in disregard of scarcity.[11]

2 If there are no registered comparables for a given area, an Officer or Committee may decide on what rent the dwelling-house might command in the open market, bearing in mind that under s 70(2), any scarcity element must be discounted.[12]

3 The exact method of assessment of a fair rent is for the Officer or Committee to decide on, as was said earlier. Nonetheless, it has been stated in the House of Lords that registered comparables, at least where available, afford the best method of assessment, and also that rigidity of approach must be avoided; and Officers and Committees may adopt any method of approach they think fit, provided that it is not unfair or unlawful.[13] This means that while they must consider all the evidence and figures placed before them, they should – and do – use their own expertise and knowledge in dealing with, for example, yield, or any other, figures.[14]

4 Subject to the above, as a check on rental values or, it seems, possibly as a last resort only, if there are no registered comparables, it is permissible to take what in the Officer's or Committee's view[15] is a fair return on the landlord's capital investment. Differences have been aired as to the desirability of this, the 'contractor's method'. It was described in the House of Lords in one case as notoriously unreliable,[16] but in an earlier case the House of Lords did not cast such disfavour on the method and it was said that the rent must be fair to the landlord as well as to the tenant.[17]

5 As was noted, s 70(2) requires that the effect of scarcity must be left out of account. This has been taken to mean that, if there is a substantial excess of persons seeking to become tenants over those willing to let in the relevant locality, s 70(2) requires an assumption of equilibrium of supply and demand – contrary to the fact – so that the registered rent is discounted from what it would otherwise be,

---

11 *Tormes Property Co Ltd v Landau* [1971] 1 QB 261, [1970] 3 All ER 653; *Mason v Skilling*, supra.

12 *Crofton Investment Trust Ltd v Greater London Rent Assessment Committee* [1967] 2 QB 955, [1967] 2 All ER 1103; *Western Heritable Investment Co Ltd v Husband* [1983] 2 AC 849, [1983] 3 All ER 65, HL.

13 *Western Heritable Investment Co Ltd v Husband*, supra.

14 *Ellis & Sons Fourth Amalgamated Properties Ltd v Southern Rent Assessment Panel* (1984) 270 Estates Gazette 39. They may, accordingly, reject the landlord's figures: *Cubes Ltd v Heaps* (1970) 215 Estates Gazette 579.

15 As opposed to the view of experts or the landlord, whose evidence they must weigh up but which they may then reject: see e g *Guppys (Bridport) Ltd v Sandoe* (1975) 30 P & CR 69.

16 *Western Heritable Investment Co Ltd v Husband*, supra per LORD KEITH at pp 857 and 69.

17 *Mason v Skilling*, supra.

owing to the scarcity factor pushing it up. The purpose of this is plain, it has been said in the House of Lords. It secures that when market rents have been pushed up in the manner described, tenants do not have to bear the increase over what would otherwise be fair due to the shortage.[18]

VI   THE REGISTER

Once a fair rent has been determined, it must be entered by the Rent Officer in an area register (s 66) and the entry must include the following: (a) the rent payable; (b) a note (where applicable) that the rates are paid by the landlord or a superior landlord (s 71(2));(c) a specification of the dwelling and (d) prescribed particulars of the tenancy[19]

The rent is inclusive of any services and furniture provided but exclusive of rates (s 71).[20] Services should be considered separately. The term includes insurance and depreciation of boilers and lifts, but not insurance of the whole building (the cost of which is relevant generally).[1] Where a tenancy provides for service charges (assuming these are exigible) these terms may be entered unless considered by the Rent Officer or Rent Assessment Committee to be unreasonable (s 71(4)). If either do consider them unreasonable, they then make up their own minds as to the correct amount.[2]

VII   EFFECT AND CANCELLATION OF REGISTRATION

General

By s 72(1) of the 1977 Act, the registration of a fair rent takes effect from the date either of registration by the Rent Officer or the date when a Rent Assessment Committee make their decision. The same rules apply where an existing registered rent is confirmed (s 72(2)).[3]

Time bar

No further single application for a registered rent may be entertained within the two years following the date the registered rent concerned

---

18 *Western Heritable Investment Co Ltd v Husband*, supra.
19 See Rent Act 1977 (Forms etc) Regulations 1980 SI 1980/1697 as amended, SI 1988/2195.
20 See *Firstcross Ltd v Teasdale* (1982) 47 P & CR 228.
1 *Property Holding and Investment Trust v London Rent Assessment Panel* (1969) 113 Sol Jo 672.
2 *Betts v Vivamat Properties Ltd* (1983) 270 Estates Gazette 849; also *Wigglesworth v Property Holding and Investment Trust plc* (1984) 270 Estates Gazette 555.
3 The date of registration/confirmation must be entered on the register (s 72(4)).

takes effect, or has been confirmed (s 67(3) and (5)).[4] So a confirmation of a previous registered rent will effectively double the life of the previous registered rent.

Reconsideration

Either party may apply alone under s 67(3) for a reconsideration of a registered rent within the two-year period. This is where there has been such a change in one of four specified circumstances such that the registered rent is no longer fair. These are any change: (a) in the condition of the dwelling-house;[5] (b) in the terms of the tenancy; (c) in the quantity, quality or condition of any furniture provided for use under the tenancy;[6] or (d) any other circumstances taken into consideration when the rent was registered or confirmed.

Once the landlord proves that a mid-term review of the registered rent is permissible, because of a change in condition such as his installing a new boiler, all the circumstances of the dwelling-house may be taken into account, not just that change in condition.[7] If a dwelling-house is let unfurnished at a given registered rent and then is re-let furnished, the previous registered rent has no application to the second letting.[8] Section 67(3) does not permit an application for re-registration of an existing registered rent at the same figure.[9]

Cancellation

In two instances, a registered rent may be cancelled.[10] The first is where a rent agreement has been entered into which takes effect more than two years after the date on which the registration took effect (s 73(1)). The second instance is where a dwelling-house is not subject to a regulated tenancy, the two-year time bar period is up, and the applicant would be the landlord if there were such a tenancy (s 73(1A)).

In neither instance will a cancellation be prejudicial to any subsequent registration applications – assuming the tenancy is regulated (s 73(7)).

---

4   As noted above, the landlord alone may apply during the last three months of the two-year period (s 67(4)) and any new rent takes effect from the end of that period.
5   Including the making of any improvements.
6   Excluding deterioration by fair wear and tear.
7   *London Housing and Commercial Properties v Cowan* [1977] QB 148, [1976] 2 All ER 385.
8   *Kent v Millmead Properties Ltd* (1982) 44 P & CR 353; *Metrobarn Ltd v Gehring* [1976] 3 All ER 178, [1976] 1 WLR 776, CA. Cf *Waddock v Cheniston Investments* [1988] 2 EGLR 136.
9   *R v Chief Rent Officer for Royal Borough of Kensington and Chelsea, ex p Moberley* [1986] 1 EGLR 168, CA.
10   The forms prescribed by Rent Regulation (Cancellation of Registration of Rent) Regulations 1980 SI 1980/1698 must be used.

D SECURITY OF TENURE

I RESTRICTIONS ON RECOVERY OF POSSESSION

On the termination of a fixed-term or periodic residential tenancy, a tenant protected by the Rent Act 1977 is entitled to remain in possession of the dwelling-house concerned, provided he pays the rent and observes the obligations of the tenancy. This is due to s 98 of the 1977 Act, which imposes additional requirements which the landlord must prove before he is able to obtain an order for possession. The county court has general jurisdiction in Rent Act possession proceedings (s 141) and is considered to be the appropriate forum for these.

The common law right of the landlord to regain possession after the expiry or determination of a contractual tenancy is severely abrogated by the 1977 Act. However, no proceedings under s 98 may be brought by the landlord unless and until he has validly and effectually determined the tenancy at common law. Thereafter, the landlord's right to possession against a Rent Act protected tenant depends on his obtaining an order of court. This is not obtainable automatically. The landlord must prove a ground or grounds as laid down in Sch 15. Grounds for possession are sub-divided into discretionary and mandatory grounds – in the former case , the court has an overriding discretion to refuse to order possession even if a ground is made out by the landlord; in the latter, it must order possession (s 98(1) and (2)). As an alternative to a ground for possession, the landlord may seek to rely on the availability of suitable alternative accommodation, but again, even if he succeeds, the court has an overriding discretion to refuse to order possession (s 98(1)).

The effect of s 98 is overriding: where a protected tenant agreed in a contract of sale not to enforce against a purchaser from the landlord any right to possession, it was held that the purchaser could not obtain specific performance of this term, due to the effect of s 98.[11] If the tenant concedes that the Rent Act does not apply an order for possession may be made without reference to the restrictions of s 98.[12] If this is not so, the landlord cannot obtain a consent order for possession.[13] Moreover, on principles discussed in Chapter 3, where a landlord creates a tenancy or joint tenancy of a flat (or house) and reserves the right to go into joint occupation, at any time, of the whole or part of the premises, with or

---

11 *Appleton v Aspin* [1988] 1 All ER 904, [1988] 1 WLR 410, CA.
12 *Barton v Fincham* [1921] 2 KB 291, CA; *Syed Hussain v A M Abdullah Sahib & Co* [1985] 1 WLR 1392, PC.
13 *R v Bloomsbury and Marylebone County Court, ex p Blackburne* [1985] 2 EGLR 157, CA.

without notice, that provision is inconsistent with the Rent Act 1977 and cannot be enforced except by an order of court under s 98.[14]

Section 98(1) provides that a court must not make an order for possession of a dwelling-house let on a protected or statutory tenancy unless the court considers it reasonable to make such an order and either

(a)   the court is satisfied that suitable alternative accommodation is available for the tenant or will be available for him when the order in question takes effect, or

(b)   the court is satisfied that the landlord has established one of the Cases for possession set out in Part I of Sch 15.

By s 98(2), if, apart from s 98(1), the landlord would be entitled to recover possession, the court must make the order for possession if the circumstances of the case fall within any of the Cases specified in Part II of Sch 15. Unlike the first set of Cases just mentioned, in Part I of Sch 15, if the landlord proves that the matter comes within a Part II Case, the court has no discretion to refuse to make an order for possession: it must do so once the facts are shown to its satisfaction.[15]

Even though the landlord establishes the ground in para (a) of s 98(1) or any one or more of the grounds under para (b), no order shall be made 'unless the court considers it reasonable to make such an order'. The judge is required to direct his mind to the question of reasonableness, and exercise his discretion in a judicial manner, 'having regard, on the one hand, to the general scheme and purpose of the Act, and, on the other, to the special conditions, including to a large extent matters of a domestic and general character'.[16] 'It is, in my opinion, perfectly clear that the duty of the judge is to take into account all the relevant circumstances as they exist at the date of the hearing. That he must do in what I venture to call a broad, common-sense way as a man of the world, and come to his conclusion giving such weight as he thinks right to the various factors in the situation. Some factors may have little or no weight, others may be decisive.'[17] And even where the ground relied on itself involves the element of reasonableness, the overall question of reasonableness must again be considered in the light of all circumstances; so under Case 9 of Sch 15 the judge must consider first whether the landlord's desire for possession is reasonable, and, then, whether it is reasonable to make an order for possession; for just 'because a wish is

---

14   *AG Securities v Vaughan*; *Antoniades v Villiers* [1988] 3 All ER 1058, HL.

15   See *Kennealy v Dunne* [1977] QB 837, [1977] 2 All ER 16, CA. The landlord must prove a genuine case.

16   *Chiverton v Ede* [1921] 2 KB 30 at 45 per McCardie J; therefore, environmental matters may be taken into account: *Redspring Ltd v Francis* [1973] 1 All ER 640, [1973] 1 WLR 134, CA.

17   *Cumming v Danson* [1942] 2 All ER 653 at 655 per Lord Greene MR.

reasonable, it does not follow that it is reasonable in a court to gratify it'.[18]

The judge must consider all the relevant circumstances in relation to both the landlord and the tenant, the premises and the interests of the public.[19] Anything which may cause hardship to the landlord or the tenant is relevant,[20] but there is no question of applying a rule of greater hardship.[1] The conduct of the parties is relevant,[2] eg an expressed intention to continue in breach of covenant,[3] false testimony on a material point,[4] the assignment of a fixed-term tenancy just before its expiry so as to give rise to a statutory tenancy,[5] etc. Generally speaking, it is easier to establish reasonableness when suitable alternative accommodation is available than when it is not.[6] However, if the suitable alternative accommodation is part of the house which the tenant occupies exclusively, preventing him from living with other occupants of his own choosing, it may be unreasonable to make the order for possession.[7] Likewise, it was held in order for a judge, in his overriding discretion, to refuse to order possession, because he was entitled to take into account the personal attachment of the tenant to her existing flat, where she had lived for 35 years.[8] Where the judge has heard the relevant evidence, it will be assumed that he has directed his mind to the question,[9] but not otherwise, and the Court of Appeal will not interfere with his discretion;[10] his decision will not be set aside unless it can be shown that he had misdirected himself by omitting some point of substance or by taking account of something which should not properly have been considered.[11] The judge is bound to consider the overriding issue of reasonableness and the question is general, not just having regard to the suitability of any accommodation.[12] It is implicit in the reasonableness requirement that the onus of satisfying the court as to reasonableness is on the landlord.[13]

---

18 *Shrimpton v Rabbits* (1924) 131 LT 478 at 469 per ACTON J.
19 *Cresswell v Hodgson* [1951] 2 KB 92 at 97.
20 *Williamson v Pallant* [1924] 2 KB 173.
1   *Syms v Dean* [1929] EGD 16.
2   *Upjohn v Macfarlane* [1922] 2 Ch 256.
3   *Bell London and Provincial Properties v Reuben* [1947] KB 157, [1946] 2 All ER 547.
4   *Yelland v Taylor* [1957] 1 All ER 627, [1957] 1 WLR 459.
5   *Regional Properties v Frankenschwerth and Chapman* [1951] 1 KB 631.
6   *Cumming v Danson*, supra.
7   *Yoland Ltd v Reddington* (1982) 263 Estates Gazette 157.
8   *Battlespring Ltd v Gates* (1983) 268 Estates Gazette 355, CA.
9   *Tendler v Sproule* [1947] 1 All ER 193.
10 *R F Fuggle Ltd v Gadsden* [1948] 2 KB 236, [1948] 2 All ER 160.
11 *Darnell v Millwood* [1951] 1 All ER 88 at 90.
12 *Minchburn Ltd v Fernandez* [1986] 2 EGLR 103, CA; *Roberts v Macilwraith-Christie* [1987] 1 EGLR 224, CA.
13 *Smith v McGoldrick* (1977) 242 Estates Gazette 1047, CA.

II   SUITABLE ALTERNATIVE ACCOMMODATION

The onus of proof that suitable alternative accommodation is available for the tenant, or will be, is upon the landlord. By virtue of Part IV of Sch 15 to the Act, a certificate of the local housing authority that they will provide such accommodation for the tenant by a date specified in the notice is conclusive evidence for the purpose of establishing this ground (para 3). In the absence of such a certificate, accommodation that the landlord can show to be available will be deemed to be suitable if it consists of either:

(a)   premises comprising a separate dwelling so as to be let on a protected tenancy (other than one on which the landlord might recover possession under one of the Cases in Part II of Sch 15 (mandatory re-possession Cases));

(b)   premises to be let as a separate dwelling on such terms as will, in the opinion of the court, afford to the tenant the same security of tenure as under a protected tenancy.[14]

Further, the accommodation must, in the opinion of the court, be reasonably suitable to the needs of the tenant and his family as regards proximity to place of work, and either:

(a)   similar as regards rental and extent to the accommodation afforded by any housing authority for persons whose needs as regards extent are, in the opinion of the court, similar to those of the tenant and of his family; or

(b)   reasonably suitable to the means of the tenant and to the needs of the tenant and his family as regards extent and character (para 5);

and if any furniture was provided for use under the protected or statutory tenancy in question, furniture is provided for use in the accommodation which is either similar to that so provided or is reasonably suitable to the needs of the tenant and his family. The alternative accommodation is not to be deemed suitable, if occupation by the tenant's family would result in overcrowding (para 6). 'Family' bears the same meaning for present purposes as it does in the case of statutory tenancies.[15]

It is not necessary for the landlord to *offer* accommodation which satisfies the above requirements of Part IV of Sch 15, but clearly, if he is in a position to do so, he can more easily discharge his burden of proof. Otherwise he must prove that it exists; and in either case, he must show that the tenancy will be granted to the tenant, and that the

---

14   Sch 15 Part IV para 4 (other than a tenancy with mandatory re-possession).
15   *Kavanagh v Lyroudias* [1985] 1 All ER 560, CA (friend not 'family').

accommodation will, if not already, be available for him at the date of the hearing.[16]

Whether the alternative accommodation is suitable often gives rise to a dispute which must be settled by the court, but it must be remembered that even if the court is satisfied that it is suitable, the question of the reasonableness of an order for possession must still be considered.[17] The fact that the accommodation offered was unsuitable for the tenant to entertain business acquaintances and had no garden for the tenant's child has been held to be relevant,[18] as was the fact that the proposed accommodation would not enable the tenant to carry out his profession as an artist because it lacked a studio.[19] So too has the fact that it would not accommodate the tenant's furniture,[20] but not that it had no garage.[1] Shared accommodation is not suitable,[2] but the dwelling under the current tenancy *minus* one room (as where the landlord lives in the same house and requires an additional room for his own family) may be suitable, depending on the needs of the tenant;[3] indeed, where the tenant has sub-let part of the premises under the tenancy, it would be difficult for him to show that it was not suitable.[4] 'Family' does not include a resident housekeeper and her own family.[5] 'Place of work' does not necessarily refer to a single place of work: an area in which the tenant travels to carry out his profession may itself constitute the 'place of work'.[6]

In deciding whether proposed accommodation is suitable as regards 'extent and character', the court will have regard to the particular tenant's housing needs, not to other ancillary advantages enjoyed with the present accommodation, nor to the tenant's own peculiar wishes and desires.[7] The court may, in dealing with 'character', compare the present environment of the tenant and that offered in the alternative accommodation on an objective basis.[7] Environmental factors are relevant to this

---

16 *Nevile v Hardy* [1921] 1 Ch 404.
17 *Hill v Rochard* [1983] 2 All ER 21, [1983] 1 WLR 478, CA; *Battlespring Ltd v Gates* (1983) 268 Estates Gazette 355, CA; also *Gladyric Ltd v Collinson* (1983) 267 Estates Gazette 761, CA.
18 *De Markozoff v Craig* (1949) 93 Sol Jo 693.
19 *McDonnell v Daly* [1969] 3 All ER 851, [1969] 1 WLR 1482, CA.
20 *McIntyre v Hardcastle* [1948] 2 KB 82, [1948] 1 All ER 696.
1 *Briddon v George* [1946] 1 All ER 609, CA.
2 *Barnard v Towers* [1953] 2 All ER 877, [1953] 1 WLR 1203, CA.
3 *Mykolyshyn v Noah* [1971] 1 All ER 48, [1970] 1 WLR 1217.
4 *Thompson v Rolls* [1926] 2 KB 426; *Parmee v Mitchell* [1950] 2 KB 199, [1950] 2 All ER 872, CA.
5 *Darnell v Millwood* [1951] 1 All ER 88, CA.
6 *Yewbright Properties Ltd v Stone* (1980) 40 P & CR 402, CA (hence, a tenant's difficulty in travel from the proposed accommodation to various places of work was relevant).
7 *Hill v Rochard* [1983] 2 All ER 21, [1983] 1 WLR 478, CA.

question, so that accommodation was not suitable where it was situated in a busy road with a nearby hospital and fish and chip shop, in place of the tenant's quiet residential flat.[8] However, such factors can only be taken into account if they relate to the character of the property itself as opposed to personal factors such as alleged loss of friends or culture due to the move away from the present accommodation.[9]

III   DISCRETIONARY GROUNDS FOR POSSESSION

Part I of Sch 15 sets out nine grounds for possession (expressed as Cases) on which the court *may* order possession, with or without proof of the availability of suitable alternative accommodation. The landlord may establish any one or more of them; and an agreement by the landlord not to rely on any particular ground is ineffective.[10] Where a statutory tenancy arises under Part I of the Landlord and Tenant Act 1954, any liability other than for non-payment of rent, rates and insurance, or for immoral or illegal uses, under the former long tenancy is extinguished, s 10 of that Act, and no order may be made under Cases 1–3 in respect of any act or fault that occurred before the statutory tenancy began.

Case 1: breach of obligation

Where any rent lawfully due from the tenant has not been paid or any obligation of the tenancy has been broken or not performed.

No order can be made if rent is tendered before commencement of the proceedings,[11] if rent is paid after the commencement of proceedings, an order can be made, and in practice, even if arrears are still unpaid at the time of the hearing, the court will rarely made an absolute order unless the arrears are substantial or there are other special circumstances, such as the tenant's bad record for non-payment.[12] A statutory tenant by succession is not liable for arrears of rent owed by his predecessor at the time of his death.[13]

As regards breaches of other obligations under the tenancy, neither s 212 of the Common Law Procedure Act 1852, nor s 146 of the Law of Property Act 1925, applies to a statutory tenancy,[14] nevertheless, on the

---

8   *Redspring Ltd v Francis* [1973] 1 All ER 640, [1973] 1 WLR 134, CA; *Warren v Austen* [1947] 2 All ER 185, CA.
9   *Siddiqui v Rashid* [1980] 3 All ER 184, [1980] 1 WLR 1018, CA.
10   *Havard v Shears* (1967) 203 Estates Gazette 27.
11   *Bird v Hildage* [1948] 1 KB 91, [1947] 2 All ER 7.
12   *Dellenty v Pellow* [1951] 2 KB 858, [1951] 2 All ER 716.
13   *Tickner v Clifton* [1929] 1 KB 207.
14   *Brewer v Jacobs* [1923] 1 KB 528.

question of reasonableness of the order, the court will take into account the fact that the tenant has remedied the breach at the time of the hearing or that he is willing to give an undertaking in respect of it. Case I applies to breaches which are of a continuing or of a once and for all nature. It therefore was held to apply to a breach of covenant against business user[15] and to sub-lettings without the landlord's consent.[16] A landlord cannot rely on a breach that he has waived, but the common law doctrine of waiver cannot strictly apply to a statutory tenancy; but the landlord may lose the right to rely on this ground by continued acceptance of the rent in knowledge of the breach without qualification and undue delay in commencing proceedings.[17] If the presence of an occupier is consistent with there being no breach of covenant, as where reasonable grounds exist for thinking that the occupier is a lodger of the tenant's, rather than a sub-tenant of his, it is not waiver for the landlord to continue to accept rent with knowledge of the occupier's existence – unless there is something further to put him on inquiry.[18]

Case 2: Nuisance, etc

Where the tenant or any person residing or lodging with him or any sub-tenant has been guilty of conduct which is a nuisance or annoyance to adjoining occupiers, or has been convicted of using the dwelling-house, or allowing it to be used, for immoral or illegal purposes.

'Annoyance' has a wider meaning than 'nuisance', which generally requires some physical act of interference. Any behaviour which is likely to trouble any ordinary person is an annoyance, and it may be inferred without evidence from adjoining occupiers.[19] 'Adjoining' means 'neighbouring' and the premises of the complainant need not necessarily be physically contiguous to or even on the same floor as the offending tenant.[20] Conviction of immoral or illegal user is sufficient for this ground to be relied on, without evidence of nuisance or annoyance, and if the purpose of the tenant's user is illegal or immoral, a single offence is sufficient,[1] but, the fact that the crime committed on the premises is

---

15 *Florent v Horez* (1983) 48 P & CR 166, CA.
16 *Roberts v Macilwraith-Christie* [1987] 1 EGLR 224, CA.
17 *Oak Property Co Ltd v Chapman* [1947] KB 886, [1947] 2 All ER 1; *Henry Smith's Charity Trustees v Willson* [1983] QB 316, [1983] 1 All ER 73, CA.
18 *Roberts v Macilwraith-Christie*, supra.
19 *Frederick Platts & Co Ltd v Grigor* [1950] 1 All ER 941n; e g substantial business user of the tenant's residential flat: *Florent v Horez* (1983) 48 P & CR 166, CA.
20 *Cobstone Investments Ltd v Maxim* [1985] QB 140; [1984] 2 All ER 635, CA; Lyons [1985] Conv 168, nor is the sub-tenant of the tenant himself included as an 'occupier': *Chester v Potter* [1949] EGD 247.
1   *Schneider & Sons v Abrahams* [1925] 1 KB 301.

incidental to the crime itself, however, e g using a portable television set without a licence, is not enough.[2] So where the tenant was convicted of being in unlawful possession of cannabis resin, the drugs having been found on the premises, the Court of Appeal held that possession without knowledge did not constitute using the dwelling for illegal purposes; though presumably it would have been otherwise if it had been used for storing the drugs.[3] Even if the nuisance has abated, it may be reasonable for an order for possession to be made.[4]

Case 3: Deterioration by waste or neglect

> Where the condition of the dwelling-house has deteriorated owing to acts of waste by, or the neglect or default of, the tenant, any sub-tenant or any lodger, and if caused by a sub-tenant or lodger, the court is satisfied that the tenant has not taken all reasonable steps to remove him.

'Waste' includes unauthorised alterations to the premises such as putting in new doors, enlargement of rooms, etc and also demolishing any part of the premises.[5] Likewise, failure by the tenant to take reasonable precautions to look after the premises causing deterioration to them, such as deterioration due to want of firing and airing in winter[6] or due to frost damage, will presumably suffice within this ground.

Case 4: Deterioration of furniture by ill-treatment

> Where the condition of any furniture provided for use under the tenancy has deteriorated owing to ill-treatment by the tenant or any person residing or lodging with him or any sub-tenant of his, and, in the case of lodgers of the tenant or any sub-tenant of his, the court is satisfied that the tenant has not, before the making of the order for possession, taken reasonable steps to remove the lodger or sub-tenant.

Case 5: Tenant's notice to quit

> Where the tenant has given notice to quit, and in consequence of that notice, the landlord has contracted to sell or let the dwelling-house, or has taken any other steps as a result of which he would be seriously prejudiced if he could not obtain possession.

---

2 See *Waller & Son Ltd v Thomas* [1921] 1 KB 541.
3 *Abrahams v Wilson* [1971] 2 All ER 1114.
4 *Florent v Horez* (1983) 48 P & CR 166, CA.
5 *Marsden v Edward Heyes Ltd* [1927] 2 KB 1, CA.
6 *Robertson v Wilson* 1922 SLT (Sh Ct) 21, or even allowing a garden to grow totally uncontrolled: *Holloway v Povey* (1984) 271 Estates Gazette 195, CA.

This ground may be relied upon where the tenant gives an undertaking that he will give up possession, though not strictly in terms of a notice to quit; it does not apply to surrender.[7] Where a contractual tenant gave a notice to quit, and after its expiry changed her mind, the Court of Appeal held that the tenant was thereupon a statutory tenant, and that since, on the facts, the landlord only intended to sell and had not contracted to sell, he could not rely on this ground.[8]

Case 6: Assignmment or sub-letting

Where, without the consent of the landlord, the tenant has assigned or sub-let the whole of the dwelling-house or sub-let part of the dwelling-house, the remainder being already sub-let. This applies for most regulated tenancies, to assignments or sub-lettings since 8 December 1965.[9]

Case 6 is available to the landlord whether the tenancy is contractual or statutory, and whether or not there is a covenant against assignment or sub-letting in the head tenancy.[10] Even if there is a sub-tenant who is 'lawful' within s 137 the court may order possession against the sub-tenant under Case 6, as the sub-tenancy is vulnerable to s 98(1) of the 1977 Act.[11]

'Consent', however, need not be in writing, but may be implied, but must be given to a particular tenant.[12] and it will be sufficient if it is given at any time before the proceedings are commenced.[13]

Case 8: Dwelling required for landlord's employee

Where the dwelling-house is reasonably required for occupation as a residence for an employee or prospective employee either of the landlord or of some tenant from him, provided that the existing tenant was formerly a service tenant of the landlord or a previous landlord, but has ceased to be employed by him and the dwelling-house was let to him in consequence of that employment.

This ground may be relied upon even though another house is available for the employee.[14] Where the dwelling is required for a prospective

---

7 *Standingford v Bruce* [1926] 1 KB 466. Nor to an agreement to surrender: *De Vries v Sparks* (1927) 137 LT 441.
8 *Barton v Fincham* [1921] 2 KB 291.
9 Special rules exist for other tenancies, in particular, the relevant date for furnished tenancies being 14 August 1974.
10 *Regional Properties Co Ltd v Frankenschwerth and Chapman* [1951] 1 KB 631, [1951] 1 All ER 178; CA; also *Pazgate Ltd v McGrath* (1984) 272 Estates Gazette 1069, CA.
11 *Leith Properties Ltd v Byrne* [1983] QB 433, [1982] 3 All ER 731, CA.
12 *Regional Properties Co Ltd v Frankenschwerth*, supra.
13 *Hyde v Pimley* [1952] 2 QB 506, [1952] 2 All ER 102.
14 *Lowcock & Sons Ltd v Brotherton* [1952] CPL 408.

employee, he must have entered into a contract of employment which is conditional upon housing being provided, and started work by the date of the hearing unless reasonably prevented from doing so by reason of his absence on holiday or through illness.[15] In such a case, it might be reasonable to make a suspended order in case he should give notice. The employment must be full-time, but although the former employee *ex hypothesi* must have been a service tenant, it is not necessary that the person for whom the dwelling is required should take it in that capacity; and it will be sufficient if he is merely a service occupier.[16]

Section 102 provides for payment of compensation if a landlord obtains an order for possession on this ground by misrepresentation or concealment of material facts (applicable also to Case 9, below).

Case 9: Dwelling required for landlord

Where the dwelling-house is reasonably required by the landlord for occupation as a residence for:

(a)   himself, or
(b)   any son or daughter of his over eighteen years of age, or
(c)   his father or mother, or
(d)   in the case of a regulated tenancy, his father-in-law or mother-in-law,

provided that the landlord did not become landlord by purchasing the dwelling-house or any interest therein after 23 March 1965 (or 8 March 1973, in the case of tenancies which on that date became regulated) or 24 May 1974 (in the case of furnished tenancies).

Part III of Sch 15 (para 1) further provides that:

a court shall not make an order on an application based solely on Case 9 if the court is satisfied that, having regard to all the circumstances of the case, including the question whether other accommodation is available for the landlord or the tenant, greater hardship would be caused by granting the order than by refusing to grant it.

'Become landlord by purchasing' limits the availability of this ground in two important respects. First, the landlord seeking an order for possession under the head must have 'purchased' his interest in the dwelling-house after whichever of the three dates specified is applicable to the tenancy. 'Purchasing' is used in its popular sense, i e 'the buying for money',[17] as opposed to acquiring under the terms of a will,[18] or a deed

---

15   *R F Fuggle Ltd v Gadsden* [1948] 2 KB 236, [1948] 2 All ER 160.
16   *UBM Ltd v Tyler* (1949) 99 LJ 723.
17   *HL Bolton (Engineering) Co Ltd v TJ Graham & Sons Ltd* [1957] 1 QB 159 at 169, 170, per DENNING LJ.
18   *Baker v Lewis* [1947] KB 186, [1946] 2 All ER 592.

of gift, or by the voluntary surrender of a tenancy.[19] Taking a tenancy of the reversion is not 'purchasing', it would appear, unless on payment of a premium[20] (in a lump sum or by instalments).[1] The date of 'purchase' is the date of the contract of purchase, and not completion.[2] Secondly, it is by virtue of that purchase that the landlord must have become the landlord of the person whom he is seeking to evict (i e the tenant), and not by virtue of some other transaction, such as an assignment of the tenancy to the present tenant or the grant of a tenancy to the present tenant. In other words, this ground cannot be relied on if the landlord bought his interest after the relevant date with the present tenant as 'sitting tenant'; it can be relied on however, if the landlord had vacant possession, and then granted a tenancy to the present tenant.

Whether the dwelling is 'reasonably required' is a question of fact; there must be a genuine need at the time of the hearing,[3] i e something more than desire but something much less than absolute necessity.[4] The onus of proof of 'reasonably required' is on the landlord.[5] He does not have to show that he requires possession at once, provided that it is reasonably required in the ascertainable and not distant future.[6] 'Reasonably required' would include proximity to work[7] and need not necessarily involve a genuine need for the whole house.[8] The fact that the person for whom the dwelling is required already has a house is clearly relevant,[9] but it is not conclusive.[10] However, Case 9 does not apply if the landlord's intention to reside is uncertain, as where he may well sell.[11] If the reversion is held by two or more joint landlords, Case 9 may be claimed only if both or all the landlords are able to prove an intention to reside in the dwelling-house.[12] This rule has no application to Case 11 – thereunder, only one joint landlord needs to satisfy the residence requirement.[13] It is also not applicable where the landlord

---

19 See footnote 17, supra.
20 See *Lucas v Lineham* [1950] 1 KB 548 at 552.
1 *Littlechild v Holt* [1950] 1 KB 1 at 7.
2 *Emberson v Robinson* [1953] 2 All ER 755, [1953] 1 WLR 1129.
3 *Williamson v Pallant* [1924] 2 KB 173; *Alexander v Mohamedzadeh* [1985] 2 EGLR 161, CA.
4 See *Aitken v Shaw* 1933 SLT (Sh Ct) 21; *Kennealy v Dunne* [1977] QB 837, [1977] 2 All ER 16, CA.
5 *Epsom Grand Stand Association Ltd v Clarke* (1919) 35 TLR 525, CA.
6 *Kidder v Birch* (1982) 126 Sol Jo 482, CA.
7 *Jackson v Harbour* [1924] EGD 99.
8 *Kelley v Goodwin* [1947] 1 All ER 810, CA.
9 *Duffield v Grinshaw* (1947) 150 Estates Gazette 322; also *Kennealy v Dunne* [1977] QB 837, [1977] 2 All ER 16, CA.
10 *Nevile v Hardy* [1921] 1 Ch 404.
11 *Rowe v Truelove* (1976) 241 Estates Gazette 533, CA; also *Ghelani v Bowie* [1988] 2 EGLR 130, CA.
12 *McIntyre v Hardcastle* [1948] 2 KB 82, [1948] 1 All ER 696, CA.
13 *Tilling v Whiteman* [1980] AC 1, [1979] 1 All ER 737, HL.

holds the legal estate as sole owner but would be bound on demand to transfer the title into the joint names of himself and another beneficiary.[14] Trustees or personal representatives cannot claim possession under Case 9 for the benefit of a beneficiary[15] but they may rely on it if able to show that they themselves intend, without breach of trust, to reside in the house.[16]

In considering the question of greater hardship, the judge must take into account all the relevant circumstances of the case, including, for example, the financial means of both parties,[17] the length of time for which the parties have respectively been landlord and tenant, and the effect an order would have on persons other than the parties. The judge must consider hardship to all who may be affected by the grant or refusal of an order for possession – relatives, dependents, lodgers, guests and the stranger within the gates – but should weigh such hardship with due regard to the status of the persons affected and their 'proximity' to the tenant or the landlord, and the extent to which, consequently, hardship to them would be hardship to him.[18] The judge must also have regard to the longer-term effects of a possession order, as, after all, the short-term effect is always to cause some hardship to the tenant.[19] The onus of proof of greater hardship is on the tenant and the judge's decision is conclusive.[20] The Court of Appeal will interfere if, however, it is shown that the judge misdirected himself in law, or based his decision on a finding of fact for which there was no evidence.[1] An example of misdirection occurred where a judge placed the burden of proof of greater hardship on the landlord.[2] Where there is an error of law, and the Court of Appeal has sufficient evidence to resolve the issue of greater hardship, it will do so; otherwise, a remit must take place.[3] However, the mere fact that the Court of Appeal might have arrived at a different result to that of the judge is no sufficient ground for interfering with his decision.[4]

If the tenant admits that the landlord's claim is well-founded, and there is no doubt about it, the court may order possession without

---

14 *Bostock v Tacher de la Pagerie* [1987] 1 EGLR 104, CA.
15 *Parker v Rosenberg* [1947] KB 371, [1947] 1 All ER 87, CA.
16 *Patel v Patel* [1982] 1 All ER 68, [1981] 1 WLR 1342, CA (personal representatives also parents of infant beneficiaries).
17 *Kelley v Goodwin* [1947] 1 All ER 810.
18 *Harte v Frampton* [1948] 1 KB 73 at 79.
19 *Manaton v Edwards* [1985] 2 EGLR 159, CA.
20 *Sims v Wilson* [1946] 2 All ER 261, CA.
1   *Smith v Penny* [1947] KB 230, [1946] 2 All ER 672, CA.
2   *Manaton v Edwards*, supra.
3   *Alexander v Mohamedzadeh* [1985] 2 EGLR 161, CA; also *Coombs v Parry* (1987) 19 HLR 384, CA.
4   *Hodges v Blee* [1987] 2 EGLR 119, CA.

investigating further, but if the tenant does not concede his case, this course of action is inadmissible.[5]

Case 10: Sub-letting of part at an excessive rent

Where the court is satisfied that the rent charged by the tenant –

(a) for any sub-let part of the dwelling-house let on a protected or subject to a statutory tenancy is or was in excess of the maximum rent recoverable for that part, having regard to Part III of the 1977 Act, or

(b) for any sub-let part as above where there was a restricted contract, was in excess of the lawful maximum rent laid down by Part V of the 1977 Act.

This head applies only where there is a sub-letting of part, which is itself a regulated tenancy within the Act; it does not apply to an arrangement for sharing living accommodation at an excessive rent,[6] nor where the part sub-let is furnished.

IV MANDATORY GROUNDS FOR POSSESSION

The landlord of a regulated tenant may recover possession under Cases 11 to 20 of Part II of Sch 15 to the 1977 Act, mandatorily. If the landlord makes out one of these grounds for possession then the court must, by s 98(2), order possession, and cannot further consider any question of reasonableness.[7] The onus of proof falls on the landlord as regards the basic facts of, and compliance with, a given ground.[7]

A speedy procedure for obtaining possession under these grounds by originating summons is available.[8] The applicant must file an affidavit in support of his claim setting out the evidence he relies on; the period of notice required between service of notice of application and hearing is shorter than the usual procedure and the matter may be heard by a registrar and in chambers.

Case 11: The landlord is an 'owner-occupier'

Where the person (the 'owner-occupier') who let the dwelling-house on a regulated tenancy had, at any time before the letting, occupied it as his residence, and

---

5 *R v Newcastle upon Tyne County Court, ex p Thompson* [1988] 2 EGLR 119.
6 *Kenyon v Walker* [1946] 2 All ER 595.
7 *Kennealy v Dunne* [1977] QB 837, [1977] 2 All ER 16, CA.
8 Rent Act (County Court Proceedings for Possession) Rules 1981, SI 1981/139. See *Minay v Sentongo* (1982) 45 P & CR 190, CA.

(a) not later than the 'relevant date' (usually the commencement of the tenancy)[9] the landlord gave notice in writing to the tenant that possession might be recovered under Case 11; *and*

(b) the dwelling-house has not, since one of three specified dates, been let on a protected tenancy not subject to a Case 11 notice; *and*

the court is satisfied that *one* of the following conditions is complied with:

(a) the dwelling-house is required as a residence for the owner or any member of his family who resided with the owner when he last occupied the dwelling-house as his residence; *or*

(b) the owner has died and the dwelling-house is required as a residence for a member of his family who was residing with him at the time of his death; *or*

(c) the owner has died and the dwelling-house is required by a successor in title as his residence or for the purpose of disposing of it with vacant possession; *or*

(d) the dwelling-house is subject to a mortgage by deed granted before the commencement of the tenancy, and the mortgagee is entitled to exercise his express or statutory power of sale and requires possession to dispose of the dwelling-house with vacant possession; *or*

(e) the dwelling-house is not reasonably suitable to the needs of the owner, having regard to his place of work, and he requires it to dispose of it with vacant possession to use the sale proceeds to acquire a more suitable dwelling-house.[10]

Although Case 11 cannot, in general, be relied on unless a written notice is served on the tenant, not later than the grant of the tenancy, the court has a power to dispense with the notice requirement if it is just and equitable to do so. This dispensation power also applies to the requirement that all lettings must be under tenancies governed by a Case 11 notice.

Where a landlord sent a Case 11 notice to the tenant but it was never received (and the tenant must receive the notice for Case 11 to be satisfied in this respect), the dispensation power was exercised in the landlord's favour because she honestly believed that due notice was given.[11] Where a landlord let on a tenancy which, at that time, he did not intend to be subject to Case 11, and later decided to rely on Case 11, he failed to invoke the dispensation power, and it was held that Case 11

---

9 Rent Act 1977 Sch 15 Part III para 2.
10 See *Bissessar v Ghosn* (1985) 18 HLR 486, CA.
11 *Minay v Sentongo* (1983) 45 P & CR 190, CA.

only applied to lettings originally intended to fall within its terms.[12] The words 'just and equitable' require the adoption of a broad view and the court must look at all the circumstances.[13] Where a landlord gave an oral notice, the dispensation power was, exceptionally, exercised: the tenant knew the landlord was an owner-occupier.[14]

One of two joint landlords who originally let subject to it, is entitled to rely on Case 11, even though only one of them requires the dwelling-house as his residence, or for another permitted purpose within the Case, as the emphasis of Case 11 is on occupation.[15]

The opening words of Case 11 are given as amended by the Rent (Amendment) Act 1985, whose effect has been held to be retrospective.[16] Therefore, Case 11 may be relied on, not only by a person who was, immediately prior to the grant of the tenancy concerned, an 'owner-occupier', but also by someone who has let on a series of tenancies – provided all tenancies comply with Case 11 and are subject to the relevant notices. The 1985 Act was passed to reverse a decision to the effect that occupation by the landlord immediately before the grant of the actual tenancy, the subject-matter of proceedings, was required.[17] Case 11 does not necessarily require that the landlord must occupy the dwelling-house concerned as his only or main residence after regaining possession: if he has another home, abroad for example, all that is required is that he requires the dwelling-house for use as an intermittent residence.[18] But where a landlord intended to let for gain and not to return to the house, her claim failed.[19]

Case 12: Retirement home

The landlord must show that he intends to occupy as his residence the dwelling-house, when he retired from regular employment; that he let it prior to retirement, and:

(a) not later than the commencement of the tenancy he served on the tenant a notice in writing that possession might be recovered under Case 12; *and*

(b) that at no time since 14 August 1974 has the dwelling-house been let on a tenancy not subject to a Case 12 notice; *and*

---

12 *Bradshaw v Baldwin-Wiseman* (1985) 17 HLR 260, CA.
13 Ibid.
14 *Fernandes v Parvardin* (1982) 264 Estates Gazette 49, CA, as explained in *Bradshaw v Baldwin-Wiseman*, supra.
15 *Tilling v Whiteman* [1980] AC 1, [1979] 1 All ER 737, HL.
16 *Hewitt v Lewis* [1986] 1 All ER 927, [1986] 1 WLR 444, CA.
17 *Pocock v Steel* [1985] 1 All ER 434, [1985] 1 WLR 229, CA.
18 *Naish v Curzon* [1985] 1 WLR 229, CA (twice-yearly visits by landlord to UK sufficient); *Davies v Peterson* (1988) 21 HLR 63, CA (frequent visits to UK sufficient).
19 *Ghelani v Bowie* [1988] 1 EGLR 130, CA.

(c)   that owner has retired as above and requires the dwelling-house as a residence for himself, *or* that conditions (b) to (d) inclusive listed under Case 11 above, apply.

Case 13: *Out of season lettings*

The dwelling-house must be let for a term certain not exceeding eight months and:

(a)   not later than the commencement of the tenancy, the landlord gave notice in writing to the tenant that possession might be recovered under Case 13; *and*

(b)   that at some period within the last 12 months ending with the commencement of the tenancy, the dwelling-house was occupied under a right to occupy it for a holiday.

There is no apparent reason why the landlord should not obtain possession under this Case by proving that he himself had, prior to the grant of the tenancy, occupied the dwelling-house for his own holiday.[20] The obvious aim of Case 13 is to encourage off-season lettings of dwelling-houses used, in season, for holiday lettings.

Case 14: *Short tenancies of student accommodation*

Where the dwelling-house is let for a term certain not exceeding 12 months and:

(a)   not later than the commencement of the tenancy the landlord gave notice in writing to the tenant that possession might be recovered under Case 14; *and*

(b)   at some time in the 12 months ending on the commencement of the tenancy, the dwelling-house was subject to a student letting.

The object of this Case is to facilitate vacation lettings of student accommodation which falls within s 8.

Case 15: *Dwelling-house required for minister of religion*

Where the dwelling-house is held for the purposes of being available for occupation by a minister of religion as a resident from which to perform the duties of his office and:

(a)   not later than the 'relevant date'[1] the tenant was given by the

---

20   See in favour: Farrand and Arden *Rent Acts and Regulations* p 199; against, Jill E Martin *Security of Tenure under the Rent Act* p 87.

1   I e the commencement date of the tenancy.

landlord notice in writing that possession might be recovered under Case 15; *and*

(b) the court is satisfied that the dwelling-house is required for occupation by a minister of religion as such a residence.

Cases 16 to 18: Dwelling-houses once occupied by persons in agriculture

If the dwelling-house is not a tied cottage (dealt with in Section G below) but was either once occupied by an agricultural employee, or is a redundant farm house at the time of the letting, and is required for an agricultural employee in all cases, then possession may be recovered under the relevant Case provided that at the start of the tenancy the requisite notice is given of intention to recover possession.[2]

Case 19: Protected shorthold tenancies

This is dealt with in Section H of this chapter.

Case 20: Lettings by servicemen

This is available for lettings after 28 November 1980 by a person who at the time of the letting was a member of the armed forces; who at the time he acquired the dwelling-house and also at the time when he let it was a member of the armed forces; that at the commencement of the tenancy at the latest, the owner gave notice in writing to the tenant that possession might be recovered under Case 20, and that at no time since, has the dwelling-house not been subject to Case 20 tenancies. Provided all these conditions are met the owner may recover possession if:

(a) the dwelling-house is required as his residence; *or*

(b) conditions (b) to (e) as stated for Case 11 apply.

There is, under this Case, no requirement of prior residence at any time in the dwelling-house concerned.

V ORDER FOR POSSESSION

In any claim for possession under s 98 other than one made on any of the grounds in Part II of Sch 15, the court has extensive discretionary powers under s 100 on the one hand to adjourn the proceedings, and on the other, to stay or suspend the execution of an order or postpone the date of possession, either on the making of the order or at any time before execution of the order, in relation to a protected or statutory

---

2 See *Fowler v Minchin* (1987) 19 HLR 224, CA (written notice required).

tenancy (s 100(1) and (2)).[3] On any such adjournment, stay, suspension or postponement, the court must impose conditions with regard to the payment by the tenant of arrears of rent and rent and mesne profits, unless it considers that to do so would cause exceptional hardship to the tenant or would otherwise be unreasonable, and may impose such other conditions as it thinks fit (s 100(3)).[4] If such conditions as are imposed are complied with, the court may discharge or rescind the order (s 100(4)).

The court may adjourn proceedings, for example, and make no order, where the tenant gives an undertaking for the future to abide by certain specified conditions; and if the tenant breaks those conditions, the landlord will be free to apply for an order for possession.[5]

Where an order for possession is made, it may be absolute or conditional. An absolute order is clearly unconditional; its operation may, however, be suspended or postponed, but that must not be confused with a conditional order, which may be discharged if the condition is complied with. An absolute order has the effect of terminating the tenancy forthwith, and should the tenant die before execution of the order, there is no tenancy to be transmitted to a successor under Sch 1;[6] under a conditional order, on the other hand, the tenancy continues.[7] An absolute order cannot be discharged as such, but may first be made conditional, and then discharged.[8]

Where an order for possession is made under one of the mandatory grounds above, a stricter set of rules applies. By s 89(1) of the Housing Act 1980, the giving up of possession cannot be postponed to a date later than 14 days after the order is made, unless it appears to the court that exceptional hardship would be caused. In any event, the giving up of possession cannot be postponed to a date later than six weeks after the making of the order.[8A]

VI   STATUTORY TENANCIES

A statutory tenancy may arise in one of two ways. After the termination of a protected tenancy, the person who, immediately before its termination, was the protected tenant, becomes the statutory tenant of the dwelling-house, if and so long as he occupies it as his residence

---

3   The court cannot make an order under s 100 after an order for possession has been executed: *Scott-James v Chehab* [1988] 2 EGLR 61, CA.
4   Special rules exist in Rent Act 1977 s 100(4A) and (4B) enabling the tenant's spouse to apply to the court to exercise its suspensory etc powers.
5   *Mills v Allen* [1953] 2 QB 341, [1953] 2 All ER 534.
6   *American Economic Laundry v Little* [1951] 1 KB 400, [1950] 2 All ER 1186.
7   *Sherrin v Brand* [1956] 1 QB 403, [1956] 1 All ER 194.
8   *Payne v Cooper* [1958] 1 QB 174, [1957] 3 All ER 335.
8A This provision does not apply to High Court, as opposed to county court proceedings: *Bain & Co v Church Comrs for England* [1989] 1 WLR 24, 21 HLR 29.

(s 2(1)(a) of the 1977 Act). Alternatively, after the death of a protected or statutory tenant, a succession may be claimed (under Sch 1) by the surviving spouse or by a family member of the deceased tenant, and, on the death of a successor, one further succession may be allowed. The succession rules differ in details, depending on whether the death occurred before or after the commencement of Part I of the Housing Act 1988 (15 January 1989). If the previous tenancy was not protected, as where it was granted by a resident landlord, no statutory tenancy can ever arise.[9]

Statutory tenancy on expiry of protected tenancy

A protected contractual tenancy, fixed-term or periodic, automatically becomes a statutory tenancy if and so long as, from the termination of the previous protected tenancy, the tenant occupies the dwelling-house as his residence (s 2(1)(a)).[10] The statutory tenancy will continue unless it is terminated in accordance with s 98 and Sch 15, or unless the tenant ceases to comply with the residence requirement.[11]

If the tenant gives notice to quit and leaves, he cannot claim a statutory tenancy; if he remains in occupation after such notice has expired, he becomes a statutory tenant, but the landlord may be able to terminate his occupation.[12] Similarly, if the previous protected tenancy has been forfeited, a statutory tenancy arises under s 2(1)(a), but the landlord may find that he is able to establish a ground for possession which corresponds to the breach giving rise to the forfeiture.[13] If a protected tenant goes bankrupt, no statutory tenancy can arise.[14]

A statutory tenant is conferred a purely personal right of continuing occupation of the dwelling-house, provided he continues to comply with the residence requirement of s 2(1)(a); he has no estate in the land concerned.[15] However, perhaps inconsistently, this right includes the right to retain possession and enjoyment against all the world unless possession is ordered by the court under s 98, and hence, the right to treat any person entering without his permission as a trespasser.[16] The

9   *Landau v Sloane* [1982] AC 490, [1981] 1 All ER 705, HL.

10 See *Remon v City of London Real Property Co Ltd* [1921] 1 KB 49, CA.

11 As to loss of a statutory tenancy by cesser of residence, see below.

12 Under Sch 15 Part I Case 5.

13 *Tideway Investment and Property Holdings v Wellwood* [1952] Ch 791, [1952] 2 All ER 514, CA. If this is not possible, a forfeiture will not entitle the landlord to possession: s 98(1).

14 *Smalley v Quarrier* [1975] 2 All ER 688, [1975] 1 WLR 938, CA. If a statutory tenant goes bankrupt, this is not *ipso facto* a ground for possession: *Sutton v Dorf* [1932] 2 KB 304.

15 *Jessamine Investment Co v Schwartz* [1978] QB 264, [1976] 3 All ER 521, CA; also *Portman Registrars and Nominees v Latif* [1987] CLY 2239. This view has been severely criticised: see passim Hand [1980] Conv 351.

16 *Keeves v Dean* [1924] 1 KB 685 at 694, CA.

rights of occupation of a statutory tenant were protected by the court as against a mortgagee whose claim for possession, which had nothing to do with protecting her security, was treated as unenforceable in equity.[17] Whilst any assignment inter vivos of a statutory tenancy causes the loss of security, owing to s 2(1)(a), the court has power to direct an assignment of a statutory tenancy in matrimonial proceedings,[18] and assignments are possible, with the landlord's agreement, to a third party.[19]

If the statutory tenant sub-lets the whole dwelling-house, he loses his status of statutory tenant as he cannot comply with the statutory residence requirement.[20] If the statutory tenant sub-lets part only of the dwelling-house, generally he retains security.[1] Loss of security also follows if the dwelling-house ceases for whatever reason to be occupied by the statutory tenant personally.[2]

A limited company which holds a tenancy cannot claim a statutory tenancy.[3] If the actual person in occupation is a licensee of the company, provided the arrangement is genuine and not a sham, the occupier will lack any statutory protection.[4]

On the other hand, if a protected tenancy is granted originally to two persons as joint tenant and, on termination of the contractual tenancy, only one of the persons is in occupation, he may still claim to be the statutory tenant.[5]

Finally, a tenant holding over after expiry of a protected tenancy is a statutory tenant, and the grant of a new contractual tenancy will be inferred from payment and acceptance of rent with reluctance: there must be other circumstances than the mere termination of the previous contractual tenancy to warrant this inference.[6]

Succession: pre-Housing Act 1988 rules

In relation to deaths *before* the commencement of Part I of the Housing Act 1988, the rules in Sch I to the 1977 Act[7] apply in their pre-1988 Act form and, very briefly, are as follows.

Two successions are allowed for, one on the death of the original

---

17 *Quennell v Maltby* [1979] 1 All ER 568, [1979] 1 WLR 318, CA.
18 Matrimonial Homes Act 1983 s 1.
19 Rent Act 1977 Sch 1 para 13.
20 *Haskins v Lewis* [1931] 2 KB 1, CA; *Skinner v Geary* [1931] 2 KB 546, CA.
1   *Berkeley v Papadoyannis* [1954] 2 QB 149, [1954] 2 All ER 409, CA.
2   *Metropolitan Properties Co v Cronan* (1982) 126 Sol Jo 229, CA.
3   *Hiller v United Dairies (London) Ltd* [1934] 1 KB 57, CA.
4   *Firstcross Ltd v East-West (Export/Import) Ltd* (1980) 41 P & CR 145, CA. Also *Hilton v Plustitle Ltd* [1988] 3 All ER 1051, CA.
5   *Lloyd v Sadler* [1978] QB 774, [1978] 2 All ER 529, CA.
6   *Marcroft Wagons Ltd v Smith* [1951] 2 KB 496, [1951] 2 All ER 271, CA; *Dealex Properties v Brooks* [1966] 1 QB 542, [1965] 1 All ER 1080, CA.
7   References in this section are to Sch 1 prior to the 1988 Act amendments.

tenant and one on the death of his or her successor. On either occasion, a succession may be claimed by a surviving spouse or, if there is none, a member of the deceased's family.

The surviving spouse must have resided in the dwelling-house immediately before the death of the original tenant or the first successor, as the case may be, and will succeed, provided that he or she occupied the dwelling-house as his or her residence (Sch 1 para 2 and 6). In the case of a family member, the individual concerned must have resided with the deceased tenant or first successor immediately before his death and for six months before then (paras 3 and 7).[8]

Succession where death occurs after Housing Act 1988

Where the original tenant, or his or her first successor, die *after* the commencement of the Housing Act 1988 (15 January 1989), the above rules are modified.[9]

The general principle is that the surviving spouse of the original tenant obtains a succession to a Rent Act statutory tenancy; but, if on the death of the original tenant, there is no surviving spouse, and only a family member, the latter obtains a succession to an assured periodic tenancy under Part I of the 1988 Act. Where a first successor to a statutory tenancy, who was a surviving spouse, dies after the commencement of the 1988 Act rules, any succession, which is by a family member (including a surviving spouse), is to an assured periodic tenancy under the 1988 Act.[10]

The precise amendments to the succession scheme to implement the new regime for post-1988 Act deaths are as follows. The distinction between surviving spouse and family member is preserved, but, as noted, only a surviving spouse of the original tenant is entitled to succeed to a statutory tenancy.[11] Family members succeed to an assured periodic tenancy under the 1988 Act.

1   A person living with the original tenant as his or her wife or husband is treated as the spouse of the former (and no length of residence is specified).

---

8   If there is more than one claimant, the succession is to be resolved by agreement or, in default, by the county court. The six-month residence period is *only applicable* where the death of the tenant/first successor was *before* the commencement of the 1988 Act amendments.
9   By amendments to Rent Act 1977 Sch 1 by Housing Act 1988 Sched 4, applied by ibid s 39.
10 Rent Act 1977 Sch 1 paras 2 and 6, as amended by Housing Act 1988 Sch 4.
11 A double succession is allowed, therefore, post the 1988 Act, only where there is a surviving spouse of the original tenant. Therefore, if T dies and is succeeded by his wife W, their daughter Z, provided she satisfies the residence requirements, will succeed on W's death to a statutory assured tenancy; if W predeceases T, Z will succeed as above on T's death, and there will be a single succession only.

2   A family member cannot succeed to the original tenant's statutory tenancy, unless he or she has resided in the dwelling-house immediately before the original tenant's death (as opposed to 'with him') and for a minimum period of two years immediately before then.[12]

3   A family member claiming a first succession will obtain, as noted, an assured periodic tenancy under the Housing Act 1988.[13]

4   On the death of a first successor, who was a surviving spouse,[14] any member of the latter's family, who was also a member of the original tenant's family, is entitled to claim a succession, which is to an assured periodic tenancy. If there is more than one claimant, the succession is to be by agreement or by decision of the county court. The family member (which includes the deceased's spouse), must have resided in the dwelling-house with the first successor immediately before his or her death and for a minimum period of two years before then.[15]

Further principles applicable to succession at any date

Where a claimant had a permanent home elsewhere, the claim to succeed to a statutory tenancy failed, and the residence of the claimant in the tenant's home was found to be transient, given that the claimant continued to maintain her other home.[16]

The word 'family' in Sch 1 was, prior to the 1988 Act, held to include cohabitees, whether male or female, of the deceased tenant, provided that the relationship was permanent, as where there was a long cohabitation, or where the parties held themselves out as married, or had children.[17] In relation to post-1988 Act deaths, cohabitees will claim as surviving spouses.

The term 'family' is to be interpreted in the popular sense and is not confined to blood relatives: accordingly, it has been held to include not just adopted children, but also those accepted into the tenant's family.[18]

---

12   If the tenant dies within 18 months of the commencement of Part I of the 1988 Act, a residence from July 15, 1988 is deemed to satisfy the two-year requirement.

13   As modified by Housing Act 1988 s 39(6).

14   Where the first successor was a family member, the succession will have been to a statute-implied assured tenancy (1988 Act s 39) and the tenant will not be statutory within Sch 1 para 5.

15   Rent Act 1977 Sch 1 para 6 (substituted by Housing Act 1988 Sch 4 para 6). The same deeming rule applies where a successor dies within 18 months of the commencement of Part I of the 1988 Act as applies to a first succession.

16   *Swanbrae Ltd v Elliott* (1986) 131 Sol Jo 410, CA.

17   *Dyson Holdings Ltd v Fox* [1976] QB 503, [1975] 3 All ER 1030, CA; *Watson v Lucas* [1980] 3 All ER 647, [1980] 1 WLR 1493, CA; *Chios Property Investment Co v Lopez* (1987) 20 HLR 120, CA. These principles may apply to post-1988 Act claims.

18   *Brock v Wollams* [1949] 2 KB 388, [1949] 1 All ER 715, CA.

An adult who is in no sense related to the tenant may well find it hard to claim a succession, as long residence is insufficient by itself.[19] Therefore, a person treated by the tenant as her so-called 'nephew', and who formed part of her household, failed in a succession claim,[20] as did a resident housekeeper.[1]

Succession under the 1977 Act takes precedence over the rights of any person entitled under the deceased tenant's will,[2] or in his intestacy. If a person entitled to succeed is also entitled to inherit the contractual tenancy, there is a presumption that he takes the latter by inheritance.[3]

VII TERMS AND CONDITIONS OF STATUTORY TENANCIES

By s 3(1), so long as he retains possession, a statutory tenant is bound to observe and is entitled to the benefit of all the terms and conditions of the original contract of tenancy,[4] so far as consistent with the provisions of the Act. It is a condition of a statutory tenancy, by s 3(2), that the tenant must afford to the landlord access to the dwelling-house and all reasonable facilities for executing any repairs which he is entitled to execute.[5]

Section 3(1) imports into the statutory tenancy all express obligations which run with the land and, indeed, any covenant which is of any benefit to the parties as such, for example, for the provision of personal services to the tenant.[6] Therefore, express and implied repairing obligations of either party are carried into the statutory tenancy, as are landlords' statute-implied repairing obligations under ss 11–16 of the Landlord and Tenant Act 1985. A tenant's right to renew was held to be imported into the statutory tenancy.[7] Purely personal covenants which are collateral to the tenancy are not imported into the statutory tenancy.[8] Covenants which are capable of being construed as limited to the contractual (i e protected) tenancy will not be carried into the statutory tenancy by s 3(1), an example being a tenant's option to

---

19 *Sefton Holdings Ltd v Cairns* [1988] 2 FLR 109, CA (almost 50 years insufficient).
20 *Carega Properties SA (formerly Joram Developments Ltd) v Sharratt* [1979] 2 All ER 1084, [1979] 1 WLR 928, HL.
1   *Darnell v Millward* [1951] 1 All ER 88, CA.
2   *Moodie v Hosegood* [1952] AC 61, [1951] 2 All ER 582, HL.
3   *Whitmore v Lambert* [1955] 2 All ER 147, [1955] 1 WLR 495, CA.
4   I e the protected tenancy immediately before the statutory tenancy.
5   This corresponds to s 148 (protected tenancies). It imports the landlord's liabilities under s 4 of the Defective Premises Act 1972.
6   *Engvall v Ideal Flats Ltd* [1945] KB 205, [1945] 1 All ER 230, CA.
7   *McIlroy v Clements* [1923] WN 81.
8   *Boyer v Warbey* [1953] 1 QB 234, [1952] 2 All ER 976, CA (where a covenant to pay £40 towards redecoration of a flat was held to bind a statutory tenant).

purchase exercisable 'at any time' during the tenancy.[9] Statutory (and for that matter protected) tenants are subject to special consent rules in relation to improvements: absolute prohibitions thereon are banned, and the landlord cannot unreasonably withhold his consent to an improvement. If he does withhold his consent, he must prove that he had reasonable grounds for doing so.[10] If the terms of the statutory tenancy do not expressly prohibit it, a statutory tenant may, without loss of security, sub-let part of the dwelling-house, but not if he has already sub-let the remainder.[11] If the tenant sub-lets part, but retains part of the premises and may at some future date re-occupy the parts sub-let, he will not lose security.[12]

VIII   TERMINATION OF STATUTORY TENANCIES

A statutory tenant retains his status only, by s 2(1)(a), 'if and so long as he occupies the dwelling-house as his residence'. For this reason, as noted above, if a statutory tenant sub-lets the whole dwelling-house, or if he first sub-lets part, followed by the remainder, he loses his status as statutory tenant.

There are three other ways in which the status of statutory tenant may be lost by non-compliance with the residence requirement and each of these is examined in what follows.[13]

(a)   Occupation by tenant's spouse or ex-spouse

Where the tenant ceases permanently to occupy the dwelling-house, occupation by his wife has been held to be sufficient for the purposes of s 2(1)(a), and the tenant remains statutory tenant, even if the parties are separated.[14] This will not apply if the house was never the matrimonial home.[15] Therefore, where a statutory tenant left, and eventually returned, leaving his wife in occupation of the house in between, he retained his statutory tenancy, in the absence of evidence of a surrender of it.[16]

---

9   *Longmuir v Kew* [1960] 3 All ER 26, [1960] 1 WLR 862.
10   Housing Act 1980, ss 81–83.
11   *Crowhurst v Maidment* [1953] 1 QB 23, [1952] 2 All ER 808, CA (where the tenant never resided and never intended to reside, in the premises sub-let).
12   *Berkeley v Papadoyannis* [1954] 2 QB 149, [1954] 2 All ER 409, CA.
13   The onus of proof in each case is on the landlord: see e g *Roland House Gardens Ltd v Cravitz* (1974) 29 P & CR 432, CA.
14   *Brown v Draper* [1944] KB 309, [1944] 1 All ER 246, CA; *Hoggett v Hoggett* (1979) 39 P & CR 121; see now Matrimonial Homes Act 1983 s 1(6).
15   *Hall v King* [1988] 1 FLR 376, CA.
16   *Hulme v Langford* (1985) 50 P & CR 199, CA.

If the parties are divorced, or judicially separated (in either case by court order) an occupation by the statutory tenant's ex-wife is not his occupation, and if he is out of occupation, with no intention to return, security is lost.[17] The same rule applies in the case of a statutory tenant's mistress.[18] The difference between wives and divorced wives or mistresses is this: the occupation of a wife is deemed to be that of the tenant; that of a divorced wife etc, cannot be so deemed, and the occupier is a mere licensee. In the case of wives, the court has power in divorce, nullity or judicial separation proceedings, to transfer a statutory tenancy to the wife.[19]

(b) Permanent absence of tenant

Where a landlord proves that the tenant is permanently absent from the dwelling-house with no intention to return, the tenant ceases to be a statutory tenant. A sufficiently prolonged absence, without any objective evidence of the necessary intention, such as the presence of the tenant's furniture, will enable the court to infer an abandonment of occupation, but it is open to the tenant to show an intention to return, backed by objective indicia such as the occupation of the house by his relatives (see below).[20] The question of intention to return is one of fact, and does not depend merely on the number of years concerned, but there must be a real hope of return coupled with a practical possibility of its fulfilment within a reasonable time.[1] In one case,[2] a tenant who was absent for seven years and who also held the freehold of other premises, was held to have lost his status of statutory tenant. However, a finding that a tenant had a genuine intention to return after 10 years enabled him to retain his statutory tenancy.[3] It is not too much to conclude from this that if a county court judge makes a finding of fact that the tenant genuinely intends to return, the Court of Appeal will interfere with his decision only if it is perverse. Moreover, there is a difference between cases where the tenant is voluntarily absent, and those where he is absent

---

17 *Metropolitan Properties Ltd v Cronan* (1982) 44 P & CR 1, CA.
18 *Colin Smith Music Ltd v Ridge* [1975] 1 All ER 290, [1975] 1 WLR 463, CA, where the statutory tenant had, effectually, surrendered the tenancy.
19 Matrimonial Homes Act 1983, Sch 1, as extended by Matrimonial and Family Proceedings Act 1984, s 22 to financial relief proceedings. The 1983 Act powers are not retroactive: *Lewis v Lewis* [1985] AC 828, [1985] 2 All ER 449, HL.
20 *Brown v Brash and Ambrose* [1948] 2 KB 247, [1948] 1 All ER 922, CA; applied in *Robert Thackery's Estates Ltd v Kaye* [1988] EGCS 158.
1 *Gofor Investments Ltd v Roberts* (1975) 29 P & R 366, CA.
2 *Duke v Porter* [1986] 2 EGLR 101, CA.
3 *Gofor Investments Ltd v Roberts*, supra; also *Brickfield Properties Ltd v Hughes* [1987] 20 HLR 108, CA (eight-year absence not sufficient to cost tenant security where he satisfied judge that he might well retire to the dwelling-house concerned); Bridge [1988] Conv 300.

due to factors he cannot control, or where he is away for, say, an extended but finite absence.[4] In the latter instances, it may be easier for the tenant to retain security, as the court may more readily infer a genuine intention to return. For example, a tenant retained his statutory tenancy despite being in prison,[5] and also while detained in hospital due to insanity.[6] In all cases, as said, there must be some objective evidence of intention to return, such as retained furniture, or the presence of a relative in the premises to look after them, to back up the tenant's inward intention to return.[7] It need hardly be said, in view of the foregoing, that a statutory tenant will not lose his status merely if he is temporarily absent.

(c) Two-home tenants

A third way in which security may be lost is if the landlord is able to prove that the tenant has another home and he is using the house of which he is statutory tenant as a convenient resort only.[8] But the fact that the tenant has another home is, apparently, certainly not enough of itself to deprive him of his statutory tenancy.[9] Therefore, a person may even occupy his own home for most of the time and the house held under a statutory tenancy more rarely or for a limited purpose: where this is so, it is a question of fact and degree whether the second house is occupied as his second home and, therefore, whether it remains held under a statutory tenancy.[10]

If, by contrast, the tenant holds two adjoining houses, originally from the same landlord, and lives in one and sleeps in the other (or divides his living activities in some other way between the two houses), it is a question of fact whether he, as s 2(1)(a) requires, resides in both houses as one complete unit, in which case he has security, or whether each unit is self-contained and occupied separately, in which case the tenant has no statutory tenancy in respect of either unit of habitation.[11]

---

4   See e g *Richards v Green* (1983) 268 Estates Gazette 443, CA.
5   *Maxted v McAll* [1952] CPL 185, CA.
6   *Tickner v Hearn* [1961] 1 All ER 65, [1960] 1 WLR 1406, CA.
7   See *Brown v Brash and Ambrose*, supra.
8   As in *Regalian Securities Ltd v Scheuer* (1982) 47 P & CR 362, CA.
9   *Langford Property Co v Tureman* [1949] 1 KB 29, CA, approved in *Hampstead Way Investments Ltd v Lewis-Weare* [1985] 1 All ER 564, [1985] 1 WLR 164, HL.
10   *Hampstead Way Investments Ltd v Lewis-Weare*, supra; Wilkinson (1985) 135 NLJ 357; P F Smith [1985] Conv 224. With respect, it is not the policy of the 1977 Act to protect a second home, still less a second home of convenience. Cf *Walker v Ogilvy* (1974) 28 P & CR 288, CA (holiday homes outside Rent Acts).
11   *Wimbush v Cibulia* [1949] 2 KB 564, [1949] 2 All ER 432, CA; *Kavanagh v Lyroudias* [1985] 1 All ER 560, CA.

(d) Further points

A statutory tenant may surrender his statutory tenancy by express or implied surrender, and the common law rules as to this apply. If the premises are destroyed and the tenant has no intention to return to them, the statutory tenancy ends.[12]

The tenant also has the right to terminate the statutory tenancy by a written notice of the requisite length, which means a notice sufficient to terminate his previous protected tenancy (s 3(3)) and the minimum period of the notice must be four weeks, by s 5 of the Protection from Eviction Act 1977. Where the landlord obtains possession by an order of court, no notice to quit to the statutory tenant is required (s 3(4)). If no notice was required under the protected tenancy, because it was fixed-term, then the tenant may terminate the statutory tenancy by a notice of not less than three months (s 3(3)).

E PREMIUMS

I PROHIBITION OF PREMIUMS ON GRANT OF PROTECTED TENANCIES

There would be no point in controlling the rent of protected tenancies if a landlord were able to charge a low rent and then take a capital sum from the tenant at the commencement of a protected tenancy. Hence Part IX of the Rent Act 1977, which prohibits devices of this sort. In relation to tenancies not originally within the 1977 Act, but brought into protection subsequently, a premium on assignment may, in principle, be taken (see Section II).

Section 119(1) of the 1977 Act makes it an offence for any person to require the payment of any premium, in addition to the rent, as a condition of the grant, renewal or continuance of a protected tenancy. By s 119(2), it is an offence for any person to receive such a premium in addition to the rent.[13] The convicting court may order the offender to repay any premium (s 119(4)).

'Premium' has a wide definition in s 128(1), to counteract avoidance schemes. It includes any fine or other like sum, and any other pecuniary consideration in addition to rent. It also includes any sum paid as a deposit. If the sum does not exceed one-sixth of the annual rent and is reasonable in relation to the potential liability in respect of which it is paid, it is allowable; if these conditions are not satisfied, the whole sum is

---

12 *Ellis & Sons Amalgamated Properties Ltd v Sisman* [1948] 1 KB 653, [1948] 1 All ER 44, CA.
13 The penalty for contravention of s 119(1) and (2) is a fine not exceeding level 3 on the standard scale (s 119(3)).

prohibited. Therefore, sums, within these two conditions, which are, typically, returnable deposits to cover rent arrears and breakages, are permitted despite the general prohibition on premiums.

The making of any loans, secured or unsecured, is prohibited by s 119(1), and such loans are recoverable on demand. These prohibitions are reinforced by s 123, which relates to premiums in connection with furniture and is discussed in III below.

On the construction of s 119(1), 'any person' obviously includes the landlord but is not limited to him: it includes anyone who requires or receives a premium, such as an agent, or any tenant receiving a sum for, for example, fixtures, as consideration for the surrender of a previous tenancy.[14] A money payment is the most obvious example of a premium prohibited by Part IX; but the term 'premium' (within s 128(1)) has been held to include any consideration expressed in terms of money whereby there is a benefit to the landlord or a detriment to the tenant.[15] Accordingly, it included a case where a prospective tenant was required by the landlord's agents, as a condition of the grant of a protected tenancy of a flat, to sell his house to a named third party connected with the landlord for £500 less than its market value.[16] Perhaps the most apt point on the scope of the premium prohibitions is that they apply to any sum which is not properly rent.[17] The question of whether a payment is a premium or commuted rent is one of substance and if a payment is commuted rent it will be treated as additional rent.[18]

Any part of a contract which requires the payment of a prohibited premium is void. The tenant (or other payor) is entitled to recover the premium from the payee (s 125(1)) and, as was noted, the court has power, on conviction, to order the offender to repay the sum concerned to the payor (s 119(4)). These recovery rules are mutually exclusive (s 128(2)). Any part of a contract which does not fall foul of Part IX of the 1977 Act may, at discretion, be severed and enforced.[19]

II RESTRICTIONS ON PREMIUMS ON ASSIGNMENT

It is, by s 120(1) and (2), an offence for any person[20] to require or receive the payment of any premium or the making of any loan (secured or

---

14   *Farrell v Alexander* [1977] AC 59, [1976] 2 All ER 721, HL; *Saleh v Robinson* [1988] 2 EGLR 126, CA.

15   *Elmdene Estates Ltd v White* [1960] AC 528, [1960] 1 All ER 306, HL.

16   *Elmdene Estates Ltd v White*, supra.

17   Farrand and Arden, *Rent Acts and Regulations* p 153.

18   *Samrose Properties v Gibbard* [1958] 1 All ER 502, [1958] 1 WLR 235, CA (payment of £35 as a condition of grant of one-year lease at low rent treated as commuted rent – tenancy then not at low rent and within Acts).

19   *Ailion v Spiekermann* [1976] Ch 158, [1976] 1 All ER 497.

20   See *Farrell v Alexander* [1977] AC 59, [1976] 2 All ER 721, HL.

unsecured) as a condition of the assignment of a protected tenancy. The penalties for contravention of this prohibition, which is absolute in the case of tenancies which are protected from the date of their grant, are the same as for s 119, discussed above.

As a concession, a protected tenant may require the payment of certain sums from his assignee, including, notably, a sum not exceeding the cost reasonably incurred by the outgoing tenant in carrying out structural alterations, or in providing or improving landlords' fixtures (s 120(3)(b)). In any dispute as to whether the money spent on these matters is reasonable, an examination of each item of expenditure will be necessary.[1]

In the case of statutory tenancies, s 120 does not apply, but there are restrictions on sums recoverable on assignments.[2]

Where, at the date of its grant, a tenancy was not protected because the rent was less than a market rent, but was also not a low rent within s 5 of the 1977 Act, special rules apply (s 120(5)). These also apply to tenancies which are both protected tenancies and long leases within Part I of the Landlord and Tenant Act 1954 (s 127 as amended by s 115 of the Housing Act 1988). A premium calculated in accordance with Sch 18 Part I may be recovered by the tenant, on assignments in either case, so as to enable him to realise the capital value of his tenancy.[3] Where a tenancy, which when granted was not protected, was brought within the Rent Act 1977 as a consequence of the 1973 rates revaluation, a premium calculated in accordance with Sch 18 Part II is recoverable by the tenant, on an assignment of the tenancy (s 121).

III FURTHER PROVISIONS

Furniture

The premium provisions are backed up by s 123 of the 1977 Act, which catches an excessive price charged for the purchase of furniture as a condition of the grant, renewal, continuance or assignment of a protected tenancy. The excess over the reasonable price is treated as a premium. The word 'excess' means the excess over the reasonable price of the furniture fitted and situated on the premises, as opposed to its auction-room price.[4] Attempts to obtain a disguised premium in

---

1 As in *Nock v Munk* (1982) 263 Estates Gazette 1085, and see also *Adair v Murrell* (1981) 263 Estates Gazette 66.
2 Rent Act 1977 Sch 1 Part II paras 12 and 14. The aim and effect of these rules is similar to s 120.
3 The tenant will have had to pay a capital sum prior to or on the grant of his lease, and it is considered that it would be unjust not to enable him to recover that sum on any assignment.
4 *Eales v Dale* [1954] 1 QB 539, [1954] 1 All ER 717, CA. This is a question of fact: *Nock v Munk*, supra.

connection with furniture purchase by a prospective tenant are caught by s 124(1). The devices caught by this provision include offering the furniture at a price which the offeror knows or ought to know is unreasonably high (s 124(1)(a)). Local authorities have exceptionally draconian powers of enforcement (s 124(2)–(7)).

Advance payments of rent

Advance payments of rent are caught by s 126. If a protected tenancy is granted, continued or renewed, a requirement that the rent is to be payable before the beginning of the rental period in respect of which it is payable is void, however imposed (s 126(1)(a)). Likewise void is any requirement that rent must be paid earlier than 6 months before the end of the rental period in respect of which it is payable, if the rental period is more than 6 months (s 126(1)(b)). Rent payments prohibited by s 126 are irrecoverable from the tenant (s 126(3)) who has a right of recovery from the landlord who received the payment, exercisable within two years of the payment concerned (s 126(5)). Any contravention of s 126 is an offence (s 126(4)).

F   MISCELLANEOUS PROVISIONS

I   SUB-TENANCIES

Protection of certain sub-tenants

By s 137(1) of the Rent Act 1977, the determination in proceedings for possession of a head tenancy of a dwelling-house let to a protected or statutory tenant or protected occupier[5] on a statutorily protected tenancy will not automatically determine any lawful sub-tenancy of the whole or any part. By s 137(2), where a head tenancy of a dwelling-house is determined in possession proceedings by the court, any lawful sub-tenant of the dwelling-house or any part is deemed to hold directly from the head landlord on the same terms as if the head statutorily protected tenancy had continued.[6] Generally, by s 137(5), long tenancies at a low rent come within the deeming effect of s 137(2).[7]

Where there is a sub-tenancy of a dwelling-house which forms part only of the premises let as a whole under a superior tenancy which is not

---

5   Within the Rent (Agriculture) Act 1976.
6   'Statutorily protected tenancy' is defined by s 137(4) as meaning: (a) a protected or statutory tenancy under the 1977 Act; (b) a protected occupancy or statutory tenancy under the Rent (Agriculture) Act 1976 and (c) in certain cases, a tenancy of an agricultural holding within the Agricultural Holdings Act 1986.
7   For exceptions to this, see s 137(6).

a statutorily protected tenancy, on termination of that superior tenancy, the sub-tenant will, in principle, retain such protection as s 137 offers him, by the statutory fiction that the dwelling-house subject to the sub-tenancy is deemed to be let separately from the remainder of the premises at a rent equal to the just proportion of the rent under the superior tenancy (s 137(3)). The superior letting must, however, be of a dwelling-house within the 1977 Act, before s 137(3) applies.[8] The notional separate lettings are taken as made to the superior tenant: where the rateable value of one of two such lettings fell within the Rent Acts, a sub-tenant of that letting was protected by this provision.[9]

Further aspects

Section 137(1) protects sub-tenants of Rent Act protected tenants where the court orders possession against the head tenant on one of the discretionary grounds (Sch 15 Part I). If it orders possession on a mandatory ground, s 137(1) has no application, and any sub-tenancy falls with the head tenancy.

Both s 137(1) and (2) imply that, if the head tenant sub-lets the *whole* dwelling-house at a time when he is *statutory* (rather than protected) tenant, then, as the residence requirement of s 2(1) of the 1977 Act is not satisfied, the sub-tenancy cannot be statutorily protected at all and so s 137 will not apply to it.[10] Likewise, the same result follows, where for some other reason, such as the sub-tenant holding under a head tenant who is a resident landlord, there is no protected (sub-) tenancy in the first place.

However, the view has been expressed that, though a sub-letting of the whole dwelling-house causes a statutory tenancy to cease, and the head tenant loses the protection of the 1977 Act, the sub-tenant, if the sub-tenancy is lawful, falls within s 137 in any case, though he is vulnerable to Case 6 of Sch 15 Part I to the 1977 Act.[11] There is much support in dicta for this plausible alternative view.[12] The problem remains that, given

---

8   *Maunsell v Olins* [1975] AC 373, [1975] 1 All ER 16, HL. This does not apply where the superior letting is of an agricultural holding within the 1986 Act (s 137(3)) but the general rule remains intact. See *Pittalis v Grant* (1989) Times, 23 March, CA (head-lease for business purposes; when surrendered, residential sub-lessee of part outside s (137)(3)).

9   *Earl Cadogan v Henthorne* [1956] 3 All ER 851, [1957] 1 WLR 1; also *Legge v Matthews* [1960] 2 QB 37, [1960] 1 All ER 595, CA.

10 *Stanley v Compton* [1951] 1 All ER 859 at 863, CA. The date at which the status of the sub-tenant is decided is that of the determination of the head tenancy: *Jessamine Investment Co v Schwartz* [1978] QB 264, [1976] 3 All ER 521, CA.

11 J Martin *Security of Tenure under the Rent Act* p 125.

12 See *Henry Smith's Charity Trustees v Willson* [1983] QB 316, [1983] 1 All ER 73 at 333 and 87, CA (Ormrod LJ).

that a statutory tenancy is not a proprietary interest, presumably a statutory tenant has nothing to sub-let.[13]

At all events, s 137(2) has the effect that, where the head tenant's protected tenancy is determined, in proceedings based on discretionary grounds, by the landlord, any lawful sub-tenant continues to be 'tenant' under the 1977 Act, and his position must be considered separately. He is still vulnerable to a discretionary order for possession under s 98(1) and Sch 15 Part I.[14] Therefore, if the tenant has gone, the landlord will have to prove any such grounds separately against the sub-tenant. It must be stresed, however, that even if s 137 applies to a sub-tenant, it does not alter the nature of his rights.[15]

Requirement that sub-tenancy must be lawful

No part of s 137 applies unless the sub-tenancy itself is lawful. This matter is by no means free from difficulty, but it imposes a significant limit on the scope of the provision.

A sub-letting in breach of an absolute covenant in the head tenancy is not lawful.[16] If the head tenancy prohibits any sub-letting merely in a fully qualified form, a sub-letting which amounts to a breach, i e to which the landlord could reasonably object, is unlawful. If the covenant is in form absolute and contains a limited exception, it is a matter of construction in the light of the surrounding circumstances whether the sub-letting concerned is lawful, by falling within the exact terms of the exception, or unlawful. For example, an absolute covenant against sub-letting allowed only consensual sub-lettings for a term not exceeding six months in any year: it was held that any sub-lettings apart from these must be unlawful, including a six-month periodic sub-tenancy.[17] Likewise, where sub-lettings of part were absolutely prohibited, except on terms providing for a substantial part of the rent to represent payments for furniture, a sub-letting without sufficient furniture to enable the place to be lived in was unlawful.[18] As part of the surrounding circumstances, the court in one case examined the quality of furniture

---

13 See *Milmo v Carreras* [1946] KB 306, [1946] 1 All ER 288, CA. In *Trustees of Henry Smith's Charity v Willson*, supra, Slade LJ, ibid at 325 and 80, found conflicting provisions in the 1977 Act as to whether a statutory tenant could lawfully sub-let.

14 *Leith Properties Ltd v Springer* [1982] 3 All ER 731 at 736, CA. See passim J Martin [1983] Conv 155.

15 Rent Act 1977 s 138 enables a head landlord (arising under s 137(2)) by notice to avoid, subject to conditions, any obligations of the erstwhile head tenant as furnished landlord and in respect of services.

16 *Oak Property Co Ltd v Chapman* [1947] KB 886, [1947] 2 All ER 1, CA.

17 *Henry Smith's Charity Trustees v Willson* [1983] QB 316, [1983] 1 All ER 73, CA.

18 *Patoner Ltd v Alexandrakis* (1984) 272 Estates Gazette 330, CA.

provided with a view to ascertaining whether it was within a requirement for high-class furnished sub-lettings only.[19]

An initially unlawful sub-letting in breach of covenant could become lawful by the date of the hearing, if the landlord by then has waived the breach. The strict common law doctrine of waiver is not applied in the case of s 137 where the head tenancy is statutory; and so a rent demand on the head tenant for future rent is not necessarily waiver, even if the landlord has full knowledge of the breach, as he has no choice but to accept the rent, owing to the effect of s 3(3) of the 1977 Act, and so the demand is not regarded as unequivocal.[20] Still, if any danger of waiver is to be avoided when making a rent demand, the landlord must make it clear at the time of the demand that it is without prejudice to his right to ask for possession; and he should follow up his demand with a summons for possession within a reasonable time. This is because the question of whether the acts of the landlord amount to a condonation of the absence of consent and an unequivocal affirmation of the sub-tenancy is one of fact.[1] In the case of protected head tenancies, the manner in which waiver is judged, and the requisite degree of knowledge required to be imputed to the landlord, correspond more nearly to those at common law.[2]

Notification of sub-lettings by protected or statutory tenant

If a protected or statutory tenant sub-lets any part of the dwelling-house let under a protected tenancy, he must, under s 139(1) of the 1977 Act, within 14 days of the sub-letting, supply the landlord with a written statement of the sub-letting, giving particulars of the occupancy, including the rent, unless the particulars would be the same as in the last statement supplied with respect to a previous letting.[3]

II DISTRESS

Section 147(1) of the Rent Act 1977 prohibits any distress for rent of any dwelling-house let on a protected or statutory tenancy except with the

---

19 *Patoner Ltd v Lowe* [1985] 2 EGLR 154, CA.
20 *Oak Property Co Ltd v Chapman*, supra; *Henry Smith's Charity Trustees v Willson*, supra.
1 *Oak Property Co v Chapman*, supra.
2 See e g *Metropolitan Properties Ltd v Cordery* (1979) 39 P & CR 10, CA; *Chrisdell Ltd v Johnson* [1987] 2 EGLR 123, CA.
3 For penalties, see Rent Act 1977 s 139(3) and for definitions, s 139(4).

leave of the county court; and, on applications for leave to distrain, the powers of adjournment etc in s 100 are applicable.[4]

III   IMPLIED CONDITION OF ACCESS FOR REPAIRS

It is made on condition of a protected tenancy, under s 148, that the tenant must afford to the landlord access to the dwelling-house and all reasonable facilities for executing therein any repairs which the landlord is entitled to execute. The same condition is implied by s 3(2) in relation to statutory tenancies.

IV   JURISDICTION OF THE COUNTY COURT

Section 141(1) confers on the county court jurisdiction with regard to proceedings relating to a dwelling. The county court is, accordingly, the main forum for Rent Act matters, and s 141(1) lists particular questions over which the county court is to have jurisdiction. These include, for example, the question whether a tenant is protected or statutory and as to the rent limit.[5]

Section 141(3) gives the county court jurisdiction to deal with any claim or other proceedings arising out of any of the provisions listed in s 141(5) even though the amount of such claim would otherwise take it out of the jurisdiction of the court or the court would for some other reason lack jurisdiction. The list in s 141(5) broadly covers most claims under the Rent Act.

G   AGRICULTURAL TIED COTTAGES

I   INTRODUCTION

Occupiers under a tenancy or relevant licence of agricultural tied cottages who are agricultural workers are governed, in principle, by one of two statutory codes.

If the occupation arose under an agreement entered into before the commencement of Part I of the Housing Act 1988, it will be governed by

---

4   An adjournment will be granted if the tenant shows a bona fide dispute as to the amount of rent arrears: *Townsend v Charlton* [1922] 1 KB 700.

5   See *Tingey v Sutton* [1984] 3 All ER 561, [1984] 1 WLR 1154, CA (no power in county court to fix a rent).

the Rent (Agriculture) Act 1976.[6] If the occupation arose under an agreement entered into after such commencement, it will be an assured agricultural occupancy under Chapter III of Part I of the Housing Act 1988 (see Chapter 18). Essentially, this latter form of occupancy is treated as an assured tenancy.

II KEY DEFINITIONS

It is only to protected occupiers that the 1976 Act applies. A protected occupier is, by s 2(1), either a qualifying worker, or a person who has been a qualifying worker at any time during the licence or tenancy. The worker must have been employed in agriculture or forestry, which is defined in s 1. It includes, for example, dairy farming, livestock breeding and keeping, production of consumable produce and using land for grazing. Excluded from this definition was a gamekeeper who reared pheasants for shooting, as the 1976 Act does not contemplate sporting activity.[7] On the other hand, a tenant who used the dwelling-house to run his builder's business did not lose statutory protection automatically.[8]

No worker will qualify for protection unless his occupancy complies with strict rules as to the time worked and as to the nature of his work. He must have worked whole-time in agriculture or as a permit worker, for not less than 91 out of the last 104 weeks (Sch 3 para 1). Certain periods are left out of account and will not reduce the total number of qualifying weeks, such as periods of occupancy but non-work due to incapacity to work at all, or where there is illness or accidental injury (Sch 3 para 2) and also, periods of holiday are left out of reckoning (para 4(4)). It is a requirement that the amount of work done in a given week should be for at least 35 hours in that week (para 12(1)).

Once a person is a qualifying worker, then, in relation to his initial contract of tenancy or licence, he is regarded as a protected occupier in his own right; upon termination of such contract or licence, he automatically becomes a statutory tenant in his own right (s 2(4)) provided that he occupies the dwelling-house as his residence at all material times (s 4(1)).

A single succession to a tenancy or relevant licence is allowed under the 1976 Act.[9] If the original occupier dies after the commencement of Part I of the Housing Act 1988, leaving no surviving spouse, but a family

---

6 Housing Act 1988 s 34(4) – which also contains transitional provisions for the 1976 Act rules. Part I of the 1988 Act commenced on 15 January 1989.
7 *Earl of Normanton v Giles* [1980] 1 All ER 106, [1980] 1 WLR 28, HL.
8 *Durman v Bell* (1988) 20 HLR 340, CA (he might be in breach of Sch 5).
9 1976 Act ss 3 and 4. The rules are to be read as amended, in relation to deaths after the commencement of Part I of the Housing Act 1988, by Sch 4 Part II to that Act.

member who has resided in the dwelling-house for two years before the death, then the succession of the family member is to an assured agricultural occupancy under the 1988 Act.[10]

A statutory tenancy will come into being not only where the original tenancy or licence expires or is terminated, but where a notice of increase of rent is served (s 16); but, succession cannot be avoided by the landlord re-granting a new contractual tenancy or licence to an occupier of the same land or wholly or partly different land (ss 3(4) and 4(4)).

III   SCOPE OF THE 1976 ACT

The 1976 Act applies to any contract under which a protected occupier occupies a dwelling-house exclusively as a separate dwelling; and the contract may be a licence or a tenancy (Sch 2 para 1). If the contract is a licence, it must be for exclusive occupation (para 1). If a tenancy, then certain modifications to the Rent Act 1977 qualifying conditions apply, so that, provided the above general rule is satisfied:

(a)   a tenancy will qualify for protection under the 1976 Act, even if at a rent of less than two-thirds the rateable value of the dwelling-house on the appropriate day; and, self-evidently, though it is of premises comprised in an agricultural holding (para 3(2)); and

(b)   while a tenancy is outside the 1976 Act if it is a bona fide term of it that the landlord provides board or attendance, meals provided in the course of the tenant's employment do not constitute board; and attendance must be substantial for the purposes of the exception (para 3(3)).

Apart from these special qualifications, the basic qualifying condition for protected tenancies laid down in s 1 of the Rent Act 1977, applies to all contracts granted to protected occupiers, whether tenancies or licences.

The 1976 Act rules governing sharing (s 23) are broadly similar to those already outlined earlier in this Chapter in relation to protected tenancies, with some slight modifications.

Certain contracts are outside the 1976 Act because of the nature of the landlord: the relevant rules of the 1977 Act are expressly applied, with slight modifications, by Sch 2 to the 1976 Act.

---

10   Housing Act 1988 Sch 4 Part II para 11, amending 1976 Act s 4. Other amendments to the 1976 Act rules are also in relevant respects identical to those to the 1977 Act succession scheme.

IV RENT AND OTHER TERMS OF THE STATUTORY TENANCY

Rent

The rent of any statutory tenancy may be agreed between the parties (s 11(1)) and an agreement is in fact essential as a prerequisite of any occupier's liability to pay rent. If a rent is registered after an agreement, under Part IV of the Rent Act 1977[11] that rent (calculated as the weekly or other periodical equivalent of the registered rent) is the rent limit (s 11(4)). If the registered rent is more than the actual rent, it may, by a s 14 notice of increase, be increased to that level. If no rent is registered, the rent limit is the weekly or other periodical equivalent of one and a half times the rateable value of the dwelling-house (s 12(9)). The rent may be increased up to this latter limit by a notice of increase (s 12(2)).[12] Rent is payable, under a weekly statutory tenancy, weekly in arrears (s 10(3)).

Other terms

The statutory tenancy starts as soon as the protected occupancy terminates (s 4(1)) and statutory terms apply, set out in Sch 5. If the original contract was a licence, the statutory tenancy is weekly (para 3).

The following are the principal terms, but generally, all burdens and benefits of the original contract continue to apply to the statutory tenancy (para 2).

1 Any services or facilities provided by the landlord but not under the original contract, such as electricity or water supplied from his own installations, must continue to be provided (para 5).
2 Section 11 of the Landlord and Tenant Act 1985 applies (para 6).
3 The tenant may only use the dwelling-house as a private dwelling and cannot assign, sub-let or part with the possession of it (para 7).
4 The tenant must give the landlord a minimum of four weeks' notice to quit where the original contract was a licence or a tenancy which failed to make provision in that regard (para 10).

By agreement, the parties have the right to vary any of the terms of a statutory tenancy (express, implied or statutory). Not variable by this means are certain matters, notably, the application of the 1985 Act, and a substantial addition to the land or premises which the tenant is entitled

---

11 Applied to the 1976 Act by s 13.
12 As with phasing of rent in respect of statutory tenancies under the Rent Act 1977, phasing of rent increases under the 1976 Act (s 15 and Sch 6) was prospectively abolished as from 4 May 1987 by the Rent (Relief from Phasing Order) 1987, SI 1987/264.

to occupy, and agreements as to rent must be in accordance with s 11 (para 12).

V RECOVERY OF POSSESSION

The 1976 Act confers security of tenure in a similar manner to that conferred on protected and statutory tenants by the Rent Act 1977. The landlord of a protected occupier is only able to recover possession on proof of one of a number of statutory grounds (s 6 and Sch 4).

The grounds for possession are, as with the Rent Act 1977, divided into discretionary and mandatory grounds. As with the 1977 Act, in the case of a discretionary ground, the court cannot make an order for possession under the 1976 Act unless it is reasonable to do so (s 7(2)). In those cases the court has a discretionary power to adjourn proceedings (s 7(2A)).[13]

The discretionary grounds (Sch 4 Part I) resemble corresponding Rent Act 1977 grounds.[14] Separate treatment of these is, therefore, not required, though Case III, which relates to breaches of obligation, includes not just breaches of the express terms of the tenancy or licence, but also breaches of statute-implied terms of any statutory tenancy.[15] In the case of the mandatory grounds (Sch 4 Part II) there is, as with the 1977 Act, no overriding discretion in the court to refuse to make an order for possession once a ground is made out by the landlord (s 7(1)). These grounds are: recovery of possession by the landlord as an owner-occupier following a notice to the tenant (Case XI);[16] a retirement ground (Case XII) and an overcrowding ground (Case XIII).

The landlord may also recover possession under a discretionary ground (Case I) where he is able to show that suitable alternative accommodation is available to the tenant. The general requirements as to suitability correspond to those in the Rent Act 1977 Sch 15 Part IV.

Where the landlord wishes to obtain possession of the dwelling-house with a view to housing an employee of his in agriculture, and that person's family, and no other suitable accommodation can be provided by the landlord by reasonable means, he may apply to the relevant

---

13 In any event, the court has a general power to impose conditions and must generally require the payment of rent arrears and payment of future rent (s 7(4)).

14 See Sch 4 Part I Cases III–X. The date as from which the purchase condition for 'reasonably required' owner-occupation (Case IX) is 12 April 1976.

15 See also *Durman v Bell* (1988) 20 HLR 340, CA (significant business user not automatically a breach of Sch 5 implied terms).

16 Under Case XI the landlord must prove that the original occupier was, prior to granting the tenancy, occupying the dwelling-house as his residence and that the dwelling-house is required as a residence for that occupier or a family member resident with him when he last occupied the dwelling-house. There must have been no lettings except under this Case since the date of the first tenancy.

housing authority (usually a local authority) for alternative accommodation to be provided for the occupier under s 27.[17] This applies if the authority ought, in the interests of efficient agriculture, to provide this facility (s 27(1)(c)). The authority may then obtain the advice of an agricultural dwelling advisory committee for the area[18] under s 28. This advice may also be sought and obtained both by the landlord and by the occupier (s 28(3)). If, in due course, following a detailed procedure, which must be carefully followed.[19] the authority decides to provide alternative accommodation, either the present occupier accepts this or the landlord will bring proceedings under Case II of Sch 4 to the 1976 Act. This ground will be satisfied if, in general, either:

(a) the housing authority offered in writing suitable accommodation to the tenant, giving him at least 14 days from the offer to accept it, *or*

(b) the housing authority notified the tenant in writing that they received an offer of suitable accommodation, which the tenant duly accepted in time, *or*

(c) that the landlord shows that no offer was accepted and that this attitude of the tenant's was unreasonable.

Sub-tenants

Sub-tenants are covered by s 9 of the 1976 Act; in general terms, their position corresponds to that for protected or statutory sub-tenants under the Rent Act 1977 s 137 which applies to them (Chap 14). Hence, where a statutory tenancy is terminated for whatever reason, whether or not by an order for possession, a sub-tenant who is lawfully sub-let the dwelling-house or any part thereof, and who qualifies as a protected occupier or statutory tenant, becomes directly the tenant of the landlord on the same terms as the head tenancy (s 9(2)).

H PROTECTED SHORTHOLD TENANCIES

I GENERAL RULES

Old-style shorthold tenancies are the product of the Housing Act 1980 (ss 51–55).[20] The aim of these tenancies, labelled 'protected shorthold

---

17 This provision also applies where the dwelling-house has been let, after the commencement of Part I of the Housing Act 1988, on an assured agricultural occupancy (1988 Act s 26(1)).

18 I e the agricultural wages committee for the area: s 29.

19 *R v Agricultural Dwelling-House Advisory Committee for Bedfordshire, Cambridgeshire and Northamptonshire, ex p Brough* [1987] 1 EGLR 106, where, owing to procedural irregularities, a report was quashed.

20 See passim P F Smith [1982] Conv 29.

tenancies' (PSTs) was to encourage short lettings of residential premises, giving the landlord the right to recover possession mandatorily after expiry of the shorthold tenancy.

After the commencement of Part I of the Housing Act 1988, PSTs were replaced by assured shorthold tenancies (ASTs). This replacement was subject to transitional provisions,[1] but the basic rule is that as from the commencement of Part I of the 1988 Act, any newly-granted shorthold tenancies will necessarily be ASTs. Some treatment of PSTs is still required, as PSTs existing when the 1988 Act was passed are still governed by the old set of rules.

Formalities

A PST is a protected tenancy granted for a term certain of not less than one nor more than five years (s 52(1) of the 1980 Act). The term certain, to qualify as a PST, must be such that, first, it cannot be brought to an end by the landlord before its expiry date except by a provision for forfeiture or re-entry for non-payment of rent or breach of any other obligation of the tenancy (s 52(1)(a)). One reason for this provision is to prevent a landlord from inserting a break clause in the term certain: hence a term entitling the landlord to re-enter in the event of the tenant's bankruptcy was held, on a liberal construction of s 52(1)(a), to fall within 'obligation of the tenancy' and it did not disqualify as a PST.[2]

Secondly, the landlord must, before the grant of the tenancy, give the tenant a notice in the prescribed form[3] stating that the tenancy is to be a PST (s 52(1)(b)).

If the requirement of s 52(1)(a) as to forfeiture and re-entry provisions is not complied with, the tenancy cannot be a PST and is fully protected. If the notice requirement of s 52(1)(b) is not complied with, again the tenancy cannot be a PST and will be protected[4] but, by s 55(2), in proceedings for possession based on Case 19, the court may, if it is just and equitable to do so, treat the protected tenancy as a PST. It seems that this dispensation power cannot be exercised if the landlord, at the time of the letting, had no intention of granting a PST, and in any case all the circumstances, including what the tenant understood he was obtaining at the time of the grant, must be considered.[5]

---

1   Housing Act 1988 s 34(2) and Sch 18, prospectively repealing Housing Act 1980 s 52.
    If a pre-1988 Act PST expires post the 1988 Act, it should be replaced, where relevant,
    by an AST, but a shorthold tenancy granted under a pre-1988 Act contract is a PST
    not an AST.
2   *Paterson v Aggio* [1987] 2 EGLR 127, CA.
3   Protected Shorthold Tenancies (Notice to Tenant) Regulations 1987, SI 1987/267.
4   See *Dibbs v Campbell* (1988) 20 HLR 374, CA (one-year tenancy held a protected
    tenancy for non-compliance with s 52(1) but on facts validly surrendered).
5   Cf *Bradshaw v Baldwin-Wiseman* [1985] 17 HLR 260, CA (Rent Act 1977 Sch 15
    Part II Case 11).

At no time is it possible for a landlord to grant a PST to a tenant if he was, immediately prior to the purported grant, an existing protected or statutory tenant (s 52(2)). This presumably refers to a letting of the same accommodation as before.[6]

PSTs are subject to rent control under the relevant provisions of the Rent Act 1977; but special rules requiring, a registration of, or application for, a fair rent prior to the grant of a PST have been repealed.[7]

If a PST is followed, after its expiry, by a periodic tenancy, the latter is a protected tenancy (s 52(5)) but it will still be possible for the landlord to bring proceedings for possession under Case 19: however, any Case 19 appropriate note must not expire before the periodic tenancy could be brought to an end by a notice to quit served by the landlord on the same day (Sch 15 Part II Case 19(ii)).

II SPECIAL STATUTORY TERMS

Assignments

A shorthold tenancy and also any protected tenancy derived from it of the same dwelling-house cannot be assigned at all (s 54(2)).[8] This means that the total prohibition on assignments applies for the whole period that the landlord would be able to serve a Case 19 notice. It is thought that the prohibition covers only voluntary (e g contractual) assignments and does not apply to invalidate, as against third parties, involuntary assignments such as the death or bankruptcy of the tenant.[9] The prohibition on assignments ends only when either:

(a) no person is in possession as protected or statutory tenant; or
(b) a protected tenancy is granted to a totally new tenant, as opposed to any person who is, immediately before the grant, a protected or statutory tenant of the dwelling-house.

Sub-lettings

There is no statutory prohibition on sub-letting by a shorthold tenant of the whole or any part of the dwelling-house; but, since s 137 of the Rent Act 1977 is excluded in the case of shortholds for the same period as the

---

6 Cf *Gluchowska v Tottenham Borough Council* [1954] 1 QB 438, [1954] 1 All ER 408.
7 Protected Shorthold Tenancies (Rent Registration) Order 1987, SI 1987/265, repealing 1980 Act s 52(1)(c) from 4 May 1987.
8 Save under an order pursuant to Matrimonial Causes Act 1973 s 24.
9 Cf *Re Riggs, ex p Lovell* [1901] 2 KB 16; *Marsh v Gilbert* (1980) 256 Estates Gazette 715.

prohibition on assignments (s 54(1)), if a landlord becomes entitled to possession against the tenant, he becomes entitled also to possession against any sub-tenant, though he will have to take separate proceedings against this latter person.[10]

Termination of shorthold tenancy by tenants' notice

A shorthold tenant has an absolute right, which cannot be contracted out of in the tenancy and cannot be avoided by any term in the tenancy or otherwise, which would impose a penalty or disability on the tenant, if he gives a notice (s 53(2)), to terminate the shorthold term. This is by written notice and the right only applies for as long as the shorthold term itself lasts (s 53(1)). The notice must be of the appropriate length, and its effect is to terminate the shorthold before its due date of expiry and to turn it into a statutory tenancy.[10A] The appropriate length is:

(a) one month if the shorthold term is two years or less; and
(b) three months is it is more than two years in duration (s 53(1)).

III   RECOVERY OF POSSESSION BY THE LANDLORD

The landlord of a shorthold tenant is entitled to recover possession in proceedings, under the mandatory Case 19 in Sch 15 Part II to the Rent Act 1977 (s 55(1) of the 1980 Act). Case 19 applies where either of the following conditions is present:

(a) there has been no grant of a further tenancy of the dwelling-house since the end of the shorthold tenancy; or
(b) if there has been such a grant, it was to a person who was not, immediately before the grant, in possession as protected or statutory tenant.

Further conditions must nonetheless be complied with as a condition precedent to the landlord obtaining possession. The landlord must have served a prescribed warning notice on the tenant before the grant of the protected shorthold tenancy and, where applicable, have complied with any registration of rent requirements, for, if not, the tenancy will not be within Case 19; but, as indicated above, these two requirements may be waived by the county court. Where the initial shorthold term certain expires, and is followed by a periodic tenancy, the latter is a protected tenancy (s 52(5)) not a PST, but, it is still terminable under Case 19. The

---

10   Protection from Eviction Act 1977 ss 1 and 3.
10A *Griffiths v Renfree* (1989) Times, 4 March, CA (tenant still liable for rent, his estranged spouse occupying premises).

same result has been held to follow where, a PST having been granted, the tenant held over under the terms of the original tenancy agreement after it expired – again, the subsequent protected tenancy was subject to Case19.[11]

The landlord must, if he is to obtain possession under Case 19, give at least three months advance notice of his intention to bring proceedings, and also must show that he has served an appropriate notice on the tenant, and begin proceedings not later than three months after its expiry.

Appropriate notice requirements

There are a number of detailed requirements which must be met if a notice is to be appropriate for Case 19 purposes. These are:

(a) it must be in writing and state that after its expiry, Case 19 proceedings may be brought; and

(b) it must expire not earlier than three months after it is served; and

(c) if, at the date of service, the tenancy is periodic, the notice cannot be served to expire any earlier than the periodic tenancy could have been terminated by a common law notice to quit served on the same day.

Not only must the landlord satisfy these complex requirements before he is able to obtain possession: the notice must always be an appropriate notice and it must be served either:

(a) within the three months period immediately before the expiry date of the initial shorthold term; or, if not, then

(b) where the date has passed, within the three months immediately before any anniversary date of such expiry.

One special rule applies to past notices. There is a sort of tacking device: if a previous but lapsed appropriate notice was served by the landlord, a further notice is capable of being subsequently served and of being appropriate for Case 19, if it is served not earlier than three months after the expiry date of the stale and previous notice.

---

11 *Gent v de la Mare* (1987) 20 HLR 199, CA.

Chapter 18

Assured tenancies

A DEFINITION OF ASSURED TENANCY

1 INTRODUCTION

Assured and assured shorthold tenancies were introduced by Part I of
the Housing Act 1988, which came into force two months from the date
on which it was passed.[1]

The general interrelationship between Part I of the Housing Act and
the Rent Act 1977 has been analysed in Chapters 16 and 17, and
reference should also be made to those chapters for a discussion, first, of
the general aims and objects of Part I of the 1988 Act and secondly,
concerning the transitional provisions to implement the new regime.

Old-style assured tenancies converted

Assured tenancies in their present form have replaced the old-style
assured tenancies granted under ss 55–58 of the Housing Act 1980,
which have been repealed.[2] Old-style assured tenancies were governed
by Part II of the Landlord and Tenant Act 1954, so enabling an assured
tenant to apply to the court for a new tenancy. Old-style assured
tenancies in existence at the commencement of Part I of the 1988 Act
were converted, generally, by s 1(3) into new-style assured tenancies.[3]
Until the commencement of the 1988 Act, only approved body landlords
(i e landlords approved by the Secretary of State in regulations), could
grant assured tenancies. This requirement has been totally removed.

---

1 Housing Act 1988 s 141(3). Part I came into force on 15 January 1989, the 1988 Act
   having been passed on 15 November 1988. See Webb (1989) NLJ 252, 288; Kenny
   (1989) 86 LS Gazette No 2, 14, No 5, 19, No 6, 20.
2 Housing Act 1988 s 37(1) and Sch 18.
3 For transitional provisions for tenancies, which were continuing under Part II of the
   1954 Act, where, before the commencment of Part I of the 1988 Act, the tenant applied
   for a new tenancy, see s 37(2). Where a new tenancy is ordered by the court, it is
   deemed to be a new-style assured tenancy (s 37(3)). For further transitional rules for
   pre-1988 contracts see s 37(5).

Any private sector landlord is capable of granting an assured tenancy, whether he is an institution or a private person, unless the landlord lacks capacity under Sch 1 to the 1988 Act.

Independent codes

There are similarities and differences between protected tenancies and assured tenancies, which have been alluded to in Chapter 16. It is thought that the two sets of codes should generally be considered independently of one another: where provisions are similar, as with the scope of the assured tenancies rules, sharing provisions or main exclusions from protection, however, it may well be that similar principles of interpretation would apply to each.

II   BASIC DEFINITIONS

Meaning of assured tenancy

Section 1(1) of the Housing Act (hereafter the '1988 Act') provides that an assured tenancy is a tenancy under which a dwelling-house is let as a separate dwelling, if and so long as two main conditions apply. These are:

(a)   the tenant, or each of the joint tenants (where applicable), is an individual; and

(b)   the tenant or at least one of a number of joint tenants, occupies the dwelling-house as his only or principal home.

Since 'tenancy' includes an agreement for a tenancy (s 45(1)), equitable as well as legal tenancies are capable of being assured. If a tenancy falls within certain categories, listed in Sch 1 and discussed below, it cannot be assured (s 1(1)(c)).

On the meaning of the words 'dwelling-house is let as a separate dwelling', reference should be made to the discussion in Chapter 17 of the same words in s 1 of the Rent Act 1977. It is thought, in the absence of authority, that they should be similarly understood in relation to both codes. The aim of s 1 of the 1988 Act is to confer some protection on most private sector residential tenants, though the motive behind its passing was, unlike the Rent Acts, to free housing for rent, not to give a cast-iron security and rent control to tenants.

Assured tenancies may be granted to and held by, individuals only, and, therefore, if a residential tenancy is granted to a company, it would appear to be outside Part I of the Housing Act 1988 for that reason. Moreover, if a joint tenancy is granted to A, an individual, and B, a company, as joint tenants, it cannot be assured, owing to s 1(1)(a), which requires that *each* joint tenant must be an individual. Whether this will

lead to wholesale avoidance of the 1988 Act is a question to which time
alone will supply the answer.

Cannot be granted to protected/statutory tenants

An assured tenancy cannot be granted to a person who, immediately
before the grant, was a protected or statutory tenant under the Rent Act
1977. It makes no difference that the size of the accommodation offered
under the new tenancy varies from that held under the former tenancy.
The rule applies if the tenancy was granted by a person who, at the date
of the grant, was the landlord (or one of joint landlords) under the
protected or statutory tenancy (s 34(1)(b)). If the grantee (A) was
protected tenant of a house with two others (B & C) jointly, and the
landlord grants A alone a new tenancy, A has, it seems, a protected
tenancy under the Rent Act 1977, not an assured tenancy, owing to the
words of s 34(1)(b) 'alone or jointly with others'.

Sub-tenancies

Since 'tenancy' expressly includes sub-tenancy and 'let' the word 'sub-let'
(s 45(1)), an assured tenancy may exist where a mesne landlord grants a
sub-tenancy to an individual of a house or flat. In this respect, the
position resembles that of the Rent Act 1977. There is a special rule for
sub-tenancies aimed at the problem which arises where a superior
tenancy comes to an end. Under s 18(1) of the 1988 Act, where there is a
lawful assured sub-tenancy,[4] and the landlord is a superior tenant, the
assured sub-tenant will thereafter hold direct from the head landlord.[5]

If the landlord grants a reversionary tenancy to begin on or after the
date a previously periodic or granted statutory periodic tenancy ends or
would by notice to quit end, the reversionary tenancy is subject to the
prior periodic tenancy (s 18(3)). If the landlord grants a tenancy to T2,
knowing that T1's existing fixed-term assured tenancy will be determined, s 18(3) will not render T2's tenancy subject thereto (s 18(4)). This
is because no statutory periodic tenancy arises if the previous fixed-term
tenancy has been determined (s 5(21)).

Where an assured tenant sub-lets part but not the whole dwelling-
house, he does not lose security of any part of the house or flat simply
because the sub-tenant is entitled to share accommodation with the
tenant (s 4(1)). This is without prejudice to the fact that, as against the

---

4   'Lawful' presumably is to be construed as for Rent Act 1977 s 137: see ch 17.
5   If the superior tenant holds from a landlord and the superior tenancy is not assured,
     the sub-tenant is in no better a position than the superior tenant and his interest is not
     statutorily protected against the head landlord: s 18(2).

sub-tenant, the head tenant may well be able to claim that the sub-tenancy is, for example, excluded by s 3A of the Protection from Eviction Act 1977 (s 4(2)).

B SCOPE OF PART I OF 1988 ACT

I GENERAL

The assured tenancies regime applies to residential individual tenants only (s 1(1)).[6] The following points arise.

Tenancy

There must be a tenancy of a dwelling-house, which must be let as a separate dwelling. 'Dwelling-house' may, by s 45(1), be a house or part of a house, thus flats are included within assured tenancies, as are self-contained living units of a house, provided that in neither case the landlord is resident, in which case the tenancy cannot be assured. Subject to what follows, it is thought that similar principles will govern the meaning of the opening words of s 1(1) as apply to those of s 1 of the Rent Act 1977. The same problems where there are mixed user premises, part business, part residential, will presumably affect assured tenancies as affect protected tenancies. Also, genuine non-exclusive licences will lie outside s 1 of the 1988 Act and cannot be assured tenancies, and the lease-licence distinction will continue to be relevant, provided some owners show a continuing wish to avoid tenant protection, even in a more limited form. See Chapter 3.

Post-1988 Act

The tenancy must be granted on or after the commencement of Part I of the 1988 Act, which was 15 January 1989. If it precedes that date, it will either be a protected or statutory tenancy or a restricted contract, in which case various forms of security under the Rent Act 1977 will apply (Chapter 17). In relation to protected or statutory tenants, there is an obvious incentive to landlords to try to evict them, or to persuade them to accept assured tenancies instead of their existing tenancies. To try to head off the dangers posed by this situation, there are penalties on

---

6 A tenancy granted under re-housing arrangements under the Housing Act 1985 by a private landlord is not assured for its first 12 months unless the landlord notifies the tenant to the contrary (s 1(6)). For a special rule where an old-style assured tenancy granted by a fully mutual housing association prior to the commencement of Part I of the 1988 Act, and converted by s 1(3) into a new assured tenancy, see s 1(5), required because, as a rule, such tenancies cannot be assured.

landlords who harass existing protected or statutory tenants (see s 27, discussed in Chapter 19). In addition, as noted, sitting protected or statutory tenants cannot be granted new assured tenancies, even after the commencement of Part I of the 1988 Act, by the person who was landlord under the protected or statutory tenancy (s 34(1)(b)).

Fixed-term and periodic

As with the Rent Act 1977, security under an assured tenancy applies whether the tenancy is fixed-term or periodic. A weekly tenancy is just as much capable of being an assured tenancy as is a lease for a term of 25 years. 'Fixed-term tenancy' for the purposes of the Act means any tenancy other than a periodic tenancy – however short its duration (s 45(1)).

Joint owners

On joint landlords and joint tenants, s 45(3) provides that, in the absence of contrary provisions, any reference to the landlord or tenant is to all joint landlords or tenants. However, an exception to this rule is provided by s 1(1)(b), where only at least one of a number of joint tenants is required to satisfy the condition of occupation of the dwelling-house as his only or principal home. If, therefore, a landlord grants, after the commencement of Part I of the 1988 Act, a tenancy to A, B and C as joint tenants, only one of them needs to occupy the house concerned at any one time, yet A, B and C will all retain security. Moreover, this will be so, even if, say, initially, A is the sole occupier, but later, he leaves, and C occupies. The tenancy remains assured. This is a very generous provision.

Abandonment of residence

Section 1(1)(b) of the 1988 Act provides that a tenancy is assured only if and so long as the tenant or at least one joint tenant occupies the dwelling-house or flat as his only or principal home. With this may be compared the residence requirement for statutory tenants under s 2 of the Rent Act 1977 ('if and so long as he occupies the dwelling-house as his residence'). A complete, irrevocable, abandonment by a single assured tenant or all the joint assured tenants, will enable the landlord to regain possession in proceedings, but the same questions as to what amounts to abandonment of possession and as to what is the 'only or principal home' of the tenant, will arise under assured tenancies as have arisen in other contexts. Some possible guidance may be found by referring to s 81 of the Housing Act 1985, which contains similar requirements. For the sake of simplicity, it is assumed in what follows that an assured tenancy was granted to one single tenant.

In relation to s 81 of the 1985 Act, it has been held that a tenant may have a 'home', even though he is not in actual physical occupation of the premises, provided that there is some sign of occupation, such as the presence of his furniture there.[7] If this were to apply to s 1(1)(b) of the 1988 Act, a tenant with a town house held under an assured tenancy, who spent most of his time in another house, could retain security provided that he thought of his town house as his principal home – assuming, again, that the question is not to be judged solely by reference to the time spent in each house.[8] However, if the landlord could prove that the tenant owned one house or flat where he spent most of his time, and only used the tenanted home, held under an assured tenancy, occasionally, or rarely, or for limited purposes, it is at least arguable that the statutory requirement of occupation as the tenant's 'only or principal home' requires that he should lose security, in contrast to the position of a statutory tenant, where the question whether he occupies the second (tenanted) house as his second home is one of fact and degree.[9]

The position where an assured tenant leaves the house or flat concerned and remains absent for a long time remains to be determined, and it could be that, since, as noted, s 1(1)(b) requires occupation by the tenant of the house as his only or principal home, where he is living away from the rented house in a different house, provided his absence is permanent, it may not be possible to retain security simply by the tenant stating that he intends to return some day, leaving furniture and/or licensees or sub-tenants on the premises.[10] Section 1(1)(b) of the 1988 Act, in contrast to s 2(1)(a) of the Rent Act 1977, refers to the 'only or principal home' of the tenant as the subject-matter of protection. It is submitted, in the absence of authority, that it cannot be the policy of Parliament either to protect two-home tenants, or long-term absentee tenants.

Where an assured tenant leaves the dwelling-house, but his wife continues to reside there, and there are divorce, nullity or judicial separation proceedings, the court has power to transfer the tenancy to the wife.[11]

---

7 *Crawley Borough Council v Sawyer* (1987) 20 HLR 98, CA.
8 Cf *Frost v Feltham* [1981] 1 WLR 452 (income tax).
9 *Hampstead Way Investments Ltd v Lewis-Weare* [1985] 1 All ER 564, [1985] 1 WLR 164, HL.
10 Cf *Brickfield Properties Ltd v Hughes* (1987) 20 HLR 108, CA and see further ch 17.
11 Matrimonial Homes Act 1983 Sch 1, as extended by Housing Act 1988 Sch 17 para 34, which applies also to assured agricultural occupancies.

II   NON-ASSURED TENANCIES: BASIC RULES

General

The following is a list of tenancies which cannot be assured, as specified in Schedule 1 to the Housing Act 1988. In addition to this list, it should be remembered that if a tenancy is held by a company, it is not assured (s (1)(a)). Licences which do not confer exclusive possession and which are genuine, not artificial devices to avoid Part I of the 1988 Act, cannot be assured tenancies (see further Chapter 3).

TENANCIES WHICH CANNOT BE ASSURED TENANCIES

1   Tenancies entered into before the commencement of the Housing Act 1988.
2   Tenancies of dwelling-houses with high rateable values.
3   Tenancies at a low rent.
4   Business tenancies.
5   Tenancies of licensed premises.
6   Tenancies of agricultural land.
7   Tenancies of agricultural holdings.
8   Student lettings.
9   Holiday lettings.
10   Tenancies granted by resident landlords.
11   Crown tenancies.
12   Tenancies granted by local authorities and other bodies.
13   Transitional cases.

Some of these exceptions are familiar, as they appear in the Rent Act 1977; some are not. Before dealing with the details of each exception, the question of tenancies granted after the commencement of Part I of the 1988 Act which are not assured or assured shorthold tenancies must be considered.

Non-assured tenancies – status

A tenancy granted after the commencement of Part I of the 1988 Act which is within one of the above exclusions cannot be assured or assured shorthold. Unlike the position with the Rent Act 1977, which attaches the label 'restricted contract' to some, but not all, non-protected tenancies, there is no special label given in the 1988 Act to tenancies within Sch 1 to the 1988 Act. The protection offered to such tenants is very minimal indeed. Section 3 of the Protection from Eviction Act 1977 will, in principle, apply to the tenant.[12] The effect of s 3 is discussed in Chapter 19: broadly, it requires the landlord to enforce his right to recover possession in court proceedings. On the other hand, in such proceedings, no grounds for possession will need to be made out: determination of the tenancy at common law, by forfeiture, if fixed-term, or a sufficient notice to quit, if periodic, must be shown. The minimum length of a notice to quit must be four weeks, since s 5 of the Protection from Eviction Act 1977 will apply. Unlike restricted contracts under the Rent Act 1977, however, there is no control of the rent payable. A tenant excluded by Sch 1 to the 1988 Act from assured status is also entitled to statutory protection against unlawful eviction and harassment[13] and to remedies in contract and tort.

Excluded tenancies

Where a tenancy which is not an assured tenancy, as where it is granted by a resident landlord, is also an excluded tenancy, neither s 3 nor s 5 of the Protection from Eviction Act 1977 applies (1988 Act, s 30(1) and 32(2)), and the tenant (or occupier) is protected under the criminal law, as forcible evictions are an offence.[14]

The tenant will also have civil redress, under s 1 of the Protection from Eviction Act 1977, as an excluded tenancy is not excluded from that provision; and he may be able to claim in contract or tort for breach of the implied covenant for quiet enjoyment or trespass or nuisance, as the case may be.

What he cannot do, is to claim security of tenure. Excluded tenancy is defined by s 3A of the 1977 Act.[15] The intention of s 3A is to enable an owner to let off (or licence) rooms in his home, and, provided any part of the accommodation is shared with, for example, the landlord/owner, he may enforce his right to recover possession without proceedings.

C TENANCIES WHICH CANNOT BE ASSURED TENANCIES

I GENERAL

Detailed provisions are made by Sch 1 to the Housing Act 1988 with regard to tenancies excluded from being assured. In some cases, the

---

12 Owing to Protection from Eviction Act 1977 s 8(e), added by Housing Act 1988 s 33(2). As a Sch 1 tenancy is not, therefore, statutorily protected, it falls within s 3 of the 1977 Act, unless it is excluded, qv.
13 Protection from Eviction Act 1977 s 1 (ch 19).
14 Criminal Law Act 1977 s 6.
15 Added by Housing Act 1988 s 31. See further Chapter 19.

exceptions are clearly based on Rent Act 1977 exceptions, as with tenancies at a low rent, business tenancies, and tenancies granted by resident landlords, and where this is so, similar principles of interpretation would appear to apply under the 1988 Act as apply under the 1977 Act (Chapter 17).

Under the 1988 Act, tenancy includes sub-tenancy (see s 45(1)) so that, if a sub-tenant is granted a tenancy by a tenant who is not assured, because he holds from the Crown, for example, there would appear to be no reason why the sub-tenancy should not, as against the superior tenancy, be assured, even though, because of s 18(2), on determination of the superior tenancy, the sub-tenant loses all further security under the 1988 Act.

II SHARING PROVISIONS

Where a tenant holds some accommodation separately and, under the tenancy, some in common with other persons, not being or including the landlord, the separate accommodation is deemed to be held on an assured tenancy, and terms modifying his use of the shared accommodation are of no effect (s 3(1) and (3)). This rule is akin to s 22 of the 1977 Act and reference should be made to Chapter 17 accordingly. Very different principles apply where the tenant shares accommodation with the landlord or a member of his family: in that case, the tenancy is not assured and may be excluded in addition, see below.

III THE EXCLUSIONS

(a) Pre-commencement tenancies

A tenancy which was entered into before, or under a contract made before Part I of the 1988 Act came into force, which was on 15 January 1989, cannot be an assured tenancy.[16] This exclusion emphasises the fact that until the commencement of the 1988 Act Part I, no assured tenancies may be granted and the Rent Act 1977 and associated rules will continue to apply to pre-1988 Act protected or statutory tenancies. However, succession is treated differently from grant: a family member who becomes entitled to succeed to a statutory tenancy after the 1988 Act Part I is in force, succeeds to an assured tenancy: see Chapter 17.

---

16 Housing Act 1988 Sch 1 para 1.

(b) Dwelling-houses with high rateable values

A tenancy cannot be an assured tenancy if the rateable value for the time being of the dwelling-house exceeds £1,500 if the house is in Greater London or £750 if it is elsewhere.[17] There is no statutory presumption that a dwelling-house falls within these limits – unlike with the Rent Act 1977, s 4(3).[18]

(c) Tenancies at a low rent

Tenancies under which either no rent is payable or the rent payable is less than two-thirds of the rateable value of the dwelling-house for the time being are not assured.[19]

(d) Business tenancies

A tenancy to which Part II of the Landlord and Tenant Act 1954 applies cannot be an assured tenancy.[20]

No guidance is given in the 1988 Act as to determining whether a mixed residential and business user tenancy is assured or within Part II of the 1954 Act. It is thought, because the present exclusion resembles Rent Act 1977 s 24(3), that similar considerations would apply here as apply to protected tenancies: please refer to the discussion in Chapter 17.

Presumably, as with the Rent Act 1977, if an assured tenant sub-lets part of the premises wholly for business purposes, the sub-tenancy is not protected by the 1988 Act *vis-à-vis* the head tenant.

(e) Licensed premises

A tenancy under which the dwelling-house consists of or includes premises licensed for the sale of intoxicating liquors for consumption on the premises cannot be assured.[1]

(f) Tenancies of agricultural land

A tenancy under which agricultural land, exceeding two acres, is let together with the dwelling-house cannot be an assured tenancy.[2]

---

17 Sch 1 para 2. Rateable values are to be ascertained under Sch I Part II: para 15 of which is akin to Rent Act 1977 s 25, but the appropriate day base for ascertainment of RVs has gone.

18 Note that Local Government Finance Act 1988 s 119 confers on the Secretary of State a regulatory power to delete references in legislation to rateable value limits. This is owing to the introduction of the community charge. Future limits will, it seems, be fixed by reference to rental value limits.

19 Sch 1 para 3(1). The computation of a low rent is in accordance with para 3(2), which corresponds to Rent Act 1977 s 5(4).

20 1988 Act Sch 1 para 4.

1   1988 Act Sch 1 para 5.

2   Ibid, para 6(1). 'Agricultural land' is as defined by s 26(3)(a) of the General Rate Act 1967.

This exclusion must be read with s 2(1) of the 1988 Act,[3] under which, where a dwelling-house is let together with[4] other land:

(a)   if and so long as the main purpose of the letting is the provision of a home for the tenant (or at least one of a number of joint tenants) the other land is treated as part of the dwelling-house;

(b)   if and so long as the main purpose of the letting is not the provision of a home as above, the tenancy is not assured.

Therefore, if agricultural land exceeding two acres is let together with a dwelling-house, the tenancy cannot in any event be assured. If a dwelling-house is let together with other land, as an adjunct to the house, the tenancy will be assured only if and so long as the purpose of the letting is the provision of a home for the tenant or at least one joint tenant. In that case, the land is treated as part of the house (s 2(1)(a)). If the purpose of the tenancy is not to provide a home as above, the tenancy cannot be assured (s 2(a)(b)), as where a dwelling-house and land are let for non-residential purposes. This may require the court to discover the purpose of the tenancy from the terms of the lease, or, if this is not possible, from the intentions of the parties and the circumstances at the date of the tenancy. Unlike s 26(1) of the Rent Act 1977, there is no presumption that agricultural land under 2 acres let with a dwelling-house is within the 1988 Act. If the letting is mainly for residential purposes, the tenancy will be assured even though subsidiary agricultural activities are carried out on the land. If residential occupation is abandoned, during the tenancy, since the residence condition of s 1(1) will not be complied with, the tenancy will cease to be assured.

(g)   Tenancies of agricultural holdings

A tenancy under which a dwelling-house is comprised in an agricultural holding as defined in the Agricultural Holdings Act 1986 cannot be an assured tenancy if the dwelling-house is occupied by the person responsible for the control (as tenant, servant or agent of the tenant) of the farming of the holding.[5]

Tenancies of agricultural holdings are protected by the 1986 Act, which is why they cannot be assured. Tenants of tied cottages whose tenancies are granted on or after the commencement of the 1988 Act are assured agricultural occupancies – a variant of assured tenancies (see later in this Chapter).

---

3   Which is subject to Sch 1 para 6 above.
4   This expression presumably has the same meaning as in ss 6 and 26 of the Rent Act 1977.
5   Sch 1 para 7. Cf Rent Act 1977 s 10.

(h) Lettings to students

A tenancy granted to a person following or intending to follow a course of study provided by a specified educational institution, granted by that institution or by another specified institution or body cannot be assured.[6] This exclusion corresponds to s 8 of the Rent Act 1977.

If a specified, or any other, landlord lets out of term time, he will be able to recover possession from any assured tenants under a mandatory ground, provided the landlord complies with a notice requirement and the tenancy is for a fixed-term not exceeding 12 months.[7]

(i) Holiday lettings

A tenancy whose purpose is to confer on the tenant the right to occupy the dwelling-house for a holiday is not an assured tenancy.[8] This exclusion corresponds to s 9 of the Rent Act 1977.

Where the landlord lets off-season, he may recover possession mandatorily from any assured tenants,[9] provided he complies with a notice requirement and the letting is for a term certain not exceeding eight months. A holiday letting is an excluded tenancy (s 3A(7)).[10]

Since the terms of the holiday lettings exclusion are the same as those used in s 9 of the Rent Act 1977, which applies to protected tenancies, please refer to the discussion of s 9 in Chapter 17, which, in the absence of authority, would appear to apply to the 1988 Act rules.

(j) Resident landlords

A tenancy granted by a resident landlord cannot be an assured tenancy.[11] Certain conditions must, however, be complied with: if not, the tenancy will be assured.

The conditions are in most respects identical to those which apply under s 12 of the Rent Act 1977, and similar rules to those in Sch 2 to the 1977 Act apply where the resident landlord sells his reversion to another person, or where, following the death of a resident landlord, his executors sell the reversion to a third party.[12]

Accordingly, reference should be made to the discussion in Chapter 17 of s 12 and Sch 2 to the 1977 Act, which applies to the present exception, subject to the modifications below, and to its construction. This is

---

6 Sch 1 para 8(1). See Assured and Protected Tenancies etc Regulations 1988 SI 1988/2236.
7 Sch 2 Part I ground 4.
8 Sch 1 para 9.
9 Sch 2 Part I ground 3.
10 Protection from Eviction Act 1987 s 3A(7) added by 1988 Act s 31.
11 Sch 1 para 10.
12 Sch 1 Part III. The relevant disregard periods are the same as for the Rent Act 1977.

particularly so, it is thought, with regard to the meaning of the word 'building'; and the operation in law of the statutory disregard periods (which are the same in length as for s 12 of the 1977 Act).

Some detailed rules under the present exception differ from the position under the Rent Act 1977.

1 In the first place, the resident landlord, described as an 'individual', must occupy the house or flat concerned as his only or principal home at the time the tenancy was granted.[13] If the landlord has another house where he resides permanently, it may be impossible for him to claim that, for the purposes of the exception, a convenience residence on occasions in the house or flat concerned is sufficient – in which case, since the condition is not complied with, the tenancy will be assured. If he has two residences and divides his time between the two, it will presumably be a question of fact and degree, whether the residence in the tenanted premises is in his 'only or principal home' for the purposes of this exemption: if it is not, then any tenancies he grants of the latter premises will be assured.

2 The rule for joint tenants is that if the reversion is held by two or more persons as joint tenants, only any one of them need satisfy the residence requirement at the date of the grant of the tenancy.[14] The same applies to the requirement that the landlord must be a resident landlord throughout: it needs only to be satisfied by any one of a number of joint landlords. If A and B are joint landlords and A is resident in the statutory sense at the date of the grant of a tenancy to X and later B becomes resident and A leaves, the tenancy remains non-assured because the residence requirement at the date of the grant was satisfied by A and later by B.

3 Where a resident landlord dies and the executors vest the reversion within the two-year period in a further resident landlord, where the landlord is a joint landlord, of whom at least one must be an individual, the tenancy is not assured provided that at least one of the joint landlords occupies the house or flat as his only or principal home.[15]

4 Where the reversion is held on trust for sale, while disregard periods apply during the occupation of a beneficiary, occupation by any one of a number of beneficiaries will qualify. If an occupying beneficiary dies, a two-year period of disregard runs from the date of his death until another beneficiary occupies, during which time the tenancy is not assured.[16]

---

13 As opposed to 'as his residence' in s 12(1)(b) of the 1977 Act.
14 Sch 1 para 10(2).
15 Sch 1 Part III para 17(1) and (2).
16 Sch 1 para 18(1)(2).

Further, where a tenancy falls within the resident landlord exemption, it may also be an excluded tenancy. If the landlord or a member of his family shares accommodation (i e use it in common) with the tenant, then the tenancy may be excluded, as to which see Chapter 19. Sharing of a kitchen will suffice. Sharing of storage areas, or a staircase, passage or corridor, is insufficient.[17] Where a flat is occupied by a resident landlord and tenant, it will commonly be an excluded tenancy and also not assured; where different self-contained accommodation in the same building is so occupied, the tenancy will simply not be assured.

The difference is that, where a tenancy is within the first category, neither ss 3 nor 5 of the Protection from Eviction Act 1977 will apply to it; but where it is within the second category, those provisions will apply. However, in neither case will the tenant have any security of tenure, nor will he be able to refer the rent.

(k) Crown tenancies

Tenancies under which the interest of the landlord belongs to the Crown or to a government department or is held in trust for the Crown by a government department cannot be assured tenancies. If the interest of the Crown is managed by the Crown Estate Commissioners, the tenancy may be assured.[18] This is akin to s 13 of the Rent Act 1977.

(l) Local authority etc tenancies

Tenancies granted by the following landlords cannot be assured: local authorities,[19] the Commission for the New Towns, the Development Board for Rural Wales, an urban development corporation, a development corporation, waste disposal authorities, a residuary body, a fully mutual housing association and a housing action trust established by Part III of the Housing Act 1988.[20]

(m) Transitional cases

The following are necessarily excluded from being assured tenancies: protected tenancies within the Rent Act 1977, a housing association tenancy within Part VI of that Act, a secure tenancy and a relevant tenancy of a protected occupier within the Rent (Agriculture) Act 1976.[1]

---

17 Protection from Eviction Act 1977 s 3A (added by Housing Act 1988 s 31).
18 Sch 1 para 11.
19 As listed in Sch 1 para 12(2).
20 Sch 1 para 12(1).
 1 Sch 1 para 13.

D SECURITY OF TENURE: GENERAL PRINCIPLES

I INTRODUCTION

General

The security of tenure regime applicable to assured tenancies, whether fixed-term or periodic, is new as respects the methods of termination, but, as with the Rent Act 1977, an assured tenancy is determinable only by a court order, and to obtain a court order the landlord must prove one or more grounds for possession (s 7(1)). For these purposes the court is to be the county court (s 40). The rules presuppose that the tenancy, fixed-term or periodic, has expired or been validly determined by forfeiture (or other method of determination) or notice to quit, as the case may be.

Some grounds for possession are mandatory and some discretionary, as with the Rent Act 1977. A novel feature of assured tenancies is that a new mandatory ground for possession on the landlord's proving an intention to redevelop is given, which corresponds, broadly, to s 30(1)(f) of the Landlord and Tenant Act 1954.

The procedures depend on the fact, in the main, that, where an assured tenancy is fixed-term, after it expires, or is determined, a statutorily implied periodic tenancy arises, on terms governed by the 1988 Act, and this may be terminated by the court on various grounds.

In the case of an assured shorthold tenancy, which is considered later in this Chapter, the landlord may if he so wishes, seek possession on one or more of the grounds for possession, which apply to all assured tenancies, but there is a specific termination procedure for assured shorthold tenancies. No doubt, this will be the principal route for termination in this instance.

Forfeiture

By s 7(6)(a), forfeiture, re-entry or termination by notice of a fixed-term assured tenancy is only effective in three sets of circumstances. This is because the court cannot make an order for possession of a dwelling-house to take effect at a time when it is let on an assured fixed-term tenancy, except where the landlord:-

(a) is within one of the discretionary grounds for possession:[2]

---

2 Except where the ground is suitable alternative accommodation (ground 9) or an employee ground (ground 16).

(b)   is a mortgagee seeking possession; or he proves –
(c)   that there are serious rent arrears.[3]

Where any of the three above matters apply, forfeiture, re-entry etc. is the first step only to obtaining an order for possession, as, once the fixed-term tenancy has been forfeited, by s 5(2) the tenant is entitled to retain possession under a statute-implied periodic tenancy, determinable only on proof of one or more of a number of statutory grounds. Where the landlord seeks possession on a mandatory ground, other than those relating to mortgagees and serious rent arrears, a fixed-term tenancy cannot be determined by forfeiture. Only after its expiry will the landlord be able to seek possession on a mandatory ground (s 7(7)). Any statute-implied periodic tenancy then expires on the day the order takes effect. Moreover, the court cannot order possession, even where forfeiture may ultimately lead to an order for possession, unless the terms of the tenancy make provision for termination on the ground in question, by forfeiture or otherwise (s 7(6)(b)).

An assured fixed-term tenancy may be ended by exercise of a landlord's express power to do so, as with a break-clause allowing for redevelopment. In that event, a statutory periodic tenancy arises under s 5(2) and this is only determinable on proof of a relevant ground for possession.

Periodic tenancies – general

A periodic assured tenancy, including a periodic tenancy following a fixed-term tenancy which has expired or been validly determined, may be terminated on various grounds, both mandatory and discretionary but only by a court order (ss 5(2) and 7(1)). The service of a landlords', but not a tenants', notice to quit is of no effect (s 5(1)). What the landlord must do, as a condition precedent to seeking re-possession, is to comply with the notice procedure laid down by s 8.[4] It should be remembered that a periodic assured tenancy arises under s 5 only after a fixed-term assured tenancy comes to an end. An order of court puts an end to a statute-implied periodic tenancy (s 7(7)).

In the case of fixed term and periodic tenancies, no proceedings for possession may, in addition, be entertained, unless the landlord has served on the tenant a prescribed form notice under s 8. However, in the case of a s 8 notice served during a fixed-term tenancy, this is valid also for the statute-implied periodic tenancy arising under s 5 (s 8(6)).

---

3   These last two grounds are mandatory grounds for possession, qv.
4   For forms etc, see Assured Tenancies and Agricultural Occupancies (Forms) Regulations 1988, SI 1988/2203.

II   SECURITY FOR FIXED-TERM TENANTS

Surrender etc by tenant

An assured fixed-term tenancy may be ended by the tenant surrendering it, or by 'some other action' of his, by s 5(2)(b). In that case, no security in the form of a statute-implied periodic tenancy arises. It is clear that surrender includes both express surrender and implied surrender, such as an abandonment of possession for a long time in such circumstances that it is clear that the tenant never intends to return.[5] 'Other action' of the tenant is not so clear, but it presumably is intended to cover cases of abandonment of the dwelling-house or flat which fall short of what might be required to establish surrender. In either event, the tenant loses security under the 1988 Act. The landlord will not have to prove a ground for possession in this instance.

Security on termination

An assured fixed-term tenancy cannot be brought to an end by the landlord except by obtaining an order of the court under Sch 2 (s 5(1)), but if the tenancy is an assured shorthold tenancy, there is a specific means of regaining possession (s 21). In the case of assured tenancies, the court is only entitled to order possession on certain grounds (s 7(1)). As will be seen, these are either mandatory or discretionary. If a mortgagee brings proceedings for possession, the statutory restrictions do not apply, if the mortgagee lent money on the security of an assured tenancy (s 7(1)).[6]

In the case of a fixed-term tenancy, if the tenancy contains a power in the landlord to determine the tenancy in certain circumstances, this will, if properly exercised, bring the assured fixed-term tenancy to an end (s 5(1)). The tenant will be entitled to remain in possession, at least for the time being, under the statute-implied periodic tenancy which arises automatically after the determination of an assured fixed-term tenancy (s 5(2)). Also, since the landlord cannot enforce his right to possession except by obtaining a court order, the tenant has security unless or until such an order is made, because if a fixed-term tenancy is forfeited, a statute-implied periodic tenancy arises automatically, determinable on statutory grounds only. If the landlord's power to determine is exercisable on the ground of redevelopment, for example, its exercise at

---

5   Cf *Preston Borough Council v Fairclough* (1982) 8 HLR 70, CA.
6   Where the mortgage was granted before the beginning of an assured tenancy, the restrictions will apply but the mortgagee will be entitled to invoke mandatory ground 2 of Sch 2.

common law would be the first step to regaining possession, as the landlord will then need to invoke ground 6 in Sch 2.

Limits where fixed-term tenancy not expired

The court cannot generally make an order for possession to take effect at a time when the dwelling-house is let on an assured fixed-term tenancy which has not expired by effluxion of time or been forfeited or determined at common law (s 7(6)). There are exceptions to this rule, as to which, see above. The whole object is to give an assured tenant security, by requiring the landlord to prove statutory grounds as a condition precedent of obtaining possession.

In cases of, for example, re-possession proceedings for serious rent arrears and for most other discretionary grounds,[7] the landlord is entitled to bring possession proceedings based on a s 8 notice (see below) under the 1988 Act, even though the fixed-term tenancy has not expired by effluxion of time. In such cases, the landlord must, if the tenancy had some years to run, first re-enter, or forfeit at common law and then proceed under the 1988 Act.

If the matter falls outside the above discretionary grounds, and is covered by most mandatory grounds,[8] such as the landlord wishing to redevelop the premises, his wishing personally to re-occupy them, or the bankruptcy of the tenant, to take three examples, he will, to obtain possession, first have to await the expiry of the tenancy or validly determine the tenancy at common law under an express power, which he may well not be entitled to do if there is no breach of obligation complained of. He will also have to serve a s 8 notice, during the fixed-term tenancy or after it, on the tenant, and prove the ground concerned. In due course, the court may order the ending of the statute-implied periodic tenancy which will then arise, if the landlord's case is made out. There is nothing expressly in s 7(6) to prevent the court from ordering possession on a mandatory ground other than ground 2 or 8, where the fixed-term tenancy has not expired, but the order cannot take effect until after the date the tenancy expires.

Powers of court

The court has power to order possession of a dwelling-house or flat on grounds which relate to an assured fixed-term tenancy which has ended, and the effect of an order for possession is also to determine the statute-implied periodic tenancy on the day specified in the court's order. No further notice will be required in such a case (s 7(7)). Moreover, any s 8

---

7   Except suitable alternative accommodation and the employee ground, see above.
8   Except, as noted, re-possession by mortgagees or serious rent arrears.

notice served by the landlord during the fixed-term tenancy has effect for any statute-implied periodic tenancy (s 8(6)). The grounds for possession are in Sch 2, and are discussed when dealing with periodic tenancies, as are the terms of s 8. Obviously, a landlord seeking possession from a tenant under a fixed-term tenancy which has expired or otherwise been determined must prove one or more discretionary or mandatory grounds for possession, and must fully comply with s 8 as to notices, and the court's discretionary adjournment powers in s 9 apply.

Statute-implied periodic tenancy

Once a statutory periodic tenancy has arisen, which, as was said, automatically takes place after termination for whatever reason of the fixed-term tenancy, it is only terminable by an order of court (s 5(1) and (2)). A surrender or other action by the tenant prevents a statute-implied fixed-term tenancy from arising. Also, no statute-implied periodic tenancy arises if the tenant is granted a new tenancy, fixed-term or periodic, of the same or substantially the same dwelling-house[9] as was let to him under the previous fixed-term tenancy (s 5(4)). On expiry or determination of the further tenancy, whether fixed-term or periodic, a statute-implied tenancy comes into being under s 5(2). The effect of s 5 cannot be avoided by means of undated surrenders, actual surrenders entered into before the statute-implied tenancy comes into being, or by any other means (s 5(5)).

The terms of the statute-implied periodic tenancy, which may only be determined by the court on proof by the landlord of one or more statutory grounds, are as follows, by s 5(3):

(a)   it takes effect immediately on the coming to an end of the fixed-term tenancy;

(b)   it is deemed to have been granted by the person who was landlord under the fixed-term tenancy immediately before it came to an end, to the tenant under that tenancy;

(c)   the premises let are the same as under the fixed-term tenancy;

(d)   the periods of the tenancy are those for which rent was paid under the fixed-term tenancy;

(e)   the other terms are the same as those of the fixed-term tenancy immediately before it came to an end.[10] While the tenancy remains

---

9   'Substantially': presumably this allows for minor modifications to the extent of the accommodation offered, as where the tenant has no use for an attic room or part of his garden. Cf *Mykolyshyn v Noah* [1971] 1 All ER 48, [1970] 1 WLR 1217, CA.

10   If these have been varied by agreement during the fixed-term tenancy, it will be the terms as varied, not originally granted, which will be the initial terms of the statutory periodic tenancy.

assured, provisions for determination by the landlord will have no effect.

Regarding para (a), it is similar in effect to continuation under s 24(1) of the Landlord and Tenant Act 1954. The effect of s 5 is automatic, and cannot be contracted out of (s 5(5)). A statute-implied periodic tenancy can only be ended by order of the court. No provision is made in s 5 for an interim rent. The terms above discussed may be varied under s 6 or, in the case of rent, raised under s 13.

For the sake of convenience, the terms of s 6 are here discussed. The landlord has one year, running from the first anniversary of the day when the former tenancy ended, to serve a s 6 notice on the tenant, proposing new terms. If he lets this date slip, he cannot propose such variations at all, and the terms as laid down by s 5 will apply.

It is not clear from s 5 whether personal covenants in the original fixed-term tenancy will survive into the statute-implied periodic tenancy. While s 5(3)(e) is apparently general ('the other terms'), it is possible that personal covenants may survive into the statute-implied periodic tenancy.[11] Certainly, if the landlord was, under the fixed-term tenancy, under the statute-implied obligation to repair under s 11 of the Landlord and Tenant Act 1985, this will be carried forward into the statutory periodic tenancy.

Alteration of implied terms

This is governed by s 6, which applies also to rent in so far as an alteration in the rent is necessitated by an adjustment in the terms, but rents are mainly governed by s 13, as to which, see below.

Section 6 only applies where a fixed-term tenancy is followed by a statutorily arising periodic tenancy (s 6(1)(a)), and it enables either landlord or tenant to propose new terms for the tenancy. The landlord or the tenant may propose terms by a notice served on the other party; the notice must be in the prescribed form;[12] the terms referred to in the notice are different terms to the terms implied by s 5 above (s 6(2)). Crucially, the notice must be served not later than the first aniversary of the day the former tenancy came to an end (s 6(2)). If the party serving the notice considers it appropriate, he may also propose an 'adjustment' of the rent to take account of the proposed terms (s 6(2)).

After an alteration notice, as one might call it, has been served by the landlord or tenant, the party receiving it has three months as from the date of service in which to refer the notice to a rent assessment

---

11 Cf *Engvall v Ideal Flats* [1945] KB 205, [1945] 1 All ER 230, CA.
12 Assured Tenancies and Agricultural Occupancies (Forms) Regulations 1988, SI 1988/2203.

committee – in a prescribed form (s 6(3)(a)). A referral must be made
within this time. If it is not, then the terms proposed in the notice become
the terms of the tenancy in substitution for any implied terms dealing
with the same subject-matter, and the rent is to be varied in accordance
with any adjustment proposed in the notice. This takes effect from such
date as is specified in the notice, which cannot be any sooner than the
three-month period allowed for a referral to a rent assessment committee
(s 6(3)(b)).[13] The idea of the three-month period may be to give the
parties time for negotiations. If so, the tenant could fall into a trap. If he
fails to refer his notice in time, he will be bound by what the landlord
originally proposed, if the parties fail to agree on new terms – in the
absence, possibly, of waiver or estoppel.

These provisions may be quite drastic in their effect. If neither party
serves a notice in the prescribed form proposing different terms to those
implied by s 5, within one year of the day the fixed-term tenancy ends,
then no notice may ever be served and the statute-implied terms take
effect for the rest of the life of the periodic tenancy. The rent may still be
increased, it would appear, under s 13, owing to s 13(1)(a). If a party on
whom a notice is served fails, within the three month period for referral,
to refer it to a rent assessment committee, he has to accept the proposed
new terms, however harsh these may be. So, if the landlord proposes in a
notice that the tenant will cease to have the use of a particular room, or
will pay rent at more frequent intervals than under the current tenancy,
and the tenant fails to refer the notice (assuming the parties fail to agree),
he will be bound by those terms.

Nothing is said in s 6 as to what is to happen if a notice is served on the
tenant (or the landlord) which is not in the prescribed form and the
tenant refers it, or accepts it. The answer may possibly lie in analogies
with business tenancies, so that if a party accepts an otherwise invalid
notice, he may have waived his right to ignore it for formal invalidity.[14]
Presumably a tenant served with a notice not in the prescribed form is
entitled to ignore it.[15]

Duty of rent assessment committee

Where a notice is referred within the three-month period above, the
committee have various powers on a reference (s 41). They must
consider the terms proposed in the notice and decide whether the terms,

---

13   It may be taken that if a landlord or tenant proposes more than one new term, the start
     date for the new terms must be the same, not different dates for each term.
14   Cf *Morrow v Nadeem* [1987] 1 All ER 237, [1986] 1 WLR 1381, CA. In this case,
     however, a prescribed form was used, with an error.
15   S 6 does not, in contrast to Landlord and Tenant Act 1954 s 25(1), allow for a notice
     to be valid which is substantially to the same effect as a notice in exactly the prescribed
     form. This omission may have been deliberate.

or some other terms, dealing with the same subject-matter, are such as, in their opinion, 'might reasonably be expected to be found in an assured periodic tenancy of the dwelling-house' (s 6(4)). The assumptions which must be made are that the tenancy begins as from the ending of the former fixed-term tenancy; and that it is granted by a willing landlord on the same terms as those implied by s 5 except in relation to the matters covered by the proposed terms (s 6(4)). The committee must also, whether or not the notice proposes rent adjustments, specify any adjustment in the rent where they determine new terms, if they consider this appropriate (s 6(5)). In adjusting the rent, the effect of there being a sitting tenant is to be disregarded (s 6(6)).

The terms determined by the committee, after a referral which is not withdrawn (by joint written notice (s 6(8)) become the terms of the statutory periodic tenancy in substitution for s 5 terms dealing with the same matter; the rent is adjusted accordingly. This operates as from whatever date the committee direct but they cannot direct a date earlier than that originally specified in the landlord's or tenant's notice for new terms to start (s 6(7)).

III SECURITY FOR PERIODIC TENANTS

In what follows, security provisions which apply to assured periodic tenants are examined, together with all provisions common both to assured periodic and fixed-term tenancies.

Basic rules

The basic security rule for periodic tenants is the same as for fixed-term tenants. By s 5(1), an assured periodic tenancy may only be brought to an end by the landlord obtaining an order of court, on proof of grounds (s 7 – see further below).

An assured periodic tenancy cannot be effectually determined by a common-law notice to quit, and under s 5 it will continue, unless and until it is determined in proceedings by the court, and the landlord must accordingly comply with the s 8 procedure. The rent may be increased under s 13, as to which see below.

Notice procedure

A special notice procedure (s 8) – an essential preliminary without which no possession proceedings can be entertained by the court – applies both to periodic tenancies, and to fixed-term tenancies and statute-implied periodic tenancies following them. If a s 8 notice is served when the dwelling-house is let on a fixed-term tenancy, or in relation to events occurring during an expired fixed-term tenancy, it is effective even though the tenant holds or held under a statutory periodic tenancy (s 8(6)). This is no doubt to save the landlord the necessity of serving two notices. The s 8 notice must be in the prescribed form – not, it is thought, some version nearly or approximately corresponding thereto.[15A] If s 8 is not followed, and no notice is served, or it is not served in the prescribed form, the court cannot entertain the possession proceedings (s 8(1)). The court has a power to dispense with the notice requirement if it considers it just and equitable to do so (s 8(1)(b)). The dispensation power is not available in the case of serious rent arrears (s 8(5)).

The requirements may be summarised as follows.

1   The landlord, or at least one joint landlord, must have served on the tenant a notice in the prescribed form, and proceedings must be begun within the time-limits given in the notice (s 8(1)(a) and (3)).

2   The notice must specify the ground or grounds on which possession will be sought. If a ground is not specified, the court cannot order possession on that ground (s 8(2)). The court may grant leave to alter or add to the grounds specified.

3   The notice must be in the prescribed form exactly and it must inform the tenant, by s 8(3):
    (a) that the landlord intends to bring proceedings for possession on one or more grounds specified in the notice;
    (b) proceedings will begin not earlier than at least two weeks nor later than 12 months from the date of service of the notice, which date must be specified in the notice.

4   If, and only if, the notice specifies certain grounds[16] the date for beginning proceedings must not, by s 8(4), be earlier than two months from the date of service of the s 8 notice; and if, in this, the tenancy is periodic, as well as the two months requirement, the s 8 notice cannot specify a date for beginning proceedings any earlier that the earliest lawful date for determination of the tenancy by a common-law notice to quit.

Discretion of court

The court has a number of discretionary powers in possession proceedings, but these do not apply to mandatory grounds for possession nor where the court is asked to order possession after an assured shorthold tenancy has expired (s 9(6)). The powers, in s 9, resemble closely those conferred by Rent Act 1977 s 100 (Chapter 17).

15A See Assured Tenancies etc (Forms) Regulations 1988, SI 1988/2203.

16 I e where the landlord was owner-occupier, a mortgagee seeks vacant possession, occupation for a minister of religion, redevelopment, devolution of periodic tenancy, suitable alternative accommodation and employee-tenant whose employment has ceased.

Shared accommodation

Where the tenant has the right under his tenancy to share some accommodation with other persons, but not the landlord, (i e where s 3 applies) the court cannot order possession of the shared accommodation unless it orders possession of the accommodation which the tenant occupies exclusively (s 10(2)). The court may, on the landlord's application, order the termination or modification of the tenant's right to occupy shared non-living accommodation (s 10(3)) except where the tenancy itself enables this to be done (s 10(4)).[17]

E GROUNDS FOR POSSESSION

I INTRODUCTION

The court (normally the county court, s 40) cannot make an order for possession of a dwelling-house let on an assured tenancy except on one or more of a number of grounds in Sch 2 to the 1988 Act (s 7(1)).[18] As with the Rent Act 1977, the grounds for possession are divided into mandatory and discretionary grounds. In all cases, no doubt, the onus of proving a ground will fall on the landlord. In the case of a mandatory ground the court must order possession if it is established (s 7(3)), subject, however, to one exception. If the dwelling-house is, at the relevant time, let on an assured fixed-term tenancy, the court cannot make a possession order take effect on a mandatory ground before the end of the tenancy, unless ground 2 or ground 8 is made out (s 7(6)), and the terms of the tenancy make provision, by a forfeiture clause or in some other way, for the tenancy to be brought to an end on the ground concerned – i e re-possession by a mortgagee or for serious rent arrears. In other cases, where there is a fixed-term assured tenancy, the earliest date on which an order for possession will be able to take effect is a date after the contractual expiry date of the tenancy (s 7(7)).

Once a mandatory ground has been made out, and subject, in the case of fixed-term tenancies, to the above, the court will have no overriding discretion to refuse an order for possession. Also, the powers of adjournment, etc, conferred by s 9, do not apply to mandatory grounds (s 9(6)(a)). Nor do they apply to the specific procedures for termination by the court of assured shorthold tenancies (s 9(6)(b)).

---

17 See the discussion of Rent Act 1977 s 22 in ch 17. On 'living accommodation' see s 3(5) of the 1988 Act.

18 A mortgagee lending money on the security of an assured tenancy is not bound by these restrictions (s 7(1)). The grounds apply to assured shorthold tenancies, but these are subject to special re-possession rules, as to which see below.

The point about discretionary grounds is that, first, the court has powers of adjournment, etc, conferred by s 9. These are similar to s 100 of the Rent Act 1977. Secondly, the court has, as with the 1977 Act, an overriding discretion to refuse to order possession, since it may only make an order if it is reasonable to do so (s 7(4)). No guidance is given in the 1988 Act as to the manner of the exercise of this discretion, and so, in the absence of authority, it may be taken that similar principles govern the matter, as would apply to s 98(1) of the 1977 Act. Therefore, the issue of reasonableness must be given separate consideration by the court, and merely because it may be reasonable for a landlord to require possession, it does not follow that it is reasonable for the court to gratify it. If the judge acts in a broad, commonsense way, taking all relevant factors into account, it may be assumed that the weight of any given factor is for him alone,[19] and it would be reasonable, if appropriate, to take into account personal, environmental and domestic factors. For some further considerations, please refer to Chapter 17. Presumably, even apart from s 5(1), as with the Rent Act 1977 s 98, no power in an assured tenancy which would, if exercised, deprive the tenant of his security, can be enforced except following an order of the court under s 7.[20]

Some individual grounds for possession resemble, to a greater or lesser extent, the cases for possession under the Rent Act 1977. Some grounds are new, or revised, notably, in the mandatory grounds, a revised owner-occupier ground (ground 1); and, very importantly, a ground enabling the landlord to obtain possession for redevelopment (ground 6); and also a mandatory ground based on proof of serious rent arrears (ground 8). A new discretionary ground is a general rent arrears ground (ground 10).

Grounds 1 to 5 inclusive in the mandatory grounds depend on prior notices from the landlord to the tenant. Any notice must be in writing, and must, where there are joint landlords, be given by at least one of them.[1] In these grounds, the notices have to be given 'not later than the beginning of the tenancy': this means 'not later than the day the tenancy was entered into'.[2] Where a landlord gives a notice as required, the notice has effect in relation to any later tenancy which starts immediately after the ending of the earlier tenancy.[3] These notice requirements must

---

19   Cf *Cumming v Danson* [1942] 2 All ER 653. CA.
20   *AG Securities v Vaughan; Antoniades v Villiers* [1988] 3 All ER 1058, HL.
1   Sch 2 Part IV para 7.
2   Ibid, paras 8 and 11, overriding s 45(2).
3   Ibid para 8(1). The tenant must be the same as the immediately preceding tenant, and the dwelling-house must be 'substantially the same' (para 8(2)). This rule does not apply if the landlord serves a further written notice on the tenant that the ground concerned is not applicable: para 8(3).

be complied with in addition to the requirement of a s 8 notice to begin proceedings.

A provision which is quite novel is s 12, under which, where a landlord obtains an order for possession and subsequently it is proved that the order was obtained by misrepresentation or concealment of material facts, the court must order the landlord to pay to the former tenant 'such sum as appears sufficient as compensation for the damage or loss sustained by that tenant as a result of the order'. The section does not give any further guidance, so it may be assumed that the quantum of an award is entirely at the discretion of the court: one wonders if it could legitimately order the landlord to pay to the tenant the value of the tenant's interest as sitting tenant, or his 'nuisance value'. One remedy which the tenant does not have, under s 12, is re-instatement in the premises.

II MANDATORY GROUNDS FOR POSSESSION

These are as follows: if the landlord makes out a mandatory ground, and has complied with preliminary notice requirements and also with s 8, the court cannot refuse to make an order for possession.

Ground 1 – *Owner-occupation*

Not later than the beginning of the tenancy the landlord gave the tenant notice in writing that possession might be recovered on this ground[4] and:

(a) at some time before the beginning of the tenancy,[5] the landlord seeking possession or, in the case of joint landlords, at least one of them, occupied the dwelling-house as his only or principal home; OR

(b) the landlord seeking possession or, in the case of joint landlords, at least one of them, requires the dwelling-house as his or his spouse's only or principal home *and* neither the landlord nor any one joint landlord (where appropriate) nor any person deriving title under the landlord who gave the notice acquired the reversion on the tenancy for money or money's worth.

Some points of construction arise out of this ground, but, plainly, it is

---

4 The court may dispense with the notice requirement if it is just and equitable to do so.
5 I e not later than the day on which the tenancy is entered into (Sch 2 Part IV para 11). It may be advisable for *any* private landlord letting on an assured tenancy to serve a ground 1 notice.

aimed at the same landlords as in Case 11 of Sched 15 to the Rent Act 1977.

1   'At some time before the beginning of the tenancy' appears to indicate that occupation by the landlord concerned, need not necessarily have been immediately before the beginning of the tenancy – an occupation several years previously would presumably suffice, apparently, whether or not before the commencement of Part I of the 1988 Act.
2   Once sufficient previous occupation is proved within para (a) above, the landlord does not have to prove that he requires to occupy the house personally, as with the owner-occupier grounds in the 1977 Act.
3   The previous occupation by the landlord must have been as his only or principal home. A tenant who could show that, at the relevant time, the landlord had a second home, which he treated as his principal home, might be able to defeat a claim based on para (a): but presumably in such a case, an alternative claim could be made under para (b).
4   Where the landlord was not previously an owner-occupier, he will have to rely on para (b) of ground 1, which is mandatory, unlike a similar discretionary ground in the 1977 Act (Case 9), but it is narrower with regard to the types of person whom the landlord can claim for.[6] Unlike Case 9, the strict joint landlord rule does not apply the present ground, as only one joint landlord need require occupation as a residence.

Ground 2 – Repossession by mortgagee

The dwelling-house is subject to a mortgage or charge granted before the beginning of the tenancy,[7] and –

(a)   the mortgagee (or chargee) is entitled to exercise a power of sale conferred by the mortgage or by s 101 of the Law of Property Act 1925; and
(b)   the mortgagee requires possession of the dwelling-house to dispose of it with vacant possession; and
(c)   the landlord gave a notice as required under ground 1 or the court dispenses with that requirement.

This ground is akin to the corresponding Rent Act 1977 mandatory ground.[8]

---

6   A reasonable requirement of occupation by certain members of the landlord's family is sufficient for Case 9. There is no equivalent to Cases 12 and 20 of 1977 Act Sch 15.
7   Defined, Sch 2 part IV para 11, above.
8   Sch 15 Part II Case 11(d).

Ground 3 – Out of season lettings

> The tenancy is a fixed-term tenancy for a term not exceeding eight months and –
>
> (a) not later than the beginning of the tenancy[9] the landlord gave notice in writing to the tenant that possession might be recovered on this ground: and
> (b) at some time within the period of twelve months ending with the beginning of the tenancy, the dwelling-house was occupied under a right to occupy it for a holiday.

This ground is to enable a landlord who lets houses or flats on holiday lettings, which are not assured tenancies, to let on a fixed-term assured tenancy or series of fixed-term assured tenancies not exceeding eight months in all and recover possession mandatorily and is similar to a corresponding Rent Act 1977 ground.[10] If a notice is served as required, before the first tenancy, and a second or subsequent tenancy is granted, the notice will be effective for that tenancy, if it is off-season, and the beginning of the tenancy is deemed to run from the beginning of the tenancy for which the notice was given.[11]

Ground 4 – Short tenancies of student accommodation

> The tenancy is a fixed-term tenancy for a term not exceeding twelve months and –
>
> (a) not later than the beginning of the tenancy,[12] the landlord gave notice in writing to the tenant that possession might be recovered on this ground; and
> (b) at some time within the twelve months ending with the beginning of the tenancy, the dwelling-house was let on a student letting within Sch 1 para 8.

This ground is similar to a corresponding ground for possession under the Rent Act 1977.[13] The object of this ground is, therefore, to facilitate vacation lettings of student accommodation.

Ground 5 – Minister of religion

This enables a landlord to recover possession on the ground that the dwelling-house is held for the purpose of occupation by a minister of

---

9 Sch 2 Part IV para 11 above.
10 Rent Act 1977 Sch 15 Part II Case 13.
11 Sch 2 Part IV para 10. The same rule applies to ground 4, below.
12 Sch 2 Part IV para 11, above.
13 1977 Act Sch 15 Part II Case 14.

religion as a residence from which to perform his duties; and the court is satisfied that the dwelling-house is so required. The ground is subject to a preliminary notice requirement.

Ground 6 – Redevelopment by landlord

This is a new ground and may well turn out to be a very important one. It corresponds, with some differences of detail, to s 30(1)(f) of the Landlord and Tenant Act 1954.

Under it, the landlord[14] or, if the landlord is a registered housing association or charitable housing trust, a superior landlord, intends to demolish or reconstruct the whole or a substantial part of the dwelling-house or to carry out substantial works on the dwelling-house or any part thereof or any building of which it forms part AND –

(a) the intended work cannot reasonably be carried out without the tenant giving up possession of the dwelling-house because –

  (i) he is not willing to agree to a variation of the terms of his tenancy so as to give access or other facilities to permit the intended work to be carried out; OR

  (ii) the nature of the intended work is such that no such variation is practicable; OR

  (iii) the tenant is not willing to accept an assured tenancy of a reduced part of the dwelling-house leaving the landlord in possession of so much of the dwelling-house as would be reasonable to enable him to carry out the intended work and would give access and other facilities over the reduced part to permit the work to be carried out, OR

  (iv) the nature of the work is such that such a tenancy is not practicable; and

(b) EITHER the landlord acquired his interest in the dwelling-house before the grant of the tenancy[15] OR his interest was in existence at the time of the grant and neither the landlord or any joint landlord nor any other person who has acquired the landlord's interest since the grant of the tenancy acquired it for money or money's worth; and

(c) the assured tenancy did not come into being under a succession

---

14   Described as the 'landlord who is seeking possession' so as to enable one of joint landlords to rely on the ground.

15   If the tenant (or any joint tenant) was in possession under an earlier assured tenancy, this means the grant of the earlier tenancy.

to a former statutory tenancy under the Rent Act 1977 or the Rent (Agriculture) Act 1976.

The purchase condition will not prevent a landlord who acquires the reversion under a will or intestacy or by surrender for no consideration from relying on this ground. This ground is new in residential tenancies, and enables a landlord or superior landlord with redevelopment plans to regain possession mandatorily of a dwelling-house let on an assured tenancy. If the tenancy is fixed-term, however, because the court cannot make an order for possession take effect until the contractual expiry date of the tenancy, a landlord intent on redevelopment will not be able to evict the tenant until after that date. If the fixed-term tenancy contains a break clause entitling the landlord to determine it for redevelopment, then, by analogy with Part II of the 1954 Act, it is thought that the clause, if duly exercised, will be effective to determine the fixed-term tenancy, and an order for possession may thereafter be sought on ground 6.[16]

The policy of this ground is, therefore, similar to s 30(1)(f) of the Landlord and Tenant Act 1954. It would seem that the relevant date for deciding on the landlord's intention is that of the hearing; and if the landlord intends to sell the reversion, he cannot rely on this ground, but if he intends to let the premises on a building lease, he may. Para (a)(i) will allow the tenant to retain security if he agrees to a variation of the terms of the tenancy to allow the landlord access and other facilities to do the work, but the landlord can resist this if the work is such that no such variation is practicable.[17] The question of whether a variation is practicable will presumably depend, in part, on the extent of the proposed work and if demolition of the whole dwelling-house is intended, a variation would be presumably not practicable. The landlord (not the tenant) has the choice of work, it would appear: so, even if a tenant could show that if a different scheme were adopted, he could retain possession of the dwelling-house with suitable access terms, the landlord would succeed if his own genuine proposed work involved the demolition of the premises. See further the consideration of s 30(1)(f) and 31A of Part II of the 1954 Act in Chapter 25. Where the court orders possession under this ground, the landlord must pay the tenant his reasonable removal expenses (s 11(1)).[18]

---

16 Cf *Weinbergs Weatherproofs v Radcliffe Paper Mill Co* [1958] Ch 437, [1957] 3 All ER 663.
17 Cf Landlord and Tenant Act 1954 s 31A: the work must not, with an access term, interfere to a substantial extent or for a substantial time with the tenant's use of the holding. It may be that the practicability test will be held to have the same effect. If so, if the landlord could show an interruption lasting for more than a very few weeks, he could defeat a defence based on para (a) of ground 6.
18 If the parties cannot agree an amount, this will be determined by the court (s 11(2)) and in any event the sum is recoverable as a civil debt (s 11(3)).

Ground 7 – Devolution of periodic tenancy

This ground enables mandatory recovery of possession following the death of an assured periodic tenant – assuming that there has been no succession to the tenancy (see below).

> The tenancy is a periodic tenancy (including a statutory periodic tenancy) which has devolved under the will or intestacy of the former tenant. Proceedings for possession must be begun no later than twelve months after the death of the former tenant, or, if the court directs, after the date the landlord or any one joint landlord became aware of the tenant's death.

It is specifically provided that for the purpose of this ground, acceptance by the landlord of rent from a new tenant, after the death of the former tenant, is not to create a new periodic tenancy, unless the landlord agrees in writing to a change in the amount of the rent, the period of the tenancy, the premises which are let, or any other term.

This is designed to overcome the danger, which there might otherwise be, of implied re-grant of a periodic tenancy to a person not entitled to succeed, but who remains in occupation of the premises after the former tenant's death.

Ground 7 is not applicable where there is a succession to the assured periodic tenancy on the death of the tenant, under s 17. Where there is a succession, the tenancy does not devolve within the present ground (s 17(1)). It applies where the person occupying the dwelling or flat is not the tenant's spouse or cohabitee, but a member of his or her family, or a friend or other person.

Ground 8 – Serious rent arrears

> Both at the date of service of the s 8 notice and at the date of the hearing –
>
> (a) at least 13 weeks' rent is unpaid, where rent is payable weekly or fortnightly;
> (b) at least three months' rent is unpaid, where the rent is payable monthly;
> (c) at least one quarter's rent is more than three months in arrears, where the rent is payable quarterly;
> (d) at least three months' rent is more than three months in arrears, where the rent is payable yearly.

'Rent' means rent lawfully due from the tenant, which presumably bears the same meaning as under Case 1 of Sch 15 to the Rent Act 1977.

The present ground is mandatory, and if rent arrears are proved within the above requirements, the court has no discretion to refuse to make an order for possession. Moreover, if the tenancy is fixed-term, this ground is one of the exceptional mandatory grounds whereunder the court is entitled to make its order for possession take effect before the contractual expiry date of the tenancy: rent arrears of a significant kind are clearly viewed as sufficient to imperil the security offered to an assured fixed-term tenant.

However, the rent must be in arrears in the prescribed sense both at the date of service of the s 8 notice and at the date of the hearing, and so, if the tenant repays all the arrears and (presumably) costs, between the date of service of the s 8 notice and that of the hearing, the landlord cannot regain possession on this ground, irrespective of the tenant's past record. If a landlord has a tenant whom he thinks might pay off a particular set of arrears in this way, to avoid re-possession under ground 8, he might consider an alternative claim in his s 8 notice under the discretionary ground 11, which enables the court to order possession for persistent delay in paying rent, even if no rent is currently in arrears.

III   DISCRETIONARY GROUNDS FOR POSSESSION

As mentioned above, in the case of discretionary grounds, the court may only make an order for possession if it considers it reasonable to do so (s 7(4)), and the significance of the court's overriding discretion has been discussed. The court has powers of adjournment etc which apply to discretionary grounds (s 9).

The court has power to make an order for possession take effect before the expiry date of an assured fixed-term tenancy in the case of most discretionary grounds (s 7(6)) provided that the terms of the tenancy enable the landlord to terminate the tenancy on that ground, by forfeiture or otherwise (see further above). Therefore, as with the Rent Act 1977, the landlord will, in such cases, first have to determine the tenancy at common law and then proceed under the 1988 Act. In no case, as noted, is the court entitled to order possession unless the landlord has served a notice under s 8 on the tenant, or the court has dispensed with this requirement. In particular, the ground relied on must be specified in the s 8 notice.

Ground 9 – Suitable alternative accommodation

Suitable alternative accommodation is available for the tenant or will be available for him when the order for possession takes effect.

This ground is similar in most material respects to the corresponding provision in the Rent Act 1977.[19] One new feature of the present ground

---

19   It is supplemented by Sch 2 Part III, which is akin to Rent Act 1977 Sch 15 Part IV, with due modifications.

is that where the landlord obtains possession, he is bound to pay the tenant's reasonable removal expenses (s 11(1)). Otherwise, reference should be made to the appropriate parts of Chapter 17.

Ground 10 – *Rent lawfully due*

Some rent lawfully due from the tenant is unpaid on the date on which the proceedings for possession are begun and is in arrears at the date of service of a s 8 notice, except where service of a s 8 notice is dispensed with.

This corresponds in material respects to Case 1 of Sch 15 to the Rent Act (Chapter 17) to which reference may be made.

Ground 11 – *Persistent delay*

Whether or not any rent is in arrears on the date on which proceedings are begun, the tenant has persistently delayed paying rent lawfully due.

Under this ground, the tenant's past record may be examined: even if he currently is punctual with his rent payments, if his past record is bad enough, the landlord may obtain possession.

The ground is in many respects akin to s 30(1)(b) of Part II of the 1954 Act, though in this precise form it is new for private sector tenancies, and hence, reference may be made to the discussion in Chapter 25.

Ground 12 – *Breach of obligation*

Any obligation of the tenancy (other than as to rent) has been broken or not performed.

In general, this ground is akin to Case 1 of Sch 15 of the Rent Act 1977, discussed in Chapter 17.

Ground 13 – *Waste, neglect etc*

The condition of the dwelling-house or any of the common parts[20] has deteriorated owing to acts of waste by, or the neglect or default of, the tenant or any other person residing in the dwelling-house and, in the case of an act of waste by, or the neglect or default of, a lodger of the tenant or a sub-tenant, the tenant has not taken such

---

20 I e parts of the building which the tenant is entitled under the terms of the tenancy to use in common with other dwelling-house occupiers of, in effect, the same landlord.

steps as he ought reasonably to have taken for the removal of the lodger or sub-tenant.

While in most respects this ground corresponds to Case 3 of Sch 15 to the Rent Act 1977 (Chapter 17), ground 13 refers, in addition, which is new, to the common parts, so that if the tenant or those claiming under him actively injure a common staircase or damage the lighting in common passageways, for example, the landlord could invoke the present ground.

Ground 14 – *Nuisance, annoyance, etc*

The tenant or any other person residing in the dwelling-house has been guilty of conduct which is a nuisance or annoyance to adjoining occupiers, or has been convicted of using the dwelling-house or allowing it to be used for immoral or illegal purposes.

This corresponds to Case 2 of Sch 15 to the Rent Act 1977, discussed in Chapter 17.

Ground 15 – *Deterioration of Furniture*

The condition of any furniture provided for use under the tenancy has, in the court's opinion, deteriorated owing to ill-treatment by the tenant or any other person residing in the dwelling-house and, in the case of ill-treatment by a lodger or sub-tenant, the tenant has not taken reasonable steps for the removal of the lodger or sub-tenant.

Again, this corresponds to Case 4 of Sch 15 of the Rent Act 1977 and calls for no further comment here.

Ground 16 – *Employee of landlord*

The dwelling-house was let to the tenant in consequence of his employment by the landlord or a previous landlord under the tenancy and the tenant has ceased to be in that employment.

This ground is based on the same general idea as Case 8 of Sch 15 to the Rent Act 1977, but is greatly simplified. The landlord seeking possession will have to prove either that the assured tenancy was granted by him to the tenant, as his former employee, or that the tenant was the former employee of any predecessor in title. The tenancy must be in consequence of the employment, but the tenant need not necessarily be occupying the house for the better performance of his duties. No doubt, if alternative accommodation is available for the tenant, it will be easier to persuade the court to order possession in its overriding discretion.

F   SUCCESSION PROVISIONS

A limited succession scheme is provided for by s 17. The scheme works in a fairly orthodox way and may be summarised as follows.

1   Where a sole periodic assured tenant dies and immediately before the death, the tenant's spouse (which includes a person living with the tenant as his or her husband or wife (s 17(4)) occupied the dwelling-house as his or her only or principal home,[1] the tenancy vests in the spouse or other person (s 17(1)). Vesting operates the succession provisions (s 17(1)(c)) and a single succession only is allowed for.

2   If the tenant was a successor then there is no succession. A tenant is a successor if the tenancy vested in him under s 17 or under the will or intestacy of a previous tenant (s 17(1)). These events operate the succession provisions, and the same result follows where the tenancy was a joint tenancy and the current tenant becomes sole tenant by the right of survivorship and where the tenant holds under an assured tenancy which vested in him on the death of a statutory tenant (s 17(2)).

3   The succession provisions are also operated, and there can be no further succession, where:
    (a)   before the current tenancy (the 'new tenancy') was granted to the tenant, he held as successor to an earlier tenancy of the same or substantially the same dwelling-house; and
    (b)   at all times since the succession he has held as tenant under, in effect, the same or substantially the same accommodation (s 17(3)).

G   RENT PROVISIONS

I   GENERAL RULES

An important aspect of the legislation governing assured and assured shorthold tenancies is the absence of any rent regulation during the life of a fixed-term tenancy.[2] After expiry of an assured fixed-term tenancy, the rent of a statutorily-implied periodic tenancy which follows it may be increased under s 13, and if a proposed rent increase is referred by the tenant under s 14, the rent will be that determined by a rent assessment committee. These provisions also apply to any assured periodic tenancy.

---

1   Disputes where there is more than one qualifying person are to be settled by the county court if agreement cannot be reached (s 17(5)).
2   Excessive rents under assured shorthold tenancies are referable to a rent assessment committee, see part I of this Chapter.

If the terms of a statutory periodic tenancy are changed under s 6, then the rent will have to be adjusted (as noted earlier in this Chapter). Apart from these provisions, rents for assured fixed-term, assured periodic and assured shorthold tenancies are governed, in principle, by whatever rent the parties agree on. In an assured fixed-term tenancy for a substantial length of time, therefore, there is nothing to preclude the parties from inserting rent review provisions. There is no 'rent limit' based on a fair rent, unlike the position with Part III of the Rent Act 1977. The idea is that the tenant will pay a market rent, but this is a concept which is given legislative force only indirectly,[3] given that rent controls have, for the most part, been abolished.

There are no provisions in Part I of the 1988 Act corresponding to the anti-premium provisions of the Rent Act 1977, considered in Chapter 17. Whether this will lead to widespread abuse remains to be seen. It is true that the premium provisions of the 1977 Act are designed to preclude evasion of rent controls by the taking of capital sums, so that it was presumably thought that since rent controls have gone, there was no need for anti-avoidance rules.

Fixed term tenancies

There is no direct rent regulation in Part I of the 1988 Act of the maximum amount of rent lawfully chargeable to an assured tenant, and the provisions (ss 13 and 14) which enable the rent to be increased by notice and for referral of a rent apply only to periodic or statutory periodic tenancies. Therefore, the inference is that, under a fixed-term tenancy, the parties may agree on any rent they like; the rent cannot later be referred to any body; the tenancy may include regular rent reviews; but, subject to that, if the landlord wishes to increase the original rent, he will have to await the end of the fixed-term tenancy and the automatic coming into existence of a statutory periodic tenancy. On that event, he will be able to proceed with a notice of increase. In the case of a statutory periodic tenancy, the general requirements as to the service of a notice apply, but the landlord does not have to delay the start of the period for the proposed new rent for one year from the commencement of the periodic tenancy – which he must do in the case of an assured periodic tenancy (s 13(2)(b)). All he must do is to serve his notice during the final year of the fixed-term tenancy, giving a minimum period for the coming into effect of the new rent, which will depend on the intervals at which rent is payable under the tenancy (s 5(3)(d)). Further increases in rent will be governed by the provisions which apply to periodic tenancies.

---

3   Housing Act 1988 s 14(1) refers to the 'rent . . . in the open market' in connection with a reference of an excessive rent, see also s 22.

Periodic tenancies

The landlord may increase the rent of a periodic or statutory periodic assured tenancy by a notice under s 13. If there is a rent review provision in a periodic tenancy, however, it will govern rent increases to the exclusion of the statutory procedure (s 13(1)(b)). The statutory procedure is without prejudice to the right of either party to vary the rent by agreement (s 13(5)).

To follow the statutory procedure, the landlord must serve a notice on the tenant in the prescribed form[4] which proposes a new rent (s 13(2)). The new rent may take effect as from a 'new period of the tenancy specified in the notice' – so if it is not specified, presumably, though the section does not so state, the notice is void. The minimum life of a new rent will run for one year from the date the increased rent took effect (s 13(2)(c)). The minimum periods below, run as from the date of service of the notice (s 13(2)(a)).

The 'minimum period' by s 13(2) and (3)), from which the new rent begins,[5] is not to begin earlier than:

(a)   in the case of a yearly tenancy, six months;
(b)   in the case of a tenancy where the period is less than a month, one month;
(c)   in any other case, the period of the tenancy.

Each of the above runs from the date of service of the s 13 notice. In addition, no new rent period can begin except from the end of the first anniversary of the date in which the first period of the tenancy began (s 13(2)(b)), but, as noted, this requirement does not apply where there was a fixed-term tenancy and it is followed, automatically, by a statutory periodic tenancy. If the rent has been previously increased by a s 13 notice or a s 14 determination by a rent assessment committee, no further notice of increase can be served until one year after the increased rent takes effect (s 13(2)(c)).

Once the period specified in the notice expires, assuming it was correctly specified, unless the tenant has referred the notice to a rent assessment committee, by an application in the prescribed form,[6] or the parties have agreed on a different rent, the new rent takes effect as specified in the notice (s 13(4)). The tenant must refer the notice, if he is going to do so, before the beginning of the 'new period' specified in the notice: if he does not, and a different rent has not been agreed, then he

4   Assured Tenancies and Agricultural Occupancies (Forms) Regulations 1988, SI 1988/2203.
5   And within which the tenant must refer the proposed rent under s 14 (s 13(4)).
6   Assured Tenancies and Agricultural Occupanices (Forms) Regulations 1988, SI 1988/2203. As to the duties of a rent assessment committee on a reference, see Rent Assessment Committees (England and Wales) (Amendment) Regulations 1988, SI 1988/2200 amending SI 1971/1065.

will have to pay the new rent, however steep an increase has been proposed. Whether this is a reasonable result, may be questioned, except that a periodic tenant who dislikes a new rent may always, by a notice to quit, determine his tenancy.

It is not stated in s 13 what is to happen where a tenant who receives a void notice of increase, because it is not in the prescribed form, or because it fails to specify the correct period as from which the new rent is to begin, decides to pay the increase and then finds out that the notice is void. There is no express right to recover excess overpayments of rent from the landlord, nor is there a provision that the increase is irrecoverable from the tenant,[7] and whether such a right be implied is an open question. The fact that such an important matter appears to have been left out of consideration is notable, although the omission may have been deliberate. If the tenant receives a void notice, it may be that he is simply entitled to ignore it.

Landlords will have to be careful about the dates in notices of increase. There is, as noted, a rule that in the case of periodic assured tenancies, no notice of increase may require an increase of rent to take effect until the expiry of the first anniversary date of the commencement of the first period of the tenancy. There might be room for disagreement as to when that period was. This rule has no application where a statutory periodic tenancy follows a fixed-term tenancy. In that case, a s 13 notice of increase, as implied above, could be validly served during the final year of the tenancy. Landlords will have correctly to specify the 'new period' as from which the rent increase is to take effect, which varies with the periods laid down in s 13(3), which may be based on common law dates for valid determination of a periodic tenancy by notice to quit. For example, if L has a yearly periodic assured tenant T, commencing in January 1990, it seems that L can serve a notice of increase in July 1990 with the new rent to start in January 1991, which is one complete year from the start of the first period of the tenancy and also the six months' minimum period for the start of the new rent. If T held a monthly tenancy, commencing in January 1990 as above, no rent increase will be effective until January 1991 for reasons advanced, but the s 13 notice may be served in December 1990 to take effect in January 1991.

II   DETERMINATION BY RENT ASSESSMENT COMMITTEE

General

Where a tenant refers a rent increase notice to a rent assessment committee, which must be in a prescribed form application and before the beginning of the period from which the new rent is to commence

---

7   As there is in the case of determinations of an excessive rent of an assured shorthold tenancy, see s 22(4)(b).

(s 13(4)) the committee must consider the reference under s 14.[8] Committees have powers to obtain information from both landlord and tenant (s 41). Specified information must be kept by the president of every rent assessment panel as to rents of assured and assured shorthold tenancies (s 42).[8A] Both parties may, by written notice, withdraw a reference (s 14(8)). Rent does not include a service charge (s 14(4)),[9] but the committee must consider, nevertheless, sums payable for furniture and also sums payable for services, repairs, maintenance or insurance or the landlord's costs of management.[10]

The rent assessment committee must then determine the rent at which they consider the dwelling-house might reasonably be expected to be let in the open market by a willing landlord under an assured tenancy on the following assumptions (s 14(1)).

(a) The tenancy is periodic with the same periods as the current tenancy.
(b) It begins at the beginning of the period from which the new rent is payable, specified in the s 13 notice.
(c) The terms are those of the current tenancy (other than as to rent).
(d) Notices under Sch 2 grounds 1 to 5 have, where relevant, been given to the tenant.

Statutory disregards

While the rent must be determined as a market rent, the committee must make the following disregards (s 14(2)):

(a) Any effect on rent of there being a sitting tenant.
(b) Any increase in the value of the dwelling-house or flat attributable to certain improvements carried out by the person who, at the time he carried it out, was the current tenant. The improvement must have been carried out otherwise than under an obligation to the immediate landlord, or carried out under an obligation to the immediate landlord, following a consent to the improvement. Moreover, the improvement cannot be disregarded unless either it was carried out during the current assured tenancy, or unless the conditions are satisfied which closely resemble those imposed by s 34(2) of the Landlord and Tenant Act 1954 (s 14(3)).

---

8 Where a committee have concurrent references under s 6(2) and s 13(2) relating to the same tenancy, and the date specified in the s 6(2) notice is not later than the first day for the rent increase to start, the committee are empowered to hear the two references together, but beginning with the s 6(2) reference, and the terms as varied thereunder become the terms for the purpose of the s 13(2) reference (s 14(6)).
8A See Assured Tenancies etc (Rent Information) Order 1988 SI 1988/2199.
9 As defined by Landlord and Tenant Act 1985 s 18.
10 As to rates borne by the landlord or a superior landlord, the determinations made as if these were not so borne (s 14(5)).

Date rent takes effect

The rent as determined by a rent assessment committee takes effect as from the beginning of the new period specified in the landlord's s 13 notice unless the committee are satisfied that this would cause undue hardship to the tenant, in which case a later date may be directed by the committee, which cannot be any later than the date the committee determine the rent (s 14(7)).

H   MISCELLANEOUS TERMS OF ASSURED TENANCIES

I   INTRODUCTION

Part I of the Housing Act 1988 makes provision for specific terms and conditions of assured tenancies, much in the same way as there are specific provisions in the Rent Act 1977 and Part IV of the Housing Act 1985, in the case of protected, statutory and secure tenancies.

Section 3, dealing with shared accommodation and with the payment by the landlord of the tenant's removal expenses in certain cases and succession have already been dealt with in this Chapter. Part I of the 1988 Act has specific provisions dealing with assignment and sub-letting, access for repairs, protection of sub-tenants and distress, which apply to all assured tenancies, including, where appropriate, assured shorthold tenancies.

II   ASSIGNMENT AND SUB-LETTING

An assured periodic tenancy, including a statutory periodic tenancy following a fixed-term assured tenancy, is subject to a statutory prohibition, in the form of an implied term, on assignments and sub-lettings without the landlord's consent (s 15(1)).

In the case of an assured periodic tenancy which is not a statutory periodic tenancy, i e a tenancy which was periodic from the start, the tenant may be under a less strict prohibition because the statutory prohibition does not apply, by s 15(3)(1) if there is a provision in the tenancy (or collaterally to it) under which the tenant is prohibited, or allowed, conditionally or absolutely, to assign, sub-let or part with the possession of the tenancy. The statutory prohibition is also excluded, by s 15(3)(b), if a premium (defined by s 15(4)) is required to be paid on the grant or renewal of the tenancy. This is, presumably, to allow the tenant to realise any capital value on an assignment.

The statutory prohibition, which excludes s 19 of the Landlord and

Tenant Act 1927 (s 15(2)), is that it is an implied term of the periodic tenancy that the tenant will not, without the consent of the landlord:

(a)   assign the tenancy in whole or in part; or
(b)   sub-let or part with the possession of the whole or of any part of the dwelling-house (s 15(1)).

The prohibition is qualified but since s 19 of the Landlord and Tenant Act 1927 is excluded where the statutory prohibition applies (s 15(2)), the statutory prohibition is not rendered fully qualified and consent may be refused on any grounds, reasonable or not. Any voluntary and unwaived breach of the prohibition will entitle the landlord to require possession under the discretionary Ground 12 of Sch 2. It is presumed that involuntary assignments are not within s 15; but in the case of the death of an assured tenant who is not a successor, there may be a succession; if not, the landlord can require possession under the mandatory ground 7 of Sch 2.

III   REPAIRS

Under s 16 it is an implied term of every assured tenancy that the tenant will afford the landlord access to the dwelling-house and all reasonable facilities to execute any repairs which the landlord is entitled to execute. This provision resembles s 3(2) of the Rent Act 1977, which applies to statutory tenancies. No doubt, in the case of many assured tenancies, the provision reflects the fact that, if the tenancy is for a term of less than seven years, s 11 of the Landlord and Tenant Act 1985 (Chapter 9) will oblige the landlord to keep the structure, exterior and installations in repair. The landlord is entitled to the facilities, but not, in terms, his servants or agents: one hopes that this omission will not cause difficulties. Many assured fixed-term tenancies will no doubt expressly provide for access rights in whatever terms the landlord requires. If so, these will presumably be carried into any statute-implied periodic tenancy by s 5(3)(c). It is presumed that, in such a case, reliance on s 16 will be unnecessary.

IV   REVERSIONS AND DISTRESS

Reversions

To a limited extent, an assured sub-tenant is protected by s 18, which has much the same object as s 137 of the Rent Act 1977. Section 18 applies where a dwelling-house or flat is lawfully let on an assured tenancy granted by a mesne landlord, and the superior tenancy comes to an end – whether by effluxion of time, surrender, forfeiture, or for any other reason (s 18(1)). The assured (sub-) tenancy continues, in principle, held direct under the superior landlord. Were it not for s 18(1), the ending of the head tenancy would entitle the superior landlord to possession, as the sub-tenancy would fall with the head tenancy.[11] The provision only applies where for the time being the house or flat is 'lawfully' let, and, as with s 137 of the 1977 Act, s 18(1) is excluded, and the superior landlord entitled to possession as against the sub-tenant, where the sub-tenancy was granted in breach of a covenant against sub-letting.

If the interest which the superior landlord holds is such that the tenancy cannot be assured, then the sub-tenant is not protected by s 18(1), and this is so where the new landlord is a landlord who cannot grant an assured tenancy (s 18(2)) – as to which, see Sch 1. Therefore, if the superior landlord is a resident landlord, or the Crown, for example, the sub-tenant is not protected by s 18.

If the landlord, having granted an assured tenancy for a fixed term, grants a reversionary tenancy to commence as from, or after, the date the previous contractual tenancy (defined by s 18(4)) ends by effluxion of time, and the fixed-term tenancy continues by virtue of s 5 as a statutory periodic tenancy, the reversionary tenancy is subject to the statutory periodic tenancy (s 18(3)). A similar rule applies where a periodic assured tenancy is granted and a reversionary tenancy is granted to commence on or after the date when the periodic tenancy could be ended at common law by a landlord's notice to quit (s 18(3)).

Distress for rent

Under s 19(1) of the 1988 Act, no distress for rent of any dwelling-house let on an assured tenancy may be levied except with the leave of the county court, which has the adjournment and other powers which apply to possession actions.[12]

V PRE-COMMENCEMENT PUBLIC SECTOR TENANCIES

In general, a tenancy granted before the commencement of Part I of the 1988 Act could not be assured, but might be protected or secure. As a result of s 38(1) and (2), a number of pre-commencement tenancies granted by such landlords as local authorities, housing associations or a housing action trust, where, after the commencement of Part I of the

---

11 See e g *Moore Properties (Ilford) Ltd v McKeon* [1977] 1 All ER 262, [1976] 1 WLR 1278.
12 This prohibition does not apply to distress levied under s 102 of the County Courts Act 1984 (s 19(2)).

1988 Act, the landlord's interest is transferred to the private sector, are capable of being assured tenancies. They cannot in any event be protected by the Rent Act 1977 or secure within Part IV of the Housing Act 1985. Consequently, where, for example, a council estate is privatised under Part IV of this Act, and sold off to the private sector, the tenants of the private sector landlord will cease to hold secure tenancies, even if their tenancies were granted before the commencement of the 1988 Act, and will, in all likelihood, be assured tenancies (s 38(3)(b)).

I   ASSURED SHORTHOLD TENANCIES

I   DEFINITION AND BASIC SCOPE OF PROVISIONS

Introduction

As from the commencement of Part I of the Housing Act 1988, assured shorthold tenancies (ASTs) are created. After then, it will not be possible to grant a protected shorthold tenancy.[13] PSTs in existence immediately before the commencement of the 1988 Act Part I will continue to be governed by the special provisions applicable to them, discussed in Chapter 17. As PSTs end, any new shorthold tenancies, even to sitting tenants, will be governed by the new regime.[14]

Assured shorthold tenancies are assured tenancies (s 20(1)). Therefore, all the provisions which apply to assured tenancies, save as modified by specific rules to be discussed, apply to ASTs. When, therefore, a fixed-term AST expires, a statutory periodic tenancy will come into being – though it will be terminable under special procedures. The rent increase provisions will apply in full[15] – subject, again, to a specific further provision enabling the tenant to refer the rent of an AST – a privilege denied to ordinary assured tenants. The specific terms which apply to assured tenancies, such as to assignment and sub-letting, distress and access for repairs, apply with equal force to ASTs. What is now discussed is the special legislative framework for ASTs. An AST cannot be granted to a tenant who was previously the tenant, or one of the tenants, under an assured tenancy which was not an AST (s 20(3)(a)). This applies where the landlord is the same as under the assured tenancy (s 20(3)(b)). The new tenancy is assured.

---

13   Housing Act 1988, s 34(1), (2)(a) and Sch 18.
14   Where a PST ends before the commencement of Part I of the 1988 Act, see s 34(2)(b) and 34(3) – the new AST rules generally apply to any new tenancy.
15   Including the right of an assured tenant to refer a landlord's notice of increase to a rent assessment committee (s 20(7), applying s 14).

Definition and conditions of grant

An assured shorthold tenancy is an assured tenancy which is granted for
a term certain of not less than six months (s 21(1)(a)). If the landlord has
a power to determine the tenancy, it cannot be exercisable during the
first six months of the tenancy – if it can, the tenancy is not an AST, and
will presumably be assured.[15A] There is no maximum upper limit on the
term which may be granted, unlike with PSTs. A preliminary statutory
notice must have been served by the landlord[16] before the tenancy is
entered into (s 20(1)). This presumably means the date of the tenancy.
The statutory notice must be in the prescribed form:[17] served by the
intending landlord on the intending tenant; stating that the assured
tenancy in question is to be an AST (s 20(2)). There is no power in the
court to dispense with this preliminary notice requirement: and if it is not
complied with, the tenancy will, though the Act does not say this, be an
assured tenancy. Likewise, if any of the other conditions precedent are
not complied with, the tenancy cannot be an AST and will presumably
be assured. While it is possible for a periodic tenancy granted after the
termination of an initial AST to be an AST, it is impossible for a periodic
tenancy to qualify as an AST at the outset: an initial minimum six-month
fixed term must be granted. On termination of the initial term certain by
effluxion of time, a periodic statutory tenancy will come into being, and
will be terminable under a special procedure.

If, when the initial term certain of an AST ends, a new AST of the same
or substantially the same premises comes into being, with the same
landlord and tenant as at the end of the previous AST, then the new
tenancy is an AST provided that the tenancy is an assured tenancy
(s 20(4)). It makes no difference that it is periodic or fixed-term, and
there is no requirement of service of a preliminary statutory notice. The
words of s 20(4) are 'comes into being', and appear to refer to a case both
where a periodic assured tenancy is expressly granted to follow a fixed-
term AST and where an initial AST for a fixed-term is followed
automatically by a statutory periodic tenancy. However, s 20(4) may be
excluded by a notice served on the tenant by the landlord[18] that the new
tenancy is not to be a shorthold tenancy (s 20(5)). The notice must be
served before the new assured tenancy is entered into, or, if a statutory
periodic tenancy has arisen, before it takes effect in possession.

15A It has been argued (Clarke (1989) 139 NLJ 84) that the only valid AST is one whose
   forfeiture clause cannot operate during the first six months. The picture is confused –
   see e g s 45(4) of the 1988 Act.
16 In the case of joint landlords, only one needs to serve the notice (s 20(6)(a)).
17 Assured Tenancies and Agricultural Occupancies (Forms) Regulations 1988, SI
   1988/2203.
18 In the case of joint landlords, this means at least one of them (s 20(6)(b)).

II   RECOVERY OF POSSESSION

The general grounds for possession, which apply to all assured tenancies, apply with equal force to ASTs (s 21(1)). There is also a quite specific procedure for the recovery of possession. This arises once the initial fixed-term tenancy has expired, and no further assured tenancy (AST or not) exists, except a statutory periodic tenancy (s 21(1)(a)). The landlord, or at least a number of joint landlords, must have given the tenant a notice of not less than two months stating that he requires possession (s 21(1)(b)). The notice requiring possession may not only be given, once the initial term certain has expired; it may be given before or on the expiry date (s 21(2)). This is much less complicated than the position with regard to PSTs, which there was occasion to criticise for excessive uncertainty, and a landlord may time his termination notice so that it may expire on the contractual termination date of the initial term certain, provided it is served not less than two months before then.

The court (generally, the county court) must make an order for possession, and has no discretion at all, if it is satisfied that the AST has come to an end, and no further assured tenancy other than a statutory periodic tenancy is in existence, and also that the landlord has complied with the two months notice requirement (s 21(1)). Where possession is ordered, any statute-implied periodic tenancy coming into being on expiry of the initial term certain ends automatically on the day the order takes effect (s 21(3)). If an initial AST was followed by a periodic tenancy to the same tenant under s 20(4), the court has the same jurisdiction to make an order for possession on the grounds of expiry under s 21(1) as it has after expiry of a fixed-term AST. The court is bound to order possession against the periodic tenant (s 21(4)) if satisfied that the landlord, or at least one joint landlord, gave the tenant a notice stating that, after a specified date, possession of the dwelling-house is required under s 21. The date specified in the notice must be the last day of a period of the tenancy and also not earlier than two months after the date it is given. The court must also be satisfied that the date specified in the notice is no earlier than the earliest day on which the tenancy could be brought to an end by a landlords' notice to quit. It is noticeable that there is no prescribed form of termination notice, although there is a requirement of a prescribed form[19] for the landlord's initial notice prior to the grant of an AST. This follows the position with PSTs. Unlike PSTs, however, the tenant under an AST has no right by notice to terminate the fixed-term tenancy early, and the omission of this right is rather unfortunate.

---

19   Assured Tenancies and Agricultural Occupanices (Forms) Regulations 1988, SI 1988/2203.

III   RENTS

The tenant under an AST may refer the rent to a rent assessment committee (s 22(1)).[20] This must be by an application in the prescribed form.[21] The committee must then determine the rent which, in its opinion, the landlord might 'reasonably be expected to obtain'. The tenant is only able to refer a rent where he has been served by the landlord with an AST notice under s 20(2) in the prescribed form. If an initial fixed-term AST is followed by a periodic AST, the rent of the latter, no matter how high, cannot be referred by the tenant (s 22(2)(b)). Also, if a rent has previously been determined under s 22, the tenant cannot refer the rent (s 22(2)(a)). The committee cannot make a determination unless, by s 22(3), they consider that:

(a)   there is a sufficient number of similar dwelling-houses in the locality let on assured tenancies (shorthold or not); and

(b)   the rent payable under the assured shorthold tenancy is 'significantly higher' than the rent which the landlord might reasonably be expected to be able to obtain under the tenancy, having regard to the level of rents payable under the tenancies in the locality of similar dwelling-houses.[1]

A rent as determined takes effect from whatever date the committee direct, but no earlier than the date of the application (s 22(4)(a)). Any excess rent over that determined is irrecoverable from the tenant as from the date the determination takes effect (s 22(4)(b)).[2] The landlord cannot serve a notice of increase of rent under s 13(2) until one year from the date of the determination taking effect (s 22(4)(c)).

This particular provision is really based on the exactly converse policy of the rent regulation provisions in Part III of the Rent Act 1977, which is, no doubt, quite deliberate. If there is a scarcity of dwellings let on assured tenancies, the committee cannot consider any application for a reduction in the rent, even if it is very high for that reason (s 22(3)(a)). Even if there is no scarcity, the landlord will only have to face a determination if the tenant can prove that the rent is significantly higher than the landlord might reasonably obtain under the tenancy, regard being had to the general rent level in the locality (s 22(3)(b)). If the general rent level is forced up by the market in a given case, then it is

---

20   The Secretary of State has power, by regulations, to order that s 22 is not to apply to specified cases or tenancies of dwelling-houses in such areas or other circumstances as may be specified (s 23).

21   See Assured Tenancies etc (Forms) Regulations 1988, SI 1988/2203.

1   By s 22(5), s 14(4), (5) and (8) apply to a determination under s 22.

2   The information, procedural and publicity of determinations rules apply to ASTs as to any assured tenancy (ss 41 and 42).

presumably more than arguable that a landlord could reasonably expect to obtain a rent reflecting the scarcity factor, against which a shorthold tenant is given no shield at all, this being the reverse of the position which, it has been held, applies to regulated tenants.[3] On the question of comparing rents, which the rent assessment committee are required to do, obviously, as assured tenancies are new, there may, initially, be no comparables: presumably, if so, they will be entitled to rely on their own expertise, but bearing in mind the statutory requirements and conditions precedent to their jurisdiction. No doubt, the exact manner in which a given committee will deal with any relevant comparables will be a matter for its own expertise.

J   ASSURED AGRICULTURAL OCCUPANCIES

I   GENERAL NATURE AND TERMS

Chapter III of Part I of the Housing Act 1988 creates a new regime for agricultural workers, assured agricultural occupancies. A tenancy or licence granted to an agricultural worker on or after the commencement of Part I of the 1988 Act, 15 January 1989, cannot, with a limited number of exceptions,[4] be within the Rent (Agriculture) Act 1976. A tenancy or licence within the 1988 Act is an assured agricultural occupancy, the general principle being that assured agricultural occupancies are governed by the same rules as assured tenancies (s 24(3)).[5] There are certain modifications of the assured tenancies rules in matters of detail, by s 24, as follows:

1   The tenancy must be assured and not assured shorthold.
2   A tenancy may be an assured agricultural occupancy even though it is at a low rent or of an agricultural holding.
3   A licence will qualify as an assured agricultural occupancy provided it is exclusive and provides for the occupation of a dwelling-house as a separate dwelling.
4   If no rent is payable under a fixed-term tenancy or licence, then, when a statutory periodic tenancy arises under s 5, the periods of the tenancy will be monthly beginning on the day following the coming to an end of the fixed-term tenancy (s 25(1)(b)).

---

3   *Western Heritable Investment Co Ltd v Husband* [1983] 2 AC 849, [1983] 3 All ER 65, HL.
4   Housing Act 1988 s 34(4): the exceptions are (a) pre-commencement contracts and (b) the grant of a tenancy or licence to a sitting 1976 Act occupier.
5   In particular, s 14 (determinations of rent by a rent assessment committee) is specifically applied (s 24(4)).

5 If the tenant gives notice to terminate his employment, notwithstanding anything in the occupancy agreement or otherwise, the notice is not a notice to quit the assured agricultural occupancy (s 25(4)).

II AGRICULTURAL WORKER CONDITION

In all cases, the occupier must comply with a specific agricultural worker condition. If this condition is at any time not complied with, the occupier loses security (s 25(1)(a)). The same rules as those which apply under the Rent (Agriculture) Act 1976, apply in the case of assured agricultural occupancies, to determine whether a person is a qualifying worker, whether he is incapable of whole time work in agriculture, and whether the dwelling-house is in qualifying ownership.[6]

The agricultural worker condition itself is governed by specific rules,[7] which may be summarised as follows.

1 The condition is satisfied that the dwelling-house has been in qualifying ownership at any time during the current tenancy or licence, and the occupier, or, where there are joint occupiers, at least one of them, is or was a qualifying worker at any time during such tenancy or licence.[8]
2 The above condition is also fulfilled if the qualifying occupier died, and the new occupier is the occupier's qualifying widow/widower or a qualifying member of his or her family.[9]
3 The agricultural worker condition is satisfied if the tenancy or licence was granted to the occupier in consideration of his giving up possession of another dwelling-house where he, or he and other joint occupiers, held that house under a qualifying tenancy or licence, and, immediately before giving up possession, the agricultural worker condition was fulfilled.
4 If an occupier is granted a new tenancy or licence of the same dwelling-house and he, solely or as one of a number of joint occupiers, immediately beforehand satisfied the agricultural worker condition, the condition will be satisfied under the new tenancy or licence.

---

6 Housing Act 1988 Sch 3 para 1.
7 Ibid Sch 3 paras 2–5.
8 Or was incapable of full-time work in agriculture or as a permit worker due to a qualifying injury or disease.
9 Broadly, this requires, in the case of a widow etc, occupation of the dwelling-house as a residence immediately before the previous occupier's death; in the case of a family member, occupation at death and for two previous years is required. Only one family member may be taken into account.

K   TENANCIES GRANTED BY HOUSING ASSOCIATIONS AND OTHER BODIES

Some consideration is appropriate of the position of housing associations and certain other bodies, with regard to the assured tenancies scheme.

Housing associations

It is quite clear that the quasi-public sector is to be encouraged to grant assured tenancies. Where a registered housing association, for example, grants assured tenancies, the same rules apply to regulate the relationship of the landlord and tenant as apply to any other parties.[10]

Part II of the Housing Act 1988[11] enlarges the range of permissible objects which a housing association may engage in, and yet still be eligible for registration with the Housing Corporation. The advantage of registration is eligibility for loan or grant aid. Housing associations may, therefore, for example, apply for registration if their purposes or objects are: providing land, amenities, or services, or providing, constructing, repairing or improving buildings for the benefit of the association's residents, exclusively or with other persons. They may also include among permissible objects such matters as managing leasehold houses.[12]

These enlargements are designed to enable registered housing associations to take over the running of council estates, among many other things, and if a housing association takes over a council estate under the so-called 'pick a landlord' scheme (Part IV of the 1988 Act), the existing tenants become assured, as opposed to secure; and new tenancies will be assured, not secure.

Housing action trusts

The Housing Act 1988 Part III set up Housing Action Trusts. The essential idea behind this scheme is that Housing Action Trusts will be designated[13] in relation to designated land and will have a limited life, and will, it is hoped, revive derelict and run-down Inner City areas.

---

10   If the housing association is fully mutual (ie the rules of the association limit membership to tenants of the association) then it cannot grant assured tenancies. Sch 1 para 12.

11   See s 48, substituting new s 4(3) and (4) of Housing Associations Act 1985.

12   New s 36A of the Housing Associations Act 1985 (added by s 49 of the Housing Act 1988) provides for the issuing of guidance by the Housing Corporation as to the management of housing by registered housing associations, with particular regard to the terms of tenancies and rents, and standards of repair.

13   There is a consultation and publicity procedure (s 61).

Tenancies granted by HATs are capable of being secure tenancies within Part IV of the Housing Act 1985 (s 83(1)) but HATs cannot grant assured tenancies.[14] In due course, they will avail themselves of a statutory power to dispose of their land (s 79), and such disposals have to be to private sector landlords. These disposals have to be with the consent of the Secretary of State and a set consultation procedure has first to be followed where the houses concerned have secure tenants (s 84). Nevertheless, it is quite possible for Housing Action Trusts to dispose of land in such a way that any secure tenants will become assured, by reason of a transfer into the private sector. In all events, HATs must secure that their objects are achieved as soon as practicable (s 88).

'Privatisation' or 'pick a landlord'

In Part IV of the 1988 Act, there are provisions for the wholesale privatisation of council estates. If these are operated in any particular case, existing secure tenants of the local authority as at the time of the transfer to a private sector landlord will become assured tenants. See further Chapter 37.

---

14   1988 Act Sch 1 para 12.

Chapter 19

Special residential tenancies provisions

A UNDER THE PROTECTION FROM EVICTION ACT AND ALLIED LEGISLATION

I AGENTS' FEES

Under s 1 of the Accommodation Agencies Act 1953 it is an offence for an agent to demand or accept payment for registering or undertaking to register the name or requirements of any person seeking a residential tenancy, or for supply or undertaking to supply addresses or particulars of houses to let, or to issue any advertisement, list or other document describing any house as being to let without the authority of the owner. It is not, however, an offence for an agency to charge a person an agreed sum for the finding of accommodation of which the person then becomes a tenant. On the other hand, if an agreement provides for the payment of money, before or after the supplying of addresses, the fact that it is a payment labelled as a deposit (returnable if no tenancy results) will not bring it within the exceptions in s 1 and an offence may be committed by anyone who demands or accepts such a payment.[1] The Act does not apply, however, except where a tenancy is sought; it does not prohibit an agent from charging fees in respect of flat-sharing arrangements, for example.

II RENT BOOKS

Where a tenant has the right to occupy premises as a residence in consideration of a rent payable weekly, the landlord must, by s 4(1) of the Landlord and Tenant Act 1985, provide a rent book or similar document.[1A] Tenant includes a statutory tenant and a person with a

---

1 *Saunders v Soper* [1975] AC 239, [1974] 3 All ER 1025, HL.
1A This duty does not, by s 4(2) of the 1985 Act, apply where the rent includes a payment in respect of board where the value thereof forms a substantial proportion of the whole rent.

contractual right to occupy the premises (s 4(3)). Therefore, the statutory duty applies to occupation of a residence at a weekly rent whether under a common-law tenancy, or statutorily protected tenancy including protected or assured tenancies and also under licence.

However, the rent must be payable weekly, or the duty does not apply, but the length of the tenancy need not necessarily be weekly, so that if a tenant holds under a monthly tenancy with the rent payable weekly, the duty applies; if it happens that the rent is payable monthly, it does not. If there is a term of years and the rent is payable weekly, then the duty to provide a rent book applies. The operation of the duty is thus quite fortuitous.

If a rent book has to be supplied, it must contain such information as is laid down in regulations (s 5(1)).[2] In all cases, the rent book must state the name and address of the landlord. If the landlord is a company, and the tenant serves a written request on the landlord, then the landlord must give the tenant written particulars of the name and address of every director and of the secretary of the company (s 6(1)).[3]

It is a summary criminal offence not to comply with any of the above duties (s 7(1)) carrying the penalty of a fine not exceeding level 4 on the standard scale of penalties. It is a defence for a landlord or his agent (for example) to show that he did not know and had no reasonable cause to suspect that any statutory requirement was not complied with. If any person demands or receives rent on behalf of the landlord, and the duty to supply a rent book or to provide the prescribed information has not been complied with, this is an offence, subject to the same statutory defence as above (s 7(2)). If any landlord or other person convicted of an offence continues in default for over 14 days, this constitutes a separate offence with the same penalty as just stated.

III NOTICES TO QUIT

By virtue of s 5(1) of the Protection from Eviction Act 1977, no notice by a landlord or a tenant to quit any premises let as a dwelling is valid unless it is in writing and is given not less than four weeks before the date on which it is to take effect. Moreover, the notice, if served by either side, must contain prescribed information[4] (which relates particularly to security of tenure for tenants under the Rent Act 1977). By s 5(1A),[5] the

---

2 Rent Book (Forms of Notice) Regulations 1982, SI 1982/1474 as amended, SI 1988/2198.
3 For rules as to service of the tenant's request see s 6(2). If a request is served on an agent of the landlord named in the rent book, it must be forwarded to the landlord as soon as may be: if not, an offence is committed (s 6(2) and 7(3)).
4 See Notices to Quit (Prescribed Information) Regulations 1988, SI 1988/2201.
5 Added by Housing Act 1988 s 32(2), which applies to licences granted before and after the passing of the 1988 Act.

same rule applies to licensors and licensees. But it does not apply to excluded tenancies or licences (see below) nor, it is thought, to tenants at will.[6]

IV PROTECTION AGAINST UNLAWFUL EVICTION, HARASSMENT AND EVICTION

The Protection from Eviction Act 1977 protects residential occupiers, which includes protected and statutory tenants under the Rent Act 1977, licensees and others, against both unlawful eviction and harassment and also against eviction without due process of law.

Unlawful eviction

By s 1(2) of the Protection from Eviction Act 1977, it is an offence for any person unlawfully to deprive a residential occupier of any premises, of his occupation of the premises or of any part of them; it is further an offence to attempt any such deprivation.[7] The person accused has a defence if he is able to prove that he believed with reasonable cause that the residential occupier had ceased to reside on the premises.

'Any person' includes both landlord and licensor. The term 'residential occupier' is defined (s 1(1)) as a person occupying the premises as a residence, whether under a contract, statute or rule of law. It therefore includes tenants, licensees,[8] lodgers and statutory tenants under the Rent Act 1977 and assured and excluded tenants under the Housing Act 1988.

The offence of unlawful eviction carries the following penalties. On a summary conviction, either a fine of up to £2,000 or up to six months imprisonment, or both (s 1(4)(a)); on conviction on indictment, either an unlimited fine or up to two year's imprisonment, or both (s 1(4)(b)). It is moreover provided in effect by s 1(5), that civil remedies remain available to a residential occupier who is unlawfully evicted (as they do in the case of harassment, below). These remedies would include for example, actions for trespass or breach of the covenant, express or implied, for quiet enjoyment; and in trespass actions, if the conduct of the tortfeasor is outrageous enough, damages may be exemplary.[9]

The sole lawful means in these cases to obtain possession is by order of the court (below) or by peaceable re-entry. On the termination of a tenancy, moreover, forcible entry is a criminal offence.[10]

---

6 See *Crane v Morris* [1965] 3 All ER 77, [1965] 1 WLR 1104, CA.
7 This means a deprivation unlawfully with the character of an eviction: *R v Yuthiwattana* [1984] Crim LR 562, CA. On s 1 see Hill [1987] Conv 265.
8 Not however a licensee whose licence has expired: *R v Blankley* [1979] Crim LR 166.
9 See e g *Drane v Evangelou* [1978] 2 All ER 437, [1978] 1 WLR 455, CA.
10 Criminal Law Act 1977 s 6.

Damages for occupier

A residential occupier (a term to be understood as for s 1 of the Protection from Eviction Act) has the right to claim damages under statute in two cases, by s 27 of the Housing Act 1988, which applies to any event after 9 June 1988. The following provisions are designed to act as a deterrent to landlords who might otherwise wish to pressure their existing Rent Act protected or statutory tenants into quitting, in view of the introduction of assured tenancies.

The first case is where the landlord[11] or any person acting on his behalf unlawfully deprives the occupier of his occupation of the whole or part of the premises (s 27(1)). The second applies where these persons are guilty of an attempt unlawfully to deprive the occupier of his occupation (as above); or are guilty, in effect, of knowing harassment, as a result of which the occupier gives up occupation of the premises as a residence (s 27(2)). The acts of harassment are described as acts calculated to interfere with the peace or comfort of the residential occupier or members of his household, or persistent withdrawal or withholding of services. The acts must be done with an intent akin to that required for the offence of harassment (below). The sort of conduct here envisaged might include intimidation of the kind which is also capable of constituting a breach of the implied covenant for quiet enjoyment (Chapter 6).

If the former occupier is reinstated as residential occupier before proceedings to enforce the liability are finally disposed of, then, in principle, there is no statutory liability (s 27(6)(a)); this is also the case where the court, at the request of the occupier, orders his reinstatement (s 27(6)(b)). No doubt, where either of these events takes place, the occupier, if a tenant, might be able to claim in contract (under the implied covenant for quiet enjoyment), for example, for any losses suffered during the period he was out of occupation. The court, by s 27(7), may reduce the damages to such amount as it thinks appropriate, if:

(a) prior to the event concerned, the conduct of the occupier or a person living with him is such that it is reasonable to mitigate the damages for which the landlord is liable; or

(b) before proceedings were begun, the landlord offered reinstatement and it was unreasonable for the occupier to refuse it, or, if offered alternative accommodation before that offer, that it was unreasonable to him to refuse the offer if he had not obtained the accommodation.

---

11 'Landlord' means the person entitled, but for the occupation, to recover possession of the premises (s 27(9)(c)).

Where there is liability, the landlord is liable to pay the former occupier damages 'in respect of his loss of the right to occupy[12] the premises in question as his residence' (s 27(3)). Liability is in the nature of a tortious liability, and is additional to any other liability in contract or tort (s 27(4)). But damages cannot be awarded for the same loss both under s 27 and under common-law liability (s 27(5)). The person liable has a statutory defence similar to that as under s 1 of the Protection from Eviction Act 1977 (s 27(8)).

Damages are based, by s 28(1), on the difference in value, as at the time immediately before the residential occupier ceased to occupy the premises as his residence, between:

(a)   the value of the landlord's interest[13] on the assumption that the occupier has a continuing right of occupation; and

(b)   the value of the landlord's interest on the assumption that the occupier ceased to have that right.

Valuations for the purpose of assessing damages are to be based on objective criteria set out in s 28(3), which are: that the landlord is assumed to be selling his interest on the open market to a willing buyer, that neither the occupier nor any member of his family[14] wishes to buy, and that any substantial development (defined by s 28(6)) or demolition of the building is unlawful.

Harassment

Under s 1(3) of the 1977 Act, it is an offence, if any person with intent to cause the residential occupier (as defined above) of any premises either:

(a)   to give up the occupation of the premises or any part thereof; or

(b)   to refrain from exercising any right or pursuing any remedy in respect of the premises or part thereof –

does acts likely to interfere with the peace or comfort of the residential occupier or members of his household, or persistently withdraws or witholds services reasonably required for the occupation of the premises as a residence.[15]

It is an offence under s 1(3A)[16] for the landlord[17] of a residential occupier or his agent to:

---

12   This term expressly includes, by s 27(9)(b), any right to occupy under, for example, a statutory tenancy.

13   I e the landlord's interest in the whole building (s 28(2)), not just the part occupied by the occupier, if less than the whole.

14   As defined in Housing Act 1985 s 113, applied by s 28(5)).

15   The act must be calculated to interfere with the occupier's peace and comfort, intended to cause him to give up possession: *R v Yuthiwattana*, supra.

16   Inserted by Housing Act 1988 s 29.

17   As defined, s 1(3C).

(a) do acts likely to interfere with the peace or comfort of the residential occupier or members of his household, or

(b) persistently to withdraw or withhold services reasonably required for the occupation of the premises as a residence,

and in either case he knows or has reasonable cause to believe that the conduct is likely to cause the residential occupier to give up the occupation of the whole or part of the premises or to refrain from exercising any right or pursuing any remedy in respect of the whole or part of the premises.[18]

The penalties for harassment are the same as for unlawful eviction (see above) and, similarly, civil remedies in respect of it are expressly preserved (s 1(5)). For example, there may be a contractual action for breach of the covenant, express or implied, for quiet enjoyment; and an occupier may even be granted a mandatory injunction to ensure access to and occupation of the premises, pending trial of the main action.[19]

Restriction on re-entry without due process of law

Section 2 of the 1977 Act provides that, where any premises are let as a dwelling on a lease which is subject to a right of re-entry or forfeiture, it is unlawful to enforce that right save by proceedings in court, while any person is lawfully residing in the premises or part of them.

Prohibition on eviction without due process of law

Under s 3(1) of the 1977 Act, where any premises have been let as a dwelling under a tenancy which is *not* a statutorily protected tenancy nor an excluded tenancy[20] and:

(a) the former tenancy has come to an end; but

(b) the occupier continues to reside in the premises or part of them,

then it is unlawful for the owner to enforce against the occupier his right to regain possession of the premises, otherwise than by proceedings in court. The term 'occupier' is widely defined (s 3(2)) so that it means any person lawfully residing in the premises at the termination of the former tenancy; and, by s 3(2A), the above restriction is extended to a restricted contract under the Rent Act 1977 which creates a licence. By s 3(3), the general prohibition of s 3(1) applies where an owner has the right to recover possession after the death of a statutory tenant under the Rent Act 1977 or the Rent (Agriculture) Act 1976, as the case may be.

These rules apply to residential licences, provided that the licence is

---

18 Under s 1(3B) if the person proves that he had reasonable grounds for his actions, he is not liable.

19 *Luganda v Service Hotels Ltd* [1969] 2 Ch 209, [1969] 2 All ER 692, CA.

20 This includes for example, – a protected tenancy under the Rent Act 1977.

not excluded but whether entered into before or after the commencement of Part I of the Housing Act 1988 (s 3(2B)).[1]

Section 3 does not apply to any excluded tenancy or licence. The result is to render it easier for landlords to recover possession of residential premises which are shared with the occupier by him or his family. This is because no security is enjoyed as an excluded tenancy cannot be assured, since the landlord must be resident, and s 3 of the 1977 Act is also not applicable. Eviction without a statutory requirement of legal process is possible in the case of excluded tenancies and licences.

By s 3A(2) and (3)[2] a tenancy or licence is excluded where:

1   The occupier shares accommodation with the landlord or licensor and, immediately before the grant and when the tenancy or licence ends, the landlord occupied as his only or principal home the shared accommodation, or that plus other accommodation.[3]

2   The occupier shares accommodation with a member of the landlord's or licensor's family (as defined in s 3A(5)) and, immediately before the grant and also when the tenancy etc ended, the family member occupied as his only or principal home the shared accommodation, or that plus other accommodation, and, immediately before the grant of the tenancy etc and when it ends, the landlord occupied as his only or principal home premises in the same building. If the building is a purpose-built block of flats (defined as for the resident landlord exclusion from assured tenancies) the tenancy etc is not excluded.

A tenancy or licence is also excluded from s 3 if it was granted as a temporary expedient to a trespasser (s 3A(6)) and also where it confers on the tenant or licensee the right to occupy the premises for a holiday or if it is granted gratuitously (s 3A(7)).[4]

Special rules for certain agricultural employees

Section 4 of the 1977 Act confers special protection on agricultural workers who cannot claim a statutory tenancy under the Rent (Agriculture) Act 1976.

---

1   Added by Housing Act 1988 s 30(2).
2   Added by Housing Act 1988 s 31. By Protection from Eviction Act 1977 s 5(1B), added by s 32(2), the four week minimum notice to quit requirement does not apply to an excluded tenancy or licence.
3   Accommodation within these rules does not include storage areas, passages, corridors or other means of access nor staircases.
4   Licences for the occupation of certain types of hostel are excluded by s 3A(8).

B UNDER LANDLORD AND TENANT ACT 1987

The Landlord and Tenant Act 1987 conferred important new rights on residential tenants of flats. These are summarised in what follows, except for the provisions of Part II and VI.[5]

I TENANTS' RIGHT OF FIRST REFUSAL

Part I of the Landlord and Tenant Act 1987[6] confers on qualifying tenants of residential flats a right to a first refusal where the landlord disposes of his interest in the premises. Examples of disposals caught are: conveyances of the freehold, or the grant of reversionary leases, or assignments of the landlord's interest, if it is leasehold.

Scope of Part I

The premises must consist of the whole or part of a building containing two or more flats held by qualifying tenants; the number of such flats must exceed half the total number of flats in the premises (s 1(2)). A tenant qualifies if he is a flat tenant under most types of residential tenancy (s 3(1)).[7]

Part I does not apply where; in particular:

1   The premises concerned are not occupied for residential purposes and the internal floor area of the non-residential parts is over 50 per cent of the internal floor area of the whole premises (s 1(3)).[8]
2   The landlord is either exempt (e g a local authority) or resident (s 58(2)).
3   The disposal by the landlord is outside Part I (s 4) – for example, it is under a will or intestacy, or by mortgage, or in matrimonial proceedings, or insolvency, or compulsory purchase, or is a gift within the landlord's family or to charity, or to an associated company of the landlord. Also excluded from Part I is any disposal in pursuance of an option or right of pre-emption binding on the landlord.

---

5   Discussed in chs 9 and 8 respectively. The 1987 Act implements, with changes, the recommendations of the Nugee Committee; Hawkins [1986] Conv 12; Percival (1988) 51 MLR 97. The text is as amended by Housing Act 1988 Sch 13.
6   In force on February 1, 1988: Landlord and Tenant Act 1987 (Commencement No 1) Order 1987 SI 1987/2177. See generally Rodgers [1988] Conv 122.
7   Shorthold, business, assured, and employment-terminable tenants are excluded.
8   This figure is variable by regulations (s 1(5)).

Notice procedures

Landlord's offer notice   Where the landlord of premises within Part I of the 1987 Act proposes to make a disposal caught thereby, he must serve an offer notice under s 5 on all, or at least 90 per cent, of the qualifying tenants of the flats concerned (s 5(1) and (4)(a)). If there are fewer than ten qualifying tenants, a notice should be served on all but one of them (s 5(4)(b)). The notice must comply with formalities: it must, for example, include particulars of the principal terms of the proposed disposal, give a minimum two-month period for acceptance of the offer and specify a further two-month period after the end of the acceptance period, for nomination by the qualifying tenants of a person to acquire the landlord's interest (s 5(2)).

Tenants' acceptance notice   Service on the landlord of an acceptance notice (s 6) is one of the options open to a requisite majority of qualifying tenants.[9] The notice must be served within the period specified for acceptance in the landlord's offer notice. Once validly served, an acceptance notice precludes the landlord from disposing of the 'protected interest' (i e the interest he proposes to dispose of, such as his freehold interest by assignment) from the date of service of the acceptance notice until either the end of the period specified by the landlord's offer notice for appointing a nominated person (s 6(2)(a)), or, if a person is nominated, for that period plus a further three months (s 6(2)(b)).[10] If no person is nominated, though an acceptance notice was served, then the landlord has a 12 month period, from the end of the period of nomination, to dispose as he thinks fit of the interest concerned for a consideration not less than that specified in the offer notice (s 6(3)). If no acceptance notice is served within the minimum two-month period, the landlord has freedom to dispose of the 'protected interest' for 12 months from the end of that period subject to the same restriction as above (s 7(1)).

Counter-notice   The requisite majority of qualifying tenants may elect to serve a counter-notice on the landlord in reply to his offer notice, within the period specified in the offer notice for acceptance, and in this case, they make a counter-offer which the landlord may then accept or reject (s 7(2)). If the landlord accepts by notice, s 6 above applies (s 7(4)); if he rejects by notice, he has, in principle, freedom to dispose of his interest (s 7(1) and (5)). The landlord may also by notice in reply to a

---

9   The requisite majority is ascertained by s 5(6), and is, essentially, 50 per cent or more of the qualifying tenants – one vote per flat.

10   The landlord must use his best endeavours to obtain any necessary consents to the disposal (s 6(7)).

tenants' counter-notice state that his notice is a fresh offer – in which case similar rules to s 6 apply (s 8).

Enforcement

The county court has general enforcement powers in relation to the various duties (e g to serve notices and replies) under Part I (s 19(1)) – but only after service of a further notice and non-compliance with it for more than 14 days (s 19(2)).

If the landlord disposes of his interest where Part I applies, without complying with it, the requisite majority of qualifying tenants have the right to serve a notice on the assignee requiring information as to the disposal (s 11). Thereafter, they may operate a purchase notice procedure (s 12) which requires the assignee to transfer the interest concerned to a person nominated by the tenants (s 12). In this case, the assignee must be compensated for any rise in the value of the property since the original disposal date; and if three months elapse from the service of a purchase notice on him and no further steps are taken by the nominated person, the assignee may by notice end the procedure and Part I will not apply to the disposal concerned (s 17(3)). Prospective purchasers have powers under s 18 to obtain information from any tenants whom they think might be within Part I.

Further provisions

Where a person is nominated to acquire the landlord's interest, he may at any time withdraw; and must do so if he becomes aware that there is no longer a requisite majority of qualifying tenants (s 9(1) and (3)). The landlord then regains freedom of disposition for 12 months as above. If the premises cease to be covered by Part I (for example, the number of tenants drops below the requisite majority) there are provisions for lapse of Part I in relation to the disposal (s 10(1)) which must be activated by the landlord, or Part I continues to apply (s 10(3)). If the landlord genuinely fails to obtain necessary consents, or the period for acceptance by the nominated person has passed with no acceptance, he regains his freedom of disposition for the disposal concerned for 12 months as above (s 10(4)).

II COMPULSORY ACQUISITION

Tenants of residential flats held on long leases i e, generally, for a term exceeding 21 years (s 59(3)) have the right to acquire compulsorily the landlord's interest under Part III of the Landlord and Tenant Act

1987.[11] This procedure applies where the landlord is in unremedied breach of his covenant to repair.

Scope of Part III

Business tenancies to which Part II of the Landlord and Tenant Act 1954 applies are, in particular, excluded from Part III of the 1987 Act (s 26(1)). The block of flats or building must contain two or more flats held by qualifying tenants (s 25).[12] A requisite majority of qualifying tenants are eligible to serve notices.[13] Property held under a resident landlord and charities is excluded from Part III (s 26(5)).

Notices

The right to acquire the landlord's interest, which is, generally, by county court order, applies if one of two conditions is satisfied. No application may be made at all unless the qualifying tenants or a requisite majority (s 27(4)) of them have first served on the landlord a notice complying with s 27.[14] The court may dispense with this requirement (s 27(3)). The conditions are *either*:

(a)   A notice has been served by the qualifying tenants under s 27; a reasonable period has expired (as specified in the notice) and no remedy by the landlord of breaches of his covenant to repair, maintain, insure or to manage the premises has taken place and the tenants then applied to the court for an acquisition order under s 28 (s 29(1)). Moreover, in this case, the tenants must show that the appointment of a manager under Part II of the 1987 Act would not be appropriate, and the breach must be shown to be likely to continue (s 29(2)) *or*;

(b)   At the date of the application as above, and for the whole of three years immediately preceding it, a Part II order appointing a manager was in force (s 28(2)).

As noted above, these conditions are alternatives. If the landlord has remedied the breaches concerned following the service of a s 27 notice on

---

11   In force on 18 April 1988: Landlord and Tenant Act 1987 (Commencement No 2) Order 1988, SI 1988/480.

12   Where the part or parts of the premises concerned are occupied otherwise than for residential purposes *and* the internal floor area of the premises as a whole, excluding that of any 'common parts' (defined s 60(1) so as to include the structure and exterior of the building) exceeds 50 per cent, Part III is excluded: s 25(4).

13   Ascertained by a 50 per cent rule (s 27(4)) similar to that applicable for Part I.

14   The notice must comply with the requirements of s 27(2) and must, in particular, recite the intention of the tenants to apply for a Part III order; and allow a reasonable time for the landlord to remedy the breaches.

him, then no Part III order may be applied for, provided the remedy is within the reasonable time there specified (s 28(2)).

Terms of order

The order will provide for a nominated person (or company) to acquire the landlord's interest in the premises specified (s 30(1)) on agreed terms or as determined by a rent assessment committee in default. The court may, at discretion, suspend any order (s 30(2)). One function of a rent assessment committee (a 'leasehold valuation tribunal' for the purpose) is to determine the price of the landlord's interest, which is, essentially, the open market price (s 31(2)). The landlord may obtain a discharge of the order on various grounds, notably, where the nominated person has failed, within a reasonable time, to carry out the acquisition (s 34(1)).

III VARIATION OF LONG LEASES OF FLATS

Part IV of the 1987 Act[15] enables the court, generally the county court, to make an order varying the provisions of an individual long lease of a flat (defined as for Part III) on various grounds, where the lease fails to make satisfactory provision with respect to:

(a) the repair or maintenance of the flat or of the building containing the flat or of any land or building let to the tenant under the lease or in respect of which rights are conferred on him under it (s 35(2)(a));
(b) the insurance of the flat or building or land (s 35(1)(b));
(c) the repair or maintenance of any installations (in the same building as the flat or not) which are reasonably necessary to ensure that occupiers of the flat enjoy a reasonable standard of accommodation[16] (s 35(1)(c));
(d) the provision or maintenance of services necessary to ensure the above standard (s 35(1)(d));
(e) the recovery by one party from another of expenditure incurred or to be incurred by him for the benefit of that party or him and others (s 35(1)(e));
(f) for the computation of service charges (s 35(1)(f)).

No application may be made if Part II of the Landlord and Tenant Act 1954 applies to the long lease in question (s 35(7)).

An application may be made by one party or by two or more parties in

---

15 In force on 18 April 1988: SI 1988/480, supra.
16 As defined in s 35(3) – these may include the safety and security of the flat and that and other factors relevant to the common parts (defined s 60(1) so as to include the structure and exterior of the building).

respect of their leases – as opposed to an individual application under s 35. In this case, the leases need not be in the same building, nor drafted identically (s 37(2)). To protect other tenants, the application cannot be made unless a majority of the tenants concerned consent.[17]

The court has a general power to vary the lease (or leases) the subject-matter of the application, whether individual or collective, in such manner as specified in the order (s 38(1)). If grounds are established for some but not all leases, then the court only has power to vary the leases in respect of which grounds have been established (s 38(4)). As an alternative to variation orders, the court may direct the parties to vary the lease as specified (s 38(8)). If the variation would be likely to prejudice any respondent or any person not a party and an award of financial compensation under s 38(10) would not be adequate, the court cannot order variation (s 38(6)). Special rules limit the power of the court in relation to any variation of the insurance provisions of the lease (s 38(7)).

A variation order will bind third parties and their predecessors in title (s 39(1)) and any surety who has guaranteed performance of any leasehold obligation (s 39(2)).

The service of notices on respondents and on any person whom the applicant knows or has reason to believe will be affected by the application will be governed by rules of court (s 35(5)). If a person entitled to a notice does not receive one, he is both entitled to an action for damages for breach of statutory duty and to apply to the court for cancellation or modification of the variation (s 39(3)).

In the case only of insurance and the recovery of insurance costs, where a long lease of a dwelling fails to make satisfactory provision for these matters, Part IV applies with certain modifications (s 40(1)).

Part IV of the 1987 Act is presumably intended to enable the curing of defects in the repairing or maintenance obligations under leases, which are necessary in the interests of the proper management of the block of flats as a whole.

IV MANAGEMENT PROVISIONS

Apart from service charges rules (see below), the 1987 Act enhances the rights of recognised tenants' associations where the landlord employs a managing agent. By the Landlord and Tenant Act 1985 s 30B[18]

---

17   As ascertained by s 37(5). If one party applies for variation, any other party to the lease may request the court to make a similar order for other leases specified in the application (s 36). For amendments to rules of court, see SI 1988/298.

18   Added by Landlord and Tenant Act 1987 s 44.

recognised tenants' associations are given consultation and information rights. These follow service on the landlord by the association of a notice.

If, at the time of the service of the notice, no managing agent is employed, the landlord must, before appointing one, serve a notice on the association which: notifies it of the name of the agent, specifies the landlord's obligations which the agent is to manage and allows a minimum period of one month for the association to make observations (s 30B(2)). If a managing agent is, at the date of service of the notice, employed by the landlord, he has one month from such service to serve a notice on the association; this must specify: (a) the obligations of the landlord which the managing agent is required to discharge and (b) a reasonable period for observations as to the manner in which the agent has discharged his obligations and as to the desirability of his continuing to discharge them (s 30B(3)).

A landlord who has been served with a s 30B(1) notice must, at least once every five years, serve a further notice on the association informing them of any changes in the duties of the managing agent (s 30B(4)(a)). Whenever the landlord proposes to change his agent, he must serve a notice complying with s 30B(2) on the association (s 30B(4)(b)).

If the reversion is assigned, any s 30B(1) notice served by the association ceases to have effect (s 30B(6)) and a fresh notice will be required.

C SERVICE CHARGES

I IN GENERAL

Special rules exist, mainly in statute, concerning service charges for flats, payable as part of the rent. Such charges cover for example the cost of services provided by the landlord or the carrying out of repairs. The amount of service charges may well be decided by the landlord's managing agent or surveyor; and where the latter two persons are merely the landlord in a different capacity, any certificate of the latter will be struck down if it is shown that the scale of charges is not fair and reasonable.[19] The basis of calculation is subject to an implied condition that it is fair and reasonable and not extravagant, at all times; if originally fair and reasonable but later unfair and unreasonable due to a change in the circumstances, again, only a reasonable amount of the charges may be recovered.[20]

---

19 *Finchbourne Ltd v Rodrigues* [1976] 3 All ER 581, CA. The landlord's surveyors cannot finally determine a disputed amount: *Concorde Graphics Ltd v Andromeda Investments SA* (1982) 265 Estates Gazette 386.
20 *Pole Properties Ltd v Feinberg* (1981) 43 P & CR 121.

A term purporting to provide that a surveyor's certificate is to be conclusive cannot oust the jurisdiction of the court.[1] Interest on borrowed money to cover the cost of works is only recoverable from the tenants if expressly sanctioned in the lease.[2] Charges for repairs cannot, in the absence of clear terms, be extended to include those for improvements.[3] Whether payment of service charges is conditional on the repairs first being executed is a question of construction of the lease.[4]

In the case of tenants of two or more dwellings, including flats, s 42(2) and (3) of the Landlord and Tenant Act 1987 require that service charges paid to the landlord or some person such as his managing agent must, together with all other service charges, be held by the payee as a single fund or as separate funds, on trust to pay for the matters covered; subject to this, on trust for the contributing tenants for the time being. The fund is not claimable in whole or in part, by any tenant whose lease ends (s 42(6)); it is held on trust for the benefit of tenants from time to time and if there are no remaining contributing tenants, the fund will vest in the landlord or payee for his own use and benefit (s 42(7)).[5]

II STATUTORY CONTROLS

Special rules are laid down by the Landlord and Tenant Act 1985 ss 18 and following[6] with regard to service charges information and other matters. These rules apply to tenants of dwellings, including flats. The main aspects may be summarised as follows.

1 *Dual limit*   There is a dual limit on recoverable costs: these must be reasonably incurred and works or services must be provided to a reasonable standard (s 19(1)). Any excess above this amount is irrecoverable. This applies whether the landlord seeks to charge for work done or for estimates for work to be done; but nothing prevents a landlord from recovering estimated charges, if reasonable[7] nor from

---

1   *Re Davstone Estates Ltd's Lease* [1969] 2 Ch 378, [1969] 2 All ER 849; *Rapid Results College v Angell* [1986] 1 EGLR 53, CA.
2   *Boldmark Ltd v Cohen* (1985) 130 Sol Jo 356, CA.
3   *Mullaney v Maybourne Grange (Croydon) Management Co* [1986] 1 EGLR 70; but see *Sutton (Hastoe) Housing Association v Williams* (1988) 20 HLR 321, CA.
4   *Yorkbrook Investments Ltd v Batten* [1985] 2 EGLR 100, CA.
5   If the terms of the lease provide differently for the destination of the fund, these prevail (s 42(8)) but otherwise, s 42 overrides the lease except in the case of express trusts created prior to its commencement (s 42(9)).
6   As amended by Landlord and Tenant Act 1987 Sch 2 from 1 September 1988: SI 1988/1283.
7   In this case there is provision for any appropriate re-adjustments after the expenditure is actually incurred (s 19(2)).

recovering charges in respect of management costs, subject to the same condition.

2   *Determining reasonableness*   What is reasonable is a question of fact and degree.[8] Any agreement relating to the determination of any question of reasonableness or standards in relation to service charges is void, except for arbitration agreements under the Arbitration Act 1950 (s 19(3)). The county court has power to declare that an amount is or is not reasonable, and as to the standard of services or works (s 19(4)).[9]

3   *Estimates etc*   Where the cost of qualifying works[10] exceeds £25 multiplied by the number of dwellings or £500 (whichever is greater)[11] the excess is disallowed unless consultation rules are complied with by the landlord, though the county court may dispense with them on proof that the landlord acted reasonably (s 20(9)). They are more detailed if the tenant is represented by a recognised tenants' association.[12] (There may be only one such association per relevant block of flats.[13]) For example, the secretary of the association must be given a specification of the proposed works, as must each tenant, and at least two estimates must be obtained, one from a person wholly unconnected with the landlord (s 20(5)).[14] Non-urgent works cannot be started before the specified date for their commencement (s 20(5)(g)), and that is generally a one-month minimum period from the date of the notice to the tenants and the landlord must have regard to the observations of the tenants. In the case of tenants not represented by a tenants' association, the landlord has lighter duties: for example, while two estimates are required, a notice with a copy thereof may be displayed in one or more places where it is likely to come to the notice of all the tenants (s 20(4)(d)).

4   *Costs*   Any tenant may by notice require the landlord to supply him with a written summary of costs incurred in the 12 months ending with the date of the request (s 21).[15] If the landlord demands payment of costs

---

8   *Russell v Laimond Properties Ltd* (1983) 269 Estates Gazette 947.
9   A person who takes proceedings in the High Court under these provisions who could have taken them in a county court will be disentitled to costs (s 19(5)).
10   As defined in s 20(2).
11   These amounts are variable by regulations.
12   Defined in s 29.
13   *R v London Rent Assessment Panel, ex p Trustees of Henry Smith's Charity Estate* [1988] 1 EGLR 34.
14   Tenants have the right to copies of a detailed specification of the works, and to make representations (s 20(5)(d)).
15   If there are more than four dwellings in the building, the summary must be certified by a qualified accountant (defined s 28) as fair and sufficiently supported (s 21(6)).

incurred over 18 months before the demand, the tenant is not liable (s 20B(1)) unless the tenant was notified within these 18 months that the costs have been incurred and will be demanded later (s 20B(2)).

5   *Insurance*   Detailed rules apply regarding information as to the insurance cover on the relevant building, and as to other matters such as tenants' notification of damage, where the cost of insurance forms part of a service charge or service charges rent.[16]

---

16   Landlord and Tenant Act 1985 Sch, added by Landlord and Tenant Act 1987 s 43(2) and Sch 3.

Chapter 20

Long residential tenancies

A   THE LANDLORD AND TENANT ACT 1954 PART I

I   INTRODUCTION

For various reasons, long residential tenancies were governed by the general law until the passing of the Landlord and Tenant Act 1954 Part I. This meant that, whereas a tenant under even a short periodic tenancy enjoyed, upon termination, full Rent Act protection, a tenant under a long tenancy whose lease expired with no prospect of a negotiated new lease had to quit. Following upon recommendations,[1] Rent Act style protection was extended to long tenancies on their termination by Part I of the Landlord and Tenant Act 1954. Since then, further rights in the form of enfranchisement or an extended lease have been granted to tenants under a long tenancy by the Leasehold Reform Act 1967. There remain those who cannot or are not able to take advantage of the 1967 Act, and to them, Part I of the 1954 Act remains relevant.

Briefly, tenancies protected by Part I are automatically continued after the contractual tenancy comes to an end by effluxion of time, unless or until it is terminated in one of the ways prescribed, on the same terms and therefore at the same rent as under the original tenancy. The landlord is given the opportunity to get possession on any one of a number of specified grounds, or to offer a statutory tenancy; meanwhile, the tenancy will be to all intents and purposes a regulated tenancy. The Act further makes special provisions in respect of dilapidations for which the tenant would have been responsible at the end of his tenancy.

II   APPLICATION OF PART I OF THE 1954 ACT

To qualify for protection under Part I, a tenancy must be a long tenancy at a low rent and must satisfy what is called 'the qualifying condition' (s 2).

---

1   Leasehold Committee Final Report 1950 (Cmd 7982).

'Long tenancy'

For the purposes of the Act, a long tenancy is one that was originally granted for a term exceeding 21 years whether or not it has subsequently been extended by the parties or by any enactment (s 2(4)).[2] 'Long tenancy' does not include a tenancy which is, or may become, terminable before the end of the term by a landlord's notice to the tenant (s 2(7)). To fall within Part I of the 1954 Act, the tenant must be entitled to claim that, subject to early termination initiated by himself (as with a tenant's option to determine), he is entitled to remain as tenant for an initial period of over 21 years.[3] Where the tenancy is at a low rent but is not a long tenancy, it will nevertheless be treated as if it were so, if immediately before it commenced, the tenant had had such a tenancy of the whole or part of the property (s 19(1)). This can be applied to any number of successive tenancies; and thus, even a periodic tenancy (which may be an implied tenancy) can be so brought within the definition of 'long tenancy' (s 19(2)).

'At a low rent'

Section 2(5) defines this as meaning an annual rent which is less than two-thirds of the rateable value, which in turn is defined as that which would be taken as its rateable value for the purposes of s 5 of the Rent Act 1977, dealt with in Chapter 17.

Where there is a progressive rent, s 2(5) requires the calculation to be based on the maximum rent payable; sums payable by the tenant for rates, services, repairs, maintenance, or insurance must, in general, be disregarded in calculating the rent.[4]

'The qualifying condition'

The qualifying condition (s 2(1)) is that the circumstances must be such in relation to the tenancy, that on termination, the tenant would, had the tenancy not been a long tenancy at a low rent, be entitled to retain possession under a statutory tenancy under the Rent Act 1977, of the whole or part of the relevant premises. There must therefore be a tenancy of a separate dwelling occupied by the tenant as his residence.[5] The essential question to decide, in dealing with the extent of property protected by Part I of the 1954 Act, is whether the tenant is entitled to lawful possession of the whole dwelling, whether this is a single entity or sub-divided into flats; and, where part has been sub-let, with the tenant

---

2   Except under the Leasehold Reform Act 1967.
3   See *Roberts v Church Comrs for England* [1972] 1 QB 278, [1971] 3 All ER 703, CA.
4   Rent Act 1977 s 146(1).
5   *Haines v Herbert* [1963] 3 All ER 715, [1963] 1 WLR 1401, CA.

in occupation of the rest at the term date, the qualifying condition is satisfied, so long as the tenant remains in possession of the whole just before the term date, or, being in occupation of part then intends to regain eventual possession of the whole.[6] The reason why the tenant must be in occupation of the whole or part at the term date is that this is laid down in s 2(6); and he must also be in occupation in this sense at the time a notice to terminate takes effect.

A landlord can protect himself, however, against resumption of occupation by the tenant just in time to qualify for protection, by applying to the county court, not more than 12 months before the term date, for a declaration under s 2(2) that the tenancy is not one to which Part I applies; and the court must make such an order if it is 'satisfied that the condition is not likely, immediately before the term date', to be fulfilled. The court cannot be satisfied that the condition is not likely to be fulfilled if, for example, the tenant can establish that he intends to resume possession. The tenant cannot claim protection, however, by resuming possession after an order has been given.

Where the condition is satisfied immediately before the term date, and the tenancy is continued by s 3(1), the tenancy will nevertheless continue until it is terminated in accordance with the Act, notwithstanding that subsequently the condition ceases to be satisfied.

III CONTINUATION OF TENANCIES UNDER s 3

As in the case of Part II of the 1954 Act, the provisions of Part I alter the general law in relation to tenancies to which it applies only on the coming to an end of the contractual tenancy. Section 3 automatically continues the tenancy beyond the term date unless or until it is terminated in accordance with the provisions of Part II; and, as has been explained above, it will do so even if the qualifying condition ceases to be satisfied after the term date. A continuing tenancy is neither a new tenancy nor a statutory tenancy, but merely an indefinite statutory extension of the contractual tenancy upon the same terms, and therefore at the same rent as before the term date, at least if the whole of the premises qualify for protection (s 3(2)(a)). If on the other hand, only part of the premises qualify for protection, as where the tenant has sub-let part of the premises, or uses part of the premises for business purposes, the tenancy will be continued in respect of that part which qualifies and the rent payable will be duly apportioned (s 3(2)(b)). The premises qualifying for protection are the aggregate of those which, if the tenancy

---

6　*Herbert v Byrne* [1964] 1 All ER 882, [1964] 1 WLR 519, CA; *Regalian Securities Ltd v Ramsden* [1981] 2 All ER 65, [1981] 1 WLR 611, HL.

were not a long tenancy at a low rent, the tenant could have retained possession of as statutory tenant (s 3(3)). Any question as to the extent of the part that qualifies, the amount of the apportioned rent or other terms of the tenancy will be settled by the county court, if the parties cannot agree (s 3(4)). Where a tenancy so continues beyond the expiry date of a superior tenancy, the interest immediately expectant upon the reversion of the expiring tenancy becomes the interest in reversion upon the continuing tenancy (s 65).

The tenancy may be terminated by the tenant, either by surrender with the landlord's consent (s 17), or by not less than one month's notice in writing given to his immediate landlord to expire on the term date or any date thereafter, regardless of the fact that the landlord has already served on him a notice to terminate on some later date (s 5). Any agreement (apart from surrender by the tenant) purporting to contract out of Part I is void.[7] Termination by the landlord is a lengthier and more complex matter. If the landlord seeks to terminate the tenancy by re-entry for forfeiture, the tenant has special rights to relief under s 16 (in addition to those under s 146 of the Law of Property Act 1925) except in relation to non-payment of rent, or rates, failure to insure, and using the premises for illegal or immoral purposes. In other cases, no order may be made when less than seven months are left to run under the tenancy, and the tenant applies for relief, and if there are more than seven months to run, the tenancy will be treated as having only seven months left to run, whereupon it will be continued by s 3 unless terminated by the landlord in accordance with the Act, i e by a notice under s 4.

IV   TERMINATION BY THE LANDLORD UNDER s 4[8]

The landlord may terminate the tenancy either on the term date or any later date by giving not more than 12 but not less than six months' notice (i e before what the Act calls the 'termination date', in order to distinguish it from the 'term date') to the tenant in one of the two forms prescribed.[9] Both forms of notice must invite the tenant to notify the landlord within two months whether he is willing to give up possession and specify the premises which the landlord believes to be, or to be likely to be, the premises qualifying for protection. The appropriate forms,

---

7   See *Re Hennessey's Agreement, Hill v Davison* [1975] Ch 252, [1975] 1 All ER 60 (landlord's option to purchase following notice procedure struck down).

8   Part I of the 1954 Act substitutes a statutory mode of termination for the contractual mode; *Magdalen and Lasher Charity Trustees, Hastings v Shelower* (1968) 19 P & CR 389, CA.

9   Landlord and Tenant (Notices) Regulations 1957, SI 1957/1157. Service on the tenant's agent is permissible within s 4: *Galinski v McHugh* [1988] NLJR 303, CA.

however, depend on whether the landlord wishes to resume possession which he may do by establishing any one of the grounds specified in s 12, or whether he is prepared to offer a statutory tenancy.

Where the tenant is a sub-tenant, 'the competent landlord'[10] in this context[11] is not necessarily the person who is his immediate landlord under the tenancy, but is the next superior landlord whose interest will last at least five years longer than the tenant's (s 21(1)). Where 'the competent landlord' is not the immediate landlord, the interests of 'mesne landlords' (i e those landlords with interests between the tenant's and the competent landlord's) and 'superior landlords' (i e those with interests superior to the competent landlord's) are protected by detailed provisions in the Fifth Schedule. Under s 18, the immediate landlord or any superior landlord may, in the last two years of a contractual tenancy, or during a period of continuation under s 3, require[12] the tenant or any sub-tenant to give him certain specified information about his own tenancy or any sub-tenancy.

Landlord's notice to resume possession

This notice (Form 2) must inform the tenant that if he is not willing to give up possession (i e if he elects to retain possession), the landlord proposes to apply to the court for possession on any one or more of the grounds under s 12. The grounds are set out in Sch 3 to the 1954 Act and correspond to those in Cases 1 to 9 of Sch 15 Part I to the Rent Act 1977;[13] plus a ground that, where the landlord is a local authority or certain other type of public sector landlord, he proposes to redevelop the premises on the termination of the tenancy.

If within two months, the tenant does not elect to retain possession, or the qualifying condition is not satisfied at the end of that time, the landlord will be entitled to possession on the termination date. Otherwise, the landlord will be entitled to apply to the court for possession, in which case he must apply within two months of the tenant's election (if any), or within four months of the service of his original notice if the tenant has not elected to retain possession. If it is satisfied that the landlord has established one or more grounds for possession and that it is reasonable that the landlord should be granted possession, the court will order the tenant to give up possession on the termination date (s 13(4)); alternatively, where the landlord's ground is based on his intention to redevelop, the court may order possession (at

---

10 Cf 'the competent landlord' for the purposes of Part II: s 44(1).
11 I e except as regards the giving of a notice to quit by the tenant under s 5: s 21(2).
12 But, like s 40, the section imposes no penalty.
13 The details of the relevant Rent Act Cases are discussed in ch 17 and it would be otiose to repeat them, though slightly modified here.

the request of the landlord) up to one year after the termination date if it is satisfied that the landlord could establish that ground then, even though he cannot do so at the time of the application (s 13(3)). Under s 55, the tenant is entitled to apply to the court to order the landlord to pay him reasonable compensation, if he can subsequently show that the landlord obtained an order for possession by misrepresentation or concealment of material facts.

If, however, the landlord fails to make his application to the court within the time prescribed, or he fails to establish a ground for possession, his notice under s 4 will lapse, and the tenancy will continue as before under s 3. If he fails to establish a ground (or if he had withdrawn his notice) he may under s 14, serve on the tenant within one month a notice proposing a statutory tenancy, in respect of which the termination date may be not less than three months later (as opposed to the usual six months under s 4).

Landlord's notice proposing a statutory tenancy

This notice (Form 1) must contain his proposals for a statutory tenancy in respect of the matters specified in s 7, i e;

(a)   what premises are to constitute the dwelling house;
(b)   the rent, the rental periods and whether rent is to be payable in advance or in arrear;
(c)   the carrying out and payment of initial repairs;
(d)   responsibility for repairs during the statutory tenancy; and
(e)   any other terms proposed.

If the parties cannot reach agreement on these matters, the landlord must apply to the county court to have them determined. The court has a wide discretion. The state of affairs existing at the date of the hearing is of primary importance, and while the terms of the contractual lease will be considered, they will not necessarily be incorporated into the statutory tenancy, in view of the latter's potentially indefinite life. Hence, a tenant's future intention to sub-divide the house and use it as a source of income was disregarded, and a power enabling him to do so in the contractual lease was not incorporated into the statutory tenancy.[14] A prohibition in qualified form against assignment, sub-letting etc by the tenant was replaced by an absolute prohibition in the statutory tenancy order, for the landlord's protection against any sub-tenancy; but a prohibition on sharing proposed was disallowed as being unreasonable, new and imprecise, on the facts.[15] Unless application is made not less than two

---

14   *Lagens Properties Ltd v Bandino* [1965] EGD 69.
15   *Etablissement Commercial Kamira v Schiazzano* [1985] QB 93, [1984] 2 All ER 465, CA.

months before the date of termination, the landlord's original notice will lapse; but it cannot be made less than two months after the landlord's notice was served (or one month if the tenant elected to take possession). If the notice lapses, the tenancy will not terminate, but will continue under s 3 as before. If on the other hand the tenant had failed within two months to elect to retain possession or the qualifying condition had ceased to be fulfilled at the end of that time, the tenant's rights will be lost, and the tenancy will come to an end on the termination date.

Section 9 gives statutory guidance as to the terms relating to repairs. By s 9(1) the court cannot without the consent of landlord and tenant, require initial repairs to be carried out in excess of what is required to bring the house into good repair or the carrying out of repairs not specified by the landlord as those he is willing to carry out. By s 9(4) repairs under the statutory tenancy are those only required to keep the house in the state it would be in after completion of initial repairs.[16]

Generally, once the statutory tenancy starts, all liability of the tenant under the former tenancy is extinguished (s 10) except for liability to pay rent, rates or for insurance in particular.

V THE STATUTORY TENANCY

Where the terms of the statutory tenancy have been duly agreed between the parties at least two months before the termination date specified, or determined by the court, the long tenancy will continue until the termination date or for three months after the application to the court has finally been disposed of and any time for appealing or further appealing has expired, whichever is the later (s 64). The statutory tenancy thereupon takes effect by virtue of s 6(1) as a statutory tenancy under the Rent Act 1977, as if the former tenancy had been a tenancy of the dwelling-house on the terms agreed between the parties or agreed by the court. And if the court has to determine what premises shall be within the meaning of 'dwelling-house' before the term date, it can only specify such premises as are likely to qualify at the term date (s 6(3)). There can be no statutory tenancy, however, if after two months after the landlord's notice was served, the qualifying condition was not satisfied unless the tenant had elected to retain possession (s 6(2)). Where the Rent Act does apply,[16A] the tenant is entitled to its protection as long as he remains in possession. The rent is such as may be agreed upon between the parties,

---

16   By s 8 of the 1954 Act, the landlord is entitled to compensation for initial repairs he carries out, necessitated by earlier tenants' breaches of covenant.

16A It is thought that, in the absence of any specific provision in the Housing Act 1988, where a statutory tenancy takes effect on or after 15 January 1989, it will necesarily be an assured tenancy, thanks to s 34 of the Housing Act 1988, and the rent will not be statute-controlled.

and if they cannot agree, it will be the rent payable immediately prior to the termination of the long tenancy. In that event, it will be open to the landlord to have a fair rent registered.

B   THE LEASEHOLD REFORM ACT 1967

I   INTRODUCTION

The Leasehold Reform Act 1967 gives a tenant under a long lease of a house at a low rent, either the right to acquire the freehold or to obtain an extended lease. All subsequent references in this part of the Chapter are to the 1967 Act as amended.

II   APPLICATION OF THE 1967 ACT

Section 1 confers on 'a tenant of a leasehold house, occupying the house as his residence, a right to acquire on fair terms the freehold or an extended lease of the house and premises' where the following conditions are satisfied:

(i)   the tenancy is a long tenancy at a low rent;
(ii)   at the relevant time (i e when the tenant gives notice under the Act of his desire to have the freehold or to have an extended lease, as the case may be), he has been a tenant of the house under a long tenancy at a low rent, and occupying it as his residence, for the last three years or for periods amounting to three years in the last ten years.

These conditions are complicated by the fact that they must each be satisfied at different times. The second condition is more complicated still, because it must be satisfied at all times throughout the three-year qualifying period, during which time there may well have been more than one tenant and more than one tenancy; and there may have been changes not only in the rent and the rateable value but also in the premises comprised in the tenancy.

Rateable value

The house must fall within the relevant rateable value limits on the appropriate day. The original such day was 23 March 1965, and the original limits £200 or £400 if the house was in Greater London (s 1(1)(a)). A house will also be caught where the tenancy was created *on or before* 18 February 1966, and rated separately before 1 April 1973, if its rateable value does not exceed £750 or £1,500 (Greater London) – under s 1(6). A tenancy created *after* 18 February 1966 but rated only after 1 April 1973, is then subject to limits of £500 or £1,000 as the case may be (s 1(5)). Tenancies created *on or before* 18 February 1966 but not rated until on or after 1 April 1973, are subject as a rule to limits of £750 and £1,500.

The rateable value must be apportioned where the house and premises form part only of the relevant valuation list; equally, if they form a number of separately rated units, there has to be aggregation.[17] The county court may determine a reduction in the rateable value if it is shown by the tenant that the limits were exceeded by reason of structural alterations, extensions or additions carried out by the tenant.[18] A reduction in the rateable value limits, which is backdated to the appropriate day in question, is to be taken into account in determining whether the house in question falls within, or outside, the statutory limits.[19]

'Tenant'

There must be a 'tenancy', which is defined by s 37 as including a legal or equitable tenancy, but not a tenancy at will, a mortgage-term nor an interest under a settlement.[20] 'Tenant', however, is not as such defined, but is given specific meanings in various provisions of the Act. Under s 1(1) it is 'the tenant' who must satisfy the condition as to occupation and who has the right to claim the rights under the Act. Normally they will be the same person, but not necessarily. Thus, under s 5, a tenant who has established a right under the Act, by giving a notice of intention, may assign that right together with the tenancy, and the assignee will be entitled to enforce that right without himself having to satisfy the condition as to occupation; so too may executors or administrators of a tenant who dies after establishing his right. Similarly, trustees for sale have the same rights as a beneficiary under the trust for sale would have had if he had been the tenant (s 6); and the widow (and certain other members of a deceased tenant's family), who succeeds to the tenancy, will be treated as having been the tenant during any period before the tenant's death when she was resident in the house during which the tenant was in occupation of the house as his residence (s 7). Members of

---

17 Rent Act 1977 s 25.
18 Leasehold Reform Act 1967 s 1(4A) and Housing Act 1974 Sch 8.
19 *Macfarquhar v Phillimore* [1986] 2 EGLR 89, CA. Whether backdating has this effect depends on all the circumstances: see *Rendall v Duke of Westminster* [1987] 1 EGLR 96, CA.
20 Mortgage term means a subsisting term, not one sold to the tenant under the mortgagee's power of sale: *Re Fairview, Church Street, Bromyard* [1974] 1 All ER 1233, [1974] 1 WLR 579.

the tenant's family who so qualify include his or her spouse, parents-in-law, son, daughter, son-in-law, daughter-in-law, step-children, illegitimate and adopted children and their respective spouses.

A sub-tenant may qualify for rights under the Act unless his sub-tenancy was unlawfully granted out of a superior tenancy, which was not itself a tenancy at a low rent, and that breach has not been waived (s 5(4)).

'Long tenancy'

By virtue of s 3(1) this means a tenancy (or sub-tenancy unless created out of a tenancy which was not itself a long tenancy) granted for a fixed-term exceeding 21 years,[1] whether or not it was terminable within that time by notice (i e a break-clause exercisable by either party), by re-entry, forfeiture or otherwise, except on death or marriage with special provisions in this latter case. Certain tenancies granted under the 'right to buy' provisions of the Housing Act 1985 are treated as falling within the 1967 Act even though they may be granted for less than 21 years (1985 Act s 173). Shared ownership leases granted under these provisions are excluded from the 1967 Act, however (1985 Act s 174). Where a long lease provided that it should cease in certain events, including the lease not being held by a member of a certain housing association, it was held still to be within s 3(1) as 'terminable' therein includes (a) determination by act of the parties and (b) determination by a specified event prior to the term date.[2] A tenancy continuing under s 3 or s 24 of the 1954 Act is within the definition (s 3(5)), but not a statutory tenancy under that Act. Where the original tenancy was not for more than 21 years with a covenant for renewal without premium (but not for perpetual renewal) and by one or more renewals the total term exceeds 21 years, the Act applies as if from the outset there had been a long tenancy (s 3(4)). Where the tenant takes a new tenancy of the property (or part of it) at the end of a long tenancy at a low rent, the later tenancy (and any later tenancy) will be deemed to be a long tenancy irrespective of its terms (s 3(2));[3] and where the tenant takes a new long tenancy (whether or not by virtue of s 3(2)) of the property, or part of it, on the coming to an end of a long tenancy, the Act will apply, as if there had been a single tenancy beginning with the earlier tenancy and expiring with the later tenancy (s 3(3)).[4] Where the tenant holds parts of a house

---

1   See *Roberts v Church Comrs for England* [1972] 1 QB 278, [1971] 3 All ER 703.
2   *Eton College v Bard* [1983] Ch 321, [1983] 2 All ER 961, CA.
3   Section 3(2) applies also to assigns of the tenant: *Austin v Dick Richards Properties Ltd* [1975] 2 All ER 75, [1975] 1 WLR 1033, CA.
4   See *Bates v Pierrepoint* (1978) 37 P & CR 420, CA (two leases granted in 1961 and 1973 at same rent treated as single term).

(any of which may include other premises occupied with the house) under separate tenancies from the same landlord, the separate parts and other premises will be treated as being under a single tenancy corresponding to the duration of the tenancy comprising the house (s 3(6)).

'Low rent'

The tenant cannot claim the benefit of the 1967 Act unless the tenancy is at all times during the qualifying period at a low rent, i e not exceeding two-thirds of the rateable value, on the relevant appropriate day (see above). However, if the tenancy (other than a building lease) was granted between the end of August 1938 and the beginning of April 1963, the test is applied by reference to the rent and letting value at the beginning of the tenancy. 'Letting value' includes the actual rent plus any decapitalised value of a premium,[5] and means the best annual return obtainable in the open market for the grant of a long lease: this may be in the form of a rack rent or a lower rent plus a premium.[6] This proviso ensures that tenancies granted during that period at what were then rack rents, did not come within the Act merely as a result of the increased rateable values shown in the valuation list in 1965. Rent means the rent reserved as such, disregarding any deduction allowed in the event of damage to the property or any penalties in the event of breaches of obligation and any sums expressed to be payable for repairs, maintenance or insurance to be effected by the landlord or a superior landlord (s 4(1)(b)).

Section 1(1)(b) requires that the condition as to low rent be satisfied not only at the 'relevant time' (i e when the tenant serves his notice of intention) but also throughout the qualifying period of three years. The tenant cannot make up the relevant period of years by adding to an insufficient period of occupation at a low rent, earlier periods at a rack rent.[7] If during this time the property comprised in the tenancy (whether or not that includes a new tenancy under s 3(3)) has remained the same, no problem arises in applying the test, since the rateable value will not have changed, though an increase in rent under a variable rent clause may have taken the rent reserved above the two-thirds limit. What may cause considerable difficulty, however, is where there has been an alteration in the premises during the qualifying period, which may have affected both the rent and the rateable value. Section 4(1) provides in effect that whenever the question arises whether a tenancy is or was a

---

5 *Manson v Duke of Westminster* [1981] QB 323, [1981] 2 All ER 40, CA.
6 *Johnston v Duke of Westminster* [1986] AC 839, [1986] 2 All ER 613, HL; also *Hembry v Henry Smith's Charity Trustees* [1987] 2 EGLR 109, CA.
7 *Harris v Plentex Ltd* (1980) 40 P & CR 483.

tenancy at a low rent, the question shall be determined by reference to the rateable value of the premises as a whole, whether or not the property then occupied with the house is the same in all respects as that comprised in the house and premises for the purposes of the claim. 'Premises' here does not include any premises let to the tenant but not occupied by him for the purposes of his claim, but which under s 2(4) the landlord can require him to take (s 4(4)), but the meaning of 'as a whole' is not explained. In view of s 4(4), it would seem that the rent and rateable value of premises which he is entitled to claim must be those at the time in question, any apportionment of rent being made in accordance with s 4(6), i e 'as is just according to the circumstances existing at the date of the severance giving rise to the apportionment'. In the case of a 'house' consisting of two (or more) units, the relevant rateable value limits are ascertained as at the first date when the unit concerned is first shown as a separate hereditament on a valuation list: the aggregate of the values so shown is then taken.[8]

'House'

A house to which the Act applies is defined by s 2(1) as including any building designed or adapted for living in and reasonably so called, notwithstanding that the building is not structurally detached, or was or is not solely designed or adapted for living in,[9] or is divided horizontally into flats or maisonettes, and:

(a) where a building is divided horizontally, the flats or other units into which it is so divided are not separate 'houses', though the building as a whole may be; and

(b) where a building is divided vertically the building as a whole is not a 'house' though any of the units into which it is divided may be.

A house which is not structurally detached, and of which a material part lies above or below a part of the structure not comprised in the house, is excluded from the above definition by s 2(2).

'Structurally detached' means detached from any other structure: where part of a tenant's rooms were above garages sub-let by him, the rooms fell outside s 2(1) since they were not detached from the rest of a structure not comprised in the house.[10] Section 2(2) therefore excludes suites of rooms and other horizontally divided parts of buildings erected

---

8 *Dixon v Allgood* [1987] 3 All ER 1082, [1987] 1 WLR 1689, HL.
9 See *Lake v Bennett* [1970] 1 QB 663, [1970] 1 All ER 457 where part of the building had been converted into business premises.
10 *Parsons v Viscount Gage (Trustees of Henry Smith's Charity)* [1974] 1 All ER 1162, [1974] 1 WLR 435, HL.

on stilts or platforms.[11] A house above an archway which gave access to mews behind was held not to be structurally detached.[12]

Flats created by horizontal divisions had to be excluded from the Act, as regards enfranchisement, at least, because of the unenforceability of positive covenants except under a lease. Separate flats are totally excluded, however, by para (a), even as regards a 50-year extension; the whole building, horizontally divided into separate flats, may doubtfully constitute a 'house', where the tenant of the building, for example, has converted it, and lives in part of it, the other flats being let off separately.[13] Conversely, para (b) excludes, for example, a row of terraced houses, but allows each one to qualify separately on its own merits.

The essential requirements are that these should be a building, which is designed or adapted for living in, and which can be called a house in the broad sense by a reasonable man. Therefore, a purpose-built shop with living accommodation above it generally falls within the notion of 'house' as tenants of such premises are fully within the intendment of the 1967 Act; and the question is not just one of fact. Thus, a mixed-user building which may reasonably be called a house (and this is a question of law) falls within the 1967 Act unless exceptional circumstances are shown.[14] A building consisting of two floors, with a flat on each floor, there being access between the two floors, which was used as a single dwelling, was held to be a 'house'.[15]

'Premises'

Where the qualifying conditions have been satisfied, a claim under the Act may be made in respect of the 'house and premises'. 'Premises' means any garage, outhouse, garden, yard and appurtenances which are let to the tenant with the house and are occupied with, and used for the purposes of, the house or any part of it by him or by another occupant (s 2(3)). A strip of land at the back of a house was not part of the premises, where it was let separately and was not closely connected with the lease of the house;[16] the term 'appurtenances' includes land let with the house; what falls within that is a question of fact.[17]

---

11   *Woodfall* para 3–0960.
12   *Cresswell v Duke of Westminster* [1985] 2 EGLR 151, CA.
13   See *Peck v Anicar Properties Ltd* [1971] 1 All ER 517, CA, and *Wolf v Crutchley* [1971] 1 All ER 520.
14   *Tandon v Trustees of Spurgeons Homes* [1982] AC 755, [1982] 1 All ER 1086, HL.
15   *Sharpe v Duke Street Securities NV* [1987] 2 EGLR 106, CA.
16   *Gaidowski v Gonville and Caius College, Cambridge* [1975] 2 All ER 952, [1975] 1 WLR 1066, CA.
17   *Methuen-Campbell v Walters* [1979] QB 525, [1979] 1 All ER 606, CA (paddock not within s 2(3) on facts, though a valuable amenity).

In addition to premises which the tenant occupies, there may be other premises under the tenancy which, because he does not occupy them, he is not entitled to claim. Section 2(4) entitles the landlord to require that they be treated as part of the house and premises. Conversely, s 2(5) entitles him to have excluded from the house and premises any part of them lying above or below other premises (not consisting only of underlying mines or minerals). As regards underlying minerals, the landlord can require them to be excluded, if proper provision is made for the support of the house and premises.

'Occupying'

Occupation of the house by the tenant as his residence is a condition to be satisfied not only at the time when he makes his claim, but also throughout the qualifying period of three years. He must be in occupation of the house as his only or main residence (whether or not he uses it for other purposes) (s 1(2)). Tenants of houses comprised in agricultural holdings, however, are in effect precluded from acquiring rights under the Act by such occupation under s 1(3)(b). Occupation 'in part only' is sufficient, and this requirement has been held by the Court of Appeal to have been satisfied by the tenant occupying a basement flat, the remaining three floors being sub-let unfurnished as separate flats.[18] The part occupied, however, must be viewed in relation to the whole, for under the definition of 'house' (see above) the building must be what could reasonably be called a house; moreover, under s 1(3)(a), a tenant cannot acquire rights under the Act by occupying a house let with land or premises to which the house is ancillary. Whether the house is the tenant's only or main residence is a question of fact;[19] and it has been held that a husband and wife can each have a main residence.[20] The condition must normally be satisfied by the tenant personally, and accordingly, under s 37(5), no company or other artificial person, nor any corporation sole is capable of occupation.[1] He must normally occupy *qua* tenant, but there are exceptions in the case of assignment (s 5), settlements and trusts for sale (s 6) and succession of certain members of the tenant's family on his death (s 7). Where the tenant is temporarily absent, he will not for that reason cease to be in occupation;

---

18 *Harris v Swick Securities Ltd* [1969] 3 All ER 1131.
19 *Byrne v Rowbotham* (1969) 210 Estates Gazette 823; *Baron v Phillips* (1978) 38 P & CR 91, CA.
20 *Fowell v Radford* (1969) 21 P & CR 99, CA.
1 If the occupation by the tenant is as bare trustee for a company but with its permission, then, though he has the legal estate as against the landlord, he is not within s 2(1) as he does not have the right to occupy as a residence; the 1967 Act does not extend to a company: *Duke of Westminster v Oddy* (1984) 270 Estates Gazette 945, CA.

prolonged absence with no intention to resume physical occupation, or absence due to legal inability to do so, disqualifies the tenant.[2]

III LIMITATIONS ON RIGHTS UNDER THE ACT

In addition to the cases mentioned above of tenants who cannot acquire any rights under the Act, e g tenants of agricultural holdings, companies, corporations sole, etc, there are a number of special cases where the rights under the Act are either excluded entirely or are restricted, even though all the conditions above have been satisfied.

(a) *Special categories of landlord* Tenants of the National Trust cannot enfranchise (s 32). Specific rules, the details of which lie outside this book, deal with special landlords, such as the Crown (s 33) and with reservation of development and other rights by local authorities (ss 28 and 29). If a landlord cannot be traced, there is a special rule that, after a claim procedure, the court deals in effect with the enfranchisement process (s 27). Tenancies granted by local authorities, or registered housing associations, at a premium are, subject to conditions, outside the 1967 Act.[3]

(b) *Loss of rights by the tenant* Any claim by a tenant is void under s 22 and the Third Schedule, if he has already given notice to terminate the tenancy (e g by notice to quit, or a notice under ss 5, 26 or 27 of the 1954 Act), or if he has been granted a new tenancy under s 28 of that Act. Conversely, such a notice is of no effect if it is given whilst a claim under the 1967 Act subsists. Secondly, a tenant loses his rights under the Act, if within two months of being given notice to terminate by the landlord, he does not himself give notice of his intention to claim enfranchisement or an extension under the Act. Thirdly, he may serve a notice under s 9(3)[4] within one month of the price being fixed stating that he is unable or unwilling to take the freehold at that price; he will thereupon be liable for the landlord's costs, and will not be entitled to make another claim to enfranchise within the next three years. Fourthly, a tenant's rights may be lost by forfeiture, but after notice of a claim has been given, forfeiture proceedings may be commenced only with the leave of the court, and leave will not be granted unless the court is satisfied that the claim was not made in good faith,[5] i e in order to avoid

---

2 *Poland v Earl Cadogan* [1980] 3 All ER 544, CA.
3 Housing Act 1980 s 140 and Housing (Exclusion of Shared Ownership Tenancies) etc Regs 1982, SI 1982/62.
4 The tenant may instead claim an extension.
5 Sch 3 para 4(1).

forfeiture.[6] Once a tenancy has been extended, the tenant has no further rights under the 1954 or 1967 Acts.

(c)   *Landlord's claim for possession*   Where the tenancy is extended, or the tenant claims an extension, the landlord may apply to the court for possession under s 17(1) (not more than one year before the term date of the original tenancy) on the grounds that he intends to redevelop the whole, or a substantial part, of the premises; in certain circumstances, the tenant will then have a right to claim enfranchisement. Also, where the tenant has claimed enfranchisement or an extension, the landlord may apply to the court for possession under s 18 on the ground that he reasonably requires possession for occupation either by himself or an adult member of his family. The court shall not make an order for possession under s 18 if having regard to all the circumstances of the case, including the availability of other accommodation for the landlord or the tenant, the court is satisfied that greater hardship would be caused by making an order than by refusing an order for possession. The landlord cannot seek possession on this ground, if he acquired his interest in the house after 18 February 1966. In both cases, the tenant is entitled to compensation.

IV   ENFRANCHISEMENT

Where the necessary conditions are satisfied, and the tenant has duly notified the landlord of his desire to acquire the freehold, the landlord is bound to make, and the tenant to accept, a conveyance of the freehold of the house and premises at a price to be fixed in accordance with the Act (s 8).

The tenant's notice[7]

The tenant's notice of intention may be served[8] on the landlord at any time, provided that all the conditions have been satisfied. He may serve it even though the original contractual tenancy has come to an end, e g under a tenancy continuing under s 3 of the 1954 Act; in practice, however, he would lose his rights on the creation of a statutory tenancy, by virtue of the rent which is then unlikely to be a 'low rent'. Once served,

---

6   See *Central Estates (Belgravia) Ltd v Woolgar; Liverpool Corpn v Husan* [1972] 1 QB 48, [1971] 3 All ER 647.

7   For provisions where the tenant is a sub-tenant, see Leasehold Reform Act 1967 Sch 1, identifying the 'reversioner' as the person with whom the sub-tenant deals.

8   In the form prescribed by the Leasehold Reform (Notices) Regulations 1967, SI 1967/1768.

the tenant's notice creates a binding contract of sale (in effect).[9] Time runs, for limitation purposes, for 12 years from the service of the s 8 notice.[10] Under s 5(5) the notice is registrable as a Class C(iv) Charge under the Land Charges Act 1972, or may be the subject of a notice or caution under the Land Registration Act 1925, in the case of registered land.[11] The tenant may, after service of a s 8 notice, abandon or contractually release the right to enfranchise; but mere failure to pursue a disputed claim following a s 8 notice is not sufficient for this purpose, because any release has to be mutual, and arise out of mutual contract, representation or estoppel.[12]

The price

1 *Houses with rateable values below £1,000 or £500*

The levels of rateable values for the purposes of price determination, are those at the date of service of the tenant's notice.[13] The general principles on the calculation of the price are laid down in s 9(1). The price is the amount which at the date of the notice, the house and premises might be expected to realise, if sold in the open market by a willing seller, with the tenant and members of his family residing in the house, not buying or seeking to buy. The following statutory assumptions must be made (s 9(1)):

(a) that the vendor is selling an estate in fee simple subject to the tenancy; that the Act did not confer a right to acquire the freehold; that the tenancy was extended by the tenant for 50 years subject to the landlord's right to resume possession under s 17 (for redevelopment purposes);

(b) that, apart from the incumbrances for which the tenant would be liable until the determination of the tenancy, it is being sold subject to the same rent charges as in the sale to the tenant;

(c) that it is being sold subject to the same rights and burdens as in the sale to the tenant.

The general principles of valuation which result from the above assumptions are that there is a hypothetical sale in the open market by a willing seller of the freehold reversion upon a lease which is deemed to be

---

9 The terms are governed by Leasehold Reform (Enfranchisement and Extension) Regulations 1967, SI 1967/1874.
10 *Collin v Duke of Westminster* [1985] QB 581, [1985] 1 All ER 463, CA.
11 The tenant's right cannot constitute an overriding interest under s 70(1) LRA 1925: s 5(5).
12 *Collin v Duke of Westminster* [1985] QB 581, [1985] 1 All ER 463, CA.
13 Leasehold Reform Act 1967 s 9(1) and (1A).

extended for 50 years under s 14 of the 1967 Act. In addition, the following factors govern the ascertainment of the value of the reversion:

(a)   the value of the present rent;
(b)   the value of the ground rent for the site only;[14]
(c)   the value of the right to resume possession under s 17 for redevelopment purposes;
(d)   the value of the freehold reversion in possession at the end of the (deemed) 50 years' extension lease;
(e)   the length of the existing term.[15]

No allowance is here made for 'marriage value', that is, the benefit to the landlord of other adjacent or neighbouring sites owned by him, even though enfranchisement will preclude him from comprehensive redevelopment which would enhance the value of each individual site.

2   *Houses with rateable values above £1,000 or £500*

In this case the principles differ somewhat. First, there is no assumption that the tenant is granted a 50 year extension lease; and secondly, s 9(1A) involves, in particular, the following special assumptions in calculating the price payable:

(a)   there is a deemed continuation of the tenancy under Part I of the 1954 Act;
(b)   it is to be assumed that the vendor is selling the freehold subject to the tenancy, but that the Act did not confer a right to acquire the freehold or an extended lease, and, where the tenancy has been extended under the 1967 Act, that the tenancy will terminate on the agreed date;[16]
(c)   that the tenant is assumed to have no liability to carry out any repairs, maintenance or redecorations at any time;
(d)   the price must be treated as diminished by any increase in the value of the house and premises due to an improvement carried out by the tenant or his predecessors in title at their own expense.

Otherwise the general assumptions to be made are the same as those laid down in s 9(1) for the lower rateable values. In valuing the price, however, it is to be noted that an allowance may be made for 'marriage values' so that an allowance may be made for the higher bid which the sitting tenant would make (as compared to any investor) due to the extra value to him of buying the reversion.

---

14   See *Official Custodian for Charities v Goldridge* (1973) 26 P & CR 191, CA.
15   See *Gallagher Estates Ltd v Walker* (1973) 28 P & CR 113, CA.
16   1967 Act s 9(1A) as amended by Housing and Planning Act 1986 s 23, reversing *Mosley v Hickman* [1986] 1 EGLR 161, CA.

3 *Miscellaneous*

In the event of any dispute as to the price payable, it being initially supposed that the parties are to agree to it, the price must be determined by the leasehold valuation tribunal, which has jurisdiction also to determine any ancillary questions such as the terms of the conveyance (s 21).

The tenant has the right to resile by notice to the landlord once the price has been determined (s 9(3)) but this ends his rights under the relevant notice and no further rights may be claimed under the 1967 Act for three further years (s 9(3)).

The conveyance

The landlord's obligation under s 8(1) is to convey to the tenant the house and premises in fee simple, subject to the tenancy and incumbrances on the leasehold interest created by the tenant (e g sub-tenancies, mortgages etc), but otherwise free from incumbrances. Incumbrances attaching to the freehold (e g rights of beneficiaries under the Settled Land Act 1925) are to be overreached, and for that purpose, the tenant is, in any event, to be treated as a purchaser for valuable consideration. Rights binding upon the land, such as easements and restrictive covenants, cannot be defeated, except by virtue of the general law, and the liability of the tenant is expressly preserved in relation to burdens originating in tenure and burdens in respect of the upkeep or regulation for the benefit of any locality of any land, building, structure, works, ways or water courses.[17]

Unless the tenant agrees otherwise, or they are excluded to protect the landlord's existing interest in tenant's incumbrances, the rights under ss 62 and 63 of the Law of Property Act 1925, will be implied in the conveyance (s 10(1)). Additionally, the tenant is entitled to have the benefit, so far as the landlord is capable of granting them, of easements that he had under the tenancy (including rights of support, light and air, the passage of water or gas, sewage, drainage, and the use of maintenance of electricity, telephone or television cables; and conversely the burden of such easements may be imposed on the tenant for the benefit of other land (s 10(2)). Rights of way necessary for the reasonable enjoyment of the house by the tenant (or of other property retained by the landlord) are to be included in the conveyance (s 10(3)), as are covenants restrictive of user for the purpose of ensuring that existing covenants remain enforceable, of indemnifying the landlord in respect of

---

17 While the tenant acquires any intermediate interest superior to his (s 5(4) and Sch 1), if he holds the freehold already, he is not given the right to acquire intermediate leasehold interests: *Gratton-Storey v Lewis* [1987] 2 EGLR 108, CA.

any breaches, or of enhancing the value of the house of the tenant or land of the landlord (s 10(4)).

The tenant is liable for the landlord's legal and other professional fees incurred in verifying the tenants claim, having the house valued and executing the conveyance (s 9(4)). The landlord has a lien in respect of the purchase price, his costs, arrears of rent and any other sums due under the tenancy up to the date of the conveyance (s 9(5)).

Rights of assigns

The rights of a tenant to enfranchise or to an extended lease, after a tenant's notice, are, by s 5(2), assignable with, but not apart from, the tenancy of the entire house and premises. An assignment without the benefit of the notice nullifies the notice, as does an assignment of the tenancy of one part only of the house and premises, to another person.

V EXTENSION OF THE LEASE

The tenant's right to claim an extension of his lease for 50 years under s 14 is dependent upon all the conditions having been satisfied and the service of a valid notice of intention by the tenant.

Extension

The 50-year extension runs from the date on which the existing tenancy would have come to an end (i e the term date). In effect, the new tenancy will be substituted for any rights of continuation under Part I of the 1954 Act. The Rent Act 1977 does not apply to an extended lease (s 16(1A)). The tenant is liable to pay the landlord's legal and other professional fees and costs incurred in verifying the tenant's claim, executing the lease, and valuing the house and premises for the purpose of fixing the rent (s 14(2)), and the landlord is not bound to execute the lease until such costs have been paid, together with any arrears of rent or other sums due under the existing tenancy (s 14(3)).

Where he would otherwise have had the right, the tenant may claim enfranchisement at any time before the term date of his existing tenancy, even though he first claimed an extension, but once the extended tenancy has commenced, he loses all further rights under the Act, and any rights he would have had under the 1954 Act, or under the Rent Act 1977 (s 16(1)): and a sub-tenancy granted by a tenant under an extended lease cannot acquire any rights under the Act (s 16(4)), nor under the 1954 Act, nor under Part VII of the Rent Act 1977 (s 16(1)).[18]

---

18 Presumably, a similar rule applies to Part I of the Housing Act 1988 (no express provision is made in that Act).

Terms of the extended tenancy

Section 15(2) provides in effect that the rent payable under the extended tenancy shall be a modern ground rent for the site only, to be determined not more than 12 months before the new rent becomes payable. A rent review clause exercisable after 25 years, on notice, may be inserted, if the landlord so requires. In fixing the rent, regard must be had to any changes in the property to be comprised in the new tenancy, or in the terms of the new tenancy; further, costs of services, repairs, maintenance, etc, may be added (s 15(3)).

The other terms of the tenancy will generally be the same as under the existing tenancy, except in so far as they need to be modified as a result of changes in the property, etc (s 15(1)). Options to purchase and options to renew contained in the existing lease or in a collateral agreement will not be included, however, nor any right to terminate the tenancy before the term date other than for breach of covenant (s 15(5)). Either party may under s 15(7) require the modification or exclusion of any terms under the existing tenancy that it would be unreasonable to include unchanged in view of changed circumstances since they were imposed. The landlord's right to resume possession under s 17 must be reserved (s 15(8)).

PART E
BUSINESS TENANCIES

Chapter 21

Introduction

The relationship of landlord and tenant of business premises is governed by the general law until the contractual tenancy expires, or the landlord serves a notice to quit or otherwise terminates the tenancy at law. Thereafter, Part II of the Landlord and Tenant Act 1954 applies, and it is only possible to regain possession as laid down in the Act.

The following is a summary of the main effects of the 1954 Act.

1   Business tenants are given security initially by the continuation, despite termination of the contractual term, of the tenancy (s 24).
2   Continuation is on the same terms as the contractual tenancy: and may be prevented or terminated only as provided in the 1954 Act.
3   The landlord may prevent, or set in motion, the termination of continuation by a strict notice procedure (s 25): if he wishes to regain possession where the tenant is unwilling to give it up, he may do so only on the grounds in s 30. This procedure generally overrides the common law methods: certain of these are specially preserved (s 24(2)) such as forfeiture and tenants' notice to quit.
4   If the landlord has not served a s 25 notice, the tenant may request by notice a new tenancy (ss 26 and 24(1)(b)). If the landlord has served a s 25 notice, the tenant must first, if he wishes a new tenancy, state his unwillingness to give up possession and then apply to court for a new tenancy (ss 24(1)(a) and 29(2)). In both cases, the landlord may resist the new tenancy on one of a number of grounds in s 30.
5   In the event that the court orders a new tenancy (on the basis of guidelines in ss 32–35) the tenancy may be for up to 14 years and is for a term certain.
6   Should the landlord make out a ground of opposition to the grant of a new tenancy and the tenant quits, he may be entitled to compensation for quitting and also for qualifying improvements (these latter being dealt with by Part I of the Landlord and Tenant Act 1927).

These procedural rules have to be most carefully followed and yet it is thought that a key policy of Part II of the 1954 Act is to encourage the parties to agree on matters out of court.[1] It is for this reason that the time-limits laid down in the Act must strictly be adhered to.

The policy of Part II of the 1954 Act has been described as follows by the Law Commission.[2] Part II recognises that a business tenant stands to lose any goodwill he has built up, and much of the value of his equipment and stock, if he has to leave when his tenancy expires. So, as a rule, he is able to obtain a renewal of his tenancy, or, failing that, compensation.

Part II of the 1954 Act generally works well and it is likely that, despite a need for some minor reforms, it will continue in its present form for some time.[3] Some difficulties on particular points of detail in the Act may at once be noted.

1   In the case of joint tenants, all must together apply for a new tenancy under the Act, otherwise the application will fail.[4] This rule has been modified for partnership tenancies (s 41A of the 1954 Act).
2   Difficulty has been experienced in balancing the interests of landlord and tenant where the terms of a new tenancy are reviewed by the court. It is generally thought that the House of Lords decision in *O'May v City of London Real Property Co Ltd* [5] precludes any modernisation of the form of the lease by the court under s 35. (The parties may agree to modernisation.)
3   The compensation provisions applicable where the landlord succeeds on one of any of three mandatory grounds for possession under s 30 (see Chapter 26) are linked to the rateable value of the premises concerned. It has been said that they should be linked to the tenant's actual loss.[6]
4   A tenant holding a lease of business premises personally may lose security under the 1954 Act Part II if he incorporates his business. In *Cristina v Seear* [7] the tenants ran a business and held the lease in their personal names, and later they incorporated the business, the lease continuing to be held by them personally. As a result, it was held that since the tenants traded through a company, they could not obtain a

---

1   The normal rule applies in this context that either party may resile from an agreement for a new tenancy 'subject to contract': *Derby & Co Ltd v ITC Pension Trust Ltd* [1977] 2 All ER 890.
2   Law Com No 141 (1985) para 7.22.
3   For suggested reforms see Law Com No 162 (1987), also Fogel and Freedman (1985) 275 Estates Gazette 118, 227; and below.
4   *Jacobs v Chaudhuri* [1968] 2 QB 470, [1968] 2 All ER 124, CA.
5   [1983] 2 AC 726, [1982] 1 All ER 660, HL. See ch 27.
6   Law Com No 162 (1987) para 4.58.
7   [1985] 2 EGLR 128, CA.

renewal of the lease under the Act, as they were not in occupation within s 23.[8]

Towards the end of 1988, the Law Commission published a working paper asking for views on proposed reforms.[9] Some of the main areas were: (1) the rules as to companies; (2) whether the landlord should be able to terminate a lease in relation to part of the premises; (3) whether periodic tenants should be able to request a new tenancy; (4) the rules as to time-limits; (5) the rules as to surrenders and agreements for surrender; (6) the current 14-year maximum limit on a new tenancy ordered by the court; (7) whether the tenant should be able to apply for an interim rent.

---

8 Occupation by trust beneficiaries is treated as within the Act by s 41 and groups of companies are specially treated by s 42. The present gap is hard to justify.
9 Law Com W/P No 111. The responses were asked for by the end of March 1989. See D W Williams 1988/48 Estates Gazette 61.

Chapter 22

Application of Part II of the 1954 Act

I TENANCIES PROTECTED BY PART II

Section 23(1) provides that Part II applies 'to any tenancy where the property comprised in the tenancy is or includes premises which are occupied by the tenant and are so occupied for the purposes of a business carried on by him or for those and other purposes'. It should be noted that Part II therefore applies to *any* 'business' tenancy, irrespective of the rental or rateable value of the premises, unless it falls within the list of tenancies specifically excluded.

'Tenancy'

There must be a *tenancy*, which is defined by s 69(1) as meaning 'a tenancy created either immediately or derivatively out of the freehold, whether by lease or underlease, by an agreement for a lease or underlease or by a tenancy agreement or in pursuance of any enactment (including this Act), but does not include a mortgage term or any interest arising in favour of a mortgagor by his attorning tenant to his mortgagee'. While it does not make any difference whether the agreement is by deed, written, oral, or implied, there must be an agreement for a lease or tenancy, and, as a result, licences are excluded from Part II of the 1954 Act.[1] In addition, express and implied tenancies at will are outside statutory protection.[2] In doubtful cases, where there is no clear lease agreement, the existence of statutory protection becomes a relevant factor in the evaluation of the parties' intentions in accepting rent, so that where an occupier was granted a series of extensions to his lease, pending abortive

---

1   *Shell-Mex and BP Ltd v Manchester Garages Ltd* [1971] 1 All ER 841, [1971] 1 WLR 612, CA; *Dresden Estates Ltd v Collinson* (1987) 55 P & CR 47, CA; cf *Essex Plan Ltd v Broadminster Ltd* [1988] 43 EG 84: see further ch 3.
2   *Manfield & Sons Ltd v Botchin* [1970] 2 QB 612, [1970] 3 All ER 143; *Hagee (London) Ltd v Erikson and Larson* [1976] QB 209, [1975] 3 All ER 234, CA (express); *Wheeler v Mercer* [1957] AC 416, [1956] 3 All ER 631, HL (implied).

negotiations for a new lease, which was to take effect outside the 1954 Act, it was held that even though rent was paid and accepted, the occupier was a tenant at will and outside Part II.[3] Sub-tenancies are expressly within the definition, and even unlawful sub-tenancies, e g granted without the landlord's consent, have been held to be within the Act.[4]

'The property comprised in the tenancy'

The meaning of this phrase is, as it suggests, the whole of the premises let to the tenant under the tenancy; but its use here must be distinguished from the technical sense of 'the holding'[5] which is defined by s 23(3) as being 'the property comprised in the tenancy' minus any parts of the premises let which are not occupied by the tenant or by any employee of the tenant for the purpose of the tenant's business. The most important result of the distinction is that since a tenant is entitled to apply for a new tenancy of only the property comprised in the 'holding' (s 23), he will not be *entitled* to apply for (but the landlord may require him to take (s 32(2))) a new tenancy in respect of any parts which, for example, he has ceased to occupy personally or through an employee in connection with his business.[6] Nevertheless, this will not prevent the current tenancy of the whole of the premises from continuing under s 24 (in similar circumstances) since that section applies to the property comprised in the tenancy which is or includes premises which are occupied by the tenant for the purposes of his business.

'Occupied by the tenant for the purposes of a business'

These words are important in two different contexts: a tenant must satisfy this condition in s 23 in order to qualify for statutory continuation and for the right to apply for a new tenancy; and the landlord must be able to satisfy a similar, but not identical condition if he wishes to oppose an application for a new tenancy on the ground specified in s 30(1)(g).

'Occupied'

Occupation imports elements of control and user, e g physical occupation; it is a question of fact and degree whether in a given case it

---

3   *Cardiothoracic Institute v Shrewdcrest Ltd* [1986] 3 All ER 633, [1986] 1 WLR 368. Neither party intended the creation of a periodic tenancy in the interim period.
4   *D'Silva v Lister House Development Ltd* [1971] Ch 17, [1970] 1 All ER 858.
5   See *Heath v Drown* [1973] AC 498, [1972] 2 All ER 561.
6   *Narcissi v Wolfe* [1960] Ch 10, [1959] 3 All ER 71.

exists.[7] Occupation need not always be personal,[8] exclusive[9] nor physical;[10] the condition must be satisfied at the right time. It was held in *I & H Caplan Ltd v Caplan (No 2)*[11] to be a continuing condition of a tenant's right to a new tenancy that he should, throughout the proceedings and at the date of the order, be in occupation of the premises. Where a tenant carried on the business of proprietor of lock-up garages and sub-let most of them, retaining merely a nominal presence on the land, it was held that the tenant was not in occupation for the purposes of s 23: as with occupation by a government department, there must, for s 23 to be satisfied, be a significant degree of control and physical presence by the tenant.[12] If the tenant exercises regular control over the premises, visits them regularly and provides all facilities, then the fact that other persons occupy the premises will not prevent the tenant from being in occupation within s 23.[13] Even a sub-letting will not take the tenant out of s 23, provided he retains a physical presence on the premises, as by installing a resident manager,[14] or by personally occupying part of the premises. In all cases, the question of whether there is retained a sufficient degree of control and physical presence on the tenant's part is one of fact and degree. Occupation cannot be considered in isolation from *business user*, and intention may sometimes exist for some kind of nexus between the two. Such a nexus is established where the premises were such that they were capable of seasonal occupation only, provided there is continuity about successive occupations,[15] or where temporarily, the tenant abandoned trading but intended to resume it as a different business if granted a new tenancy.[16]

---

7   See e g *Hancock and Willis v GMS Syndicate Ltd* (1982) 265 Estates Gazette 473, CA.
8   In *Hills (Patents) Ltd v University College Hospital Board of Governors* [1956] 1 QB 90, [1955] 3 All ER 365, the Court of Appeal held that the Board of Governors of a hospital, as landlord, could establish the ground of objection specified in s 30(1)(g), they being capable of occupation as managers, on behalf of the Minister of Health; *Groveside Properties Ltd v Westminster Medical School* (1983) 267 Estates Gazette 593, (degree of control is vital); also *Linden v Department of Health and Social Security* [1986] 1 All ER 691, [1986] 1 WLR 164 (Secretary of State in occupation, having sufficient control over employee flats).
9   The Crown is capable of 'occupation': *Town Investments Ltd v Department of the Environment* [1978] AC 359, [1977] 1 All ER 813, HL.
10 See *I & H Caplan Ltd v Caplan (No 2)* [1963] 2 All ER 930 at 936–939, per Cross J.
11 Ibid. See also *Aspinall Finance Ltd v Viscount Chelsea* [1989] 09 EG 77.
12 *Trans-Britannia Properties Ltd v Darby Properties* [1986] 1 EGLR 151, CA.
13 *Linden v Department of Health and Social Security* [1986] 1 All ER 691, [1986] 1 WLR 164.
14 *Lee-Verhulst (Investments) Ltd v Harwood Trust* [1973] QB 204, [1972] 3 All ER 619, CA.
15 *Teasdale v Walker* [1958] 3 All ER 307, [1958] 1 WLR 1076, CA.
16 *I & H Caplan Ltd v Caplan* [1961] 3 All ER 1174, [1962] 1 WLR 55, HL; *I & H Caplan v Caplan (No 2)* [1963] 2 All ER 930, [1963] 1 WLR 1247. Or where occupation temporarily is abandoned after a fire: *Morrison Holdings Ltd v Manders Property (Wolverhampton) Ltd* [1976] 2 All ER 205, [1976] 1 WLR 533, CA.

There is no nexus where the occupation is in breach of covenant.[17] Where the tenants held personally a lease of business premises, and subsequently ran the business through the medium of a company, it was held that, after the incorporation, the tenants, who continued to hold the lease personally, were no longer in occupation of the premises and could not apply for a new tenancy.[18]

Part business part residential user

In the event that the premises are used partly for business and partly for residential user, difficult issues arise, as where a professional man uses part of his home as an office.[19] The following facts are relevant:

(a) If the premises are mainly used for residential purposes and the de facto business user is purely incidental, s 23 will apply to no part of the premises.[20]

(b) If it is shown that the object of the tenancy is to use the premises (or part) for business purposes, then the tenancy is for business purposes (or partly for those purposes) and s 23 prima facie applies.[1]

(c) If the lease prohibits any business user in the whole or any part of the premises, de facto business user cannot of itself attract s 23 of the 1954 Act.[2]

Should a lease restrict user to business purposes, that means that the tenancy is for business purposes; and so, if business user ceases the tenancy is not then covered by Part II of the 1954 Act nor by any other code (such as the Rent Act 1977).[3] Therefore, it seems that a business tenant using part for residential purposes who then ceases business user is outside the protection of either the business or residential code.

It appears that if in a wholly residential tenancy, a substantial business user later develops, s 23(1) will then apply and the tenancy will cease to qualify for Rent Act 1977 or Housing Act 1988 Part I protection, as the case may be.[4]

---

17 *Bell v Alfred Franks & Bartlett Co Ltd* [1980] 1 All ER 356, [1980] 1 WLR 340, CA (keeping of business cars and storage of business materials in garage in breach of covenant).

18 *Cristina v Seear* [1985] 2 EGLR 128, CA; also *Nozari-Zadeh v Pearl Assurance plc* [1987] 2 EGLR 91, CA.

19 As in *Royal Life Saving Society v Page* [1979] 1 All ER 5, [1978] 1 WLR 1329, CA.

20 *Lewis v Weldcrest Ltd* [1978] 3 All ER 1226, [1978] 1 WLR 1107, CA.

1 *Cheryl Investments Ltd v Saldanha* [1979] 1 All ER 5, [1978] 1 WLR 1329, CA.

2 *Bell v Alfred Franks & Bartlett Co Ltd*, supra.

3 *Pulleng v Curran* (1980) 44 P & CR 58, CA; *Henry Smith's Charity Trustees v Wagle* [1989] 11 EG 75, CA; and see J Martin [1983] Conv 380.

4 *Cheryl Investments Ltd v Saldanha*, supra; *Henry Smith's Charity Trustees v Wagle*, supra.

General limits on 'occupation'

So far as general limits on occupation are concerned, 'occupied' does not include the enjoyment, in isolation, of an incorporeal right such as an easement, as it refers to rateable occupation;[5] but incorporeal hereditaments such as a right of way may be 'occupied' along with premises such as land and buildings.[6]

'By the tenant'

The tenant must generally satisfy the condition as to occupation personally, but the Act contains three provisions to cover cases where the current tenancy is vested in some other person than the occupant who is actually carrying on the business, for whose benefit the rights under the Act are required:

(a)   Section 41(1) provides that where a tenancy is held on trust,[7] occupation by all or any of the beneficiaries under the trust for business purposes shall be treated as occupation by the tenant for the purposes of s 23.

(b)   Section 41A enables one of two or more joint tenants (e g partners in a firm), in whom the tenancy is vested, to apply for a new tenancy where the same partnership no longer exists.

(c)   Section 42(2) provides that where a tenancy is vested in one member of a group of companies, occupation by any member of the same group of companies shall be treated as occupation by the tenant for the purposes of s 23. By virtue of s 42(1), two companies are members of a group only if one is a subsidiary of the other, *or* both companies are subsidiaries of a third.

'For the purposes of'

This means something more than 'in connection with', but it has the effect of not requiring the tenant to be actually carrying on the business on the premises; e g a storage of stock in connection with the business.

'Business'

Business is defined by s 23(2) as including 'a trade, profession or employment', and including 'any activity carried on by a body of persons whether corporate or unincorporate'. 'Business' has a wider meaning

---

5   *Land Reclamation Co Ltd v Basildon District Council* [1979] 2 :All ER 993, [1979] 1 WLR 767, CA.

6   *Nevill Long & Co (Boards) Ltd v Firmenich & Co* (1983) 47 P & CR 59, CA (and this is so even if the reversion on the land etc and the right of way is severed later).

7   As in *Morar v Chauhan* [1985] 3 All ER 493, [1985] 1 WLR 1263, CA.

than 'trade'; the latter implies buying or selling, whereas 'business' extends to any activity which is done for payment. The words of definition in relation to a tenant who is an individual as opposed to a body corporate, are exhaustive of the term 'business'.[8] 'Activity' is correlative with the rest of the definition and casual user such as dumping waste on the relevant premises is excluded.[9] The definition is wide enough to cover offices, shops, garages, warehouses, factories, laboratories, hotels, cinemas, a doctor's surgery and clubs. The activities of the governors of a hospital, though non-profitmaking, have been held to be a 'business',[10] as has the running of a members' tennis club[11] but not a Sunday school for one hour each week.[12] A property company has been held to be running a 'business' in sub-letting residential flats in a block which it holds itself under a tenancy, but nevertheless, not to be entitled to protection under the Act since it could not be said to be 'in occupation'.[13]

Where a director of the tenant company lived in the basement and devoted his whole time to running sub-let flats, the occupation and business conditions were satisfied.[14] The difference between the two cases lies in the fact that in the second, the tenant was physically present, providing full-time services on the premises.[15] The question is ultimately one of degree.

A business carried on in breach of a general prohibition of use for business purposes covering the whole premises is outside the Act unless the immediate landlord or his predecessor in title consented to the breach, or the immediate landlord acquiesced (s 23(4)). A business carried on in breach of a prohibition of use for specified purposes will qualify (s 23(4)). Acquiescence means a passive non-objection; consent is a positive act such as written or oral acceptance or conduct.[16]

As to the question of part user of premises for business, part for residential purposes, see above. Part-time user of premises for business

---

8 *Lewis v Weldcrest Ltd* [1978] 3 All ER 1226, [1978] 1 WLR 1107, CA.
9 *Hillil Property and Investment Co Ltd v Naraine Pharmacy Ltd* (1979) 39 P & CR 67, CA.
10 *Hills (Patents) Ltd v University College Hospital Board of Governors* [1956] 1 QB 90, [1955] 3 All ER 365; *Town Investment Ltd v Department of the Environment* [1978] AC 359, [1977] 1 All ER 813, HL; *Parker v Westminster Roman Catholic Diocese Trustee* (1978) 36 P & CR 22, CA.
11 *Addiscombe Garden Estates Ltd v Crabbe* [1958] 1 QB 513, [1957] 3 All ER 563, CA.
12 *Abernethie v AH & J Kleiman Ltd* [1970] 1 QB 10, [1969] 2 All ER 790; also *Lewis v Weldcrest Ltd* [1978] 3 All ER 1226, [1978] 1 WLR 1107, CA.
13 *Bagettes Ltd v GP Estates Co Ltd* [1956] Ch 290, [1956] 1 All ER 729.
14 *Lee-Verhulst (Investments) Ltd v Harwood Trust* [1973] QB 204, [1972] 3 All ER 619, CA; also *William Boyer & Sons Ltd v Adams* (1975) 32 P & CR 89.
15 *Trans-Britannia Properties Ltd v Darby Properties Ltd* [1986] 1 EGLR 151, CA.
16 *Bell v Alfred Franks & Bartlett Co Ltd* [1980] 1 All ER 356, [1980] 1 WLR 340, CA.

purposes will not, due to the words 'or for those and other purposes', exclude Part II of the 1954 Act. If premises are occupied by the tenant's servants, only if this is a necessary part of their contractual duties is it ancillary to the business occupation of the tenant, and thus within Part II of the 1954 Act.[17]

II   TENANCIES EXCLUDED FROM PROTECTION

There are excluded from the protection of Part II:

(a)   Agricultural holdings: s 43(1)(a)

'Agricultural holding' is given s 69(1) the same meaning as under the Agricultural Holdings Act 1986 s 1, and therefore any letting which is brought within that Act, is excluded from the protection of Part II.

(b)   Mining leases: s 43(1)(b)

'Mining lease' is given (s 46) the same meaning as under the Landlord and Tenant Act 1927 s 25(1).

(c)   Wholly residential tenancies

Wholly residential tenancies are excluded from Part II of the 1954 Act. If the tenancy is a protected or statutory tenancy under the Rent Act 1977 (s 24(3)), or an assured tenancy under the Housing Act 1988 (Sch 1 para 4), it cannot be a tenancy to which Part II of the 1954 Act applies. If the tenant uses the demised premises partly for business and partly for residential purposes, the discussion earlier in this Chapter applies to the determination of whether the business or the 1977 or 1988 residential code applies.

(d)   Tenancies of on-licensed premises: s 43(1)(d)

Section 43(1)(d) excludes any tenancy of public houses, with exceptions. Premises such as restaurants and hotels, with a licence to sell intoxicating liquor, are within Part II of the 1954 Act, provided that a substantial proportion of the business consists of transactions other than the sale of alcohol;[18] so are other places of public entertainment, subject

---

17 *Chapman v Freeman* [1978] 3 All ER 878, [1978] 1 WLR 1298, CA; *Groveside Properties Ltd v Westminster Medical School* (1983) 47 P & CR 507, CA.

18 See *Grant v Gresham* (1979) 252 Estates Gazette 55, CA; also *Ye Olde Cheshire Cheese Ltd v Daily Telegraph plc* [1988] 3 All ER 217, [1988] 1 WLR 1173 (44 per cent of sales of non-alcoholic provisions held, on facts, substantial); Lee and Luxton [1989] Conv 59.

to the same condition, and railway refreshment rooms. Off-licensed premises fall within Part II of the 1954 Act.

(e) Service tenancies: s 43(2)

The distinction between a service tenancy and a service occupancy is the same as between a tenancy and a licence, a service occupancy therefore would not in any event be protected by Part II as being, in effect, no more than a licence.[19] Service tenancies, as well as 'tenancies granted by reason that the tenant is holder of an office or appointment from the grantor', are excluded from Part II by this subsection; however, tenancies which were created after 1 October 1954, are excluded *only* if they were granted by an instrument in writing expressing their purpose. The statement of purpose required may be gathered from any part of the tenancy or lease, but it must be clear that the tenant is to hold a service occupier rather than as a business tenant: if not, the present exclusion will not apply.[20]

(f) Tenancies for a fixed term not exceeding six months: s 43(3)

Tenancies granted initially for a term certain not exceeding six months are excluded, unless they contain provision for renewal or extension beyond six months, or the tenant has been in occupation for a total period exceeding 12 months (inclusive of any period during which his predecessor in title was in occupation). It should be noted that s 43(3) refers to tenancies for a term certain, i e for a fixed term, not exceeding six months. There is no reference to periodic tenancies, and weekly, monthly and quarterly tenancies, for example, are *not* excluded; indeed they enjoy full protection of Part II from the time they are granted.

In addition to the tenancies expressly excluded, there are a number of other cases where the tenant's rights to protection under Part II are excluded or restricted, and these are next discussed.

(g) Exclusions authorised by the court: s 38(4)

Section 38(4)(a) makes provision for the court to authorise the grant of a tenancy for a fixed-term longer than six months which will not attract the protection of Part II. Section 38(4)(b) makes similar provision in respect of agreements to surrender which would otherwise be void under s 24(2)(b). (See further Chap 23.)

---

19 *Shell-Mex and BP Ltd v Manchester Garages Ltd* [1971] 1 All ER 841, [1971] 1 WLR 612, CA.
20 *Davies v Thrift Building Society* (14 May 1987, unreported).

(h)   Agreement for a new tenancy: s 28

Section 28 is fundamental to the operation of Part II: once the landlord has agreed, in writing (s 69(2)),[1] to grant a new tenancy of the holding, on terms and from a date specified in that agreement, the current tenancy will continue until that date and no longer, and the tenant will have no further rights under Part II in respect of the current tenancy. An enforceable contract accomplishes the main object of the Act,[2] whose protection is thereby rendered unnecessary to the tenant, at least, for the duration of the tenancy agreed. In negotiation as to terms, neither party is in any stronger position than he would be if, on failure to agree, they went to court; the court's powers, and the tenant's indefeasible right of access to the court, are as much a balancing force that is conducive to a voluntary settlement as they are a sanction.

(i)   Premises certified as requisite for public and other purposes: ss 57 and 60

Part II applies generally to tenancies granted by the Crown and public authorities (s 58) but if the relevant Minister certifies that the premises are required by the Crown or public authority for public purposes, the certificate will deprive the tenant of his rights to apply for a new tenancy (s 57(3)(a)), or reduce the length of tenancy for which he may apply (s 57(3)(b)), depending on the operative date of the certificate. Section 60 makes special provisions in respect of certain premises in areas specified as 'development areas' or 'intermediate areas'.

(j)   Premises certified as required in the interests of national security: s 58

A certificate that premises are required in the interests of national security will similarly restrict or exclude a tenant's rights to a new tenancy. This section is available only if the landlord is a government department.

Finally, the current tenancy (i e the contractual tenancy or, as the case may be, the tenancy continuing under s 24) will come to an end and the tenant will lose any rights he would otherwise have had under *that* tenancy by reason of the circumstances listed below.

---

1   I e the immediate landlord: *Bowes-Lyon v Green* [1963] AC 420, [1961] 3 All ER 843, HL.
2   See *RJ Stratton Ltd v Wallis Tomlin & Co Ltd* [1986] 1 EGLR 104, CA (letters construed as binding agreement).

(k) Notice to quit: s 24(2)(a)

The giving of a notice to quit by the tenant, which is valid under the common law rules, is effective to terminate a periodic tenancy under the Act, and automatically deprives the tenant of the rights he would otherwise have had. To ensure that it is given voluntarily, s 24(2) precludes the tenant from giving such a notice until he has been in occupation under the tenancy for at least one month.

(l) Surrender: s 24(2)(b)

Voluntary surrender is preserved as a mode of terminating a tenancy under the Act, but to be valid, neither the surrender nor the agreement for surrender must have been made before the tenant has been in occupation under the tenancy for at least one month.[3] An agreement that would be vitiated by this provision, however, may be authorised by the court under s 38(4). (See further, Chapter 23.)

(m) Forfeiture: s 24(2)

Forfeiture of a tenancy for breach of covenant or condition and destruction of a sub-tenancy by forfeiture of a superior tenancy are governed by the general law, and s 24(2) specifically retains that position. But if the tenancy, though forfeited, has a pending application for relief against forfeiture, it is outside s 24(2).[4]

(n) Termination by certain fixed-term tenants: s 27

To prevent statutory continuation of his tenancy after the term date under s 24(a), a fixed-term tenant must give his immediate landlord (i e not necessarily the 'competent' landlord) a notice not less than three months before the term date. Termination of a continuing tenancy is by not less than three months' notice on any quarter day. In neither case is the notice valid if given before the tenant has been in occupation under the tenancy for at least one month.

(o) Tenant's failure to comply with s 29(2)[5]

Where the landlord serves a notice to terminate the tenancy in accordance with s 25, the tenant is required by sub-section (5) *within two*

---

3 See *Watney v Boardley* [1975] 2 All ER 644, [1975] 1 WLR 857 (notice to exercise option to purchase not within s 24(2)(b)).

4 *Meadows v Clerical, Medical and General Life Assurance Society* [1981] Ch 70, [1980] 1 All ER 454. Likewise, s 24(2) will not prevent s 24(1) applying where a vesting order could have been granted under LPA 1925 s 146(4): *Cadogan v Dimovic* [1984] 2 All ER 168, [1984] 1 WLR 609, CA.

5 No special form of notice is required here: *Lewington v Trustees of the Society for the Protection of Ancient Buildings* (1983) 45 P & CR 336, CA.

months to notify the landlord whether or not, at the date of termination, he will be willing to give up possession of the premises. If he fails to comply strictly with this provision, the court will be precluded by s 29(2) from entertaining any application for a new tenancy that he may make, and thus he will have lost all further rights under Part II, and the s 25 notice to terminate will take effect on the date specified in it. Since neither the court nor the parties[6] have any discretion to extend the two-month time limit, its observance is vital to preserve the tenant's rights.

(p)   Tenant's failure to comply with s 29(3)

Similarly, the court is precluded by s 29(3) from entertaining any application for a new tenancy unless an application is filed[7] not less than two months nor more than four months after the landlord's notice under s 25 is given, or, as the case may be, the tenant's request under s 26 is made. The court has no discretion to extend these time-limits either way,[8] but the House of Lords has held[9] that they being merely procedural and for the benefit of the landlord, he, but only he, may waive them, either expressly or impliedly, if he is so minded. The period of four months elapses on the corresponding day of the month of expiry, no account being taken of the fact that some months are longer than others.[10]

---

6   *Price v West London Investment Building Society* [1964] 2 All ER 318, [1964] 1 WLR 616, CA.

7   The County Court Rules make provision for late filing, if the County Court Office is closed on the last possible day; CCR 1981 Ord 6 r9(6), *Hodgson v Armstrong* [1967] 2 QB 299, [1967] 1 All ER 307, CA.

8   *Dodds v Walker* [1981] 2 All ER 609, [1981] 1 WLR 1027, HL.

9   *Kammins Ballrooms Co Ltd v Zenith Investments (Torquay) Ltd* [1971] AC 850, [1970] 2 All ER 871.

10   *Dodds v Walker* [1981] 2 All ER 609, [1981] 1 WLR 1027, HL.

Chapter 23

Restrictions on contracting out

Contracting out of Part II of the 1954 Act by means of a contract for the surrender of the tenancy is void. The court (usually the county court) is empowered to authorise the granting of tenancies to which the statutory termination procedures do not apply. These matters are dealt with in this Chapter.

Tenancies at will and genuine non-exclusive licences are other permitted methods of contracting out of the Act. On licences, it will be remembered that the essential issue is whether the agreement confers exclusive possession, at a rent, for a term – though the payment of rent is not an essential prerequisite of a tenancy if there is exclusive possession.[1] The agreement, if described as a 'licence' or 'management agreement', must not be a sham: if it is, it will be treated as a tenancy and within the 1954 Act.[2]

I SECURITY OF TENURE

Section 38(1) renders void any agreement (whether contained in the instrument creating the tenancy or not) in so far as it purports to preclude the tenant from requesting or applying for a new tenancy, or provides for the termination or surrender of the tenancy in the event of his making such application or request or for the imposition of any penalty or disability on the tenant in that event.[3]

'Purports' in s 38(1) means 'has the effect of precluding the tenant'.[4] Where the tenant held under a lease with a fully qualified prohibition on assignments which also provided that, if the tenant wished to assign, he

---

1 *Ashburn Anstalt v Arnold* [1988] 2 All ER 147, CA; also *Dresden Estates Ltd v Collinson* (1987) 55 P & CR 47, CA. See ch 3.
2 See *Dellneed Ltd v Chin* (1986) 53 P & CR 172.
3 See *Stevenson & Rush (Holdings) Ltd v Langdon* (1978) 38 P & CR 208, CA (payment of all landlord's costs clause a penalty).
4 *Joseph v Joseph* [1967] Ch 78, [1966] 3 All ER 486, CA.

must first offer the landlord a surrender of the lease, it was held that s 38(1) rendered an agreement to surrender the lease under this clause void.[5] This was because, if the agreement had been carried out (in fact the tenant withdrew from it), he would have been precluded from applying for a new tenancy under the Act. Similarly, a letter stating that the tenant would quit within 28 days, released from rent arrears, was held to be invalidated by s 38(1) as part of a contract for a surrender enforceable in equity.[6] However, s 38(1) is limited to agreements for a surrender, and was held not to apply to an actual surrender of a tenancy pursuant to a consent order in repossession proceedings.[7] Section 38(1) does not, moreover, invalidate surrender-back clauses in covenants against assignment.[8]

However, the tenant is enabled validly to give a notice to quit the holding under s 24(2)(a), or, in the case of a term certain, a notice to the effect that he does not desire the tenancy to be continued (under s 27); in both instances the tenant must have been in occupation under the tenancy for at least one month. Further, the tenant may, subject to the same condition, execute, under s 24(2)(b), an instrument of surrender. It must be immediately effective: a contract for a future surrender is caught by s 38(1).[9]

Section 43(3) allows tenancies for a fixed term of up to six months to be granted without attracting the provisions of the Act, unless they contain provision for renewal or extension beyond six months. However, a tenancy that is excluded from protection at the start will, nevertheless, lose that exemption if the tenant stays in occupation longer than 12 months, and any period during which a predecessor in title was in occupation will count towards that total.

The court – generally the county court – is empowered by s 38(4)(a) to authorise agreements for a term certain[10] which exclude ss 24 to 28 of the Act. It also has power, under s 38(4)(b), to authorise agreements for a surrender of the tenancy on such date, in such circumstances and on such terms, as may be specified. The parties must make a joint application in both cases.[11] The agreement must be contained in or endorsed on the

---

5   *Allnatt London Properties Ltd v Newton* [1981] 2 All ER 290; affd on this aspect [1984] 1 All ER 423, CA.
6   *Tarjomani v Panther Securities Ltd* (1982) 46 P & CR 32.
7   *Hamilton v Sengray Properties* (6 March 1987, unreported), CA.
8   *Allnatt London Properties Ltd v Newton, supra.*
9   *Tarjomani v Panther Securities Ltd* (1982) 46 P & CR 32.
10 This includes a term for six months: *Re Land and Premises at Liss, Hants* [1971] Ch 986, [1971] 3 All ER 380.
11 Where the parties intended to apply under s 38(4) but did not, and the tenant held over under interim extensions, paying rent, he had no security under Part II during the extensions: *Cardiothoracic Institute v Shrewdcrest Ltd* [1986] 3 All ER 633, [1986] 1 WLR 368.

instrument creating the tenancy or other instrument specified by the court. To come within s 38(4)(a), any lease must be granted conditionally on the court sanctioning the contracting out of ss 24 to 28; an unconditional grant, with blanks to be filled in for the date of the order and other matters, conferred full security on the tenant.[12] An agreement authorised by the court took effect, however, even though it was not contained in or indorsed on a formal lease, since the tenant continued in possession and paid an increased rent under the terms of the new agreement.[13]

It has been claimed that the county court will invariably approve s 38(4) applications by business persons, acting with legal advice,[14] but the case must be clear, and there must be no suggestion of coercion or oppression of the tenant.[15]

II COMPENSATION

Section 38(2) prohibits agreements modifying or excluding future rights of the tenant to compensation for disturbance where there has been continuity of the same business carried on by the tenant (and, as the case may be, by the person previously in occupation) for a total period of five years; but, once those rights have accrued, the amount of compensation payable may be varied by agreement. These restrictions do not apply where the relevant period is shorter, s 38(3), and therefore, where, for example, a tenancy is granted for a fixed-term of three years, the agreement may exclude the rights under s 37. Such exclusion will become void, however, once the tenant has been in occupation for five years, as where his tenancy is statutorily continued.

---

12 *Essexcrest Ltd v Evenlex Ltd* (1987) 55 P & CR 279, CA; Sparkes [1988] Conv 445.
13 *Tottenham Hotspur Football and Athletic Co Ltd v Princegrove Publishers Ltd* [1974] 1 All ER 17, [1974] 1 WLR 113.
14 *Hagee (London) Ltd v A B Erikson and Larson* [1975] 3 All ER 234 at 236, CA.
15 *Practice Direction* [1971] 2 All ER 215, [1971] 1 WLR 706 (Chancery Masters); CCR 1981 Ord 43 r 15(2) (county courts).

Chapter 24

Continuation and termination of tenancies under Part II

By s 24(1), a tenancy to which Part II of the Act applies is not to come to an end unless terminated in accordance with Part II of the Act. This is the principle of statutory 'continuation' of a business tenancy, whether fixed-term or periodic. The principle is further considered below.

Three common law methods of termination of a business tenancy are fully effective (s 24(2)) and where they apply, there is no continuation or no further continuation, and statutory security does not apply. The first is a tenant's notice to quit, in the case of a periodic tenancy: therefore, the tenant has the right to prevent, or to stop further, continuation by means of service on the immediate landlord of a notice to quit which is valid at common law. The second effective method is surrender, and the third forfeiture (see Chapter 13). In connection with forfeiture, a business tenancy ended by forfeiture but subject to a subsisting application for relief is still continued by s 24(1).[1]

Where the parties agree in writing on a new tenancy, which has the effect of terminating the current tenancy as from the commencement date of the new tenancy, the current tenancy continues until that date but no longer – Part II does not apply to the new tenancy (s 28).

Part II provides for various statutory methods of terminating a continuing tenancy, by means of statutory notices. The following is a list: details are given below.

1   The tenant has the right to terminate a fixed term tenancy, prior to the start of continuation or during continuation, by notice under s 27.
2   The landlord has the right to terminate a fixed-term or periodic tenancy by a notice in the prescribed form under s 25.
3   The tenant may request a new tenancy under s 26, by a notice in the prescribed form, where the current tenancy (i e the contractual term)

---

1   *Meadows v Clerical, Medical and General Life Assurance Society* [1981] Ch 70, [1980] 1 All ER 454; *Associated Deliveries Ltd v Harrison* (1984) 50 P & CR 91, CA. There is a twilight period, after which the lease may, despite notional re-entry, be restored.

is a fixed-term tenancy exceeding one year, continued by s 24(1) or not. In the case of fixed terms for less than one year and periodic tenancies, the tenant cannot request a new tenancy under s 26 unless he is given a landlords' s 25 notice.

I CONTINUATION UNDER S 24

But for s 24(1), a fixed-term tenancy (referred to as a 'contractual' term) would end by effluxion of time. Owing to s 24(1), despite the ending of a tenancy, fixed-term or periodic, at common law,[2] it is continued unless or until it is terminated in one of the ways laid down by the Act. Continuation is, in principle, of the contractual term and the continuation tenancy is, subject thereto, fully assignable. The contractual tenancy and the continuation tenancy are treated as the current tenancy for statutory purposes.

However, a landlord's common law notice to quit or notice to determine the tenancy, which are not in accordance with s 25, are still effective to terminate the contractual term. They will start continuation as from the date of expiry of the notice concerned.[3] Once, therefore, the contractual term is ended by either common law method, the landlord may terminate the tenancy by means of a s 25 notice. The landlord may also, with a notice to quit or to terminate, serve a s 25 notice, with a termination date identical or not much later than that given in his common law notice, but the minimum and maximum periods of the s 25 notice must always comply with the statutory time-limits (see below). He may even serve a single notice, which will suffice to terminate the tenancy both at common law and under Part II of the 1954 Act, provided that it both complies with s 25 and with any contractual requirements as to termination.[4]

On the nature of a continuation tenancy, purely personal obligations cease to be enforceable as from the termination of the contractual tenancy. Covenants which run with the land will be fully enforceable during continuation.[5] A right in the tenant or sub-tenant to remove

---

2   Except where one of the three methods outlined earlier applies.
3   *Weinbergs Weatherproofs v Radcliffe Paper Mill Co* [1958] Ch 437, [1957] 3 All ER 663, approved in *Scholl Manufacturing Co v Clifton (Slim-Line)* [1967] Ch 41, [1966] 3 All ER 16, CA.
4   *Keith Bayley Rogers & Co v Cubes Ltd* (1975) 31 P & CR 412 (combined s 25 notice and notice to break at common law upheld).
5   This is because the contractual term is extended with a statutory variation as to the mode of termination: *GMS Syndicate Ltd v Gary Elliott Ltd* [1981] 1 All ER 619 at 624.

tenants' fixtures extends into continuation,[6] as do rights of way enjoyed under the contractual tenancy,[7] but not, in the absence of clear words, a guarantor's possible liability in respect of rent.[8]

Where the current tenancy, being a sub-tenancy, is continued beyond the term of the superior tenancy, s 65 provides for the superior tenancy to be kept alive for the duration of its term, but then to be deemed to have been surrendered under s 139(1) of the Law of Property Act 1925, and the sub-tenant will become the tenant directly of the superior landlord.

Section 24 further makes special provision for tenancies which during their currency either ceases to be, or become , business tenancies within the Act. Where a tenancy ceased to be a business tenancy to which Part I applies during the period of continuation, it may be terminated by the landlord,[9] subject to the terms of the contractual tenancy on not less than three nor more than six months' notice in writing; s 24(3)(a). Conversely, a periodic tenancy which was not a tenancy within the Act when the landlord served a notice to quit cannot become protected by subsequently becoming such a tenancy: s 24(3)(b).

II TERMINATION OF A FIXED-TERM TENANCY BY THE TENANT UNDER S 27

A tenancy for a fixed-term will be continued beyond its contractual term date automatically under s 24 unless steps are taken to prevent it by the tenant under s 27(1) (or by the landlord under s 25). He is required to give his immediate landlord,[10] not less than three months before the tenancy would otherwise have expired, notice in writing that he does not want the tenancy to be continued. Alternatively, under s 27(2) he can terminate a tenancy that is continuing (i e after the term-date) by giving not less than three months' notice in writing expiring on any quarter day, but in any event, not sooner than the original term-date.

No special form of notice is prescribed, but in neither case can the notice validly be given by the tenant before he has been in occupation under the tenancy for one month (ss 24(2) and 27). Once notice is validly given the tenant will lose any further rights under the Act, and the current tenancy will be terminated on the date specified in the notice.

---

6 *New Zealand Government Property Corpn v HM & S Ltd* [1982] QB 1145, [1982] 1 All ER 624, CA.

7 *Nevill Long & Co (Boards) v Firmenich & Co* (1983) 47 P & CR 59, CA.

8 *Junction Estates Ltd v Cope* (1974) 27 P & CR 482; *A Plesser & Co Ltd v Davis* (1983) 267 Estates Gazette 1039.

9 I e the common law landlord: *William Skelton & Son Ltd v Harrison & Pinder Ltd* [1975] QB 361, [1975] 1 All ER 182.

10 I e not the 'competent landlord'.

Suppose that from 1 November 1987, T takes a lease of business premises from L for one year certain. Should T wish to quit at the end of his term, i e 1 November 1988, he must serve a notice under s 27(1) at any time between 1 December 1987 and 31 July 1988. If he wishes to stay in possession until 1 December 1988, he must serve a notice under s 27(2) at any time between 1 December 1987 and 24 September 1988, expiring on 25 December 1988. (The curious result of s 27(2) tying statutory notices thereunder to quarter days is that T cannot avoid remaining in possession for three and a half weeks longer than he requires.)

III   TERMINATION OF THE TENANCY BY THE LANDLORD UNDER S 25

A landlord's notice under s 25

A landlord's only way to terminate a tenancy to which Part II applies, other than by granting a new tenancy, or by forfeiture, is by giving the tenant a notice to terminate under s 25. This applies to all periodic tenancies (including weekly tenancies) and tenancies for a fixed term exceeding six months, whether or not they are continuing under s 24(1). The landlord's notice must comply strictly with the provisions of s 25:

(a)   *Form*   The notice must be in writing, in the prescribed form,[11] or in a form 'substantially to the like effect'. Therefore, a notice which gives the real substance of the required information will be valid, even if it omits certain immaterial details.[12] Minor errors will be ignored. Hence, an otherwise correct notice in which the space for the date and signature was left blank was held valid.[13] Serious errors cannot be condoned. A notice which failed to state correctly the name and address of the competent landlord was held invalid.[14] It may be that an error in a landlord's notice is such as to put any reasonable tenant on inquiry regarding who in fact is the correct landlord: if so, the notice might be valid; and while the tenant may waive the invalidity of a notice, if he serves a counter-notice this is not so.[15]

---

11   Landlord and Tenant Act 1954 Part II (Notices) Regulations 1983, SI 1983/133.
12   *Tegerdine v Brooks* (1977) 36 P & CR 261, CA (immaterial prescribed notes omitted: notice valid).
13   *Falcon Pipes Ltd v Stanhope Gate Property Co Ltd* (1967) 117 NLJ 1345; also *British Railways Board v A J A Smith Transport Ltd* (1981) 259 Estates Gazette 766 (notice omitting rateable value limits of county court's jurisdiction likewise valid).
14   *Morrow v Nadeem* [1987] 1 All ER 237, [1986] 1 WLR 1381, CA; also *Morris v Patel* [1987] 1 EGLR 75, CA.
15   *Morrow v Nadeem*, supra.

(b)   *Date of termination*   The notice must specify[16] the date on which the current tenancy is to come to an end (the date of termination). The date specified must not be earlier than the date on which, in the case of a fixed-term tenancy, it would have expired by effluxion of time (s 25(4)),[17] or, in the case of a periodic tenancy, it must be not earlier than the earliest date on which the current tenancy could have been brought to an end by a notice to quit served by the landlord (s 25(3)(a)). It is not necessary for the date of termination for s 25 purposes to fall on the correct day at common law.[18] Therefore, a s 25 notice may validly be given for any later date.[19]

(c)   *Giving of a s 25 notice*   A s 25 notice may be given by the landlord, not less than six nor more than 12 months, before the termination date specified in it (s 25(2)). Where the tenancy requires a period of notice above six months, the time-limit is extended from 12 months to a period equal to the period required under the tenancy plus six months (s 25(3)(b)). One of two joint landlords may serve a s 25 notice.[20]

On the service of s 25 notices, s 23 of the 1927 Act applies (s 66(4)). This provision resembles s 196 of the Law of Property Act 1925. If, therefore, a s 25 notice is sent by recorded delivery or registered post, the tenant will be deemed to have received it in the ordinary course of the post, irrespective of whether he actually sees it.[1]

An important limit on s 25 is that a notice served thereunder must relate, generally, to the whole holding and not just to part; a notice served as to part only is invalid.[2] Even if a common law notice to quit or to break may validly be served in relation to part of the holding, s 24 will continue the tenancy of the whole unless a s 25 notice relating to the whole is served on the tenant, which may be impossible if the reversion has been severed since the grant of the

---

16   Ambiguities in the date are resolved in favour of validity if possible: *Germax Securities Ltd v Speigal* (1978) 37 P & CR 204, CA; *Safeway Food Stores Ltd v Morris* (1980) 254 Estates Gazette 1091.

17   See *Re Crowhurst Park, Sims-Hilditch v Simmons* [1974] 1 All ER 991, [1974] 1 WLR 583.

18   *Hogg Bullimore & Co v Co-operative Insurance Society Ltd* (1984) 50 P & CR 105.

19   A notice failing (as required) to specify a date of termination on the front is valid if it specifies such a date on the back: *Sunrose Ltd v Gould* [1961] 3 All ER 1142, [1962] 1 WLR 20, CA.

20   *Leckhampton Dairies Ltd v Artus Whitfield Ltd* (1986) 130 Sol Jo 225.

1   *Italica Holdings SA v Bayadea* [1985] 1 EGLR 70. Section 23 does not prevent common law rules of service operating outside its terms: *Galinski v McHugh* [1988] NLJR 303, CA.

2   *Southport Old Links Ltd v Naylor* [1985] 1 EGLR 66, CA.

tenancy.[3] If in substance, there are two separate leases in one document, a s 25 notice served in respect of the premises demised by one of the leases will be valid.[4] Generally, a s 25 notice must refer to all the demised premises, and this may be of importance where a tenant occupies premises which are physically not contiguous, as with an office-floor and ground-floor storage facilities.[5]

(d) *Competent landlord*   The notice must be served by the person who is identified by s 44(1) as being the 'competent landlord'. No problem arises where the tenant's landlord is the owner of the premises in fee simple, but where there is a chain of tenancies, the landlord under the relevant contractual tenancy may not be the landlord who is the 'competent landlord' for the purposes of giving and being given any of the statutory notices and counter-notices under the Act. In such a case, 'the landlord' is the person next above the tenant in the chain of tenancies who has a reversion of at least 14 months' duration, i e because he is owner in fee simple, or himself a tenant with an unexpired tenure of at least 14 months. Even if the immediate landlord is such a tenant, he will nevertheless be the 'competent landlord' if his tenancy is protected by Part II and he has not himself been given a s 25 notice. Thus, a tenant whose tenancy is statutorily continuing under Part II may be 'the landlord' *vis-à-vis* a sub-tenant, within the meaning of s 44(1),[6] but not a statutory tenant under the Rent Act 1977.[7] Section 40 imposes duties on landlords and tenants to supply information necessary to each other.

A head-landlord may terminate at one and the same time both the tenancy and any sub-tenancies derived out of it where the tenant is himself protected by Part II.[8] Within two months, in effect, of becoming the 'competent landlord' *vis à vis* the sub-tenants (e g by serving a s 25 notice upon the tenant), the landlord may withdraw any s 25 notices already given to the sub-tenants by

---

3   As in *Dodson Bull Carpet Co Ltd v City of London Corpn* [1975] 2 All ER 497, [1975] 1 WLR 781 (tenancy of two properties not determinable by s 25 notice from landlord of severed part of reversion).

4   *Moss v Mobil Oil Co Ltd* [1988] 1 EGLR 71, CA.

5   *Herongrove Ltd v Wates City of London Properties plc* [1988] 1 EGLR 82.

6   See *Green v Bowes-Lyon* [1961] 1 All ER 13, applying *Cornish v Brook Green Laundry Ltd* [1959] 1 QB 394, [1959] 1 All ER 373, CA. In *Shelley v United Artists Corpn Ltd* [1989] 08 EG 115, a mesne landlord who served a s 26 request on the head landlord was not the 'competent' landlord of a sub-tenant, applying s 26(5).

7   *Piper v Muggleton* [1956] 2 QB 569, [1956] 2 All ER 249, CA.

8   Landlord and Tenant Act 1954 Sch 6 paras 6 and 7; *Lewis v MTC (Cars) Ltd* [1975] 1 All ER 874, [1975] 1 WLR 457, CA (competent landlord may determine business sub-tenancy before mesne tenancy expired).

the tenant and may proceed *de novo* to terminate the sub-tenancies himself.

(e)   *Tenant's counter-notice*   The landlord's notice must require the tenant, within two months after the giving of the notice, to notify the landlord in writing whether or not, at the date of termination specified in the landlord's notice, he will be willing to give up possession. This provides, in effect, for the service of a counter-notice by the tenant.

(f)   *Landlord's opposition*   The landlord's notice must, under s 25(6), state whether or not the landlord would oppose an application to the court by the tenant for a new tenancy, and, if so, on what grounds he intends to rely. The grounds on which he is entitled to oppose an application are limited to those set out in paragraphs (a) to (g) of s 30(1) – see Chapter 25. They fall roughly into two categories, ie breach of obligation by the tenant, and the landlord requiring possession for certain specified purposes. The landlord should consider these carefully, because at a later stage in the proceedings he (or his successor in title) may find himself bound by whatever was stated in his s 25 notice. He may rely on any one or more of the grounds specified, but in stating them he must appreciate that he will have to substantiate them; further, he should bear in mind that if he satisfies the court on any one of the grounds specified in paragraphs (a) to (d), the tenant will be precluded from claiming compensation for disturbance under s 37(1). He need not, at this stage, set out in full[9] the paragraphs relied on; it is sufficient to identify them either by reference to the letter in the paragraph,[10] or by language clear enough to indicate the particular paragraph intended.[11] 'Under paragraph (f)' and 'intends to demolish and reconstruct' are therefore in fact sufficient; and having once identified the particular ground, the landlord's statement will be liberally construed, so that he will be allowed to rely on any facts falling within that paragraph, even though he omitted them.[12] The paragraphs stated, however, cannot subsequently be changed;[13] nevertheless the court is not precluded from taking into account generally, conduct of the tenant, for example, which would have constituted a ground under s 30(1), but which was not stated in the s 25 notice.

---

9   See *Boltons (House Furnishers) Ltd v Oppenheim* [1959] 3 All ER 90.
10   *Biles v Caesar* [1957] 1 All ER 151.
11   *Philipson-Stow v Trevor Square Ltd* (1980) 257 Estates Gazette 1262.
12   *Biles v Caesar* [1957] 1 All ER 151.
13   See *Betty's Cafés Ltd v Phillips Furnishing Stores Ltd* [1957] Ch 67, [1957] 1 All ER 1; *Hutchinson v Lamberth* (1983) 270 Estates Gazette 545, CA.

If at the date of the hearing, either party so conducts himself that he cannot rely on the invalidity of a s 25 or s 26 notice or request, as the case may be, he may be estopped from setting up the invalidity, as with a clear, unequivocal representation intended to be acted on and in fact acted on.[14]

A tenant's counter-notice under s 25(5)

The tenant's reply to a landlord's s 25 notice to terminate may conveniently be referred to as 'the tenant's counter-notice' under s 25(5) to distinguish it from 'the tenant's request for a new tenancy' under s 26 (discussed below). No special form is prescribed for the tenant's counter-notice, but it must express unequivocally the tenant's refusal to give up possession.[15]

This stage in the procedure is vital if the tenant is to preserve his right to apply to the court for a new tenancy, for if he fails to give the landlord the required counter-notice within the two months, he will lose that right altogether.[16] On the other hand, if he does give the landlord the required counter-notice in time, it will have precisely the same effect as a tenant's request for a new tenancy under s 26 (see below), i e it will entitle him to apply to the court to order a new tenancy if the parties cannot reach agreement for one themselves.

IV TENANT'S REQUEST FOR A NEW TENANCY UNDER S 26

A tenant's request under s 26

Whereas *any* tenant who has been given a s 25 notice by his landlord is, by virtue of serving the requisite counter-notice, entitled to apply for a new tenancy (as explained above), only tenants under a tenancy originally granted for a term of years certain (i e a fixed term) exceeding one year (or a term of years certain and thereafter from year to year) are entitled to request a new tenancy under s 26 upon the expiry of their

---

14 *Bristol Cars Ltd v RKH (Hotels) Ltd* (1979) 38 P & CR 411, CA; *British Railways Board v A J A Smith Transport Ltd* (1981) 259 Estates Gazette 766.

15 *Smale v Meakers* [1957] JPL 415. An informal notice making plain the tenant's intention suffices: *Lewington v Trustees of the Society for the Protection of Ancient Buildings* (1983) 45 P & CR 336, CA. Not a letter seeking to purchase the reversion: *Mehmet v Dawson* (1983) 270 Estates Gazette 139, CA.

16 S 29(2); the statutory timetable must generally be strictly adhered to but it is not absolutely mandatory and the court has a sparing discretion to allow service out of time: *Baxendale v Davstone (Holdings) Ltd* [1982] 3 All ER 496, [1982] 1 WLR 1385, CA.

original tenancy, or during its continuance under s 24(1).[17] The procedure under s 26, however, cannot be used by a tenant who has already been given a s 25 notice (or has himself already given a s 27 notice or notice to quit);[18] conversely, a landlord cannot serve a s 25 notice if the tenant has already made a request under s 26 (s 26(4)). The two procedures are mutually exclusive, even though they take much the same course and will eventually bring about the same situation, i e either an agreement for a new tenancy, an application to the court for a new tenancy or the tenant voluntarily quitting the premises because he is satisfied that the landlord has incontestable grounds for getting possession. If the landlord serves an invalid s 25 notice, the tenant may ignore it and serve a s 26 request; if the request is valid, the tenant acknowledges the invalidity of the s 25 notice.[19]

Short-term and periodic tenants are precluded from initiating the s 26 procedure; they have the right to apply for a new tenancy only when the landlord serves a s 25 notice. If it were otherwise a weekly tenant, for example, would have the right, from the first week of his tenancy, to request a fixed-term tenancy for up to 14 years.

Unlike a tenant's counter-notice under s 25(5), which may be informal, a tenant's request under s 26 must comply with the following requirements:

(a) *Form*   The notice must, under s 26(3), be in writing, in the form prescribed,[20] i e Form 8, or in a form 'substantially to the like effect'.

(b) *Competent landlord*   It must be served on the person who is identified by s 44(1) as being 'the competent landlord' in relation to the tenancy (see above).

(c) *Proposed terms of the tenancy requested*   Section 26(3) requires that in his notice, the tenant should set out his proposals in respect of the tenancy requested, as follows:

   (i) the property to be comprised in the new tenancy, which may not necessarily comprise all of the premises held under the current tenancy;

   (ii) the length of the new tenancy;[1]

---

17   See *Watkins v Emslie* (1982) 261 Estates Gazette 1192, CA.

18   A common law notice to quit would be sufficient to terminate a tenancy for a term of years certain and thereafter from year to year.

19   *TS Investments Ltd v Langdon* (13 February 1987, unreported), CA.

20   Landlord and Tenant Act 1954 Part II (Notices) Regulations 1983 SI 1983/133.

1   It was held in *Bolsom (Sidney) Investment Trust v E Karmios & Co (London) Ltd* [1956] 1 QB 529, [1956] 1 All ER 536 that the same length as under the current tenancy may be *implied* as the term proposed, where the notice fails to mention the duration expressly, but provides otherwise for renewal upon the same terms as under the current tenancy.

    (iii) the rent payable under the new tenancy;
    (iv) the other terms of the new tenancy.

(d) *Commencement of the tenancy requested* The notice must, under s 26(2), specify the date on which the proposed tenancy shall commence, which in any event must not be earlier than the date on which the current tenancy would otherwise have expired by effluxion of time or could have been brought to an end by notice to quit given by the tenant (i e depending on whether or not the contractual tenancy was for a fixed-term or for a fixed-term and thereafter from year to year); and the request must be made to the landlord at least six, but not more than 12 months before the date specified for the commencement of the proposed tenancy. Thus it may be the date on which the contractual tenancy is due to come to an end, or *any* later date. The time-limits may be waived by the landlord[2] e g by applying for an interim rent.[3] Service of a request under s 26 is governed by s 23 of the 1927 Act (s 66(4)).

Once the tenant has made a request under s 26 for a new tenancy, it cannot unilaterally be withdrawn and followed by a fresh application merely because the original request was not followed up, within the four months laid down in s 29(3), by an application for a new tenancy.[4] In such a case all right to a new tenancy is lost.[5]

A landlord's counter-notice under s 26(6)

With regard to a tenant's request under s 26, the notice does not have to require the landlord to make any reply corresponding to a tenant's counter-notice under s 25(5), but the notes in Form 8 (i e the tenant's request) indicate sufficiently clearly to him his rights under the Act. Under s 26(6), he may, if he wishes, reply to the tenant's request within two months stating that he intends to oppose any application to the court for a new tenancy on any one of the grounds specified in paragraphs (a)–(g) of s 30(1). This part of the procedure under s 26 corresponds to the statement of intention to oppose contained in a landlord's notice to terminate under s 25(6), and the same considerations apply. Thus, a landlord will be limited to opposing any application subsequently made to the court on those grounds, and those grounds only, that he has indicated sufficiently clearly in his counter-notice; so too, he will lose any right to oppose an application if he fails to serve a counter-notice within the time allowed.

---

2 *Zenith Investments (Torquay) Ltd v Kammins Ballrooms Co Ltd (No 2)* [1971] 3 All ER 1281, [1971] 1 WLR 1751, CA.
3 *Bristol Cars Ltd v RKH (Hotels) Ltd* (1979) 38 P & CR 411, CA.
4 *Polyviou v Seeley* [1979] 3 All ER 853, [1980] 1 WLR 55, CA.
5 *Stile Hall Properties Ltd v Gooch* [1979] 3 All ER 848, [1980] 1 WLR 62, CA.

V   INTERIM RENT UNDER S 24A

The landlord may apply to court, if he has given a s 25 notice, or following a s 26 tenant's request for a new tenancy, to determine an interim rent, i e a rent which it would be reasonable for the tenant to pay during continuation (s 24A(1)). The court has a discretion: it is not obliged to fix an interim rent. The interim rent is deemed to be payable either from the date on which the application was made to the court; or, if later, the date specified in the landlord's s 25 notice or the tenant's s 26 request, whichever of the two is later (s 24A(2)). The basis of an interim rent is, by s 24A(3), that it is an open market rent, taking into account the disregards laid down in s 34; but for a notional tenancy from year to year starting from the date when the interim rent is payable. Therefore, the interim rent may be less than the market rent but more than the existing rent, to which, by s 24A(3), regard must be had.[6] It has been held that regard must be had to the state of the premises, in determining interim rent, at the time when the relevant period starts; if they are then out of repair, the interim rent may be differential, effective only once repairs are done.[7] Withdrawal of the tenant's application for a new tenancy does not affect an application for an interim rent, once made.[8]

The court may, when fixing an interim rent, allow a reduction or discount in the market rent for the notional yearly tenancy, but this is not obligatory. The idea behind this is to shield the tenant from too steep a jump in the rent from its old level to the market level. The amount of any reduction is at the discretion of the court, and the Court of Appeal has stated that it will only interfere with a county court judge's decision if it is obviously wrong.[9] A 50 per cent reduction has been allowed, but this was exceptional.[10] More modest reductions of the order of 6 to 10 per cent have properly been made.[11] In fixing an interim rent, it has been held that any obligation of the tenant as to repairs may be taken into account if this involves expense during continuation.[12] It is implicit in

---

6 *English Exporters (London) Ltd v Eldonwall Ltd* [1973] Ch 415, [1973] 1 All ER 726; *Ratners (Jewellers) Ltd v Lemnoll* (1980) 255 Estates Gazette 987; *UDS Tailoring Ltd v BL Holdings Ltd* (1981) 261 Estates Gazette 49.
7 *Fawke v Viscount Chelsea* [1980] QB 441, [1979] 3 All ER 568, CA.
8 *Michael Kramer & Co v Airways Pension Fund Trustees Ltd* (1976) 246 Estates Gazette 911; *Artoc Bank and Trust Ltd v Prudential Assurance Co plc* [1984] 3 All ER 538, [1984] 1 WLR 1181. Nor does the assignment, after a s 24A application, of the reversion: *Bloomfield v Ashwright Ltd* (1983) 47 P & CR 78, CA so that once the old landlord has applied for an interim rent and the application is not withdrawn, the new landlord obtains the benefit of any subsequent order.
9 *Halberstam v Tandalco Corpn NV* [1985] 1 EGLR 90, CA.
10 *Charles Follett Ltd v Cabtell Investment Co Ltd* (1987) 55 P & CR 36, CA.
11 As in *Janes (Gowns) Ltd v Harlow Development Corpn* (1979) 253 Estates Gazette 799 (10 per cent).
12 *Woodbridge v Westminster Press Ltd* [1987] 2 EGLR 97.

s 24A(3) that an interim rent must be a market rent throughout the whole period that it is payable, and so, where proceedings were delayed for some three years and the interim rent was fixed at 330 per cent above the old rent, the decision was upset on appeal, since for the earlier part of the three-year period, the rent was above the market rent.[13]

VI OUT-OF-COURT NEGOTIATIONS

The procedures for the service of notices and counter-notices within the strict time-limits explained above are designed to bring matters to a head as soon as possible. In fact, within two months of the original notice being served (whether under s 25 or s 26), the issues will be clearcut on both sides. Precisely the same position is reached by either procedure. If the tenant is satisfied that the landlord has incontestable grounds of opposition, he may decide to quit, and not to make an application to the court. In that event, his current tenancy will come to an end on the date specified in the landlord's notice, or the tenant's request, as the case may be; and he may nevertheless be entitled to claim compensation under s 37. Assuming, however, that the tenant wants a new tenancy, it is now left open to the parties to negotiate and, if possible, to reach an agreement, out of court, on the grant of a new tenancy and on all the terms under it. The tenant is in a fairly strong bargaining position, for if they fail to reach agreement, the court has the power, in the last resort, to order a new tenancy or to settle any terms which are in dispute. Moreover, s 29(3) imposes a time-limit, in effect, on the negotiations, in so far as the tenant's application to the court must be made not more than four months, but not less than two months,[14] after the original notice was served. Two months means exactly that (the period ends on the corresponding date in the relevant month).[15] If a new tenancy is agreed upon within that time, no further steps need be taken, for the current tenancy is continued until the new tenancy commences, but without any further rights under Part II (s 28). If, on the other hand, negotiations break down completely at an early stage, the tenant will have no alternative but to apply to the court under s 24(1) as soon as he

---

13   *Conway v Arthur* [1988] 2 EGLR 113, CA.
14   The time-limits are procedural and the landlord may waive them: *Zenith Investments (Torquay) Ltd v Kammins Ballrooms Co Ltd (No 2)* [1971] 3 All ER 1281, [1971] 1 WLR 1751, CA; a tenant's application was struck out where it was so late that the date for a new tenancy was to start after the existing tenancy ended under s 26(5): *Meah v Sector Properties Ltd* [1974] 1 All ER 1074, [1974] 1 WLR 547, CA. But see CCR Ord 7, r 20 (power of county court to allow extended time); *Ali v Knight* (1984) 272 Estates Gazette 1165, CA.
15   *E J Riley Investments v Eurostile Holdings Ltd* [1985] 3 All ER 181, [1985] 1 WLR 1139, CA.

can, i e two months after the service of the original notice. Where a tenant applied, in time, for a new tenancy, but for part of the holding, she was given leave in the court's discretion under CCR Ord 15 r 2, outside the two-month period, to amend her application so as to relate to the whole of the holding in view of the substantial detriment she would otherwise suffer.[16] That said, the tenant must on no account allow the four-month period for making application to the court to pass without filing an application.[17]

VII TENANT'S RIGHT TO APPLY TO THE COURT FOR A NEW TENANCY UNDER S 24(1)

A tenant can apply to the court for a new tenancy under s 24(1) within the time specified, unless an agreement for one is reached between the parties. No application can be entertained unless it is made not less than two nor more than four months after the service of the s 25 or s 26 notice, whichever initiated the proceedings (s 29(3)), nor, in the case of a s 25 notice, unless the tenant has, within the two months, served a counter-notice stating his unwillingness to give up possession on the termination date (s 29(2)).

The court to which an application should be made is the county court where the rateable value of the holding does not exceed £5,000, and the High Court in all other cases (s 63(2)); s 63(3) allows jurisdiction to be transferred from the High Court to a specified county court, and *vice versa*. The county court has power under s 43A to make any declaration required in connection with proceedings under Part II.

Application to the county court is by originating application and the procedure is governed by Order 43 of the County Court Rules 1981. Application to the High Court is by originating summons in the Chancery Division under Order 97 of the Rules of the Supreme Court. The originating application is not necessarily a nullity if it contains at any rate minor defects only.[18] A single application may validly be made so as to request two new tenancies, in, at least, adjoining premises.[19]

If, after an application to the court has been made, but before the hearing, agreement is reached between the parties for the grant of a new tenancy, either the tenant may withdraw his application or the parties may ask the court to order a new tenancy on the terms agreed.

---

16 *Bar v Pathwood Investments Ltd* (1987) 54 P & CR 178, CA.
17 If this is done, then a failure of negotiations outside the four-month period will not disentitle the tenant from pursuing an application.
18 *Williams v Hillcroft Garage Ltd* (1971) 22 P & CR 402, CA.
19 *Curtis v Galgary Investments Ltd* (1983) 47 P & CR 13, CA (where single application clearly requested two tenancies of neighbouring premises).

Where the tenant decides to quit after receiving a landlord's counter-notice relying on grounds (e) to (g) or one of them, having applied for a new tenancy, and seeks leave to discontinue that application, leave will generally be given unconditionally in the absence of intervening prejudice to the landlord; and even if the landlord withdraws his opposition, he cannot in these circumstances avoid paying compensation to the tenant.[20]

---

20 *Lloyds Bank Ltd v City of London Corpn* [1983] Ch 192, [1983] 1 All ER 92; also *Fribourg & Treyer Ltd v Northdale Investments Ltd* (1982) 44 P & CR 284.

Chapter 25

Grounds of opposition

The landlord is entitled to oppose the tenant's application to the court for a new tenancy only if he notified the tenant of his intention to oppose either in his s 25 notice or in his s 26(6) counter-notice, and indicated with sufficient clarity any one or more grounds upon which he intends to rely. Under s 31(1), the court must dismiss the tenant's application if it is satisfied that the landlord has established any one or more grounds stated in his notice. The grounds upon which he may oppose the tenant's application are set out in s 30(1), as follows:

para (a): breach of repairing obligations:

> that the tenant ought not to be granted a new tenancy in view of the state of repair of the premises caused by the tenant's breach of any repairing obligation under the current tenancy.

It is not sufficient for the landlord to prove simply that the tenant is in breach of a repairing obligation: he must satisfy the court that the breach is so serious that the tenant 'ought not' to be granted a new tenancy.[1] Thus, the court has a discretion, and, therefore, an undertaking by the tenant to remedy the breach would be taken into account by the court in the exercise of its discretion.[2] It has been stated that the question is whether it would be unfair to the landlord, having regard to the tenant's past conduct, to grant the latter a new tenancy, and where the past breaches were serious and the tenant openly neglected his covenant to repair, a new tenancy was refused.[3]

para (b): persistent delay in paying rent:

> that the tenant ought not to be granted a new tenancy in view of his persistent delay in paying rent due under the current tenancy.

---

1 *Nihad v Chain* (1956) 167 Estates Gazette 139.
2 *Lyons v Central Commercial Properties Ltd* [1958] 2 All ER 767, CA; *Betty's Cafés Ltd v Phillips Furnishing Stores Ltd* [1957] Ch 67 at 82, 83, per Birkett LJ.
3 *Lyons v Central Commercial Properties Ltd*, supra.

'Persistent delay' means a course of conduct over a period of time, and the court will consider the frequency and the extent of the delays,[4] and the steps the landlord was obliged to take to secure repayment and the question of how the landlord may be secured in any new tenancy against future breaches of this covenant.[5]

para (c): other substantial breaches:

that the tenant ought not to be granted a new tenancy in view of other substantial breaches of obligations under the current tenancy, or for any other reason connected with the tenant's use or management of the holding.

The court is directed to consider the seriousness of any breach alleged, and would take into account whether or not it is a continuing breach, and in the case of a remediable breach, whether or not it has been remedied, and whether or not the breach has been waived. Paragraph (c) provides a reason for opposing an application based on fault, which goes beyond breach of any obligation towards the landlord. Therefore, the landlord may rely on the fact that the tenant's continued user of the holding would be in breach of a planning enforcement order.[6] In exercising its discretion, when considering making an order for possession, the court looks at all circumstances, such as personal matters and the general conduct of the tenant[7] provided that these are shown to cause a prejudice to the landlord's interest.[8] The Court of Appeal will only interfere with a county court judge's exercise of discretion under para (c) if it is vitiated by an error of law.[9]

para (d): suitable alternative accommodation:

that the landlord has offered and is willing to provide suitable alternative accommodation for the tenant on terms which are in all the circumstances reasonable.

The landlord must have made a *bona fide* offer, which he is still able and willing to honour. The premises must be suitable for the tenant's requirements (including the preservation of goodwill attaching to his business), having regard to the nature and class of his business and to the

---

4 *Hopcutt v Carver* (1969) 209 Estates Gazette 1069, CA.
5 *Rawashdeh v Lane* [1988] 2 EGLR 109, CA; also *Hurstfell Ltd v Leicester Square Property Co Ltd* [1988] 2 EGLR 105, CA.
6 *Turner and Bell (trading as Avro Luxury Coaches) v Searles (Stanford-le-Hope) Ltd* (1977) 33 P & CR 208, CA.
7 *Eichner v Midland Bank Executor and Trustee Co Ltd* [1970] 2 All ER 597, [1970] 1 WLR 1120; *Hutchinson v Lamberth* (1983) 270 Estates Gazette 545.
8 *Beard v Williams* [1986] 1 EGLR 148, CA.
9 *Jones v Jenkins* [1986] 1 EGLR 113, CA.

situation, size and other facilities of the premises under the current tenancy. By analogy with residential sector provisions, if the landlord's offer is of part only of the whole accommodation, it must be proved by him that the part in question is sufficient for the tenant's business purposes as at the date of the hearing. Paragraph (d) is not expressed in discretionary terms; if the landlord establishes this ground, the application must be dismissed.[10] Thereafter, the tenant must either accept the landlord's offer or run the risk of its being withdrawn, whereupon he will have to quit the premises without any compensation for disturbance.

para (e): possession required for letting or disposing of property as a whole:

> that the tenant ought not to be granted a new tenancy in view of the fact that the current tenancy was created by a sub-letting of only a part of the premises let under a superior tenancy by the landlord, that he might reasonably expect to re-let more advantageously as a whole, and that on the termination of the current tenancy, the landlord requires possession for the purpose of re-letting, or otherwise disposing of the property as a whole.

Paragraph (e) necessarily envisages the situation where he, as superior landlord, has by virtue of s 44(1), become 'the competent landlord' *vis-à-vis* a sub-tenant of part of the premises. Since the landlord's requirement of possession must arise on the termination of the current tenancy, i e the tenancy held by the tenant requesting a new tenancy, if the landlord is a head landlord, and the tenant a sub-tenant, the landlord must, to come within para (e), prove that the intermediate tenancy will come to an end by the termination date of the sub-tenancy. Or, he may prove, which is sufficient for para (e), that the intermediate tenancy will come to an end within the period specified as sufficient to entitle him to a s 31 declaration.[11] In exercising its discretion, the court would presumably take into account the fact that the landlord had consented to the sub-letting, for instance, as required under the tenancy. The landlord must show that the total rents for the whole of the property would be substantially higher if it were re-let as a whole than if it were re-let in parts; but his reason for requiring possession is not limited to re-letting: he is entitled to rely on this ground, for instance, if on the termination of the current tenancy, he intends to sell the property with vacant possession.

---

10 *Betty's Cafés Ltd v Phillips Furnishing Stores Ltd* [1957] Ch 67 at 84, [1957] 1 All ER 1 at 8.
11 *Woodfall* 1–0716.

para (f): landlord intends to demolish or reconstruct:

> that on the termination of the current tenancy the landlord intends to demolish or reconstruct the whole or a substantial part of the premises, or to carry out substantial work of construction on the holding or part, and that he cannot reasonably do so without obtaining possession of the holding.

Where the landlord opposes on this ground, he must establish two separate things, namely, his intention and his need for possession.

Landlord's intention   The court will require more than a mere hope: there must be a clear intention. It must have moved out of the zone of contemplation and have moved into the valley of decision, as Asquith LJ said in *Cunliffe v Goodman*.[12] Evidence of intention can be given by showing, for example, that plans have been drawn up, that tenders have been sought, that the requisite finance will be available and in every possible way, short of actually doing the work, that this is what the landlord is going to do, once he has been given possession. In other words, the landlord must prove that his project is viable and has a reasonable prospect of being carried out.[13] But it is not essential to show that binding contracts have been entered into in connection with the work.[14] If the landlord intends an outright sale, para (f) will not be satisfied, but he need not necessarily prove an intention to carry out the demolition or reconstruction personally, and para (f) was, accordingly, satisfied where the landlord definitely intended to grant a long building lease to a developer, who would execute the work.[15] The time at which the relevant[16] intention must be proved is at the time of the hearing,[17] and if the landlord subsequently changes his mind when he has gained possession, the tenant has no remedy.[18] Intention to reconstruct need

---

12   [1950] 2 KB 237 at 253–254; the test is whether the landlord really intends to do the work by a method suitable to him, even if another means is available that would not involve the tenant quitting: *Decca Navigator Co Ltd v Greater London Council* [1974] 1 All ER 1178, [1974] 1 WLR 748, CA.

13   *Capocci v Goble* [1987] 2 EGLR 102, CA.

14   *A Levy & Son Ltd v Martin Brent Developments Ltd* [1987] 2 EGLR 93.

15   *P E Ahern & Sons Ltd v Hunt* [1988] 1 EGLR 74, CA; *Spook Erection Ltd v British Railways Board* [1988] 1 EGLR 76, CA.

16   Where a s 25 notice was served by the landlords (as joint tenants) and one of them died before the application was heard, the survivor's intention was held to be the relevant intention; *Biles v Caesar* [1957] 1 All ER 151, [1957] 1 WLR 156, CA; note that if the tenant's delaying tactics are the only obstacle to the landlord's intention, possession will be ordered: *A J A Smith Transport Ltd v British Railways Board* (1980) 257 Estates Gazette 1257.

17   *Betty's Cafés Ltd v Phillips Furnishing Stores Ltd* [1959] AC 20, [1958] 1 All ER 607.

18   *Reohorn v Barry Corpn* [1956] 2 All ER 742.

not be the primary purpose;[19] this may make it possible for a landlord to get possession, even though his primary purpose is to carry on his own business on the premises (under para (g)), but he is precluded from opposing under that paragraph by the five-year rule.

The intention must be to demolish, etc, 'on the termination of the current tenancy', but in view of the fact that if the landlord succeeds in his opposition, he may get possession little more than three months after the hearing (s 64), this presumably can be taken to mean 'within a reasonably short time after the termination'.[1] In any event, it should not be taken to mean longer than a few weeks, since s 31(2) (which applies equally to paras (d) and (e) as well as to para (f)) provides that where the court would have been satisfied on this ground, but for the date of termination, the tenant may claim to have the termination date specified in the statutory notice postponed by up to one year to the date indicated by the court as being satisfactory.

'*Construction*' does not include the removal of material, infilling and landscaping.[2] The court will have regard to the nature and extent of the proposed works in deciding whether they involve 'substantial' work of reconstruction. A plan to build an extension over a period of nearly four months, at a cost of upwards of £8,000, which would considerably improve the premises, fell within para (f).[3] Para (f) is irrelevant if, the landlord having obtained possession due to the tenant quitting voluntarily, the tenant's premises have ceased to exist as a separate entity due to works of reconstruction.[4]

Landlord's need for possession Paragraph (f) must be considered in the light of s 31A. Section 31A(1) provides that the landlord cannot establish that he reasonably requires possession of the holding under s 30(1)(f):

(a) if the tenant is willing to have included in the terms of the new tenancy a reservation giving the landlord access and other facilities reasonably necessary and sufficient for carrying out the proposed work; or

(b) if the tenant is willing to accept a new tenancy of an economically separable part of the holding,[5] provided that the landlord can

---

19 *Betty's Cafés Ltd v Phillips Furnishing Stores Ltd* [1959] AC 20, [1958] 1 All ER 607.
1 Plans to start the work within three months of termination has been held sufficient: *Livestock Underwriting Agency v Corbett and Newsom* (1955) 165 Estates Gazette 469.
2 *Botterill and Cheshire v Bedfordshire County Council* [1985] 1 EGLR 82, CA.
3 *Morar v Chauhan* [1985] 3 All ER 493, [1985] 1 WLR 1263, CA.
4 *Aireps Ltd v City of Bradford Metropolitan Council* [1985] 2 EGLR 143, CA (new tenancy refused to tenants).
5 See s 31A(2): the aggregate of rents obtainable on separate lettings of that part, after completion of the work, plus those from the rest of the premises, must not, for para (b) to apply, be substantially less than the rent from letting the whole premises.

reasonably carry out the intended work by having possession of the remainder (if necessary, with rights reserved, as in (a) above, over the parts retained by the tenant).

For s 31A(1)(a) to apply, the landlord must be shown to be able to carry on the work without interfering to a substantial extent or for a substantial period of time with the tenant's business.[6] The question of interference under s 31A(1)(a) is ultimately one of fact and degree, and the court looks at the physical effects of the work on the use of the holding for the purposes of the tenant's business.[7] Where, therefore, work which the landlord could not do without obtaining possession was shown to require the closure of the tenant's shop for a mere two weeks, s 31A(1)(a) was satisfied.[8] The longer the interrruption, however, the less likely is it that the provision will apply to protect the tenant. So, where it was proved by the landlord that he required possession of the premises for 12 weeks, the tenant failed to resist a para (f) claim under s 31A(1)(a).[9]

The work intended within s 31A(1)(b) means that work which the landlord in fact intends to do; once the landlord shows that the work will involve occupying the whole premises, the tenant cannot then establish that by a different method, part only of the premises would have been occupied.[10] Regard is to be had to the physical effects of the work.[11]

'Possession' in s 31A means legal possession: if the tenancy agreement allows the landlord a right of access to do the work, and the tenant shows that the operations may be carried out without physical possession of the whole holding, provided a right of access is included in any new tenancy, then the tenant may be able to defeat a landlord's claim under s 30(1)(f) by means of s 31A(1)(a). A qualification to this is that the premises should remain substantially as before, once the work is carried out.[12] If the right of access is wide enough to enable the landlord to complete the work, as where it refers to improvement, alteration and addition, and this is all the landlord intends to do, s 31A(1)(a) will preclude reliance on para (f).[13] If the work goes outside the terms of the right of access, as with total rebuilding such that the tenant's user contemplated in the lease is thereafter impossible, then para (f) may be relied on.[14]

---

6   *Redfern v Reeves* (1978) 37 P & CR 364, CA; also *Mularcyzk v Azralnove Investments Ltd* [1985] 2 EGLR 141, CA.
7   *Cerex Jewels Ltd v Peachey Property Corpn plc* (1986) 52 P & CR 127, CA.
8   *Cerex Jewels Ltd v Peachey Property Corpn plc*, supra.
9   *Blackburn v Hussain* [1988] 1 EGLR 77, CA.
10   *Decca Navigator Co Ltd v Greater London Council* [1974] 1 All ER 1178, [1974] 1 WLR 748, CA.
11   *Redfern v Reeves*, supra.
12   *Heath v Drown* [1973] AC 498, [1972] 2 All ER 561, HL.
13   *Price v Esso Petroleum Ltd* (1980) 255 Estates Gazette 243, CA.
14   *Leathwoods Ltd v Total Oil (Great Britain) Ltd* (1986) 51 P & CR 20, CA.

Determining the dividing line between the two types of case is difficult, and if the right of access is wide enough for part of the work but not the whole, the court must decide which part falls within and which without the access right; then, in relation to the latter work, the effect of the work on the tenant's business must be considered and whether s 31A(1)(a) applies to preclude reliance on para (f) by the landlord.[15]

Section 31A diminishes the significance of 'substantial' in s 30(1)(f). Since however 'substantial' means solid or big, para (f) covers work involving amalgamation of two shops by substantial removal of a party wall and other major structural alterations;[16] but not putting in a new staircase and a new floor.[17]

para (g): landlord's intention to occupy the premises:

> that on the termination of the current tenancy the landlord intends to occupy the premises for the purposes of a business to be carried on there by him, or as his residence, provided that his interest in the holding was not purchased or created within the previous five years.

Intention   The general test on sufficiency of intention is similar to that for para (f); it is objective and a reasonable prospect of the landlord's carrying out his intention must be shown.[18] This requires proof by the landlord of his firm and settled intention to occupy.[19] The question is ultimately one of fact for the county court.[20] The relevant time is the date of the hearing, and it is not necessary to adduce evidence that the relevant intention existed before then.[1] The question of who is likely to occupy is more difficult where this is not the person who gave the s 25 or s 26(6) notice. In certain cases legislation imposes a solution:

(a)   *Trusts:*   by s 41(2), if the landlord's interest is held on trust[2], the

---

15   *Cerex Jewels Ltd v Peachey Property Corpn plc* (1986) 52 P & CR 127, CA.

16   *Bewlay (Tobacconists) Ltd v British Bata Shoe Co Ltd* [1958] 3 All ER 652, [1959] 1 WLR 45, CA.

17   *Percy E Cadle & Co Ltd v Jacmarch Properties Ltd* [1957] 1 QB 323, [1957] 1 All ER 148, CA.

18   *Gregson v Cyril Lord Ltd* [1962] 3 All ER 907, [1963] 1 WLR 41, CA. If the tenant is a local authority, it is assumed that any planning application by the landlord with a genuine intention, under para (g), to occupy, will succeed and that he will obtain possession, though he intends a change of user: *Westminster City Council v British Waterways Board* [1985] AC 676, [1984] 3 All ER 737, HL.

19   *Europark (Midlands) Ltd v Town Centre Securities plc* [1985] 1 EGLR 88; *Capocci v Goble* [1987] 2 EGLR 102, CA.

20   *Elizabeth Claydon & Co v Johnson* (14 January 1987, unreported), CA; also *Cox v Binfield* [1989] 01 EG 69.

1   *J W Thornton Ltd v Blacks Leisure Group plc* (1986) 53 P & CR 223, CA.

2   Where a landlord was trustee of a family trust he could rely on para (g): *Morar v Chauhan* [1985] 3 All ER 493, [1985] 1 WLR 1263, CA. Any beneficiary may oppose under para (g), provided the trust complies with the five-year rule: Ibid.

intention of any beneficiary to occupy is sufficient for para (g) purposes; and

(b) *Groups of companies:* by s 42(3), where the landlord's interest is vested in one member of a group of companies, the intention of any member of the group is similarly enough.[3]

Once a sufficient intention is shown by the landlord, it is not necessary to show that he intends to make physical use of the entire holding.[4]

Occupation   The landlord must intend to 'occupy' the whole premises, but need not necessarily intend user of the whole for business purposes. Where, however, the landlord simply intended, having obtained possession, to re-let the whole premises, para (g) was held inapplicable, even though, during planned works of conversion, the landlord would (temporarily) be in occupation.[5] The landlord may 'occupy' within para (g) through an agent.[6] Para (g) cannot be relied on where the landlord intends to demolish existing buildings and put new buildings on the site in their place.[7] Yet para (g) was held to be available where the site was vacant and the landlord intended erecting a building on part of it as the object of para (g) is evidently to hand the landlord back his land if he wants to carry on his own business on it.[8]

Paragraph (g) was also held available to a landlord who intended to demolish partition walls between his present premises and those of the tenant, and then to occupy the whole (enlarged) premises for the purposes of his business.[9] Therefore, if the holding consists of a building and no surrounding land, and the landlord intends to demolish the building, he cannot be within para (g). If he occupies business premises, and wishes to expand his business into the tenant's adjoining premises, and, as a result, the landlord will of necessity require to carry out some demolition or reconstruction works, para (g) will be applicable.[10] Apparently, where the landlord proves sufficient intention, it is assumed that he will 'intend' from the date of the order for possession until termination of interim continuation under s 64.[11]

---

3   For one-man companies, see Landlord and Tenant Act 1954 s 30(3) and *Tunstall v Steigmann* [1962] 2 QB 593, [1962] 2 All ER 417.

4   *Method Development Ltd v Jones* [1971] 1 All ER 1027, [1971] 1 WLR 168, CA.

5   *Jones v Jenkins* [1986] 1 EGLR 113, CA.

6   *Skeet v Powell-Sheddon* [1988] 2 EGLR 112, CA.

7   *Nursey v P Currie (Dartford) Ltd* [1959] 1 All ER 497, [1959] 1 WLR 273, CA. The landlord seems able to invoke para (g) where, on a part built-on site, he intends to demolish the buildings and construct others.

8   *Cam Gears Ltd v Cunningham* [1981] 2 All ER 560.

9   *J W Thornton Ltd v Blacks Leisure Group plc* (1986) 53 P & CR 223, CA.

10 *Cam Gears Ltd v Cunningham*, supra; *Leathwoods Ltd v Total Oil (Great Britain) Ltd* (1986) 51 P & CR 20, CA; Wilkinson (1987) 137 NLJ 71.

11 *Espresso Coffee Machine Co Ltd v Guardian Assurance Co* [1958] 2 All ER 692, [1958] 1 WLR 900; affd [1959] 1 All ER 458, [1958] 1 WLR 250, CA; *Chez Gerard Ltd v Greene Ltd* (1983) 268 Estates Gazette 575, CA.

The five-year-rule   The right of a landlord to oppose under paragraph (g) is subject to the important qualification contained in s 30(2), which precludes him from doing so:

(a)   if his interest in the property was purchased or created[12] within the five years preceding the termination date specified in the original notice under s 25 or request under s 26; and

(b)   if throughout that period there has been a tenancy or succession of tenancies of the holding, to which Part II applies.

In other words, if the landlord has purchased, i e acquired for money,[13] the freehold or a tenancy (whether by grant or by assignment),[14] within the five-year period, he cannot rely on this ground under paragraph (g), unless there was a time during that period when there was no business tenancy of the holding in being. Where the landlord's interest is leasehold, a succession of tenancies are treated as a single continuing tenancy for the purpose of determining when the landlord acquired his interest.[15]

---

12   The landlord's interest is created on the date of execution of the lease and not that of commencement of the term, if different: *Northcote Laundry Ltd v Frederick Donnelly Ltd* [1968] 2 All ER 50, [1968] 1 WLR 562, CA.

13   *H L Bolton (Engineering) Co Ltd v T J Graham & Sons Ltd* [1957] 1 QB 159, [1956] 3 All ER 624, CA.

14   But not by surrender (i e merger) without payment of consideration, for that is not 'purchased or created': *Frederick Lawrence Ltd v Freeman, Hardy and Willis* [1959] Ch 731, [1959] 3 All ER 77.

15   See *Artemiou v Procopiou* [1966] 1 QB 878, [1965] 3 All ER 539, CA.

Chapter 26

Dismissal of tenant's application

I TERMINATION OF THE CURRENT TENANCY

The court is precluded by s 31(1) from ordering a new tenancy to be granted if the landlord establishes any one or more of the grounds of opposition under s 30(1) to its satisfaction; otherwise, the court will order a new tenancy. In either event, the current tenancy will continue until the date of termination specified in the original notice or for three months after the application has been determined and any time for appealing or further appealing has expired (s 64), whichever is the later.[1]

If, however, the landlord would have established any of the grounds specified in paragraphs (d), (e) and (f) to the satisfaction of the court, but for the date specified in the original notice, the court must make a declaration to that effect, stating the ground of opposition, and the date (being a date not more than one year later than the date originally specified) on which that ground would be established to its satisfaction. The court is precluded from ordering a new tenancy, but the tenant may, within 14 days, require the court to substitute the date specified in the declaration, for the date specified in the landlord's notice to terminate or the tenant's request (s 31(2)).

II COMPENSATION FOR DISTURBANCE

Where the tenant can subsequently show that the court was induced to refuse an order for a new tenancy by misrepresentation or concealment of material facts, the court may order the landlord to pay 'sufficient' compensation to the tenant for damage or loss sustained by him as a result of the refusal (s 55). This provision relates to the position when the application is heard; it affords the tenant no remedy if the landlord

---

1 The termination date will not be postponed by s 64 where the application was filed outside the time-limits imposed by s 29(3): *Zenith Investments (Torquay) v Kammins Ballrooms Co Ltd (No 2)* [1971] 2 All ER 901.

establishes a *bona fide* ground of opposition, and subsequently changes his mind.

In certain circumstances, a tenant who fails to get a new tenancy under Part II may be entitled to compensation for disturbance under s 37. For him to qualify, the landlord must have established any of the grounds of opposition specified in paragraphs (e), (f) or (g) of s 30(1), and no others,[2] or, if the tenant made no application for a new tenancy or withdrew his application,[3] the landlord must have specified in his notice under s 25 (or, as the case may be, in his counter-notice under s 26(6)) any of those grounds, and no others. The amount of compensation is the product of the appropriate multiplier and either (a) the rateable value of the holding or (b) twice the rateable value thereof (s 37(2)). The multiplier is fixed at 3[4] so that compensation is either at the lower rate of 3 or the higher rate of 6 times the rateable value of the holding. By s 37(3) the higher rate is only available where the premises have been used for business purposes throughout the preceding 14 years by the occupier and any predecessor of his in the same business. The tenant will be entitled to the higher rate of compensation if he or a predecessor in title have occupied part only (say one floor) of the present holding in question for the continuous period of 14 years. This is because the premises required by s 37(3)(a) to be occupied must be 'comprised' in the holding.[5] However, to qualify for the higher rate of compensation, the tenant's occupation must be for the full period of 14 years from taking possession: any period short of that, by no matter how small a margin, qualifies for the lower rate only.[6] The period of occupation is to be calculated up to the date specified in the original notice under s 25, or request under s 26,[7] as the case may be. Therefore the effect of interim continuation under s 64 is ignored and cannot increase compensation (s 37(7)). In general the relevant date for assessing compensation is that when the tenant quits.[8] The rateable value is the annual value of the premises as it appears in the valuation list in force at the time when the original notice was given or the request made.

---

2   A certificate to that effect may be required by the tenant of the court: s 37(4).

3   Where a tenant obtained leave to withdraw, the court imposed a condition that he should not seek compensation under s 37: *Fribourg and Treyer Ltd v Northdale Investments Ltd* (1982) 44 P & CR 284.

4   Landlord and Tenant Act 1954 (Appropriate Multiplier) Regulations 1984 (SI 1984/1932).

5   *Edicron Ltd v William Whiteley Ltd* [1984] 1 All ER 219, [1984] 1 WLR 59, CA.

6   *Department of the Environment v Royal Insurance plc* (1986) 54 P & CR 26.

7   *Edicron Ltd v William Whiteley Ltd*, supra.

8   *Cardshops Ltd v John Lewis Properties Ltd* [1983] QB 161, [1982] 3 All ER 746, CA; *Sperry Ltd v Hambro Life Assurance Ltd* (1982) 265 Estates Gazette 223.

Chapter 27

Court order of a new tenancy

I POWERS OF THE COURT AS TO TERMS

Where the tenant has applied to court for a new tenancy, the court must, by s 29(1), make an order for the grant of a new tenancy in accordance with ss 32–35 of the 1954 Act. The court cannot do this where:

(a) the landlord successfully establishes one or more grounds of opposition under s 30; or

(b) the court is precluded by s 31(2) from ordering a new tenancy.

Where the parties have been negotiating for a new tenancy by agreement, and it is only in so far as terms are not agreed that the court has power to order any, the court cannot order the grant of a new tenancy based on a draft agreement 'subject to contract'.[1]

Property to be comprised in the holding (s 32)

The parties may agree on what is to constitute the holding; if not, s 32(1) requires the court to designate the holding with regard to the circumstances existing at the date of the order. The tenant's application must relate only to the premises or part, occupied by him for business purposes. If the tenant's originating application is defective, for example, it fails to cover the whole holding, the court has a discretion to allow subsequent corrections.[2] The landlord may insist under s 32(2), that all property comprised in the current tenancy be included in the new tenancy.[3] In addition, the court has the power, under s 32(1A), to order a new tenancy in respect of the part of the premises of which the tenant has indicated[4] that he was willing to accept a tenancy; but the tenant

---

1 *Derby & Co Ltd v ITC Pension Trust Ltd* [1977] 2 All ER 890.
2 *Bar v Pathwood Investments Ltd* (1987) 54 P & CR 178, CA.
3 Even if he cannot offer vacant possession of the property over and above the holding: *Re No 1, Albermarle Street W1* [1959] Ch 531, [1959] 1 All ER 250.
4 See s 31A(1)(b) and ch 25; this would follow a s 30(1)(f) application by the landlord.

cannot be forced to accept the landlord's offer of a tenancy of part only of the business premises where he cannot obtain the grant of a new tenancy of the whole and he will be given leave to withdraw his application.[5]

Section 32 distinguishes between property to be comprised in the new tenancy and 'rights enjoyed in connection with the holding', such as purely contractual rights (e g to erect advertising signs),[6] fixtures, easements and quasi-easements such as would pass under s 62 of the Law of Property Act 1925, unless expressly excluded. Such rights as were enjoyed by the tenant under the current tenancy will be included in the new tenancy except as otherwise agreed between the parties, or in default of agreement, as determined by the court.[7]

Duration (s 33)

The parties themselves are free to agree upon whatever length or period of tenancy they choose; but if this is in dispute, the court is limited, in the case of a fixed-term tenancy, to a term not exceeding 14 years. The period or term, however, must in all the circumstances, be reasonable. Thus, relative hardship may be a relevant factor, or that the landlord would in a matter of months be able to establish the ground specified in s 30(1)(g) or (f).[8] The length of the current tenancy, the nature of the business, the age and the state of the property and its prospects of redevelopment are all material circumstances.

Therefore, if the landlord is able to show a *bona fide* intention to redevelop, which is not capable of immediate realisation, the court may order a tenancy for a given period with a break clause on suitable terms to enable him to terminate the lease and redevelop if and when able to do so.[9] Equally, where the tenant requested a one-year term and the landlord sought a 14-year term, a one-year term was granted, giving the landlord time in which to find new tenants.[10] Essentially, the length of the term is at discretion: in one case a tenant was given a longer lease than he would have liked.[11]

To prevent long appeals prolonging a term, the court may well direct

---

5   *Fribourg and Treyer Ltd v Northdale Investments Ltd* (1982) 44 P & CR 284.

6   *Re No 1 Albemarle Street W1* [1959] Ch 531, [1959] 1 All ER 250; *G Orlik (Meat Products) Ltd v Hastings and Thanet Building Society* (1974) 29 P & CR 126, CA.

7   Evidence is admissible to show the true extent of the intended demise if the parcels clause is incorrect: *I S Mills (Yardley) Ltd v Curdworth Investments Ltd* (1975) 119 Sol Jo 302, CA.

8   See *Upsons Ltd v E Robins Ltd* [1956] 1 QB 131, [1955] 3 All ER 348, CA.

9   *McCombie v Grand Junction Co Ltd* [1962] 2 All ER 65n, [1962] 1 WLR 581, CA; *Adams v Green* (1978) 247 Estates Gazette 49, CA; *Amika Motor Ltd v Colebrook Holdings Ltd* (1981) 259 Estates Gazette 243, CA.

10   *CBS United Kingdom Ltd v London Scottish Properties Ltd* [1985] 2 EGLR 125.

11   *Re Sunlight House, Quay St, Manchester* (1959) 173 Estates Gazette 311.

that the term should start from the final disposal of the application and end on a specified date.[12]

The discretion of the county court regarding the term is wide and generally the Court of Appeal will not interfere in the absence of error of law.[13] Special rules exist to order the grant of any necessary reversionary leases where required because the new tenancy extends beyond the immediate landlord's interest.[14]

Rent (s 34)

In the event of non-agreement as to the rent payable under the new tenancy, s 34(1) provides that the court shall determine it as that at which, having regard to the terms of the current tenancy (other than those relating to rent), the holding might reasonably be expected to be let in the open market by a willing lessor.

Both ss 34 and 35 (below) direct the court to have regard to the terms of the current tenancy; the court must first consider other terms before deciding on the new rent: if any new term is added or if any existing term is altered or excluded in the new tenancy, this may well have an effect on the new rent.[15] If a party seeks a departure from the terms of the current tenancy, the onus of justifying the departure is on him; hence the court refused both to relax a user clause where the effect would be to raise the rent[16] and to narrow a user clause where the effect would be to depress it.[17] Where the county court altered a covenant against assignment or underletting so as to incorporate a surrender-back clause after fixing the new rent, the case was remitted to enable reconsideration of the rent.[18]

Since s 34(1) postulates an open market rent, this must be decided on the basis, preferably, of expert evidence from a surveyor experienced in current values for comparable neighbourhood property, taking into account the terms of the new tenancy.[19] The rent of neighbouring property is relevant, however, only to compare the relative trading position of the premises.[20] If there are no comparables, general rent

---

12 *Chipperfield v Shell UK Ltd* (1980) 42 P & CR 136, CA.
13 *Upsons Ltd v E Robins Ltd* [1956] 1 QB 131, [1955] 3 All ER 348, CA.
14 Landlord and Tenant Act 1954, s 44 and Sch 6 para 2, which applies both where the parties agree on duration and where it is fixed by the court.
15 *O'May v City of London Real Property Co Ltd* [1982] 1 All ER 660 at 665, HL (Lord Hailsham LC).
16 *Charles Clements (London) Ltd v Rank City Wall Ltd* (1978) 246 Estates Gazette 739.
17 *Aldwych Club Ltd v Copthall Property Co Ltd* (1962) 185 Estates Gazette 219.
18 *Cardshops Ltd v Davies* [1971] 2 All ER 721, [1971] 1 WLR 591, CA.
19 *Woodfall* Vol 2, 2–0740; cf *English Exporters (London) Ltd v Eldonwall Ltd* [1973] Ch 415, [1973] 1 All ER 726. Also *Khalique v Law Land plc* [1989] EGCS 9, CA (allowance for increases in value from date rent fixed to court order).
20 *Rogers v Rosedimond Investments (Blakes Market) Ltd* (1978) 247 Estates Gazette 467, CA.

increases in the area may be applied.[1] The matter is, at the end of the day, at the general discretion of the judge.[2] There is no general rule that the tenant is bound to disclose the trading accounts of his business.[3] The tenant cannot set up his own breaches of covenant to repair in reduction of the rent under s 34(1).[4] In contrast, the court has power, under s 34(1), to order that the rent is not to commence, or is to commence at a lower rate, until repairs are carried out, where it is the landlord who is in breach of a covenant to repair under the contractual term.[5] Since an assessment of the rent is objective, s 34 does not allow a rent below the market level to be fixed simply because the tenant cannot afford the new rent.[6]

It is provided (s 34(1)) that four matters must be disregarded in assessing the rent for a new tenancy:

(a) Any effect on rent attributable to occupation by the tenant (or a predecessor in title) of the holding. Therefore, the tenant is not protected against the open market rent by the fact that he is a sitting tenant.[7]

(b) Any goodwill attaching to the premises by reason of the business carried on by the tenant or any predecessor in title of his in the same business.

(c) Any increase in value attributable to certain improvements carried out by the person who was current tenant other than in pursuance of an obligation to his immediate landlord.[8] The following conditions apply to this, by s 34(2):

   (i) that the improvement was completed either during the current tenancy or not more than 21 years before the application for a new tenancy;

   (ii) that the holding or the part improved was at all times since completion of the improvement, subject to tenancies to which Part II applies; and

   (iii) that on the termination of any tenancy the tenant did not quit.

---

1 *National Car Parks v Colebrook Estates Ltd* (1982) 266 Estates Gazette 810.
2 *Turone v Howard de Walden Estates Ltd* (1982) 262 Estates Gazette 1189, CA; *Oriani v Dorita Properties Ltd* [1987] 1 EGLR 88, CA; *Khalique v Law Land plc*, supra.
3 *W J Barton Ltd v Long Acre Securities Ltd* [1982] 1 All ER 465, [1982] 1 WLR 398, CA.
4 *Family Management v Gray* (1979) 253 Estates Gazette 369, CA.
5 *Fawke v Viscount Chelsea* [1980] QB 441, [1979] 3 All ER 568, CA.
6 *Giannoukakis Ltd v Saltfleet Ltd* [1988] 1 EGLR 73, CA.
7 *O'May v City of London Real Property Co Ltd* [1982] 1 All ER 660 at 665, HL.
8 If the improvement is carried out under a licence prior to the lease, the disregard will not apply: *Euston Centre Properties Ltd v H & J Wilson Ltd* (1981) 262 Estates Gazette 1079. If under a licence to improve, disregard is a question of construction: *Godbold v Martin the Newsagents Ltd* (1983) 268 Estates Gazette 1202.

As with rent review, it is not possible to treat the premises as though no improvement had ever been made, as a matter of valuation.[9]

(d) In the case of licensed premises, the increase in value attributable to the licence, if its benefit is to be regarded as the tenant's.

The court has power, under s 34(3), to include a rent review clause in the new tenancy on such terms as it thinks fit. By reason of s 35, there is power in the court to include a term dealing on a fixed or variable basis, with service charges.[10]

As to the date from which the new rent is payable: if the parties agree on the commencement date for the new tenancy, they may provide that rent is payable from the date of commencement, even if this precedes execution of the lease.[11] If there is no agreement as to a commencement date, the relevant date is that of the hearing.[12]

Other terms (s 35)

The court is enabled by s 35, in the absence of agreement between the parties, to determine any other terms under the new tenancy, having regard to the terms of the current tenancy and to all relevant circumstances.

As was seen above, the courts will be reluctant to impose, without good reason, new terms and the party seeking to do this must justify a change as fair, reasonable, and adequately compensated for.[13] Hence, where under the current tenancy the landlords were responsible for all maintenance, repairs and services, without recourse to the tenants, and sought to impose a term in a new tenancy on the tenants providing for service charges in respect of these items, in return for a small cut in the overall basis of calculation of the rent payable, the House of Lords refused to force this proposal on the tenants as it was a significant, unjustified and inadequately compensated for change.[14] A change in the terms of the current tenancy will be allowed if essentially fair with adequate compensation to the party adversely affected by the change.[15] For example, the court refused to insert a tenants' option to purchase the freehold in a new tenancy where the option in the current tenancy had expired.[16] Nor is the court able to enlarge the current holding by

---

9   Cf *Estates Projects Ltd v Greenwich London Borough* (1979) 251 Estates Gazette 851.

10 *Hyams v Titan Properties Ltd* (1972) 24 P & CR 359, CA.

11 *Bradshaw v Pawley* [1979] 3 All ER 273, [1980] 1 WLR 10.

12 *Lovely and Orchard Services Ltd v Daejan Investment (Grove Hall) Ltd* (1977) 121 Sol Jo 711.

13 *O'May v City of London Real Property Co Ltd* [1983] 2 AC 726, [1982] 1 All ER 660, HL.

14 Ibid.

15 *Gold v Brighton Corpn* [1956] 3 All ER 442, [1956] 1 WLR 1291, CA.

16 *Kirkwood v Johnson* (1979) 38 P & CR 392, CA.

incorporating against the landlord's will, easements or rights over his own land not hitherto enjoyed by the tenant.[17] As to user clauses, see the text dealing with s 34. Where the residue of a business lease was assigned subject to a newly imposed term on assignment that the tenant would obtain a guarantor of his obligations under the lease, it was held that the court could, on a ten-year new tenancy order, impose the like guarantee requirement, even though it would last for ten years rather than, under the contractual term, one year.[18] However, the court should not impose a term on the tenant requiring him to pay the landlord's costs of preparing the new tenancy.[19] Where the original leases of business premises contained break-clauses exercisable in the event of the landlord's wishing to redevelop, new leases were granted for fixed terms with break-clauses in each after five years.[20] The result of the above considerations may be that there is very little scope for 'modernising' leases under s 35.[1]

II EFFECT OF THE ORDER

Carrying out of the court's order (s 36)

Even though the court makes an order for the grant of a new tenancy, on the application of the tenant, the tenant is not bound to take the tenancy and the parties may agree not to act on its terms. First, the tenant is entitled under s 36(2) to apply to the court within 14 days for the revocation of the order, and the court is bound to revoke it.[2] In that event, the parties may agree, or the court may determine, that the current tenancy shall continue beyond what otherwise would have been its date of termination (i e the date specified in the original notice or a later date by virtue of s 64) for such period as is 'necessary to afford to the landlord a reasonable opportunity for reletting or otherwise disposing of the premises which would have been comprised in the new tenancy'. This provision is necessary for the protection of a tenant who cannot afford

---

17 *G Orlik (Meat Products) Ltd v Hastings and Thanet Building Society* (1974) 29 P & CR 126, CA.

18 *Cairnplace Ltd v CBI (Property Investment) Co Ltd* [1984] 1 All ER 315, [1984] 1 WLR 696, CA.

19 Ibid. Otherwise the tenant would lose the protection of the Costs of Leases Act 1958 s 1.

20 *J H Edwards & Sons Ltd v Central London Commercial Estates Ltd* (1983) 271 Estates Gazette 697. The landlords did not have any firm proposals: hence the measure of security given to the tenants. Cf *Leslie & Godwin Investments Ltd v Prudential Assurance Co Ltd* [1987] 2 EGLR 95.

1   See further Law Com No 162 (1987) paras 4.54–4.56.

2   There is no discretion in the court not to revoke: *Broadmead Ltd v Corben-Brown* (1966) 201 Estates Gazette 111.

the rent, for example, or accept the terms, as finally determined by the court, for where these were matters in dispute, he was not necessarily to be sure of their outcome when he made the application; nevertheless, the court has a discretion to order costs, or vary an order for costs, in the original application, as well as to order costs in the revocation (s 36(3)), which will tend to discourage abuses on the part of tenants. Secondly, the parties are free to modify or exclude any of the terms determined by the court which may suit neither of them.

Those two cases apart, the landlord is bound to execute and the tenant bound to accept, a lease or agreement for a tenancy of the holding embodying the terms as agreed between them or determined by the court; and the tenant may be required by the landlord to execute a counterpart of the instrument. Default in execution is not only a contempt of court; compliance may be enforced by specific performance.[3] Until then, equity treats the parties as landlord and tenant.[4]

Termination of the current tenancy

The current tenancy will continue until the new lease or binding agreement for a new lease takes effect. Where the court determines the duration of the new tenancy under s 33, that will commence on the date specified in the original notice, or a later date by virtue of s 64. Where the parties have themselves agreed upon the duration of the new tenancy, however, there appears to be nothing in s 33 to prevent them from agreeing to some other date, except possibly that if the agreed date were earlier, it is arguable that this would be a surrender of the current tenancy, which in turn would have to be authorised under s 38(4)(b). Once there is a binding agreement for a new tenancy, the tenant loses all his rights under Part II in relation to the current tenancy.

3   *Pulleng v Curran* (1980) 44 P & CR 58.
4   *Greaves Organisation Ltd v Stanhope Gate Property Co Ltd* (1973) 228 Estates Gazette 725.

Chapter 28

Compensation for improvements

I APPLICATION OF PART I OF THE 1927 ACT

Holdings within the Act

A tenant's rights to compensation for improvements are governed by Part I of the Landlord and Tenant Act 1927, and Part III of the 1954 Act. The 1927 Act applies to holdings other than an agricultural holding under a lease (which is defined by s 25 as including any under-lease) other than a mining lease, used wholly or partly for carrying on thereat any trade or business, whether created before or after the commencement of the Act (s 17(1)). Service tenancies created after 25 March 1928 are excluded as long as the tenant's employment or appointment continues if the contract is in writing and expresses the purpose for which the tenancy is created (s 17(2)). Trade or business is defined as including any profession regularly carried on upon the premises, but not the business of sub-letting premises as residential flats (s 17(3)); but beyond that, there is no definition of trade, business or profession, which are open to the same meanings as under the 1954 Act. Where premises are used partly for other purposes, the right to compensation is limited to improvements in relation to trade or business (s 17(4)). Tenancies of on-licensed premises are not excluded, and therefore a tenant is entitled to compensation for improvements under the 1927 Act.

Improvements within the Act

Under s 1, a tenant is entitled to claim compensation for improvements (including the erection of any building but not trade or other fixtures which he is entitled to remove) on his holding made by him or his predecessors in title, which add to the letting value of the holding. 'Tenant' is defined by s 25(1) as 'any person entitled in possession to the holding under any contract of tenancy'; hence, 'predecessor in title' receives a wide construction and includes an improving sub-lessee assigning to an assignee.[1] Improvements made before 25 March 1928 do not qualify for compensation, nor improvements made pursuant to any contract for valuable consideration including a building lease (s 21(1)), whenever made, and whether the agreement was made between the tenant and his landlord or a sub-tenant.[2] Improvements made after the passing of the 1954 Act pursuant to any statutory requirements qualify for compensation (s 48 of that Act). An improvement made less than three years before the termination of the tenancy and begun on or after 1 October 1954, qualifies for compensation.[3] Section 49 of the 1954 Act renders void any agreement purporting to contract out of the 1927 Act, unless made before 10 December 1953 for valuable consideration. There is no general definition of 'improvement': it may include the erection, demolition and rebuilding of buildings, whether for the same or a different business;[4] but does not include any trade or other fixture which the tenant is entitled to remove.

II QUALIFYING CONDITIONS

In order to qualify for the right to claim compensation on quitting on the termination of the tenancy, the tenant must observe certain conditions laid down in s 3. Before making the improvement,[5] the tenant must under s 3(1) first serve on his landlord a notice of his intention to make it, together with a specification[6] and plan showing the proposed improvement and any part of the premises affected thereby, and if the landlord raises no objections, the tenant may proceed with the work. However, the landlord is, within three months, entitled to serve on the tenant a notice of objection, and if he does, the tenant must apply to the court (i e the county court or, if the rateable value of the holding exceeds £5,000, the High Court, by virtue of s 63 of the 1954 Act) to certify that the proposed improvement is a 'proper improvement'. On such an application, any superior landlords are notified and are entitled to be heard, and the court must give a certificate if it is satisfied that the improvement:

(a) is of such a nature as to be calculated to add to the letting value of the holding at the termination of the tenancy; and

---

1 *Pelosi v Newcastle Arms Brewery (Nottingham) Ltd* (1981) 43 P & CR 18, CA.
2 *Owen Owen Estate v Livett* [1956] Ch 1, [1955] 2 All ER 513.
3 Landlord and Tenant Act 1954 s 48(2).
4 *National Electric Theatres Ltd v Hudgell* [1939] Ch 553, [1939] 1 All ER 567.
5 The following does not apply to statutory improvements, where the tenant may proceed as soon as he gives notice of intention to the landlord.
6 See *Deerfield Travel Services Ltd v Wardens etc of the Leathersellers of the City of London* (1982) 46 P & CR 132, CA.

(b)   is reasonable and suitable to the character thereof; and
(c)   will not diminish the value of any other property belonging to the same landlord or any superior landlord from whom the immediate landlord or tenant holds.

In certifying the improvement, the court may make such modifications to the plans and specifications proposed by the tenant, as it thinks reasonable. No certificate will be given, however, if the landlord can prove that he has offered to make the proposed improvement himself in consideration of a reasonable increase in rent, or of an increase to be determined by the court, unless he has failed to carry out such an undertaking. As regards the reasonableness and suitability of the proposed improvement the court is directed by s 3(2) to have regard to any evidence adduced by the landlord or superior landlord (but no one else) to show that the improvement is calculated to injure the amenity or convenience of the neighbourhood. Where the landlord serves no notice of objection, or the improvement is certified as proper, the tenant may execute the improvement in accordance with the plans and specifications (s 3(4)), and on completion within the time agreed with the landlord, or determined by the court, is entitled to require of the landlord a certificate of completion, to be issued at the tenant's expense; and if the landlord fails to give one within one month, the tenant may apply for one to the court.

III   THE TENANT'S CLAIM FOR COMPENSATION

The claim

A tenant's claim for compensation for improvements in respect of which the qualifying conditions are satisfied must, under s 1(1) of the Act,[7] be made in the prescribed manner[8] in writing, and signed by the tenant or his agent. It must specify the holding and the business and state the nature of the claim, the cost and other particulars of the improvement, the date when it was completed, and the amount claimed.[9] The claim must be served on the landlord in accordance with s 23 of the Act[10] within the strict time limits imposed by s 47 of the 1954 Act:

---

7   As amended by Landlord and Tenant Act 1954 s 47(5).
8   County Court Rules 1981, Ord 43, or RSC Ord 97.
9   It is vital to state the amount claimed: *British and Colonial Furniture Co Ltd v William McIlroy Ltd* [1952] 1 KB 107, [1952] 1 All ER 12.
10   See *Sector Properties Ltd v Meah* (1973) 229 Estates Gazette 1097, CA (service at place of business a proper method).

1 Within three months of the giving of a notice to quit or a notice to terminate (or if the tenancy is terminated under s 26 of the 1954 Act, within three months of the landlord's counter-notice);
2 not more than six but not less than three months before the termination of a tenancy that will expire by effluxion of time;
3 within three months of the effective date of an order for possession in forfeiture proceedings, or within three months of re-entry without an order for possession.

Service of the claim must be made within the requisite time-limits and these limits cannot be extended.[11]

The importance of Part I of the 1927 Act has been greatly reduced since 1954, in relation to claims for compensation, since under s 1(1) of the 1927 Act the right to compensation arises only if the tenant quits the holding on the termination of the tenancy. However, it is nevertheless important that a tenant should satisfy the qualifying conditions in respect of improvements which he proposes to make, in order not only to get compensation should the landlord establish a ground for possession in due course, but also to have their added value disregarded in fixing the rent under s 34 in respect of any new tenancy granted under Part II within the next 21 years.

The amount of compensation

In the absence of agreement between the parties, all questions as to the right to compensation are determined by the court (s 1(3)); and under s 1(1) the amount shall not exceed:

(a) the net addition to the value of the holding as a whole which may be determined to be the direct result of the improvement; or
(b) the reasonable cost of carrying out the improvement at the termination of the tenancy, subject to a deduction of an amount equal to the cost (if any) of putting the works constituting the improvement into a reasonable state of repair, except so far as such cost is covered by the liability of the tenant under any covenant or agreement as to the repair of the premises, whichever is the less.

In determining the amount under (a), regard must be had to the purposes for which it is intended to use the premises after the termination of the tenancy, and if it is shown that it is intended to demolish or to make structural alterations in the premises or any part of them or to use the premises for a different purpose, regard must be had to the effect of such demolition, alteration or change of user on the additional value attributable to the improvement, and to the length of time likely to elapse between the termination of the tenancy and the

---

11 *Donegal Tweed Co v Stephenson* (1929) 98 LJKB 657.

proposed changes (s 1(2)). If the claim for compensation is on that account reduced, by the court, the tenant may later make a further application to the court to vary the amount originally determined, if he can show that the landlord has not carried out his intentions within the time specified. Further, the amount is to be reduced by any benefit received by the tenant or his predecessor in title from the landlord 'in consideration expressly or impliedly of the improvement' (s 2(3)). On the question as to what constitute 'benefits', there is little authority, and it is arguable that any reductions in rent under successive tenancies by virtue of s 34(2) of the 1954 Act, might be set off against the tenant's claim. In practice, a tenant's claim is most frequently reduced or indeed defeated by virtue of s 1(2).

IV REFORM

The Law Commission is currently reviewing the question of compensation for improvements and has made the following provisional recommendations.[12]

1   The present system of compensation of business tenants' improvements should continue with some amendments. These would seek, in particular, to integrate more fully the compensation and consent rules.
2   The tenant would still have to notify the landlord of any proposed improvement. Unlike at present, this duty would be complied with by a request for consent under the lease, or a simple notification.
3   A landlord's refusal of consent to a proposed improvement would be regarded as reasonable, if he undertook to carry out the improvement, whether or not in return for a rent increase.
4   There would be no compensation for an improvement carried out on other premises than the demised premises, and none where an improvement was carried out in breach of covenant, unless such breach was waived or consent was given prior to the making of the improvement.
5   The tenant should be under an obligation to pay the landlord compensation for an improvement which diminishes the value of the landlord's reversion, to be based on the lesser of: (a) the diminution in the value of the reversion and (b) the cost of reinstatement. This notion is quite novel.
6   A radical departure from the present rules is the provisional proposal that in the event of a renewal of the tenancy, for example under the 1954 Act, compensation rights should be carried forward.

---

12   Law Com Working Paper No 102 (1987). It is understood that a Report is likely to appear during 1989.

PART F
AGRICULTURAL HOLDINGS

Chapter 29

Introduction and terms of the tenancy

I CUSTOM OF THE COUNTRY AND MODERN POLICY

Until about 100 years ago, the relationship of landlord and tenant of an agricultural holding was governed by the common law. The parties could agree on a written tenancy agreement if they so wished: but if there was no such agreement, then local custom supplied terms by implication, and these varied as between different parts of the country. These customs, in their varied forms, were given the force of the common law in the implied obligation by the tenant of agricultural land to manage and use it in a husband-like manner in accordance with the custom of the country.

The significance of customary obligations is much reduced today. First, it is usual for there to be a written tenancy agreement (indeed under the statute it may be secured and arbitrated upon). Secondly, many aspects of the relations of landlord and tenant of an agricultural holding are regulated by detailed and complex statutory provisions. These are broadly designed to secure the following aims:

1 A measure of compensation to tenants on quitting for improvements, disturbance and other matters;
2 A degree of security of tenure for agricultural tenants. This has been enhanced by succession provision so that certain relatives of a tenant of an agricultural holding may succeed to the tenancy on his death; since 1984, the scope of these provisions has been drastically curtailed;
3 To enable the tenant of an agricultural holding to secure a written tenancy agreement and to make provision to supplement deficient tenancy agreements with regard to obligations to repair and maintain;
4 To provide for the settlement of disputes by arbitration procedures, whether the dispute relates to rent or other matters.

The first general Act dealing with agricultural holdings was the

Agricultural Holdings (England) Act 1875, giving a statutory right to compensation for certain improvements. Later these rights were extended and made impossible to contract out of. Compensation for improvements was extended to yearly tenants of market gardens in 1913. Compensation for disturbance was steadily extended from 1914.

Security of tenure was first seriously tackled in the Agriculture Act 1947, notable for setting up Agricultural Land Tribunals.

The code applicable to all agricultural tenancies, whenever created, is the Agricultural Holdings Act 1986. This consolidated a number of earlier enactments.[1]

II APPLICATION OF THE ACT

The Agricultural Holdings Act 1986 applies to contracts of tenancy of agricultural holdings. By s 1(1) 'agricultural holding' is defined as meaning 'land (whether agricultural land or not) comprised in a contract of tenancy which is a contract for an agricultural tenancy', provided that such land is not 'let to the tenant during his continuance in any office, appointment or employment held under the landlord'; and for this purpose, 'agricultural land' is defined by s 1(4) as meaning 'land used for agriculture which is so used for the purpose of a trade or business and includes any other land which . . . is agricultural land within the meaning of' the Agriculture Act 1947, i e land so designated by the Minister.[2] By virtue of the definition in s 96(1) 'agriculture' includes 'horticulture, fruit growing, seed growing, dairy farming and livestock breeding and keeping, the use of land as grazing land, meadow land, osier land, market gardens and nursery grounds, and the use of land for woodlands where that use is ancillary to the farming of land for other agricultural purposes', and 'livestock' includes any creature for the production of food, wool, skins or fur or for the purpose of its use in the farming of land or the carrying on in relation to land of any agricultural activity.

Land used for agriculture, etc

Land is used for agriculture and is 'so used for the purposes of a trade or business' if the use itself is agricultural, even though the trade or business is not. Thus, the tenancy of a field let for the grazing of horses from a riding school has been held to be within the Act,[3] but not the tenancy of a racehorse stud farm, nor the stabling of a horse or pony to be used for

---

1   See Law Com No 153; Rodgers [1987] Conv 177; also passim, Rodgers, *Agricultural Tenancies* (1985) Butterworths.

2   Under s 109 of the 1947 Act.

3   *Rutherford v Maurer* [1962] 1 QB 16, [1961] 2 All ER 775.

pleasure, nor pigeon-keeping[4] since no agricultural use was made of the land. 'Land used for agriculture' also includes land forming part of an agricultural unit,[5] which includes 'any dwelling-house or other building occupied by the same person for the purposes of farming the land',[6] e g a cottage and its garden let for use in connection with a farm,[7] and any other land designated as such by the Minister.

Section 1(2) deals with the question of deciding whether a contract of tenancy is within s 1. A contract of tenancy relating to any land is a contract for an agricultural tenancy if, having regard to three factors, the whole of the land comprised in the contract is let for use as agricultural land – subject to such exceptions only as do not substantially affect the character of the tenancy. The three factors are:

(a) the terms of the tenancy;
(b) the actual or contemplated use of the land at the time of the conclusion of the contract and subsequently; and
(c) any other relevant circumstances.

On para (a) above, it appears that if the tenancy contemplates user for a particular purpose, this will be an essential factor in initially deciding whether the 1986 Act applies.[8] In relation to actual initial and subsequent user (para (b)), note that where an inn was let with 12 acres of agricultural land, and the tenant used the inn as an inn and as a farmhouse, the whole formed an agricultural holding.[9] If a tenancy is originally within the 1986 Act, and agricultural activity is wholly or substantially abandoned during the tenancy, even without the consent of the landlord, the 1986 Act will cease to apply; but a tenancy cannot alternate between being within and outside the 1986 Act as minor changes of user take place. Strong evidence of abandonment of agricultural user is required.[10]

---

4 *Hickson & Welch Ltd v Cann* (1977) 40 P & CR 218n, CA. But if there is mainly agricultural user, such as grazing, use of the land for incidental non-agricultural purposes e g as a stud farm, will not take the tenancy out of the 1986 Act: *McClinton v McFall* (1974) 232 Estates Gazette 707, CA.
5 S 96(5) of the 1986 Act.
6 S 109(2) of the 1947 Act.
7 *Blackmore v Butler* [1954] 2 QB 171, [1954] 2 All ER 403. Cf *Darby v Williams* (1974) 232 Estates Gazette 579, CA, where a cottage was let under separate contract from the land; see however Rent (Agriculture) Act 1976, ch 17.
8 *Russell v Booker* (1982) 263 Estates Gazette 513, CA.
9 *Dunn v Fidoe* [1950] 2 All ER 685, CA; but not where a nursery garden was let with a shop selling only partly agricultural produce of which only a small portion was from the nursery: *Lord Monson v Bound* [1954] 3 All ER 228, [1954] 1 WLR 1321.
10 *Wetherall v Smith* [1980] 2 All ER 530, [1980] 1 WLR 1290, CA; also *Short v Greeves* [1988] 1 EGLR 1, CA (fact that over half the turnover was from produce not grown on the land did not deprive tenant of 1986 Act protection). See Wilkinson (1988) 138 NLJ 329; Rodgers [1988] Conv 430.

It is further provided by s 1(3) that a change in user of the land subsequent to the conclusion of the contract of tenancy which involves any breach of the terms of the tenancy is to be disregarded for the purpose of determining whether a contract not originally for an agricultural tenancy has subsequently become one unless it is effected with the landlord's permission, consent or acquiescence. The reverse side of this coin is that if land is originally let on an agricultural tenancy, unilateral change by the tenant to some other user will not of itself take the tenancy into some other code and the 1948 Act will cease to apply to the tenancy.[11]

The Minister has powers under the Agriculture Act 1947, to designate as agricultural land, any land which in his opinion ought to be brought into use for agriculture. No designation may extend, however, to land:

(a)   used as pleasure grounds, private gardens or allotment gardens, or

(b)   kept or preserved mainly or exclusively for the purposes of sport or recreation, except that where the Minister is satisfied that its use for agriculture would not be inconsistent with its use for those other purposes and it is so stated in the designation.[12]

Contract of tenancy

'Contract of tenancy' is defined by s 1(5) of the 1986 Act as meaning a 'letting of land, or agreement for letting land, for a term of years or from year to year', and for the purposes of this definition a lease for life, etc, which is converted into a lease for 90 years by virtue of s 149(6) of the Law of Property Act 1925, is deemed to be a letting for a term of years. Section 2(1) and (2) of the Act further provide that any letting of land for use as agricultural land for an interest less than a tenancy from year to year, or any licence to occupy such land shall take effect, with the necessary modifications, as if it were an agreement for the letting of the land for a tenancy from year to year. Section 2 applies to any agreement unless:

(a)   the agreement was made in contemplation (express or implied) of the use of the land only for grazing or mowing during some specified period of the year; or

(b)   the lessor's (or licensor's) interest is itself an interest in land less than from year to year, and has not by virtue of this section taken effect as such a tenancy.

In deciding whether an agreement is for an interest less than a tenancy from year to year, the court looks at the tenant's interest in the land as

---

11   *Russell v Booker*, supra.
12   S 109(1) of the 1947 Act.

actually granted by the agreement: and if a tenant when taking possession is then entitled to such an interest, s 2 applies; moreover, since s 2 is mandatory, even if the tenant knows that the landlord did not intend the 1986 Act to apply, he may properly invoke s 2 if it applies and the rule cannot be overridden by any estoppel.[13]

Under s 2(4) any dispute with regard to the operation of s 2(1) must be determined by arbitration.

By s 3, a tenancy granted for two years or more is converted into an annual tenancy at the end of the term certain. If either party, not more than two years and not less than one year before the termination date of the fixed term, gives effective notice to terminate, then no such conversion will take place. By s 4,[14] if the tenant or last surviving tenant dies one year or more prior to the expiry of the fixed term, the tenancy expires, without continuation beyond the term date, on that date. If the tenant or surviving tenant dies within the last year of the fixed term, without any notice having been given, the only continuation is for 12 months from the term date. Section 5 enables the parties to an agricultural tenancy for not less than two nor more than five years certain to contract out of s 4, prior to the grant of the tenancy, with Ministerial approval (after a joint application).

Main exceptions under s 2

(a) *Grazing or mowing*

A requirement that the tenant cultivate the land, in the agreement, prevents the exception in s 2 from applying.[15] The fact that the tenancy includes the use of outbuildings is not sufficient to exclude s 2[16] provided (as in any case) the agreement is genuinely intended to fall within the exception: and if an agreement contemplates use of the land only for the season when grazing or mowing is possible, it may fall within s 2 as this is a sufficient specification of a period under the exception.[17] Any agreement granting grazing or mowing rights will be construed objectively though the conduct of the tenant is a relevant factor.[18] An arrangement for seasonal grazing which does not refer to specific dates

---

13   *Keen v Holland* [1984] 1 All ER 75, [1984] 1 WLR 251, CA.
14   The compensation provisions on quitting apply: s 4(3).
15   *Lory v London Borough of Brent* [1971] 1 All ER 1042, [1971] 1 WLR 823.
16   Cf *Avon County Council v Clothier* (1977) 75 LGR 344, CA.
17   *Stone v Whitcombe* (1980) 40 P & CR 296, CA. Cf *James v Lock* (1977) 246 Estates Gazette 395. A series of agreements giving the tenant several years, granted him a tenancy under the Act in *Short Bros (Plant) v Edwards* (1978) 249 Estates Gazette 539, CA.
18   *Chaloner v Bower* (1983) 269 Estates Gazette 725. If the agreement is express, written or not, its terms will be gone behind only if shown to be a sham: ibid.

falls within the present exception; the onus of proving that it does is on the landlord; in this, the court is entitled to have regard to what was in fact done on the land and to the conduct of the parties subsequent to the agreement.[19]

(b)   *Licences*

The security provisions of the 1986 Act apply, by s 2(2)(b), to licences of agricultural land. An agreement will be construed as a tenancy if it confers exclusive possession, at a rent, for a term, of agricultural land.[20]

If an agreement is a licence, it will only attract the security umbrella of the 1986 Act if it grants the licensee, for consideration, exclusive occupation rights for agricultural purposes, as against the licensor or any person authorised by him; if the licensor genuinely retains the right to make whatever concurrent or co-extensive or contemporaneous use or control of the land he wishes, the licence is outside the statutory umbrella.[1] A sham agreement will be treated as a tenancy.[2] The reservation of a limited right of access to the land is not inconsistent with the grant of exclusive occupation or possession to the occupier.[3]

(c)   *Miscellaneous*

1   Fixed-term tenancies for a term of more than one year but less than two years fall outside the protection of the 1986 Act: s 2(1) does not apply, as they are not interests for less than from year to year[4] and they lie outside s 3, which applies only to tenancies for two to five years.

2   For protection to apply, the agricultural holding must be comprised in a single contract of tenancy.[5]

3   There are no lower acreage limits on the application of the Acts.[6]

---

19   *Watts v Yeend* [1987] 1 All ER 744, [1987] 1 WLR 323, CA.
20   *University of Reading v Johnson-Houghton* [1985] 2 EGLR 113; *Harrison v Wing* [1988] 2 EGLR 4, CA; Rodgers [1986] Conv 275.
1   *Bahamas International Trust Co Ltd v Threadgold* [1974] 3 All ER 881, [1974] 1 WLR 1514, HL; *Stone v Whitcombe* (1980) 40 P & CR 296, CA; *Collier v Hollinshead* (1984) 272 Estates Gazette 941.
2   Cf *South West Water Authority v Palmer* (1983) 268 Estates Gazette 357, CA, and *Street v Mountford* [1985] AC 809, [1985] 2 All ER 289, HL. See further ch 3.
3   *Lampard v Barker* (1984) 272 Estates Gazette 783, CA. The reservation of concurrent rights of grazing (for example) would presumably be a different matter.
4   *Gladstone v Bower* [1960] 2 QB 384, [1960] 3 All ER 353, CA.
5   *Blackmore v Butler* [1954] 2 QB 171, [1954] 2 All ER 403, CA.
6   *Look v Davies* [1952] EGD 17; *Stevens v Sedgeman* [1951] 2 KB 434, [1951] 2 All ER 33, CA.

III SECURING A WRITTEN AGREEMENT

Where there is no written agreement between the landlord and tenant of an agricultural holding, or, there is, but it fails to contain the basic statutory terms dealt with in Section IV of this chapter, then either party, by s 6(1), may refer the terms of the tenancy to arbitration, provided he has first requested the other party to enter into a written agreement embodying the basic terms as above but no such agreement was concluded. On a reference, the arbitrator must, in his award, specify the existing terms of the tenancy, subject to any variations agreed between the parties, and make provision for all the matters specified in Sch 1, in such a manner as is agreed between the parties or, in default of agreement, as appears to the arbitrator to be reasonable and just between them (s 6(2)). No provision inconsistent with the statute may be included. The award may include, by s 6(2), any further provisions, apart from those in Sch 1 and relating to repairs, which may be agreed between the parties.

With a view to protecting the landlord against assignment sub-letting or parting with possession during the period from a landlord's request for arbitration, or agreement, and ending with an award or agreement, in a case where no provision is made in the tenancy, s 6(5) precludes the tenant from assigning, sub-letting or parting with the possession of the holding or any part of it without the landlord's written consent while an agreement or arbitration is pending. A transaction contravening s 6(5) is void.

IV TERMS OF A WRITTEN AGREEMENT

The matters for which provision is to be made in a written tenancy agreement under s 6(2), either by agreement or, in default of agreement, by the arbitrator, are set out in Sch 1 to the Act, as follows:

1 The names of the parties.
2 Particulars of the holding with sufficient description, by reference to a map or plan, of the fields and other parcels of land comprised therein, to identify the extent of the holding.
3 The term or terms for which the holding, or different parts thereof, is or are agreed to be let.
4 The rent reserved and the dates on which it is payable.
5 The incidence of the liability for land tax and rates (including drainage rates).
6 A covenant by the tenant in the event of destruction by fire of harvested crops grown on the holding for consumption thereon, to return to the holding the full equivalent manurial value of the crops

destroyed, in so far as that is required in accordance with the rules of good husbandry.

7   Except where the tenant is a Government Department, or the tenant has made alternative provision with the approval of the Minister, a covenant by the tenant to insure all dead stock on the holding, and all such harvested crops as aforesaid, against damage by fire.

8   A power to the landlord to re-enter on the holding in the event of the tenant not performing his obligations under the agreement.

9   A covenant by the tenant not to assign, sub-let or part with the possession of the holding or any part thereof without the landlord's consent in writing.

V   LIABILITY FOR MAINTENANCE, REPAIR AND INSURANCE OF FIXED EQUIPMENT

The effect of s 7(1) of the 1986 Act is to incorporate the provisions of the Schedule to the Agriculture (Maintenance, Repair and Insurance of Fixed Equipment) Regulations 1973,[7] into the terms of the tenancy. However, any express term in a written contract of tenancy which is inconsistent with the model clauses will prevail over the latter in relation to any aspect covered by the express term. Unless and until a party avails himself of his statutory right to arbitration, an express, inconsistent, term will continue to prevail.[8]

Part I: Rights and liabilities of landlord

The landlord is, broadly, liable to repair the structure and exterior of the farmhouse, cottages and farm buildings, including the roofs, chimney stacks and pots, eaves-guttering and downpipes, main walls and exterior walls, including walls and fences of open and covered yards and garden walls, plus any interior repairs made necessary as a result of structural defects. He must also repair floors, floor joists, ceiling joists and timbers, exterior and interior staircases, fixed ladders, doors, windows and sky-lights. In the case of repairs to, e g floorboards, interior staircases, doors and windows, eaves-guttering and downpipes, the landlord may recover half the reasonable cost from the tenant (see para 1(1) generally).

The landlord must also replace anything which it was under para 5 the tenant's responsibility to repair which has become worn out or otherwise incapable of further repair unless by virtue of para 6(2), the tenant is liable to replace it because it has worn out or otherwise become

---

7   SI 1973/1473 as amended, from 24 March 1988, by SI 1988/281.
8   *Burden v Hannaford* [1956] 1 QB 142, [1955] 3 All ER 401, CA. This does not apply to *oral* tenancies.

incapable of repair if its condition has been brought about by or is substantially due to the tenant's failure to replace it.

The landlord is liable also for external decoration when required to prevent deterioration and in any case at intervals of not more than five years (para 3) but he may recover half the reasonable cost from the tenant of certain items.

The landlord is not, by para 4, liable:

(a)   to execute repairs etc to buildings which are the tenant's property; nor

(b)   to execute repairs etc rendered necessary by the wilful act or negligence of the tenant or any members of his household or his employees.

The landlord must keep the farmhouse, cottages and farm buildings insured to their full value against loss or damage by fire (para 2(1)).

As to other things apart from buildings, the landlord must (para 1(2)) execute all repairs and replacements to underground water supply pipes, wells, bore-holes and reservoirs and all underground installations connected therewith and to the sewage disposal systems, including septic tanks, filtering media and cesspools.

If the landlord fails to execute repairs, other than repairs to an underground water pipe,[9] within three months of receipt of a written notice from the tenant specifying the repairs, the tenant may then carry out the repairs and recover the reasonable cost from the landlord. A similar right applies to replacements, except that there is an upper limit of £2,000 or the annual rent of the holding, whichever is the less (para 12(1)(3) and (4)). If the landlord wishes to contest his liability for any repairs or replacements specified in the tenant's notice, he must serve a written counter-notice on the tenant, within one month of the service of the tenant's notice, specifying the items of which he denies liability and requesting arbitration. Once a counter-notice is served, the tenant's right to recover the cost of the work arises only if the question of liability is decided in his favour by the arbitrator (para 12(5)).

Part II: Rights and liabilities of the tenant

The tenant is liable, so far as the buildings, farmhouse and cottages are concerned, to repair and keep and leave clean and in good tenantable repair, order and condition, those parts which do not fall to the landlord. The duty extends to all fixtures and fittings. The duty is to carry out interior repairs on the farmhouse, cottages and farm buildings; plus the full maintenance of drains, sewers, gulleys, grease-traps, manholes and

---

9   In the case of these latter repairs, the period concerned is one week (para 12(2)).

inspection chambers, electrical and water supply systems and fittings so far as above ground, and hydraulic rams (above or below ground). The tenant is responsible for maintenance of the following on the land: fences, hedges, field walls, stiles, gates and posts, cattlegrids, bridges, culverts, ponds, watercourses, sluices, ditches, roads and yards in and on the holding (para 5).

The tenant must keep clean and in good working order all roof valleys, eaves-guttering and downpipes, wells, septic tanks, cesspools and sewage disposal systems (para 5).

The tenant must redecorate at least every seven years the inside of the farmhouse, cottages and farm buildings (para 7) and must renew all broken or cracked tiles or slates and replace all slipped tiles or slates from time to time as the damage occurs, up to an annual limit of £100 (para 8). He must cut, trim or lay a proper proportion of the hedges in each year of the tenancy so as to maintain them in good and sound condition (para 9) and dig out, scour and cleanse all ponds, watercourses, ditches and grips as may be necessary to keep them at sufficient width and depth and to keep clear and free from obstruction all field drains and their outlets (para 10).

Failure by the tenant to comply with any of these duties means that the landlord may serve a written notice on him and if he does not start within two and complete within three months, the landlord may enter, execute the repairs and recover the reasonable cost from the tenant forthwith (para 4(2)). The tenant may within one month of this notice contest liability by a counter-notice, which refers the disputed items to arbitration and this suspends the landlord's notice until the arbitration is terminated (para 4(3)).

Part III: General provisions

By para 13(1), if at any time either landlord or tenant is of the opinion that any item of fixed equipment is redundant, either may serve a two months notice on the other requiring arbitration (if no agreement can be reached). If the arbitrator decides that the item is redundant to the farming of the holding, he must so award, and then neither party is under any obligation to maintain, replace or repair that item.[10] With regard to redundant and obsolete buildings para 13 applies but para 14(2) adds a category to redundancy following an award (as for fixed equipment) viz that there is no liability to execute work which is impossible except at prohibitive or unreasonable expense by reason of subsidence of the land or the blocking of outfalls not under either party's control.

---

10 As to guidelines to the arbitrator, see para 13(2) of the 1973 regulations.

VI MISCELLANEOUS STATUTORY PROVISIONS IN RESPECT OF THE TENANCY

(a) Compensation for damage by wild animals

Section 20 provides for payment by the landlord of compensation where the tenant has sustained damage to his crops from any wild animals or birds, the right to kill and take which is vested in the landlord or anyone claiming under the landlord (other than the tenant), which are not wild animals or birds which the tenant has permission in writing to kill. Such compensation is payable only if (s 20(2)):

(a) the tenant gave notice of the damage to the landlord, in writing, within one month of first becoming aware of it (or of the time that he ought reasonably to have become aware of it), and gave the landlord a reasonable opportunity to inspect the damage, i e before harvesting or removing the crops; and

(b) the tenant gave notice in writing of the claim, with particulars, to the landlord within one month of the expiration of the year in respect of which the claim is made.

The amount of compensation is settled by agreement after the damage has been caused, or in default of agreement, by arbitration (s 20(4)); and where the rights in respect of the wild animals or birds that did the damage are vested in someone other than the landlord, he is entitled to be indemnified by that person against all claims for compensation under this section (s 20(5)).

(b) Restriction on landlord's remedies for breach of contract of tenancy

Section 24 restricts the amount of extra rent or liquidated damages recoverable by the landlord against the tenant for breach of obligation (by distress or otherwise) to the extent of the damage actually suffered by him in consequence of the breach.

(c) Record of condition of the holding

Section 22(1) entitles either party at any time to require the making of a record of the condition of the fixed equipment on the holding and the general condition of the holding itself (including any parts not under cultivation); and the tenant may, at any time during the tenancy, make a similar request in relation to:

(a) existing improvements executed by him or in respect of which, with the landlord's consent, he paid compensation to an outgoing tenant; and

(b)   any fixtures or buildings which, under s 10 of the Act, he is entitled
      to remove.

Such a record, the cost of which is borne in equal shares unless they agree
otherwise (s 22(3)) is vital to the tenant's claim for compensation under
s 70 (special systems of farming). Any record is to be made, in default of
any agreement between the parties, by a person appointed by the
Minister and this person may enter the holding at all reasonable times
for the purpose of making such a record (s 22(2)).

(d)   Landlord's powers of entry

Under s 23, the landlord, or any person authorised by him, is given the
right to enter upon the holding at all reasonable times for the purpose of:

(a)   viewing the state of the holding;
(b)   fulfilling the landlord's responsibilities to manage the holding in
      accordance with the rules of good estate management; or
(c)   providing or improving fixed equipment for the holding otherwise
      than in fulfilment of those responsibilities.

(e)   Distress for rent

On distress generally, see Chapter 8. It should be noted here that any
compensation found due to the tenant prior to a distress, is to be set off
against the rent, and distress may be only levied for the balance, if any
(s 17).

Chapter 30

Variation of the terms of the tenancy

I RENT

Arbitration of terms of tenancies as to rent

If the parties cannot agree on a rent then by s 12(1) of the 1986 Act the landlord or tenant may by notice in writing served on the other, demand that the rent payable as from the next termination date be referred to arbitration. By s 12(4) this means the next day, following the date of the demand, on which the tenancy of the holding could have been determined by notice to quit on the date of demand. The earliest date for the new rent will be 12 months after the demand for arbitration.

There is a limit on the frequency of arbitrations. The general rule is (Sch 2 para 4(1))[1] that no demand for arbitration is valid if the next termination date after the date of the demand is earlier than three years from any of the following dates:

(a) the commencement of the tenancy; or
(b) the date from which a previous increase or reduction in rent took effect under s 12 or otherwise; or
(c) the date from which a previous arbitrator's direction that the rent should continue unchanged took effect under s 12.

In calculating the dates under exception (b) above, there are by para 4(2) three disregards to be made:

(a) the date of an increase or reduction in rent under s 6(3) or 8(4) of the Act;

---

1 A special rule applies where a new tenancy commences between the same tenant and a landlord entitled to a severed part of the reversion and the rent is a proportion of the old. Sch 2, para 5 relates back references to the commencement of the tenancy or to rent to the start of the tenancy of the original holding or the last agreement, arbitration etc, as to rent, as the case may be.

(b)   the date of an increase of rent under s 13(1) or (3);[2]
(c)   the date of a reduction of rent under s 33.

An arbitration notice lapses on the next termination date after the date of the demand (s 12(3)) unless before then either an arbitrator has been appointed by agreement or an application has been made under s 84 to appoint an arbitrator. If, after a landlord's arbitration notice, the tenant duly applies for the appointment of an arbitrator, the landlord is precluded from unilaterally withdrawing his notice.[3]

Note that the s 12 procedure merely revises the rent and does not operate to determine the tenancy.[4]

Determination of a proper rent

The general rule is that by s 12(2), the arbitrator must determine a rent properly payable for the holding at the date of the reference and must then increase or reduce the previous rent or direct that it continue unchanged. The new rent takes effect, generally, 12 months from the date of the demand.

Under Sch 2 para 1(1), the rent is to be that at which the holding might reasonably be expected to be let by a prudent and willing landlord to a prudent and willing tenant, taking into account all relevant factors and including:

(i)   the terms of the tenancy including rent;
(ii)   the character, situation and locality of the holding; and
(iii) its productive capacity and its related earning capacity.[5]

The arbitrator must also take into account the current level of rent for comparable lettings. This means any available evidence of rents currently paid or likely to become payable for other tenancies of agricultural holdings on similar terms other than terms fixing the rent (para 1(3)). From this figure there are three disregards:

---

2   Also (para 4(2)(b)) there is disregarded any reduction in rent agreed between the parties in consequence of any change in the fixed equipment provided on the holding by the landlord.

3   *Buckinghamshire County Council v Gordon* [1986] 2 EGLR 8.

4   See further Agricultural Holdings Act 1986 Sch 2 para 6. An agreement adjusting the boundaries of the holding or varying any term apart from rent does not determine the tenancy nor cause the three-year time bar to start running afresh. If solely due to these things, the rent is adjusted, the same result follows.

5   Defined on the assumption that the holding is occupied by a competent tenant practising a suitable system of farming taking fixed equipment and any other facilities on the holding into account (productive capacity); or the extent to which, in the light of this, a competent tenant could reasonably be expected to profit from farming the holding (related earning capacity) (para 1(2)).

(a) any appreciable scarcity element in the comparables;
(b) any element in the rent due to the fact that the tenant or a person tendering for a comparable holding occupies land in its vicinity conveniently capable of occupation with the holding; and
(c) any effect on rents due to allowances or reductions due to the charging of premiums.

The arbitrator must also disregard (para 2) any increases or, as the case may be, decreases, in the rental value due to:

(a) tenant's improvements or fixed equipment[6] other than those executed or provided under tenants' obligations in the tenancy;
(b) landlord's grant-aided improvements;
(c) the effect of the tenant's occupation; and
(d) the effect of dilapidation or deterioration of or damage to buildings or land caused or permitted by the tenant.

On the general approach to be taken, any enhancement of rental values due to a scarcity of farms available for letting must be discounted from the open market value; but if there is sufficient evidence of a balanced market, the full open market value prevails.[7]

Tenant's improvements mean, in effect, improvements executed on the holding wholly or partly at his expense (grant-aided or not) but without any allowance or benefit in return from the landlord in consideration thereof (para 2(2). If the tenant held a previous tenancy of the holding, then this disregard extends to those improvements executed under that tenancy and the same extended disregard applies to tenant's fixed equipment if any (para 2(3)). Again, excluded from the extended disregard are tenant's improvements or fixed equipment for which the tenant received any compensation on termination of that or any other tenancy.

A special rule is in para 2(4): if the tenant continuously adopted a system of farming more beneficial than that required or customary, this is an improvement for these purposes on his part.

Increases of rent for landlord's improvements

Section 13 entitles the landlord to an increase in rent on account of any improvement carried out by him on the holding, whether or not compensation for it would be payable under the Act, provided he serves on the tenant a six month written notice after completion of the works.

---

6 Tenant's fixed equipment means (para 2(3)) fixed equipment provided by the tenant during the current or a previous tenancy. On 'improvements', cf *Tummon v Barclays Bank Trust Co Ltd* (1979) 39 P & CR 300 (no necessity that these be agricultural).
7 *Aberdeen Endowments Trust v Will* 1985 SLT (Land Ct) 23; Muir Watt (1985) 275 Estates Gazette 1076.

Only however those improvements carried out at the request of or in agreement with the tenant or under a s 67(5) notice (where the landlord elected to carry out an improvement which the tenant had applied to the Agricultural Land Tribunal to execute), qualify.

The amount of the increase is the increase in rental value attributable to the improvement: if grant-aided then the scale of the increase is reduced proportionately (s 13(4)). By s 13(3), there will be no increase in rent if before the six month period of any notice is up, the parties agree on an increase in rent or other benefit to the landlord, in respect of the improvement.

II   MAINTENANCE, REPAIR AND INSURANCE OF FIXED EQUIPMENT

There has been noted the terms prescribed in the Agriculture (Maintenance, etc) Regulations 1973, which by s 7(1) of the 1986 Act are to be incorporated into the terms of every tenancy of an agricultural holding, except in so far as there are written terms of the tenancy to the contrary. Where such written terms exist, and they impose substantial modifications in the operation of the regulations, s 7(2) entitles either party to refer to arbitration the terms of the tenancy relating to the maintenance, repair and insurance of fixed equipment, provided that he has first requested the other party to vary the agreement so as to bring it in conformity with the regulations, and no agreement has been reached on the request. Where there has been a previous reference to arbitration under this section, no further reference may be made within three years of the date on which the award on the previous arbitration came into effect.

On a reference, the arbitrator must consider whether (disregarding the rent payable) the modifications affected by the terms of the tenancy are justifiable, having regard to the circumstances of the holding, and of the landlord and the tenant. If he determines that they are not, he may by his award vary the terms referred to arbitration in such manner as appears to him reasonable and just between the landlord and the tenant (s 8(3)); and if by reason of such variation, he thinks that the rent should be varied, he may do so accordingly (s 8(4)).

Where the terms are varied under s 8 so as to conform with the regulations, and liability for the repair and maintenance of fixed equipment is transferred from the tenant to the landlord, s 9(1) provides that the landlord may, within the prescribed period[8] following the date on which the transfer of liability took effect, require that he be paid by

---

8   Agriculture (Time-Limit Regulations) 1988, SI 1988/982. The period is 3 months: Ibid.

the tenant any compensation for which the latter would have been liable under s 71(1) or (3) (i e for deterioration of the holding), if the tenant had quitted the holding on the termination of the tenancy at the date of the transfer of liability. Correspondingly, where liability is transferred from the landlord to the tenant, the tenant may, within the prescribed period,[9] require that any claim of his in respect of any previous failure by the landlord to discharge his liability under the terms of the tenancy, be determined by arbitration (s 9(3)).

III   PERMANENT PASTURE

Where the terms of the tenancy provide for the maintenance of specified land, or a specified proportion of the holding, as permanent pasture, either party may, by notice in writing served on the other, demand a reference to arbitration under s 14 of the question whether it is expedient in order to ensure the full and efficient farming of the holding that the amount of land required to be maintained as permanent pasture should be reduced (s 14(2)). On such a reference, the arbitrator may by his award:

(a)   vary the terms of the tenancy as to the land which is to be maintained as permanent pasture or is to be treated as arable land, and as to cropping, and

(b)   if he gives a direction reducing the area of land to be maintained as permanent pasture, order the terms of the tenancy to be modified so as to require the tenant, on quitting the holding on the termination of the tenancy to leave a specified amount of land as permanent pasture or as temporary pasture sown with a seeds mixture of a specified kind.

---

9   See footnote 8 above.

Chapter 31

Notices to quit and succession

I GENERAL RULES

Agricultural tenancies are subject to special statutory rules governing the length and consequences of notices to quit. Section 25(1) of the Agricultural Holdings Act 1986 provides that, notwithstanding any provision in the tenancy to the contrary, a notice to quit an agricultural holding or part of it is invalid if it purports to terminate the tenancy before the expiration of 12 months from the end of the current year of tenancy.[1] There are certain exceptions to this rule.[2] These include:

(a) where the tenant is insolvent;

(b) where notice to quit is given under a provision in the tenancy authorising the resumption of possession of the whole or part of the holding for a specified and non-agricultural purpose;

(c) where a tenant gives a sub-tenant notice to quit;

(d) where a notice of one month is given to a tenant holding under a lease for life or lives to which s 149(6) of the Law of Property Act 1925 applies;

(e) where an arbitrator has specified a date for the termination of the tenancy on the failure of the tenant to do work after a notice to remedy or where the time under a notice to remedy has been extended;

(f) where on a reference under s 12 of the 1986 Act the arbitrator determines an increase in rent (s 25(3)).[3] In this case, a six months' notice may validly be given by the tenant, though it terminates the tenancy immediately before the increase in rent is effective.

---

1 The tenant may waive his right to a 12 month notice: *Elsden v Pick* [1980] 3 All ER 235, [1980] WLR 898, CA.

2 Agricultural Holdings Act 1986 s 25(2) and Agricultural Holdings (Arbitration on Notices) Order 1987, SI 1987/710.

3 This overrides any term in the tenancy (s 25(5)).

II TENANT'S COUNTER-NOTICE

General rules

By s 26(1) of the 1986 Act, if within one month of the giving of the landlord's notice to quit, whether it relates to the whole or any part of an agricultural holding, the tenant serves on the landlord a counter-notice in writing requiring that s 26(1) is to apply, the notice to quit takes effect only if the Agricultural Land Tribunal for the area consents to its operation. Section 26 does not expressly prohibit contracting out, but it has been held to be mandatory and to override any contrary stipulation in the tenancy.[4] If, therefore, A grants a tenancy to B and C and they as tenants agree with A as landlord that they will not serve a counter-notice without A's consent, this condition is void.[5] A counter-notice served by one of two individual joint tenants is of no effect.[6] If one of the joint tenants is also the landlord, possibly a notice served by all the tenants except for the landlord-tenant is valid.[7] Where the tenancy is a trust asset, the landlord (if a partner) may be compelled to join in the service of a counter notice, where this is requisite to preserve the tenancy.[8] Where, with a view to evading the 1986 Act, a landlord let a farm to his wife, who at once sub-let to the tenant, it was held that, in substance, an agricultural tenancy, stripped of security, had been granted; as this grant contravened the Act, the tenancy was terminable only in accordance with the Act and not at common law.[9]

Where the landlord serves a notice to quit which does not specify any of the various grounds for possession and a tenant's counter-notice follows, the landlord has one month from service of the latter to apply for the consent of the Agricultural Land Tribunal to the operation of his notice.[10] If his notice specifies a ground then no counter-notice is possible.

Consent of Agricultural Land Tribunal to unspecified notice to quit

The landlord must establish one of five grounds to obtain the consent of the Tribunal. Even then, it may withhold its consent if, by s 27(2), in all the circumstances, it appears to it that a fair and reasonable landlord would not insist on possession. The grounds are:

---

4 *Johnson v Moreton* [1980] AC 37, [1978] 3 All ER 37, HL.
5 *Featherstone v Staples* [1986] 2 All ER 461, [1986] 1 WLR 861, CA.
6 *Newman v Keedwell* (1977) 35 P & CR 393.
7 *Featherstone v Staples,* supra.
8 *Sykes v Land* (1984) 271 Estates Gazette 1264, CA.
9 *Gisbourne v Burton* [1988] 3 All ER 760, CA; J Martin (1988) 138 NLJ 792.
10 S 27(1) and Agricultural Land Tribunals (Rules) Order 1978, SI 1978/259. The one month period is inflexible: *Parrish v Kinsey* (1983) 268 Estates Gazette 1113, CA.

(a)   *Good husbandry* (s 27(3)(a)):   that the carrying out of the purpose for which the landlord proposes to terminate the tenancy is desirable in the interests of good husbandry as respects the land to which the notice relates, treated as a separate unit. This means that, under the landlord's proposals, the land would be farmed better, comparing the merits of each party.[11]

(b)   *Sound estate management* (s 27(3)(b)):   that the carrying out of the above purpose is desirable in the interests of sound management of the estate of which the land in question forms part or which that land constitutes. The question must be considered in relation to the land to which the notice relates and any other relevant land.[12] The purpose must be connected with the way in which the estate is managed by the tenant.[13] A scheme to sell off parts of the holding and to apply the sale proceeds to improving the fixed equipment on what remained might suffice.[14]

(c)   *Agricultural research etc* (s 27(3)(c)):   that the carrying out of the above purpose is desirable for the purposes of agricultural research, experiment or demonstration, or for the purposes of enactments relating to smallholdings or allotments.

(d)   *Greater hardship* (s 27(3)(d)):   that greater hardship would be caused by withholding than by giving consent to the operation of the notice. The fact is that this matter is up to the discretion of the Tribunal.[15] The financial result to the parties from a decision is always important.[16] The tenant's poor performance, if any, as a farmer is a relevant factor.[17] Where the landlord wished to manage the farm assisted by his son, the Tribunal accepted that he proved greater hardship from the refusal of consent compared to the hardship to the tenant by granting it and yet the landlord was refused consent under the Tribunal's discretion because the tenant was found more experienced than the landlord and so the productivity of the holding would suffer.[18] Hardship to third parties may be taken into account.[19]

---

11   *Davies v Price* [1958] 1 All ER 671, [1958] 1 WLR 434, CA.
12   *Evans v Roper* [1960] 2 All ER 507, [1960] 1 WLR 814.
13   *National Coal Board v Naylor* [1972] 1 All ER 1153, [1972] 1 WLR 908.
14   *Lewis v Moss* (1961) 181 Estates Gazette 685.
15   *Wickington v Bonney* (1982) 47 P & CR 655.
16   *Purser v Bailey* [1967] 2 QB 500, [1967] 2 All ER 189, CA.
17   *R v Agricultural and Land Tribunal for the South Eastern Area, ex p Parslow* (1979) 251 Estates Gazette 667.
18   *Jones v Burgoyne* (1963) 188 Estates Gazette 497.
19   *Addington v Sims* (1952) 159 Estates Gazette 663.

(e) *Non-agricultural use* (s 27(3)(e)): that the landlord proposes to terminate the tenancy for the purpose of the land being used for a use, other than for agriculture, not falling within Case B (below).

Section 27(4) empowers a Tribunal, if it gives consent, to impose any conditions requisite to secure that the land will be used for the purpose in question. If necessary, it may revoke or vary any condition on the landlord's application.

III EXCLUSION OF TENANT'S RIGHT TO SERVE A COUNTER-NOTICE

If any of the Cases below apply (Sch 3) then the tenant cannot serve a counter-notice, but the landlord's notice to quit, for this to apply, must specify at least one of Cases A to H. Reliance on a Case renders the notice incontestable but the tenant may refer notices relying on Cases A, B, D or E to arbitration.[20]

Case A: Smallholdings

This is where the holding was let as a smallholding by a smallholdings authority or the Minister on or after 12 September 1984 and:

(a) the tenant has attained 65, and
(b) if the notice would deprive him of living accommodation occupied under the tenancy, suitable alternative accommodation[1] is available or will be available to him, when the notice takes effect, and
(c) the tenancy acknowledges that Case A applies.

The notice to quit must state that it is given under Case A and it is referable to arbitration within one month of service.

Case B: Planning consent

The notice to quit is given on the ground that the land is required for a non-agricultural use, for which planning permission has been given or for which such permission is not required, and the fact is stated in the notice. The landlord gives a 12 month notice of intention to rely on Case B but the tenant may contest this by a counter-notice, served within one month of the notice to quit, requiring arbitration.[2]

---

20 Agricultural Holdings (Arbitration on Notices) Order 1987, SI 1987/710 art 9.
1   As determined in accordance with Sch 3 Part II paras 2–7.
2   Agricultural Holdings (Arbitration on Notices) Order 1987, SI 1987/710; art 9. See *Cawley v Pratt* [1988] 2 EGLR 6, CA.

Case C: *Certificate of bad husbandry*

Not more than six months before the notice to quit was given, the Tribunal granted a certificate under Sch 3 para 9 that the tenant was not fulfilling his responsibilities to farm in accordance with the rules of good husbandry, and that fact is stated in the notice.[3]

The landlord may apply to the Tribunal for a certificate of bad husbandry but its power to grant a certificate is limited (Sch 3 para 9): it must disregard any practice adopted by the tenant under any provision of the tenancy or otherwise agreed with the landlord, indicating its object to further any of three things:

(a) conservation of flora or fauna or geological etc features of special interest;

(b) protection of buildings etc of archaeological, architectural or historic interest;

(c) conservation or enhancement of the natural beauty or amenity of the countryside, or promoting public access.

Case D: *Non-compliance with notice to pay rent or to remedy breaches*

This is that at the date of the notice to quit the tenant had failed to comply with a landlord's written notice in the prescribed form requiring him –

(a) within two months of the service of the notice, to pay any rent due; or

(b) within a reasonable period specified in the notice, to remedy any breach by the tenant capable of being remedied by him of the terms and conditions of the tenancy.[4]

Rent   Once the tenant fails to pay all the rent due within two months of the landlord's notice to pay, then the notice to quit becomes indefeasible.[5] The sole means of contesting a notice to pay is to require arbitration (Sch 4) and if none is sought, no relief is possible.[6]

---

3   For procedure, see Agricultural Land Tribunals (Rules) Order 1978, SI 1978/259. By s 25(4), the Tribunal may specify in the certificate a minimum period of at least two months notice instead of the usual 12 months: if a notice to quit states this fact and is for at least that period it will be valid.

4   Compliance with an agreement listed in Sch 3 para 9(2) to the 1986 Act is not a ground for a Case D or E notice for failure to farm in accordance with the good husbandry rules: paras 10(1) and 11(2). For forms of notice see Agricultural Holdings (Forms of Notice etc) Regulations 1987, SI 1987/711.

5   *Stoneman v Brown* [1973] 2 All ER 225, [1973] 1 WLR 459, CA.

6   *Magdalen College, Oxford v Heritage* [1974] 1 All ER 1065, [1974] 1 WLR 441, CA; *Harding v Marshall* (1983) 267 Estates Gazette 161, CA; *Parrish v Kinsey* (1983) 268 Estates Gazette 1113, CA.

On the other hand, the landlord must strictly comply with the following to enforce a notice to pay: he must correctly state his name,[7] correctly state the rent due,[8] and if applicable, serve the notice on all joint tenants.[9]

The requirement that all the rent due must be paid by the stated date is capable of waiver by agreement, express or implied, e g where the landlord indicates preparedness to accept a cheque posted by the due date.[10] Where a tenant presented two cheques which were not acepted by the landlord and which became outdated by the date of service of a Case D notice, the tenant had not discharged his obligation to pay.[11] Not all joint owners of the reversion on a periodic tenancy need be parties to a Case D notice.[12]

Other breaches The following points should be noted. First, a notice to remedy other breaches must be in the prescribed form and must specify the period for remedy of the breach.[13] Then, if the notice requires any work of repair, maintenance or replacement, it must be in Form 2 of the Regulations. If the tenant wishes to contest a reason stated he must within one month of service of the landlord's notice to do work, serve a notice specifying the items in respect of which he denies liability and requiring arbitration.[14] The landlord's notice must describe the items of repair, maintenance or replacement required and must allow at least six months in which the tenant is to do the work specified.

Generally speaking, the arbitrator may modify the notice by deleting any unnecessary or unjustified item; he may substitute a different method or material for that required if the latter would involve undue difficulty or expense (art 5). The arbitrator has power to extend the time for work, by specifying a date of termination for the tenancy if the tenant fails to do the work within the extended time (art 7). The arbitrator may also extend the time to do the work given in the notice even if reasonable (art 6) and may also extend it if satisfied that an event prior to expiry of that time renders it unreasonable (art 14).

The notice to do work must (eventually) be complied with in full subject to s 28(5): substantial compliance is insufficient as a defence to a later notice to quit.[15] If the failure to comply is due to non-supply of materials to be provided by the landlord, this is excusable,[16] yet if more

---

7   *Pickard v Bishop* (1975) 31 P & CR 108, CA.
8   *Dickinson v Boucher* (1983) 269 Estates Gazette 1159, CA.
9   *Jones v Lewis* (1973) 25 P & CR 375, CA.
10 *Beevers v Mason* (1978) 37 P & CR 452, CA.
11 *Official Solicitor v Thomas* [1986] 2 EGLR 1, CA.
12 *Parsons v Parsons* (1983) 47 P & CR 494.
13 Agricultural Holdings (Forms of Notice etc) Regulations 1987, SI 1987/711.
14 Agricultural Holdings (Arbitration on Notices) Order 1987, SI 1987/710, art 3.
15 *Price v Romilly* [1960] 3 All ER 429, [1960] 1 WLR 1360.
16 *Shepherd v Lomas* [1963] 2 All ER 902, [1963] 1 WLR 962, CA.

than one breach is to be remedied, a reasonable time must be allowed for all breaches to be remedied.[17]

Despite non-compliance with a notice to do work, the tenant may under s 28, by counter-notice within one month of the landlord's notice or arbitration award, require the consent of the Tribunal to the Case D notice. By s 28(5)[18] the Tribunal must consent to the operation of the notice unless it appears to them that a fair and reasonable landlord would not insist on possession, having regard to:

(a)   the extent of the tenant's failure to comply with the notice to do work;
(b)   to the consequences of his failure to comply in any respect; and
(c)   the circumstances surrounding the failure.

Case E: Irremediable breaches

This is that at the date of giving the notice to quit the landlord's interest has been materially prejudiced by the tenant committing an irremediable breach of a term or condition of his tenancy, if it is a term not inconsistent with his responsibilities to farm in accordance with the rules of good husbandry. The notice must specify this ground if relied on. The tenant may then require an arbitration within one month of the service of the notice.[19]

The tenant cannot validly contract out of his right to serve an arbitration notice (under this nor where applicable any other Case): to enforce a covenant not to require arbitration is contrary to public policy.[20] Where the parties in negotiations and dealings both assumed that, contrary to the fact, a tenancy did not restrict assignments, and went to arbitration on the rent on their joint false assumption, it was held that the landlords were estopped by convention from invoking Case E.[1]

Case F: Insolvency

It is a ground for possession, which must be stated as a reason in the notice, that at the date of giving the notice to quit the tenant had become insolvent (defined, s 96(1)).

Case G: Death of tenant

Under this it is provided that the notice to quit is given:

(a)   following the death of a person who immediately before his death

---

17   *Wykes v Davis* [1975] QB 843, [1975] 1 All ER 399, CA.
18   See also *Clegg v Fraser* (1982) 264 Estates Gazette 144.
19   Agricultural Holdings (Arbitration on Notices) Order, supra, art 9.
20   *Johnson v Moreton* [1980] AC 37, [1978] 3 All ER 37, HL.
 1   *Troop v Gibson* [1986] 1 EGLR 1, CA.

was the sole (or sole surviving) tenant under the contract of tenancy; and

(b) not later than three months beginning with the date of any relevant notice;

and it is stated in the notice to quit that it is given by reason of that person's death.

The date of any relevant notice in (b) above means either (1) the date of service of a written notice on the landlord by or on behalf of an executor or administrator of the tenant's estate informing the landlord of the tenant's death; or (2) the date on which the landlord is given notice by virtue of s 40(5) an application for a succession to the tenancy.

If both of the above events occur then the three month period above runs from the first to occur.

There is no provision for arbitration on a Case G notice; even though it may state the death as the reason for the notice, it will take effect where a succession is applied for. The notice to quit will only be effective if, after an application, no person is determined by the Tribunal to be suitable, or they consent to the operation of the notice in relation to the whole or part of the holding (s 43). As will be seen, however, in the case of the death of a tenant under most tenancies granted on or after 12 July 1984, no succession applications are possible (s 34). If the tenancy of the deceased was granted prior to 12 July 1984, or if the tenancy falls within one of the excluded classes from the removal of successions, then persons who think themselves eligible to succeed may still apply to the Tribunal and in the case of success, the Case G notice will have no effect. See Section V of this chapter.

Case H: Ministerial certificates

This is that the Minister has certified that the notice to quit is given by him to enable him to use or dispose of the land to effect an amalgamation under s 26(1) of the Agriculture Act 1967 or the re-shaping of any agricultural unit, and the tenancy itself contains an acknowledgment signed by the tenant that Case H is to apply.

IV NOTICE TO QUIT PART OF THE HOLDING

The tenancy may enable the landlord under an express term to serve a notice to quit part of the holding. If it does not, a notice to quit part only is void. By s 31 of the 1986 Act a notice to quit part of the holding is valid if given for the purpose of adjusting the boundaries between agricultural units or amalgamating agricultural units or parts; or if given for a list of purposes in s 31(2) for which it is intended to use the land, such as the erection of cottages or other houses for farm labourers, the provision of gardens for cottages etc. By s 32 the tenant may within 28 days of a notice to quit part of the holding accept it as notice to quit the whole and notify the landlord. By s 33 where notice to quit part is given, the tenant is entitled to a reduction in rent proportionate to the part lost and to any depreciation in value to the rest and if the amount of any reduction cannot be agreed, it will be settled by arbitration.

V   SUCCESSION TO AGRICULTURAL TENANCIES

It is possible for there to be a double succession to an agricultural tenancy by limited classes of relatives of a deceased tenant. However, the succession scheme, by means of both routes outlined below, applies only to any tenancy originally granted before 12 July 1984, and, in time, the scheme's significance will slowly diminish, because it is not available, in principle, to any tenancy granted on or after 12 July 1984. In what follows, the scheme is outlined.

Outline of scheme

There are two routes to a succession for a tenancy created before 12 July 1984.

1   After the death of the tenant of an agricultural holding, an applicant may apply to the Agricultural Land Tribunal for a direction entitling him to succeed, but he may only obtain a direction if he is both eligible and suitable to succeed. If the applicant succeeds on both these points, the Tribunal directs the grant of a new tenancy and consent to any Case G notice served by the landlord is refused.
2   If the tenant decides to retire he may by notice nominate one person (who must be eligible) to succeed to the tenancy from a specified date. The nominated successor then applies to the Tribunal within one month of the retirement notice and if he is successful, there is a deemed succession.[2]

Eligibility to succeed

A person eligible to succeed (i e any surviving close relative of the deceased) may apply, under s 36(1) of the 1986 Act, for a direction under s 39, to the Tribunal, within three months of the death of the tenant. The following persons are eligible as 'close relatives':

(a)   the wife or husband of the deceased;

---

2   Agricultural Holdings Act 1986 ss 49–58 and Sch 6 Part II. The Tribunal must decide whether the nominated successor is suitable.

(b)   a brother or sister of the deceased;
(c)   a child of the deceased;
(d)   certain persons treated as children of any marriage of the deceased's.

The Tribunal must be satisfied that the applicant has not ceased to be eligible since the date of the death (s 39(2)).

An eligible person must show that he is not the occupier of a commercial unit of agricultural land (s 36(3)(b)).[3] He must also show that in the seven years ending with the death, his only or principal source of livelihood for a continuous period of five years or for two or more discontinuous periods amounting to five years, was derived from his agricultural work on the holding or on a unit of which it forms part (s 36(3)(a); in the case of the deceased's wife, the work may be hers, or the deceased's, or both (s 36(4)).[4]

Occupation by the survivor (subject to the above) must be shown. If a close relative is occupier (in effect) though the right to occupy is wholly or partly vested in another person or company, detailed rules decide what is or is not occupation for the purposes both of eligibility and the commercial unit rules.[5] Moreover:

(a)   Joint occupation by a close relative of the deceased and others is treated as occupation by the former of the whole land, with a right of apportionment of income if the former's share of income falls below that attributable to a commercial unit.[6]

(b)   Occupation by a close relative under a list of short and other interests, such as licences and tenancies for grazing or mowing, will not, of itself, debar a succession.[7]

(c)   If a close relative has already a tenancy of a holding under a Tribunal direction, he is in deemed occupation of the first-mentioned holding: if that is a commercial unit, he cannot succeed to the second.[8]

(d)   Occupation by the spouse of a close relative of the deceased or by a body corporate controlled by a close relative of the deceased counts as occupation by the latter.[9]

---

3   Defined, Sch 6 para 3(1): 'a unit of agricultural land which is capable, when farmed under competent management, of producing a net annual income of not less than the aggregate of the net average earnings of two full-time, male agricultural workers aged twenty or over'.

4   See *Trinity College, Cambridge v Caines* (1983) 272 Estates Gazette 1287 (money spent on ordinary living costs to be included); also *Bailey v Sitwell* [1986] 2 EGLR 7.

5   1986 Act Sch 6 paras 9 and 10. The rules noted here and immediately below apply to the nomination provisions: Sched 6 Part II.

6   Sch 6 para 7.

7   Sch 6 para 6.

8   Sch 6 para 8.

9   Sch 6 para 9.

Suitability to succeed

The Tribunal must decide whether an eligible applicant is suitable to succeed. In relation to this, s 39(8) requires the Tribunal to have regard to all relevant matters, including the training and practical experience in agriculture of the applicant, his age, health and financial standing and the landlord's views. If the Tribunal decides that the applicant is suitable, they must give a direction entitling him to a tenancy of the holding within three months from the day after date of death (s 39(1)). If there are two or more applicants, each person's eligibility and suitability must be separately determined (s 39(3)). The landlord may consent to accept a joint tenancy of up to four applicants (s 39(9)). After a direction, the landlord is deemed to grant the applicant(s) a new tenancy or joint tenancy (s 45). The terms of the new tenancy are generally the same as those of the old, except as varied by agreement or arbitration (ss 47 and 48)). It will generally be granted to run as from 12 months immediately after the end of the year in which the deceased tenant died (s 46(1)).

Landlord's application for consent to Case G notice

Before giving a direction, the Tribunal must allow the landlord to apply for its consent to the operation of any Case G notice (s 44). They may consent to the operation of such notice in relation to the whole or part of the holding. If the applicant agrees (s 39(10)) to a tenancy of part only of the holding the Tribunal may consent to the operation of the notice in respect of the excluded part (ss 44(5) and 43(2)).[10] If no application for a tenancy is made, or if no person has been determined as suitable, and the Tribunal consents to the operation of the notice, it takes effect in relation to the whole holding (s 43(1)).

Excluded cases

Even in relation to a tenancy granted before 12 July 1984, no succession is possible where, in particular:

(a) At the date of the death, the tenancy is subject to a valid notice to quit within s 26 or subject to a Case B to F notice (s 38).
(b) Where two succesions have already occurred (s 37). This may be either where the Tribunal has made a direction (s 37(6)) or where the landlord granted a tenancy to an eligible person who is a close relative without any Tribunal direction (s 37(1)).

---

10 By s 44(6) and (7), the Tribunal may, on the tenant's application, delay the notice to quit consented to for up to three months from its original date, or from the date on which they consent to the notice, whichever is later.

(c) The landlord and the current tenant agree on a new tenancy of the holding or a related holding to be granted to a close relative of the tenant: this operates the succession rules, no matter whether a single or joint tenancy is granted, and the agreement need not, for this to be so, necessarily relate to the whole holding (s 37(2) and (4)). Likewise, an assignment to an eligible person of an existing tenancy operates the succession rules (s 37(2) and (4)).

No succession where tenancy granted on or after 12 July 1984

The succession scheme only applies to tenancies granted before 12 July 1984. There are four cases where, in relation to tenancies granted on or after 12 July 1984, the succession scheme will apply, but apart from these it is excluded.

Exceptional cases of succession for tenancies on or after 12 July 1984

In the following cases only, by s 34(1), the succession scheme will apply for tenancies granted on or after 12 July 1984. First, where the tenancy was obtained under a Tribunal direction under s 39. Secondly, where the landlord granted the tenancy under s 45(6) to a person or persons entitled, after a Tribunal direction, to a tenancy. Thirdly, the tenancy is written and the parties agree that the succession scheme is to apply to it. Lastly, the tenancy was granted to a person who, immediately before 12 July 1984, was tenant of the whole or a substantial part of the land comprised in the holding.

Chapter 32

Rights on termination

I LANDLORD'S RIGHTS

The landlord may have claims for damage or dilapidation from the tenant after quitting, and these fall under three heads.

Claim under contract of tenancy

By s 71(3) of the 1986 Act, the landlord may claim damages for dilapidation, deterioration or damage due to the tenant's failure to farm in accordance with the rules of good husbandry, under the written contract of tenancy.[1] In no case, by s 71(4), is the amount of compensation to exceed the amount, if any, by which the value of the landlord's reversion is diminished by the breach in question.[2]

Claim under statute

The landlord may, alternatively, claim under s 71(1) for breaches of the implied obligation of the tenant to farm in accordance with the rules of good husbandry. This right applies only on the tenant's quitting the holding. The amount of compensation in this case is (s 71(2)) the cost, as at the date of quitting, of making good the dilapidation, deterioration or damage. This is subject to the ceiling on claims imposed by s 71(5), above.

General deterioration

There is an additional right in the landlord under s 72 to claim, not later than one month before the termination of the tenancy, for general

---

1 This head of claim may also be made during the currency of the contract of tenancy: *Kent v Conniff* [1953] 1 QB 361, [1953] 1 All ER 155, CA.
2 Similar considerations presumably apply to s 71(4) as apply to Landlord and Tenant Act 1954 s 18(1), ch 9 above.

deterioration. The amount recoverable is that by which the value of the holding has been reduced.

No claim can be made under s 71 nor s 72 above, unless an arbitration notice is given under s 84 within two months of the termination of the tenancy. On arbitration, it has been held that the terms of the tenancy are always relevant.[3] In the case of s 72 claims, additionally, there must be a preliminary notice of intention to claim compensation served by the landlord not later than one month prior to termination.[4]

II TENANT'S RIGHTS

(a) Emblements

The position is governed by s 21 of the 1986 Act, which substitutes security of tenure for the right to emblements in the rare cases where the tenant would have been entitled to them, i e a tenant at a rack rent whose landlord has only an interest for life, or some other uncertain interest. Section 21(1) provides that instead of a claim to emblements, the tenant shall continue to hold and occupy the holding until his tenancy is terminated by a 12 months' notice to quit. By s 21(2), the succeeding landlord is entitled to rent as from the cesser of the estate of the previous landlord, and by s 21(3), until termination of the tenancy, he and the tenant have all the same rights and are subject to all the same terms, conditions and restrictions as would have been the previous landlord and the tenant.

(b) Fixtures

A tenant's right to remove fixtures at any time during the tenancy or on quitting the holding on termination of the tenancy is dealt with in Chapter 15.

(c) Other claims

As to the tenant's right to remove agricultural fixtures, see Chapter 15 above. Four further claims are dealt with in Chapter 33, i e:

(a) Improvements;
(b) 'Tenant-Right';
(c) Special systems of farming;
(d) Disturbance.

---

3 *Barrow Green Estate Co v Walker's Executors* [1954] 1 All ER 204, [1954] 1 WLR 231, CA.

4 On the relationship between ss 71 and 72, see *Evans v Jones* [1955] 2 QB 58, [1955] 2 All ER 118 (landlord entitled to recover for specific failures under s 71 plus a s 72 claim for any general depreciation over and above that).

Chapter 33

Tenant's rights to compensation

I IMPROVEMENTS

(a) Rights to compensation

At common law, as has been explained, an agricultural tenant had no rights to compensation for any improvements which he had acquired or carried out at his own expense. In time, such rights came to be established by custom of the country, and local customary rights were often incorporated expressly in the terms of the tenancy. The 1986 Act supersedes customary rights, except that in the case of 'old improvements', a claim may be made, in the alternative, under custom or agreement. 'Old improvements' mean those begun before 1 March 1948 (s 64(4) and Sch 9 Part I). 'New improvements' refer to those begun on or after 1 March 1948 (see below).

The statutory rights to compensation are available to any tenant of agricultural land (including land belonging to the Crown (s 95)). A tenancy for less than a year is within the 1986 Act, as it takes effect under s 2 as a tenancy from year to year, and by s 1(5) a 'contract of tenancy' means a letting for a term of years or from year to year. Moreover, 'term of years' includes a term for less than a year.[1]

The tenant's rights to compensation arise on his quitting the holding on the termination of his tenancy, and therefore a tenant who is granted a new tenancy is not entitled to compensation on the termination of the earlier tenancy, but such rights as he would have had will be preserved until ultimately he quits (Sch 9 Part I). A tenant who on entry, and with the written consent of the landlord, paid any compensation to the outgoing tenant for improvements, may, on quitting the holding, claim the same compensation as the outgoing tenant would have been entitled to claim, if he had remained in occupation and was now quitting.

---

1 *Re Land and Premises at Liss, Hants* [1971] Ch 986, [1971] 3 All ER 380.

(b) Compensation for 'old improvements'

'Old improvements' are defined by s 64(4) as improvements specified in Schedule 4 begun before 1 March 1948. Schedule 9 is divided into two parts:

Part I improvements for which compensation is payable if written consent of the landlord was obtained before they were carried out (permanent improvements such as the erection of buildings).

Part II improvements for which compensation is payable if notice was given to the landlord before they were carried out (i e drainage).

'Old improvements' may be claimed either under the Act, or under custom or agreement, but not both. The measure of compensation is an amount equal to the increase attributable to the improvement in the value of the holding as such, having regard to its character and situation and the average requirements of tenants reasonably skilled in husbandry (para 2(1)), subject to any deductions permitted under para 2(2) in respect of benefits allowed by the landlord to the tenant in consideration of the improvement and the manurial value of crops sold or removed from the holding within the last two years of the tenancy.

(c) Compensation for 'new improvements'

'New improvements' are defined by s 64(1) as improvements specified in Sch 7 and Part I of Sch 8 to the Act, which were begun on or after 1 March 1948. Rights to compensation in respect of them are governed by ss 64–69 of the Act.

Improvements within Part I of Sched 7 may only be carried out by the tenant with the landlord's written consent (s 67(1)). Improvements within Part II of Sch 7 require either the consent of the landlord, or, if it is refused, the consent of the Agricultural Land Tribunal (s 67(1)). It is therefore advisable for the tenant to obtain the requisite consents before embarking on an improvement within Sch 7.

SEVENTH SCHEDULE

LONG-TERM IMPROVEMENTS BEGUN ON OR AFTER 1 MARCH 1948, FOR WHICH COMPENSATION IS PAYABLE

PART I

IMPROVEMENTS TO WHICH CONSENT OF LANDLORD REQUIRED

1 Making or planting of osier beds.

2   Making of water meadows.
3   Making of watercress beds.
4   Planting of hops.
5   Planting of orchards or fruit bushes.
6   Warping or weiring of land.
7   Making of gardens.
8   Provision of underground tanks.

PART II

IMPROVEMENTS TO WHICH CONSENT OF LANDLORD OR APPROVAL OF THE
TRIBUNAL REQUIRED

9   Erection, alteration or enlargement of buildings, and making or improvement of permanent yards.
10 Carrying out works in compliance with an improvement notice served, or an undertaking accepted, under Part VII of the Housing Act 1985 or Part VIII of the Housing Act 1974.
11 The creation or construction of loading platforms, ramps, hard standings for vehicles or other similar facilities.
12 Construction of silos.
13 Claying of land.
14 Marling of land.
15 Making or improvement of roads or bridges.
16 Making or improvements of water course, culverts, ponds, wells or reservoirs, or of works for the application of water power for agricultural or domestic purposes or of works for the supply, distribution or use of water for such purposes (including the erection or installation of any structures or equipment which form part of or are to be used in connection with operating any such works).
17 Making or removal of permanent fences.
18 Reclaiming of waste land.
19 Making or improvement of embankments or sluices.
20 Erection of wirework for hop gardens.
21 Provision of permanent sheep-dipping accommodation.
22 Removal of bracken, gorse, tree roots, boulders or other like obstructions to cultivation.
23 Land drainage (other than mole drainage and works carried out to secure the efficient functioning thereof).
24 Provision or laying-on of electric light or power.
25 Provision of facilities for the storage or disposal of sewage or farm waste.

26 Repairs to fixed equipment, being equipment reasonably required for the proper farming of the holding, other than repairs which the tenant is under an obligation to carry out.

27 The grubbing up of orchards or fruit bushes.

28 Planting trees otherwise than as an orchard and bushes other than fruit bushes.

The measure of compensation for improvements under Schedule 7 is not the cost of the improvements,[2] but an amount equal to the increase attributable to the improvement in the value of the holding, having regard to the character and situation of the holding and the average requirements of tenants reasonably skilled in husbandry (s 66).

EIGHTH SCHEDULE

SHORT-TERM IMPROVEMENTS BEGUN ON OR AFTER 1 MARCH 1948, AND OTHER MATTERS, FOR WHICH COMPENSATION IS PAYABLE

PART I

IMPROVEMENTS (TO WHICH NO CONSENT IS REQUIRED)

1 Mole drainage and works carried out to secure the efficient functioning thereof.

2 Protection of fruit trees against animals.

3 Clay burning.

4 Liming of land.

5 Application to land of purchased manure (including artificial manure).

6 Consumption on the holding of corn (whether produced on the holding or not) or of cake or other feeding stuff not produced on the holding by horses, cattle, sheep, pigs or poultry.

By s 68(1), a tenant is not entitled to compensation for an improvement under para 1 above (mole-drainage), unless he notified the landlord of his intention to carry out the work at least one month before doing so. The landlord cannot elect to do the improvement himself, however, and there would seem little point in this requirement.

The measure of compensation for improvements set out in the Eighth Schedule is their value to an incoming tenant, calculated in accordance

---

2 See *Re Duke of Wellington's Parliamentary Estates, King v Wellesley* [1972] Ch 374, [1971] 2 All ER 1140.

with regulations.[3] The landlord is entitled to make certain deductions in respect of benefits allowed to the tenant and improvement grants or local government grants paid to the tenant (s 66(5), as is the case of 'old improvements'.

II   TENANT-RIGHT

Part II of the Eighth Schedule sets out 'tenant right matters' in respect of which the tenant is entitled to compensation by virtue of the Act. Where the tenant was in occupation on 1 March 1948, the tenant may claim statutory compensation if he elects to do so during the currency of the tenancy, by notice in writing served on the landlord; and if he fails to make that election within one month of being required to do so during the running of a notice to quit by the landlord, he loses his statutory rights (Sch 12 para 8). The measure of compensation for improvements under Part II of the Eighth Schedule is the same as for those under Part I (see above), unless the parties have agreed in the contract of tenancy that it should be calculated in some other way (s 66(4)).

PART II

TENANT–RIGHT MATTERS

7   Growing crops and severed or harvested crops and produce, being in either case crops or produce grown on the holding in the last year of the tenancy, but not including crops or produce which the tenant has a right to sell or remove from the holding.

8   Seeds sown and cultivations, fallows and acts of husbandry performed on the holding at the expense of the tenant (including the growing of herbage crops for commercial seed production).

9   Pasture laid down with clover, grass, lucerne, sainfoin or other seeds, being either –
(a) pasture laid down at the expense of the tenant otherwise than in compliance with an obligation imposed on him by an agreement in writing to lay it down to replace temporary pasture comprised in the holding when the tenant entered thereon which was not paid for by him; or
(b) pasture paid for by the tenant on entering on the holding.

---

3   Agriculture (Calculation of Value for Compensation) Regulations 1978, SI 1978/809; as amended.

10 Acclimatisation, hefting or settlement of hill sheep on hill land.
11 In areas of the country where arable crops can be grown in an unbroken series of not less than six years and it is reasonable to grow them on the holding or part, the residual fertility value of the sod of the excess qualifying leys on the holding, if any.

III SPECIAL SYSTEMS OF FARMING

The tenant may claim compensation under s 70, whereby he is entitled to an amount equivalent to any increase in the value of the holding as a result of his continued adoption of a special system of farming during his tenancy. In order to establish such a claim, the tenant must show that the system adopted was more beneficial than the system of farming required by the terms of the tenancy, or if none was specified, then the system of farming normally practised on comparable agricultural holdings. Section 70(2) further requires that:

(i) the tenant has, not later than one month before the termination of the tenancy, given the landlord notice in writing of his intention to claim compensation under this head, and
(ii) a record has been made under s 22 of the Act of the condition of the fixed equipment on the holding and of the general condition of the holding.

Compensation under s 70 is not payable in respect of matters arising before that record was made (or the first of them), nor of improvements for which compensation has, or should have been, claimed separately under any other head.

IV DISTURBANCE

Where the tenancy of an agricultural holding is terminated by reason of:

(a) a notice to quit given by the landlord, or
(b) a counter-notice given by the tenant under s 32 after being given notice to quit part of the holding,

and in consequence, the tenant quits, he is entitled to compensation for disturbance unless the notice to quit specified and the landlord makes out Cases C–G (s 61). Compensation is restricted by s 63(3) where the tenant serves a counter-notice after a notice to quit[4] part of the holding,

---

4 I e a notice given by the original landlord or any other person entitled to a severed part of the reversion: s 63(4).

which enlarges the notice to cover the whole holding which the tenant then quits. If the notice related to less than one quarter of the holding and the rest was reasonably capable of being farmed as a separate unit, then compensation for disturbance is for that relating to the original part to which the notice related. On the other hand, a tenant who becomes liable to pay compensation for disturbance to a sub-tenant, in consequence of being served with a notice to quit by his own landlord, is not debarred from claiming compensation under this head against his landlord by reason only that he cannot strictly be said to 'quit' the holding on the termination of his tenancy, owing to the fact that he was not in occupation of the holding (s 63(2)). Section 63(1) gives a sub-tenant the right to claim compensation for disturbance, on quitting after termination of his sub-tenancy consequent on termination by operation of law of the head tenancy after notice or counter-notice.

The amount of compensation payable is the amount of loss or expense directly attributable to the tenant's quitting the holding, which is unavoidably incurred by him on sale or removal of household goods, implements of husbandry, fixtures, farm produce or stock; and it includes expenses reasonably incurred by him in preparation of his claim for compensation, but not costs incurred as a result of a reference to arbitration (s 60(5)). The minimum compensation under this head is one year's rent of the holding and this is payable without proof of loss or expense. If, however, the tenant considers that his losses or expenses exceed that figure, he may claim up to the maximum of two years' rent, provided that at least one month before the termination of the tenancy he has given the landlord notice in writing of his intention to make a claim under this head, and before selling any of the goods, etc, he has given the landlord a reasonable opportunity of making a valuation thereof.

Compensation is payable under s 60 notwithstanding any agreement to the contrary (s 78(1)).

Additional compensation for disturbance

Section 60[5] enables the tenant to obtain additional compensation: this is the payment to him of a further sum to assist in the reorganisation of his affairs, notwithstanding any agreement to the contrary. The sum payable under this head is an amount equivalent to four times the annual rent of the holding (or four times the apportioned part of the annual rent, where the tenant quits part of the holding), at the rate at which the rent was payable immediately before the termination of the tenancy (s 60(4)).

---

5   This applies (s 74(3)) where compensation is payable by a person entitled to a severed part of the reversion.

In certain cases there is no right to claim additional compensation, listed in s 61 and, in summary, these are:

(a) Where the Agricultural Land Tribunal consent to the notice for reasons of good husbandry, sound estate management, agricultural research or greater hardship, and the notice stated that it was given on one of these grounds.

(b) The reason stated in the notice was based on Case A or H of Sch 3.

However, contracting out of the tenant's right is forbidden by s 78(1).

Chapter 34

Market gardens

I APPLICATION OF THE ACTS

Where an agricultural holding is let or treated as a market garden, the tenant has three specific rights (s 79(2)(4) and (5)):

(a) Before the termination of the tenancy, the tenant may remove all fruit trees and fruit bushes planted by him (but not permanently set out), but if he leaves them, he will not be entitled to compensation.

(b) An incoming tenant may claim compensation for improvements which he purchased, although the landlord did not consent in writing.

(c) Improvements listed in Sch 10 begun before 1 March 1948 are to be treated as if they were included in Part I of Sch 8. Those begun after that date are treated as if included in Part II of Sch 9, with the result that the amount of compensation is the value to an incoming tenant.

The tenant of a market garden has the right to remove any fixture or building, erected on the holding before 1st January 1884 and acquired by him since then for the purposes of his trade as market gardener (s 79(3)). He is also entitled to remove all fixtures, including buildings, irrespective of whether he is entitled to compensation under the 1986 Act, but this right relates only to fixtures erected or acquired for the purpose of his trade or business as a market gardener (s 79(3)).

Where the tenant wishes to have his holding treated as a market garden, for the purpose of being entitled to compensation under Sch 10, and the landlord refuses, the Agricultural Land Tribunal have powers under s 80 to make a direction to that effect, on an application by the tenant, if they are satisfied that the land is suitable for that purpose, and also to direct what provisions of Sch 10 are to apply to the letting.

Where any such direction is given and the tenancy is determined by notice to quit given by the tenant or by reason of the tenant's insolvency, he loses any rights to compensation, unless within one month thereof he produces to the landlord an offer in writing (which must remain open for

three months) from a substantial and otherwise suitable person to accept
a tenancy of the holding as from the termination of the tenancy, and to
pay the tenant the amount of compensation due to him, and the landlord
fails to accept that offer within the three months (s 80(3)). If the landlord
accepts the offer, the incoming tenant must pay on demand all sums due
to the landlord from the outgoing tenant, which sums the incoming
tenant is entitled to deduct from any compensation he is liable to pay to
the outgoing tenant (s 80(5)). These provisions as to compensation,
known as the 'Evesham custom', may be substituted for the provisions as
to compensation which would otherwise be applicable to a tenancy of
land agreed to be let or treated as a market garden (s 81(2)).
Nevertheless, the parties are free to contract out of the provisions of the
Act relating to compensation for improvements, provided that the
compensation agreed is fair and reasonable (s 81(1)).

II   SCHEDULE 10 IMPROVEMENTS

1   Planting of standard or other fruit trees permanently set out.
2   Planting of fruit bushes permanently set out.
3   Planting of strawberry plants.
4   Planting of asparagus, rhubarb and other vegetable crops which
    continue productive for two or more years.
5   Erection, alteration or enlargement of buildings for the purpose of
    the trade or business of a market gardener.

Chapter 35

Arbitration

I CLAIMS ON TERMINATION OF THE TENANCY

Section 83(1) provides for any claim, of whatever nature, arising between the parties to a tenancy of an agricultural holding to be determined by arbitration, if the claim arises:

(a) under the Act or any custom or agreement; and
(b) on or out of the termination of the tenancy of the holding or part of the holding.

In order to preserve such a claim, the claimant must serve a notice in writing on the other party within two months after the termination of the tenancy, of his intention to make the claim. The notice must specify the nature of the claim, if only by reference to the statutory provision, custom, or term of an agreement under which it is made (s 83(2),(3)).

The parties are given eight months after the termination of the tenancy within which to reach agreement in writing upon the matters of the claim (s 83(4))[1] If the claim has not been settled when the time-limit expires it is to be determined by arbitration under the 1986 Act (s 70(4)).[1]

II CLAIMS ARISING DURING A TENANCY

Claims arising on or out of the termination of a tenancy are compulsorily referable to arbitration, in default of agreement between the parties under s 83. Settlement of a number of claims arising during the currency of a tenancy are also made referable to arbitration, e g rent (s 12), increases of rent for certain improvements carried out by the landlord (s 13(7)), variation of terms as to permanent pasture (s 14), assessment of the tenant's farming methods in proceedings for an injunction (s 15(6)), disputes as to any amount of fair value payable by the landlord to the tenant in relation to fixtures of buildings (s 10(6)), compensation for

---

1 See *Hallinan v Jones* (1984) 272 Estates Gazette 1081.

damage by wild animals or birds (s 20(4)). There is nothing to prevent the parties from agreeing to refer other matters to arbitration, which would otherwise be the subject of litigation, but it is doubtful whether the parties may agree to invoke the special arbitration procedures under the Agricultural Holdings Act 1986 in such cases; consequently, they would be subject to the Arbitration Act 1950.

III PROCEDURE ON A REFERENCE

Section 84(1) provides that any matter which by virtue of the Act or regulations made under the Act is required to be determined by arbitration under the Act, must be determined by a single arbitrator in accordance with Sch 11, and not in accordance with the Arbitration Act 1950. The arbitrator is either appointed by agreement between the parties or in default of agreement, by a person appointed by the Minister on the application of one of the parties, from a panel (Sch 11 para 1). Appointment by the Minister must be made by him as soon as possible after receiving the application; where the application is referable to a demand for arbitration under s 12 (rent) an appointment must not in any event be made earlier than four months before the next termination date following the date of the demand as defined in s 12(4).

The detailed procedure to be followed by an arbitrator is laid down in Sch 11 and regulations deal with ancillary aspects.[2]

In particular, it may be noted that there is a statutory requirement that reasons for the award be given whether the arbitrator is appointed by agreement or not (para 21). Also that the county court may remove an arbitrator for misconduct (para 27) and it may remit the award or any part to the arbitrator for reconsideration; and in the case of error of law on the face of the award, the county court may, as an alternative to remission, vary the award itself (para 28). An example of an error of law of the latter kind was where an arbitrator misconstrued a tenant's covenant to pay rent as conditional on the landlord's compliance with his covenant to repair certain items.[3] The parties must deliver a statement to the arbitrator of their respective cases, with all necessary particulars within 35 days of his appointment (para 7), and no amendments, except with his consent, are allowed. Leave to amend should be given to the arbitrator, despite this time-limit, which is not mandatory and inflexible, if no undue prejudice will result to the other side.[4]

---

2 Agricultural Holdings Rules 1948 SI 1948/1943 as amended SI 1985/1829.
3 *Burton v Timmis* [1987] 1 EGLR 1, CA.
4 *E D & A D Cooke Bourne (Farms) Ltd v Mellows* [1983] QB 104, [1982] 2 All ER 208, CA.

Chapter 36

Smallholdings and allotments

I SMALLHOLDINGS

Part III of the Agriculture Act 1970 constitutes local authorities as 'smallholdings authorities' (s 38)[1] The authorities are required by s 39, having regard to the general interests of agriculture and of good estate management, to make it their general aim to provide opportunities for persons to be farmers on their own account by letting holdings to them. There was an upper limit of 50 acres under the earlier Acts, but by s 39(2), a holding is to be treated as within the upper limit, if in the opinion of the Minister, it is capable of providing full-time employment for not more than two men (including the person to whom it is let) with or without additional part-time employment of another man. Smallholdings may be let only to a person who is to farm the holding, and either:

(a) is regarded by the authority as being qualified by reason of his agricultural experience to farm the holding on his own account, or

(b) is a person in respect of whom the authority are satisfied that within a reasonably short time he will become eligible to be so regarded (s 44(2)).

More than one smallholding may be let to several similarly qualified persons proposing to farm the land together on a co-operative system (s 44(3)). In determining the rent at which a smallholding should be let, the authority are required by s 45(1) to have regard to the rent which, in their opinion, might reasonably be expected to be determined by arbitration under the 1986 Act in respect of a tenancy of that land if it were let as an agricultural holding on the same terms as under the proposed letting.

---

1   Upon the abolition of the Greater London Council by Local Government Act 1985 s 1, no provision was made for any authorities to act as smallholdings authorities, and there is no statutory warrant for assuming that London Boroughs or the London Residuary Body are such authorities.

Section 46 of the 1970 Act gives the authorities the necessary powers to equip smallholdings. Note that no person claiming to succeed to a tenancy of a smallholding granted before or after Part III of the 1970 Act was passed may claim a succession to it under the succession scheme (s 38(4) of the 1986 Act).

II ALLOTMENTS

The tenant of an allotment, which is defined by s 1 of the Allotments Act 1922, as any parcel of land, whether attached to a cottage or not, of not more than two acres in extent let as a farm or a garden, or partly as a garden and partly as a farm, is entitled by s 3(2) of that Act (which cannot be contracted out of), on the termination of his tenancy, to compensation for:

(a) crops, including fruit, growing upon the land in the ordinary course of cultivation and for labour expended upon and manure applied to the land; and

(b) fruit trees or bushes provided and planted by the tenant with the landlord's prior consent in writing, and for drains, outbuildings, pigsties, fowl-houses, or other structural improvements made or erected by and at the expense of the tenant on the land with such consent.

The measure of compensation is the value to an incoming tenant (s 22(3)), and the amount is subject to deductions in respect of any arrears of rent, breach of the terms of the contract of tenancy and of any wilful or negligent damage caused or permitted by the tenant (s 3(3)). If the parties cannot agree on the amount payable, the dispute is settled by a person appointed by the county court (s 6(1)). By s 3(5), the tenant may claim either under the 1922 Act or under the 1986 Act if that Act applies to the allotment.

Under s 23 of the Smallholdings and Allotments Act 1908, parish councils have a duty to provide allotments or allotment gardens (i e allotments not exceeding forty poles), depending upon the size of the population, if there is sufficient demand from local residents, and they have power to acquire land for the purpose.

III ALLOTMENT GARDENS

By s 22(1) of the Allotments Act 1922, the expression 'allotment garden' means an allotment not exceeding 40 poles in extent, which is wholly or mainly cultivated for the production of vegetables or fruit for consumption by the tenant or his family. On quitting the land on the termination of his tenancy by the landlord, the tenant is entitled, by s 2(3), notwithstanding any agreement to the contrary, to compensation for crops growing upon the land in the ordinary course of the cultivation of the land as an allotment garden and for manure applied to the land.

He may remove his fruit trees and bushes, and any erection or improvement made by him, before the end of his tenancy; and in addition, he may be entitled to claim compensation for disturbance (amounting to one year's rent), provided that his tenancy is terminated:

(a) by re-entry under the Allotments Act 1922;
(b) where the landlord is himself a tenant by the termination of *his* tenancy; or
(c) where the landlord is a local authority which has let the land under s 10 of the 1922 Act, by the termination of the authority's right of occupation.

Termination must generally be by a 12 months' notice to quit expiring on or before the sixth day of April or on or after the twenty-ninth day of September. Under s 1 of the 1922 Act, re-entry may be made on three months' notice, however, where the land is required for certain statutory purposes. On re-entry for non-payment of rent, bankruptcy or other breach of obligation, there are no rights to compensation.

PART G
SECURE TENANCIES

Chapter 37

Secure tenancies

I INTRODUCTION

Landlord condition

Security of tenure for public sector tenants is conferred by Part IV of the Housing Act 1985. Security arises where the landlord condition is satisfied (s 80), and tenancies of dwelling-houses granted by any of the following landlords satisfy that condition: a local authority, a new town corporation, an urban development corporation, a housing action trust, the Development Board for Rural Wales and certain housing co-operatives.[1] The landlord condition will not be satisfied if one of two joint landlords complies with it: it is essential that both landlords satisfy s 80.[2] Where the landlord's interest is transferred from one of the above public sector landlords to a private sector landlord, any tenancies granted by the public sector landlord will cease to be secure unless the landlord's interest reverts to a relevant public sector landlord (Housing Act 1988 s 38). Thereafter, if the conditions precedent for assured tenancies apply, the tenancies will become assured.

Basis of security rules

The general basis of the statutory rules governing secure tenancies is different from the Rent Act regime. This is because, it has been said, Part IV of the 1985 Act simply gets rid of the common-law methods of terminating fixed-term and periodic tenancies and provides that on termination of, for example, a fixed-term secure tenancy, a statute-implied periodic tenancy automatically arises, which is only determin-

---

1 The rules are given as from the commencement of Part I of the Housing Act 1988. For transitional provisions see s 35(4) and (5). Until the 1988 Act was passed, the Housing Corporation and housing associations within Rent Act 1977 s 15(3) could grant secure tenancies.
2 *R v Plymouth City Council and Cornwall County Council, ex p Freeman* (1987) 19 HLR 328, CA.

able as laid down in the Act.[3] On the other hand, the security of tenure provisions in Part IV of the 1985 Act resemble, in many respects, those in Part I of the Housing Act 1988 for assured tenancies.

II   SCOPE OF SECURE TENANCY PROVISIONS

General

Security of tenure is conferred where both the landlord condition and the tenant condition are satisfied, and where, in addition, there is a tenancy under which a dwelling-house is let as a separate dwelling (s 79(1)). A dwelling-house may be a house or part of a house (s 112(1)).[4] Land let together with a dwelling-house is within the protection of the Act unless it is agricultural land exceeding two acres (s 112(2)).

The landlord condition (s 80) means that secure tenancies may only be granted by the landlords listed in section I of this Chapter. The tenant condition is, by s 81, that the tenant must be an individual who occupies the dwelling-house as his only or principal home. Two houses may be occupied at the same time as a home and actual physical occupation is not, it seems, always necessary to satisfy this condition.[5] Where the tenancy is a joint tenancy, s 81 relaxes the strict joint tenancies rule, by providing that each of the tenants must be individuals and that at least one of them must occupy the dwelling-house as his only or principal home. The tenant condition requires continuing occupation by the tenant or one of a number of joint tenants, and where, therefore, a sole tenant abandoned occupation permanently, leaving no possessions, and the landlords re-let the premises, security was lost by implied surrender of the tenancy.[6]

Excluded tenancies

A tenancy cannot in any event be secure if:

1   It falls within any of the exclusions in Sch 1.
2   It comes within s 90(3).
3   It contravenes either s 91 or s 93.
4   The landlord is no longer a public sector landlord, by reason of the transfer of the landlord's interest to the private sector.

---

3   *Hammersmith and Fulham London Borough v Harrison* [1981] 2 All ER 588, CA; P F Smith [1982] Conv 218.
4   Similar rules to determine the scope of ss 79 and 112 apply as for Rent Act 1977 s 1: see, therefore, ch 17.
5   *Crawley Borough Council v Sawyer* (1987) 20 HLR 98, CA.
6   *R v London Borough of Croydon Council, ex p Toth* (1987) 20 HLR 576, CA.

Licences

Section 79(3) provides that the security provisions apply to a licence to occupy a dwelling-house (whether granted for a consideration or not) as they apply to a tenancy. By s 79(4), however, this rule does not apply, and there will be no security, where there is a licence granted as a temporary expedient to a person who entered the dwelling-house or other land as a trespasser (whether or not before the grant, another licence to occupy that or another dwelling-house had been granted to him).

In any event (as with agricultural holdings) the main anti-licence provision is fairly narrow: it certainly brings exclusive licences within the secure tenancies rules.[7] In this, the presence or absence of exclusive possession in the conditions of tenancy under which the occupier holds is the crucial factor.[8] It would, however, appear that, in spite of the fact that s 79(3) refers simply to a 'licence to occupy', non-exclusive licences to occupy are outside the statutory umbrella.

Tenancies which cannot be secure

The following tenancies are excluded from security by Sch 1 to the 1985 Act.

(a) *Long leases* (para 1)

A long tenancy (i e a tenancy granted for a term certain exceeding 21 years[9]) is not a secure tenancy.

(b) *Premises occupied in connection with employment* (para 2)

If the tenant is the employee of certain landlords, in particular a local authority, and his employment requires him to occupy the dwelling-house for the better performance of his duties, the tenancy cannot be secure. Certain other employee-tenants cannot have a secure tenancy, such as employee-tenants holding from a fire authority or the police – special rules apply in these cases.

(c) *Land acquired for development* (para 3)

A tenancy is not secure if the dwelling-house is on land acquired for development and the dwelling-house is used by the landlord, pending development, as temporary living accommodation.

---

7   *Family Housing Association v Miah* (1982) 5 HLR 94, CA; also *Kensington and Chelsea Royal Borough Council v Hayden* (1984) 17 HLR 114, CA.
8   *Eastleigh Borough Council v Walsh* [1985] 2 All ER 112, [1985] 1 WLR 525, HL; cf *Street v Mountford* [1985] AC 809, [1985] 2 All ER 289, HL; and see ch 3.
9   Housing Act 1985 s 115(1); also tenancies with a right to perpetual renewal.

(d)   *Accommodation for homeless persons* (para 4)

A tenancy granted to certain classes of homeless persons is not secure for the first twelve months from notification of a decision on homelessness, unless before the expiry of the twelve months, the landlord notifies the tenant that the tenancy is to be regarded as secure. A tenancy within para 4 is not deemed by s 79(3) to be secure, as it can only become secure, in certain circumstances, after a specified lapse of time.[10]

(e)   *Temporary accommodation for persons taking up employment* (para 5)

A tenancy is not secure for one year from its grant if it is granted to a person not previously resident in the local housing authority's district, who, prior to the grant of the tenancy, obtained employment or an offer thereof in the district or in the area of any district surrounding it. The tenancy must be granted to enable the person to meet his need for temporary employment and to enable him to find permanent accommodation in the district or its surrounding area. The landlord must, in addition, notify the tenant of the circumstances of the exception and if, before the year expires, the landlord further notifies the tenant that the tenancy is to be regarded as secure, it will become secure.[11]

(f)   *Short-term arrangements* (para 6)

If the dwelling-house has been leased to the landlord itself, with vacant possession, for use as temporary housing accommodation and the lessor is able, under the head lease, to obtain vacant possession from the landlord on the expiry of a specified period or when required, and the lessor is not a local authority or other landlord within s 80, and has no interest in the dwelling-house other than as lessor or mortgagee, the tenancy is not secure.

(g)   *Temporary accommodation during works* (para 7)

A tenancy is not a secure tenancy if the dwelling-house was made available to the tenant or to a predecessor in title of his, for occupation by him while works are carried out on a dwelling-house previously occupied as his home. If the tenant or predecessor (this seems to mean *any* predecessor) was a secure tenant of the other dwelling-house at the

---

10   *Eastleigh Borough Council v Walsh* [1985] 2 All ER 112, [1985] 1 WLR 525, HL; also *Kensington and Chelsea Royal Borough Council v Hayden* (1984) 17 HLR 114, CA.

11   Otherwise it remains non-secure. Para 5 does not in terms state as from what date the tenancy becomes secure if the landlord so notifies the tenant; this could be as from the date of notification of the date of expiry of the year referred to. The former date seems preferable.

date of cesser of occupation as his home, the tenancy of the temporary house will be secure.

(h) *Miscellaneous* (paras 8–12)

The following tenancies are excluded from secure status. Since similar considerations apply to these as apply to the corresponding private sector grounds discussed in part D of this book, no details are here given.

1 Agricultural Holdings (para 8).
2 Licensed Premises (para 9).
3 Student Lettings (para 10).
4 1954 Act tenancies (para 11).
5 Almshouses (para 12).

III   NOTE ON PRIVATISATION OR 'PICK A LANDLORD'

Under Part IV of the Housing Act 1988, there are rules to enable the disposal of public-sector estates to private sector landlords, including, no doubt, housing associations. Once these procedures have been gone through, existing tenants cease to be secure and may be assured tenants: new tenancies will be assured. Provisions will be made in regulations to require the old landlord to determine any tenancies or licences granted after the date of the new landlord's application to buy the freehold. Such tenancies or licences are not capable of being secure (s 101).[12]

Scope of Part IV

Part IV applies to approved private sector landlords only, i e landlords approved by the Housing Corporation (s 94). These will be able to acquire the fee simple in relevant buildings occupied by 'qualifying tenants' of the public sector landlord. 'Qualifying tenant' means, by s 93(3), generally, a secure tenant of a public sector landlord who holds directly under him.[13] Part IV applies to residential buildings and to property reasonably required for occupation with them. The right is exercisable against: a local authority, a new town corporation, a housing action trust and the Development Board for Rural Wales.

Exclusions

A building is excluded by s 95(1) from Part IV if, at the date of the application to acquire:

---

12 Part II of the 1954 Act does not apply either, and every such tenancy or licence is terminable by four weeks' notice.
13 For exceptions, see s 93(4).

(a)   any part or parts of the building are occupied or intended to be occupied otherwise than for residential purposes; and

(b)   the internal floor area of that part or parts exceed 50 per cent of the internal floor area of the building taken as a whole.

A part of the building occupied with the dwelling-house, used for purposes connected therewith, or used in connection with the provision of services to a residential building, are included within Part IV (s 95(2)). There are certain further exclusions from Part IV, however, notably where there are two or more flats in a building occupied by non-qualifying tenants and the total so occupied at the date of exercise of the right to acquire is over half the total number of flats (s 95(3)).[14]

The price and other procedures

1   There are a number of initial procedures which have to be gone through, including the need for a prescribed form of application to exercise the right to buy out the local authority, etc, from the applicant (s 96).

2   Within four weeks of the date of the application, the landlord must serve a notice on the applicant. This must inform the applicant of the names and addresses of every tenant or licensee in the building or buildings, and will specify the general nature of his tenancy or licence (s 97(1)). As from four weeks after service of this notice, the applicant has the right to access to any part of the property not subject to a tenancy and to inspect and take copies of documents reasonably required to pursue the application (s 97(2)).

3   Within 12 months of the date of the application, the landlord must serve a further notice on the applicant, which will state what, if any, buildings are excluded from the application for whatever relevant reason, e g that they are not occupied by qualifying tenants. This notice must specify any rights the landlord wishes to retain over the property to be acquired for the maintenance of retained land of his; any other proposed terms of the conveyance, and prescribed particulars (s 98(1)). If the applicant does not accept any matters, he has four weeks from service of this notice to notify the landlord (s 98(4)).

4   The price is decided by means of a further notice served by the landlord on the applicant, s 99, usually within eight weeks of the service of the s 98 notice. The s 99 notice will specify the price payable, which is to be the open market price as at the date of the

14   Also where a building is the subject-matter of another Part IV application (s 95(5)).

application (s 99(2))[15] with the following principal statutory assumptions.

(a) The property is sold subject to subsisting tenancies at the date of the application to acquire, otherwise with vacant possession.

(b) It is to be conveyed with the same rights and burdens as it would be in pursuance of the right of acquisition.

(c) The only bidders in the market are approved persons and the applicant would, within a reasonable period, carry out works necessary to comply with the landlord's repairing obligations.

If the applicant has matters which he does not accept in the price notice, he must notify the landlord (s 99(4) and (5)).

Consultation and later procedures

The applicant must consult with all qualifying tenants in the prescribed manner (s 102) but subject to that, the applicant may serve notice of his intention to proceed (s 103).[16] After that, the landlord must convey the fee simple to the applicant – a duty enforceable by injunction (s 104).[17] Rent due up to the date of the conveyance is recoverable by the old landlord (s 104(5)).

Subsequent disposals by the applicant require the consent of the Secretary of State (s 105). No notice to proceed is possible if less than 50 per cent of the qualifying tenants give notice of their wishes in the prescribed manner, or the number of tenants who gave notice as above, and who indicate that they wish to continue with their existing landlord, exceeds 50 per cent of the total number of qualifying tenants (s 103(2)).

IV SPECIAL PROVISIONS

Section 90(3)

Where a secure tenant entitled to a fixed-term tenancy dies, the tenancy will eventually devolve on the beneficiary or beneficiaries under his will, having first vested in his personal representatives and unless there is a beneficiary who would be qualified to succeed to the tenancy if it had

---

15 If the property could not, having regard to these assumptions, fetch a price, there is a deemed disposal cost, i e excess of cost of works over the price of the building after the works are carried out (s 99(3)).

16 The period for consultation runs from either the notification of the district valuer's determination or the service of the landlord's notice, and within two weeks from the end of this period, the landlord may serve his notice of intention to proceed (s 102(1) and 103(1)).

17 As to title registration and related matters see Sch 12.

been periodic (in which case the tenancy remains at all times secure), s 90(3) provides that security is lost by reason of the above events (except where an order under s 24 of the Matrimonial Causes Act 1973 is made).

Section 91

A secure tenancy granted on or after 5 November 1982 whether periodic or fixed term, and any fixed-term secure tenancy granted before that date cannot be assigned (s 91(1)) and if it is assigned, it simply ceases to be a secure tenancy. To this rule there are three exceptions.

(a) Assignments under s 24 of the Matrimonial Causes Act 1973.[18] Such assignments cause the succession provisions (below) to operate if the other party to the marriage was a successor (s 91(3) and 88(2)).

(b) An assignment to a successor to the secure tenancy under s 91(3) or an assignment to a person who would have succeeded to the tenancy had the tenant died immediately prior to the assignment. This exception applies so that the tenancy, fixed-term or periodic, remains secure in the hands of the successor-assign (provided qualified to succeed, e g the tenant's wife or daughter). This is so even if the tenancy itself prohibits assignments, because s 91 is an overriding provision; but, at the same time, if the tenancy itself prohibits assignments, the landlord may proceed against the successor for the previous tenant's breach of covenant.[19] The succession provisions are operated by a s 91 assignment: on the death of the assign, there will be no further succession (s 88(1)(d)).

(c) Where s 92 applies to the assignment: this is where a secure tenant assigns the tenancy by way of exchange with another secure tenant, in both cases with the landlord's written consent, so that both tenancies remain secure. Where consent is applied for, only on one or more statutory grounds[20] is it possible for the landlord to withhold consent and if consent is withheld otherwise, it is treated as given (s 92(3)).[1] The succession provisions only operate if the tenant receiving an assignment of a tenancy was a successor in relation to the tenancy he himself assigned (s 88(3)).

---

18 Where a suspended possession order was made and the tenant failed to comply with its terms, from that moment, the tenancy ended and there was nothing for s 24 of the 1973 Act to operate on: *Thompson v Elmbridge Borough Council* [1987] 1 WLR 1425, CA.

19 *Peabody Donation Fund v Higgins* [1983] 3 All ER 122, [1983] 1 WLR 1091, CA. Such circularity seems rather absurd.

20 Housing Act 1985 Sch 3. To rely on any ground, the landlord must give the tenant a 42-day statutory notice (s 92(4)).

1 By Housing Act 1985 s 92(5), if rent is in arrear or other covenants are broken by the tenant, consent may, exceptionally, be conditional on remedy by the tenant; but no other conditions may be imposed on a consent required by s 92 (s 92(6)).

Section 93(2)

This provision enacts that if a secure tenant parts with the possession of the dwelling-house or sub-lets the whole of it (or sub-lets first part of it, then the whole) security of tenure is lost. Once that happens, security cannot be regained. This rule is excluded if the first two exceptions to s 91 apply; but not where s 92 applies.

V   SUCCESSION RULES

Secure tenants for a fixed term

On the death of the tenant, the tenancy vests in his personal representatives and remains secure until it is vested or otherwise disposed of in the administration of his estate, or until it is known that when vested or disposed of, it will not be secure (s 90(2) and (3)). If the tenancy is vested in a person qualified to succeed (qv), it remains secure throughout (s 90(3)(b)).

Secure periodic tenants

On the death of a secure periodic tenant,[2] the tenancy will vest, if appropriate, in any person qualified to succeed;[3] and if there is more than one such person, s 89(2) provides that the tenant's spouse has the prior claim: as between other competing family claimants, there must be an agreement for one of them to succeed or, failing that, a selection by the landlord. Where there is no person qualified to succeed, the tenancy ceases to be secure (s 89(3)). In the case both of fixed-term and periodic tenancies, if the tenancy is vested or disposed of under s 24 of the Matrimonial Causes Act 1973, it remains secure.

Meaning of 'qualified to succeed'

By s 87, a person is qualified to succeed if he occupied the dwelling-house as his only or principal home at the time of the tenant's death, and is either the tenant's spouse, or another member of the tenant's 'family' (very widely defined in s 113) residing with the tenant throughout the 12 months ending with the tenant's death.[4] The 12 months must be

---

2   If the tenant dies intestate, any landlord's notice to quit must be served on the President of the Family Division: *Wirral Borough Council v Smith* (1982) 43 P & CR 312, CA.

3   The onus of proof is on any would-be successor: *Peabody Donation Fund Governors v Grant* (1982) 264 Estates Gazette 925, CA.

4   On 'family' see *Reading Borough Council v Ilsley* [1981] CLY 1323; also *Harrogate Borough Council v Simpson* [1986] FLR 91, CA (lesbian co-resident with tenant not a member of her 'family'). 'Residing with': i e spending a significant part of one's time with the person concerned: *Peabody Donation Fund Governors v Grant*, supra.

spent in the premises concerned and so, where five months only were spent by the claimant and deceased tenant in the premises, the residence requirement was not satisfied, even though the parties had cohabited for well over 12 months.[5] Only one succession is allowed under these rules.

Successor

After the death of any successor to a secure tenancy, security ends. For this purpose, 'successor' is accordingly defined by s 88 as including the person in whom the tenancy vests because of that person being qualified to succeed. A succession also takes place where a joint secure tenant becomes sole tenant on the death of the other joint tenant(s). A deemed succession takes place where the first two exceptions to s 91 apply.[6] If the tenant is a successor to the tenancy and within six months of its coming to an end, the same tenant becomes tenant under another tenancy, either of the same landlord or the same dwelling-house or both, and both tenancies are secure periodic tenancies, the tenant is treated as a successor in relation to the second tenancy (i e it cannot further be succeeded to) unless the contrary is provided in the agreement creating the second tenancy (s 88(4)).

VI   SECURITY OF TENURE

Fixed-term tenancies

Where a fixed-term tenancy comes to an end by effluxion of time or by a court order under s 82(3), a periodic tenancy arises automatically under s 86(1), unless the tenant is granted another fixed-term or periodic tenancy of the same dwelling-house to begin when the first tenancy ends. The periods, parties and terms of the statute-implied secure tenancy are governed by s 86(2): the periods are those for which rent was last payable under the first tenancy and the parties and terms are the same as those at the end of the first tenancy, but confined to terms compatible with a periodic tenancy and excluding forfeiture provisions. The court cannot order forfeiture of a secure fixed-term tenancy but if it decides to terminate it, it will make a termination order in respect of the secure tenancy on the date fixed in its order (s 82(3)). In that case, s 86 applies.

The statute-implied periodic tenancy which follows the ending or termination of a secure fixed-term tenancy must be terminated in accordance with a statutory procedure and on specified grounds and in

---

5   *South Northamptonshire District Council v Power* [1987] 3 All ER 831, [1987] 1 WLR 1433, CA.

6   I e assignments under s 24 of the Matrimonial Causes Act 1973 and to a successor to a secure tenancy: see above.

no other way.[7] Therefore, in any event, the s 83 notice procedure will apply to a fixed-term tenancy, as it does to the periodic tenancy which arises under statute on termination of a fixed-term tenancy, except that where a statutory notice is served with respect to a fixed-term tenancy, it applies automatically to the statute-implied periodic tenancy arising on termination of the fixed-term tenancy (s 83(5)).[8]

Periodic tenancies

By s 82(1), a periodic tenancy of any length cannot be brought to an end by a landlord's notice to quit. The landlord must obtain an order for possession (in the county court (s 110)) and the tenancy ends on any date specified in that order. To obtain possession, the following steps must be gone through by the landlord.

1 He must serve a notice under s 83(2) on the tenant. This statutory notice must be in force when proceedings are begun (s 83(4)) after a date, which must be specified in the notice, as from which possession proceedings may be begun (s 83(3)(a)).[9] The statutory notice cannot purport to specify a date earlier than the earliest date at which the tenancy could have been terminated at common law (s 83(3)).
2 The statutory notice must be in the prescribed form,[10] and it must also specify the ground relied on by the landlord (s 83(2)(b)) and give particulars of that ground (s 83(2)(c)).

It is not sufficient, for the purposes of the specification requirement, for a notice to repeat a ground for possession or part: a statement must be given which tells the tenant of the details of his alleged breaches: for example, any rent arrears must be stated, or any breaches of covenant to repair must be specified; and the particulars required by s 83 must be such as to indicate to the tenant the particular head (or heads) of claim the landlord intends to pursue.[11] If the statutory requirements are not complied with, the notice will be bad and no proceedings may be based on it. It is implicit in these provisions that, as a statutory notice is a warning to the tenant, if he remedies the alleged breaches, possession will be refused.

The above rules as to notices have no application to tenants' notices to quit: if a tenant serves a notice to quit, he cannot later rely on the security

---

7 See *Hammersmith and Fulham London Borough v Harrison* [1981] 2 All ER 588 at 597–598, CA.
8 Where this is to, it is not necessary for the statutory notice to specify a date for commencing proceedings and also, it will not lapse 12 months after that date (s 83(5), excluding s 83(3) and s 83(4)).
9 Statutory notices relating to periodic tenancies have a 12-month life: s 83(3)(b).
10 Secure Tenancies (Notices) Regulations 1987, SI 1987/755.
11 *Torridge District Council v Jones* [1985] 2 EGLR 54, CA.

provisions.[12] If, moreover, a secure tenant permanently leaves the premises owing rent, it seems that he will lose security, having ceased to comply with the statutory residence requirement.[13]

Grounds for possession

The county court cannot make an order for possession against a secure tenant except on proof by the landlord of one or more grounds for possession as laid down in Sch 2. If a ground is not specified in the landlord's statutory notice, it cannot be relied on (s 84(3)).[14] Grounds 1 to 8 are subject to the overriding requirement that it must be reasonable to make an order for possession (s 84(2)(a)).[15] Grounds 9 to 11 are subject to a requirement that when the order takes effect, suitable alternative accommodation will be available to the tenant (s 84(2)(b)).[16] Grounds 12 to 16 are subject to *both* requirements.

The grounds for possession are these.

1   Tenant's failure to pay rent or breaches of covenant (ground 1).
2   Tenant's nuisance, annoyance etc (ground 2).
3   Deterioration of dwelling-house due to tenant's waste (ground 3).
4   Deterioration in condition of furniture due to tenant's or other's ill-treatment (ground 4).[17]
5   The landlord was induced to grant tenancy by false statement made knowingly or recklessly by the tenant (ground 5).
6   The tenancy was assigned to tenant or family member who was predecessor in title to tenant under s 92 and a premium was paid on one or other assignment (ground 6).
7   The tenant lives in part of (or within the curtilege of) a building not mainly used for housing purposes and holds the tenancy as employee of the landlord and the tenant or a resident with him is guilty of conduct such that it would not be right to allow him to continue in occupation (ground 7). If the landlord reasonably requires the dwelling-house as a residence for an employee of his, possession may be mandatorily recovered from the tenant subject to certain conditions (ground 12).
8   The dwelling-house was available for occupation during works on

---

12   *Greenwich London Borough Council v McGrady* (1982) 81 LGR 288, CA.
13   *Preston Borough Council v Fairclough* (1982) 8 HLR 70, CA; also *R v Croydon London Borough Council, ex p Toth*, supra.
14   The county court has a discretion to allow alterations or additions to grounds: s 84(3). No consent order is possible: *Wandsworth London Borough Council v Fodayami* [1987] 3 All ER 474, [1987] 1 WLR 1473, CA.
15   Similar considerations apply as apply where Rent Act 1977 s 98(1) applies. See e g *Woodspring District Council v Taylor* (1982) 4 HLR 95, CA; *Second WRVS Housing Society v Blair* (1986) 19 HLR 104, CA (personal factors relevant).
16   See Housing Act 1985 Sch 2 Part IV; cf Rent Act 1977 Sch 15 Part IV; and see *Enfield Borough Council v French* (1984) 83 LGR 750, CA.
17   As to these grounds, identical rules apply to Rent Act 1977 Sch 15 Cases.

tenant's previous dwelling-house of which he was secure tenant, and the works have been completed (ground 8).

9 The dwelling-house is overcrowded such as to constitute an offence (ground 9).

10 The landlord intends, within a reasonable time of obtaining possession, to demolish or reconstruct the building or part comprising the dwelling-house, or to carry out work on the building or land let with it, and cannot reasonably do so without obtaining possession (ground 10).[18]

11 The landlord intends to redevelop the land in which the dwelling-house is situated under an approved scheme (ground 10A).

12 The landlord is a charity and the tenant's continuing occupation would conflict with its purposes (ground 11).

13 The landlord[19] proves that he requires the dwelling-house for occupation by tenants with special needs, i e disablement (ground 13), persons with special circumstances (ground 14) or social priority needs (ground 15).

14 The accommodation provided in the dwelling-house is too extensive for the current tenant's reasonable requirements, and the latter is a successor (ground 16). In this case, the court must take particular factors into account in exercising its discretion whether to make an order.[20]

In relation to grounds 1 to 8 and 12 to 16, s 85 confers on the county court very wide powers of adjournment, staying or postponement in relation to any order for possession.[1]

VII FURTHER TERMS OF SECURE TENANCIES

In what follows, there are discussed special terms dealing with lodgers, improvements, repairs, management and variation.

Lodgers and sub-letting

By s 93(1)(a), it is a term of all secure tenancies that the tenant may allow lodgers to reside in the dwelling-house. Section 93(1)(b) provides that no

---

18 Cf Landlord and Tenant Act 1954 s 30(1)(f): similar considerations apply to ground 10, except that the tenant lacks the protection of 1954 Act s 31A. See *Wansbeck District Council v Marley* (1987) 20 HLR 247, CA.

19 In the case of Grounds 14 and 15, the landlord must (in effect) be a landlord which lets to these particular kinds of tenants.

20 These are: the age of the tenant, the period of his occupation and the financial support given to the previous tenant.

1 See ch 17. As from any failure by the tenant to comply with a suspended possession order, it becomes effective to terminate the tenancy: *Thompson v Elmbridge Borough Council* [1987] 1 WLR 1425, CA.

secure tenant may, without the landlord's written consent, sub-let or part with possession of part of the dwelling-house. Consent cannot be unreasonably withheld: if it is, it is treated as given (s 94(2)). The burden of proof of reasonableness is on the landlord (s 94(2)) but certain factors are statutorily listed as material, namely, the likelihood of overcrowding or the effect of proposed works on the accommodation to be offered to a possible sub-tenant (s 94(3)). Conditional consent is treated as unconditional (s 94(5)). If the tenant applies in writing for a consent and it is refused, the landlord must state his reasons in writing. If he fails to act at all, consent is treated as withheld (s 94(6)). However, consent may be given by the landlord following an action requiring it (s 94(4)).

Improvements: consent rules

Special consent rules apply to secure tenants. By s 97(1), it is a term of every secure tenancy that the tenant will not make any improvement without the written consent of the landlord. 'Improvement' is widely defined by s 97(2). Consent cannot be unreasonably withheld: if it is, it is treated as given (s 97(3)). The onus of proving the reasonableness of a withholding of consent is on the landlord (s 98(1)). Guidance is given to the county court by s 98(2) as to matters to be taken into account in determining reasonableness. These are: the extent to which the improvement would be likely to make the dwelling-house or other premises less safe for occupiers, or to cause the landlord unnecessary expenditure or to reduce the market or the letting value of the dwelling-house. If consent is refused following a tenant's written application, identical deeming rules apply, by s 98(4), as apply to lodgers (see above). However, the landlord has a power, when giving consent, to impose a reasonable condition (s 99(1)).[2] The landlord must show that any condition is reasonable (s 99(3)) and the imposition of an unreasonable condition is equivalent to refusing consent (s 99(2)).

Improvements: other rules

Section 100 of the 1985 Act enables the landlord, in certain circumstances, at the end of the tenancy, to make a discretionary payment to the tenant on account of tenants' improvements begun on or after 3 October 1980. The improvement must have added to the open market price or rental value of the dwelling-house and it must have been carried out with the landlord or his predecessor's written consent. Section 101 protects the tenant and his 'qualifying successors' (defined in s 101(3)) against any rent increases due to the effect of tenants' improvements.

---

2   Failure to satisfy such a condition is treated by s 99(4) as a breach of the tenancy obligations.

Repairs

The obligations of the parties under a secure tenancy are governed by the general law.[3] Under s 96 of the 1985 Act, regulations have been made as to repairs by secure tenants.[4] The scheme enables secure tenants to carry out landlords' repairs and to recover the cost from the landlord.

Management and variation

Landlords letting on secure tenancies are obliged by ss 104 to 106 of the 1985 Act to make and maintain arrangements to consult and inform secure tenants on such matters as housing management.

The terms of a secure tenancy may be varied, but only as laid down by s 102. Agreement between landlord and tenant is one permitted method of variation, but merely to circulate a booklet to tenants which mentions varied terms is not even an offer by the landlord to be contractually bound by the terms of the booklet, in so far as they differ from the current terms of the tenancy.[5]

---

3 See ch 9.
4 Secure Tenancies (Right to Repair) Scheme Regulations 1985, SI 1985/1493. See Maughan-Pawsey (1986) 136 NLJ 829.
5 *Palmer v Metropolitan Borough of Sandwell* (1987) 20 HLR 74, CA (landlord not bound by statement in booklet, which differed from existing terms, that landlord would remedy design faults).

Index

Business tenancy—*contd*
notices—*contd*
tenant, by,
improvements, intention to make,
499
notice to quit, 461, 464, 466
terminate, to, 469–473
premises,
national security, required for, 460
public purposes, required for, 460
proposed reforms, 451, 502
protected tenancy, whether, 273, 291,
304
reservation of rights, 48
security of tenure, 227, 463–465
service tenancies excluded, 459
Street v Mountford rulings, application
to, 42, 44, 50
sub-tenancy,
continuation of, 468
protection of, 304, 453
termination of, 471–472
termination of, 11, 225, 461–462, 466,
468 *et seq.*
agreement for new tenancy, by, 460,
466
compensation for misrepresentation
etc., 489
current tenancy, 489, 497
fixed-term tenants, by, 461, 466,
468–469
forfeiture, by, 461, 466
landlord's notice, by, 466, 469–473
competent landlord, 471–472
intention to oppose, statement of,
472–473, 474, 480
interim rent, application for,
476–477
sub-tenancies, 471
tenant's counter-notice, 472, 473
notice to quit by tenant, 461, 464,
466
notices to terminate, 469–473
out-of-court negotiations, 477–478
statutory notices, by 466–467
surrender, 461, 464
tenant's failure to comply with
s 29(2), (3), 461–462
tenant's request for new tenancy,
466–467, 473–475
interim rent, application for,
476–477
landlord's counter-notice, 475
requirements of, 473–475
wholly residential tenancy excluded,
458

Certificate
business tenancy, improvements,
499–500
Charge
covenant against charging, 118
Charitable housing trust
tenancy not protected, 303
College
capacity to lease, 21
Commission for New Towns
tenancy,
assured, cannot be, 371
not protected, 303
Company
business tenancy, 487
capacity to lease, 22
groups of, 487
liquidator, disclaimer of onerous lease
by, 238
notice to quit, service on, 233
statutory tenancy, cannot claim, 334
Compensation
agricultural holding. *See*
AGRICULTURAL HOLDINGS
allotment garden holders, 550
allotment holders, 549
business tenancies. *See* BUSINESS
TENANCY
change of user of premises, for, 130
Compulsory acquisition
residential flats by tenants on long
leases, 417–419
Compulsory purchase
repair, breach of covenant, and
damages, 194
Condition
breach of, re-entry on, right of, 71, 79,
162, 239
covenant distinguished, 79–80
Contract
collateral,
covenant distinguished, 81–82
enforceability, 83
frustration, 226
lease, for, 52. *And see* AGREEMENT FOR
LEASE
privity of contract between parties,
84–86
restricted,
abolition of, 275, 278
circumstances where arises, 279
furniture, 279
Housing Act 1988, effect of, 279
meaning, 279
rent controls, 279–280
resident landlord, 279